The Body Reader

The Body Reader

Essential Social and Cultural Readings

IIIIIIIIIIIIIIIIIIIIIIIIIIIIIIIIIIIIIIIIIIIIIIIIIIIIIIIIIIIIIIIIIIIIIIIIIIIIIIIIIIIIIII

EDITED BY

Lisa Jean Moore and Mary Kosut

IIIIIIIIIIIIIIIIIIIIIIIIIIIIIIIIIIIIIIIIIIIIIIIIIIIIIIIIIIIIIIIIIIIIIIIIIIIIIIIIIIIIIII

NEW YORK UNIVERSITY PRESS

NEW YORK AND LONDON

NEW YORK UNIVERSITY PRESS
New York and London
www.nyupress.org

Library of Congress Cataloging-in-Publication Data

The body reader : essential social and cultural readings /
edited by Lisa Jean Moore and Mary Kosut.
p. cm.
Includes bibliographical references and index.
ISBN-13: 978–0–8147–9565–1 (cl : alk. paper)
ISBN-10: 0–8147–9565–X (cl : alk. paper)
ISBN-13: 978–0–8147–9566–8 (pb : alk. paper)
ISBN-10: 0–8147–9566–8 (pb : alk. paper)
1. Human body—Social aspects. I. Moore, Lisa Jean, 1967– II. Kosut, Mary.
HM636.B653   2010
306.4—dc22   2009035181

New York University Press books are printed on acid-free paper,
and their binding materials are chosen for strength and durability.
We strive to use environmentally responsible suppliers and materials
to the greatest extent possible in publishing our books.

Manufactured in the United States of America
c   10 9 8 7 6 5 4 3 2 1
p   10 9 8 7 6 5 4 3 2 1

For Paisley, LJM

With Mike in mind, MK

Contents

Acknowledgments

Writing and assembling this book has been a terrific experience of collaboration. We are grateful to many generous and talented friends and colleagues.

For their careful reading of and expert commentary on the introduction to this volume, we thank Paisley Currah and Monica Casper, as well as the anonymous reviewers.

At Purchase College, we are very lucky to have magnificent colleagues who support and inspire us—Matthew Immergut, Chrys Ingraham, Rudi Gaudio, Shaka McGlotten, John Forrest, Ahmed Afzal, and Jason Pine in particular—as well as a supportive dean, Suzanne Kessler. Mary is especially grateful to be awarded a Purchase College Junior Faculty Development Grant, which afforded her time to devote to the completion of this project.

Our undergraduate students are among the most talented and engaging. Those who inspired us in this work are Lara Rodriguez, Maggie Cavallo, Emily Dyett, Ben Harnick, and Nathan Baron.

Lisa would like to thank her family, Paisley, Grace, Georgia, and Greta, for their patience, support, and dance parties. Mary is indebted to Mike for his enthusiastic participation in an often-pleasing life sentence, and to her mother, Elizabeth Jesella, for her unflagging support. She would also like to thank Johanna for her astute feedback, Alisoun for being delightfully inappropriate, as well as Sean, Fakir, and the other extraordinary bodies who inspire and provoke her.

Finally, working with NYU Press has been a wonderful experience. Invaluable editorial assistant Aiden Amos was always at the ready to help us with the preparation of the manuscript. Our executive editor, Ilene Kalish, is truly the best, and we are fortunate to have benefited from her acumen and expertise.

Introduction: Not Just the Reflexive Reflex
Flesh and Bone in the Social Sciences

Mary Kosut and Lisa Jean Moore

Seeing the Body: The Goals of Our Book

Sociologist Arthur Frank elegantly describes the body as follows: "the body is not mute, but it is inarticulate; it does not use speech, yet begets it."[1] When an academic tells a theoretical story about the body or bodies, she must listen closely to hear her own body speaking from within it. If she is able to hear this body, she then must translate its communication into an imperfect language.

As we reflect on this complicated process, we are forced to confront our own embodiment and the pleasures and dangers of revealing our bodies. If we trot out the usual demographic information to our multiple audiences, including our gender, race, ethnicity, age, sexual orientation, reproductive status, physical ability, grooming rituals, body modification practices—what might this enable the reader to glean about us? And how might such a practice of self-reflection enrich the contents of this book? For women, this practice of "sharing" these embodiments has become a necessary yet risky rite of passage into the academic right (and requirement) to produce knowledge. Importantly, this rite of passage is not equally mandated for our academic colleagues who inhabit bodies that are both physically and symbolically different from ours.

The body is the medium or raw material through which we navigate the world, but it is also an entity that is invested with meanings. Outing our bodies, speaking of and through them, is not only a subjective individual act but is also a political and cultural act. This is the case because bodies can convey a range of statuses, ranks, and relationships. Bodies may be read aesthetically, as things to be beautified, fixed, fetishized, and adorned. Or bodies can be registered bureaucratically and demographically via binary categories like male or female, black or white, and straight or gay. Bodies may convey national pride, as in the case of Olympic athletes who symbolically represent the fittest and the best. Or, conversely, bodies can communicate the effects of institutional racism, abandonment, and neglect as seen in the media images of poor black Hurricane Katrina victims stranded on rooftops begging for water and rescue. We may consider the body through the medical-scientific lens of a microscope or through the ideologies of religion. Clearly, the body is not neutral—it is the entry point into cultural and structural relationships, emotional and subjective experiences, and the biological realms of flesh and bone.

Sociologists Simon J. Williams and Gillian Bendelow have called for an "embodied sociology," one that rejects theorizing "*about* bodies in a largely disembodied, typically male way" in favor of a "new mode of theorizing *from* lived bodies."[2] Approaching the body as lived, rather than as an abstract object or social construct, allows us to begin to understand the subjectivities of the flesh, and how bodies themselves hold an unspoken knowledge. Where possible, we have encouraged our "authors" to confront their own embodiment in the construction of their essays. In this way the "lived body" is made to be more alive and accountable in their work.

We define the body as the fleshy, verdant, carnal, sensate, engaged organism that is composed of bones, blood, organs, and fluids, as well as statuses, hopes, fears, and anxieties. It is the ultimate location of the division in sociology between structure and agency. What we mean is that the body is our first introduction to the performance of the self and identity—our expression of agency, while at the same time its structural location in stratified worlds that limit that very agency.

Bodies are sites of contradictions. The body, in this text, is that entity that both enables us with great potential and profoundly limits us. It is both material and symbolic. The flesh is inscribed with meaning both from ourselves with our consent and by others against our will. It is our possession and our prison, while at the same time it is out of our control as it leaks, fails us, and gives us away (Moore, this volume). Our bodies may not wholly belong to ourselves—particularly in the case of labor, reproductive and otherwise (Slavishak, this volume).

The everyday experiences and practices of living inside the body must not be overlooked or trivialized. As sociologist Anne Witz argues, it is imperative that we not only recuperate the body within sociology but also continue to forge *new* ways of thinking about the body that will be helpful to those working in a variety of disciplines.[3] This framework advances beyond simplistic dualisms (such as the Cartesian mind/body distinction) in an effort to explicitly recognize the somatic, subjective, and social components of embodiment and how they interrelate.

Now that we have recovered the body, we must make sense of it. Sociologist Bryan Turner's conception of different orientations to the body—having a body, doing a body, and being a body—is particularly salient in fleshing out the body's multifaceted nature.[4] We need to be cognizant of the somatic, subjective, and social components of embodiment and how they entangle within continually changeable cultural (and global) webs. We must be aware of the relationship between the body and the self, remembering that when we speak of such things as the unconscious, identity, and the mind, we are invariably talking about the body, as they are one and the same. We must consider the uniqueness of modern embodiment but remember that our understandings don't exist in a vacuum—a rich field of work reminds us of the historicity of bodies. And finally, it is imperative that we remember that the body is in praxis—undeniably shaped by society but simultaneously marking the world through the negotiation of everyday life.

Our book examines key concepts and theories of the body throughout each of its four sections: "Vulnerable Bodies," "Bodies as Mediums," "Extraordinary Bodies," and

"Bodies in Media." Rather than organize the book around the familiar categories of gender, race, class, ability, and sexuality, we take the significance of these status variables as a given and highlight them throughout the volume. As an alternative, we present readings within larger thematic frameworks that are both salient and topical, paying special attention to bodies that are at risk, contemporary embodied practices and regimes, bodies that challenge norms, and representations of the body in mass media. While roughly half of the chapters in the book are previously unpublished and have been written with the intent to bring the "lived body" into focus, we also include previously published works from authors such as Sander Gilman, among others. Such germinal works have clearly shaped the field of body studies, and much contemporary work on the body draws from and expands such studies. Each section begins with a brief introduction that defines some key terms and concepts that run through the section's essays. It is our hope that these mini introductions will enable the reader, both students and teachers, to make further connections between chapters. While we have organized the book in these four sections, clearly there is a bleed among sections as scholarship on the body, like the body itself, traffics across borders and boundaries. Overall, the diverse studies in this book point to the significance of bodies, as objects invested with social meanings and as embodied actors that challenge and transgress the boundaries of culture and the flesh.

The section that follows, "Social and Cultural Studies Come to the Body," is meant to provide a general introduction to key readings and theories on the body, particularly within the field of sociology. In addition, we highlight the importance of interdisciplinary fields such as disability studies and science and technology studies, because of their valuable contributions to understanding the complexity of embodiment. We also place the body within the context of contemporary culture to show why and how the body matters at this particular historical moment.

Social and Cultural Studies Come to the Body

The assertion that the human body has historically been overlooked within social theory, and largely unseen within the broader discipline of sociology, is a well-worn truism. The reason why the body wasn't adequately theorized by sociologists is appreciable given the development of the field and its early substantive foci—making sense of major historical, political, industrial, and ideological changes in Europe during the late eighteenth and early nineteenth centuries. Juxtaposing traditional with nascent industrial societies and tracing the fading import of religion, the rise of democracy and capitalism, and the emergence of the metropolis are all macrosociological, structural, or, more colloquially put, *society* questions. Furthermore, we suggest that part of the reason why bodies have been so absent from sociological theory and practice is that the disciplinary origins were limited by masculinist perspectives. Sociological scholarship and practice were created by men who privileged male ways of knowing and male prerogatives and thus constructed institutions of male domination. Ideologically, women embodied (or imprisoned) in the feminine flesh are positioned in a dichotomous fashion in relationship to men. Historically, female bodies were posited as entirely fleshy, leaky, and linked to the primitive, whereas male bodies were associated with the mind, logic, rationality, and civility. We argue that the simultaneity of barriers to women's participation as producers of knowledge and epistemological beliefs that relegated bodies to obdurate binary dualisms severely hampered a rich sociological tradition of engagement with the body.

Additionally, the project of establishing sociology as a legitimate and distinct field of study (fueled by the efforts of Emile Durkheim and Auguste Comte) necessitated drawing boundaries that would distinguish sociology from the biological sciences and the field of psychology. This constellation of historical forces effectively eclipsed the individual bodies that constitute the basis of society itself. In order to be accepted as a legitimate disciplinary field, early sociological work made a strategic decision to privilege the social and relinquish the human body to other sciences. Over the past few decades, sociologists and feminist scholars have worked to bring the body back in.

Embodiment, despite recent attention to "the body," remains as conceptually problematic as it is riveting. One of the most interesting aspects of this discourse is how awkward and difficult it is to talk (or write) about embodiment and its consequences and implications, and how little shared vocabulary exists. This, of course, is no accident, as the "scientific revolution" of modernity was predicated on the denial of embodiment.[5] The science of the past few centuries, which required disembodied knowers and producers of knowledge (constituted through the erasure of bodies, actual work practices, and the messiness of life itself), produced very partial official knowledges, particularly stunted about embodiment in general and sexual, gendered, raced embodiments in particular (Frank, Kroll-Smith and Floyd, this volume). Through discourse and disciplinary analyses of a now very wide array of media, sciences, and technologies, feminist scholars have elucidated the "othering" and racialization of women, girls, females, the feminine, and many if not most aspects of bodies, including gender, sexualities, and reproduction (Patton, Collins, this volume).

The reasons why social and cultural theorists brought the body into sharper focus in the last decades of the twentieth century are complex. Yet, if we reflexively observe the world around us we can see how bodies do indeed matter, to paraphrase philosopher Judith Butler, albeit in historically unparalleled ways. The rise of media culture has brought new visualizations of the body that suggest which bodies are normal, healthy, and worthy (Huggins, this volume). For example, consider how bodies have recently been represented in the mass media in television shows like *The Biggest Loser* or *Extreme Makeover* (Kosut, this volume). Obese bodies and those deemed physically unattractive in myriad ways are displayed, analyzed, medicalized, and ultimately (if they are lucky and hard-working), these bodies are transformed as millions watch the process, some even discussing the merits and success of such transformations within the blogosphere. Bodies are endlessly mediated by our cultural commentary. Take for example, Thomas Beattie, a 34-year-old transgender man (with a beard and so-called baby bump), who garnered mass media attention by coming out as a "pregnant father." By sharing Oprah's couch with his wife, Beattie defied the long-standing cultural belief that anatomy always dictates a person's gender. Beattie's body, like those who have undergone an *Extreme Makeover*, provides a new set of understandings and meanings about what it means to have and be a body and to reproduce a body. These media representations and the discourses surrounding them disseminate an amended and fluid embodied cultural blueprint that can take us beyond the confines of the flesh as we have previously understood it. And we are constantly bombarded by a dizzying number of opinions and expert reflections on these enhanced bodies.

Cyberculture and new media technologies have expanded and extended the way the body looks and functions as the interface between the real and the virtual, and the human and the machine, overlap and merge. Since the Internet has become a common public sphere of social interaction, networking, and recreation, the constitution and definition of the body has become even more liquid in cyberspace. While computer-mediated interactions do not require physical copresence, they do allow for a visual and virtual bodily exchange that is a tangible embodied experience. For example, televideo cybersex or more mundane video teleconferencing via Skype transpires as participants embody themselves in the mediated image (see Waskul, this volume). People feel, through their bodies, the pleasures and pitfalls that may occur through the process of virtual communication. Virtual spaces, such as Second Life, free the body from its physical limitations, as it can be rewritten through the avatar or visual representation of the user. However, studies suggest that the physical appearance of an avatar may be transferred to the person behind it.[6] Nonetheless, in an embodied encounter we are bound within our fleshy exterior (gender, height, race, age), whereas in a mediated environment our avatar, or virtual body, may be unbound from biological and social status variables. Televideo interactions and cyber-representations (avatars) both call attention to the murky interface between the real and the virtual body.

Indeed, what gets to count as a body—a normal, healthy, functioning body—is contested by medical professionals, the state, clergy, and lay people alike. Clearly, beauty and health products are marketed that prey on our insecurities about our bodily vulnerabilities—just as prenatal genetic tests are recommended to anxious parents to ensure the "normality" of the fetus (Karlberg, this volume). But these very vulnerabilities are undergirded by a complex system of physicalism, the practice of "rating an individual's social value solely on his or her muscular, sensory, and/or mental prowess."[7] Over the past few decades, disability studies, an interdisciplinary field of academic inquiry and political activism, has produced scholarship and advocacy that examine the heterogeneous and transhistorical meanings of disability.[8] Even though 15 percent of the population is made up of people with disabilities, these bodies are rendered invisible in social spaces, political arenas, and intellectual endeavors. Bodies of all abilities are at some point recalcitrant; for example, they may break, ache, or bleed. However, those deemed permanently *disabled* are demanding to be seen in myriad environments regardless of how they are categorized (Peace, this volume).

In the everyday realm, the emergence of new life-saving and life-prolonging technologies make novelist William Gibson's cyborg less fictitious and science-studies scholar Donna Haraway's cyborg more feasible. This prevalence of the cyborg, an integrated circuit of flesh and technology, a blending of the "natural" and the "social," redefines the very notions of humanness and the distinctions of animate and inanimate. As a result, when life begins and ends, once historical givens that were empirically observable (either when the baby emerged or when the body went cold), are today rendered ambiguous and opaque events as medicine continues to breach previous technological boundaries. The case of 41-year-old severely brain-damaged Terry Schiavo, whose body became the center of an infamous right-to-die case in 2005, reminds us that what defines a living body, one that is truly *alive*, is open to question. Similarly, in recent years the congressional and popular debates over the use of human embryos in stem cell research have kindled arguments over exactly when a life starts. These kinds of cases illustrate that when bodies, or even parts of the body, are viewed and treated through a medical and scientific lens, conflicting moral, ethical, and religious viewpoints come into focus. As we know more about the body's biological workings, and arguably, for the most part, our lives are improved and extended, we are forced to ponder where the tangible and intangible meet.

In addition to new medical technologies, the growth of consumer culture, including the worlds of commercial beauty and fashion, the ubiquity of plastic surgery, and the arrival of the fitness and diet industries have also significantly shaped the way we recognize and experience our bodies in contemporary Western society (Kent, Dias, Gilman, Immergut, this volume). It can be argued that for certain people, particularly those with creativity and imagination, life inside the body has drastically changed. Depending upon one's economic and social capital, the body may be increasingly malleable and protean. French performance artist Orlan, who beginning in 1990 radically altered her body in unprecedented ways in live "surgery performances" epitomizes this notion. Orlan used plastic surgery to transform her face and body using iconic images of women in the Western art canon such as the *Mona Lisa* or *Venus*, as her template. While Orlan's work shocked those both inside and outside of the art world, almost twenty years later such radical surgical modification appears less scandalous and extreme. The rise of surgical and nonsurgical cosmetic surgeries in the West hints at the normalization of procedures like breast implants and liposuction. Cosmetic-surgery television shows like *Nip/Tuck* and *The Swan*, as well as media coverage of celebrity surgeries and advertising for nonsurgical products like Botox and Restylane have played a part in redefining cosmetic surgery as an acceptable and even mundane means to improve the body's appearance. Some people have become so obsessed with cosmetic surgery that they have been described as "surgery junkies" and "plastaholics."[9] While Orlan and plastaholics are examples of extreme cases, the larger message conveyed in the media is clear. If you have the means and the desire, your body can be potentially made more perfect than its natural or embryonic state (Vannini and McCright, this volume).

In the academic realm, the (re)emergence of feminism in the 1960s–1970s problematized sex, sexuality, and gender, effectively challenging conservative and functionalist views of the female body as posited by American sociological forefather Talcott Parsons and many others. Much of the best work in this area focuses on how the socialization process transforms male and female into masculine and feminine, directly leading to the subjugation of women in various spheres. According to feminist social theory, claims about bodies are part of the social arrangements and cultural beliefs that constitute the gendered social order. Men's physical capabilities are, for the most part, considered superior to women's. As bodies prone to illness and early death, as well as higher infant mortality rates and lower pain thresholds, men's are actually more fragile than women's, and feminist analysis has tried to tease the physiological from the social, cultural, and environmental in illness and death rates. For example, in the United States in 2005, women's life expectancy was 5.2 years greater than men's.

Significant contributions and interventions into studies of the body have come from feminist science and technology studies, or feminist STS. A primary objective of feminist STS has been to explore the construction of gender/sex differences both within and across transdisciplinary borders, flowing through both the humanities and the social and natural sciences. In these studies, reproductive anatomy and sexual physiology are skillfully investigated, illuminating their reliance on beliefs of embodied differences.[10] Scholars of science, technology, and medicine also examine understandings of female and male embodied sexual pleasure, as well as pharmaceutical enhancements like Viagra. This work reveals how the orgasm, the natural locus of pleasure, is mediated by many layers of bodily tissue and morphology.[11]

The vulnerability of certain bodies is also apparent within the context of globalization, specifically with regard to a rise in global organ trafficking in which the human body is viewed as a pure commodity.[12] The most socially disadvantaged citizens of impoverished countries sell organs and other body tissues to affluent people, often foreigners, who do not want to wait through the sanctioned means of a donor list (Haddow, this volume). This phenomenon has spawned "transplant tourism," wherein buyers from the United States and Europe travel to developing countries in search of cheap kidneys and other body parts, sometimes via post mortem harvesting. The global capitalist economy has also fueled female sexual slavery, sexual tourism, and the trafficking of women and children, particularly from countries in the global south.[13] Both female bodies and impoverished bodies are increasingly dissected, mutilated, tortured, and sold to assure the health and pleasure of others. These invisible exploited populations provide a tangible example of the way real bodies are fundamentally shaped through a powerful web of technological, economic, political, and cultural conditions (Masters, this volume).

The rise of subdisciplines within the field, such as the sociology of sport, aging, and the life course, and postmodernism in general have also influenced the need to take the body seriously as a cultural construction, symbol, and conduit of social processes. The body is increasingly being recognized as a central concern not only within sociological subfields—medicine, sexuality, race, media—but within the discipline as a whole. Likewise, many scholars working outside of the social sciences, particularly in the areas of anthropology, history, English, media and communication studies, and philosophy, have also begun to highlight the body and its significance, many focusing on gender and sexuality issues in particular, including scholars such as Judith Butler,

Judith Halberstam, and Eve Kosofsky Sedgwick. The relationship between race and the body has also been called attention to by scholars such as bell hooks, Patricia Hill Collins, and Dorothy Roberts. If one looks carefully, it becomes clear how important the physical body is within much contemporary research. Whether focusing on the reproduction of social stratification in systems of education[14] or the urban underground economy[15] these diverse types of studies share a commonality—a concern with the way the classification and treatment of the body due to race, ethnicity, class, or gender affect our life chances and the paths we take. The body is clearly no longer peripheral, but rather an increasingly central and problematic issue within social and cultural studies.

Early Sociological Theory

Approaches to theorizing the body are divergent in scope, methodology, and content, sometimes eluding categorical classification. For example, under the rubric of feminist theory, there is little agreement about how to theorize the relationships among gender, sex, and embodiment, nor is there a consensus regarding how these terms should be defined. There is also a surplus of body classification schemas. For example, in *The Body and Society*, sociologist Bryan Turner (1984) posits four types of bodies, while Arthur Frank (1991, 1995) advances a "typology of body use in action" that narrows the body into four abstract types. Sociologist John O'Neill (1985) develops a theory of *Five Bodies* and anthropologists Nancy Scheper-Hughes and Margaret Lock (1987) posit three bodies—individual, social, and political.

However, before we explore contemporary perspectives on the body, it is important to make clear that the "founding fathers" of sociology and anthropology did not entirely omit bodies from their work. Georg Simmel (1858–1918) explicitly considers the body in the essay "Adornment" and offers a more implicit treatment in his seminal work *The Metropolis and Mental Life*. According to Simmel, we adorn the body for the sake of the individual self, yet cannot accomplish the act (the reception of egoistic pleasure) without society. Simmel believes that this activity "is one of the strangest sociological combinations" because it is simultaneously egoistic and altruistic.[16] Wearing adornment, whether it is jewelry or a particular hair style, singles out the wearer by embodying a kind of self-feeling. Notwithstanding, bodily gratification is directed towards society because the wearer can enjoy it only insofar as she mirrors herself within it. While there is not an explicit discussion, there is a suggestion of a reflexive body-self within Simmel's analysis.

Although Karl Marx is criticized for his overdeterministic material analysis of history in which the individual is treated as a passive being (possessing agency only when subsumed within a class analysis), at the core of Marx's work one finds corporeal beings. In the *Economic and Philosophic Manuscripts of 1844*, Marx analyzes humanity's universal relationship to nature and our inherent need to produce, or labor for our survival. In order to survive *physically* as a species, humanity needs products of nature, i.e., food, shelter, clothing, housing, etc. Thus, nature provides the "means of life" for human beings. Marx maintains that because we live on nature, nature is, in essence, our body. Notwithstanding, the human species holds a very distinctive relationship to nature because we are sentient creatures. It is precisely this consciousness or cognizance, our "species being," that distinguishes humans from animals. Humans emerge as a species being when we labor in the objective world.

Because human beings are capable of transforming their relation to nature (and to other human beings), Marx views humanity as inherently creative. Humanity creates itself as the product of its own labor, ultimately objectifying itself through the work it performs. Marx's regard for the bodies of the working class underscores his concept of alienation and alienating labor. He argues that with the emergence of capitalist production, the worker's mind and body become increasingly machinelike. For example, in the *Communist Manifesto* the proletariat "becomes an appendage of the machine, and it is only the most simple, most monotonous, and most easily acquired knack that is required of him."[17] According to Marx, alienating mechanized labor erodes and jeopardizes our species being—that which makes us humans. Even though Marx's focus was not specifically on the body, an acknowledgment of the corporeal undergirds some of his most influential writings.

An implicit approach to embodiment is found in the work of Max Weber, particularly his work on rationalization and religion. Unlike Marx, who had a passionate concern for the way (some) bodies are subjugated under inhumane capitalist labor, Weber is concerned, in his treatment of the body, with the way religious ideology and rationalization led to rigid corporeal control and denial of pleasure. For Weber, the emergence of modern capitalist society signaled an abnegation of the body's sexual drives. In *The Protestant Ethic* Weber outlines the way Calvinist asceticism (involving a combination of both hard work and negation of sexual pleasure) represented a devout spiritual commitment functioning to ward off "moral unworthiness."[18] Forsaking corporeal pleasure, the Protestant ethic emphasized intense commitment to hard work, frugality, and moderation as the only paths to salvation for Protestant devotees. Weber further expands on rationalization and the body in *Religious Rejections*, positing that because erotic passions cannot be calculated and thus rationalized, the tension that exists between the spheres of religion and eroticism is profound in modern life. Originally, sex and religion shared an intimate relationship due to the ideals and rituals surrounding magic orgiasticism, in which "every ecstasy was considered holy."[19] According to Weber, a tension between religion and sex arrived with the "cultic chastity of priests."[20] Priests renounced sex as a sign of their ability to resist temptation by the devil. Hence, the passionate nature of eroticism came to be viewed as inherently nonrational and therefore as something that must be denied. Within Weber's treatment of religion and rationalization one finds a self-controlled and self-regulated modern body.

Unlike Marx and Weber, Emile Durkheim's treatment of the body encompasses debates over mind/body dualism and the relationship between individuals and social structure. Much as in his dichotomous self-society and profane-sacred conceptualizations, the individual body is treated as secondary to the social body. For example, in *The Elementary Forms of Religious Life,* Durkheim asserts that the soul (sacred) is always opposed to the body (profane). Society necessitates that we sacrifice our embodied selves for the greater good of the collective. Durkheim contends that "our nature is double" as "there truly is a parcel of divinity within us, because there is a parcel of the grand ideas that are the soul of collectivity."[21] It is society, not the body, that gives us life and humanity. Durkheim's lack of concern with corporeality is further evidenced in *Suicide*. Suicide, the ultimate catastrophic embodied act, is reduced to statistical categories of gender, race, and age. Here Durkheim's primary focus is on the relationship between society and its subjective effects on individuals. Suicide, the death of the body, becomes entirely disembodied. In Durkheim's work the body is sacrificed for, and subsumed within, the social landscape.

Like Durkheim, George Herbert Mead also neglects to seriously consider embodiment, instead focusing on the relationship between self and society. In *Mind, Self, and Society*, Mead theorizes society as a dynamic process between individual actors and the social world. Although explicit recognition of embodiment is absent, Mead offers an important conceptualization of self (and how it develops from childhood to adulthood). The self consists of two aspects, or what Mead calls "distinguishable phases"— the "I" and the "me."[22] The "I" is the spontaneous, uncalculated self and the "me" is the part of us that has internalized society's norms and structures. When a person says to herself, "I can't believe I did that last night," the "me" is reflecting back on the transgressions of the "I." These two aspects of the self arise in social interaction. For Mead, the self is ultimately a social construct rather than a biological entity or a derivative of the soul.

These early nineteenth- and twentieth-century sociological theories demonstrate how the body was sometimes hidden in plain sight. The tangible flesh and blood subject was symbolically covered by economics, religious ideology, statistical analysis, and societal concerns, and, in some cases, was completely absent. As will become evident in the next section, the body became increasingly important in theoretical analyses, occupying a key role in some of the most influential works of the mid- to late-twentieth century.

Socially Constructed and Civilized Bodies: Class, Power, and Control

The writings in this section cover a broad range of topics; sexuality, consumption, bodily control, institutionalization, and even table manners. However, these theories have a common thread. They show how social structures can, to greater and lesser degrees, shape the way bodies look, feel, and are expected to act. Whether the setting is an insane asylum or a medieval dining table, it is apparent that since early human history all bodies have been subject to powerful discourses and knowledges, both in formal institutional settings or within the familiar landscapes of everyday life.

In *Distinction: A Social Critique of the Judgement of Taste*, sociologist Pierre Bourdieu posits that the body is a conveyor of symbolic value that reproduces "the universe of the social structure."[23] Although *Distinction* is not explicitly about bodies, it takes the body seriously as bearer of social values and was one of the first major sociological works to emphasize the growing importance of the body in the late twentieth century. Bourdieu places bodies within modern stratified consumer culture, arguing that the body bears the imprint of social class based on habitus, taste, and social location. According to Bourdieu, "the body is the most indisputable materialization of class taste" in that one's hairstyle, clothing, diet, and even gait function as signs within a larger system of social positions.[24] Bourdieu acknowledges that bodies are biological, yet stresses that they are inherently unfinished, becoming transformed (imbued with marks of social class) within society. Arguably, Bourdieu's most significant contribution to body theory is his conception of the body as a form of physical capital. As such, the body is a resource to greater or lesser degrees, and can be converted into economic, cultural, and social capital.

While Bourdieu approaches the body through a lens of culture and class, French social constructionist Michel Foucault underscores the notion of social power in a different way. Foucault asserts that the body is "directly involved in a political field: power relations have an immediate hold upon it; they invest it, mark it, train it, torture it, force it to carry out tasks, to perform ceremonies, to emit signs."[25] In essence, the Foucauldian body is a creation of culture and is modified as it is governed by various forms of power and manufactured through discourse.

In *Discipline and Punish*, Foucault outlines how a "history of bodies" is subjected to disciplinary systems that produced "docile" subjects. Using historical comparative analysis, Foucault illustrates how the body changed as a target of discourse. For example, in the sixteenth and seventeenth centuries, punishment was a public and physical spectacle that relied upon burning, ripping, and mutilation of the flesh—acts that reinforced institutional authority and power. However, by the beginning of the nineteenth century, "the old partners of the spectacle . . . the body and the blood, gave way" to the penitentiary system.[26] Foucault argues that the development of prisons ushered in control not only of the bodies but, more importantly, of the minds and "souls" of criminals. Thus, as new sources of institutional knowledge and power emerged to constrain subjects, discourses shifted in focus from the body to the mind.

Similarly, in *The History of Sexuality*, Foucault traces the way Christian confession as a discursive ritual shifted in focus from the sexual activities of individuals to their intentions. Foucault asserts that sexuality is not a "stubborn drive" but an "especially dense transfer point for relations of power."[27] The sexual body is not a biological body but rather a product of a complicated network of social control. Foucault posits that four strategic sexually based categorizations emerged in the nineteenth century as foundations for knowledge and discourse: the hysterization of female bodies, the pedagogization of children's sex, a socialization of procreative behavior, and a psychiatrization of perverse pleasure. From these designs sprung the archetypal nervous woman, masturbating child, Malthusian couple, and perverse adult, all of whom are products of discursive strategies that utilize the sexuality of women, men, and children. After appropriately being typed and classified, the Foucauldian body is governed by experts—psychiatrists, gynecologists, educators, therapists, and social scientists—who serve to reinforce institutions of power.

Even though Foucault recognizes the malleability of the body, he never acknowl-edges the way individuals create or change discourse/culture. As sociologist Bryan Turner (1984) asserts, if we are determined by what we are permitted to know, then there is no theoretical space for human resistance to discourse. Another limitation of Foucault's theoretical treatise is that his bodies are disembodied. Simply put, the bio-logical or material dimension of the body is suspended in discussions of discursive power. Although he explains how the target of discourse shifted from the corporeal body to the mindful body, he fails to acknowledge the obvious relationship between the two, that is, that the mind resides inside the body. The subjectivity of life inside the body—the personal, the particular, and the idiosyncratic dimension that each of us experience in our everyday lives—is missing here. Notwithstanding, Foucault's work is invaluable to the field because of its persuasive analysis of the way culture (power/discourse) constrains and invests human bodies. His enormous contribution is evidenced by his influence on many authors, such as historian Thomas Laqueur (1990), sociologist Barbara Duden (1993), anthropologist Emily Martin (1989, 1994), and countless others. In particular, Foucault's work points out the surveillance bod-ies experience in mundane ways, and the conceptual utility of the normalizing gaze. For example, feminist Susan Bordo (1993) uses a genealogical approach to explore the creation of docile female bodies, exposing the medical labels and social discourses that create the image of woman.

Like Foucault, American sociologist Erving Goffman also examines the body in terms of social structures and ideologies that are external to the body. However, even though he focuses on the way bodies are socially constrained, Goffman views the body as something that individuals have some control over to varying degrees. Goffman ac-knowledges the agentic quality that humans possess in terms of attempting to manage and control their bodies in different social contexts, from eating in a restaurant to go-ing to the doctor's office. Unlike Foucault, Goffman assigns significance to embodied subjective experience. Our ability to interact in society and to achieve desired out-comes within specific social contexts depends upon the management of our bodies.

One of the central themes threading through Goffman's work is his treatment of bodily control and appearance as a central component in mundane everyday encoun-ters among people. In *The Presentation of Self* (1959) Goffman uses a theatrical anal-ogy to describe how self-controlled individuals attempt to follow cultural scripts that dictate appropriate behaviors in the presence of other people. According to Goffman, any successful social "performance" hinges on expressive control to keep inconsis-tent moods and signs from disrupting it. In order to achieve a semblance of reality or authenticity one must master the art of "impression management," a highly nu-anced technique of constant reflexive self-examination (this involves both mind and body). Goffman asserts that "the impression of reality fostered by a performance is a delicate, fragile thing that can be shattered by very minor mishaps" such as a belch, a stutter, or flatulence.[28] In order to prevent embarrassment and disruption in social in-teraction we must learn to manage our body, including its demeanor, noises, smells, and facial expressions. Any agency in Goffman's theory is based on how we choose to act within different circumstances. Yet, it is important to note that all of the scripts that constitute a successful social performance, as it were, stem from an internalization of social texts. If we fail to keep our bodies in check, we risk public embarrassment and social stigmatization. Thus, ultimately Goffman presents the body as socially constructed.

In addition to mundane contexts, Goffman also examines the role of the body in institutional environments. *Asylums* (1961) chronicles the way in which prisoners' and psychiatric patients' bodies are reconstructed and often mistreated during the institutionalizing process as part of destroying or degrading self-worth and self-autonomy. For example, upon entering an institution the individual is stripped of his or her "identity kit"— clothing, combs, hair products, accessories, and other items that differentiate a person as unique. As a result, the individual suffers a "personal defacement."[29] Goffman asserts that the self (preinstitutional) is often whittled away through defilement of the body. *Asylums* is a notable early contribution to body theory because it makes an explicit connection between the way changes in the body relate to changes in self within extreme institutional contexts.

Much akin to *Asylums*, *Stigma* (1963) examines the way we categorize others during social interaction by assessing attributes that may be read as "discrediting." Within *Stigma* is the implicit idea that everyone has at one time felt stigmatized in the presence of others. There are three different types of stigma: physical deformities or "abominations of the body," negative character traits such as "weak will" or "dishonesty," and "tribal" characteristics such as "race, nation and religion."[30] As opposed to "normals," stigmatized persons face discrimination and reduced life chances. Here Goffman focuses specifically on the moment when a stigmatized person and a "normal" are brought together within social situations. Because of the known stereotypes, both parties feel extremely apprehensive when faced with each other and often try to avoid, rather than manage, these interactions. Although Goffman is concerned with both stigmas of the body (such as blindness and scars) and stigma resulting from behaviors and actions (like being institutionalized or unemployed), he observes that the "social information" that each of us carries is embodied.

One of the most convincing social constructionist theories of the body is found within Norbert Elias's *Civilizing Process*. By tracing historical documents describing manners and etiquette, Elias identifies the processes that facilitated the emergence of the modern self within a civilized (controlled) body and the way this development relates to state formation. While the human body is not the principal focus of Elias's theory of the civilizing process, it does play a significant role. *The Civilizing Process* is particularly important within the field of body theory because it merges Foucault's historical and structural approach with Goffman's primarily micro or interactionist perspective. Elias demonstrates that different modes of behavior such as bodily carriage, bodily functions, and table manners change as part of an ongoing interactive process between individuals and larger structural formation. Elias adroitly illustrates the mind/body/society relationship by employing a microsociological, macrosociological, and historical lens.

According to Elias, from about the Renaissance onward "civilizational self-controls" became internalized, causing people to notice not only themselves but also others.

Civilité is dependent upon seeing and being seen by others and behaving properly in social situations. *The Civilizing Process* reveals that socially acceptable behavior is connected to social structure and the emergence of a self-controlled individual. Manners and bodily etiquette originated from the upper social strata, eventually filtering down to the daily interactions of people from all social classes. Elias shows how social control was mild in courtly medieval society as compared with later eras. For example, courtly table etiquette dictated that people could spit while eating (being sure to refrain from spitting across the table) and could eat from others' plates as long as they refrained from "falling on the dish like a pig, and from dripping bitten food into the communal space."[31] Centuries later, table manner etiquette changed rather significantly, as social controls became more exacting for the individual within public space. The civilized body is physically separate from others ("my" space), self-reflective, controlled, and aware of the way it must behave in any given social context—in both public and private realms.

Goffman's dramaturgical body and Elias's civil body are comparable in that they examine the way individuals must conform to modes of socially acceptable behavior or risk public (and private) embarrassment and shame. In everyday life and civil society it is necessary to monitor one's self and body, as well as the bodies of others. A main link between Goffman and Elias is an interest in examining how the body is controlled—both individually and socially. However, Elias's and Goffman's theories are also quite different in a number of ways. Most obviously, Elias's scope (breadth and depth) and methodological framework are more sophisticated than Goffman's, and it is also important to distinguish that Elias carefully considers the biological component of embodiment, which Goffman treats only peripherally. The evolution of human history and the process of "civilizing" the body contain at their core the unequivocal interdependence between the biological and the social.

Body Projects and Consumer Culture

Recent scholarship seeks not only to bring the body back "in" to social and cultural studies, as it were, but also to place the body within the context of contemporary society or what sociologist Anthony Giddens refers to as "late modern culture." Much of this work is in conversation with postmodern debates focusing on a variety of subjects, from the propensity to question scientific facts, experts, and the grand narrative (Lyotard 1984) to the proliferation of imagery and simulations (Baudrillard 1994) in contemporary culture.

In *Modernity and Self-Identity* Giddens argues that the complex and ambiguous characteristics of late modernity (erosion of science, changes in the family, occupation, etc.) have led to an increase in individual reflexivity and new problems with attributing meaning to one's life. In this context, Giddens contends that the body as an "action system" within everyday life has become an increasingly essential part of sustaining a consistent sense of self-identity.[32] Because contemporary individuals cannot rely on traditional institutional moorings (marriage) or roles (wife) to ground the self, we focus on what we know best—the body. As the self is embodied, "the reflexivity of the self extends to the body."[33] Giddens maintains that the contemporary reflexive body-self is continually worked on through diet, exercise regimes, implants, and so on. We can see evidence of these practices and routines in the cases of "man-scaping" and "extreme" body modification (Immergut, Kosut, this volume.)

Notwithstanding, Giddens's theory of a reflexive body/self has some limitations. Although Giddens attempts to link the self with the body, "it is the unconscious that receives more play than embodiment."[34] Furthermore, Giddens maintains that the body is an "action system" and a "mode of praxis" but does not adequately address the everyday experiential aspect of embodiment (life in the body). However, Giddens's work is still useful in that it provides a conceptual framework for beginning to think about contemporary bodies and whether or not the body is somehow experienced in a significantly different way than in previous historical periods. Giddens's theory raises a number of questions and ultimately creates a conceptual space for us to think in new ways about whether or not there is such an entity as a uniquely late-modern body. And if so, how do we begin to theorize it?

Much in the same vein as Giddens, sociologist Mike Featherstone also regards the emphasis on the self-body's surface as a phenomenon particular to contemporary society. However, Featherstone examines the overly surface-oriented body within the framework of consumer culture. He argues that the proliferation of stylized (idealized) images of the body via the media (advertisements, fashion magazines, popular film, television) constantly and relentlessly inundate individuals like never before. This process reinforces the ideology that if the body is maintained cosmetically, it will reap a number of rewards such as thinness, beauty, increased sexual potency, and overall healthiness. Unlike Weberian asceticism's ultimate eternal reward (heaven), the reward for consumeristic asceticism "ceases to be spiritual salvation or even improved health, but becomes an enhanced appearance and more marketable self."[35] Discipline and hedonistic pleasure are not antithetical; the subjugation of the body (through diet, exercise, and other health regimes) is necessary if one is to obtain "the look" that can guarantee a sexy, exciting, leisure-filled life.

Featherstone acknowledges that body maintenance regimes are not unique to contemporary Western culture; however, what is divergent is the propensity to view the body as a machinelike product. He argues that we are maintaining our bodies much in the same way as we maintain our cars. The goods we consume affect the way we think and act and this extends to the treatment of the body. Just as one would want to extend the life of one's car by waxing and polishing, changing the oil, and so on, so too do bodies "require servicing, regular care and attention to preserve maximum efficiency."[36] While Featherstone's neo-Weberian theory is creative and sophisticated—establishing a relationship among production, consumption, belief systems, and the body—he leaves very little space for human agency. It is also important to take seriously the way the dimension of social class affects the consumeristic body. Shiatsu, nail polish, herbal remedies, plastic surgery, and thigh masters are products and services that require discretionary income. The consumer body's success hinges upon its economic resources and presupposes the availability of choice.

The development of contemporary body theory requires an inherent task—seriously engaging the concepts of consumerism, globalization, and global culture. The advent of electronic media, the expansion of the tourist industry, and global migration have significantly changed the way we think about culture in general and thus will have some direct or indirect influence on the way we think about our bodies. For example, research on the modern primitive body modification movement provides us with an example of the way some contemporary Americans are appropriating ancient non-Western rituals, practices, and ideologies centered on the body.[37] Increasingly, we are witnessing hybrid "globalized" bodies on the horizon.

Challenging the "Natural" Body: Feminist Contributions

When asked about the inequities between men and women with respect to social power, we have often heard our students say, their voices exasperated, "women's and men's bodies are just different." These presumed differences are presented as evidence for why our culture is organized in certain ways. Importantly, feminist scholars of the body have worked to reveal how these "self-evident" differences are actually culturally produced. Certain bodies survive and thrive according to economic resources and social power. For example, men's bodies are at risk of military, athletic, and industrial exploitation and, for disadvantaged men, imprisonment, while women's bodies are controlled by institutions dominated by men, namely, medicine and religion.

Through the discourse of science and medicine these differences are recast as natural, physical, universal, transhistorical, and permanent truths. It is commonly understood in tautological fashion that men's and women's bodies are different because they were born that way. Feminist activism and scholarship have increased awareness of the way bodies are gendered by making visible the cultural and social dynamics that produce difference and dominance out of the flesh of male and female bodies. However, before discussing feminist critiques and contributions, it is important to discuss naturalistic approaches to the body.

In general, naturalistic approaches to the body hold that humans are constrained and/or enabled by their birth-given characteristics (sex, skin color, height, etc.). Correspondingly, social relationships, institutions, and the ideologies that support them are founded to some degree upon the biological body. Naturalistic approaches to the body have produced a highly polemicized field of work, particularly revolving around the sociology of gender and the basis for women's inequality (and social stratification in general). Some of the earliest and most controversial work in this vein emanated out of sociobiology in the 1970s, particularly the work of Harvard sociobiologist Edward O. Wilson, who received praise and publicity for his work on genetic evolution and social behavior.

According to Wilson (1975, 1978), human behavior is explained by and encoded within the gene. Wilson attempted (many argue unsuccessfully) to link genetic structures in animals to those in humans to establish a biological basis for human behavior. For example, in *Sociobiology: The New Synthesis* (1975), Wilson deduces that slavery is part of the natural evolutionary order because there is a species of "slavemaking" ants that use "propaganda substances" and "engineering rules."[38] He conveniently ignores the reality that slavery is fundamentally an economic relationship. Wilson (1978) also professes that homosexuality is genetic (because it is common among animal species) and that racial differences have a biological basis. The insupportable but extraordinarily recalcitrant search for the "race" gene or the "gay" gene persists to this day. Of course, one of the major problems with Wilson's biological reductionist argument is the notion that evolution is synonymous with improvement and progression. His theories begin from within mainstream contemporary American society—racist, homophobic, patriarchal, ethnocentric—and serve to justify and maintain the status quo (social inequality).

Sociobiology developed simultaneously with the rise of the women's movement, particularly radical feminism. Not surprisingly, Wilson maintains that women's social subordination was natural because "women as a group were less assertive and physically aggressive" due to their genetic makeup.[39] Sociobiology quickly became a useful way to undermine the increase in feminist discourse and the call for gender inequality in both lay and academic communities. Nonetheless, other social theorists have attributed female inequality to biology, as in the case of Parson's AGIL system (1964), which posits women (expressive role) as different than men (instrumental role) due to their child-bearing capacity. For Parsons, woman is an inherently natural creature (best suited for reproductive work), while man, the more cultured being, belongs in the public sphere (the world of production). He further maintains that female discrimination in the workplace is functional to society because occupational equality was "incompatible with any positive solidarity in the family."[40] For Wilson and Parsons the "woman question" is conveniently answered in one word—biology.

Like functional and neo–social Darwinist theories, some early feminist theory also prioritized corporeal analyses in explanations of patriarchy and women's position in society (see Rich [1976] and Chodorow [1978] for two distinctive approaches that consider reproduction and reproductive work, i.e., mothering). Radical feminist Shulamith Firestone's *Dialectic of Sex* (1970) serves as a prime example of feminist biological reductionism. While Firestone recognizes that social institutions assist in maintaining patriarchy, ultimately the foundations of male dominance reside in women's reproductive capabilities. Both functionalist and feminist arguments that emphasize biology are highly problematic as the social construction of gender is typically neglected or absent altogether.

A notable and useful work on body and biology within the sex/gender debate is Thomas Laqueur's *Making Sex* (1990), a historical account of the medical, political, and cultural construction of sex from ancient Greece to the Enlightenment. Unlike the above arguments that place gender differences as a result of biology (sex), Laqueur traces the way medical knowledge and common understandings of sex and sexuality were based on cultural discourse rather than biology. To simplify, he illustrates how our biology was, and continues to be, culturally determined. According to Laqueur, the corporeal body (visible flesh and blood) cannot be regarded as the "real" foundation for cultural claims about sex and gender. This assertion is evidenced in the rather extraordinary one-sex model of the body that held sway as a biological given until the end of the seventeenth century. Galen's "mole model or unborn penis model" stated the "obvious," that women had an unborn penis inside their bodies, thus proving biologically women's lesser perfection. His work reminds us that our duty as social scientists and historians is to understand how the "real" (biology) is only an expression of other, more pervasive, culturally constructed truths.

While Laqueur elucidates the way past scientific truths are infused with cultural assumptions, others have explored the way *current* scientific ideas regarding biology are culturally constructed and exist in a historical continuum. Sociologist Barbara Duden's *Disembodying Women* (1993) examines the historical process in which pregnancy has been transformed from a personal experience—between woman and child/fetus—to an impersonal and even public concern via technological advancements in medicine and shifts in discourses. Ethical and religious arguments surrounding the abortion debate, and more recently governmental policy that protects a "life" or pro-tolife such as a stem cell, are evidence that women have been erased (or temporarily negated) from the experience of pregnancy (Rothman, this volume).

Within feminism, there is a long history of examining women's social location in stratified societies through examining their bodies. Early 1970s feminist theorists such as Gayle Rubin, Shulamith Firestone, and Adrienne Rich prioritized the corporeal in their explanations of patriarchy and the subjugation of women, seen as accomplished specifically through reproduction and reproductive work. Beginning with reproduction, and then subsequently through the menstrual cycle and menopause, feminists have insisted that bodies matter in all aspects of social analysis. Embodied dynamics of gender, race, class, and ability imbue the questions of who is encouraged to procreate and who is prevented, and what types of human bodies should be born. Of course, feminist work is also not solely relegated to examining female bodies. One of the paradoxical effects of male domination is that even though most men have dominance over most women, men are not a monolithic group. The ranking of culturally desirable male bodies, based on form and function, often mirrors their social standing.[41]

The self-help women's-health movement especially challenged predominant biomedical ways of constructing bodies.[42] As both consumers and scholars, many women rebelled against the hegemonic medical establishment's strategies of medicalization and mystification of female bodily functions. These challenges to "thinking as usual" within medical settings encouraged many women to wage feminist critiques against the standardization of male bodies as the model for individualism and better health. During the 1970s, *Our Bodies, Ourselves* and *A New View of a Women's Body* emerged as owners' manuals to women's bodies. As Moira Gatens (1996) argues, women are often forced to "elide" or suppress their own "corporeal specificity" to participate in liberal democracies.

Psychoanalyst and literary critic Julia Kristeva (1982) theorized an abject embodiment, referring to the point at which physical boundaries erode and the self must deal with a body that leaks unsightly fluids like blood and puss, betraying social norms and biological givens in the process. More recently, feminist postmodern theorists such as

Judith Butler (1990, 1993), Elizabeth Grosz (1994, 1995), and Donna Haraway (1991) have challenged binary sex/gender distinctions, championed queerness, and proposed a cyborg body that transcends materiality. While this feminist scholarship does not emanate from within the discipline of sociology, a critical sociology of the body acknowledges, draws from, and may seek to expand upon this ground-breaking work. Therefore any serious social and cultural scholarship on the "body" must consider the interdisciplinary contributions of certain feminists. Feminism thrust the body into focus, calling attention to its simultaneously political, biological, and cultural dimensions.

Anthropology, Phenomenology, and Cartesian Dualism

Since its beginning, the field of anthropology has generally been more observant of the body as compared with classical sociological traditions. This may in part be attributed to the anthropological focus on material culture as an object of study in its own right, as well as the employment of qualitative methods and methodology. Ethnographic fieldwork by nature presumes a degree of bodily engagement on two basic levels, primarily through the obvious interaction of a researcher and those she is studying (an exchange of and between bodies) but also in the sense that a researcher's body can be understood as a medium of data collection itself. Interactive ethnographic engagement, or what is referred to as "participant-observation," requires engagement of all of the senses. For example, listening carefully to the sounds of a particular instrument used in a ritual or discerning a difference between local dialects is by definition *embodied* fieldwork. To hear, taste, smell, and feel the tactile, material world is to experience and participate in the creating of culture. As anthropologist Thomas Csordas argues, "embodied experience is the starting point for analyzing human participation in a cultural world."[43]

Issues of embodiment have long been the staple of examining aspects of culture such as the social management of human waste, religious rituals, birth, death, nutrition, sex, and illness. Anthropologist Marcel Mauss (1935) was one of the first social scientists to stress that ordinary bodily actions—walking, running, throwing, eating—are not simply mechanical and universal in nature and should be assiduously studied and observed as "body techniques" or cultured acts that are performed by a bio-physical actor. He called attention to the fact that bodily dispositions and performances vary across both societies and generations. For Mauss, the "art of using the human body" is reflected by cultural context, even in a physical activity as mundane as swimming or chewing.

While Mauss argued that bodily techniques were culturally defined, anthropologist Mary Douglas (1970) focused on the way actions and activities deemed to be "natural" are reflections of two bodies, a bio-individual body and the social body. She asserts that the way people choose to modify their bodies can tell us about their social status and also their regard for social boundaries and control. In *Purity and Danger* (1966), Douglas directly links the body and society together in a discussion of the human propensity to maintain bodily boundaries in times of crisis and threat. Douglas argues that "we cannot possibly interpret rituals concerning (the body) . . . unless we are prepared to see the body as a symbol of society, and to see the powers and dangers credited to social structure reproduced in small on the human body."[44] In other words, the body is an obvious and readily available sign of the social system. Douglas conceptualizes the body as "a complex structure," a metaphor for society as a whole. Viewing the body as social metaphor is reminiscent of anthropologist Clifford Geertz's (1973) analysis of the Balinese cockfight as a ritual that orders, reinforces, and gives meaning to both individual social relationships and society at large. Just as the cockfight says something about society, Douglas maintains that so too does the body.

Anthropological approaches have clearly influenced the way contemporary theorists from across disciplines envision what the body is in the most abstract sense. More recent scholarship in the subfield of medical anthropology in particular has further uncovered the complex relationship between the material and the social body, moving beyond simplistic dualisms. Notably, in "The Mindful Body," anthropologists Nancy Scheper-Hughes and Margaret Lock assert that the body is "simultaneously a physical and symbolic artifact that is both naturally and culturally produced, and is securely anchored in a particular historical moment."[45] They critique the field of anthropology and the Western tradition of favoring Cartesian dualism. Based on the philosophical writings of Rene Descartes (1596–1650), Cartesian dualism refers to the radical distinction made between the mind and the body in social and philosophical inquiry. In particular, proponents of this perspective have tended to privilege and highlight mental processes, the self, and the soul as being paramount to human existence. The physical body is in effect conceptually dislodged from the mind, as if the self or the soul could exist on its own—hence this advanced the idea that the mind and body are distinct entities that should be examined as such. This binary perspective of viewing the body and mind as separate has been challenged in academia, and in the field of medicine as well (Frank, this volume). For example, it is common within the mainstream medical community to speak of curing the whole person, referring to the patient's attitude or outlook as being connected to recovery and wellness.

Medical anthropologist Emily Martin moves beyond the pitfalls of both nature/culture and mind/body dualisms in her empirically based studies of the body. Her ground-breaking *The Woman in the Body* (1987) tracks the history of menstruation, menopause, and birth (from ancient Greece to late modernity), focusing on the way expert and everyday epistemological shifts correspond with dominant forms of societal organization—from medical institutions to globalization. Martin continues these ideas in *Flexible Bodies* (1994) by examining how contemporary bodies have become increasingly medicalized. Specifically, Martin traces the way the emergence of the immune system, its "discovery" by medical experts, and its subsequent ubiquity in popular media (fueled by the AIDS epidemic) signaled a focus upon the interior of the body. She argues that an epistemological shift from the exterior to the interior of the body ultimately empowers science and medical institutions as we have less ability to control what we cannot see. She adeptly captures lived embodied experiences and links them to changes in society, from the way we approach relationships and our jobs to the way we handle illness. Martin's creative and sophisticated approach untangles the biological, the cultural, and the subjective elements of embodiment. The inclusion of subjective embodied experience or, simply, the way people themselves understand their bodies from the inside out, enables us to see the body from beyond the rubrics of nature/culture or mind/body.

French philosopher Maurice Merleau-Ponty (1962) has been particularly influential in challenging the dualistic legacy of Cartesian thought. His phenomenological analysis of perception—how we become aware of the sensory world around us—rejects the subject-object division between mind and body and the notion that the mind is the locus of subjectivity. Merleau-Ponty asserts that perception is inherently carnal and stems from an openness to the world. In other words, when our mind perceives (observes, identifies), it does so through a practical and sensual embodied location within the social realm. A practical understanding of the body accounts for a fuller understanding of the way culture, customs, norms, and routines materialize through lived experience.

Merleau-Ponty's phenomenological body is helpful in understanding the difference between studying the body as an object and the idea of *embodiment*, which refers to a perceptive way of knowing and experiencing the world through our own bodies. As embodied individuals, we all hold incarnate knowledge (Pine, this volume). For example, a professional guitar player may understand music theory, but through years of practice, her hands and fingers physically know how to achieve a particular sound by moving in a precise way. Even mundane activities such as text messaging or driving a car involve the collection of incarnate knowledge. Once we learn to text or drive *through our bodies*, we are able to "do it without thinking." This is because our body literally understands what to do. Incarnate knowledge moves beyond speaking *of* the physicality of bodies, instead speaking from *within* a body that is somatically perceptive.

NOTES

1. Frank, *The Wounded Storyteller*, p. 27.
2. Williams and Bendelow, *The Lived Body*, p. 3.
3. See Witz, "Whose Body Matters?"
4. Turner, *The Body and Society* and "The Possibility of Primitiveness."
5. See Haraway, *Simians, Cyborgs, and Women*; and Hayles, *How We Became Posthuman*.
6. See Nowak and Rauh, "The Influence of the Avatar on Online Perceptions."
7. Russell, *Beyond Ramps*, p. 15.
8. See, for example, Garland-Thomson, *Extraordinary Bodies*; Davis, *The Disability Studies Reader*; and McRuer, *Crip Theory*.
9. Pitts-Taylor, *Surgery Junkies*.
10. See, for example, Kessler, "The Medical Construction of Gender"; and Moore and Clarke, "Clitorial Conventions and Transgressions."
11. See, for example, Tuana, "Coming to Understand"; and Loe, *The Rise of Viagra*.
12. See, for example, Cohen, "The Other Kidney"; Scheper-Hughes, "Commodity Fetishism in Organ Trafficking"; and Tober, "Kidneys and Controversies in the Islamic Republic of Iran."
13. Ehrenreich and Hochschild, eds., *Global Woman*.
14. Willis, *Learning to Labour*.

15. Wacquant, *Body and Soul.*
16. Wolff, *The Sociology of Georg Simmel*, p. 339.
17. Tucker, *The Marx-Engels Reader*, p. 479.
18. Weber, *The Protestant Ethic and the Spirit of Capitalism*, p. 158.
19. Gerth and Mills, *From Max Weber: Essays in Sociology*, p. 343.
20. Gerth and Mills, p. 344.
21. Durkheim, *The Elementary Forms of Religious Life*, p. 267.
22. Mead, *Mind, Self, and Society*, p. 178.
23. Bourdieu, *Distinction*, p. 193.
24. Bourdieu, p. 190.
25. Foucault, *Discipline and Punish: The Birth of the Prison*, p. 25.
26. Foucault, p. 16.
27. Foucault, *The History of Sexuality: An Introduction*, p. 103.
28. Goffman, *The Presentation of Self in Everyday Life*, p. 56.
29. Goffman, *Asylums*, pp. 20–21.
30. Goffman, *Stigma*, p. 4.
31. Elias, *The Civilizing Process*, p. 87.
32. Giddens, *Modernity and Self-Identity*, p. 99.
33. Giddens, p. 77.
34. Frank, "For a Sociology of the Body," p. 36.
35. Featherstone, *Consumer Culture and Postmodernism*, p. 171.
36. Featherstone, p. 182.
37. See, for example, Kleese, "Modern Primitivism."
38. Wilson, *Sociobiology: The New Synthesis*, p. 370.
39. Wilson, p. 128.
40. Parsons, *Essays in Sociological Theory*, p. 852.
41. See, for example, Kimmel, *Manhood in America*; and Klein, *Little Big Men.*
42. See, for example, Ruzek, *The Women's Health Movement*; and Lewin and Olesen, *Women, Health, and Healing.*
43. Csordas, "Somatic Modes of Attention," p. 135.
44. Douglas, *Purity and Danger*, p. 116.
45. Scheper-Hughes and Lock, "The Mindful Body," p. 6.

REFERENCES

Appadurai, Arjun. 1996. *Modernity at Large: Cultural Dimensions of Globalization.* Minneapolis: University of Minnesota Press.

Balsamo, Anne. 1995. "Forms of Technological Embodiment: Reading the Body in Contemporary Culture." In *Cyberspace/Cyberbodies/Cyberpunk: Cultures of Technological Embodiment*, edited by M. Featherstone and R. Burrows, 215–37. Thousand Oaks, CA: Sage.

Baudrillard, Jean. 1994. *Simulacra and Simulation.* Ann Arbor: University of Michigan Press.

Beauvoir, Simone de. 1972. *The Second Sex.* Harmondsworth, England: Penquin.

Biocca, Frank. 1997. "The Cyborg's Dilemma: Progressive Embodiment in Virtual Environments." *Journal of Computer-Mediated Communication*, 3(2). Retrieved October 18, 2008, from http://www.ascusc.org/jcmc/vol3/issue2/biocca2.html.

Bordo, Susan. 1993. *Unbearable weight: Feminism, Western Culture, and the Body.* Berkeley: University of California Press.

Bourdieu, Pierre. 1984. *Distinction: A Social Critique of the Judgement of Taste.* London: Routledge.

Bourgois, Phillipe. 1995. *In Search of Respect: Selling Crack in El Barrio.* Cambridge, England: Cambridge University Press.

Bruner, Ed. 1996. "Tourism in the Balinese Borderzone." In *Displacement, Diaspora, and Geographies of Identity*, edited by S. Lavie and T. Swedenberg. Durham, NC: Duke University Press.

Butler, Judith. 1990. *Gender Trouble: Feminism and the Subversion of Identity.* New York: Routledge.

———. 1993. *Bodies That Matter: On the Discursive Limits of "Sex."* New York: Routledge.

Casper, Monica J., and Lisa Jean Moore. 2009. *Missing Bodies: The Politics of Visibility.* New York: NYU Press.

Chodorow, Nancy. 1978. *The Reproduction of Mothering.* Berkeley: University of California Press.

Cohen, Lawrence. 2002. "The Other Kidney: Biopolitics beyond Recognition." In *Commodifying Bodies,* edited by L. Wacquant and N. Scheper-Hughes, 9–30. Thousand Oaks, CA: Sage.

Crossley, Nick. 1995. "Merleau-Ponty, the Elusive Body, and Carnal Sociology." *Body and Society*, 1(1): 43–63.

Csordas, Thomas. 1993. "Somatic Modes of Attention." *Cultural Anthropology*, 8 (2): 135–56.

Davis, Lennard. 2006. *The Disability Studies Reader, Second Edition.* New York: Routledge.

Douglas, Mary. 1966. *Purity and Danger: An Analysis of the Concepts of Pollution and Taboo.* London: RKP.

———. 1970. *Natural Symbols: Explorations in Cosmology.* London: Crescent.

Duden, Barbara. 1993. *Disembodying Women: Perspectives on Pregnancy and the Unborn.* Cambridge, MA: Harvard University Press.

Durkheim, Emile. 1951 (1897). *Suicide: A Study in Sociology.* New York: Free Press.

———. 1995 (1912). *The Elementary Forms of Religious Life.* New York: Free Press.

Ehrenreich, Barbara, and Arlie Hochschild, eds. 2003. *Global Woman: Nannies, Maids, and Sex Workers in the New Economy.* New York: Metropolitan Books.

Elias, Norbert. 1994. *The Civilizing Process: The History of Manners and State Formation and Civilization.* Oxford: Blackwell.

Fausto-Sterling, Anne. 1992. *Myths of Gender: Biological Theories about Men and Women.* New York: Basic Books.

Featherstone, Mike. 1982. "The Body in Consumer Culture." *Theory, Culture and Society*, 1:18–33.

———. 1991. *Consumer Culture and Postmodernism.* Thousand Oaks, CA: Sage.

Firestone, Shulamith. 1970. *The Dialectics of Sex.* London: Jonathan Cape.

Foucault, Michel. 1979. *Discipline and Punish: The Birth of the Prison.* Harmondsworth, England: Penguin.

———. 1981. *The History of Sexuality: An Introduction.* Harmondsworth: Penquin.

Frank, Arthur. 1991. "For a Sociology of the Body: An Analytical Review." In *The Body: Social Process and Cultural Theory*, edited by M. Featherstone, M. Hepworth, and B. Turner. London: Sage.

———. 1995. *The Wounded Storyteller: Body, Illness, and Ethics.* Chicago: University of Chicago Press.

Garland-Thomson, Rosemarie. 1997. *Extraordinary Bodies: Figuring Disability in American Culture and Literature.* New York: Columbia University Press.

Gatens, Moira. 1996. *Imaginary Bodies: Ethics, Power, and Corporeality*. New York: Routledge.

Geertz, Clifford. 1973. *The Interpretation of Cultures*. New York: Basic Books.

Gerth, Hans H., and C. W. Mills, eds. 1946. *From Max Weber: Essays in Sociology*. New York: Oxford University Press.

Giddens, Anthony. 1991. *Modernity and Self-Identity: Self and Society in the Late Modern Age*. Palo Alto, CA: Stanford University Press.

Gilman, Sander. 1985. *Difference and Pathology: Stereotypes of Sexuality, Race, and Madness*. Ithaca, NY: Cornell University Press.

Goffman, Erving. 1959. *The Presentation of Self in Everyday Life*. New York: Doubleday.

———. 1961. *Asylums: Essays on the Social Situations of Mental Patients and Other Inmates*. Chicago: Aldine.

———.1963. *Stigma: Notes on the Management of Spoiled Identity*. Englewood Cliffs, NJ: Prentice Hall.

Grosz, Elizabeth. 1994. *Volatile Bodies: Toward a Corporeal Feminism*. Bloomington: Indiana University Press.

———. 1995. *Space, Time, and Perversion: Essays on the Politics of Bodies*. New York: Routledge.

Haraway, Donna. 1991. *Simians, Cyborgs, and Women: The Reinvention of Nature*. New York: Routledge.

———. 1997. *Modest_Witness@Second_Millenium. FemaleMan_Meets_OncoMouse: Feminism and Technoscience*. New York: Routledge.

Hartmann, Heidi. 1976. "Capitalism, Patriarchy, and Job Segregation by Sex." *Signs: Journal of Women in Culture and Society*, 1: 137–39.

Hayles, N. Katharine. 1999. *How We Became Posthuman: Virtual Bodies in Cybernetics, Literature, and Informatics*. Chicago: University of Chicago Press.

Horne, John. 2000. "Understanding Sport and Body Culture in Japan." *Body and Society*, 6:73–86.

Hubbard, Ruth. 1990. *The Politics of Women's Biology*. New Brunswick, NJ: Rutgers University Press.

Kessler, Suzanne. 1990. "The Medical Construction of Gender: Case Management of Intersexed Infants." *Signs*, 16: 3–26.

Kimmel, Michael. 1996. *Manhood in America: A Cultural History*. New York: Free Press.

Kleese, Christian. 1999. "Modern Primitivism: Non-Mainstream Body Modification and Radicalized Representation." *Body & Society*, 5(2–3): 15–38.

Klein, Alan. 1993. *Little Big Men: Bodybuilding Subculture and Gender Construction*. Albany: State University of New York Press.

Knight, Chris. 1991. *Blood Relations: Menstruation and the Origins of Culture*. New Haven, CT: Yale University Press.

Kristeva, Julia. 1982. *Powers of Horrors: An Essay on Abjection*. New York: Columbia University Press.

Laqueur, Thomas. 1990. *Making Sex: Body and Gender from the Greeks to Freud*. Cambridge, MA: Harvard University Press.

Lewin, Ellen, and Virginia Olesen. 1985. *Women, Health, and Healing: Toward a New Perspective*. New York: Tavistock.

Loe, Meika. 2004. *The Rise of Viagra: How the Little Blue Pill Changed Sex in America*. New York: NYU Press.

Lorber, Judith, and Lisa Jean Moore. 2007. *Gender Bodies: Feminist Perspectives*. Oxford: Oxford University Press.

Lyotard, Jean-Francois. 1984. *The Postmodern Condition: A Report on Knowledge.* Minneapolis: University of Minnesota Press.

Martin, Emily. 1989. *The Woman in the Body.* Milton Keynes, England: Open University Press.

———. 1994. *Flexible Bodies: Tracking Immunity in American Culture from the Days of Polio to the Age of AIDS.* Boston: Beacon Press.

Mauss, Marcel. 1973 (1935). Techniques of the Body. *Economy & Society.* 2:70–88.

McRuer, Robert. 2006. *Crip Theory: Cultural Signs of Queerness and Disability.* New York: NYU Press.

Mead, George Herbert. 1962. *Mind, Self, and Society.* Chicago: University of Chicago Press.

Merleau-Ponty, Maurice. 2005 (1962). *Phenomenology of Perception.* London: Routledge.

Moore, Lisa Jean, and Adele E. Clarke. 1995. "Clitorial Conventions and Transgressions: Graphic Representations in Anatomy Texts, c. 1900–1991." *Feminist Studies,* 21(2): 255–301.

Nowak, Kristine L., and Christian Rauh. 2005. "The Influence of the Avatar on Online Perceptions of Anthropomorphism, Androgyny, Credibility, Homophily, and Attraction." *Journal of Computer-Mediated Communication,* 11(1), article 8. Available at http://jcmc. indiana.edu/vol11/issue1/nowak.html. Accessed August 17, 2008.

O'Neill, John. 1985. *Five Bodies: The Human Shape of Modern Society.* Ithaca, NY: Cornell University Press.

Parsons, Talcott. 1964. *Essays in Sociological Theory.* New York: Free Press.

Pitts-Taylor, Victoria. 2007. *Surgery Junkies: Wellness and Pathology in Cosmetic Culture.* New Brunswick, NJ: Rutgers University Press.

Rich, Adrienne. 1976. *Of Woman Born: Motherhood as Experience and Institution.* New York: Norton.

Rubin, Gayle. 1975. "The Traffic in Women: Notes on the 'Political Economy' of Sex." In *Toward an Anthropology of Women,* edited by Rayna R. Reiter, 157–210. New York: Monthly Reviews Press.

Russell, Marta. 1998. *Beyond Ramps: Disability at the End of the Social Contract.* Monroe, ME: Common Courage Press.

Ruzek, Sheryl. 1978. *The Women's Health Movement: Feminist Alternatives to Medical Control.* New York: Praeger.

Scheper-Hughes, Nancy. 2002 ."Commodity Fetishism in Organ Trafficking." In *Commodifying Bodies,* edited by Nancy Scheper-Hughes and Loic Wacquant, 31–62. Thousand Oaks, CA: Sage.

Scheper-Hughes, Nancy, and Margaret Lock. 1987. "The Mindful Body: A Prolegomenon to an Anthropology of the Body." *Medical Anthropology Quarterly,* 1: 6–41.

Shildrick, Margrit. 1997. *Leaky Bodies and Boundaries: Feminism, Postmodernism, and (Bio) ethics.* London: Routledge.

Shilling, Chris. 1993. *The Body and Social Theory.* 2nd ed. London: Sage.

Smith, Dorothy. 1987. *The Everyday World as Problematic: A Feminist Sociology.* Boston: Northeastern University Press.

Tober, Diane M. 2007. "Kidneys and Controversies in the Islamic Republic of Iran: The Case of Organ Sale." *Body & Society,* 13:151–70.

Tuana, Nancy. 2004. "Coming to Understand: Orgasm and the Epistemology of Ignorance." *Hypatia,* 19(1): 194–232.

Tucker, Robert, ed. 1978. *The Marx-Engels Reader.* New York: Norton.

Turner, Bryan. 1984. *The Body and Society.* Oxford: Blackwell.

———. 1999. "The Possibility of Primitiveness: Towards a Sociology of Body Marks in Cool Societies." *Body & Society*, 5(2–3): 39–50.

Van der Wijngaard, Marianne. 1997. *Reinventing the Sexes: The Biomedical Construction of Femininity and Masculinity*. Bloomington: Indiana University Press.

Wacquant, Loïc. 1995. "Pugs at Work: Bodily Capital and Bodily Labour among Professional Boxers." *Body & Society*, 1:65–93.

———. 2004. *Body and Soul: Notebooks of an Apprentice Boxer*. New York: Oxford University Press.

Weber, Max. 1992. *The Protestant Ethic and the Spirit of Capitalism*. London: Routledge.

Williams, Simon, and Gillian Bendelow. 1998. *The Lived Body: Sociological Themes, Embodied Issues*. New York: Routledge.

Willis, Paul. 1977. *Learning to Labour*. Aldershot, England: Gower Publishing.

Wilson, Edward O. 1975. *Sociobiology: The New Synthesis*. Cambridge, MA: Harvard University Press.

———. 1978. *On Human Nature*. London: Tavistock.

Witz, Anne. 2000. "Whose Body Matters? Feminist Sociology and the Corporeal Turn in Sociology and Feminism." *Body & Society*, 6:1–24.

Wolff, Kurt, ed. 1950. *The Sociology of Georg Simmel*. New York: Free Press.

||||||||||||||||||||||||||||||||||||||||||||||||||||||||||||||||||||||||||||||||

Vulnerable Bodies

Introduction to Part I

One of the supreme ironies about human bodies is that they are simultaneously powerful forces to be reckoned with, while at the same time fragile things that require constant care, maintenance, and regulation. Take, for example, the experience of athletic achievement, no matter one's ability or skill: the miraculous feeling of catching a ball with one's fingertips, the exhilaration of speeding through wind as tears stream down one's face, or the joy of propelling oneself through water. These are awesome exercises in corporeality. And so is the snap, pop, crack, or stitch that emerges and prevents our forward momentum, releasing the "oh, no" gasp all too familiar. We move from feeling infinite to being hobbled so quickly—ah, the fall from grace.

This first section of this book, "Vulnerable Bodies," attempts to straddle that space of ironic play between power and fragility. To be vulnerable is to be susceptible to attack, persuasion, or temptation. Lurking dangers expose the skin, lungs, stomach, and intestines to germs and toxins, and human and nonhuman predators threaten the once strong and hearty body. Some of us, particularly those who are younger than twenty-five, may have the sense that the intact body (a dubious claim with temporal limitations) is invulnerable. Many more of us believe or hope that this invulnerability can be achieved through consumption of certain products or through the performance of certain rituals. Medical, health, and fitness experts train us to build up our muscle mass, decrease our body mass index (BMI), lower our cholesterol, take vitamins and supplements, or seek homeopathic or allopathic treatments. We can hold off the signs of aging with wrinkle cream, we can enhance our immune system with boosters, and we can achieve peak physical performance with the aid of elixirs.

As citizens of larger social bodies (the communities and institutions our bodies populate), we are responsible for keeping our bodies functioning in the pursuit of national goals and economic agendas. One of the primary ways contemporary Western bodies are kept functioning and healthy, able to stave off vulnerability, is through processes of medicalization. Medicalization is the encroachment of medical institutions that define social life and social problems. Biomedical interpretations and meanings of social phenomena are then deemed the most legitimate, dominant, and powerful, and therefore garner the most social resources. Defining and explaining alcoholism, baldness, impotence, restless leg syndrome, hyperactivity, homosexuality, and obesity as medical problems leads to certain ways of understanding the body as an object in need of medical intervention. Sociologist Arthur Frank's excerpt from *The Wounded Storyteller* presents the consequences of bodies existing in formal, institutionalized systems of medicalization. Although the way we translate illness narratives of the body is through the discourse of pain and suffering, this very discourse cannot be easily heard by the medical industrial complexes that contain wounded bodies. Frank suggests that we consider new practices that will enable us to begin to listen to the stories of vulnerable bodies. He establishes a metanarrative of a typology of four bodies: the disciplined body, the mirroring body, the dominating body, and the communicative body. Frank concludes by imploring us to allow the communicative body to speak.

Allowing bodies to speak, however, is not as easy as one might think. Because even when they are speaking, yelling in fact, systems of medicalization have ways of silencing and stigmatizing bodies, particularly women's bodies. Vulnerable female bodies are often labeled as hysterical within medical and social contexts. Medical sociologist Barbara Katz Rothman's excerpt from *Laboring On: Birth in Transition in the United States* compares the treatment of pregnancy within the medical model and the midwifery model. Because medical models are based on the language of pathology, pregnancy and birth are perceived as health crises requiring medical management of the body. Taking us through the history of medical management of childbirth, Rothman examines the embodied differences manifested by medical intervention. The actual bodily experience of birthing a baby depends, in large part, on the ideological perspective of those aiding the pregnant woman. What might make the body vulnerable, thus, may be the very institutions that are designed to "protect" the laboring body.

Bodies might also be vulnerable because they are deemed precious for larger purposes. What we mean is that there is an investment in bodies to perform certain functions for the larger social good. For example, in the case of women's bodies, human reproduction is considered vital to the continuation of the species. Additionally, women are viewed as always, and everywhere, potentially pregnant. Notice the ubiquitous social reminders of fetal risk in warning labels on cigarettes, at bars, and on medical packaging. Prior to dental x-rays the hygienist asks female patients, of a certain age, if there is any chance they could be pregnant. Thus, not only are female bodies potentially pregnant, but they are also inherently untrustworthy. Due to technologies of seeing and testing fetuses, bodies are introduced to us through social and medical information well before these bodies are able to sustain themselves in time, space and geography. Medical sociologist Kristen Karlberg's chapter, "Am I Good Enough for my Family? Fetal Genetic Bodies and Prenatal Genetic Testing," explores the advent of new technologies that enable a more sophisticated surveillance of women's bodies. Sharing her own deeply personal reproductive narrative, Karlberg's multisited ethnography invites us into the world of prenatal genetic testing. She argues that these fetal bodies are wholly dependent on pregnant women and that the fetal body is increasingly genetized, genetization being the process by which genetic information is gleaned from body fluids to make future predictions about genetic mutations manifestations. Knowing genetic information leads women, and men, to consider what is a "good enough" fetal body to keep. These questions of worth are driven by the growth of innovative technologies that recraft the human body, or potential human body, as knowable and visible.

Bodies are also vulnerable to the physical, sexual, and emotional abuse perpetrated by other bodies. In sociologist Patricia Hill Collins's "Assume the Position: The Changing Contours of Sexual Violence," the historical legacy of sexual violence against African American women is described as institutionalized rape. When something becomes institutionalized, it becomes so embedded within the social fabric of cultural practice that it becomes part of the cultural norms. It is not necessarily seen as an outrageous act of violence against the bodily integrity of a human being, but rather as an accepted fact of daily life. Due to the attention to the public lynching of African American men, Collins argues, the institutionalized rape of African American women has been rendered invisible. While these very gendered forms of bodily punishment, discipline, and murder enable the perpetuation of systemic racism, the invisibilizing of sexual violence against African American women (and men) has consequences for the way a rape culture reverberates into all aspects of social life and diminishes the quality of life for all Black women.

Dying and dead bodies may be viewed as having surrendered, and while no longer vulnerable, are also no longer socially useful. However, as the next chapter in this section demonstrates, dead bodies may in fact just heighten the sense of vulnerability we all feel when confronting death. Just as Collins's essay is well within the realm of necropolitics, so too is science-studies scholar Gillian Haddow's essay "The Phenomenology of Death, Embodiment, and Organ Transplantation." Social theorist Achilles Mbembe uses the term "necropolitics" to mean the global expression of sovereignty in which the world is divided into those who are disposable and those who are not, those who can be wasted and those who cannot. Necropolitics provides us with structural ways to discuss death and the disposal of human bodies. In order for a body to be harvested for organs, that body must be defined as dead by those who govern decision making. Defining when someone is actually dead might not be as simple as one might think. Through a qualitative study of donor families in Scotland, Haddow establishes a theory of "disembodiment" in which the self leaves the body. This process of disembodiment and its acknowledgment by family members is a necessary step toward releasing the organs of a loved one to a transplantation team. Importantly, Haddow enables us to see how we variably value parts of the body, investing significance into specific organs. For example, human eyes are often not donated by family members, as they were seen to be related to personhood and not easy to part with in the grieving process.

Sociologists Steve Kroll-Smith and H. Hugh Floyd's excerpt from *Bodies in Protest* is about the physical and social manifestations of multiple chemical sensitivity (MCS) and environmental illness (EI). These are umbrella terms used to describe the illness experience of those who have extreme reactions to chemicals used in everyday life; these symptoms include nausea, headaches, heart palpitations, and vomiting. It is the very act of living in the social environment while being exposed to modern innovations (such as air conditioning, Xerox machines, and disinfectants) that are supposed to make life easier that, in fact, literally makes certain people sick. The very existence of MCS and EI is denied by some, as those who are afflicted report being ridiculed for claiming they are made sick by chemicals in our everyday lives. But public ridicule and disbelief do not address the fact that many individuals report embodied symptoms of illness from exposure to everyday chemicals in beauty treatments, cleaning products, and fragrances. Kroll-Smith and Floyd's work, like all the work in this section, demonstrates that vulnerability is very much about getting the larger collective conscious to see and believe your vulnerability, and understand its dire consequences as harbingers for all of us.

1

||||||||||||||||||||||||||||||||||||||||||||||||||||||||||||||||||||||||||||||

The Body's Problems with Illness

Arthur Frank

The body is not mute, but it is inarticulate; it does not use speech, yet begets it. The speech that the body begets includes illness stories; the problem of hearing these stories is to hear the body speaking in them. People telling illness stories do not simply describe their sick bodies; their bodies give their stories their particular shape and direction. People certainly talk about their bodies in illness stories; what is harder to hear in the story is the body creating the person.

Hearing the body in the speech it begets is never an easy task. Although the body has been a frequent topic of social science in recent years, no satisfactory solution has been found to avoid reducing the body to a thing that is described. Arthur and Joan Kleinman critique social science's limited concern "with *what* the body's cultural form means and *why* its representation differs in different epochs and among different people." The body becomes an object existing in different cultures, another cultural artifact to be described. Such writing ignores the complex mutual relation between the body and the culture, what the Kleinmans call infolding and outfolding.

Referring to their own field, the Kleinmans write what should become a maxim for any students of the body: "A medical anthropology unable or unwilling to examine how culture infolds into the body (and, reciprocally, how bodily processes outfold into social space) is not very likely to get far in the conceptualization and empirical study of the sociopolitical roots of illness or the cultural sources of healing."[1]

The Kleinmans' solution to this problem is to invoke the language of medical symptoms. Their empirical analysis of contemporary China uses symptoms to read how bodies have recorded the effects of half a century of trauma, from the revolutions preceding World War II through Tiananmen Square. They write: "Symptoms of social suffering, and the transformations they undergo, *are* the cultural forms of lived experience. They are lived memories. [Symptoms] bridge social institutions and the body-self" (716). Bodily symptoms are the infolding of cultural traumas into the body. As these bodies continue to live and to create history, these symptoms outfold into the social space of that history. The Kleinmans provide one of the most sophisticated analyses of the interweaving of bodies, cultures, and lives, and the limitations of their efforts to hear the body speaking reveal the dilemma that every such attempt, including my own, must struggle with.

In order to hear bodies speak, the Kleinmans have to express bodies in a language of symptoms. As descriptors of the body, the language of symptoms is not transparent; . . . it imposes its own "general unifying view" on bodies. But this language is as good as any other: the speech that the body begets *always* imposes itself on the body. The issue then becomes what language I will now impose on ill bodies, in order to understand "how bodily processes outfold" through their stories, as well as how, in these stories, "culture infolds into the body."

I begin with some basic questions about how to act as the embodied being that the Kleinmans call a "body-self." During illness, people who have always *been* bodies have distinctive problems *continuing* to be bodies, particularly continuing to be the same sorts of bodies they have been. The body's problems during illness are not new; being a body always involves certain problems. Illness requires new and more self-conscious solutions to these general problems. In earlier writing I have proposed four general problems of embodiment: control, body-relatedness, other-relatedness, and desire.[2] These problems, developed in detail in the rest of the chapter, are *general* body problems. One way or another, everyone has been resolving—if never finally "solving"—these problems throughout her life.

Each body problem is a problem of *action*: to act, a body-self must achieve some working resolution to each problem. The ways that a body-self responds to each problem are presented as a continuum or range of possible responses; thus four problems yield four continua. I emphasize that each range of possible actions, while it looks on paper like a dichotomy, is in reality a continuum of responses.

Within the matrix of these four continua, I generate four ideal typical bodies: the disciplined body, the mirroring body, the dominating body, and the communicative body. Each of these types is described in the sections that follow. The language I will use to talk about bodies thus consists of these four problems of action, the four continua of responses to these problems, and the four ideal typical bodies

This language is an imposition on bodies; real people are not ideal types. Ideal types are puppets: theoretical constructions designed to describe some empirical *tendency*.[3] Actual body-selves represent distinctive mixtures of ideal types. . . . The four ideal types of bodies prove inadequate to what is "really real" in the stories, this inadequacy is not a problem; the theory is doing what it is supposed to do. As James understood, the "really real" does not exist in order to be theorized. But theory is still useful in approaching the bewildering particularity of that really real. Ideal types provide a reflexive medium, a language, for talking about what is particular in real bodies.

Body Problems

The Problem of Control

Everyone must ask in any situation, can I reliably predict how my body will function; can I *control* its functioning?

People define themselves in terms of their body's varying capacity for control. So long as these capacities are predictable, control as an action problem does not require self-conscious monitoring. But disease itself is a loss of predictability, and it causes further losses: incontinence, shortness of breath or memory, tremors and seizures, and all the other "failures" of the sick body. Some ill people adapt to these contingencies easily; others experience a crisis of control. Illness is about learning to live with lost control.

The question of control suggests that the body is lived along a continuum from the *predictability* that may reach its highest expression in ballet and gymnastics to *contingency* at the other end. Contingency is the body's condition of being subject to forces that cannot be controlled. The infantile body is contingent: burping, spitting, and defecating according to its own internal needs and rhythms. Society expects nothing more, and infants are afforded some period to acquire control. When adult bodies lose control, they are expected to attempt to regain it if possible, and if not then at least to conceal the loss as effectively as possible.

A man described to me the social problems he experienced when he lost bladder control following surgery for prostate cancer. He was expected to conceal the contingency of his bladder; stains and smells are stigmatizing. But he also found incontinence products with him, in part, it seemed to him, because he was male (incontinence is, demographically, more a female problem) and perhaps also because he was younger than social stereotypes of incontinence allowed.

Erving Goffman's classic work on stigma shows that society demands a considerable level of body control from its members; loss of this control is stigmatizing, and special work is required to manage the lack of control.[4] Stigma, Goffman points out, is embarrassing, not just for the stigmatized person but for those who are confronted with the stigma and have to react to it. Thus the work of the stigmatized person is not only to avoid embarrassing himself by being out of control in situations where control is expected. The person must also avoid embarrassing others, who should be protected from the specter of lost body control.

Stigma imposed on the ill represents social ambivalence over what kind of contingency illness is. Parson's sick-role theory states the dominant medical ideology that persons are not responsible for being ill, but Goffman shows that they are responsible for how they present themselves and manifest the signs of their illness. While society remains ambivalent, a post-colonial affirmation of stigma has emerged. Members of Alcoholics Anonymous become less anonymous when they display bumper stickers of AA slogans. Published illness stories that reveal a variety of bodily stigmas are another affirmation of being a stigmatized body-self.[5]

Goffman defined *passing* as keeping from public view a "spoiled identity" that was otherwise invisible. When I wear the lapel pin of my own cancer support group I am

there are social standards for bodies that when one's standards divergent of these standards they are shamed for it doing a kind of reverse passing, proclaiming my identity to be spoiled even though I could easily pass. This behavior would fit the generic type "coming out," which is distinctively postmodern. But the membership pin or bumper sticker also proclaims a person who is "doing something" about a contingency that is thus defined as not entirely contingent. This "doing something" about contingency is meta-control. Turning illness into a story is a kind of meta-control, although meta-control is only one reason for storytelling.

A body's place on the continuum of control depends not only on the physiological possibility of predictability or contingency, but also on how the person chooses to interpret this physiology. The flesh cannot be denied, but bodies are more than mere corporeality. As body-selves, people interpret their bodies and make choices: the person can either seek perfected levels of predictability, at whatever cost, or can accept varying degrees of contingency. Most people do both, and strategies vary as to what is sought to be controlled, where, and how.

How any individual responds to lost predictability is woven into the dense fabric of how the other action problems of the body are managed, since the same illness provokes crises in these other dimensions as well.

Body-Relatedness[6]

Is my body the flesh that "I," the cognitive, ethereal I, only happen to inhabit, or is whatever "I" am only to be found as my body? Do I *have* a body, or *am* I a body?[7]

A friend of mine had an inflammation of lymph nodes under his arms. Physicians did not find any disease (and the years proved them correct), but they advised him to check the swelling daily for any change, tenderness, or other symptom. He told me what he disliked was "having to be embodied," which I understood to mean having to attend to his body on a daily and intimate basis, taking this body seriously as having implications for who he was. He preferred, apparently, to get his body dressed as soon as possible and then regard "it" as disappeared within his clothes. He didn't like to eat, and liquids were consumed for the pleasure of that consumption, not in recognition of the body's needs. He represents the *dissociated* end of the continuum.

I myself tend toward the opposite end, choosing to live in a body that I am compulsively *associated* with. I believe I am what I eat. I do *tai chi* exercises in order to become more aware of my body's balance and tensions. I once saw enlargements of a slide of my recently drawn blood. I think about that blood: the red cells sometimes bonding together, the white cells eating bacteria, and even the odd cancer cells, whose presence is perfectly normal. I know who I am as much in that blood as in this writing or any other activity.

But bodies are not simply associated with or dissociated from. Here as elsewhere, the continuum is not really linear; in this case the quality of association changes.

Zygmut Bauman points out a paradox of body association: the body, at least in the end that will come to us all, is the enemy of survival.[8] As long as the body is healthy and mortality is beyond the horizon of consciousness, associating the self with the body comes easily. The recognition of mortality complicates this association. Legend has it that Gautama who later became the Buddha left his palace and became an ascetic after seeing bodies that exemplified suffering, decay, and death. Until then he had been sheltered from such sights, and his association with his body was based on the illusion that bodies brought only gratification. When he learned what troubles the body is prone to, he dissociated himself from his body through asceticism.

The Buddha's later enlightenment included his renunciation of asceticism and ability to move back into his body. By then the quality of association had changed for him. His body association was no longer either tacit or hedonistic but became a moral choice to accept his lot as a body prone to suffering. Some body association is simply naïve to suffering; another level of association accepts is mortality. In the really real, the continuum of body-relatedness is not linear but spirals.

Modernist medicine does much to discourage body association. Robert Zussman in his study of intensive care units quotes one physician: "I think you don't have to look at a patient here, basically. You don't have to examine a patient. . . . The numbers, I feel, they are more reliable."[9] Such physicians then teach their patients that with respect to how they feel, the numbers, or diagnostic images, or cardiac tracings, are more reliable. Most of us, sooner or later, go to the doctor to find out how we feel, our distrust of subjective feelings being a form of dissociation.

Many healers outside of orthodox medicine, whom I will call "alternatives" for convenience, practice teaching the patient refined sensitivity to how he feels, and teaching him to trust that feeling. The shift to alternative healing—survey data suggest that more visits are made to alternative practioners than to orthodox physicians—is another indicator of crossing a postmodern divide. Again, the same baggage is brought over the divide: most people who visit alternative healers continue to see medical physicians.[10] But for people who are seeing an alternative healer, what it feels like to see the orthodox medical practitioners changes.

Other-Relatedness

[handwritten: ✗ how do you see yourself connected to other bodies]

What is my relationship, as a body, to other persons who are also bodies? How does our shared corporeality affect who we are, not only to each other, but more specifically *for* each other? Other-relatedness as an action problem is concerned with how the shared condition of being bodies becomes a basis of empathic relations among living beings. Albert Schweitzer expressed this concern in his phrase, the "brotherhood of those who bear the mark of pain."

In 1921, following both his first medical missionary expedition to Africa and a period of severe illness resulting from his internment as an enemy alien during World War I, Schweitzer wrote what became of one of his most famous passages:

> Whoever among us has learned through personal experience what pain and anxiety really are must help to ensure that those out there who are in physical need obtain the same help that once came to him. He no longer belongs to himself alone; he has become the brother of all who suffer. It is this "brotherhood of those who bear the mark of pain" that demands humane medical services. . . ."[11]

My term for the body's sense of this "brotherhood" is the *dyadic* body. Schweitzer's contemporary, Martin Buber, wrote of perceiving a tree that "it is bodied over against me and has to do with me, as I with it."[12] The dyadic relation is the recognition that even though the other is a body outside of mine, "over against me," this other *has to do with me, as I with it.*

Illness presents a particular opening to becoming a dyadic body, because the ill person is immersed in a suffering that is both wholly individual—my pain is mine alone— but also shared: the ill person sees others around her, before and after her, who have gone through this same illness and suffered their own wholly particular pains. She sees others who are pained by her pain. Storytelling is one medium, through which the dyadic body both offers its own pain and receives the reassurance that others recognize what afflicts it. Thus storytelling is a privileged medium of the dyadic body.

At the opposite end of the other-relatedness continuum is the *monadic* body, understanding itself as existentially separate and alone. A 1991 film, *The Doctor*, shows William Hurt as a surgeon who has just been told he has cancer. His wife receives the news with a "we" statement about their ability as a couple to cope with whatever comes. He corrects her, saying that *he* alone has cancer. Many, like this character, choose the monadic body when faced with illness. That the character is a surgeon is an interesting comment on cultural perceptions of where medicine places bodies on the continuum from monadic to dyadic.

Medicine encourages monadic bodies in many ways. Hospitals treat patients in close enough proximity to each another to obviate any meaningful privacy, but at just enough distance to eliminate any meaningful contact. Some friendships are formed in waiting rooms and between roommates, but in my observations of cancer centers, most contact among patients is minimal and transitory. Patients relate individually to medical staff, not collectively among themselves, and this pattern of relating seems to result from how medical spaces are designed and how movement within them is orchestrated. Modernist administrative systems not only prefer the monadic body, but the disease model that grounds medical practice has little ability to admit any other concept of the body.[13]

The monadic body of medicine articulates well with modernist society's emphasis on individual achievement in education or the marketplace. The dyadic body thus represents an ethical *choice* to place oneself in a different relationship to others. This choice is to be a body *for* other bodies.[14] Living for others means placing one's self and body within the "community of pain," to render Schweitzer's phrase contemporary.

Thus my continua are not only not linear, as the shifting nature of body association demonstrates; they are also ideal types of ethical *choices*. The choice to live as a dyadic body points toward an ethics of the body. Dyadic bodies exist *for* each other: they exist for the task of discovering what it means to live for other bodies. The dyadic body is a lived reality, not simply a conceptual ethical idea. Schweitzer writes as one who dedicated his life, and body, to actualizing the ideal of the community of pain. But acting for the other cannot proceed apart from contemplative reflection on this action: Schweitzer took considerable time away from his medical work to continue to write.

Desire

What do I *want*, and how is this desire expressed *for* my body, *with* my body, and *through* my body?

My usage of desire has its conceptual roots in the psychoanalytic theory of Jacques Lacan.[15] Lacan places desire in a triad with need and demand. The need is fully corporeal and can be satisfied at that level. The baby needs milk or a dry diaper. The expression of the need is the demand, but the demand differs from the need itself: the baby's cry is not the same as its hunger or wetness. The demand's difference from the need enlarges the context: the demand asks for more than the need it seeks to express.

Desire is this quality of *more*. When the child asks for one more of whatever at bedtime—one more story, one more drink, one more hug—that displacement of each "more" by another expresses the desire in the demand. The parents' frustration is that when they fulfill the demand, the child remains unhappy. Desire, Lacan teaches, cannot be filled: there is always more.

I read expressions of this desire constantly in people's stories. Dan Wakefield, in his widely read spiritual autobiography, expresses Lacanian desire when he writes, "I wanted—needed, it felt like—*more*."[16] Robert Coles reports a student's story about her mother's compulsive shopping; the terms are explicitly Lacanian: "Need was beside the point; she had everything. Desire was the point—to think of something she wanted. . . ."[17] Desire has to express itself as the demand for some object, but the object is not what is desired, any more than the child at bedtime desires what he demands. The point of desire is that the displacements never end: there is no final demand; desire is always wanting more.

Yet some bodies, particularly ill bodies, do cease desiring. The body's problem of desire generates a continuum between bodies that have come to *lack* desire and those that remain *productive* of desire. Illness often precipitates a condition of lacking desire. Stewart Alsop, dying of leukemia, writes of his approaching birthday that perhaps being sixty "is a good time to bow out."[18] . . . I quote it here for its commonsense quality of resignation: desire is lacking.

Malcolm Diamond, writing about his reaction to the diagnosis of multiple myeloma, expresses questions that—so far as I can tell—virtually every person facing such a disease asks: "Why buy shoes? Why have dental work done?"[19] The plot of the story centers on desire: the narrative tension is whether lost desire will be regained. The initial loss of desire is expressed in indifference to such mundane acts as keep up one's footwear and teeth. Diamond's story ends, happily, with him in a remission that is stable enough for him to want to buy shoes; he has made a transition from diagnostic shock to living with cancer. This plot of desire lost and regained informs all lives at various points, but illness demands reflection on cycles of when desire is lacking and when the body produces desire.

Just as illness almost invariably plunges the body into lacking desire, illness can instigate new reflections on how to be a body producing desire. Anatole Broyard describes critical illness as "like a great permission."[20] Part of what becomes permitted

need vs demand vs desire

is the exploration of desires. Broyard writes that he began taking tap-dancing lessons after his diagnosis with prostate cancer. These lessons, besides probably being something he always wanted to do, were part of his self-conscious attempt "to develop a style" to meet his illness: "I think that only by insisting on your style can you keep from falling out of love with yourself as the illness attempts to diminish or disfigure you." (25).

Broyard's "falling out of love with yourself" gives life to my generic notion of "lacking desire," and "insisting on your style" says more than "producing desire" can capture. Yet generic terms are needed to point to what Broyard's language is doing and suggest relations between his sense of illness and that of others such as Diamond.

Broyard concludes that "it may not be dying we fear so much, but the diminished self" (25). What diminishes the self is no longer desiring for itself. Falling out of love with yourself means ceasing to consider yourself desirable to yourself: the ill person fears he is no longer worth clean teeth and new shoes.

As desire becomes reflective, an opening exists to assume enhanced responsibility for what is desired. Although desire is always for more than the immediate object—Diamond's shoes or Broyard's tap-dancing are self-consciously metonymic of a desire that will always exceed its tokens—the immediate objects remain ethical choices. For the dyadic body, productive desire leads to what Schweitzer called service.[21] Schweitzer's community of pain expresses a productive desire grounded in the ethical choices to be a body for other bodies.

Service can take many forms, but for the person who is seriously ill, a primary possibility for service is storytelling as an act of witness. As storytellers, writers like Broyard or Diamond do not tell people *how* to be sick; their testimony is rather that you *can* be sick and remain not just in love with yourself but in love with the humanity that shares sickness as its most fundamental commonality.

Four Ideal Typical Bodies

What are the four puppets that dance, and sometimes dangle, at the theoretical ends of these four continua? What are the types of action I invent in order to speak of the bodies in illness stories?

My typology of bodies is a meta-narrative, setting up different *choices* that body-selves then act out. The emphasis on choice is a reminder that the body is, ultimately, a moral problem, perhaps *the* moral problem a person has to address. Yet choice is also a deceptive word, because the body-self is created in reciprocal processes. Selves act in ways that choose their bodies, but bodies also create the selves who act. We can observe more of the first process than of the second; how bodies create selves is scarcely understood at all.

Matters are further complicated by noting that "choice" occurs in social contexts that constrain choice: conventions of stigma are one such constraint. But the post-colonial affirmations of stigma show that constraints on bodies can also become resources for body-selves. Broyard is constrained by the social undesirability of the body he is becoming, but he chooses to take tap-dancing lessons, at least as long as the flesh allows. He then turns tap-dancing into a story about the possibilities of choice.

People, particularly ill people, may not choose their bodies, but as body-selves they remain responsible for their bodies, and they choose how to exercise responsibility. Those who observe others making choices have their own responsibility to note the conditions, both corporeal and social, that responsibility is exercised in.

The Disciplined Body

The disciplined body-self defines itself primarily in actions of *self-regimentation*; its most important action problems are those of control. The disciplined body experiences its gravest crisis in loss of control. The responses of such a body-self are to reassert *predictability* through therapeutic regimens, which can be orthodox medical compliance or alternative treatment. In these regimens the body seeks to compensate for contingencies it cannot accept.

Such single-minded pursuit of regimens transforms the body into an "it" to be treated; the self becomes *dissociated* from this "it." A self dissociated from its body will rarely seek and discover terms of association with others, so the disciplined body becomes *monadic*.

In its ideal-typical form the disciplined body *lacks* desire, and here real bodies most likely vary from the ideal type. The ideal type is most applicable in those moments of treatment when compliance becomes an end in itself. But few ill people pursue their regimens simply to demonstrate compliance to themselves or to their healers, without any desire for themselves. More often the pursuit of regimens indicates that something is desired; in Broyard's phrase, the body still loves itself. Often, but not always: Broyard offered this phrase because he recognized that many ill bodies cease to love themselves.

The disciplined body-self is not likely to tell stories about itself; rather, its stories are told through the pursuit of the regimen. Insofar as the regimen is the story, disciplined bodies can make "good patients" in terms of their medical compliance. Such a good patient is the medical equivalent of Robert Merton's ideal type, the ritualist, who has given up all hope of social success but continues to act out the prescribed norms of conduct.[22] Their demands are only in the cause of getting the regimen just right, and their expectations are surprisingly low, since performance of the regimen itself counts much more than its outcome.

The regimen need not be medical: diets, meditation programs, and exercise can complement or substitute for physicians' prescriptions. To the extent that these treatments are carried out like military drill, for the sole end of getting it right in itself, then desire is lacking and the pure ideal type is approximated. To the extent that the regimen provides pleasure—the food on the diet is preferred, the mediation or exercise are sources of relaxation and invigoration—then desire has become productive and something more than disciplined ritualism is being practiced.

Chemotherapy is perhaps the best example of the disciplined body's paradoxes of desire. Deborah Kahane narrates the story of a woman she interviewed, "Marcia."

Marcia experiences breast cancer as a "tremendous relief." "I was finally being punished," she says, "and paying the price for being a bad mother and now it was over."[23] Other aspects of her story do not fit the monadic body, but in seeing cancer as punishment, she is monadic in her self-isolation. Her phrase, "and now it was over," seems to refer to the period of awaiting punishment she believes she deserves; if desire is present, it is masochistic.

Marcia also exemplifies the disciplined body as she works to restore predictability; she prides herself on returning to work soon after her mastectomy and on using a prosthesis to give her body a "normal" appearance. Then she suffers a recurrence and undergoes chemotherapy. Chemotherapy requires becoming a different sort of disciplined body: predictability becomes imposed, and body dissociation enters Marcia's story. "My whole life was planned around chemo treatments. I was wearing a wig and feeling lousy about my body" (123).

The tension that animates Marcia's story is whether she can move away from being a disciplined body, and she does. A crucial moment is her decision to end chemotherapy sooner than her physician advises. In that break from the prescribed regimen, she ceases to be a disciplined body. She makes peace with her aging body and finds new relationships as "a grandmother type" and a "mentor" (125). At the end of her story, far from interpreting cancer as punishment, she now claims it as her own experience that has made her "more of a person for having survived" (127).

As a pure ideal type, the disciplined body is not a pleasant way to live. But most ill people experience some aspects of it: monadic self-enclosure, dissociation from a body that becomes "it," a need to restore some measure of control, and loss of desire. Marcia displays but never quite fits the ideal type of the disciplined body. Fortunately, she finally finds the terms to love herself.

The Mirroring Body

The mirroring body defines itself in acts of *consumption*. The body is both instrument and object of consuming: the body is used to consume, and consumption enhances the body: feeding it, clothing it, grooming it, and, in the consumption of medical services, curing it. This body-self is called mirroring because consumption attempts to recreate the body in the images of other bodies: more stylish and healthier bodies. The primary sense is visual: the body sees an image, idealizes it, and seeks to become the image of that image. The mirroring body thus attempts to become the image of that image. The mirroring body thus attempts to make itself exactly what the popular phrase calls "the picture of health."

Like the disciplined body, the mirroring body seeks *predictability* because it fears contingency, but the kinds of contingency that the two bodies fear differ. The disciplined body typically fears contingencies that might disrupt work routines; it then substitutes health routines. The mirroring body fears disfigurement, which some disciplined bodies might regard as signs of battles well fought. Their respective attempts to ensure predictability will also differ. The disciplined body seeks predictability of appearance. If the disciplined body marches to the commands of an internalized drill sergeant, the mirroring body grooms itself in conformity to an internalized set of ideal images.

Both mirroring and disciplined bodies are also *monadic*, but again in differing ways. The disciplined body, set on its own course, regards others either as instrumental allies or obstacles. The mirroring body finds its course in the performance expectations of others who are its audience. Both bodies act alone in a world that judges them, but the judgments are made on different grounds: performance for the disciplined body and appearance for the mirroring body. Clearly many body-selves alternate between being disciplined bodies and mirroring bodies: Marcia alternates between speaking of her need to continue her work during illness and of the effect of illness on her appearance.

The mirroring body-self is almost compulsively *associated* with its body, but the body is now a surface; again, the visual is primary. The mirroring body *produces* desires, but its desire is monadic. What the mirroring body-self wants, it wants for itself.

If the disciplined body tells its story in its regimens, the mirroring body tells itself in its image, and this image comes from elsewhere. The images this body mirrors come most often from popular culture, where image is reality. Thus in one of the most bizarre news stories generated by Jacqueline Kennedy Onassis's death, Michael Jackson, whose book she had edited, was quoted expressing opposition to her having chemotherapy to treat non-Hodgkin's lymphoma: "She's too much of a legend to risk her hair falling out."[24] Whether Jackson said this or not, the tabloid writers have a clear enough sense of their readership to realize the statement would have sufficient popular resonance to make a story.

The reality of death is less real than the image of baldness. The identity of people who would take this story seriously is what Bauman described as "for today." What counts is sustaining the image today. As I have talked to people about to begin chemotherapy, a common reaction is for fears of immediate side-effects, particularly hair loss, to be more of a topic than fears of the treatment not working. Psychologists might call this a defense mechanism: the greater fear is displaced onto the lesser. But perhaps for some people whose identity is truly "for today," the immediate side-effects are the greater fear.[25]

Neither the Michael Jackson example nor its source are simply oddities. Tabloid journalism, advertisements, made-for-TV movies, and soap operas produce the images that most bodies seek to mirror. These images include both idealized health and pitiful illness; popular culture often plays one image against the other, idealizing health in contrast to illness, and depicting illness as pitiful in contrast to idealized health. Clearly other sources of images exist: families and medicine generate images of their own, though these images are often expressed in adaptations of popular culture. Professional culture is more "popular" than is imagined: prescription drug advertisements in medical trade magazines are presented in iconography that is hard to distinguish from non-prescription ads in popular magazines.

The mirroring body does love itself, but this love is a parody of what Broyard probably meant; his point is that the body needs to be loved *with* the disfigurement brought by disease. As an ethical strategy for being ill—and each body type is an ethical strategy—the mirroring body has the same monadic limitations as the disciplined body. But consumer culture being as pervasive as sociology commonly proclaims, we are all mirroring bodies at one time or another.

Lacan's concept of the Imaginary suggests that what we call the self is always a sedimentation of images from elsewhere. These images are worn like armor, and what is within this armor is certainly less than we often believe. No self ever ceases living in the imaginary sedimentation of images from elsewhere. Thus, while the mirroring body has limited ethical possibilities, it remains as one inevitable facet of who most of us are. We can, however, complement our imaginary selves with entry into what Lacan calls the Symbolic. Here the body-self enters into symbolic exchanges: naming and being named are paradigmatic exchanges. Rather than simply appropriating others' images for itself, the body-self communicates with these others. Some exchanges with others are openings for ethical relationships; other exchanges, sadly, are not.

The Dominating Body

The dominating body defines itself in *force*. There is considerable cultural reluctance to talking about ill people, especially dying people, as being dominating bodies. Most people do not tell stories about themselves dominating others, and most certainly they do not write these stories down. Their narratives are lived, and the stories of these lives are told by others. Carole E. Andersen tells the story of the years her husband, Dick, was dying of leukemia.[26] Andersen observes that in the stories spouses tell about the death of a loved one, the dying person is invariably depicted as wise and courageous. "Bless them all," she writes, "their tales tell only one side of the story" (27).

As soon as he was diagnosed, Dick got mad. More precisely, he made anger into the narrative of his dying years, at least until the last months when his death was imminent and he did exhibit those qualities that surviving spouses idealize in their stories. But until those last months he was emotionally abusive in his possessiveness of Carole. The climax of this abuse came when he screamed her into the submissive act of giving up her part-time job writing a column in the local newspaper: "his words came as bullets; few of them missed. . . . He towered over me and let me have it—words, vile cruel words, repeated over and over again" (29). A psychologist she consults advises her to leave Dick, but she stays. Readers of her story can only hope that their last couple of months made the years worthwhile. Andersen's story is stark testimony to the reality of dominating bodies who are also ill.

The dominating body assumes the *contingency* of disease but never accepts it. Andersen tells that for twenty-seven months of the three-and-a-half years that Dick lived with leukemia, he was in remission, but the contingency of that remission, remission being defined as contingent, drove him crazy. Dick "insisted he was not afraid of death but of the wait. It was never knowing that had haunted him" (31). Where the disciplined body turns its fear of contingency into the predictability of the regimen, the dominating body displaces rage against contingency onto other people. If Dick could not control his illness, he could control Carole.

The dominating body shares the qualities of *dissociation* and *lacking* desire with the disciplined body, with the crucial difference that the dominating body is *dyadic*. When the body is dissociated from itself but linked with others, the body's will turns against the other rather than toward itself. The aggression of this turning against others may reflect the bitterness of the dominating body's loss of desire. Andersen writes that at the time of his diagnosis, Dick loved life. But when his life was rendered contingent, he lost his desire. His bitterness comes from the knowledge that this *is* a loss. Contingency militates against desire throughout his illness. Even when he was in remission, Dick could no longer take pleasure in the life he had so enjoyed. Finally when his death was certain and "once again he felt in control," Dick became the husband Carole loved.

Although the dominating body is dyadic in its other-relatedness, the ethical stance of the dyadic relation is *against* others rather than *for* others. Being dyadic toward others while dissociated from itself, and while lacking in desire, is dangerous. The disciplined and mirroring bodies turn on themselves. The dominating body turns on others. Society does not want to hear the resulting narratives of abusive force, but as Carole Andersen puts it, if both those dying within this narrative and their loved ones are to be helped, "then it's time for some honesty" (28).

The Communicative Body

The disciplined, mirroring, and dominating bodies are ideal types; no actual body fits their specifications, at least for long,[27] but these specifications provide some interpretive understanding of how bodies exist at different moments of their being. The communicative body-self is not only an idea type but also an *idealized* type. Its specifications are not only descriptive but provide an ethical ideal for bodies. Again, no actual body fits this ideal for long, though many bodies may approximate it in differing ways.[28]

The communicative body accepts its *contingency* as part of the fundamental contingency of life. The human body, for all its resilience, is fragile; breakdown is built into it. Bodily predictability, if not the exception, should be regarded as exceptional; contingency ought to be accepted as normative. The communicative body-self takes its place in Schweitzer's "brotherhood of those who bear the mark of pain."

The contingent body is fully *associated* with itself. The communicative body understands that the body-self exists as a unity, with its two parts not only interdependent but inextricable. There may be aspects of body that are not self, and *vice versa*, but just where one ends and the other begins is undecideable. Thus no distinction between corporeal disease and illness experience can be sustained: a problem within the tissues pervades the whole life.

Association and contingency are contextualized by the qualities of *being dyadic* and *producing desire*, and these qualities crystallize the body's ethical dimension. When a body that associates with its own contingency turns outward in dyadic relatedness, it sees reflections of its own suffering in the bodies of others. When the body is a desiring one, the person wants and needs to relieve the suffering of others. Here lies the sense of obligation toward the other that grounds Schweitzer's "brotherhood of those who bear the mark of pain": the dyadic desire of the communicative body means that it never belongs to itself alone but constructs its humanity in relation to other bodies.

The communicative body realizes the ethical ideal of existing *for* the other. The *communing body* might be more precise, but I retain "communicative" as the more general term. The communion of bodies involves a communication of recognition that transcends the verbal. Bodies commune in touch, in tone, in facial expression and gestural attitude, and in breath. Communication is less a matter of content than of *alignment*: when bodies sense themselves in alignment with others, words make sense in the context of that alignment. When alignment is lacking, even the best semantic content risks misinterpretation or will be unsatisfactory as a message.

The body itself *is* the message; humans commune through their bodies. Anatole Broyard wrote that he wanted "to be a good story" for his physician.[29] The phrase catches the reader off guard; conventionally, the ill person would say something like "I want him to listen to my story." Broyard incites the recognition that his ill body *is* a story, and he wants it to be a good one. The remark occurs as Broyard talks about the ill person's need to personify his illness and to "own" it, rather than allow it to be the anonymous disease that medicine depicts. Ethics seems to begin in a similar sense of ownership of situations; responsibility as an ethical person involves making a good story of the situation that self and other find themselves in and must come to own.

Like the disciplined, mirroring, and dominating bodies, the communicative body *is* a story, but a wholly different one. The communicative body *communes* its story with others; the story invites others to recognize themselves in it. Thus the communicative body tells itself explicitly in stories. Reciprocally, stories are the medium of bodies seeking to approximate the communicative type.

Human communication with the world, and the communion this communication rests on, begins in the body. "I can understand the nature of the living being outside of myself," Schweitzer wrote, "only through the living being within me."[30] This statement is an essential epigram of the communicative body-self, with its confluence of *associated* body-relatedness and *dyadic* other-relatedness. Schweitzer's joint emphases on suffering as life's inevitable *contingency* and on service as a *productive* desire to join with other bodies express the full ethical ideal of the communicative body. . . .

I reiterate several points about th[e] false appearance of neatness to emphasize the four ideal types only present rough parameters for the action choices of body-selves.

For each range of responses to action problems, the paired terms—such as predictable/contingent in relation to the problem of control—mark the ends of a continuum. Thus in the really real, bodies act not at the extremes but anywhere along these continua. Moreover, the quality of each extreme can change: thus body association can be naïve to suffering or accepting of it, and contingency can be feared or embraced.

How far along the body is placed on any continuum sometimes represents embracing that condition, as the communicative body embraces being dyadic. The body's placement can also represent a resistance to the opposite end of that continuum: the disciplined body makes itself predictable as resistance to its fundamental contingency, and the dominating body lacks desire because its contingency seems to deny what it desires to desire. The "continua" thus have a shape that defies conventional geometrical metaphors, as well as two-dimensional printing.

Clearly then the four body types cannot be either mutually exclusive or exhaustive. Other permutations certainly have descriptive force, and because the body is moving in time, the condition of any actual body represents a layering of types. Each of us is not one type or another, but a shifting foreground and background of types. The value of the types is to describe the extreme moments of these shifts, thus providing some parameters for hearing the body in the story.

Finally, because my objective is an ethics of the body, I am mixing three ideal types with one *idealized* type. My typology seeks to be normative not in a descriptive sense but in a prescriptive one. I want to show how the communicative body distinguishes itself from other body types. By specifying the communicative body as the undertaking of an ethical task, I hope to orient an ethics of the body. Reflexive monitoring requires an ideal against which the progress of the body-self can be measured. . . .

My thesis is that different bodies have "elective affinities" to different illness narratives. Bodies are realized—not just represented but created—in the stories they tell. This realization can and should be reflexive: by telling certain stories, ethical choices are made; the choices in turn generate stories. Common sense understands people as having some responsibility for their stories and for their bodies. Common sense is less accustomed to the possibility of exercising that responsibility for bodies *through* stories.

One road to the achievement of the communicative body is through storytelling. . . .

NOTES

1. Arthur Kleinman and Joan Kleinman, "How Bodies Remember: Social Memory and Bodily Experience of Criticism, Resistance, and Delegitimation Following China's Cultural Revolution," *New Literary History* 25 (1994): 710–11.

2. Arthur W. Frank, "For a Sociology of the Body: An Analytical Review" (cf. chap. 1, n. 32). See discussions in Chris Shilling, *The Body and Social Theory* (London: Sage, 1993), 93–98, and in Anthony Synnott, *The Body Social: Symbolism, Self and Society* (New York: Routledge, 1993), 239–41.

3. Alfred Schultz refers to ideal types as puppets in *Collected Papers*, vol. 2: *Studies in Social Theory*, ed. Arvid Brodersen (The Hague: Martinus Nijhoff, 1971), 17–18.

4. Erving Goffman, *Stigma: Notes on the Management of Spoiled Identity* (Englewood Cliffs, N.J.: Prentice Hall, 1963).

5. This "affirmation" may, however, be anything but affirmative. Thus a recent "thinly fictionalized, autobiographical novel" describes the author's ilestomy in terms that self-consciously underscore what Goffman calls spoiled identity: "A plastic bag full of warm shit hang[s] by my side. I hated the bag, even though it had saved my life. I feared what its odour could reveal about me." Quoted in Richard Perry's review of Donna McFarlane's *Division of Surgery*, "Dark-horse Fiction Nominee Offers Fierce Testimony," *The Globe and Mail*, Toronto, November 12, 144. McFarlane's prose preempts "the bag," regaining control by revealing more than the bag could.

6. In earlier writing I called this problem "self-relatedness." "Self-relatedness" juxtaposes more neatly to the next problem of "other-relatedness," but what I am discussing under this topic is relation to one's self as a body, hence body-relatedness.

7. For a useful review of the positions taken on this question by classical and early Christian writers, see Synott, *The Body Social*.

8. Bauman, *Mortality, Immortality*, 36 (cf. chap. 1, n. 25).

9. Robert Zussman, *Intensive Care: Medical Ethics and the Medical Profession* (Chicago: University of Chicago Press, 1992), 33.

10. For survey data on alternative medicine usage, see David M. Eisenberg et al., "Unconventional Medicine in the United States," *The New England Journal of Medicine* 328 (January 28, 1993): 246–52. For ethnographic insights, see Fred M. Frohock, *Healing Powers: Alternative Medicine, Spiritual Communities, and the State* (Chicago: University of Chicago Press, 1992). For stories of using alternative healing, see Gilda Radner, *It's Always Something* (New York: Avon Books, 1989) and David A. Tate, *Health, Hope, and Healing* (New York: M. Evans and Company, 1989).

11. Originally written in Schweitzer's *On the Edge of the Primeval Forest*. Quoted by Schweitzer in *Out of My Life and Thought: An Autobiography*, trans. Antje Bultmann Lemke (1993; New York: Henry Holt, 1990), 195.

12. Buber, *I and Thou*, 8 (cr. Chap. 1, n. 3).

13. For a sociological perspective on the disease model, see Elliot G. Mishler, "Viewpoint: Critical Perspectives on the Biomedical Model," in Elliot G. Mishler et al., eds., *Social Contexts of Health, Illness, and Patient Care* (Cambridge: Cambridge University Press, 1981), 1–23. Larry Dossey, M.D., has been most provocative in his criticisms of medicine's inability to think beyond the monadic body; see his *Meaning and Medicine* (New York: Bantam, 1991) and *Healing Words: The Power of Prayer and the Practice of Medicine* (New York: HarperCollins, 1993). For the conclusions he suggests about how much bodies have to do with each other, Dossey would be regarded as a "fringe" figure by many.

14. Cf. chap. 1, pp. 14–15.

15. Jacques Lacan, *Ecrits: A Selection*, trans. Alan Sheridan (New York: Norton, 1997) and *The Four Fundamental Concepts of Psychoanalysis*, ed. Jacques-Alain Miller, trans. Alan Sheridan (New York: Norton, 1978).

16. Dan Wakefield, *Returning: A Spiritual Journey* (New York: Penguin, 1984), 20.

17. Robert Coles, *The Call of Stories: Teaching and the Moral Imagination* (Boston: Houghton Mifflin, 1989), 142.

18. Stewart Alsop, *Stay of Execution: A Sort of Memoir* (Philadelphia: Lippincott, 1973), 288.

19. Malcolm Diamond, "Coping with Cancer: A Funny Thing Happened on My Way to Retirement," *The Princeton Alumni Weekly*, April 6, 1994, 13–16.

20. Anatole Broyard, *Intoxicated by My Illness: And Other Writings on Life and Death*, comp. and ed. Alexandra Broyard (New York: Clarkson N. Potter, 1992), 23.

21. For contemporary statements about the centrality of service to medicine, see Robert Coles, *The Call of Stories*, and David Hilfiker, *Not All of Us Are Saints: A Doctor's Journey with the Poor* (New York: Hill and Wang, 1994).

22. Robert Merton, "Social Structure and Anomie," *American Sociological Review* 3 (October 1938): 672–82.

23. Deborah H. Kahane, *No Less a Woman* (New York: Simon & Schuster, 1990), 118.

24. "Jaco & Jackie O," *Star*, April 5, 1994, 7.

25. The real trauma of hair loss should not be minimized either. Henri Nouwen describes the nearly bald head of the younger son in Rembrandt's painting, "The Return of the Prodigal Son": "When a man's hair is shaved off, whether in prison or in the army, in a hazing ritual or in a concentration camp, he is robbed of one of the marks of his individuality" (*The Return of the Prodigal Son: A Story of Homecoming* [New York: Image Books, 1994], 46). Nouwen does not include hospitals in his list of sites where hair is cut off, but the places he does mention contextualize the experience of hair loss in chemotherapy. And if he refers to a man's loss, how much greater women's loss of individuality must be.

26. Carole E. Andersen, "The Case: Another Side of Cancer," *Second Opinion* 19 (April 1994): 27–31. The original title of Andersen's story was "Some Get Mad," which I suggested based on a phrase she used in an earlier draft. The editorial shift from "Some Get Mad" to "Another Side of Cancer" exemplifies the way editing can change emphases in the stories people tell. Of course "Some Get Mad" was itself my editorial suggestion, and the "original" manuscript I saw may already have been shaped in ways that modified Andersen's experience. The anecdote suggests both that there is little unedited experience available, but also that much anger is expressly edited out of illness stories.

27. Andersen writes that among friends and outsiders, Dick would return to his charming "old" self.

28. The idealization inherent in the communicative body is specified by M. Therese Lysaught, who applies my schema of body types in "Sharing Christ's Passion: A Critique of the Role of Suffering in the Discourse of Biomedical Ethics from the Perspective of the Sick," Ph.D. diss., Duke University, 1992. Lysaught argues that the exemplar of the communicative body is Jesus, particularly in the crucifixion. This application of my work complete surprised me, and I gratefully acknowledge its importance in my present thinking.

29. Broyard, *Intoxicated by My Illness*, 45.

30. Schweitzer, *Out of My Life and Thought*, 104.

‖‖

2

Laboring Now
Current Cultural Constructions of Pregnancy, Birth, and Mothering

Barbara Katz Rothman

Visualizing the Fetus: Bringing Forth the New Patient

When I began looking at pregnancy care, back in the 1970's, the fetus was being thought of as a patient, but it was still quite an abstraction. No longer. When I give a talk about prenatal care, sometimes I ask the audience to picture a fetus, and then "draw it" in the air with their hands. You get arms waving in the air, forming a big circle for a head with a curled-up body beneath. Then I ask them to put the pregnant woman's belly button right on that fetus. Just point where it would be. And the room is still. People have no idea where that woman's belly button would be. Of course if they were to draw the pregnant woman around the fetus, she'd be standing on her head. The fetus has been turned around to a more baby-like position. Oddly, as real as the fetus is, it's the pregnant woman that has become the abstraction. Ultrasound is a near-perfect example of an ideology made real, a set of beliefs reified with a technology. Obstetricians think of fetuses as separate patients more or less trapped within the maternal environment, and ultrasound was developed as a technology to get through that maternal barrier and show the separate fetus lying within. The separate baby becomes an entirely separated image, floating free on the screen, tethered only by the umbilical cord. The woman is erased, an empty surround in which the fetus floats.

But we are not surrounds: we are living people experiencing these pregnancies, with all the contradictions the technology brings. Women are asked to take a moment of profound psychological separation and differentiation, when they first see inside themselves to the being that is growing within, and make of that a moment of attachment, a "bonding" experience. The baby on the screen is made "real," more

From *Laboring On: Birth in Transition in the United States*, pp. 29–72, by Wendy Simonds, Barbara Katz Rothman, and Bari Meltzer Norman. © 2007 Taylor & Franics Group LLC. Reprinted with permission of Taylor & Francis Group LLC.

real than the baby within, the experienced pregnancy. Making a baby, a fetus, real with ultrasounds includes, but is not limited to, "sexing" it, assigning fetal sex to the blur on the screen. "It" becomes "she," she becomes named, an abstraction becomes a baby.

I'd had my own pregnancies before this technology. So while I knew, sort of, what it must mean for women, it's nothing I really understood until I read Lisa M. Mitchell's study of the use of ultrasound in pregnancy in Quebec (2001). Quebec is the Canadian province most like the United States in its highly medicalized maternity care and in its highly politicized abortion context, and Mitchell's study made me see what women are experiencing in the U.S.

Back when I was pregnant, we did not actually have fetuses—we had pregnancies, that resulted in the birth of babies. I remember a half joking, half fantasy, dreamlike image I had of myself, the night before my first baby was born, searching around frantically for the eyebrows, the fingernails, all those details, much like the last few footnotes on an overdue paper. The baby I imagined within was amorphous, unstructured, unfinished.

Not so today's fetus. It has every little detail in place. From that grey blur on the ultrasound image, a fully formed fetus is read into being. The sonographer works to construct fetal personhood, "talking about the image and encouraging the parents to see and to bond with a sentient and acting 'baby'" (Mitchell 2001, 118). The irony, of course, is that this construction occurs in the very same moment the sonographer is looking for the signs and symptoms that would indicate the fetus is not developing normally. In that case, the woman would be encouraged to consider abortion, and the "baby" would be quickly de/reconstructed as a fetus or even a "genetic mistake," an "abnormality."

But for most women, most of the time, the fetus passes its inspection and "fetal personhood" or more accurately "babyhood" is narrated into being—with or without the participation of the mother. Some women resist: "I think we'll forget the picture. It looks like a deep sea animal," Marie Claude says during her 32-week scan. And the technician responds: "Can you see that? The foot. Little toes." And as Marie Claude and her husband peer into the screen, the technician continues "tickling" the toe on the screen, "It's so cute" (125). Who could resist?

With the routine scan, done shortly before most women would feel fetal movement, the observed fetal movement on the screen is maybe not anthropomorphized, maybe "baby-ized" would be the term. Mitchell observed technicians using terms like dancing, playing, swimming, partying or waving to describe fetal movement. A rolling fetus is "trying to get comfortable," one with an extended limb and arching back is "stretching." Not moving doesn't spare the women and her partner the process: Without movement, the fetus is described as sleeping, resting. A fetal hand near the mouth turns into "The baby is sucking his thumb," even though sonographers told Mitchell that actual thumb sucking is rarely seen. Parents, the sonographers told her, like to think that is what the baby is doing (2001, 127).

Who knows what it is parents like to think. Sonographers, along with the rest of medicine, apparently know quite well what they *should* think. In Quebec, as elsewhere, a racialized script exists: Some women (Black, first nation) "never show anything," are impassive and unemotional. Other women are too emotional, giggling loudly, shedding tears, showing "excessive" joy. Both groups are punished by silence: sonographers give them only brief descriptions (135), saving their rich descriptions that call a baby forth into being for the good mothers, the ones who respond "appropriately."

Women tend to take silence during the exam as a sign of a problem. And, for all the commercialization of the process, the pictures for sale, the souvenirs to take home and to share, ultimately searching for a problem is the reason the technology is being used. Women have reason to worry. Perhaps they ought to worry more: informed consent has been notably lacking, and many women don't even realize what the implications of having this ultrasound could be until the sonographer is suddenly silent, seeing something unexpected on the screen.

Somewhere between tickling toes on the screen and clinical coldness, there must be a way of handling the use of this technology better. But no one seems to have found it—not Mitchell, not the other social scientists who have studied the new ultrasound diagnostic technologies in pregnancy (see e.g., Summers Scholl), not the Dutch midwives I have interviewed who tried really, really hard (Rothman 2000), and not the U.S. and Canadian midwives who are working on it. In one generation we have truly changed pregnancy: from a time of "expecting" a baby, to a time of containing a fetus. And who can resist?

Prenatal Care in Sum: Two Approaches

The differences between the models of pregnancy developed by obstetrics and by the home birth movement and midwifery are based on both their underlying ideologies and their political necessities. Medicine had to emphasize the disease-like nature of pregnancy, its "riskiness," in order to justify medical management. Midwifery, on the other hand, had to emphasize the normal nature of pregnancy in order to justify nonmedical control in a society in which medicine has a monopoly on illness management.

The first major difference between the two models is that while medical management organized itself around a search for pathology, the midwifery model approached pregnancy as essentially normal and healthy, a period of psychological as well as physical growth and development. Ideologically, medicine developed as a patriarchal institution, an institution that embodied the religious and cultural views of western European society. It consequently focused on the presence of the fetus during pregnancy, and saw that fetus as the child of the man. Pregnancy then is a stress and disease-like state caused by the presence of the fetal parasite. In the midwifery model, the focus is the perspective of the woman, and pregnancy is understood as a normal condition for women. Women were not compared to a hypothetically stable, noncycling male system, but expected to always be in one or another phase of reproductive life. There is no single "normal" from which to judge deviations: ovulation, menstruation, pregnancy, lactation, menopause—these are not deviations from some abstract norm, but are themselves normal states.

Medicine thus attempted to maintain the normalcy of the mother throughout the stress of the pregnancy, viewing deviations from normal (nonpregnant) status as symptoms of disease states. This of course justified medical control. Midwifery, on the other hand, viewed the changes as demonstrating the health of the mother. Rather than seeking to change the mother back in the direction of nonpregnant normality, midwifery's goal was to provide the best possible environment in which the changes of pregnancy could occur.

In the medical model, prenatal care is the *management* of pregnancy, like the medical management of any (other) disease. How did obstetrical prenatal care come to take its current form? Much of it, as stated earlier, revolved around screening for what was called toxemia. The standard that evolved from the introduction of prenatal care, mostly by nurses and social workers, to obstetrical management called for increasingly frequent visits. By the 1970's, the pregnant woman was expected to see the obstetrician each month during the first two trimesters, twice a month for the seventh and eighth months, and weekly for the last month. No research ever showed such a schedule to be of particular value. In fact, as heretical as it may sound, it is hard to find any evidence that prenatal care improves birth outcomes (Fiscella 1995, 468).

Even now the "prenatal care" that obstetricians offer women is basically a screening program. The visits typically take ten to fifteen minutes or less, in which the woman is weighed, her blood pressure taken, and her urine tested. Blood is drawn for yet more screening and testing. She lies on an examining table and the fetal heart rate is noted, as is the position of the baby. If she has symptoms to present, these are noted, and remedies may be prescribed. As is often the case in physician visits, a prescription handed over is a way of resolving questions and terminating the interview. Time, one feels, is of the essence as the doctor moves from one examining room to the next.

The prenatal care that the midwives of the home birth movement developed grew in response to this approach. Screening for pathology is part of the care they offered, but not where the emphasis was placed. Nutrition, self care, and education were stressed, and the psychological meaning of the pregnancy was particularly important. As one midwife doing home births in the 1970's put it,

> I'm usually interested in why they wanted the pregnancy in the first place; why they want to do it at home and what that means to them, this is a decision for responsibility that they've taken; their relation as a couple; how they relate to the baby—these are the principal issues to deal with, usually at the first meeting.

The second major difference between the medical and the midwifery model is in the conceptualization of responsibility. In the medical model, responsibility is something shouldered by the doctor. This is of course not unique to obstetrics, but has long been part of the traditional clinical mindset. In the medical model, practitioners see themselves as responsible for the outcome of treatment, and since pregnancy is a disease-like state, its care comes under the treatment model. The physician "managed" the pregnancy, attempting constant, usually minor adjustments in order to bring the physiological picture of the woman back to "normal." In the midwifery model the woman herself holds the responsibility for her pregnancy and makes her own decisions The midwife sees herself as a teacher and a guide for the pregnant woman and her family.

Thus while a physician might spend ten to fifteen minutes at each prenatal visit (or even less, if ancillary staff do part of the work) a routine midwifery prenatal visit takes thirty minutes, an hour or even more. Essentially the same physical screening procedures are performed (frequently by the mother herself) but the midwives also discuss and evaluate the socio-emotional context of the pregnancy. The sense of rush and efficiency in medical care may be heightened under "managed care," and the general speedup in medicine, but it is also deeply rooted in the logic of the medical model. The job of the physician is to diagnose and to treat, and in the relatively straightforward work of pregnancy management, these routines are handled quickly.

The goals of the midwives doing home and birth center births are more time-consuming and far more complex. Getting to know women and their families, educating and sharing information, all take time and involve the midwives in the lives of clients to a greater extent than does drawing blood. As one midwife in a 1970's birth center summed up the work of prenatal care:

> We strive to create a milieu that is safe and supportive in which individuals can discover for themselves what it means to give birth. To open themselves on physical, emotional and spiritual levels to another person—to give birth.

Childbirth

The Social Construction of Birth

The first thing to remember is that obstetrics is a surgical specialty. In surgery, the ideology of technology is dominant. Perhaps more clearly than anywhere else in medicine, the body is a machine, the doctor a mechanic. In the typical surgical situation the unconscious patient is waiting, like a car upon a hydraulic lift, when the surgeon arrives, and is still in that condition as the surgeon leaves. The surgeon and the rest of the medical staff may care about the person whose body lies before them, but for the duration of the surgery, the mind-body dualism theorized by Descartes is a reality. Marcia Millman reported, in a classic study of observations of surgical wards, that when patients have been given local rather than general anesthesia for an operation and are thus awake, their serious remarks about the operation or their attempts to take part in the doctors' conversations as the surgery is underway often bring the staff to laughter (Millman 1977). To them, the talking patient is incongruous, almost as if a car had sighed while one of its flat tires was being replaced.

When women were sedated through labor and made unconscious for delivery, then the only possible description of birth is as an "operation" performed by a surgeon on a patient. And this was the basic model for birth for more than fifty years.

In the early days, scopolamine, known as "twilight sleep," was the standard anesthesia for labor, with general anesthesia used for birth. In the 1970's, the approach to anesthesia shifted towards spinal anesthesia, or the more contemporary epidural, both of which leave the woman conscious but numbed from the waist down.

Nancy Stoller Shaw described the physician-directed, in-hospital deliveries she observed in the 1970's in Boston as all following the same pattern. The patient was placed on a delivery table similar in appearance to an operating table. The majority of patients had spinal anesthesia or the epidural. The woman was placed in the lithotomy position and draped; and her hands were sometimes strapped to prevent her from "contaminating the sterile field." She could not move her body below the chest, and her "active participation" in the birth was effectively over.

This does not mean that the woman becomes unimportant, only that her body, or more specifically, the birth canal and its contents, and the almost born baby are the only things the doctor is really interested in. This part of her and, in particular, the whole exposed pubic area, visible to those at the foot of the table, is the stage on which the drama is played out. Before it, the doctor sits on a small metal stool to do his work. Unless he stands up, he cannot clearly see the mother's face, nor she his. She is separated as a person, as effectively as she can be, from the part of her that is giving birth (Shaw 1974, 84).

Much has gone on in the past few decades to "humanize" birth in hospitals, not just to let significant others be present at birth, but actually to welcome the mother back. People do talk to women giving birth now: even cesarean sections can be "family centered." Mirrors abound. So much has changed since the days of the scopolamine-drugged, leather-strapped, isolated woman of the 1950's. And yet birth itself, the actual process of laboring and delivering a baby, is believed to have remained the same, untouched by anything other than evolutionary forces. How people "manage" birth changes, but does birth?

The Birth Process

The medical literature defines childbirth as a three-stage physiological process. In the first stage the cervix, the opening of the uterus into the vagina, dilates from being nearly closed to its fullest dimension of approximately ten centimeters (almost four inches). This is referred to as "labor," and the contractions of the uterus that pull upon the cervix are known as "labor pains." In the second stage, the baby is pushed through the opened cervix and through the vagina, or birth canal, and out of the mother's body. This is the "delivery." The third stage is the expulsion of the placenta or "afterbirth."

In any situation the possibility exists for alternative definitions of the event, different versions of what is *really* happening. Which version is accepted and acted upon is a reflection of the power of the participants. Those with more power can have their definition of the situation accepted as reality. Often this involves some bargaining or negotiating between the people involved. Take, for example, a child with a sore throat who doesn't want to go to school. The parent may say the throat is not *that* sore, and the child counters with, "but my head hurts too." Might the child be experiencing some soreness and pain? Certainly. But is it bad enough that the child should stay home from school? That depends. Medical authorities may function just like the parent in this situation. Some of the classic work in medical sociology has addressed just this: how doctors and patients negotiate reality. Patients recovering from tuberculosis claim that they really are well enough to have a weekend pass (Roth 1963), and patients and doctors in mental hospitals negotiate over the patients' mental health (Goffman 1961). These are not, as we might assume, just "medical" judgments, but interpersonal negotiations.

Similarly, pregnant women frequently come to the hospital claiming that they are in labor, but by medically established judgments they are not. The state of being in labor, like any illness or any deviance, is an ascribed status; that is, it is a position to which a person is assigned by those in authority. But one can also negotiate to try to achieve that status or have one's claim to it recognized.

When people have negotiated a definition of the situation, that becomes reality for them, and they have to work within that reality. Let us take as an example a woman at term having painful contractions at ten-minute intervals, who has not yet begun to dilate. Whether she is or is not in labor will depend on whether she then begins to dilate, or the contractions stop and begin again days or weeks later. Whether a woman is in labor or "false labor" at Time One depends on what will have happened by Time Two. If she presents herself to the hospital claiming that she is in labor, and by weeping, pleading, or just because she seems educated and middle class she is admitted, the medical acknowledgment that she is in labor will have been established. If she does not begin to dilate for twenty-four hours and then twelve hours after that—thirty-six hours after her admission—she delivers, that woman will have had a thirty-six hour labor. On the other hand, if she is denied or delays admission and presents herself to the hospital twenty-four hours later for a twelve-hour in-hospital labor, she will have had a twelve-hour labor preceded by a day of discomfort. From the point of view of the institution that is "responsible" for her labor, and thus her pain, only from the time of her admission, the latter is preferable, the longer labor being easily perceived as institutional mismanagement. Yet from the point of view of the woman, the *physical* sensations in both cases are precisely the same; it is the *social* definition—calling it labor or not—that makes the difference between a terribly long labor or a pretty average labor with some strange contractions beforehand. Because medicine wanted to define labor as a situation requiring hospitalization, but at the same time wanted to avoid prolonged labor, "real" labor got defined not in terms of the sensations the woman experiences, but in terms of "progress," cervical dilation. A dilatation of 3 centimeters was generally required to be admitted.

The pregnant woman thus wants to be accurate (in medical terms) about defining the onset of labor. Otherwise, if she gains early admission she will have helped to define the situation as an overly long labor. In addition to the stress inherent in thinking oneself to be in labor for thirty-six hours, the medical treatment she will receive presents its own problems. Laboring women have been routinely confined to bed in hospitals, a situation that can be disturbing psychologically and physically. Not only is the labor perceived as being longer, but the horizontal position physically prolongs labor, as may the routine administration of sedatives during a long hospital stay. In addition to the variations in treatment during the first hours of labor, the treatment she will receive is different in the last hours, when the woman is hospitalized in either case. Women who have been in a hospital labor room for thirty hours receive different treatment than do women who have been there for only six hours, even if both are equally dilated and have had identical physical progress. Which woman, after all, is more likely to have a cesarean section for overly long labor—the one who got there just six hours ago, or the one who has been there through three shifts of nurses? What the woman experienced before she got to the hospital—how strongly, how frequently and for however long her contractions have been coming—does not enter into the professional decision making nearly as much as what the medical attendants have seen for themselves.

It is also important for the pregnant woman to be accurate in identifying labor because if she presents herself to the hospital and is denied admission, she begins her relationship with the hospital and her birth attendants from a bad bargaining position. Her version of reality is denied, leaving her with no alternative but to lose faith in her own or the institution's ability to perceive accurately what is happening to her. Either situation will have negative consequences for the eventual labor and delivery. That is why childbirth-education classes frequently spend considerable time distinguishing labor from so-called false labor.

In U.S. hospitals, until recently, first and second stages of labor were seen as sufficiently separate to require different rooms and, frequently, different staff. Women attended to by nursing and house staff throughout their labors might not have seen their own obstetricians until they got to the delivery room. When women were moved from one room to another to mark the transition from one stage of labor to another, the professional staff had to make a distinction between laboring and delivering, and then apply that distinction to the individual woman. A cut-off point had to be established at which a woman was no longer viewed as laboring, but as delivering. If the point was missed, and the woman delivered, say, in the hall on the way to the delivery room, then she was seen has having "precipped," having had a precipitous delivery. If the point was called too soon, if the staff decided that the woman was ready to deliver and the physical reality was that she had another hour to go, then concern would be aroused about the length of the second stage because she had spent that extra hour in a delivery rather than a labor room.

Even today the editors of *Williams*, in bold print, state that, "One of the most critical diagnoses in obstetrics is the accurate diagnosis of labor" (Cunningham et al. 2001, 310). Why? They offer two reasons: "If labor is falsely diagnosed, inappropriate interventions to augment labor may be made" (310). But home birth midwives do not intervene just because a clock tells them a labor is long. They look at the condition of the mother, the fetal heart tones, and if all is well, all is well. The second reason *Williams* offers is that if labor is not diagnosed, "the fetus-infant may be damaged by unexpected complications occurring in sites remote from medical personnel and adequate medical facilities" (310). The birth may, that is, occur at home.

As hospitals permit the mother to labor and birth in the same room, hospital staff pay less attention to establishing the moment of entry into second stage.

What if there were no hospital, no labor room, no delivery room? That of course has been the case for most of human history, and is what the midwives doing home births faced. There were no *institutional* demands to define labor, or to distinguish the very end of first stage from the start of second stage. If a woman is having painful contractions and feels she needs her midwife, then her needs are real, whether or not her labor is "false." If you're not moving her from one place to another, does it really matter what "stage" she is in? Can just being in any given stage for "too long" itself make a birth unsafe? For midwives in the early home birth movement, these were important questions. Those who were trained as nurse-midwives, and those who were self-taught, had very little in the way of "midwifery" knowledge to draw upon. There was only "obstetrical" knowledge. And many "facts" of obstetrical knowledge turned out to be "artifacts" of obstetrical management.

The Active Management of Labor

There is something enormously appealing about the language "active management" applied to labor. The notion that labor can be managed, is manageable—what a reassuring thought. When women face labor they often think about managing it: How will I manage, they ask, how will I cope? That question is really about managing oneself. The labor arrives, happens, unfolds, descends—and one manages or copes as best one can. "Best" here often means being a good patient, not complaining, being cooperative, not making a fuss.

When physicians think about it, they like to think of themselves as managing the labor itself: steering its course, speeding it up or slowing it down, "handling" or "managing" it much the way one "manages" a car on a highway. When you add in the word "active" you're really on to something. Then the physician can think of him/herself as managing the labor not reactively, responding to or coping with what happens, following the bends of the highway and keeping the wheels on the road, but what people now like to call "proactively," actually taking charge. Now we are not talking about fine-tuning, or steering between shoulder and side rails, but piloting in open seas, controlling the labor by taking its power into one's own hands.

Either notion of managing labor—managing one's reactions to it as a laboring woman or taking charge of it as a physician—assumes the labor itself as the object of attention. Labor, in this medical way of thinking, is something that happens to women, rather than something women *do*. This is a way of thinking about labor that encourages what is called "prepared" childbirth, preparing the woman to cope with the labor as it is managed. Labor—and its active medical management—is something that happens to a woman and she can learn to cope with it.

From the physician's perspective, when all is said and done, there is not much that can be done to "manage" labor. Doctors cannot make, produce or guarantee healthy babies or healthy mothers. The two areas they have had some success with are the management of the pain of labor, and the management of its length. One can absolutely guarantee a woman a painless labor, if one is willing to use the medications to assure it, whatever their costs. That was the direction medical management first took: from chloroform onward, they promised painless labors.

By the early 1970's the costs of pain control—both psychological and physiological—became increasingly apparent. At that point, two things happened. The most common form of pain relief switched from the sedations and general anesthesia approach, to more localized pain relief. Epidural anesthesia has become the most widely used medical form of pain relief. According to the Maternity Center Associations report, *Listening to Mothers*, 59% of women having vaginal births reported using epidural analgesia for pain relief during labor (DeClerq 2002, 1). For an epidural, a fine plastic tube is inserted in the lower back just outside of the spinal cord, and numbing drugs are dripped in. An anesthesiologist is necessary to insert the epidural, and the availability of on-site anesthesiologists is the single most significant factor in a hospital's epidural rates. Epidurals are more commonly inserted during daylight hours, and Ina May Gaskin reports that often, women accept epidurals they don't really feel they need at the time because the anesthesiologist tells them he'll be leaving shortly and it's their last chance (Gaskin 2003, 236). Epidurals have the enormous advantage of allowing the woman to be fully present mentally: she can observe the proceedings. When they work—and 15% of women do not get full pain relief from the epidural—they numb her. Some women feel pressure and an urge to push with an epidural; some do not, and then become "bystanders" to their own labors. For many women, that is the ideal situation: they can have essentially the same experience being offered their husbands: a chance to watch their baby being born. Of course it is *not* the same experience when it is your own body you are watching give birth, but epidurals absolutely do resolve the problem of "managing" the pain and the intensity of labor and birth.

The other change in medical management that occurred was a shift in energy from managing the *pain* of labor to managing its *length*. In 1968, a Dublin hospital introduced "the active management of labor" as an obstetrical approach focused on providing control over the length of labor. As long as one is prepared to stop the labor with a cesarean section, one can guarantee a labor no longer than any arbitrary time limit one chooses: twelve hours seems to have become the standard figure. In the United States today, according to the *Listening to Mothers* survey, almost half of mothers had a caregiver try to induce labor, and these inductions successfully started one third of all labors. Just over half of all the women reported that they were given drugs to strengthen (speed up) contractions, and more than half had their membranes artificially ruptured, also to speed labor (DeClerq 2002, 1).

It's All in the Timing

The standard obstetrical model of labor is best represented by "Freedman's curve," a "graphicostatistical analysis" of labor, introduced by Emanuel A. Freedman in seven separate articles between 1954 and 1959 in the major American obstetrical journal (see summary in Freedman 1959). "Graphicostatistical analysis" is a pompous name for a relatively simple idea. Freedman observed labors and computed the average length of time they took. He broke labor into separate "phases" and found the average length of each phase. He did this separately for primiparas (women having first births) and for multiparas (women with previous births). He computed the averages, and the statistical limits—a measure of the amount of variation. Take the example of height. If we computed heights for women, we would measure many women, get an average, and also be able to say how likely it was for someone to be much taller or much shorter than average. A woman of over six feet tall is a statistical abnormality.

What Freedman did was to make a connection between *statistical* normality and *physiological* normality. He used the language of statistics, with its specific technical meanings, and jumped to conclusions about physiology: "It is clear that cases where the phase-durations fall outside of these (statistical) limits are probably abnormal in some way. . . . We can see now how, with very little effort, we have been able to define average labor and to describe with proper degrees of certainty the limits of normal" (Freedman 1959, 97). Once the false and misleading connection is made between statistical abnormality and physiological abnormality, the door is opened for medical treatment. *Statistically abnormal labors are medically treated.* The medical treatments include rupturing membranes, administering hormones, and cesarean sections. Using this logic, we would say that a woman of six feet one inch was not only unusually tall, but that we should treat her for her "height condition."

How did this work in practice? Obstetrics has held very closely to these "limits of normal" for labor. The first phase of labor Freedman identified was the *latent* phase. This he said began with the onset of regular uterine contractions and lasted to the beginning of the *active* phase, when cervical dilation is most rapid. But how can one know when contractions are "regular"? There is no way to examine a particular contraction and identify it as "regular." It can only be determined retroactively, after contractions have been *regularly* occurring for a while. This brings us to the confusion over "false labor." The only difference between "false labor" and "true labor" is in what happens next: true labor pains produce a demonstrable degree of effacement (thinning of the cervix) and some dilation of the cervix, whereas the effect of false labor pains on the cervix is minimal. The difference is then one of degree: how *much* effacement and dilation, and how *quickly.*

The concept of "false labor" served as a buffer for the medical model of "true labor." Labors that display an unusually long "latent phase" or labors that simply stop can be diagnosed as "false labors." Doctors could continue to believe that labor does not stop and start, even after they have seen it happen, because they could retroactively diagnose the labor as "false." Friedman himself pointed out that the latent phase may occasionally be longer than the time limits, yet the active phase be completely normal. He explained these "unusual cases" by saying that part of the latent phase must really have been "false labor." That way his tables of what is statistically normal still work out. These are of course techniques that are used to prevent anomalies from being seen, to "normalize" events so that they conform to the medical model.

Midwives attending home births, on the other hand, see labors start and stop, see women stop in labor, be reassured in some way, and have their labors start again. Ina

May Gaskin has pointed out that doctors themselves used to know these things. They even knew that labor could reverse itself, that "progress" is not an inevitable direction. A partially opened cervix could tighten back up again. She cites a dozen medical textbooks, published between 1846 and 1901, in which doctors knew and taught that their presence, their entry into a woman's birthing room, could disturb the labor (Gaskin 2003, 140–141). By the middle of the twentieth century, that knowledge was lost. Birth had moved into the hospitals and doctors never saw the consequences of their own presence because they had nothing to compare it to. If a woman's labor appeared to stop, then the doctors decided it had never really started, it was a "false" labor. If a labor appeared to reverse itself, the cervix to close back up again, then they decided the admitting nurse had measured wrong. A fact that didn't fit into the theory was simply not a fact, just a mistaken measure.

Home birth midwives, on the other hand, saw these things happen. They saw a birth slow down when the mother was made uncomfortable, saw the effect that social and emotional factors had on labor, and began to reevaluate the medical definitions of labor itself. Eventually, in the midwifery model, strict time limits were abandoned: each labor is held to be unique. Statistical norms may be interesting, but they are not of value for the management of any given labor.

Consider too the situational politics of home birth: When a midwife has a woman at home or in a birth center, there is a very strong incentive to keep her out of the hospital. Arbitrary time limits can be "negotiated," and the midwife looks for *progress*, some continual change in the direction of birthing. It was hard for nurse-midwives who started to do home births to "let go" of their medical training. One midwife I interviewed in the 1970's expressed her ambivalence: "They don't have to look like a Friedman graph walking around, but I think they should make some kind of reasonable progress." Another expressed the concern in terms of the laboring woman's subjective experience, a more woman-centered understanding: "There is no absolute limit—it would depend on what part of the labor was the longest and how she was handling that—was she tired? Could she handle that?"

A third midwife described her technique for dealing with long labors:

> Even though she was slow, she kept moving. I have learned to discriminate now, and if it's long I let them do it at home on their own and I try to listen carefully, and when I get there it's toward the end of labor. This girl was going all Saturday and all Sunday, so that's forty-eight hours of labor. It wasn't forceful labor, but she was uncomfortable for two days. So if I'd gone and stayed there the first time, I'd have been there a whole long time; then when you get there you have to do something.

"Doing something" is the cornerstone of medical management. Every labor that takes "too long" and cannot be stimulated by hormones or by breaking the membranes will go on to the next level of medical intervention, the cesarean section. Breaking the membranes is an induction technique that is particularly interesting in this regard. The sac in which the baby and the amniotic fluid are enclosed is easily ruptured once the cervix is partially opened. Sometimes that happens by itself early on in labor, and "the waters breaking" may even be the first sign of labor. But once broken, the membranes are no longer a barrier between the baby and the outside world. The *Listening to Mothers* survey reports that 55% of women experienced artificially ruptured membranes. (*Williams* states that "If the membranes are intact, there is a great temptation even during normal labor to perform an amniotomy [rupture them]" [Cunningham et al. 2001, 315].) It is not a temptation that home birth midwives feel. Once the membranes are ruptured, the chances of infection increase, more so in hospitals with frequent vaginal examinations, but in any case more than if the membranes remained intact. Once the membranes are ruptured, it is important that the labor proceed more quickly to avoid infection. Thus the intervention, the "doing something" to speed the labor itself demands that the labor indeed be sped up.

Length of labor is not a basic, unchanging biological fact, but is subject to social and medical control. Even before the introduction of the Dublin-style "active management of labor," which guarantees a labor of no more than twelve hours, there has been a kind of "speed up" of hospital labors. Looking at *Williams* in its different editions, the reported length of labor dropped from an average first stage of labor in first births of 12.5 hours in 1948, down to 10.5; and from 7.3 hours for second and subsequent births in 1948 down to only 5 hours by the 1980 edition.

The speed-up was even more dramatic for the second stage, which dropped from an average of 80 minutes for first births in 1948 to only 50 minutes for first births, and from 30 minutes in 1948 down to 20 minutes for subsequent births. Third stage is barely measurable in time, with some obstetricians practicing "routine manual removal of any placenta that has not separated spontaneously by the time they have completed delivery of the infant and care of the cord in women with conduction analgesia" (Cunningham et al. 2001, 323). In 1980, *Williams* said that if the placenta has not separated within three to five minutes of the birth of the baby, manual removal of the placenta should probably be carried out (Pritchard and McDonald 1980, 425), and in 2001 that "Manual removal of the placenta is rightfully practiced much sooner and more often than in the past" (323). In a home birth, the birth of the baby is itself such an important event, so demanding of human response and attention, that unless there is particular cause—like excessive bleeding—midwives are content to wait a while for the woman to spontaneously expel the placenta. At home, babies are usually put to the breast, or brought up to the breast by the mother, and the suckling stimulates contractions that expel the placenta.

A midwife in the 1970's told me a story of one of her first home births. The birth went well, and the mother and baby were doing fine—but after almost an hour, the placenta had yet to appear. The midwife went into the kitchen and, barely restraining her panic, called a colleague who was far more experienced with home births. "Is there any chamomile tea in the house?" the calm voice on the phone asked. Pushing through kitchen cabinets, still clutching the phone, the midwife found a box. "Well, then, make a strong cup and sit down and drink it." The placenta, the experienced midwife assured her, will come when it's ready. It takes a few minutes, but what's the rush?

The rush is largely institutional: births in hospitals need to be meshed together to form an overarching institutional tempo. Predictability is important; timing matters, as staff moves from birth to birth, as women are moved from place to place. There have been many studies of the variations in interventions by time of day, time of week, even by football schedules: interventions increase when doctors are rushed, whatever the reason. One good, careful and recent study done of more than 37,000 live births in Philadelphia hospitals shows that women who give birth during the day are much more likely to have obstetric interventions than those who give birth during the "off peak" hours of 2 AM to 8 AM. Looking only at low-risk women admitted in active, non-induced labor, and excluding labors involving fetal distress or "prolonged, obstructed or abnormal labors," the researchers found that women who gave birth during peak hospital hours were 43% more likely to have forceps or vacuum extraction and 86% more likely to have drug-induced labors. They were also 10% more likely to have an episiotomy (Webb and Culhane 2002). The institutional tempo slows down at night and staff allow birth to take a bit longer.

"Active management": managing labor by the clock with interventions as necessary to speed it up, is part of the medical ethos. While they may often have to watch the clock the obstetricians have set for them, it is not part of the midwifery approach.

Giving Birth or Being Delivered?

As in prenatal care, the differences between the models of birth care developed by obstetrics and by the home birth movement and midwifery are based both on underlying ideology and on political necessity. Physicians control birth in hospitals because it is done in their territory, under their expertise. That control over their work space is what makes them "professional." As the senior professionals around, they obviously control all the other workers—including midwives and doulas, along with nurses, orderlies and aides. But they also control the patients. The medical management of birth means the management of birthing women: to control or to manage a situation is to control and manage individuals.

The alternative to physician and institutional control of childbirth is childbirth outside of medical institutions, outside of the medical model. In this alternative, birth is an activity that women *do*. The woman may need some help, but the help is, for the most part, in the form of teaching her how to do for herself.

The word "deliver" exemplifies the medical model: it is a service delivered. The word "birthing" clarifies the midwifery model: birthing, like swimming, singing and dancing, is something people do, not have done for them.

Home birth midwives struggled to redefine birth, but also to define their *own* role, what they did at a birth. Nancy Mills was a direct-entry midwife in the 1970's, not a nurse, but a midwife who began by helping a friend during labor. By the time she had attended over 600 births, she had come to see her role at birth as this:

> I see myself going in and being a helper, being an attendant. Sometimes I play with the kids, or I do some cooking. Sometimes I sit with the woman. Sometimes I help the husband assist the woman. Some families need more help than others, but it is easy to go in and see where you are needed and how you can fill that role. (Mills 1976, 131)

The birth is not made to fit the routine, but the attendant to fit the birth. The birth is something the mother does by herself, but: "It is important for that woman to be able to look at you, to know you are there, to hold your hand, to be reassured. I know it helps when I say to a woman, 'I know how you feel. I know it's harder than you thought it was going to be, but you can do it'" (Mills 1976, 134).

What do midwives actually do when they get to a birth at home? They come in, say hello, introduce themselves to anyone they don't know. Just as any guest in a home would do. And in that entry, in that way of entering the home, they make the statement that they are not there to "do" the birth. One midwife, when asked what she does when she first gets to a birth, said: "Nothing, first. Which is very important, because they expect me to do something, like I'm supposed to do something. But they're doing it already and that's what we're going to be doing, so I find it very important to just come in and sit down."

This approach is a radical departure from the medical model, in which the entry of the doctor signifies the start of the performance, or the admission of the woman to the hospital signifies the official start of the labor. Judy Luce, a Vermont midwife who has been practicing for over 25 years, likes to show people a birth film made in Australia. In this film, the woman is seated on a big lounge chair, and casually brushes away the midwife's hand. The camera watches as slowly, without any touching, the vagina bulges and the baby emerges. It reminds her, she says, that whatever midwives are doing or not doing with their hands and their skills, it is women who give birth.

Which is not to say that midwives don't have and use their skills. They do vaginal exams during labor, but not usually on a clocked schedule. They will, on a more regular basis, listen for fetal heart tones. The role is to keep a check on the physical changes, and not to interfere with personal interactions. Often that means that the midwife has to "support the support person," providing reassurance not only to the woman but to her support people, that labor is progressing normally, and occasionally offering advice on how to give support. People are often not fully prepared for just how painful labor can be, or how needful the laboring woman may become. The midwife provides reassurances that her condition, however distressing, is normal, and suggests positive ways of coping.

There are of course no changes in room (labor to delivery room) for the second stage of labor, but there is usually a marked change in the ambience. The end of active labor (transition), as the woman reaches full dilation, is usually quite painful for the mother and difficult for the support person. The pushing stage is usually exciting, climactic. The mother may be semi-sitting at the edge of or on a bed, braced by her support person, or she may be squatting, lying on her side, on a chair, or on her hands and knees, depending on her comfort and the suggestions of the midwife. The mother is in no way physically restrained. Sometimes the midwife encourages the woman to reach down, to push the baby out into her own hands. After the baby emerges, into either the mother's hands or the midwife's, the mother draws the baby up to her. As one of the home-birth midwives I interviewed in the 1970's said: "There are at least thirty seconds of both mother and baby looking at each other and going, 'who are you?' Then everybody usually starts climbing all over the baby and we usually back off at that point, just back off a bit and keep an eye on the placenta, what's going on."

The ability to "back off" is raised almost to an art by some midwives. One said that she never lets herself call out "it's a boy" or "it's a girl" because "all of her life a woman will remember the sound of those words, and she should hear them in a voice she loves."

After a few minutes the midwife will either cut the cord herself, or may help the father, or less commonly the mother or someone else to do so. The baby will be wrapped in warm blankets and given back to the mother to put to the breast. Suckling usually stimulates uterine contractions, and the mother will hand the baby to someone else while she expels the placenta. After checking the placenta and showing it to the mother if she is interested in seeing it, as most women are, the midwife will check the mother for tears and for excessive bleeding. In the unlikely event of a tear or an episiotomy the midwife will do the repair with a local anesthetic. If all is well, the mother might get up and bathe or shower while other people dress the baby and weigh it.

Midwives stay for some hours after birth, depending on the needs of the family and the condition of the mother and baby. Many families celebrate the birth with the traditional glass of champagne, some with birthday cake. People are frequently ready for a meal and a party atmosphere may prevail. At other births the family may just want to sleep. The midwife eventually bids goodbye; as one said:"My aim is that when I leave that family feels they birthed it. I was there and I helped, but they did it . . . so that in their whole recollection of the experience I will be very minimal. That's my goal and that's my aim." That role and that goal are very different from the role of the doctor in a hospital birth, a role that Shaw, in her observations, summed up as being "the director and the star" (1974, 87).

The Importance of Place

It is not just a matter of moving from place to place as we examine birth under different circumstances. Under different systems of care we are not just doing the same thing in a different place. Different meanings make birth a different event. Teeth, tongue, jaw, intestines are all pretty much the same thing the world over, but the meaning of a meal could not be more different as we move from a famine in a country under siege to a food court in a suburban U.S. mall, from a Passover Seder to a fast-food lunch, from a high tea to a steakhouse. So it is with childbirth: the social and cultural variation overwhelms the physiological sameness.

Institutionalization—any institutionalization—disempowers, drains power from the birthing woman and gives it to the institution itself, as it homogenizes the experience. The late Annemiek Cuppen, an extraordinarily fine midwife in the Netherlands, shared the following illustrative story. She had attended a birth in which the woman planned to give birth in the hospital. While the Netherlands has a 30% home birth rate, midwives do attend births in both places. Annemiek Cuppen came first to the woman's home for the early labor. As she came in the door she was greeted by the woman who told her husband to go and get the midwife a cup of coffee, sent her children and mother-in-law scurrying on errands, and generally kind of bossed people around and remained the center of her home. And then came the move to the hospital, a move chosen, remember, by the woman herself. As they entered the hospital room, the woman sat herself quietly on the edge of the bed. With a new demeanor now, looking up at Annemiek, the woman asked, "Uh, excuse me, do you think it would be OK if maybe we opened the window please?"

It is not only at this individual level that an institution drains power from women. Once institutionalization is inevitable for birth, once all births move as they have essentially done in the United States, out of the home and to a specialized site, that site, the institution itself, comes to seem necessary. And once it seems necessary, it seems causal, as if the birth itself depends on the institution. That is how it is now in much of the world where home birth is not so much unavailable as unthinkable. Most Americans cannot imagine home birth.

That is one reason that maternity homes or birth centers are often suggested as a compromise for places like the United States that have lost their home birth traditions. Even if there is absolutely nothing that makes a particular birth center any safer than a home birth, people who are now several generations removed from home birth can accept the possibility of a maternity home or birth center. Just going there will somehow make birth safe and possible in a way that simply staying in one's bedroom will not. Because to trust the home as a place for birth is to fundamentally trust the woman to give birth—and that is the fundamental trust that most of this country now has lost. The power that is the birthing woman's has been drained from her and given to the institution in which she is placed.

Giving birth at home returns that power to the woman.

REFERENCES

Cunningham, F. Gary, et al. *Williams Obstetrics*, 21st edition, New York: McGraw Hill, 2001.

———. *Williams Obstetrics*, 20th edition. Stamford, CT: Appleton & Lange, 1997.

———. *Williams Obstetrics*, 19th edition. Stamford, CT: Appleton & Lange, 1993.

DeClercq, Eugene R., et al. *Listening to Mothers: Report of the First National U.S. Survey of Women's Childbearing Experiences.* Conducted for the Maternity Center Association by Harris Interactive, October, 2002.

Fiscella, K. "Does Prenatal Care Improve Birth Outcomes? A Critical Review." *Obstetrics & Gynecology* 85 (1995): 468.

Freedman, Emanuel. "Graphic Analysis of Labor." *Bulletin of American College of Nurse-Midwifery* (1959): 94–105.

Friedman, Emanual A., ed. *Obstetrical Decision Making.* Trenton, NJ: B.C. Decker, Inc., 1982.

Gaskin, Ina May. *Ina May's Guide to Childbirth.* New York: Bantam, 2003.

———. *Spiritual Midwifery*, 3rd edition, Summertown, TN: The Book Publishing Company, 1990.

Goffman, Erving. *Asylums: Essays on the Social Situation of Mental Patients and Other Inmates.* Garden City, NY: Doubleday, 1961.

Millman, Marcia. *The Unkindest Cut: Life in the Backrooms of Medicine.* New York: Morrow, 1977.

Mills, Nancy. "The Lay Midwife," in *Safe Alternatives in Childbirth*, eds. David Stewart and Lee Stewart. Chapel Hill, NC: NAPSAC, 1976.

Mitchell, Lisa M. *Baby's First Picture: Ultrasound and the Politics of Fetal Subjects*. Toronto: University of Toronto Press, 2001.

Pritchard, Jack A., and Paul C. McDonald, eds. *Williams Obstetrics*, 16th edition. New York: Appleton Century Crofts, 1980.

Roth, J.A. *Timetables: Structuring the Passage of Time in Hospital Treatment and Other Careers*. Indianapolis: Bobbs-Merrill Company, 1963.

Rothman, Barbara Katz. *Spoiling the Pregnancy: The Introduction of Prenatal Diagnosis to the Netherlands*. Bilthoven, The Netherlands: Catharina Schrader Stichting of the Dutch Organization of Midwives (KNOV), 2000.

Shaw, Nancy Stoller. *Forced Labor: Maternity Care in the United States*. New York: Pergamon Books, 1974.

Webb, D. A., and J. Culhane. "Time of Day Variation in Rates of Obstetric Intervention to Assist in Vaginal Delivery." *Journal of Epidemiology and Community Health* 56 (August 2002): 577–578.

Am I Good Enough for My Family?
Fetal Genetic Bodies and Prenatal Genetic Testing

Kristen Karlberg

I was pregnant! I was certain this fetus would have Down Syndrome and I would abort. But I desperately wanted that not to be true. I had CVS, a type of prenatal genetic test, to find out if the chromosomes were normal. The women in the waiting room all looked pregnant. I was thankful I was doing this early because these women had baby bumps and I did not. When I was called back to a room, an ultrasound tech gauged the position of the fetus and dated my pregnancy—ten weeks, four days. He put the transducer on my lower abdomen and a circle with a much smaller, dark, pulsing circle inside appeared on the screen. I didn't want to see it, but I had to look. He didn't turn on the noise of the heartbeat, but I could see it beating, with the blood coursing around in there. The idea that inside my body was the beginning of another body was terrifying. Would I let it grow into my baby or stop it because of something found through this test?

The procedure itself was very odd because it involved my body, but was going to provide information about the fetus's genotype. The insertion of the four-inch long needle into my uterus felt like I expected it to, but the aspiration of the fluid was more challenging. It felt like someone was pulling on the inside of my uterus with tiny pliers. I was at the point of asking him if there was something wrong when he withdrew the needle. In reality it probably was not more than twenty seconds, but it seemed like an eternity. The sample looked like a pinkish jelly M&M candy resting in the bottom of the test tube—minuscule. But he inspected it and seemed satisfied there was enough there, so we were done. It was very anticlimactic. It was hard to believe that small tube held the future of our first pregnancy. Now we had to wait, up to two weeks.

When the genetic counselor called, my heart started pounding. She quickly said everything was fine; there wasn't even the translocation. I sobbed with relief. The reality of the fact that I would stay pregnant took time to sink in. I was almost twelve weeks pregnant.

When I was nineteen, I found out that I and four other family members carried the Robertsonian translocation that could potentially cause translocation Down Syndrome (DS) in offspring, a rare inherited type of DS. This is a chromosomal rearrangement that, when balanced like mine, causes no known medical effects and, when not balanced, results in Down Syndrome. Just as with all things genetic, this rearrangement of chromosomes can be passed through families. My risk was 10–15 percent higher than the normal risk for having a child with Down Syndrome. As a carrier, I could have a chromosomally normal child, a balanced carrier like myself, or a child with Down Syndrome. The above story was my first pregnancy. I was thirty-one.

When I was thirty-three, I wanted to have another child. Between 2003 and 2006 I had five pregnancies that resulted in first-trimester miscarriages, usually between seven and eight weeks' gestation. After the first miscarriage, I was diagnosed as having a congenitally malformed uterus, bicornuate with a septum, which has an alarmingly high 90 percent miscarriage rate. I had another two miscarriages before I had surgery to make the septum less intrusive. By my fourth miscarriage, I was fed up with believing they were caused by chromosomal or uterine issues, and decided to have genetic analysis done on the miscarried embryos. Miscarriage four was a balanced translocation carrier, so chromosomes did not contribute. Miscarriage five was trisomy four, which is lethal. As the number of miscarriages grew, I realized that my individual genetic identity as someone at reproductive risk had evolved in my mind to make me see myself as unable to carry a pregnancy, even though I had a healthy child.

My seventh pregnancy was fraught with bleeding issues, but I remained pregnant, had CVS, and, at thirty-six years of age, had a healthy child, a carrier of a balanced translocation like me. The reason I share this story is to show that my experiences have given me a deeply personal knowledge about genetic information and resulting vulnerabilities. It also illustrates how badly I wanted to have another child, but only one without Down Syndrome. I am glad I did not have to make the choice to abort that desperately desired seventh pregnancy, but I believe I would have if testing revealed that it had DS.

This essay examines how prenatal genetic testing creates fetuses as vulnerable, genetically defined bodies. I began by telling my story, a very personal one, because it is representative of many women's stories. The experience of making choices about what kind of family one desires is considered an American right: to decide whether to have children or not, and if so, how many and when. With the increasing availability of assisted reproductive and prenatal genetic testing technologies, to a certain extent one can also dictate what kind of child. I did not want a child with DS, but for someone else the criterion could be deafness or Tay-Sachs disease.

I am a feminist, one who clings to the hard-won rights of women in our society. I embrace the politics of choice and vehemently defend a woman's right to control her reproductive life. What I gleaned from my years trying to have my two children, however, is that when you're dealing with prenatal genetic testing of a desired pregnancy, it's all about the fetus. The questions and vulnerabilities that come from a pregnant woman's embodied experience relate directly to the fetus and its genetic body. So I attempt to write in such a way as to give the fetal perspective primacy, ignoring the pangs of conscience that allowing this viewpoint prompts in me, because I do not believe fetuses have rights separate from the pregnant women who carry them. Instead, I believe that fetuses are the most important part of pregnancy for a pregnant woman. Pregnant women do not ponder the legal rights of fetuses. They daydream and hope about what their child will be like.

My previous research (Karlberg 2004) was a multisited ethnography that examined genetic bodies and the way they are shaped through prenatal genetic testing technologies. I spoke with pregnant women, genetic counselors, and medical geneticists and perinatologists. I also observed genetic counseling sessions and watched the tests performed. Overall I collected data on thirty-two pregnancies among the twenty women I interviewed. There were forty-three genetic screening tests conducted on these twenty women in the first twenty-four weeks of their pregnancies. There were sixty-nine genetic-screening and diagnostic tests conducted over the course of thirty-two pregnancies, an average of 2.2 genetic tests per pregnancy. As of September 2008, there were genetic tests available for 989 unique disorders (Gene Tests 2008), not all of which can be conducted prenatally. Obviously, there is no shortage of ways to find out if there is something "wrong" with a fetus using genetic technologies. The primary reason women in my research had PGT was to get a better picture of what their babies would be like, and many of them wanted to try to prevent them from having genetic disorders.

In the first section of this chapter I clarify why fetuses do not have individual rights separate from the women who carry them. Second, I define "genetic body" and show how these kinds of bodies are vulnerable, especially fetal genetic bodies. Next, I explore prenatal genetic testing as the mechanism for labeling fetal bodies "genetic." Then I situate genetic bodies in our society through geneticization and biomedicalization. Finally, I explain three ways fetal genetic bodies are particularly vulnerable: to their own genetics, to termination, and to embryo selection. We begin, appropriately, with fetuses.

Fetal Bodies: Cyborg Babies

Through technologies, fetuses have changed over the years. Fetuses are made visible and virtually created through the use of technologies of ultrasound, PGT, and assisted reproduction. Ultrasound technologies show the outline of the fetus on a screen and include sonography, which makes audible the heartbeat of a fetus at approximately eight weeks. Hearing and seeing the fetus encourages attachment to the idea of the fetus as a "baby" and a separate entity from the mother (Taylor 2008) even though survival is impossible without the mother's uterus. Having seen many ultrasounds of embryos and fetuses of my own, I know that the identification one feels seeing a heartbeat and humanlike movements in the black void on the screen encourages one to think of this being as a person, especially when one really wants a baby.

Today many fetuses are nearly cyborg in their creation: micromanipulation of gametes uses technologies to produce embryos that are implanted in the woman's uterus to create a fetus. The assisted reproductive technologies available include artificial insemination, intracytoplasmic sperm injection (ICSI), in vitro fertilization (IVF), surrogacy, and preimplantation genetic diagnosis (PGD) with IVF. Artificial insemination occurs when a partner's sperm or donated sperm is inserted directly into the cervix. ICSI occurs when a sperm is inserted into an egg and implanted in the uterus. In vitro fertilization occurs when egg and sperm are joined in a test tube and allowed to grow to eight cells and then implanted in the uterus. Surrogacy has two types: gestational surrogacy, in which the surrogate carries a genetic embryo of the intended parents, and traditional surrogacy, in which the surrogate's egg is fertilized through artificial insemination using either the father's sperm or donor sperm. PGD with IVF involves creating an embryo to eight cells, removing a cell and conducting genetic testing to determine the genetics of the embryo, and implanting only those embryos that are genetically acceptable. It is possible for a fetus to have five parents: a surrogate birth mother, a donor egg mother, a donor sperm father, and two social parents who raise the resulting child.

Attributing personlike traits to fetuses occurs because we as a society believe in things we can see, and fetuses are visible and present through technologies. Visibility makes us forget this entity is basically a parasite of the pregnant woman—an organism living in and dependent upon another organism. The visibility and cyborg identities of fetuses are furthered by the genetic nature of their bodies, because most of these technologies (like prenatal genetic testing) provide genetic information while further personifying the fetuses they examine/create/define.

Fetal Genetic Bodies: Not without My Mama

Fetal bodies are inherently vulnerable because they are completely dependent upon pregnant women. Treating the fetus as a person gives it the same rights as someone living in the world, even though the fetus can exist only in the uterine environment. Pregnant women are responsible for the well-being of fetuses, but are they legally liable if they drink too much coffee and have a miscarriage? Who is the patient when both mother and fetus are endangered? When the fetus is granted individual status, where does that leave the pregnant woman's autonomy?

No state interest described by fetal rights advocates has enough force to override a woman's fundamental rights of privacy, bodily integrity, and self-determination. . . . Until the child is brought forth from the woman's body, our relationship with it must be mediated by her. (Gallagher 1987)

The woman's autonomy comes first. If a pregnant woman is in a situation where there is a medical or legal question about whether she or the fetus is primary, *she* is the concern. Her privacy, body, and choice are her own, not dependent upon the fetus that inhabits her. It is that simple. Except sometimes when you are the pregnant woman.

The women who carry them often grant their fetuses personhood. Through these PGT technologies and assisted reproductive technologies, women's responsibilities have grown to include providing healthy fetuses to their families. It is very difficult to exist as a pregnant woman without awareness of the entity growing inside you as something separate from you, yet part of you. In the opening story, I did not want to see the heartbeat of the embryo in my body, because I did not want to think of it as a baby, but as something separate from me because I was considering abortion if the PGT revealed DS. In my research, parenting responsibilities to the fetus were a reason cited by women who thought they might consider abortion after PGT. Tasha chose to terminate a Down Syndrome fetus and rationalized that decision, saying, "it just wasn't right to have a child knowing what we knew," implying that Down Syndrome was not an acceptable fit for a child in her family.

> All of that stuff is just really not in your control. And it was weird to be making this big, sort of powerful decision over someone's life.—Rox, 38, Arab

> I think maybe (having amnio) is sort of like you make one of the first parenting decisions early, you know, and in a sense it feels like a premonition of what's to come.— Kate, 35, Jewish

The power of making the life-or-death decision for the fetus was overwhelming to Rox, who spoke of the fetus as a vulnerable person because of PGT and potential abortion. Kate framed the decision to have PGT as a parenting decision, implying that amnio was beneficial to the fetus, despite the possibility of abortion if it was found to have something wrong. This idea that PGT is a responsible parenting decision is supported in other research (Remennick 2006) and in bioethics arguments about procreative beneficence (Savulescu 2001), the idea that parents have some kind of responsibility to bear the healthiest child possible (Sparrow 2007). What "healthy" means is increasingly defined through genetic knowledge.

Defining Genetic Bodies: Knowledge Is Power

"Genetic body" is the term I created to describe the technologically shaped and medically surveyed body of someone with knowledge about his or her genetics. Think for a moment about how many ailments are attributed to genes (breast cancer, many other cancers, Alzheimer's disease, mental illness) or illnesses the doctor asks if you have in your family (stroke, heart attack, cancer, high blood pressure, obesity). The reason a medical history is relevant is genetics. A genetic body is someone's body that has been examined through a genetic test of some kind. While genetic knowledge gleaned from this test is new to the person, the genetics were always present in the body, just not defined as "genetic." That is why genetic bodies are so fascinating: the information has been there all along, but only through these technologies can we possess it. Fetal genetic bodies are not even physically real bodies, but from conception possess the genetics that will in part determine their fate. The term "genetic body" could encompass all individuals, because all bodies have potential genetic information discoverable through genetic testing of that person. My body was geneti-cized at nineteen. One morning I did not have the translocation, and that afternoon I received the test results that I did. I was given information that made me defective on some level—I had something wrong with my genetics. It was not easy to process. It was incredibly complicated to explain to my peers. I avoided it until I had to deal with it when I wanted to become pregnant.

Knowledge of one's genetics establishes a "virtual social identity" (Goffman 1963), a "technoscientific identity" (Clarke, Shim et al. 2003) vis-à-vis genetics: you become your genes. These new identities are consequential for stigmatizing processes that la-bel and define people as "abnormal" on the basis of their genetics, making genetic bodies vulnerable. This is especially true for fetal genetic bodies, in that there is no actual body to touch, see, and examine in relation to the genetic information. To the parents and doctors, a way to know the fetus is by means of its genetics. Pregnant women and their partners who choose to have prenatal genetic testing want to know the genetics of their fetus, creating the fetal genetic body.

Prenatal Genetic Testing: Get Your Genetic Knowledge about Fetuses Here

American reproductive culture has been altered by the introduction of prenatal ge-netic testing (PGT). Our culture is increasingly biomedicalized. "Biomedicalization" (Clarke, Shim, et al. 2003) is defined, for this essay, as the medicalizing of pregnancy through technoscientific means like PGT and other assisted reproductive technolo-gies. Because of the biomedicalization of pregnancy, it is no longer a process experi-enced by women and their fetuses without medical intervention for most of the nine months. As early as 1974 and officially beginning in 1983, physicians caring for preg-nant women were advised to offer or refer their patients for prenatal genetic diagnos-tic services, making them part of routine care. PGT is diagnostic testing of amniotic fluid or fetal material to determine the discernable genetic components of the fetus. Testing can be done for specific genetic abnormalities if individual genes have been identified in the family, but standard PGT determines only fetal chromosomal ab-normalities. The most common types of PGT are amniocentesis (amnio), conducted between fifteen and twenty weeks' gestation, and chorionic villus sampling (CVS), conducted as early as nine weeks. Both tests use ultrasound to guide the doctor to remove genetic material from the uterus using a needle, and both tests have a risk of miscarriage. While in any pregnancy there is a 2–3 percent risk of miscarriage, when one has PGT the risks are slightly increased. CVS and amnio are 99 percent accurate in diagnosing chromosomal abnormalities (MOD 2005). PGT can have multiple pur-poses: detecting a fetal anomaly for pregnancy termination; allowing the couple to prepare for the birth of a potentially affected child; and, while this is extremely rare, detecting and treating a condition in utero.

PGT becoming part of routine care is a facet of the geneticization of American society. Geneticization is the attribution of genetic cause to disorders, behaviors, and physiological variations for the purpose of managing problems of health (Lippman

1991). The combination of biomedicalization and geneticization primes our social environment for the acceptability of PGT and the pursuit of genetic knowledge. PGT is more common in affluent urban areas, but is used throughout the country. One estimate I received is that about 5–15 percent of pregnancies in the United States have amnio or CVS, depending on regional variation (Berck 2008). Prenatal genetic screening techniques are often grouped within the PGT rubric, and nearly every pregnancy experiences one of those: ultrasound. If something is found through ultrasound, PGT is often recommended as a diagnostic verification of the ultrasound finding. So even though prenatal genetic *testing* is still primarily for at-risk pregnancies, prenatal genetic *screening* will usher many more women and their fetuses into the world of prenatal genetics through the ultrasound experience.

The focus on the fetus in medicine has led to a new subspecialty: maternal-fetal medicine. In 1974 the first board-certification exam for the subspecialty of maternal-fetal medicine took place. The fetus was officially a patient. Barbara Katz Rothman, another contributor to this volume and a social science researcher who specializes in pregnancy, believes that "obstetricians think of fetuses as separate patients more or less trapped within the maternal environment" (Rothman 2002:786). A recent textbook, *Fetology: Diagnosis and Management of the Fetal Patient* (2000), appropriates answers for most fetal medical problems, including extensive coverage of genetic issues. While the pregnant woman's body serves as a backdrop, the fetus is the patient. The pregnant woman is a second-hand consideration except when her life is threatened. In my research, which was conducted between 2000 and 2002, 15 percent of the women had received care from a maternal-fetal medicine specialist. The numbers are no doubt much higher now. I used the services of a maternal-fetal medicine specialist to deal with my last three miscarriages and my final pregnancy.

This increased focus on the fetus during pregnancy has evolved over time. It occurred in conjunction with the rising interest in other medical and genetic facets of health, feeding the biomedicalization and geneticization of American society.

Biomedicalization and Geneticization: Encouraging the Creation of Fetal Genetic Bodies

Biomedicalization and geneticization of pregnancy are essential to my point that pregnant women make decisions about continuing their pregnancies on the basis of genetic knowledge about their fetuses. I argue that once pregnant women perceive themselves as genetic bodies, they desire the most "normal, healthy" genetic bodies for their fetuses, attainable through PGT identifying genetic "abnormalities." For most women, the option of shaping their families genetically is an enormous, challenging responsibility, regardless of whether they opt to terminate. The pregnant women who have PGT have consciously chosen to test the genetics of their potential family member. This "choice" is possible only through the availability of prenatal genetic testing technologies and the socially accepting climate of using them in America, tenable because of biomedicalization and geneticization. Novas and Rose (2000) suggest that society is now viewed through "molecular optics," in which life itself is correlated with molecular/genetic conceptions. Rose (2001) argues that human existence is now molecularly biopolitical. PGT instantiates these assertions.

The decisions women make about aborting fetuses are dependent upon what technology can tell them about their potential child. Before PGT was available, women learned about the sex and health of their child at birth. The current state of PGT technologies lies somewhere between fate and design. There are presently three options available to pregnant women: 1) no testing and take what you get; 2) testing and know more about what you are getting; and 3) testing with the option of aborting a problematic fetus. One can also currently utilize in vitro fertilization with preimplantation genetic diagnosis to implant only those embryos with screened genetics.

The perceived biomedicalizing and geneticizing of pregnancy through the cultural normalization and routinization of PGT were obvious during my research. Some women, although they did have PGT, framed pregnancy as "natural" and PGT as disrupting naturalness, inserting science into what was once a woman's domain even though they decided to have PGT:

> Everything is so natural, just like what it's supposed to be, but then stepping into the medical realm and getting all these tests, you start to feel like you're poisoning the natural joy of it all with this clinical crap. It's like a medical procedure rather than a natural happening.—Rox, 38, Arab

Others decided that having prenatal genetic testing was *the* thing to do, so they had the tests. They experienced the normalizing and routinizing strategies of geneticization and just flowed with the socially accepted path.

> I looked at it very comfortably. Things could happen. We need more information. The information is there. The technology is there so let's take advantage of it. They're not incredibly risky tests. For me, pregnancy came relatively easy, so the risk of miscarriage wasn't that threatening like it is for some people. The positives of having the tests done far outweigh any of the negatives.—Jennifer, 35, Asian

These women were informed, and felt they knew what they were getting themselves into, but in a Foucauldian way, they were normalized through "technologies of the self" (Foucault 1988))—ways the self polices itself in society, which often seem to be natural but in reality are reflections of power, in this case the powers of biomedicalization and geneticization. Let's move now from the way fetal genetic bodies are created to, more specifically, why they are vulnerable.

Fetal Bodies as Vulnerable Genetic Bodies

It is important to consider why a fetus is a genetic body within the maternal genetic body. The fetal genetic body is unique from the pregnant woman's body in that its genetics are different. Traditionally, fetal genetics were a melding of the biological parents' genes, but more recently, donor genes often contribute to a fetus's genetic code. The genetic information available through PGT provides the lens through which the creation of the fetal genetic body occurs. There are four potential ways a fetus is granted a genetic body: (1) the parents were tested before conception for carrier status, which may be passed to the fetus, (2) the pregnant woman has CVS or amniocentesis, (3) the pregnant woman participates in a genetic screening program either through blood testing or ultrasound (the nuchal translucency screen), or (4) the pregnant woman uses IVF in conjunction with genetic screening of the egg, sperm, or resultant embryo. Most pregnant women participate in some kind of ultrasound during their pregnancies, so most fetuses are granted a genetic body through ultrasound examination revealing things potentially genetic that would otherwise not be known until birth.

As genetic bodies, fetuses suffer particular vulnerabilities because of the cyborg, tentative nature of their identities. Fetal genetic bodies are vulnerable through genetic knowledge in the following ways:

1. to luck-of-the-draw genetics through contributing gametes;
2. to termination;
3. to sex selection or selection against or for other detectable genetic traits.

Fetal Vulnerability through the Fate of Genetics

The primary way fetuses are vulnerable is the luck of the draw of genetics. The genes you are randomly given determine the genetic fitness you live with, and fetuses often expire very early in their existence because of faulty genetics that are incompatible with life. More than 10 percent of miscarriages occur naturally before eight weeks, and nearly 70 percent of miscarriages that occur in the first trimester are caused by chromosomal abnormalities. About one in twenty live-born infants is expected to have a single-gene disorder or a condition with an important genetic component by age twenty-five, about one in thirty-three will have a major birth defect, and a similar proportion will have a significant developmental disability (Botto and Mastroiacovo 2000). The fetus is vulnerable to its genetics even before the PGT examination.

Fetal Vulnerability to Termination

Fetal genetic bodies are vulnerable to the choices pregnant women make about their futures based on genetic information gleaned from PGT. When asked what they would do if something "abnormal" were detected, 75 percent of my sample stated they would have or would consider having an abortion if a genetic abnormality was detected through PGT. Fifteen percent of the women said they were not considering abortion, and 10 percent either did not know or did not say during the interview. Two of the women I interviewed had terminated pregnancies because of a genetic diagnosis.

Women expressed fear and anxiety about making decisions to abort their wanted pregnancies. Some hedged the decision, not committing to abortion prior to knowing the diagnosis:

> I know that it would've really been hard if something was wrong and I decided I did want to terminate. You see it there and you see it kicking, you know? I've always been pro-choice, but when you are actually there you kind of realize that "oh my god that really is a person" you know?—Maya, 34, Jewish

Others were certain that if there were a diagnosis that was not genetically acceptable to their idea of family, they would abort:

> It was strongly encouraged that I have the amnio done, and for my husband and I it was really a big decision because we had decided that if the baby did have a really good chance of having DS we would not have the baby.—Tiffany, 40, Caucasian

Many of the providers I spoke with reflected on the ways women make abortion decisions.

> Whether or not you chose prenatal diagnosis mostly depends upon your worldview side. [This] is where you start to bring in the religious views and the pregnancy termination. In the sense that that determines whether the other side—the abortion—is even an option. If you believe that pregnancy termination is murder, you're not going to ask for prenatal diagnosis, because you just don't want to deal with it. —Jacob, medical geneticist, 42, refused race/ethnicity

> It's an awful burden to live with, that choice to abort. Everyone relies on medical people to be the experts on medical information, so if you're saying this is a genetic condition we don't really know what it is, how helpful is that? I think abortion is an incredibly difficult process, even when it's a chosen abortion for your own reasons in the first trimester. We're talking about second trimester abortions because the baby has possible problems. There are lots of layers of things that can really haunt people for the rest of their lives. —Clarissa, genetic counselor, 35, North American

These providers believe the women go through complicated, multifaceted decision-making processes as opposed to quickly deciding to abort because they feel the resulting baby will not be a good fit for their families.

The difficulty in making a decision about aborting from a genetic diagnosis is summed up by Clarissa, who notes that without the "baby" there to judge whether this kind of person fits with the family, these decisions can be heart-wrenching:

> It's telling them [the diagnosis] and asking them to make a judgment and decision on that particular condition before they've ever had a chance to deal with what we're talking about. They don't have that child there. That's an awful burden to live with, making

the choice for abortion. It's a pretty unique form of responsibility. The only other thing that I can think of is deciding to take someone that you love off life support. This opens up a whole realm of decision making that I really feel people have never had to deal with before.—Clarissa, genetic counselor, 35, North American

The "burden" of making the choice for abortion that Clarissa mentions is a personal perception of what a pregnant woman who chooses to terminate might feel. Clarissa's framing of the decision making is in line with Rapp's (Rapp 1999) characterization of women who have prenatal genetic testing as "moral pioneers." These types of decisions that shape the family through preventing certain types of fetal genetic bodies from becoming babies are decisions loaded with personal and social consequences, and must be recognized as such.

The women themselves are the ones who may live every day with the good and bad of life with a child with a genetic disability. The women I interviewed all felt very strongly about this issue, and were clear about the ways they had struggled with making decisions about what type of fetus they would consider terminating. The women mentioned family considerations, including factoring other children into the decision to have testing, the wish to avoid a child with disabilities that would complicate family life, and parenting responsibilities to the unborn child.

> With my first two pregnancies I was hoping to be prepared, if the child needs a lot of special care. This pregnancy is very different. Now, we've been living with Peter [a nephew] and all of his special needs. We see the hardships on the family. I was like, I know this pregnancy is going to be Downs or some abnormality that's going to cause the rest of its life to be very difficult, and that's it. I knew that I would terminate the pregnancy, so it was a very different expectation.—Jennifer, 35, Asian

> We talked about it, and neither of us thought we could handle it. It was an awful thing to realize about one's self. You hear these wonderful stories of people who have these great kids, but we're just really scared. We're *so* scared.—Heather, 33, Caucasian

Jennifer's concern was for the child who might suffer from disabilities, while Heather admitted she and her partner were more focused on themselves and how a genetic disorder would affect them.

The women who cited other children as the reason they wanted PGT were thoughtful about how their existing children's lives would be altered by a sibling with disabilities. They expressed concern about weighing the responsibilities of the children without disabilities to care for those with genetic disease after the parents were gone, as well as about how the financial implications of a child with genetic disease would alter family life.

> Nissa, 36, Mexican, Irish, and Jewish, discussed her first child and how she and her husband had wondered when deciding to have the amnio, "Were we ready to sacrifice his life in that way?" —referring to her son and his potential responsibility to care for this "other child" if it suffered from Down Syndrome.

We were looking at the really life-altering aspect of it—financially devastating. We thought we couldn't do that, so we needed to know. And of course, we had to worry about it because we had both baby A and baby B.—Heather, 33, Caucasian (carrying twins)

Decisions made about termination are never easy, no matter what the context. The process of choosing abortion for a particular genetic diagnosis is extremely complex, involving consideration of family, finances, religion, health, and other factors. Fear is a component. My inclination to abort a Down Syndrome fetus was based on personal experience with translocation DS and with the limitations of my own and my husband's willingness to commit to the emotional work involved in raising a child with special needs—if we could avoid it, we wanted to. It is difficult to come to terms with these kinds of decisions, but they are increasingly common in the reproductive culture today. Fetal genetic bodies are vulnerable to pregnant women's preferences about what they believe will fit with their families.

Fetal Vulnerability to Selection through Technologies of Procreation

Another fetal genetic body vulnerability occurs before the fetus is even a fetus. Potential fetal genetic bodies may be prevented through technologies that allow parents to choose the types of embryos that are inserted into the uterus for implantation. This may sound like something from a futuristic movie, but it is possible to choose only male or female embryos, or those with only normal chromosomes, or those without specific detectable genes (like genes for cystic fibrosis or sickle cell), and have those put in the uterus. These techniques occur before conception, but shape the type of fetal genetic body created. Because of the choice involved, the fetal genetic body is subject to expectations different from one that was created the old-fashioned way.

Fetal genetic bodies are vulnerable before they become fetuses, when they survive to fetushood, and whether they are considered persons or not. The most basic vulnerability for fetal genetic bodies is their genetics and the inherent risks of the luck of the draw. Fetal genetic bodies are also made vulnerable through the possibility of termination based on genetic information. The final way fetal genetic bodies are made vulnerable is a product of their cyborg nature: through technologies of procreation that allow selection of specific types of embryos for implantation in the uterus.

Daunting Decisions for Fetal Futures

We are all potentially genetic bodies. The process of PGT creates fetal genetic bodies through the identification of individuals as genetic entities, shaped and determined by what the genetics of their cells indicate, no matter how tenuously, about their genetic health. Fetal genetic bodies are vulnerable because they are dependent upon the pregnant woman's choices in relation to their genetics. Having PGT produces vulnerability in fetuses by raising the question of whether the fetus is genetically good enough to keep. Termination questions create vulnerabilities for fetuses. New reproductive technologies create vulnerabilities for fetuses before they even exist.

Fetuses are not people, so it is impossible to effectively separate them from pregnant women. Through biomedicalization and geneticization, there has been a gradual shift in American society towards explaining health and social problems through genetics and medicine. The resulting environment enables and encourages pregnant women to have PGT, and to decide whether to continue the pregnancy on the basis of fetal genetics. In the end, it's all about how the fetus—defined by its fetal genetic body because technologies are the ways we know the fetus—fits within the pregnant woman's ideas about her future family.

My family is complete now. My seven pregnancies gave me two genetically healthy—by my definition—children. I do not look at them every day as the normal one and the balanced translocation carrier. But I know. Now they're too young to understand it, but someday they'll know too. It feels wrong on some level. Before I knew them, I knew their genetics. It is part of who they are; a small part, but present. I feel grateful that I was not faced with choosing abortion for a Down Syndrome fetus. That genetic diagnosis would have been most of what the fetus was to me. I'm 99 percent sure I would have had an abortion, but I am relieved that I will never know.

Questions not answered here but that should be addressed include the following: What emotional work is involved for women making these kinds of choices? What factors influence women's choices about what genetic information is bad or good for a fetus? How do women cope with the decision to end a desired pregnancy? Should American society regulate genetic choices through legislating the use of prenatal genetic technologies to ease this decision making for pregnant women, as do most other first-world countries (Great Britain, Canada, Japan, Australia, Germany, France, etc.), or is that state control of something personal? What role do partners play in the decision-making process? Should the woman have the primary decision-making power because she is the one whose body is impacted?

REFERENCES

Berck, David 2008. In-person conversation with Dr. David Berck, a board-certified maternal-fetal medicine specialist in Mt. Kisco, New York, on September 3.

Bianchi, D. W., T. M. Crombleholme, and M. E. D'Alton 2000. *Fetology: Diagnosis and Management of the Fetal Patient.* New York: McGraw-Hill Professional.

Botto, L., and P. Mastroiacovo 2000. "Surveillance for Birth Defects and Genetic Diseases," chapter 7, pp. 123–40 in Muin Khoury, Wylie Burke, and Elizabeth Thomson (eds.), *Genetics and Public Health in the 21st Century: Using Genetic Information to Improve Health and Prevent Disease.* New York: Oxford University Press.

Clarke, A., J. Shim, L. Mamo, J. Fosket, and J. Fishman 2003. "Biomedicalization: Technoscientific Transformations of Health, Illness, and U.S. Biomedicine." *American Sociological Review* 68: 161–94.

Foucault, M. 1988. "Technologies of the Self," in L. H. Martin, H. Gutman, and P. H. Hutton (eds.), *Technologies of the Self: A Seminar with Michel Foucault.* Amherst: University of Massachusetts Press.

Gallagher, J. 1987. "Prenatal Invasions and Interventions: What's Wrong with Fetal Rights?"*Harvard Women's Law Journal* 10: 9, 37, 57.

GeneTests: Medical Genetics Informational Resource 2008. Copyright, University of Washington, Seattle, 1995–2008. Available at http//:www.genetests.org. Accessed September 2, 2008.

Goffman, E. 1963. *Stigma: Notes on the Management of Spoiled Identity.* Harmondsworth, England: Penguin.

Karlberg, K. 2004. *Genetic Bodies and Genetic Families: Social and Material Constructions of Prenatal Genetic Testing.* Dissertation: University of California San Francisco.

Lippman, A. 1991. "Prenatal Genetic Testing and Screening: Constructing Needs and Reinforcing Inequities." *American Journal of Law and Medicine* 18(1–2): 15–50.

MOD 2005. "Pregnancy and Newborn Health Education Center. March of Dimes. Available at http://www.marchofdimes.com/pnhec/159_520.asp. Accessed 8 September 2008.

Novas, C., and N. Rose 2000. "Genetic Risk and the Birth of the Somatic Individual." *Economy and Society* 29(4): 485–513.

Rapp, R. 1999. *Testing Women, Testing the Fetus.* New York: Routledge.

Remennick, L. 2006. "The Quest for the Perfect Baby: Why Do Israeli Women Seek Prenatal Genetic Testing?" *Sociology of Health and Illness* 28(1): 21–53.

Rose, N. 2001. "The Politics of Life Itself." *Theory, Culture and Society* 18: 1–30.

Rothman, B. K. 2002. Review of Lisa Mitchell's *Baby's First Picture. Health, Illness and Medicine* 31(6): 786–88.

Savulescu, J. 2001. "Procreative Beneficence: Why We Should Select the Best Children." *Bioethics* 15(5): 413–26.

Sparrow, R. 2007. "Procreative Beneficence, Obligation, and Eugenics." *Genomics, Society and Policy* 3(3): 43–59.

Taylor, J. 2008. *The Public Life of the Fetal Sonogram: Technology, Consumption and the Politics of Reproduction.* New Brunswick, NJ: Rutgers University Press.

|||||||||||||||||||||||||||||||||||||||||||||||||||||||||||||||||||||||||||||||||||||||

4

Assume the Position
The Changing Contours of Sexual Violence

Patricia Hill Collins

At the center of the table sat a single microphone, a glass of water, and a name card: "Professor Anita Hill." I sat down at the lone chair at the table. . . . In front of me, facing me and the bank of journalists, was the Senate Judiciary Committee—fourteen white men dressed in dark gray suits. I questioned my decision to wear bright blue linen, though it hadn't really been a decision; that suit was the only appropriate and clean suit in my closet when I hastily packed for Washington two days before. In any case, it offered a fitting contrast.[1]

By now, the outcome of Anita Hill's 1991 testimony at the confirmation hearings of Supreme Court Justice Clarence Thomas is well known. In a calm, almost flat manner and before a packed room that contained twelve family members, including both of her parents, Hill recounted how Thomas had sexually harassed her when he headed the Equal Employment Opportunity Commission ten years earlier. Although she passed a lie detector test, her testimony did not affect the upshot of the hearings. The Senate Judiciary Committee simply did not believe her. Hill was no match for the fourteen White men in dark gray suits, many of whom had made up their minds before hearing her testimony. Thomas's opportunistic claim that the senators were engaged in a "high-tech lynching" sealed the outcome. Because lynching had been so associated with atrocities visited upon Black men, it became virtually impossible for the Senators to refute Thomas's self-presentation without being branded as racists. The combination of male dominance and the need to avoid any history of racism made the choice simple. Believing Thomas challenged racism. Doubting Thomas supported it. Thomas won. Hill lost.[2]

But was it really this simple? Certainly not for African Americans. For Black women and men, the Thomas confirmation hearings catalyzed two thorny questions.

Why did so many African Americans join the "fourteen white men dressed in dark gray suits" and reject Hill's allegations of sexual harassment? Even more puzzling, why did so many African Americans who believed Anita Hill criticize her for coming forward and testifying? Critical race theorist Kimberlé Crenshaw offers one reason why the hearings proved to be so difficult: "In feminist contexts, sexuality represents a central site of the oppression of women; rape and the rape trial are the dominant narrative trope. In antiracist discourses, sexuality is also a central site upon which the repression of Blacks has been premised; the lynching narrative is embodied as its trope. (Neither narrative tends to acknowledge the legitimacy of the other)."[3]

Crenshaw joins a prestigious group of African American women and men who, from Ida B. Wells-Barnett through Angela Davis, have examined how discourses of rape and lynching have historically influenced understandings of race, gender, and sexuality within American society.[4] In American society, sexual violence has served as an important mechanism for controlling African Americans, women, poor people, and gays and lesbians, among others. In the post-emancipation South, for example, institutionalized lynching and institutionalized rape worked together to uphold racial oppression. Together, lynching and rape served as gender-specific mechanisms of sexual violence whereby men were victimized by lynching and women by rape. Lynching and rape also reflected the type of binary thinking associated with racial and gender segregation mandating that *either* race *or* gender was primary, but not both. Within this logic of segregation, race and gender constituted separate rather than intersecting forms of oppression that could not be equally important. One was primary whereas the other was secondary. As targets of lynching as ritualized murder, Black men carried the more important burden of race. In contrast, as rape victims, Black women carried the less important burden of gender.

African American politics have been profoundly influenced by a Black gender ideology that ranks race and gender in this fashion. Lynching and rape have not been given equal weight and, as a result, social issues seen as affecting Black men, in this case lynching, have taken precedence over those that seemingly affect only Black women (rape). Within this logic, lynchings, police brutality, and similar expressions of state-sanctioned violence visited upon African American men operate as consensus issues in African American politics.[5] Lynching was not a random act; instead, it occurred *in public*, was sanctioned by government officials, and often served as a unifying event for entire communities. In this sense, lynching can be defined as ritualized murder that took a particular form in the post-emancipation South. In that context, through its highly public nature as spectacle, lynching was emblematic of a form of institutionalized, ritualized murder that was visited upon Black men in particular. African American antiracist politics responded vigorously to the public spectacle of lynching by protesting against it as damage done to Black men as representatives of the "race."[6] Because African American men were the main targets of this highly public expression of ritualized murder, the lynching of Black men came to symbolize the most egregious expressions of racism.

In contrast, the sexual violence visited upon African American women has historically carried no public name, has garnered no significant public censure, and has been seen as a crosscutting gender issue that diverts Black politics from its real job of fighting racism. Black women were raped, yet their pain and suffering remained largely invisible. Whereas lynching (racism) was public spectacle, rape (sexism) signaled *private* humiliation. Black male leaders were not unaware of the significance of institutionalized rape. Rather, their political solution of installing a Black male patriarchy in which Black men would protect "their" women from sexual assault inadvertently supported ideas about women's bodies and sexuality as men's property. Stated differently, Black women's suffering under racism would be eliminated by encouraging versions of Black masculinity whereby Black men had the same powers that White men had long enjoyed.

By 1991, the Thomas confirmation hearings made it painfully obvious that these antiracist strategies of the past were no match for the new racism. Ranking either lynching or rape as more important than the other offered a painful lesson about the dangers of choosing race over gender or vice versa as the template for African American politics. What is needed is a progressive Black sexual politics that not only recognizes how important both lynching and rape were in maintaining historical patterns of racial segregation but also questions how these practices may be changed and used to maintain the contemporary color-blind racism. Rather than conceptualizing lynching and rape as either race- or gender-specific mechanisms of social control, another approach views institutionalized rape and lynching as *different* expressions of the *same* type of social control. Together, both constitute dominance strategies that uphold the new racism. Both involve the threat of or actual physical violence done to the body's exterior, for example, beating, torture, and/or murder. Both can involve the threat of or actual infliction of violence upon the body's interior, for example, oral, anal, or vaginal penetration against the victim's will. Both strip victims of agency and control over their own bodies, thus aiming for psychological control via fear and humiliation. Moreover, within the context of the post–civil rights era's desegregation, these seemingly gender-specific forms of social control converge. Stated differently, just as the post-civil rights era has seen a crossing and blurring of boundaries of all sorts, lynching and rape as forms of state-sanctioned violence are not now and never were as gender-specific as once thought.

Revisiting the Foundation: Lynching and Rape as Tools of Social Control

Lynching and rape both served the economic needs of Southern agriculture under racial segregation. In the American South during the years 1882 to 1930 the lynching of Black people for "crimes" against Whites was a common spectacle—mob violence was neither random in time nor geography. Like many other violent crimes, lynchings were more frequent during the summer months than in cooler seasons, a reflection of the changing labor demands of agricultural production cycles.[7] One function of lynchings may well have been to rid White communities of Black people who allegedly violated the moral order. But another function was to maintain control over the African American population, especially during times when White landowners needed Black labor to work fields of cotton and tobacco.

Lynching also had political dimensions. This tool of gendered, racial violence was developed to curtail the citizenship rights of African American men after emancipation. Because Black women could not vote, Black men become targets for political repression. Explaining the power of lynching as a spectacle of violence necessary to maintain racial boundaries and to discipline populations, literary critic Trudier Harris describes the significance of violence to maintaining fixed racial group identities:

> When one Black individual dared to violate the restrictions, he or she was used as an example to reiterate to the entire race that the group would continually be held responsible for the actions of the individual. Thus an accusation of rape could lead not only to the accused Black man being lynched and burned, but to the burning of Black homes and the whipping or lynching of other Black individuals as well.[8]

This is why lynchings were not private affairs, but were public events, often announced well in advance in newspapers: "To be effective in social control, lynchings had to be visible, with the killing being a public spectacle or at least minimally having the corpse on display for all to witness. Whereas a murder—even a racially motivated one—might be hidden from public scrutiny, lynchings were not."[9]

The ritualized murders of lynching not *only* worked to terrorize the African American population overall but they also helped to install a hegemonic White masculinity over a subordinated Black masculinity. Lynching symbolized the type of violence visited upon African American men that was grounded in a constellation of daily micro-assaults on their manhood that achieved extreme form through the actual castration of many Black male lynch victims. Although Black women were also lynched, Black men were lynched in far greater numbers. Thus, lynching invokes ideas of Black male emasculation, a theme that persists within the contemporary Black gender ideology thesis of Black men as being "weak."[10] The myth of Black men as rapists also emerged under racial segregation in the South. Designed to contain this newfound threat to White property and democratic institutions, the sexual stereotype of the newly emancipated, violent rapist was constructed on the back of the Black buck. No longer safely controlled under slavery, Black men could now go "buck wild."

Wide-scale lynching could only emerge after emancipation because murdering slaves was unprofitable for their owners. In contrast, the institutionalized rape of African American women began under slavery and also accompanied the wide-scale lynching of Black men at the turn of the twentieth century. Emancipation constituted a continuation of actual practices of rape as well as the shame and humiliation visited upon rape victims that is designed to keep them subordinate. Black domestic workers reported being harassed, molested, and raped by their employers.[11] Agricultural workers, especially those women who did not work on family farms, were also vulnerable. In the South, these practices persisted well into the twentieth century. For example, in the 1990s, journalist Leon Dash interviewed Washington, D.C., resident Rosa Lee.

It took many conversations before Lee could share family secrets of stories of sexual abuse that had occurred in rural North Carolina. Because the experiences were so painful, she herself had learned about them only in bits and pieces from stories told to her by her grandmother and aunt. Rosa Lee came to understand the harsh lives endured by her mother Rosetta and her grandmother Lugenia at the bottom of the Southern Black class structure. Describing how White men would come and look over young Black girls, Rosa Lee recounted her family's stories:

> "You could tell when they wanted something. They all would come out there. Come out there in the field while everybody was working. And they're looking at the young girls. Her mouth. Teeth. Arms. You know, like they're looking at a horse. Feeling her breasts and everything. The white men would get to whispering."
> "And the mothers let them men do that?" Rosa Lee asked her grandmother.
> "What the hell do you think they could do?" Lugenia answered. "Couldn't do nothing!"[12]

The overseers apparently preferred light-skinned Black girls, often the children of previous rapes, but dark-skinned girls did not escape White male scrutiny. In exchange for the girls, mothers received extra food or a lighter load. The costs were high for the girls themselves. Because Rosetta developed early, her mother tried to hide her when the men came. But after a while, it was hopeless. Rosetta did not escape the rapes:

> "Your mama was put to auction so many times," Lugenia told Rosa Lee. "They just kept wanting your mother." The overseers would assign the girls they wanted sexually to work in isolated parts of the farm, away from their families. The girls would try to get out of the work detail. "It never worked," Lugenia said. "Those men always got them."[13]

Lugenia continued her tale by sharing how two White overseers had raped her when she was fourteen, and how two of her daughters, including Rosetta, had suffered the same fate. Only one daughter was spared, "because she was so fat," explained Lugenia. As for the children who were conceived, they were left with their mothers. Once a girl was pregnant, she was generally never bothered again. As Lugenia recalled: "They only wanted virgins. . . . They felt they'd catch diseases if they fooled with any girl that wasn't a virgin."[14]

These social practices of institutionalized lynching and institutionalized rape did not go uncontested. Ida B. Wells-Barnett's antilynching work clearly rejected both the myth of the Black male rapist as well as the thesis of Black women's inherent immorality and advanced her own highly controversial interpretation.[15] Not only did Wells-Barnett spark a huge controversy when she dared to claim that many of the sexual liaisons between White women and Black men were in fact consensual, she indicted White men as the actual perpetrators of crimes of sexual violence *both* against African American men (lynching) *and* against African American women (rape). Consider how her comments in *Southern Horrors* concerning the contradictions of laws forbidding interracial marriage place blame on White male behavior and power: "the miscegenation laws of the South only operate against the legitimate union of the races: they leave the white man free to seduce all the colored girls he can, but is death to the colored man who yields to the force and advances of a similar attraction in white women. White men lynch the offending Afro-American, not because he is a despoiler of virtue, but because he succumbs to the smiles of white women."[16] In this analysis, Wells-Barnett reveals how ideas about gender difference—the seeming passivity of women and the aggressiveness of men—are in fact deeply racialized constructs. Gender had a racial face, whereby African American women, African American men, White women, and White men occupied distinct race/gender categories within an overarching social structure that proscribed their prescribed place. Interracial sexual liaisons violated racial and gender segregation.

Despite Wells-Barnett's pioneering work in analyzing sexual violence through an intersectional framework of race, gender, class, and sexuality, African American leaders elevated race over gender.[17] Given the large numbers of lynchings from the 1890s to the 1930s, and in the context of racial segregation that stripped all African Americans of citizenship rights, this emphasis on antilynching made sense. Often accused of the crime of raping White women, African American men were lynched, and, in more gruesome cases, castrated. Such violence was so horrific that, catalyzed by Ida B. Wells-Barnett's tireless antilynching crusade, and later taken up by the NAACP and other major civil rights organizations, antilynching became an important plank in the Black civil rights agenda.

In large part due to this advocacy, lynchings have dwindled to a few, isolated albeit horrific events today. This does not mean that the use of lynching as a symbol of American racism has abated. Rather, Black protest still responds quickly and passionately to contemporary incidents of lynching and/or to events that can be recast through this historic framework. For example, the 1955 murder of fourteen-year-old Emmett Till in Mississippi was described in the press as a lynching and served as an important catalyst for the modern civil rights movement. The 1989 murder of sixteen-year-old Yusef Hawkins in the Bensonhurst section of New York City also was described as a lynching. When Hawkins and three friends came to their neighborhood to look at a used car, about thirty White youths carrying bats and sticks (one with a gun) immediately approached them. Furious that the ex-girlfriend of one of the group members had invited Black people to her eighteenth birthday party, the White kids thought that Hawkins and his friends were there for the party and attacked them, shooting Hawkins dead. In 1998, three White men in Jasper, Texas, chained a Black man named James Byrd, Jr. to a pick-up truck and dragged him to his death, an event likened to a modern-day lynching. Events such as these are publicly censured as unacceptable in a modern democracy. These modern lynchings served as rallying cries for the continuing need for an antiracist African American politics.

Unfortunately, this placement of lynching at the core of the African American civil rights agenda has also minimized the related issue of institutionalized rape. Even Ida Wells-Barnett, who clearly saw the connections between Black men's persecution as victims of lynching and Black women's vulnerability to rape, chose to advance a thesis of Black women's rape through the discourse on Black men's lynching. In the postbellum period, the rape of free African American women by White men subsisted as a "dirty secret" within the *private* domestic spheres of Black families and of Black civil society. Speaking out against their violation ran a dual risk—it reminded Black men of their inability to protect Black women from White male assaults and it potentially identified Black men as rapists, the very group that suffered from lynching. The presence of biracial Black children was tangible proof of Black male weakness in protecting Black women and of Black women's violation within a politics of respectability. Because rapes have been treated as crimes against women, the culpability of the rape victim has long been questioned. Her dress, her demeanor, where the rape occurred, and her resistance all become evidence for whether a woman was even raped at all. Because Black women as a class emerged from slavery as collective rape victims, they were encouraged to keep quiet in order to refute the thesis of their wanton sexuality. In contrast to this silencing of Black women as rape victims, there was no shame in lynching and no reason except fear to keep quiet about it. In a climate of racial violence, it was clear that victims of lynching were blameless and murdered through no fault of their own.

Because the new racism contains the past-in-present elements of prior periods, African American politics must be vigilant in analyzing how the past-in-present practices of Black sexual politics also influence contemporary politics. Clarence Thomas certainly used this history to his advantage. Recognizing the historical importance placed on lynching and the relative neglect of rape, Thomas successfully pitted lynching and rape against one another for his gain and to the detriment of African Americans as a group. Shrewdly recognizing the logic of prevailing Black gender ideology that routinely elevates the suffering of Black men as more important than that of Black women, Thomas guessed correctly that Black people would back him no matter what. If nothing else comes of the Thomas hearings, they raise the very important question of how sexual violence that was a powerful tool of social control in prior periods may be an equally important factor in the new racism.

African Americans need a more progressive Black sexual politics dedicated to analyzing how state-sanctioned violence, especially practices such as lynching (ritualized murder) and rape, operate as forms of social control. Michel Foucault's innovative idea that oppression can be conceptualized as normalized war *within* one society as opposed to between societies provides a powerful new foundation for such an analysis.[18] Mass media images of a multiethnic, diverse, color-blind America that mask deeply entrenched social inequalities mean that open warfare on American citizens (the exact case that lynching Black men presented in the past) is fundamentally unacceptable. Many Americans were horrified when they saw the 1992 videotape of Rodney King being beaten by the Los Angeles police. Fictional attacks on Black men in movies are acceptable, assaults on real ones, less so. Managing contemporary racism relies less on visible warfare between men than on social relations among men and between women and men that are saturated with relations of war. In this context, rape as a tool of sexual violence may increase in importance because its association with women and privacy makes it an effective domestic tool of social control. The threat of rape as a mechanism of control can be normally and routinely used against American citizens because the crime is typically hidden and its victims are encouraged to remain silent. New configurations of state-sanctioned violence suggest the workings of a rape culture may affect not just Black women but also Black men far more than is commonly realized. Given the significance of these tools of social control, what forms of sexual violence do African American women and men experience under the new racism? Moreover, how do these forms draw upon the ideas and practices of lynching and rape?

African American Women and Sexual Violence

Racial segregation and its reliance on lynching and rape as gender-specific tools of control have given way to an unstable desegregation under the new racism. In this context, the sexual violence visited upon African American women certainly continues its historical purpose, but may be organized in new and unforeseen ways. The terms *institutionalized rape* and *rape culture* encompass the constellation of sexual assaults on Black womanhood. From the sexual harassment visited upon Anita Hill and Black women in the workplace to sexual extortion to acquaintance, marital, and stranger rapes to how misogynistic beliefs about women create an interpretive framework that simultaneously creates the conditions in which men rape women and erases the crime of rape itself to the lack of punishment meted out by the state to Black women's rapists, sexual violence is much broader than any specific acts. Collectively, these practices comprise a rape culture that draws energy from the ethos of violence that saturates American society. African American essayist Asha Bandele describes the persistent sexual harassment she experienced during her teenaged years as part of growing up in a rape culture: "although the faces may have changed, and the places may have also, some things could always be counted on to remain the same: the pulling, and grabbing, and pinching, and slapping, and all those dirty words, and all those bad names, the leering, the propositions."[19] It is important to understand how a rape culture affects African American women because such understanding may help with antirape initiatives. It also sheds light on Black women's reactions to sexual violence, and it demonstrates how this rape culture affects other .groups, namely, children, gay men, and heterosexual men.

Rape is part of a system of male dominance. Recall that hegemonic masculinity is predicated upon a pecking order among men that is dependent, in part, on the sexual and physical domination of women. Within popular vernacular, "screwing" someone links ideas about masculinity, heterosexuality, and domination. Women, gay men, and other "weak" members of society are figuratively and literally "screwed" by "real" men. Regardless of the gender, age, social class, or sexual orientation of the recipient, individuals who are forcibly "screwed" have been "fucked" or "fucked over." "Freaks" are women (and men) who enjoy being "fucked" or who "screw" around with anyone. Because the vast majority of African American men lack access to a Black gender ideology that challenges these associations, they fail to see the significance of this language let alone the social practices that it upholds. Instead, they define hetero-sexual sex acts within a framework of "screwing" and "fucking" women and, by doing so, draw upon Western ideologies of Black hyper-heterosexuality that define Black masculinity in terms of economic, sexual, and physical dominance. In this interpre-tive context, for some men, violence (including the behaviors that comprise the rape culture) constitutes the next logical step of their male prerogative.

Currently, one of the most pressing issues for contemporary Black sexual politics concerns violence against Black women at the hands of Black men. Much of this vio-lence occurs within the context of Black heterosexual love relationships, Black fam-ily life, and within African American social institutions. Such violence takes many forms, including verbally berating Black women, hitting them, ridiculing their ap-pearance, grabbing their body parts, pressuring them to have sex, beating them, and murdering them. For many Black women, love offers no protection from sexual vio-lence. Abusive relationships occur between African American men and women who may genuinely love one another and can see the good in each other as individuals. Black girls are especially vulnerable to childhood sexual assault. Within their families and communities, fathers, stepfathers, uncles, brothers, and other male relatives are part of a general climate of violence that makes young Black girls appropriate sexual targets for predatory older men.[20]

Because Black male leaders have historically abandoned Black women as collective rape victims, Black women were pressured to remain silent about these and other violations at the hands of Black men. Part of their self-censorship certainly had to do with reluctance to "air dirty laundry" in a White society that viewed Black men as sexual predators. As Nell Painter points out, "because discussion of the abuse of Black women would not merely implicate Whites, Black women have been reluctant to press the point."[21] Until recently, Black women have been highly reluctant to speak out against rape, especially against Black male rapists, because they felt confined by the strictures of traditional Black gender ideology. Describing herself and other Black women rape victims as "silent survivors," Charlotte Pierce-Baker explains her silence: "I didn't want my nonblack friends, colleagues, and acquaintances to know that I didn't trust my own people, that I was afraid of black men I didn't know. . . . I felt responsible for upholding the image of the strong black man for our young son, *and* for the white world with whom I had contact. I didn't want my son's view of sex to be warped by this crime perpetrated upon his mother by men the color of him, his father, and his grandfathers."[22] African American women grapple with long-stand-ing sanctions within their communities that urge them to protect African American men at all costs, including keeping "family secrets" by remaining silent about male abuse.[23]

Black women also remain silent for fear that their friends, family, and community will abandon them. Ruth, a woman who, at twenty years old, was raped on a date in Los Angeles, points out: "You can talk about being mugged and boast about being held up at knife point on Market Street Bridge or something, but you can't talk about being raped. And I know if I do, I can't count on that person ever being a friend again. . . . People have one of two reactions when they see you being needy. They either take you under their wing and exploit you or they get scared and run away. They abandon you."[24] Black women recount how they feel abandoned by the very communities that they aim to protect, if they speak out. Theologian Traci West describes how the very visibility of Black female rape victims can work to isolate them: "When sexual violation occurs within their families by any member of 'their' community, black women may confront the profound injury of being psychically severed from the only source of trustworthy community available to them. Because of the ambiguities of their racial visibility, black women are on exhibit precisely at the same time as they are confined to the invisible cage."[25]

Contemporary African American feminists who raise issues of Black women's victimization must tread lightly through this minefield of race, gender, and sex. This is especially important because, unlike prior eras when White men were identified as the prime rapists of Black women, Black women are now more likely to be raped by Black men.[26] Increasingly, African American women have begun to violate long-standing norms of racial solidarity counseling Black women to defend Black men's actions at all costs and have begun actively to protest the violent and abusive behavior of some African American men. Some African American women now openly identify Black men's behavior toward them as abuse and wonder why such men routinely elevate their own suffering as more important than that experienced by African American women: "Black women do not accept racism as the reason for sorry behavior—they have experienced it firsthand, and for them it is an excuse, not a justification."[27]

Since 1970, African American women have used fiction, social science research, theology, and their writings to speak out about violence against Black women.[28] Many African American women have not been content to write about sexual violence—some have taken to the streets to protest it. Determined not to duplicate the mistakes made during the Thomas confirmation hearings, many Black women were furious when they found out that a homecoming parade had been planned for African American boxer and convicted rapist Mike Tyson upon his release from prison. The Mike Tyson rape case catalyzed many Black women to challenge community norms that counseled it was Black women's duty as strong Black women to "assume the position" of abuse. Within this logic, a Black woman's ability to absorb mistreatment becomes a measure of strength that can garner praise. In efforts to regulate displays of strong Black womanhood, some Black people apparently believed that prominent Black men like Mike Tyson were, by virtue of their status, incapable of sexual harassment or rape. "Many apparently felt that Washington [Tyson's victim] should have seen it as her responsibility to endure her pain in order to serve the greater good of the race," observes cultural critic Michael Awkward.[29] Rejecting this position that views sexual violence against Black women as secondary to the greater cause of racial uplift (unless, of course, sexual violence is perpetrated by White men), Black women in New York staged their own counterdemonstration and protested a homecoming celebration planned for a man who had just spent three years in prison on a conviction of rape.

Assume the Position: Black Women and Rape

Rape is a powerful tool of sexual violence because women are forced to "assume the position" of powerless victim, one who has no control over what is happening to her body. The rapist imagines absolute power over his victim; she (or he) is the perfect slave, supine, legs open, willing to be subdued or "fucked," and enjoying it. Rape's power also stems from relegating sexual violence to the private, devalued, domestic sphere reserved for women. The ability to silence its victims also erases evidence of the crime. These dimensions of rape make it a likely candidate to become an important form of social control under the new racism.

We have learned much from African American women both about the meaning of rape for women and how it upholds systems of oppression. For one, female rape victims often experience a form of posttraumatic stress disorder, a rape trauma syndrome of depression, anxiety, and despair, with some attempting suicide that affects them long after actual assault. Women who survived rape report effects such as mistrust of men or all people in general, continued emotional distress in connection with the abuse, specific fears such as being left alone or being out at night, and chronic depression that lasted an average of five and a half years after the assault.[30] This climate harms all African American women, but the damage done to women who survive rape can last long after actual assaults. Yvonne, who was molested by an "uncle" when she was eight and raped at age twelve, describes how the rape and sexual molestation that she endured as a child affected her subsequent attitudes toward sexuality: "I didn't take pride in my body after the rape. After it happened, I became a bit promiscuous. . . . Everyone *thought* I was bad; so I thought, I should just *be* bad. After the rape it was like sex really didn't matter to me. It didn't seem like anything special because I figured if people could just take it, . . . if they had to have it enough that they would take a little girl and put a knife to her neck and *take* it, . . . that it had nothin' to do with love."[31] Yolanda's experiences show how as an act of violence, rape may not leave the victim physically injured—emotional damage is key. The rape itself can temporarily destroy the victim's sense of self-determination and undermines her integrity as a person. Moreover, when rape occurs in a climate that already places all Black women under suspicion of being prostitutes, claiming the status of rape victim becomes even more suspect.

Black women are just as harmed by sexual assault as all women, and may be even more harmed when their abusers are African American men within Black neighborhoods. Gail Wyatt's research on Black women's sexuality provides an important contribution in furthering our understanding of Black women and rape.[32] Wyatt found little difference in the effects of rape on Black and White women who reported being rape victims. One important finding concerns the effects of *repeated* exposure to sexual violence on people who survive rape: "Because incidents of attempted and completed rape for Black women were slightly more likely to be repeated, their victimization may have a more severe effect on their understanding of the reasons that these incidents occurred, and some of these reasons may be beyond their control. As a consequence, they may be less likely to develop coping strategies to facilitate the prevention rather than the recurrence of such incidents."[33] Stated differently, African American women who suffer repeated abuse (e.g., participate in a rape culture that routinely derogates Black women more than any other group) might suffer more than women (and men) who do not encounter high levels of violence, especially sexual violence, as a daily part of their everyday lives. For example, being routinely disbelieved by those who control the definitions of violence (Anita Hill), encountering mass media representations that depict Black women as "bitches," "hoes," and other controlling images, and/or experiencing daily assaults such as having their breasts and buttocks fondled by friends and perfect strangers in school, the workplace, families, and/or on the streets of African American communities may become so routine that African American women cannot perceive their own pain.

Within the strictures of dominant gender ideology that depict Black women's sexuality as deviant, African American women often have tremendous difficulty speaking out about their abuse because the reactions that they receive from others deter them. Women may be twice victimized—even if they are believed, members of their communities may punish them for speaking out. As Yvonne points out, "where I lived in the South, anytime a black woman said she had been raped, she was never believed. In my community, they always made her feel like she did something to deserve it—or she was lying."[34] Adrienne, a forty-year-old Black woman who had been raped twice, once by a much older relative when she was seven and again by her mother's boyfriend when she was twelve, observes, "Black women tend to keep quiet about rape and abuse. . . . If you talk about it, the man will think it was your fault, or he'll think less of you. I think that's why I never told the men in my life, because I've always been afraid they would not look at me in the same way. We all live in the same neighborhood. If something happens to you, *everybody* knows."[35]

One important feature of rape is that, contrary to popular opinion, it is more likely to occur between friends, loved ones, and acquaintances than between strangers. Black women typically know their rapists, and they may actually love them. Violence that is intertwined with love becomes a very effective mechanism for fostering submission. Black women's silence about the emotional, physical, and sexual abuse that they experience within dating, marriage, and similar love relationships resembles the belief among closeted LGBT people that their silence will protect them. Just as the silence of LGBT people enables heterosexism to flourish, the reticence to speak out about rape and sexual violence upholds troublesome conceptions of Black masculinity. Within the domestic sphere, many Black men treat their wives, girlfriends, and children in ways that they would never treat their mothers, sisters, friends, workplace acquaintances, or other women. Violence and love become so intertwined that many men cannot see alternative paths to manhood that do not involve violence against women. Black feminist theologian Traci C. West uses the term "domestic captivity" to describe women who find themselves in this cycle of love and violence: "Although they are invisible, the economic, social, and legal barriers to escape that entrap women are extremely powerful. This gendered denial of rights and status compounds the breach with community. Being confined in a cage that seems invisible to every-one else nullifies a woman's suffering and exacerbates her isolation and alienation."[36]

As Barbara Omolade observes, "Black male violence is even more poignant be-cause Black men both love and unashamedly depend on Black women's loyalty and support. Most feel that without the support of a 'strong sister' they can't become 'real' men."[37] But this may be the heart of the problem—if African American men need women to bring their Black masculinity into being, then women who seem-ingly challenge that masculinity become targets for Black male violence. Educated Black women, Black career women, Black women sex workers, rebellious Black girls, and Black lesbians, among others who refuse to submit to male power, become more vulnerable for abuse. Violence against "strong" Black women enables some African American men to recapture a lost masculinity and to feel like "real" men. By describ-ing why he continued to financially exploit women, and why he hit his girlfriend, Kevin Powell provides insight into this process:

> I, like most Black men I know, have spent much of my life living in fear. Fear of White racism, fear of the circumstances that gave birth to me, fear of walking out my door wondering what humiliation will be mine today. Fear of Black women—of their mouths, their bodies, of their attitudes, of their hurts, of their fear of us Black men. I felt fragile, fragile as a bird with clipped wings, that day my ex-girlfriend stepped up her game and spoke back to me. Nothing in my world, nothing in my self-definition prepared me for dealing with a woman as an equal. My world said women were inferior, that they must, at all costs, be put in their place, and my instant reaction was to do that. When it was over, I found myself dripping with sweat, staring at her back as she ran barefoot out of the apartment.[38]

Powell's narrative suggests that the connections among love, sexuality, and violence are much more complicated than the simple linear relationship in which African American men who are victimized by racism use the power that accrues to them as men to abuse African American women (who might then use their power as adults to beat African American children). Certainly one can trace these relations in love relationships, but the historical and contemporary interconnections of love, sexual-ity, violence, and male dominance in today's desegregated climate are infinitely more complex.

In these contexts, it may be possible for African American women and men to get caught up in a dynamics of love, sexuality, and dominance whereby the use of violence and sexuality resembles addiction. In other words, if Black masculinity and Black femininity can be achieved only via sexuality and violence, sexuality, violence, and domination become implicated in the very definitions themselves. Once ad-dicted, there is no way to be a man or a woman without staying in roles prescribed by Black gender ideology. Men and women may not engage in open warfare, but they do engage in mutual policing that keeps everyone in check. As a form of sexual vio-lence, actual rapes constitute the tip of the iceberg. Rape joins sexuality and violence as a very effective tool to routinize and normalize oppression.

The effectiveness of rape as a tool of control against Black women does not mean that they have escaped other forms of social control that have disproportionately affected Black men. Working jobs outside their homes heightens African American women's vulnerability to other forms of state-sanctioned violence. For example, Black women are vulnerable to physical attacks, and some Black women are murdered. But unlike the repetitive and ritualized form of male lynching to produce a horrific spectacle for White and Black viewers, Black women neither served as symbols of the race nor were their murders deemed to be as significant. There is evidence that forms of social control historically reserved for Black men are also impacting Black women. For example, in the post-civil rights era, African American women have increasingly been incarcerated, a form of social control historically reserved for African American men. Black women are seven times more likely to be imprisoned than White women and, for the first time in American history, Black women in California and several other states are being imprisoned at nearly the same rate as White men. Incarcerating Black women certainly shows an increasing willingness to use the tools of state-sanctioned violence historically reserved for Black men against Black women. But is there an increasing willingness to use tools of social control that have been primarily applied to women against Black men? If institutionalized rape and institutionalized lynching constitute *different* expressions of the *same* type of social control, how might they affect Black men?

African American Men, Masculinity, and Sexual Violence

African American men's experiences with the criminal justice system may signal a convergence of institutionalized rape and institutionalized murder (lynching) as state-sanctioned forms of sexual violence. Since 1980, a growing prison-industrial complex has incarcerated large numbers of African American men. Whatever measures are used—rates of arrest, conviction, jail time, parole, or types of crime—the record seems clear that African American men are more likely than White American men to encounter the criminal justice system. For example, in 1990, the nonprofit Washington, D.C.–based Sentencing Project released a survey result suggesting that, on an average day in the United States, one in every four African American men aged 20 to 29 was either in prison, jail, or on probation/parole.[39] Practices such as unprovoked police brutality against Black male citizens, many of whom die in police custody, and the disproportionate application of the death penalty to African American men certainly suggest that the state itself has assumed the functions of lynching. Because these practices are implemented by large, allegedly impartial bureaucracies, the high incarceration rates of Black men and the use of capital punishment on many prisoners becomes seen as natural and normal.

But how does one manage such large populations that are incarcerated in prison and also in large urban ghettos? The ways in which Black men are treated by bureaucracies suggest that the disciplinary practices developed primarily for controlling women can be transferred to new challenges of incarcerating so many men.

In particular, the prison-industrial complex's treatment of male inmates resembles the tactics honed on women in a rape culture, now operating not between men and women, but among men. These tactics begin with police procedures that disproportionately affect poor and working-class young Black men. Such men can expect to be stopped by the police for no apparent reason and asked to "assume the position" of being spread-eagled over a car hood, against a wall, or face down on the ground. Rendering Black men prone is designed to make them submissive, much like a female rape victim. The videotape of members of the Los Angeles Police Department beating motorist Rodney King provided a mass media example of what can happen when Black men refuse to submit. Police treatment of Black men demonstrates how the command to "assume the position" can be about much more than simple policing.

Rape while under custody of the criminal justice system is a visible yet underanalyzed phenomenon, only recently becoming the subject of concern. Because rape is typically conceptualized within a frame of heterosexuality and with women as rape victims, most of the attention has gone to female inmates assaulted by male guards. Yet the large numbers of young African American men who are in police custody suggest that the relationship among prison guards and male inmates from different race and social class backgrounds constitutes an important site for negotiating masculinity. Moreover, within prisons, the connections among hegemonic and subordinated masculinities, violence, and sexuality may converge in ways that mimic and help structure the "prison" of racial oppression. Because prisons rely on surveillance, being raped in prison turns private humiliation into public spectacle. The atmosphere of fear that is essential to a rape culture as well as the mechanisms of institutionalized rape function as important tools in controlling Black men throughout the criminal justice system. Whereas women fear being disbelieved, being abandoned, and losing the love of their families, friends, and communities, men fear loss of manhood. Male rape in the context of prison signals an emasculation that exposes male rape victims to further abuse. In essence, a prison-industrial complex that condones and that may even foster a male rape culture attaches a very effective form of disciplinary control to a social institution that itself is rapidly becoming a new site of slavery for Black men.

Drawing upon a national sample of prisoners' accounts and on a complex array of data collected by state and federal agencies, *No Escape: Male Rape in U.S. Prisons,* a 2001 publication by Human Rights Watch, claims that male prisoner-on-prisoner sexual abuse is not an aberration; rather, it constitutes a deeply rooted systemic problem in U.S. prisons. They note, "judging by the popular media, rape is accepted as almost a commonplace of imprisonment, so much so that when the topic of prison arises, a joking reference to rape seems almost obligatory."[40] Prison authorities claim that male rape is an exceptional occurrence. The narratives of prisoners who wrote to Human Rights Watch say otherwise. Their claims are backed up by independent research that suggests high rates of forced oral and anal intercourse. In one study, 21 percent of inmates had experienced at least one episode of forced or coerced sexual contact since being incarcerated, and at least 7 percent reported being raped. Certain prisoners are targeted for sexual assault the moment they enter a penal facility. A broad range of factors correlate with increased vulnerability to rape: "youth, small size, and physical weakness; being White, gay, or a first offender; possessing 'feminine' characteristics such as long hair or a high voice; being unassertive, unaggressive, shy, intellectual, not street-smart, or 'passive'; or having been convicted of a sexual offence against a minor."[41]

As is the case of rape of women, prisoners in the Human Rights Watch study, including those who had been forcibly raped, reported that the *threat* of violence is a more common factor than actual rape. A rape culture is needed to condone the actual practices associated with institutionalized rape. Once subject to sexual abuse, prisoners can easily become trapped into a sexually subordinate role. Prisoners refer to the initial rape as "turning out" the victim. Rape victims become stigmatized as "punks": "Through the act of rape, the victim is redefined as an object of sexual abuse. He has been proven to be weak, vulnerable, 'female,' in the eyes of other inmates."[42] Victimization is public knowledge, and the victim's reputation will follow him to other units and even to other prisons. In documenting evidence that sounds remarkably like the property relations of chattel slavery, Human Rights Watch reports on the treatment of male rape victims:

> Prisoners unable to escape a situation of sexual abuse may find themselves becoming another inmate's "property." The word is commonly used in prison to refer to sexually subordinate inmates, and it is no exaggeration. Victims of prison rape, in the most extreme cases, are literally the slaves of their perpetrators. Forced to satisfy another man's sexual appetites whenever he demands, they may also be responsible for washing his clothes, massaging his back, cooking his food, cleaning his cell, and myriad other chores. They are frequently "rented out" for sex, sold, or even auctioned off to other inmates. . . . Their most basic choices, like how to dress and whom to talk to, may be controlled by the person who "owns" them. Their name may be replaced by a female one. Like all forms of slavery, these situations are among the most degrading and dehumanizing experiences a person can undergo.[43]

Prison officials condone these practices, leaving inmates to fend for themselves. Inmates reported that they received no protection from correctional staff, even when they complained.

Analyzing the connections among imprisonment, masculinity, and power, legal scholar Teresa Miller points out that "for most male prisoners in long-term confinement, the loss of liberty suffered during incarceration is accompanied by a psychological loss of manhood."[44] In men's high-security prisons and large urban jails, for example, sexist, masculinized subcultures exist where power is allocated on the basis of one's ability to resist sexual victimization (being turned into a "punk"). Guards relate to prisoners in sexually derogatory ways that emphasize the prisoners' subordinate position. For example, guards commonly address male prisoners by sexually belittling terms such as *pussy, sissy, cunt,* and *bitch*.[45] Moreover, the social pecking order among male prisoners is established and reinforced through acts of sexual subjugation, either consensual or coerced submission to sexual penetration. The theme of dominating women has been so closely associated with hegemonic masculinity that, when biological females are unavailable, men create "women" in order to sustain hierarchies of masculinity.

Miller reports that the pecking order of prisoners consists of three general classes of prisoners: men, queens, and punks. "Men" rule the joint and establish values and norms for the entire prison population. They are political leaders, gang members, and organizers of the drug trade, sex trade, protection rackets, and smuggled contraband. A small class of "queens" (also called bitches, broads, and sissies) exists below the "men." A small fraction of the population, they seek and are assigned a passive sexual role associated with women. As Miller points out, "the queen is the foil that instantly defined his partner as a 'man.'"[46] However, "queens" are denied positions of power within the inmate economy. "Punks" or "bitches" occupy the bottom of the prison hierarchy. "Punks" are male prisoners who have been forced into sexual submission through actual or threatened rape. As Miller points out, "punks are treated as slaves. Sexual access to their bodies is sold through prostitution, exchanged in satisfaction of debt and loaned to others for favors."[47] In essence, "punks" are sexual property. A prisoner's position within this hierarchy simultaneously defines his social and sexual status.

Male rape culture has several features that contribute to its effectiveness as a tool of social control. For one, in the prison context, maintaining masculinity is always in play. Miller points to the fluid nature of masculine identity: "Because status within the hierarchy is acquired through the forcible subjugation of others, and one's status as a man can be lost irretrievably through a single incident of sexual submission, 'men' must constantly demonstrate their manhood through sexual conquest. Those who do not vigorously demonstrate their manhood through sexual conquest are more apt to be challenged and be potentially overpowered. Hence, the surest way to minimize the risk of demotion is to aggressively prey on other prisoners."[48] Consensual and forced sexual contact among men in prison has become more common.[49] Because masculinity is so fluid and is a subject of struggle, it is important to note that sexual relations between men does not mean that they are homosexuals. Rather, sexual dominance matters. Those men who are treated as if they were women, for example, the "queens" who voluntarily submit to the sexual advances of other men and are orally or anally "penetrated" like women, may become lesser, less "manly" men in prison but need not be homosexuals. Moreover, those men who are forcibly penetrated and labeled "punks" may experience a subordinated masculinity in prison, but upon release from prison, they too can regain status as "men." Engaging in sexual acts typically reserved for women (being penetrated) becomes the mark of subordinated masculinity. In contrast, those men who are "on top" or who are serviced by subordinate men retain their heterosexuality. In fact, their masculinity may be enhanced by a hyper-masculinity that is so powerful that it can turn men into women.

Another important feature of male rape culture in prison concerns its effects on sexual identities. Since male prisoner-on-prisoner rape involves persons of the same sex, it is often misnamed "homosexual rape" that is thought to be perpetrated by "homosexual predators." This terminology ignores the fact that the vast majority of prison rapists do not view themselves as being gay. Rather, they are heterosexuals who see their victim as substituting for a woman. Because sexual identities as heterosexual or homosexual constitute fluid rather than fixed categories, masculinity in the prison context is performed and constructed.[50] The sexual practices associated with rape—forced anal and oral penetration—determine sexual classification as "real" men or "punks," not biological maleness. In this predatory environment, it is important to be the one who "fucks with" others, not the one who "sucks dick" or who is "fucked in the ass." As one Illinois prisoner explains it: "the theory is that you are not gay or bisexual as long as YOU yourself do not allow another man to stick his penis into your mouth or anal passage. If you do the sticking, you can still consider yourself to be a macho man/heterosexual."[51] The meaningful distinction in prison is not between men who engage in sex with men and in sex with women, but between what are deemed "active" and "passive" participation in the sexual act.[52]

Installing a male rape culture in prison has the added important feature of shaping racial identities. White men rarely rape Black men. Instead, African American men are often involved in the rape of White men who fit the categories of vulnerability.[53] One Texas prisoner describes the racial dynamics of sexual assault: "Part of it is revenge against what the non-white prisoners call, 'The White Man,' meaning authority and the justice system. A common comment is, 'ya'll may run it out there, but this is our world!'"[54] Another prisoner sheds additional light on this phenomenon: "In my experience having a 'boy' (meaning white man) to a Negro in prison is sort of a 'trophy' to his fellow black inmates. And I think the root of the problem goes back a long time ago to when the African Americans were in the bonds of slavery. They have a favorite remark: 'It ain't no fun when the rabbit's got the gun, is it?'"[55] Drawing upon psychoanalytic theory, William Pinar offers one explanation for these racial patterns: "Straight black men could have figured out many kinds of revenge, could they not: physical maiming for one, murder for another. But somehow black men knew exactly what form revenge must be once they were on 'top,' the same form that 'race relations' have taken (and continue to take) in the United States. 'Race' has been about getting fucked, castrated, made into somebody's 'punk,' politically, economically, and, yes, sexually."[56]

Yet another important feature of male rape culture in prison that shows the effectiveness of this form of sexual violence concerns its effects on male victims/survivors. Men who are raped often describe symptoms that are remarkably similar to those of female rape victims, namely, a form of posttraumatic stress disorder described as a rape trauma syndrome. Men expressed depression, anxiety, and despair, with some attempting suicide.[57] Another devastating consequence is the transmission of HIV.[58] However, because male rape victims are men, they still have access to masculinity and male power, if they decide to claim it. As one Texas prisoner described his experiences in the rape culture: "It's fixed where if you're raped, the only way you [can escape being a punk is if] you rape someone else. Yes I know that's fully screwed, but that's how your head is twisted. After it's over you may be disgusted with yourself, but you realize that you're not powerless and that you can deliver as well as receive pain."[59] Because prison authorities typically deny that male rape is a problem, this inmate's response is rational. As one inmate in a Minnesota prison points out, "When a man gets raped nobody gives a damn. Even the officers laugh about it. I bet he's going to be walking with a limp ha ha ha. I've heard them."[60]

It is important to remember that the vast majority of African American men are not rapists nor have they been raped. However, male rape in prison is a form of sexual dominance and its clear ties to constructing the masculine pecking order within prisons do have tremendous implications for African American male prisoners, their perceptions of Black masculinity, and the gendered relationships among all African Americans. First and foremost, because such a large proportion of African American men are either locked up in state and federal prisons and/or know someone who has been incarcerated, large numbers of African American men are exposed to conceptions of Black masculinity honed within prison rape culture.[61] Among those African American men who are incarcerated, those who fit the profile of those most vulnerable to abuse run the risk of becoming rape victims. In this context of violence regulated by a male rape culture, achieving Black manhood requires *not* fitting the profile and *not* assuming the position. In a sense, surviving in this male rape culture and avoiding victimization require at most becoming a predator and victimizing others and, at the least, becoming a silent witness to the sexual violence inflicted upon other men.

Second, so many African American men are in prison on any given day that we fail to realize that the vast majority of these very same men will someday be released. Black men cannot be easily classified in two types, those who are "locked up" in prison and those who remain "free" outside it. Instead, prison culture and street culture increasingly reinforce one another, and the ethos of violence that characterizes prison culture flows into a more general ethos of violence that affects all Black men. For many poor and working-class Black men, prison culture and street culture constitute separate sides of the same coin. Sociologist Elijah Anderson's "code of the streets" has become indistinguishable from the violent codes that exist in most of the nation's jails, prisons, reform schools, and detention centers. Describing young Black men's encounters with the criminal justice system as "peculiar rites of passage," criminologist Jerome Miller contends: "So many young black males are now routinely socialized to the routines of arrest, booking, jailing, detention, and imprisonment that it should come as no surprise that they bring back into the streets the violent ethics of survival which characterize these procedures."[62] For middle-class Black men who lack the actual experiences of prison and street culture, mass media representations of gangstas as authentic symbols of Black masculinity help fill the void. They may not be actual gangstas, but they must be cognizant that they could easily be mistaken as criminals. Varieties of Black masculinity worked through in prisons and on the streets strive to find some place both within and/or as respite from this ethos of violence.

Black men who have served time in prison and are then released bring home this ethos of violence and its culpability in shaping Black masculinity. Certainly these men are denied access to full citizenship rights, for example, having a prison record disqualifies large numbers of Black men from getting jobs, ever holding jobs as police officers, or even voting. But an equally damaging effect lies in the views of Black masculinity that these men carry with them through the revolving doors of street and prison culture, especially when being victims or perpetrators within a male rape culture frames their conceptions of gender and sexuality. One wonders what effects these forms of Black masculinity are having on African American men, as well as their sexual partners, their children, and African American communities.

As sociologist Melvin Oliver points out in *The Violent Social World of Black Men,* African American men live in a climate of violence.[63] Because the American public routinely perceives African American men as actual or potential criminals, it often overlooks the climate of fear that affects Black boys, Black men on the street, and Black men in prison. In his memoir titled *Fist, Stick, Knife, Gun: A Personal History of Violence in America,* Geoffrey Canada details how he and his brothers had to work out elaborate strategies for negotiating the streets of their childhood, all in efforts to arrive safely at school, or buy items at the grocery store. As children of a single mother, they lacked the protection of an older Black man, thus making them vulnerable in the pecking order among Black men.[64] All Black boys must negotiate this climate of fear, yet it often takes an especially tragic incident to arouse public protest about Black boys who victimize one another. For example, in 1994, five-year-old Eric Morse was dropped from a fourteenth floor apartment window to his death in the Ida B. Wells public housing project in Chicago. His tormentors allegedly threw him down a stairwell, stabbed him, and sprayed him with Mace before dropping him from the window. The two boys convicted of murdering him were ten and eleven years old.

The question of how the ethos of violence affects Black male adolescents is of special concern. In many African American inner-city neighborhoods, the presence of gang violence demonstrates a synergistic relationship between Black masculinity and violence. Research on Black male youth illustrates an alarming shift in the meaning of adolescence for men in large, urban areas. Autobiographical work by David Dawes on the Young Lords of Chicago, Nathan McCall recalling his youth in a small city in Virginia, and Sayinka Shakur's chilling autobiography that details how his involvement in gang violence in Los Angeles earned him the nickname "Monster" all delineate shocking levels of Black male violence.[65] As revealed in these works, many young Black men participate in well-armed street gangs that resemble military units in which they are routinely pressured to shoot and kill one another. In these conditions, it becomes very difficult for Black boys to grow up without fear of violence and become men who refuse to use violence against others.

Only recently have scholars turned their attention to the effects that living in fear in climates of violence might have both on the quality of American men's lives and on their conceptions of Black masculinity. Sociologist Al Young conducted extensive interviews with young Black men who were in their twenties, with some surprising findings. The men in his study did not exhibit the swagger and bravado associated with glorified hip-hop images of gangstas, thugs, and hustlers. Instead, these men shared stories of living in fear of being victimized, of dropping out of school because they were afraid to go, of spending considerable time figuring out how to

avoid joining gangs, and, as a result, becoming cut off from all sorts of human relationships.[66] Some suggest that Black men have given up hope, or as columnist Joan
Morgan states: "When brothers can talk so cavalierly about killing each other and
then reveal that they have no expectation to see their twenty-first birthday, that is
straight-up depression masquerading as machismo."[67]

Unlike Young's work, the effects of violence on African American men, especially
those with firsthand knowledge of a prison male rape culture, have been neglected
within social science research. Moreover, the effects of sexual violence on African
American men also generates new social problems for African American families,
communities, and American society overall. As the graphic discussion of the male
"slaves" as property within the penal system indicates, many Black men victimize one
another and strive to reproduce the same male pecking order *within* African American communities that they learn and understand as masculine within prison. These
men victimize not just women and children; they harm other men and place all in a
climate of fear.

Sexual Violence Revisited

The new racism reflects changes in mechanisms of social control of the post–civil
rights era. Lynching and rape as forms of violence still permeate U.S. society, but
because they no longer are as closely associated with the binary thinking of the logic
of segregation, these seemingly gender-specific practices of sexual violence are organized in new ways.

First, movies, films, music videos, and other mass media spectacles that depict
Black men as violent and that punish them for it have replaced the historical spectacles provided by live, public lynchings. When combined with the criminalization of
Black men's behavior that incarcerates so many men, the combination of mass media images and institutional practices justifies these gender-specific mechanisms of
control. For example, as vicarious participants in spectator sports, audience members
can watch as men in general, and African American men in particular, get beaten,
pushed, trampled, and occasionally killed, primarily in football arenas and boxing
rings. The erotic arousal that many spectators might feel from viewing violence that
historically came in attending live events (the violence visited upon the lynch victim
being one egregious example of this situation) can be experienced vicariously in the
anonymity of huge sports arenas and privately via cable television. Films and other
forms of visual media provide another venue for framing societal violence. Contemporary films, for example, the slasher horror films targeted to adolescents, produce
images of violence that rival the most gruesome lynchings of the past. Lynching is no
longer a live show confined to African American men, but, as is the case with other
forms of entertainment, has moved into the field of representations and images. Thus,
there is the same ability to watch killing, left in the safety of one's living room, with
DVD technology allowing the scene to replayed. Both of these mass media spectacles
fit nicely with the lack of responsibility associated with the new racism. Viewers need

not "know" their victims, and violence can be blamed on the "bad guys" in the film or on governmental or corporate corruption. Witnessing beatings, tortures, and murders as spectator sport fosters a curious community solidarity that feeds back into a distinctly American ethos of violence associated with the frontier and slavery. Black men are well represented within this industry of media violence, typically as criminals whose death should be celebrated, and often as murder victims who are killed as "collateral damage" to the exploits of the real hero.

Second, in this new context of mass media glorification of violence, rape of women (but not of men) along with the constellation of practices and ideas that comprise rape culture has been moved from the hidden place of privacy of the past and also displayed as spectacle. Whether in Hollywood feature films, independent films such as Spike Lee's *She's Gotta Have It,* or the explosion of pornography as lucrative big business, viewers can now see women raped, beaten, tortured, and killed. Clearly, the ideas of a rape culture persist as a fundamental form of sexual dominance that affects African American women. As feminists remind us, thinking about rape not as a discrete act of violence but as part of a systemic pattern of violence reveals how social institutions and the idea structures that surround rape work to control actual and potential victims. Not every woman needs to be raped to have the *fear* of rape function as a powerful mechanism of social control in everyday life. Women routinely adjust their behavior for fear of being raped. The workings of a rape culture, the privacy of the act, the secrecy, the humiliation of being a rape victim, seem especially well suited to the workings of routinization of violence as a part of the "normalized war" that characterizes desegregation. Rape becomes more readily available as a public tool of sexual dominance. At the same time, prison rape of men is not taken seriously and does not routinely appear as entertainment.

Third, the mechanisms of social control associated with a rape culture and with institutionalized rape might be especially effective in maintaining a new racism grounded in advancing myths of integration that mask actual racial relations of segregation. Both Black men and Black women are required to "assume the position" of subordination within a new multicultural America, and the practices of a rape culture help foster this outcome. Most Americans live far more segregated lives than mass media leads them to believe. The vast majority of men and women, Blacks and Whites, and straights and gays still fit into clearly identifiable categories of gender, race, and sexuality, the hallmark of a logic of segregation. At the same time, the increased visibility and/or vocality of individuals and groups that no longer clearly fit within these same categories has changed the political and intellectual landscape. For example, many middle-class African Americans now live in the unstable in-between spaces of racially desegregated neighborhoods; lesbian, gay, bisexual, and transgendered (LGBT) people who have come out of the closet undercut the invisibility required for assumptions of heterosexism; some working-class kids of all races now attend elite universities; and biracial children of interracial romantic relationships have challenged binary understandings of race. Crossing borders, dissolving boundaries, and other evidence of an imperfect desegregation does characterize the experiences of a substantial minority of the American population.

When it comes to African Americans, focusing too closely on these important changes can leave the impression that much more change is occurring than actually is. The record on African American racial desegregation is far less rosy. This illusion of racial integration, especially that presented in a powerful mass media, masks the persistence of racial segregation for African Americans, especially the racial hyper-segregation of large urban areas. Maintaining racial boundaries in this more fluid, desegregated situation requires not just revised representations of Black people in mass media but also requires new social practices that maintain social control yet do not have the visibility of past practices. Institutionalized rape serves as a mechanism for maintaining gender hierarchies of masculinity and femininity. But institutionalized rape and the workings of rape culture can also serve as effective tools of social control within racially desegregated settings precisely because they intimidate and silence victims and encourage decent people to become predators in order to avoid becoming victims. In this sense, the lessons from a rape culture become important in a society that is saturated with relations of war against segments of its own population but that presents itself as fair, open, and without problems.

Finally, these emerging modes of social control have important implications for antiracist African American politics generally and for developing a more progressive Black sexual politics in particular. Violence constitutes a major social problem for African Americans. State violence is certainly important, but the violence that African Americans inflict upon on another can do equal if not more damage. When confronting a social problem of this magnitude, rethinking Black gender ideology, especially the ways in which ideas about masculinity and femininity shape Black politics, becomes essential. As the Clarence Thomas confirmation revealed, African Americans' failure to understand the gendered contours of sexual violence led them to choose race over gender. Incidents such as this suggest that Black leaders have been unable to help either Black women or Black men deal with the structural violence of the new racism because such leaders typically fail to question prevailing Black gender ideology. What happens when men incorporate ideas about violence (as an expression of dominance) into their definitions of Black masculinity? Can they remain "real" men if they do not engage in violence? How much physical, emotional, and/or sexual abuse should a "strong" Black woman absorb in order to avoid community censure? Stopping the violence will entail much more than Black organizations who protest state-sanctioned violence by White men against Black ones. Because violence flows from social injustices of race, class, gender, sexuality, and age, for African American women and men, eradicating violence requires a new Black sexual politics dedicated to a more expansive notion of social justice.

NOTES

1. Hill 1997, 13.

2. African Americans may have lost far more than Anita Hill as a result of Thomas's appointment. Routinely aligning himself with its most conservative wing, Thomas's record on the Supreme Court concerning racism has been disappointing to labor organizations,

women's constituencies, and civil rights groups. Anita Hill also suffered personal loss. In the ten years following the hearings, Hill experienced hate mail, unwanted phone calls, and death threats. In contrast, Thomas has remained on the Supreme Court, enjoying its privileges. Hill was virtually run out of her job as a law professor at the University of Oklahoma and underwent persistent harassment by students, colleagues and strangers on the street (Hill 1997).

3. Crenshaw 1992, 205.

4. Wells-Barnet 2002; Davis 1978.

5. For a discussion of the consensus and cross-cutting issues within Black politics, see Cohen and Jones 1999.

6. Lynching has not always been so central to Black antiracist politics. See historian Paula Giddings' analysis of Black leadership, which initially took little action concerning lynching before Ida B. Wells-Barnett's solitary crusade (Giddings 2001).

7. Beck and Tolnay 1992, 22.

8. Harris 1984, 19.

9. Beck and Tolnay 1992, 7–8.

10. Gender analysis shed light on why castration reappears in accounts of Black male lynchings. Robyn Weigman provides a psychoanalytic analysis of lynching that examines its power in terms of national identity—the end of slavery constituted a rebirth of the nation that needed to develop new race relations. African American bodies were no longer commodities, and making this transition from slavery to the reenslavement of Jim Crow de jure segregation required a complicated process of reworking Black male sexuality and African American masculinity. Weigman suggests that lynching served as a "threat of ritualized death" that provided one means for hegemonic White masculinity to be rearticulated within the uncertainties of postemancipation. As Weigman points out, "not only does lynching enact a grotesquely symbolic—if not literal—sexual encounter between the white mob and its victim, but the increasing utilization of castration as a preferred form of mutilation for African American men demonstrates lynching's connection to the sociosymbolic realm of sexual difference. In the disciplinary fusion of castration with lynching, the mob severs the black male from the masculine, interrupting the privilege of the phallus, and thereby reclaiming, through the perversity of dismemberment, his (masculine) potentiality for citizenship" (Weigman 1993, 224).

11. Collins 2000, 53–55.

12. Dash 1996, 225.

13. Dash 1996, 226.

14. Dash 1996, 226.

15. In 1892, Ida B. Wells-Barnett learned firsthand the lengths to which some White citizens of Memphis were willing to go to maintain African American political and economic subordination. In March, Memphis Whites lynched three successful African American managers of a grocery business. Wells knew all three men, and also understood that they were resented because their store successfully competed with a White store. This painful experience of her friends' lynching was a turning point in Wells-Barnett's commitment to social justice activism. Wells-Barnett wrote an editorial that, for 1892, advanced the shocking hypothesis that not only were African American men often falsely accused of rape but also that because some White women were attracted to Black men, some sexual relationships that did occur between African American men and White women were consensual. Fortunately, when the editorial appeared, Wells-Barnett was out of town or she too might have been lynched. Memphis citizens burned down the *Free Speech* and threatened Wells-Barnett's life if she ever

returned to Memphis. This shocking catalyst marked the beginning of Ida Wells-Barnett's impressive over-twenty-year crusade against lynching that took the form of going on speaking tours, publishing editorials, preparing pamphlets, organizing community services, participating in women's and civil rights groups, and publishing *Southern Horrors, A Red Record,* and *Mob Rule in New Orleans*, three of Wells-Barnett's important pamphlets on lynching (Wells-Barnett 2002).

16. Wells-Barnett 2002, 6.

17. James 1996; Giddings 2001.

18. These ideas come from Anne Stoler's excellent analysis of Michel Foucault's ideas about race. Stoler states: "as 'private wars' were cancelled and war was made the prerogative of states, as war proper moves to the margins of the social body, as society is 'cleansed of war-like relations' . . . this 'strange,' 'new' discovery emerged, one in which society itself was conceived as an entity saturated with the relations of war" (Stoler 1995, 64–65).

19. Bandale 1999, 86.

20. See Wilson 1994 and Pierce-Baker 1998, 117–139. African American adolescent mothers also report that the fathers of their babies are much older men (Kaplan 1997).

21. Painter 1992, 213.

22. Pierce-Baker 1998, 64.

23. Cleage 1993.

24. Pierce-Baker 1998, 91.

25. West 1999, 59.

26. Because so many African American women live in large, racially segregated urban areas, Black women are more likely to be victims of rape than White women—reported rapes are 1.4 to 1.7 times higher. Yet such women are less likely to have their rape cases come to trial than White women, and they are less likely to get convictions for those cases that do come to trial. Moreover, African American women who are sexually assaulted are less likely to use rape-counseling services. It is important to stress that patterns of Black male violence against Black women occur within a broader social context in which the routinization of violence works to desensitize everyone to its effects. Viewing one's first violent movie may be shocking—viewing the fiftieth film has far less impact. The genre of stalker films that make raping and killing women a spectator sport contributes to this broader climate of violence against women. Black men whose violent behavior is targeted toward Black women are certainly not immune from these societal pressures.

27. Bell 1999, 240.

28. Childhood sexual assault (Maya Angelou's *I Know Why the Caged Bird Sings* and Toni Morrison's *The Bluest Eye*); family violence (see Alice Walker's fiction, especially *The Color Purple* and *The Third Life of George Copeland*), and the effects of rape on African American women (Gayle Jones's *Eva's Man*) have all been explored in African American women's fiction. Black women's essays examine similar themes. Statements about the pain of rape (Austin 1993), rape as a tool of political control (Davis 1978) and the pervasiveness of violence in African American civil society (Cleage 1993) all have received considerable treatment in African American women's writings. Increasingly, womanist theologians are providing a new interpretive context that encourages Black women to speak out about abuse. See Douglas 1999 and West 1999.

29. Awkward 1999, 137.

30. Wyatt 1992, 87.

31. Pierce-Baker 1998, 136.

32. Supplementing survey data with interviews with 126 African American and 122 White Women in the Los Angeles area conducted by a same-race interviewer, Wyatt investigated women's perceptions of rape. Wyatt' s interviewers also asked the question, "Why do you think you were victimized?" African American women were significantly more likely than White women to offer explanations about their victimization that involved the riskiness of their living circumstances (Wyatt 1992, 84).

33. Wyatt 1992, 85.

34. Pierce-Baker 1998, 124.

35. Pierce-Baker 1998, 161.

36. West 1999, 58.

37. Omolade 1994, 89.

38. Powell 2000, 74.

39. Miller 1996, 1–9.

40. Human Rights Watch 2001, 3.

41. Human Rights Watch 2001, 5.

42. Human Rights Watch 2001, 7.

43. Human Rights Watch 2001, 8.

44. Miller 2000, 300.

45. Material in this section is taken from Miller 2000, 300.

46. Miller 2000, 302.

47. Miller 2000, 303.

48. Miller 2000, 303.

49. Human Rights Watch 2001.

50. Sociologist R. W. Connell offers an explanation for the fluidity of gender categories: "In our culture, men who have sex with men are generally oppressed, but they are not definitively excluded from masculinity—conflicts occur between their sexuality and their social presence as men, about the meaning of their choice of sexual object, and in their construction of relationships with women and with heterosexual men" (Connell 1992, 737).

51. Human Rights Watch 2001, 70.

52. Violence targeted against gay Black men can be especially vicious, in part, because gay Black men become suitable targets for violence. Some guards view homosexuality as an open invitation to sexuality. As one prisoner, who was heterosexual, recalled: "I had an officer tell me that 'faggots like to suck dick, so why was I complaining'" (Human Rights Watch 2001, 114).

53. Pinar 2001, 1031–1046. Given the myth of the Black rapist, placing Black men in prison situations in which they are encouraged to rape other men produces the very stereotype created in the postemancipation era. Black men become dangerous, a reason to keep them locked up.

54. Human Rights Watch 2001, 169.

55. Human Rights Watch 2001, 216.

56. Pinar 2001, 1119.

57. Pinar 2001, 1053–1057.

58. Human Rights Watch 2001, 109–122.

59. Human Rights Watch 2001, 171.

60. Human Rights Watch 2001, 168.

61. African American men constituted 42 percent of those admitted to prison in 1981 and, by 1993, had become an unsettling 55 percent of those admitted (Miller 1996, 55).

62. Sociologist Elijah Anderson describes the code of the street in which demanding respect and exhibiting toughness function as important dimensions of Black masculinity within
inner-city neighborhoods (Anderson 1999). In his lengthy study of lynching and prison rape,
William Pinar identifies another connection between prison culture and masculine identity:
"Prisons are not alien womanless worlds in which men resort to unimaginable acts. Prisons
disclose the profoundly womanless worlds most men in fact inhabit, in which women are
fundamentally fictive, units of currency in a homosocial economy . . . perhaps most men 'live'
in an all-male world intrapsychically from which women are aggressively banished. It is a
sign of manhood" (Pinar 2001, 1119).

63. Oliver 1994.

64. Canada 1995.

65. McCall 1994; Shakur 1993.

66. Anecdotal, unpublished material.

67. Morgan 1999, 73.

REFERENCES

Anderson, Elijah. 1999. *Code of the Street: Decency, Violence, and the Moral Life of the Inner
City.* New York: W. W. Norton.

Austin, Regina. 1993. "Sapphire Bound!" *Feminist Jurisprudence.* Ed Patricia Smith, 575–93.
New York: Oxford University Press.

Awkward, Michael. 1999. "'You're Turning Me On': The Boxer, the Beauty Queen, and the
Rituals of Gender." *Black Men on Race, Gender, and Sexuality.* Ed. Devon W. Carbado,
128–46. New York: NYU Press.

Bandale, Asha. 1999. *The Prisoner's Wife: A Memoir.* New York: Scribner.

Beck, E. M., and Stewart E. Tolnay. 1992. "A Season for Violence: The Lynching of Blacks and
Labor Demand in the Agricultural Production Cycle in the American South." *International
Review of Social History.* 37: 1–24.

Bell, Derrick. 1999. "The Sexual Diversion: The Black Man/Black Woman Debate in Context."
Black Men on Race, Gender, and Sexuality. Ed. Devon W. Carbado, 237–247. New York:
NYU Press.

Canada, Geoffrey. 1995. *Fist, Stick, Knife, Gun: A Personal History of Violence in America.* Boston: Beacon Press.

Cleage, Pearl. 1993. *Deals with the Devil: And Other Reasons to Riot.* New York: Ballantine.

Cohen, Cathy J., and Tamara Jones. 1999. "Fighting Homophobia versus Challenging Heterosexism: 'The Failure to Transform' Revisited." *Dangerous Liaisons: Blacks, Gays, and the
Struggle for Equality.* Ed. Eric Brandt, 80–101. New York: The New Press.

Collins, Patricia Hill. 2000. *Black Feminist Thought: Knowledge, Consciousness, and the Politics
of Empowerment.* New York: Routledge.

Connell, R. W. 1992. "A Very Straight Gay: Masculinity, Homosexual Experience, and the Dynamics of Gender." *American Sociological Review* 57 (December): 735–751.

Crenshaw, Kimberle Williams. 1992. "Whose Story Is It Anyway? Feminist and Antiracist
Appropriations of Anita Hill." *Race-ing Justice, En-Gendering Power.* Ed. Toni Morrison,
402–440. New York: Pantheon Books.

Dash, Leon. 1996. *Rosa Lee: A Mother and Her Family in Urban America.* New York: Basic
Books.

Davis, Angela Y. 1978. "Rape, Racism, and the Capitalist Setting." *Black Scholar* 9, no. 7: 24–30.

Douglas, Kelly Brown. 1999. *Sexuality and the Black Church: A Womanist Perspective.* Maryknoll, NY: Orbis.

Giddings, Paula. 2001. "Missing in Action: Ida B. Wells, the NAACP, and the Historical Record." *Meridians: Feminism, Race, Transnationalism* 1, no. 2: 1–17.

Harris, Trudier. 1984. *Exorcising Blackness: Historical and Literary Lynching and Burning Rituals.* Bloomington: Indiana University Press.

Hill, Anita. 1997. *Speaking Truth to Power.* New York: Doubleday.

Human Rights Watch. 2001. *No Escape: Male Rape in U.S. Prisons.* New York: Human Rights Watch.

James, Joy. 1996. "The Profeminist Politics of W.E.B. DuBois with Respect to Anna Julia Cooper and Ida B. Wells Barnett." *W.E.B. DuBois on Race and Culture.* Ed. Bernard W. Bell, Emily R. Grosholz, and James B. Stewart, 141–160. New York: Routledge.

Kaplan, E. B. 1997. *Not our Kind of Girl: Unraveling the Myths of Black Teenage Motherhood.* Berkeley: University of California Press.

McCall, Nathan. 1994. *Makes Me Wanna Holler: A Young Black Man in America.* New York: Random House.

Miller, Jerome G. 1996. *Search and Destroy: African-American Males in the Criminal Justice System.* New York: Cambridge University Press.

Miller, Teresa A. 2000. "Sex and Surveillance: Gender, Privacy, and the Sexualization of Power in Prison." *George Mason University Civil Rights Law Journal* 10, no. 291–356.

Morgan, Joan. 1999. *When Chickenheads Come Home to Roost: My Life as a Hip-Hop Feminist.* New York: Simon & Schuster.

Oliver, William. 1994. *The Violent Social World of Black Men.* New York: Lexington Books.

Omolade, Barbara. 1994. *The Rising Song of African American Women.* New York: Routledge.

Painter, Nell. 1992. "Hill, Thomas, and the Use of Racial Stereotype." *Race-ing Justice, Engendering Power.* Ed. Toni Morriosn, 200–214. New York: Pantheon Books.

Pierce-Baker, Charlotte. 1998. *Surviving the Silence: Black Women's Stories of Rape.* New York: W. W. Norton.

Pinar, William. 2001. *The Gender of Racial Politics and Violence in America: Lynching, Prison Rape, and the Crisis of Masculinity.* New York: Lang Publishing.

Powell, Kevin. 2000. "Confessions." *MS*, April/May, 73–77.

Shakur, Saniya. 1993. *Monster: The Autobiography of an L.A. Gang Member.* New York: Atlantic Monthly Press.

Stoler, Ann Laura. 1995. *Race and the Education of Desire: Foucault's History of Sexuality and the Colonial Order of Things.* Durham: Duke University Press.

Wells-Barnett, Ida B. 2002. *On Lynchings.* Amherst, NY: Humanity Books.

West, Traci C. 1999. *Wounds of the Spirit: Black Women, Violence and Resistance Ethics.* New York: NYU Press.

Weigman, Robyn. 1993. "The Anatomy of Lynching." *American Sexual Politics.* Ed. John C. Fout, and Maura Tantillo, 223–245. Chicago: University of Chicago Press.

Wilson, Melba. 1994. *Crossing the Boundary: Black Women Survive Incest.* Seattle: Seal Press.

Wyatt, Gail Elizabeth. 1992. "The Sociocultural Context of African American and White American Women's Rape." *Journal of Social Issues* 48, no. 1: 77–91.

5

The Phenomenology of Death, Embodiment, and Organ Transplantation

Gillian Haddow

The Dead Body as a Resource

In the period immediately after the medical pronouncement of death and before bodily destruction the body becomes a valuable resource either as a teaching aid, research model or for cadaveric organ transplantation. Organs for cadaveric transplantation in the UK are not widely available and demand continues to outstrip supply. Data as of 28 December 2003 show 5,860 people awaiting a solid organ transplant (http://www.uktransplant.org.uk/statistics/latest_statistics/latest_statistics.htm). In the UK, organ procurement is based on a voluntary gifting system whereby individuals choose to donate or 'opt-in' to organ donation after suffering brain stem death (BSD). Health professionals then negotiate procuring the deceased's organs with the deceased's family. As stated in the 1961 Human Tissue Act, in the UK, health professionals always ascertain a 'lack of objection' from the family, regardless of whether the decedent had carried a donor card or had made their wishes known (written or verbally). Latest statistics demonstrate that in nearly 49 percent of cases the families will refuse to donate; this refusal rate is therefore considered one factor contributing to the current shortage (http://society.guardian.co.uk/health/news). Research with families approached by health professionals with a donation request shows that transplant removal procedures can cause difficulty, 'dissonance' and refusal or restriction of particular organs (Belk 1987, Fulton et al. 1987, Sque and Payne 1996, Wilms et al. 1987). Quantitative studies have highlighted that although the dead body is to be ultimately disposed of, some relatives refuse because, 'they did not want surgery to the body' (BACCN/UKTCA 1995). In the modern era, the transmission of cultural beliefs about the dead body takes the form of 'the symbolic meaning of showing respect for the individual who once was' (Sanner 1994b: 1148). How surgical procedures to the newly dead body are significant in organ donation refusals, when autopsies and dissection have been occurring routinely for

From *Sociology of Health & Illness* v27.i1 (2005), pp. 92–113. Reprinted with permission of Blackwell Publishing.

the last few centuries, highlights the differing levels of acceptable interference with the corpse, which some have linked to the 'symbolism of different uses' (Feinberg 1985: 31).

This article continues to address questions about why surgical transplantation procedures might cause the donor relatives difficulty through examining their perceptions of when death occurs and what a dead body is. Drawing on the findings from 19 donor family interviews, I argue that much is dependent on what an individual believes about death; death either brings about a division between the once-living self and body and the corpus left behind as an empty vehicle from which organs can be harvested. Alternatively, there exists a belief that death does not change the status of embodiment; that is, the person remains embodied at death. In this understanding, the dead body and the organs remain inseparable from the once-living relative. So this discussion is about how such different bodily representations of self-identity after death affect the relatives' decision whether to acquiesce to organ donation.

The Struggle for Hearts and Minds

Important changes have occurred over the last 100 years in not only what is done to, and with, dead bodies, but also in the definition of death itself. One of the most significant changes is from a traditional conception of death as heartbeat cessation, to one where irreversible damage to the brain, a condition known as brain stem death (BSD), has come to be recognised. In 1968, the Harvard Committee ruled BSD as death and this 'new' definition went on to supersede cardiac death. BSD was soon implemented in most countries, although for a variety of reasons, Japan and Denmark only recently recognised BSD in the early nineties (Lock 2002, Rix 1990a, Rix 1990b). There are heated ethical, legal, religious and social debates about BSD outside the scope of this article (Gervais 1986). Here, BSD is considered as analogous to decapitation, whereby damage has occurred to the brain stem and no information can be exchanged between the body and the higher brain.

Despite the UK's increasing medical reliance on the diagnosis, studies have regularly shown varying levels of confusion about BSD in both the health professional and lay population (Dejong et al. 1998, Sque and Payne 1996, Tymstra et al. 1992, Younger 1990). Research demonstrates that BSD poses a major obstacle to donation, as it can be difficult for relatives to understand brain-orientated death (Sque and Payne 1996, Tymstra et al. 1992, Fulton et al. 1987). With BSD, apparent breathing and respiration continue, resulting in an 'ambiguous entity' termed by some authors as a 'living cadaver' (Lock 2002) or described in statements such as, '[T]he patient is dead but has not died' (Hogle 1995). The appearance of brain stem dead individuals is far different from someone who has died from cardio-pulmonary causes. Colour appears normal, the body may still be warm, and the heart continues to beat, albeit with artificial assistance. These patients do not look as if they are dying or are indeed dead.

Authors have used this to suggest that fears about bodily mutilation are related to respect for the deceased; relatives are confused and, '. . . generally not able to imagine a difference between the living and the dead. The dead body was ascribed qualities that only a living individual possesses' (Sanner 1994b: 1147). Indeed, early work with donor relatives found that respondents who were unsure about whether death had transpired tended to conflate the self/body at, and after, death (Fulton et al. 1987). Remarkably, this aided donation as some relatives donated because they believed the organs carried remnants of the deceased within them. Subsequently a form of 'bodily immortality', i.e. a continuation of the decedent's identity, was gained through organ donation (admittedly only one that lasted until the recipient's death). The need to know that the deceased achieved a certain amount of bodily immortality was found to be frustrated by a lack of information about the recipient (Bartucci and Seller 1986, Pelletier 1993, Sque and Payne 1996).

Historical Ambiguity about Death

Death, it is generally supposed, separates the state of being alive from being dead; but the ambiguity that surrounds death is not unique to contemporary society. Throughout history, distrust of the medical profession and ambivalence about the diagnosis of death is frequently noted, and accounts as far back as 1740 have suggested that, 'putrefaction was [death's] only sure sign' (quoted in Lamb 1985: 51). During the 18th to 20th centuries, because of new medical technologies such as artificial resuscitation, which demonstrated that individuals previously thought dead could now be revived, there was increasing uncertainty about the diagnosis of death. This has led Pernick to suggest that 'Lay mistrust of doctors' definitions has been the historical rule rather than the exception, though such mistrust only periodically caused great alarm' (Pernick 1988: 61). The paradox, as Pernick goes on to argue, is that accompanying the advancement of scientific and technological precision of defining death come doubts about its diagnosis (Pernick 1988). Giacomini (1997: 1478) argues that death (i.e. BSD) is not solely a clinical definition, but a socially constructed one:

> Brain-dead bodies had to be created, recognised, and defined in the development of brain stem death criteria: brain stem death was socially as well as clinically constructed. The 1968 definition did not produce a more 'accurate' description of death so much as mark new delineations between the living and the dead.

With shifting and mutable definitions of death it is to be expected that relatives neither immediately nor decisively accept such 'new delineations'. Then, continuing with such a line of reasoning, BSD might cause relatives to be concerned about post-mortem bodily mutilation, as they do not understand death has occurred, and therefore they continue to conflate the living person with the dead body. . . .

Theoretical Dimension

Theoretically, the practice of, and apparent resistance to, donating organs in this country has interesting implications for the sociology of the body. The discussion that follows reflects a move within the sociology academy, from locating the body within social-structuration theories to what some have argued is a 'corporeal' sociology whereby the lived experience of embodiment is stressed (Howson and Inglis 2001, Turner and Wainwright 2003). The phenomenology of embodiment, interpreted here to mean the experience of self and body, is de rigueur though controversial in the current sociological climate (see, for example, Howson and Inglis 2001, Turner and Wainwright 2003). Although some authors use the term 'embodiment' differently, I liken it to a person's experience of the body and whether individuals feel they have a body, or the alternative of whether a person feels they are a body. For example, Turner suggests that people both 'have' and 'are' bodies at the same time (Turner 1996). I go on to demonstrate that it is precisely this that caused the difficulties for the donor families. For, as the important question in this article poses, 'What happens to an embodied identity at or after corporeal death'? The practice of removing an organ from a previous living self, in order to place it into another, raises unavoidable issues around where 'I' am located in my body and what kind of relationship I have with my body. Authors have found it difficult to locate precisely where we might be in the corpus:

> We can only give confusing answers to the curious question of where in this whole corpus we think we truly live. Science tells us the brain, and no one would naturally give such an answer. Much of the time, I think, we feel ourselves concentrated just behind the eyes; when someone says 'look at me' we look at his face—usually the eyes, expecting there to encounter the person or at least his clearest self-manifestation (Kass 1985: 23).

The common intuitive answer to 'where am I' gives contradictory answers. Am I in my brain? Or am I somewhere behind my eyes? Do I 'have' my body in the same way I 'have' a car? Or is the relationship with my corporeality more entwined? Providing answers to sociological questions about how we experience ourselves as embodied is neither a new nor an easy endeavour. Part of the problem, as I suggest, resides in a dichotomy between: having a body, a dualist image that organ transplantation depends on, or an alternative, being a body; a holistic image that stresses the inter-connected nature of self and body.

Cartesian Embodiment: Having a Body?

Philosophers have long reflected on the relationship between body and self. Descartes' methodological contemplation of whether he 'was' or 'had' a body eventually led to the Cartesianism that dominates Western medicine today, and is a legacy that advocates the separation of the non-tangible aspects of self from the body. This 'dualistic' way of viewing the self/body became historically and culturally associated with the medical profession, and was fundamental to the development of anatomical dissection and 'clinical detachment' (Richardson 1988). Cartesian thinking is not only associated with the medical realm but is also the building block for most rational, Western models of thinking about embodiment. Taking, for example, Gidden's work, he has been subject to recent criticisms of 'dualistic mind/body thinking' in that he privileges the mind over that of the body (Witz 2000). Giddens argued that the current ontological and existential insecurities regarding our status of 'who we are' relates to an era in society where individuals are increasingly 'reflexive' about their self identity (Giddens 1991). Authors counter-argued that Giddens' over-emphasis on reflexivity produces a body that is strangely disembodied from the self (Shilling and Mellor 1996).

Holistic Embodiment: Being a Body?

Contra the Cartesian ideology, and in parallel to it, a holistic view also exists that stresses the relationship between self and body as closely inter-linked; the emphasis therefore is that we are our bodies (Turner 1996). We are not platonic entities but material bodies that are intimately connected to selfhood. In a criticism of the 'choice' in Giddens' suggestion that the body/self is always under construction, one researcher suggests, '[N]either the self nor the body can be chosen because they are very often lived as though they are already there. The body is already the self. The self is already the body' (Budgeon 2003). In interviews with teenage girls, it was apparent that modifications to the body through cosmetic surgery not only produced changes in the exterior body surface, but in the interior self, for example, the person had become more confident. Hence an alternative perspective to the Cartesian one exists that highlights an inalienable 'self-in-body' (Joramelon and Cox 2003) or 'body-as-self' (Belk 1990) linkage whereby the living body is the tangible concrete expression, or manifestation, of individual identity. These terms share a common phenomenological approach to the individual's lived experience of embodiment, and henceforth will be referred to as a 'holistic' relationship between self-corporeal identity. A phenomenology of the body highlights the experience of a body/self inter-link; leading Howson and Inglis to suggest that 'the body is the subject and the subject is the body' (2001: 304).

Objective and Method of Study

The research objective was to explore whether the donor families were aware and understood that death had occurred. If they were aware that death had occurred did the relatives view the moment of death as the rite of passage that separated the once living self from the newly-dead body; a 'dis-selve' perhaps? Or did they continue to conflate the person/body? Finally, did this affect the donation decision?

During 1999–2001, interviews with 19 donor relatives from three different regions in Scotland were carried out. These families were selected only on the basis that, at some point between eight months and three years earlier, health professionals had approached them with a request to donate the organs of their deceased next of kin. Approval was gained from the local research ethics committees before the recruitment of families. Health professionals (both the respondents' GP, transplant surgeons and co-ordinators) were closely involved at different times of the study, from the design of the interview aide memoir, to the selection and contact of the families from intensive care unit records, to discussing emergent findings. A letter of introduction from health professionals, alongside a patient information sheet and consent form, was sent to the families on my behalf by health professionals. No follow-up or reminders were sent. The families returned the consent form to myself indicating whether or not they were willing to participate. In total, 46 donor families were contacted with 29 letters returned and 15 families agreeing to take part. The respondents were advised that a family member could also be present for support; then 19 relatives who were involved with the donation decision were interviewed at a time and place convenient to them. The families were given assurances of confidentiality and anonymity (pseudonyms are used in the following accounts to protect the identities of both participants and deceased. . . .)

Modern Death

The deaths of the donors were caused by an internal trauma to the brain such as a blood clot or through an external trauma caused by a fall or a car crash. The patient had been rushed to an intensive care unit where they were usually attached to a mechanical ventilator to aid breathing. If the brain injury proved untreatable, as was the case in the present study, it caused them to suffer brain stem death. Unlike death from cessation of heartbeat when we can generally tell that the person is dead or dying—these patients do not look as if they will die, or indeed are dead. Yet the majority of families in this study said that health professionals explained BSD to them, that they had understood it and also demonstrated this understanding of BSD (whilst not denying that intense grief and emotion also clouded comprehension at times). Mr. Andrews, for example, when asked what he understood by the term brain stem death, made a cutting action at the back of the neck demonstrating severance of the spinal cord and thus, 'there was nothing else I needed to know'. Eight participants recalled hearing the term brain stem death through televised medical dramas such as *ER*, *Holby City* and *Casualty* and these programmes were often mentioned, unprompted, by respondents. Unanticipated data also arose regarding the propensity of the donor families to 'make sense' of the intensive care unit technology, in order to gain some indication of a likely prognosis:

> He [husband] didn't have anything in his mouth or anything; they were just keeping his heart going. So he wasn't all wired up, but when you were sitting you could see the

numbers going down, whether it said heart beats or whatever, you could see him going down. You could see him slowly dying (Mrs. O'Neill, Donor wife).

You know in Intensive Care? You know they have this machine that measured the pressure? In the brain? And it should be whatever figure and it was much higher you know than it should be. And you become fixated that you're just looking at this machine all the time and it's going up and up and up. . . . (Mrs. Kildare, Donor mother).

Relatives searched for, assessed, interpreted and examined available information from a variety of sources, enabling them to make their own judgement regarding the potential outcome. These relatives were not passive recipients of health professional information but were active, intelligent and aware agents (Haddow 2004). Nevertheless, this is not to overstate understanding and acceptance of BSD as there were instances where respondents, mostly parents, articulated levels of difficulty:

You know if she [daughter] was totally dead, you have less concern. But the fact that she was there with the life support thing, but we know that she was not really alive, but there was a slight concern about that. You know that she was almost still alive, but she was alive but brain dead. So you think how long would the body survive? So just that, not a concern, a slight worry (Mr Roberts, Donor father).

Mr Roberts's quote demonstrates a lack of clear distinction between being 'alive' and being 'dead'. He thought his daughter was 'almost still alive' and although he goes to great lengths to stress that he is not 'concerned' about BSD, he simultaneously acknowledges that it causes him a 'slight worry'. The problem, as Hogle describes it, 'stems in part from the fact that humans have both biological and cultural bodies. The biological death event thus requires an attendant social death' (1995: 210). In the absence of such a 'moment of death' relatives identified a point when they thought death had occurred and this was before medical confirmation:

Basically, I think, my wife died, that was the Thursday the 6th February, but I'm convinced myself that she died on the Wednesday. I think she died on the Wednesday and it was only the machines that kept her going (Mr. Verble, Donor husband).

Relatives suggested that they had had a personal realisation of when death had occurred due to health professional communication, attending to the intensive care unit technology and through previous awareness of brain stem death from television medical-dramas. Based on the current findings, it would seem reasonable to suggest that 'brain stem death' is not solely existing in the medical realm, but gaining awareness and understanding in the public arena. The relatives made a judgement as to when death had occurred; a social death based on the specific environment and the previous wider lay context.

Cartesian Dualism/Holism and the Dead Body

An important point is therefore established; that is, despite the ambiguity of the dead body's appearance, there was no uncertainty about BSD evidenced in this study. We can now claim that a subsequent view of the self/body representation was not related to confusion around whether or not death had occurred. So what then of the newly dead body? As mentioned, in this sample, it emerged, somewhat unexpectedly, that seven donor families had some form of medical background. Obviously, one cannot treat the medical respondents as a homogenous group, but some appeared to offer a representation of the dead body as an empty car and, as the 'driver had got out', the parts could be legitimately salvaged. Mr Roberts was the strongest example of this:

[F]or me I just look at it like, somebody that is brain dead, whatever, is just like a broken car. A broken car itself is not going to be of use, but you can cannibalise the parts for something else (Mr Roberts, Donor father).

Opposed to the Cartesian representation, however, another image was also apparent; one that tended to emerge in the non-medical sample and emphasised the newly-dead body's integrity and previous living identity:

In fact not even so long ago it flashed in front of me that his [son] body, which I'd lain with, touched and stroked, wouldn't have looked the same. That he would have scars. That he would be cut (Mrs Evans, Donor mother).

Mr Forbes, again a non-medical respondent, explained his initial refusal to the donation request of his wife's organs and why he would not donate his own in the future. He likened the organ transplantation removal procedures to a 'butcher's shop':

I know it's not but it's too much like a butcher's shop to me. . . .
    Let's have half pound of heart, three quarters of a pound of liver. Eh, I'm afraid that's in me. I'm just trying to be as honest as I can and that's the way I feel about it. . . . (Donor husband).

In his view, organ transplantation is tantamount to treating his wife's remains like those of any other animals (despite no obvious vegetarian sympathies) and thereby negates the social identity of his deceased wife. Mr Davidson also suggested that he required reassurances about the conduct and outcome of the procedure:

Are you just going to be, this is going to be one of these 'take them out and throw them in the bucket' sort of things. And they said 'oh no, that's not it' and my sister-in-law assured me it's just like a normal operation and somebody going in and opening her up, and instead of putting something in, they're taking it out, you know. Everything is done with sort of respect, it's not just mutilation you know (Donor husband).

Most donor family respondents reported some level of concern about whether organ removal procedures would compromise the body's integrity: four initially refused because of this anxiety.

Restricting the Eyes

Such emotional and symbolic capital invested in the dead body and its parts by relatives implies that it is not altogether easily separable from the once-living self. For most of the non-medical donor respondents a continuing link between corpus and self caused concern not only about the transplantation removal procedures, but also affected what organs were to be donated. There was no evidence of anyone refusing donation of the heart as found by earlier studies (Fulton et al. 1987). But nearly a third of all respondents refused to donate the deceased's eyes when health professionals asked them (and was unrelated to the deceased's wishes). Being able to see a person's eyes when living, and presumably newly dead, was mentioned as important and hence concerns regarding the cosmetic effects of the actual removal were articulated. Another reason commonly offered was that a person's eyes were the 'windows of the soul'. In everyday interactions, the eyes play a significant role in communication, and are a visible expression of the less tangible aspects of personhood, as affected by metaphors such as, 'being able to see it in her eyes', 'he couldn't look me in the eye', etc. Hence, the eyes provide sight, but also in-sight. Respondents who did not restrict any organs suggested the following:

> Well, what's the use to her [laugh]. That's basically the idea behind it, as they say, 'they can't take it with you' so might as well use them. I mean it's *a body*. It's not really a person that you grew up with or anything like that (Mr Johns, Donor son, emphasis added).

Mr Johns' denial of any personal element attributed to the newly-dead body ('it's not really a person') allows him to stress the utility of the corpse and its parts. In this way he cultivates a degree of detachment and reserve. In addition, he states that 'you can't take it with you' and therefore the organs can serve a purpose only in this life, clearly demonstrating that the body and the self are no longer one and the same. . . .

The Dissolution of the Embodiment Dichotomy

Differences in the sample between the medical and non-medical relatives' discourse of the body are arguably symptomatic of wider ontological questions about the nature of embodiment, personhood and corporeal identity. For some donor families it is not merely a question of removing organs or 'body parts', as they are otherwise referred to in the medical literature. Yet socio-cultural beliefs about bodies, organs and their relationship to personal identity are not always amenable to medical re-conceptualisations, even by those who might have cultivated 'clinical detachment'. One should not over-emphasise the division between holistic and dualistic embodiment, as such metaphors and representations are 'entwined' (Birke 1999). There were exceptions to such a medical/dualistic and non-medical/holistic portrayal. For example, a medical respondent substantiated the 'body immortality' argument, whereby post-donation parts of the deceased may 'live on'. As Mrs Stewart, a retired nurse, suggested:

> GH: How do you feel now about the decision to donate her organs?
> MRS STEWART: Well I feel that there is a little bit of her out there somewhere.
> GH: In what way?
> MRS STEWART: Well somebody is being able to use it. You know? She's not gone. Not completely gone (Donor aunt).

Through donating, Mrs Stewart's niece continued to be present to her and she was still about 'somewhere'. In this sense, she seems to imply that her niece is not completely gone. She also articulated a fear about a potential confusion of personal identity for the recipient, and a suggestion that personal characteristics were transferred from donor to recipient although it was unclear how this transference occurred:

> MRS STEWART: But eh, I think that some people would want to know too much about the donor and then say, well if the donor, was a drunkard, well maybe 'I'll end up the drunkard'.
> GH: But I mean, what you're saying . . .
> MRS STEWART: I mean taking on the personality. I don't think that's a good thing. I think the less we know is better than knowing too much (Donor aunt).

Other non-medical respondents were interested in the whereabouts of the organs and the age of the recipient. Miss Allison, for example, asked the transplant co-ordinator whether her son's organs could stay in the area (whilst simultaneously recognising that allocation was based on matching organs with the recipient waiting lists throughout the UK). What she wanted was to:

> . . . Try here [Scotland] first. Because I don't want ever to go to Bristol thinking somebody is walking about here with David's heart. I hate Bristol. I'm not going back there. You know? I don't want that feeling. Cos it would be as though, 'well where is *he* [her son]'? (emphasis added).

For Miss Allison, it would appear that her son is co-existent with the location of his organs. Donating his body parts implies that the body/self as a whole persists. Indeed, other facets of the self, for example, national identity, appeared noteworthy. Two respondents mentioned a desire for the organs to stay in Scotland:

It was her liver or something but it did go to like an 18-year-old in Ayrshire I can remember that and thinking that 'I'm glad *it* stayed in Scotland' and her heart went to
somebody down South. One of her other kidneys, I think that went somewhere, but not
too far down South. Mid kind of way (emphasis added, Mrs Moon, Donor sister).

In these accounts the self continues to be inextricably linked with the parts that
were neither cremated nor buried. In contrast, other respondents generally denied
the organs could carry personal vestiges of the deceased and, 'it was not the person
only their organs' continuing to exist:

> MR EVANS: No it occurred to me a week later that was where his body went. But parts of
> him that were very much alive are still alive. I think eh, I felt that that was em, a
> strong consoling moment for me.
> GH: That he was still kind of alive?
> MRS EVANS: No, his organs (Donor mother and father).

Likewise, other respondents stated that irrespective of embodiment views, part of the
reason why they donated was 'once you're dead, you're dead. Eh, it's [organ dona-
tion] not going to hurt you' (Mr Davidson, Donor husband) and that the deceased
'couldn't use them [organs] any more, so why burn them?' (Mrs O'Neill, Donor wife).
More generally, the colloquial expression of 'when you're dead, you're dead' indicated
no lingering embodiment and stressed the benefit of further utility of the deceased's
body.

Continuing Social Bonds

Hence, a minority of respondents' views on the representation of the dead body
could not be easily categorised or explained. One way the dissolution of the holistic/
dualistic dichotomy arose was via a change in the medical respondents' articulation
of embodied dualistic representations. Then, the dualistic rhetoric and representation
often weakened at certain points in the donation process, primarily in relation to previous ties with the deceased. In the present study, the 'ability to let go', especially for
parents, regardless of any medical associations, appeared almost insurmountable. In
this study, Mrs. Cohen, a nurse, initially refused to donate because of fears relating to
the violation of her daughter's body:

> My initial reaction was no. I don't want to. I mean I don't have a problem with it
> [organ transplantation] for myself. If that were to happen to me I would give, I would
> donate. But when it's your child, I don't know.
> I just think the whole idea . . . Your child has died; you're in a situation, which, never
> in your wildest dreams you would have expected to happen to you. You don't expect
> your child to die before you. You kind of, you think, you know just the fact that they
> were going to cut her [daughter] open and take her heart out.

Indeed, in modern Western society, characterised by falling child mortality rates, 'you don't expect your child to die before you'. It appeared that parents in this sample had not yet relinquished a pre-existing protective bond with their child, causing a contradiction between accepting their child was dead and having to leave them 'un-protected'. Mrs Cohen found it difficult to leave the hospital, wanting to 'turn round and run back in again' to be with her daughter. Mrs Evans, a non-medical respon-dent, recalled not having any concerns regarding the procurement procedures at the time, but that she felt 'very sad, I wasn't there when they did the operation. That struck me. That he'd [son] gone through this surgery'. Recent research has also found that mothers who lost a child were more likely to suffer from psychosocial problems (Cleiren and Van Zoelen 2002).

Above then, we have two mothers articulating similar concerns about the organ transplantation procedures at different points of the donation process. What they shared was a continuation of the maternal role that they had had with the deceased and the emphasis therefore is on the previous relationship with the person and not the representation of their body. Mrs Moon, who offered to donate her sister's or-gans, would not have done the same after her mother's death, 13 years previously. She related that, 'I probably had, like, a very close relationship with my mother. Like she was my friend as well. You know what I mean? I wouldn't have liked her to have been cut or anything like that' (Donor's sister). There was a history of past tension and conflict with her sister, and Mrs Moon did not consider them to have a close relationship. Hence, fears about mutilation are not only about what the dead body is thought to represent, but appears also related to the relationship with the deceased.

Conclusion: Representation and Relationship

. . . In the current model, views of embodiment were not caused by uncertainty about whether death had occurred, or confusion produced by the 'life-like' appear-ance of a BSD individual (Table 2: ii, iii, iv). Certainly the current study challenges arguments that one is related to the other. On the contrary, the donor families in this sample said they had been previously familiar with the term 'brain stem death'; they demonstrated what it meant, and understood that death had taken place. The major-ity had even had a 'personal realisation' of death prior to medical confirmation (Sque and Payne 1996). Essentially, the patient was socially dead to them (Glaser 1966, Sud-now 1967). . . .

The Continuing Relationship

Organ transplantation is dependent on death of the body, but death does not mean the termination of the relationship with the previous embodied self. For instance, it is widely recognised that pronouncing death does not cause the immediate separation of self from body, and therefore ties to the deceased 'self' persist (Klass et al. 1996,

Mulkay and Ernst 1991, Seale 1998, Walter 1996). As Joramelon and Cox argue, death does not cause an instantaneous cutting of ties:

> . . . it is a basic human recognition that our 'self', our identity exists in the space of social relations, and that the ongoing flow of social life necessitates a gradual disaggregation of the deceased from the ties to the living that constituted the social self (2003: 30).

Although numbers are small, and more research is required, in the current study this caused particular difficulties for parents who wanted to continue the relationship with their child. This research indicates the importance and existence of ties to the dis-embodied self that are strongly related to previous corporeal existence. In agreement, other authors have suggested that it is generally assumed that when we are socially alive, we are biologically alive; when we are biologically dead we are also socially dead (Hallam et al. 1999). There is no clear-cut biological/social and death/existence division, however, and my own research provides a clear illustration of this. The majority of families demonstrated awareness that death had occurred, to the extent that they often articulated a moment of social death prior to medical confirmation of BSD. However, they also appeared to continue in the relationship they once had. The analytical value of this research suggests, quite simply, that regardless of how clinically detached one is, or purports to be, the strength of previous social/kinship relationships can prove overwhelming, especially for parents in the present study.

The Interconnection between Stable Relationships and Fluid Representations

I stress, therefore, the fluidity of changing bodily representations invoked by the dying or dead body and the stability of a continuing previous relationship. These bonds, I show, appeared to be more durable than the fluid and permeable nature of differing views of embodiment. The ties that parents had formed with their children often challenged the Cartesian representation of embodiment when faced with a donation request or when thinking over events. Richardson (1988) once wrote that historically, the cultivation of clinical detachment represented a huge adjustment to the human psyche, and there is certainly evidence of that in this study.

Thus, what I have attempted to show is that a previous medical association was generally associative with experiencing less conflict about donation and vice versa. Nevertheless, this was not always the case, and examining the reasons for the exceptions to the rule is as important as showing what the cause of it was in the first instance. Through this method, what the study adds is value and insight into discussions of 'who we are', demonstrating that it is equally important to investigate 'who we were' to those around us. It leads to a more complex but nuanced analytical representation of the different meanings around what happens to our self-identity at death and the bonds that we form as embodied beings, and how these issues impact on the lives of the bereaved. Undoubtedly, there is scope for further research on this. What has become obvious is that respecting the deceased's body is not just about dying and death, but the experience of the living, the identity of the deceased and the strength of social relationships. The meanings about identity and bodies, both in life and in death, are often complex and contradictory. Today in contemporary society, with the pace of medical and information technological change, there is ahead of us an exciting but uncertain future. But it is only through careful unpacking and scrutiny that some recognition can be given to the way that the past and present shape of personal, social and corporeal identity structures the impact modern medical progress has on our lives.

REFERENCES

BACCN/UKTCA (1995) Report of a Two-Year Study into the Reasons for Relatives' Refusal of Organ Donation, MORI Health Research Unit for the United Kingdom Transplant Coordinators Association.

Bartucci, M.R. and Seller, M.C. (1986) Donor family responses to kidney recipient letter of thanks, Transplant Proceedings, 18, 401–5. ISI.

Belk, R. (1987) Possession and the extended self, Journal of Consumer Research, 15, 139–63. CrossRef, ISI, CSA.

Belk, R. (ed.) (1990) Me and Thee versus Mine and Thine: How Perceptions of the Body Influence Organ Donation and Transplantation. Washington: American Psychological Association.

Birke, L. (1999) Feminism and the Biological Body. Edinburgh: Edinburgh University Press.

Budgeon, S. (2003) Identity as an embodied event, Body and Society, 9, 9, 35–55.

Cleiren, M. and Van Zoelen, A. (2002) Post-mortem organ donation and grief: a study of consent, refusal and well-being in bereavement, Death Studies, 26, 837–49. CrossRef, Medline, ISI, CSA.

Craib, I. (1998) Experiencing Identity. London: Sage.

Dejong, W., Franz, H., Wolf, S., Nathan, H., Payne, D. and Reitsma, W. (1998) Requesting organ donation: an interview study of donor and non-donor families, American Journal of Critical Care, 7, 1, 13–23. Medline.

Department of Health (2002) Human Bodies, Human Choices: The Law on Human Organs and Tissue in England and Wales. A Consultation Report, London.

Donaldson Report (2000) Report of a Census of Organs and Tissues Retained by Pathology Services in England by the Chief Medical Officer. London : Department of Health.

Feinberg, J. (1985) The mistreatment of dead bodies, Hastings Center Report, 15, 1, 31–37. Medline, ISI, CSA.

Fulton, J., Fulton, R. and Simmons, R. (1987) The cadaver donor and the gift of life. In Simmons, R., Klein, S.K. and Simmons, R. (eds) Gift of Life: The Effects of Organ Donation on Individual, Family and Social Dynamics. Oxford : Transaction Books.

Gervais, K. (1986) Redefining Death. New Haven and London : Yale University Press.

Giacomini, M. (1997) A change of heart and a change of mind? Technology and there-definition of death in 1968, Social Science and Medicine, 44, 10, 1465–82. CrossRef, Medline, ISI, CSA.

Giddens, A. (1991) Modernity and Self-Identity: Self and Society in the Late Modern Age. Cambridge: Polity Press.

Glaser, B.G. (1966) Awareness of Dying. Chicago : Aldine.

Haddow, G. (2004) Donor and nondonor families' accounts of communication and relations with healthcare professionals, Progress in Transplantation, 14, 1, 41–8.

Hallam, E., Hockey, J. and Howarth, G. (1999) Beyond the Body: Death and Social Identity. London : Routledge.

Hogle, L. F. (1995) Tales from the cryptic: technology meets organism in the living cadaver . In Gray, C.H. (ed.) The Cyborg Handbook. New York and London: Routledge.

Howson, A., and Inglis, D. (2001) The body in sociology: tensions inside and outside sociological thought, Sociological Review, 49, 3, 297–317. Synergy, ISI, CSA.

Independent Review Group on Retention of Organs at Post-Mortem (Scotland) (2001) Final Report, Professor Sheila McLean: University of Glasgow.

Joramelon, D., and Cox, D. (2003) Body values: the case against compensating for transplant organs, Hastings Center Report, 27–33.

Kass, L. (1985) Thinking about the body, Hastings Center Report, 20–30.

Klass, D., Silverman, R. and Nickman, S.L. (1996) Continuing Bonds: New Understandings of Grief. London: Taylor and Francis.

Lamb, D. (1985) Death, Brain Stem Death and Ethics. London and Sydney: Croom Helm.

Lock, M. (2002) Twice Dead: Organ Transplants and the Reinvention of Death. Berkeley: University of California Press.

Meikle, J. (2004) Fears over drop in organ donors, The Guardian . Accessed Thursday 15th January. (http://society.guardian.co.uk/health/news) UK transplant (http://www.uktransplant.org.uk/statistics/latest_statistics/latest_statistics.htm). Accessed 21st January 2004.

Mulkay, M., and Ernst, J. (1991) The changing position of social death, European Journal of Sociology, 32, 172–96. ISI, CSA.

Pelletier, M. (1993) The needs of family members of organ and tissue donors, Heart and Lung, 22, 2, 151–7. Medline, ISI.

Pernick, M.S. (1988) Back from the grave: recurring controversies over defining and diagnosing death in history. In Zaner, R.M. (ed.) Death: Beyond Whole Death Criteria. Dordrecht: Kluver Press.

Richardson, R. (1988) Death, Dissection and the Destitute. London and New York: Routledge.

Rix, B.A. (1990a) Danish Ethics Council rejects brain stem death as the criterion of death, Journal of Medical Ethics, 16, 5–7. Medline, ISI, CSA.

Rix, B.A. (1990b) The importance of knowledge and trust in the definition of death, Bioethics, 4, 3, 232–6. Synergy, Medline, CSA.

Sanner, M. A. (1994a) A comparison of public attitudes toward autopsy, organ donation and anatomical dissection, Journal of American Medical Association, 271, 4, 284–90. CrossRef, Medline, ISI, CSA.

Sanner, M. A. (1994b) Attitudes toward organ elevation and transplantation: a model for understanding reactions to medical procedures after death, Social Science and Medicine, 38, 8, 1142–52.

Seale, C. (1998) Constructing Death: The Sociology of Dying and Bereavement. Cambridge: Cambridge University Press.

Shilling, C. and Mellor, P. (1996) Embodiment, structuration theory and modernity: mind/body dualism and the repression of sensuality, Body and Society, 2, 4, 1–15.

Sque, M. and Payne, S. (1996) Dissonant loss: the experiences of donor relatives, Social Science and Medicine, 9, 1359–70. Medline.

Sudnow, D. (1967) Passing On: the Social Organization of Death. Englewoods Cliff, N. J: Prentice Hall.

Turner, B. (1996) The Body and Society: Exploration in Social Theory. 2nd Edition, London: Sage.

Turner, B. S. and Wainwright, S. P. (2003) Corps de ballet: the case of the injured ballet dancer, Sociology of Health and Illness, 25, 4, 269–88. Synergy, Medline, ISI, CSA.

Tymstra, T. J., Heyink, J. W., Pruim, J. and Slooff, M.J.H. (1992) Who granted or refused permission for organ donation, Family Practice, 9, 141–4. Medline, ISI, CSA.

Walter, T. (1996) A new model of grief: bereavement and biography, Mortality, 1, 1, 7–25. CSA.

Wilms, G., Keifer, S.W., Shanteau, J. and McIntyre, P. (1987) Knowledge of image of body organs: impact on willingness to donate, Advances in Consumer Research, 14, 338–42. ISI.

Witz, A. (2000) Whose body matters? Feminist sociology and the corporeal turn in sociology and feminism, Body and Society, 6, 6, 1–24.

Younger, S. (1990) Brain death and organ procurement: some vexing problems remain, Dialysis and Transplant, 19, 2–4.

|||||||||||||||||||||||||||||||||||||||||||||||||||||||||||||||||||||||||||||||||

6

Chemically Reactive Bodies, Knowledge, and Society

Steve Kroll-Smith and H. Hugh Floyd Jr.

> What will become of . . . thought itself when it is subjected to the pressure of sickness?
>
> (Nietzsche 1987, 34)

Multiple chemical sensitivity [MCS], at its core, is a dispute over knowing. It is a dispute over what will count as rational explanations of the relationship of the human body to local environments. One stake in this struggle is the privilege to render an authoritative explanation of the body and its relationship to the environment by, in part, accessing and applying the language of biomedicine; while the outcome may not change the traditional organization of rational knowledge, it will at the very least suggest an alternative. Also at stake in this dispute are the cultural understandings of what are safe and what are dangerous places. If social order depends in part on tacit agreement among participants that the world is divided into places to avoid and places to inhabit, MCS portends a reordering.

At this moment the dispute is little more than a skirmish of words waged between outlying detachments of opposing forces. The chemically reactive on one side, armed with their somatic experiences, borrowed biomedical interpretations, and a profound determination, look across the "no-man's-land" at the profession of biomedicine, armed with the authority of science and the state to control the definition of disease and pronounce bodies sick or well. Each side is supported by important confederates.

Siding with the chemically reactive are dozens of physicians who accept the idea of EI [environmental illness] in spite of the resistance of their medical societies, several biomedical researchers who are working to document the physiological basis for the disorder, and an unknowable number of ordinary people who believe local environments can make people sick. Allied with the medical profession are such powerful groups as the Chemical Manufacturers Association, the Pharmaceutical Manufactures Association, and the health insurance industry.

From *Bodies in Protest: Environmental Illness and the Struggle over Medical Knowledge*, by Steve Kroll-Smith and H. Hugh Floyd. © 1997 New York University. Reprinted with permission of New York University.

The state's interest in promoting the use of chemicals is not hard to figure out. Approximately 80 percent of the commodities in this country are manufactured through some type of industrial chemical process (Chemical Manufacturers Association 1994). Americans bought a record high of $47 billion in tobacco products in 1995 and also a record $86 billion in prescription and nonprescription drugs (*World Almanac* 1997, 150). In 1995 the U.S. Department of Commerce reported export sales of chemicals for manufacturing and chemical commercial products in excess of $50 billion. Organic and inorganic compounds alone accounted for $21 billion, while cosmetics and plastics totaled almost $19 billion (*World Almanac* 1997, 241). Also in 1995, the U.S. produced 71.16 quadrillion Btu of energy (a quadrillion is 1 with fifteen zeros behind it). Of that number, 57.40 quadrillion Btu were produced by fossil fuels (*World Almanac* 1997, 235). Finally, over a million people work in the chemical industry, including 78,400 scientists and engineers. Women make up 30 percent of the work force (*Chemical and Engineering News* 1994, 29).

Assume for the moment that society determines the knowledge claims of the environmentally ill to be true. Assume people really do become sick from exposure to a seemingly endless array of chemicals found in ordinary environments. Assume the chemicals that cause illness are present in the environment at orders of magnitude lower than current regulatory levels. Moreover, assume that exposure to one chemical compound sensitizes the body to an array of unrelated chemical compounds. Finally, assume any body system is subject to the disease. If these assumptions are true, what is at stake is more than the public right to assign a rational explanation to a human trouble. At stake in the struggle to theorize a new relationship of the body to the environment is the vast process of chemical production, disability rights legislation, housing, commercial and public building construction codes, personal habits and codes of conduct, and local, state, and federal tolerance regulations, among other significant societal changes.

Consider the account of one environmentally ill woman who struggles to reduce the number of chemical agents that trigger her symptoms:

> I stopped coloring my hair, stopped having my nails done, and stopped wearing makeup, as the petrochemicals made my eyelids swell, the tissue around my eyes dry out, and my eyelids crusty. I haven't sat on my living room chairs and couches since 1989. They are foam filled and polyester covered. I sit only on cane Breuer chairs in my own home. Shower curtains, plastic implements, plastic bags, and plastic wrap for foods are out. I avoid plastic- and polyester-covered chairs whenever possible. This, of course, is almost impossible to do in our world. . . . I gradually eliminated the restaurants and auditoriums I would normally frequent, as the chemically treated air hurt a gland in my neck. I now never go to . . . theaters, movies, concerts, or plays, or into any commercially air-cooled or heated environment. I rarely go into stores of any kind as the chemicals in the treated air cause me pain which lasts for days after, and further open me to reactions from other sources. . . .
>
> This is not an environment I can tolerate.

This account portrays a body unable to tolerate routine beauty techniques for making it attractive; a body that severely reacts to ordinary commercial furniture designed to offer it at least a modicum of rest; a body that responds violently to air passed through conventional heating and cooling systems designed to make it more comfortable; and a body that is intolerant of the seemingly countless products lining the shelves of stores and markets. It is as if this body is in protest against the products of modernity and, in its distress, is calling for a radical change in the conventional boundaries between safe and dangerous. If the built environment, in combination with any consumer item that is made with a chemical compound, renders the body chronically sick and unable to work or consume, nothing less than the transformation of material culture is warranted. Resistance to the cultural legitimation of this new and troublesome body is hardly surprising.

Moreover, if the environmentally ill body portends a social transformation in production and consumption patterns, it also threatens the delicate filigree of personal habits and tastes, and their mutual confirmation in the highly stylized world of intimate and casual relationships. In the presence of one another, we depend on a shared, unspoken sense of what may be done or said without giving offense or committing an impropriety. For the chemically reactive, however, simple expressions of good taste and regard for others may become the sources of debilitating somatic distress. A man in his early thirties remembers

asking the people in my office to stop putting on so much cologne and perfume; I asked my office partner to stop using starch in his shirts. . . . My mom was willing to use another bathroom air thing (freshener) but my dad thought all this was much too strange. . . . I know it sounds strange but these things make me sick.

Somewhat indelicately, a more assertive woman reminds people around her, "Perfume causes brain damage. Think before you stink."

The judges who decide the winner of these skirmishes are arrayed throughout society, from intimate others, friends, work associates, and strangers who encounter the chemically reactive to municipal, county, state, and federal governments that are petitioned to accommodate them. These official and unofficial judges hear both accounts, the marginalized voices of the environmentally ill and their allies on one side and the powerful voices of medicine and trade groups on the other, supported by the suasive plea of an internalized culture that pronounces the domestic environments and products of modernity "safe" for human use. The important question is whether or not people and organizations are willing to change their behaviors regarding bodies and environments based on stories by nonprofessionals who borrow from the vernacular of biomedicine to fashion explanations of the origin of their troubles. If there is change, it is in opposition to the medical profession that refuses to acknowledge the legitimacy of environmental illness as a bio-organic disorder. If there is evidence that people and especially organizations are listening to the stories of the chemically reactive and modifying social and physical environments to assist them in coping with their troubles, then an arguably new form of social learning is surfacing, one in which organizations are bypassing a profession as a source of knowledge and modifying their practices in accord with citizens' professionally discredited accounts of bodies and environments.

This complicated conflict over knowing, embedded in the controversies surrounding MCS, begins with the body. To paraphrase Lévi-Strauss, the chemically reactive body is good to think and talk; indeed, its peculiar somatic changes insist on thinking and talking. People with MCS are forced to think about why their bodies change in the presence of common consumer products and ordinary environments; and they are often forced to explain these peculiar somatic changes to skeptical others.

Two Ways of Talking and Thinking, and the Reappearance of the Subject

We can think about our bodies because we both *are* bodies and *have* bodies (Berger and Luckmann 1966). The question, "How do we have bodies?" is routinely answered in sociology with some variant of the word *symbol*. We "have" bodies because we talk about them. Indeed, bodies are fabricated in talk; they are, literally, figures of speech, tropes, embodied conversations, social constructions. Many conversations about the body are occurring simultaneously, however, some more privileged than others. The power of physicians and medical researchers is embedded in their use of biomedical talk to promote a culturally preferred account of the body and disqualify other accounts. To the profession of medicine society has given the right to author the body: to pronounce it legally alive, to name its systems and diseases, to control its capacity to labor by defining when it is sick and when it is well, and, finally, to pronounce it legally dead. From the birth certificate to the death certificate and everything in between, biomedicine is charged by the state with writing the somatic text.[1]

Consider, for example, a proud father who looks at his newborn daughter and observes, "She has my eyes and nose," and thus locates her body in his lineage. Important as this moment is in the life of the father and daughter, of equal or greater importance is the issuance of a state birth certificate signed by a physician that officially recognizes the infant body as living and legally belonging to the father who gave her the eyes and nose and the mother who birthed her. In the absence of state certification of the live body of the infant, the date of birth, and her legal father and mother, recognizing a similarity between her nose and that of an adult would not be sufficient to establish paternity.

Two strategies for knowing the body are evident in the configuration of the father, the infant, and the state that are important in understanding the epistemological controversy over MCS. The father apprehends the physical features of his child in talk that embeds them both in a familial world supported by history and emotion. In this fleeting moment, everyday language about the body links two subjects to a past, present, and future based on reciprocal feelings and expectations. This is truly *the* common language, a dramatic vocabulary creating and mediating attitudes, history, and community to fashion communal relationships governed by common sentiment and reciprocal expectations about behavior.

A state's bureau of vital statistics, on the other hand, issues a certificate that literally licenses the body but does so anonymously, abstractly, without face, if you will. It separates the persona from the soma and locates the body in demographic and numerical coordinates. This second talk about the body is guided by technical rules, not social norms. Its goal is the elimination of attitudes and other emotional factors that might complicate an objective location of the body in society. If the communal world is constructed through a dramatic vocabulary, the biomedical world is possible only by avoiding drama. When experts speak, scientific-technical talk works to eliminate emotion while providing, in Kenneth Burke's words, the "name and address of every event in the universe" (1973, 88).

While both talks are symbolic conversations, biomedical talk is presented as context-free, that is, ahistorical and apolitical, a "natural fact." It does not construct and sustain existential experiences; rather, it claims to mirror external reality. Diseases and treatments are discovered by the languages of anatomy, physiology, hematology, immunology, and so on. The body is a materialist product of these vocabularies, unencumbered by experiential or communal ways of knowing.

Alain Touraine would likely find our example of the father with his newborn and the bureau of vital statistics an apt illustration of his recent theory of modernity. The foundation of modernism, he contends, is the separation of the ordinary person from the instruments of rationality (1995, 219). Modernity, he argues, suffers from a cultural bipolarism, "a divorce between the world of nature, which is governed by the laws discovered and used by rational thought, and the world of the Subject" (57). Personal identity, biography, the emotive and affective culture of the individual are isolated from a managerial power legitimated by a claim to efficiency-based instrumental reason. When the world of technical rationality is dissociated from the world of subjectivity, "reason becomes an interest of might" and no longer the measure of a just and equitable society (5).

Touraine's Subject, the person who dissolves the chasm between instrumental rationality and communal, experiential history, figures prominently in the narratives of the environmentally ill. People who explain the origins of their somatic problems in chemically saturated environments are, to borrow an image from Geertz, constructing illness narratives "ostensibly scientific out of experiences broadly biographical" (1983, 10). A chemically reactive person invents and constructs a body by the skillful use of a technical language that helps him adapt to a world he no longer assumes is safe. The image of science joined with biography is an uncommon one in our society and is important to our account of environmental illness as a practical epistemology.

Recall the example of the father and the newborn in contrast with the bureau of vital statistics; while biography is created in ordinary speech that embeds both father and daughter in a common culture and history, in an entirely different and anonymous act the newborn is officially registered and classified as alive and belonging to a mother and father through a formal certification process that is nothing if it is not objective, rational, and independent of social involvements. What makes the illness narratives of the environmentally ill unique is their pattern of joining these two traditionally separated strategies for apprehending the world. Without exception, the illness stories of the chemically reactive collected for this book weave together the pain, loss, embarrassment, and challenge of a debilitating chronic illness not recognized by the profession of medicine, with a complex account of its etiology and pathophysiology, and frequent mention of sophisticated strategies for avoiding reactions and managing symptoms. Consider the following narrative.

An EI Narrative

Joan calls herself multiply chemically sensitive. Unable to use common cleaning products without experiencing debilitating headaches, nausea, and heart palpitations, she found baking soda comparatively nontoxic and buys it in bulk at her local grocery store:

> On one occasion I was bringing a five-pound box of baking soda to the checkout line and my body began to react violently to something or someone in the store. I responded by pulling a cotton bandanna from my pocket and wrapped it around my nose and mouth, tying it in back of my head. I approached the checkout line. Now picture this. I am trembling, my face is masked, and I am breathing hard. Several customers looked at me and stood aside, leaving me staring, with my mouth and nose covered by a black bandanna, at the cashier.
>
> I told the cashier that I was multiply chemically sensitive and my body was reacting to the store. I gave them my standard line: "I'm sorry for the confusion. I have environmental illness. Something happens to me when I get around certain chemical products. As you can see, my body shakes and my breathing becomes difficult. The mask blocks some of the toxins." I remember my symptoms steadily intensifying. Talking became difficult. My mouth refused to form the words I needed to speak. I was unable to grasp my wallet in my purse because my hands were trembling uncontrollably. I handed the purse to the cashier who found the wallet and rang up the sale.
>
> I asked the cashier to call the store manager. I tried to explain to him that I drove to the store but could not drive home. At this point in my reaction, I could not hold my package or my car keys in my fingers. The manager wanted to call an ambulance. I told him that an ambulance and an emergency room would make me more sick than I was at the moment. I told him, "This is going to sound dumb, but ambulances and hospitals are full of chemicals and I know I will get sicker. I need to get home where I can take care of myself." I asked the manager to call me a cab and ask for a smoke-free cab. He took the initiative, however, and personally drove me home.

A few days following Joan's emergency at the grocery store, she wrote the store manager a thank-you card. She remembers trying to explain her problem to him so he would understand that she was "not crazy and not blaming the store." She wrote:

> I have a new disease called environmental illness. I got it when I was exposed to the chemicals 2,4-D and Diazinon while spraying my house for fleas. The chemicals

damaged my immune system and I get reactions now to almost everything around me, but I am learning how to control them. . . . I know I acted crazy in your store, but it is due to the chemicals. I don't mean to say your store is contaminated. I just can't tolerate things like I use to. Doctors don't believe I get sick from chemicals like those in your store. But I do.

If the Cartesian revolution successfully silenced the authorial voice of the body, rendering it a mechanical thing, in a passing moment in a nondescript grocery aisle, Joan's body found a voice, its own. Giving voice to their bodies, however, is a necessity for the environmentally ill. As exemplified in Joan's predicament, the chemically reactive are frequently required to tell illness stories while in acute states of distress and dependent on the help and understanding of others. It is in this manner that illness narratives become a claim on other people by describing new and disturbing relationships between bodies and environments.

Several observations are suggested in Joan's emergency in the grocery store and her situated explanations of her body's failure to adapt to this mundane setting. First, it is possible to account for Joan's illness narrative as a theory about her body in relationship to the environment. She uses a coherent group of propositions regarding the relationship between pesticide exposures and her immune system to account for her body's inability to adapt to routine, putatively safe environments, such as grocery stores and hospitals. Grocery stores, and perhaps to a lesser extent hospitals, are not routinely experienced as sources of acute illness. While someone may question the health effects or safety of a specific item on the shelves, most people experience grocery stores as safe, domestic environments. Joan's somatic failure, of course, may be understood as having nothing to do with the store. Her symptoms suggest several possible standard biomedical explanations, including grand mal seizures, epilepsy, or hysteria, that locate the causes of her distress in the body or the mind and not the immediate environment. Joan's theory, however, stresses her belief that it was the grocery store that made her sick.

Moreover, if we examine Joan's narrative, it is possible to discern a theory of disease etiology and pathophysiology. Joan theorizes that the chemicals 2,4-D and Diazinon are the source of her illness. Her exposure to these chemicals was subclinical, or below measurable levels using standard diagnostic technology. Nevertheless, her symptoms started within a few days of treating her apartment with an aerosol flea spray. The time association was important to Joan in figuring out the source of her illness. Another factor that proved important in Joan's theorizing the source of her sickness were the accounts of other people's adverse reactions to 2,4-D and Diazinon found in newspapers and newsletters and through word of mouth. Finally, Joan clung to her etiology theory with increasing tenacity as three physicians representing three different medical specialties could find nothing physically wrong with her. When the last physician she visited suggested a psychiatric evaluation, Joan ignored the suggestion and instead joined the National Coalition against Pesticides to, in her words, "become smarter than the doctors. . . . If my explanation wasn't better than theirs I was afraid people would call me crazy like the doctors thought I was."

Joan's theory of MCS also included an account of its pathophysiology and treatment regimens that worked to reduce her symptoms. Convinced the pesticides started her illness, Joan felt she also needed to know how they adversely affected her body. She talked with a nurse who lived in her neighborhood, who suggested the problem might be in her immune system. She read a *Newsweek* article on the immune system and watched a television special on AIDS. When she heard the phrase "chemical AIDS" in a National Public Radio report on EI, she concluded that the pesticides damaged her immune system and thus weakened her body's ability to fend off chemicals. Finally, while Joan is unable to find a cure for her MCS, she has developed several strategies for managing her symptoms, most of them based on avoiding those places and things that make her sick.

Is Joan's theory of MCS defensible? Perhaps not from a strict biomedical perspective. Her exposure to the pesticides was far below the threshold for acute toxicity. Assuming for the moment that she was exposed to sufficient levels of 2,4-D and Diazinon to cause an acute response, biomedicine cannot explain her subsequent sensitization to an array of unrelated chemicals. Finally, at least a few of her symptoms invited a psychosomatic interpretation.

On the other hand, Joan's account of her body is founded on the assumption that there is a natural world that can be examined. Through careful consideration of her symptoms, her experiences, and a knowledge of the (popular) literature, she has constructed a theory of her body and its adverse relationships to what were once safe and secure environments. Finally, she has tested her theory by organizing her life to avoid these environments while developing strategies for responding to stressful situations, such as the incident in the grocery store. Joan's capacity to control the definitions, meanings, and behaviors of her disability through the reflexive use of a homespun theory is a pragmatic argument for investing some faith in her ideas about her body and environments. The important question of what criteria should be used to discern the validity of MCS illness narratives is addressed in later sections of the book. At the moment it is necessary to focus on the unique features of Joan's theory about her body and environments.

Changing the Social Location, Definition, and Consequences of Expert Knowledge

Joan's theory encompasses three interrelated ideas—*social location, social definition, and social representation*—that work together to represent the outlines of an alternative strategy for creating and politically employing instrumental, rational knowledge in modern society. As we have defined the term here, constructing a practical epistemology may be said to begin when people appropriate a language of expertise and organize their personal lives around it. It becomes a unique way of knowing insofar as people modify and change its conventional strategies for defining and organizing. Finally, a practical epistemology becomes politically interesting when sectors of society are persuaded to change policies and habits in response to languages of expertise wielded by nonexperts who claim to know something new about the world. Consider first the idea of social location and expert knowledge.

Social Location

State-sponsored theorizing about the body and its relationship to disease and the environment is the right and obligation of the medical profession. A distinction routinely made in medical anthropology between illness and disease recognizes the unequal positions of the physician and the patient in explaining and treating sick bodies (Atkinson 1995). *Disease* is a politically powerful word controlled by the profession of medicine to classify bio-organic states of the body as unable to work properly, that is, to produce a day's labor. To have a disease is to be officially certified as unable to work at full capacity, or perhaps at all. To be designated as diseased may carry a substantial social penalty (witness the AIDS pandemic), but it is more likely to demand consideration and understanding on the part of others. Disease is, in one important sense, a rhetoric of entitlement. A state-sponsored definition of a pathogenic body pressures people and organizations to relieve a person from some (if not all) social responsibilities.[2] Without a physician's certification that the body is in a state of disease, a person who claims to be sick is likely to meet with skepticism, if not charges of malingering.

If physicians control the word *disease,* sick people are said to control the word *illness,* or the subjective awareness and meanings associated with a sick body. From the vantage point of disease, illness is a residual category. It is a necessary, but rarely privileged, concomitant of the simple fact that people *are* bodies and *have* bodies. Illness is not meant to signal a theory of etiology, pathophysiology, or treatment, for these represent the fact that people are bodies; rather, it is a cluster of words that locates sickness in meaningful social and historical arrangements, an anthropological necessity based on the fact that people have bodies and thus are required to attribute a meaning to them.

While it is true that, from the position of the state, illness is of secondary or minor importance in the classification and management of disease, it nevertheless suggests that authority over the body's problem is not in the sole possession of the physician. The ideal case, of course, is one of symmetry between the physician's assignment of a disease classification and the patient's acceptance of it; here, disease and illness merge, with one becoming, for all practical purposes, indistinguishable from the other. Perhaps the general stability of the medical profession is related, at least in part, to the observation that in this case the ideal approximates the real. A less than ideal case is a physician's diagnosis that is resisted by the person; here other institutional authorities (parents, spouses, employers) may be called upon to persuade him or her to "be reasonable and follow the doctor's recommendations."

Arguably the most disquieting case of all is the person who defines himself as sick although a physician is unable to certify that a physical basis for a disorder exists. Here a request for a disease classification is officially denied, leaving the person with a choice: to accept the authoritative account that "nothing physically unusual is happening" or to maintain a "something physically unusual" stance. The first choice may or may not be troublesome for the person, but it is unlikely to become a social issue. After all, the appearance is that the doctor and patient each performed their respective roles in a respectable fashion. If the patient later dies because of the physician's failure to diagnose in time, society is able to sanction or discredit the physician while simultaneously affirming the competence of the medical profession. The choice to adhere to the "something physically unusual" claim in spite of the doctor's opinion, however, places the person in the unenviable position of scrambling to find resources to persuade others that the medical community is wrong and he is right, and, moreover, that he should be accorded the social and moral status of those who are officially recognized as suffering from a disease.

Joan visited three doctors, and each one refused to acknowledge her belief that a common consumer item had caused her sickness. In the absence of a professional diagnosis, Joan constructed her own disease theory. Joan is not simply fabricating an illness narrative to render her somatic troubles meaningful to her; she is also theorizing the etiology and pathophysiology of her sickness and prescribing treatment strategies to reduce the deleterious effects of her sickness. In short, Joan appropriates the language of biomedicine to locate her body in the nomenclature of disease and thus shifts the social location of theorizing disease from physicians to nonphysicians. It is in this fashion that Joan's illness narrative, her subjective experience of distress, begins to sound like a disease narrative, a technical account of the origins, pathways, and treatments of a legitimate biomedical disorder.

Another way of considering this shift is to visualize Joan moving a language from an expert system to a nonexpert system, from the protected sphere of a licensed profession to the more contingent and negotiated sphere of communal life. While this shift may not appear particularly important at first, it gains a measure of significance when it is situated within a defining feature of late modern life: the increasing dependence of ordinary people on abstract or expert systems (Giddens 1990, 1991; Beck 1992). An increasing number of life experiences are created and shaped by technical knowledge that remains abstruse and opaque to most people. Ordinary people who have troubling experiences are likely to seek professional or expert advice. The troubling experience is a biographical moment; the professional or expert offers an explanation of that troubled moment, creating a growing chasm between biographical moments and their subsequent explanations. The person who awakes in a house heated and cooled by electricity, motors, pumps, and thermostats, drives to work in a car with automatic transmission and cruise control, types on a word processor, and sends a message by fax to a client in another country is caught in a tangled web of dependence on expert systems. The abstract technical systems ensnaring her both created these technologies and are required when they break down.

Dependence almost always begs the question of trust, however. And the more dependent we become on abstract systems, the more complicated are the questions of trust (Giddens 1990, 1991). The trust we invest in abstract systems is less a matter of conscious choice between viable alternatives and more, in Anthony Giddens's words, "a tacit acceptance of circumstances in which other alternatives are largely foreclosed" (1990, 90).

When we require expert systems we seek out system representatives, or experts. Experts are the intersections between ordinary people and abstract knowledge systems. In these encounters, according to Giddens, expert systems become vulnerable to skepticism and lose the trust of people whose problems remain in spite of the efforts of the experts. Joan's story suggests a modification of this idea by suggesting that at these intersections the legitimacy of expert systems is less at risk than the credibility of experts. Most people are impatient when an expert representing an abstract system cannot fix a technological trouble. In the event an expert cannot repair a faulty technology, however, people are not likely to abandon the expert system or the hardware it created; rather, they are more likely to desert the expert while retaining their faith in the system.

Abandoning an expert while retaining faith in an abstract system acts to protect the legitimacy of the system. It is the person who represents the system and not the system itself that is rejected. The act of finding another expert expresses a tacit faith in the integrity of the abstract system independent of the skill of this or that expert. Joan's example, however, reveals how people lose trust in a whole class of experts, bypass them, and access the system on their own, in the absence of licensed representation.

Social Definition

It is reasonable to assume that if the environmentally ill are moving away from physician-experts while appropriating the symbols and meanings located in the biomedical-expert system, it is possible to discern the vague outlines of a new way of knowing that links (or relinks) experience with explanation and protests an important accomplishment of the Enlightenment project that successfully separated the two. People who conclude that they are suffering from MCS or EI, who construct theories about the origins of their sickness (its pathophysiology), and conceive of treatment strategies to manage a complicated array of symptoms are claiming the privilege to classify their bodies as *diseased*, not simply ill. If shifting the social location of theorizing the body as diseased from expert to nonexpert systems hints at an alternative way of knowing the world, it does so in large part because of the changes in social definition that accompany this shift. Once expert knowledge is uprooted from its location in expert cultures and placed in communal, nonexpert settings, its logics for apprehending the world might also change. Rational or technical knowledge does more than describe; it also justifies social and political arrangements (Habermas 1968). Importantly, it promotes a way of knowing that obscures its own social foundations. Rational, particularly scientific, knowledge "conceptualizes an absolute social-natural disconnection" (Wright 1992, 58). By denying its own social commitments, technical knowledge in the hands of experts can pronounce on the affairs of nature and the body as an objective, unbiased witness.

Science is important to the state in its capacity to legitimate a political economy in terms that cannot be easily recognized as social. A product of modernity, biomedicine shares with the major social institutions of the era a remarkable capacity to avoid self-examination. Paraphrasing Gellner, Wright (1992) argues that "genuine knowledge is inherently indifferent" to biography or inequality; it is, rather, "inherently scientific" (50). "Genuine explanation," Gellner writes, "means subsumption under a structure or schema made up of neutral, impersonal elements. In this sense, explanation is always 'dehumanizing,' and inescapably so" (quoted in Wright 1992, 50).

In spite of the popularity of the holistic and community health movements, the importance of scientific assumptions to modern medicine persists. Descartes might be in hiding from the postmodernists, but he is alive and well in the profession of medicine.

> It is a mistake to underestimate the force of Cartesian dualism in medicine today. In spite of a growing disaffection of a section of the populace with traditional approaches to health, the dualist philosophy is alive and well, the guiding light of almost all theoretical and clinical efforts of Western medicine. (Dossey 1984, 13; see also Young 1982; Gordon 1988; Freund and McGuire 1991)

A professor of psychiatry and medicine writes: "The biomedical model embraces both reductionism, the philosophic view that complex phenomena are ultimately derived from a single primary principle, and mind body dualism, the doctrine that separates the mental from the somatic" (Engle 1977, 130).

One observer attributes the tenacity of biomedical assumptions and practices to the continued hegemony of "naturalism" in modern culture. A domain assumption of the Enlightenment, naturalism asserts that humans are a part of nature; they are bio-organic processes that will reveal themselves to those trained in the scientific method (Gordon 1988, 21). The politics of naturalism begins with the capabilities and constraints of the biological body as the sources of individual, social, and economic relationships (Johnstone 1992). To know something from the vantage point of naturalism is to imagine it in its simplest form, uncomplicated by political or economic arrangements. Not surprisingly, the emergence of naturalism corresponded closely with the emergence of the "bourgeois individual," each cultural idea reinforcing the other. The creation story of both early and late modern capitalism "would have to begin with 'In the beginning there was the individual . . .'" (Gordon 1988, 34).

Indeed, the modern period worked to shape the human being as independent of history, "autonomous and thus essentially [a] nonsocial moral being" (Dumont 1986, 25). The person in modernity was freed from the dead "hand of custom," from the greedy grasp of local traditions; now science and its partner the state would serve to legislate the self (Bauman 1993, 83). Sontag locates the idea of the bourgeois individual in biomedicine, citing Groddeck's eighteenth-century observation that "the sick man himself creates his disease. . . . he is the cause of the disease and we need seek none other" and Karl Menninger's quite similar conclusion reached two hundred years later that "'illness is in part what the world had done to a victim, but in a larger part it is what the victim had done with his world, and with himself'" (quoted in Sontag 1989, 46–47). Consider the painful words of Katherine Mansfield, written in 1923, a year before her death: "A bad day . . . horrible pains go on, and weakness. I could do nothing. The weakness was not only physical. I must heal my self before I will be well. . . . This must be done alone and at once. It is at the root of my not getting better" (quoted in Sontag 1989, 47).

Joining naturalism with the bourgeois individual ensured that the bio-organic person would be considered prior to society and the technical proficiency of biomedicine would be based in part on its claim to mirror the natural, not the social, world. Only by claiming to identify and explain somatic troubles in the absence of politics and history can biomedicine claim its privileged access to natural processes. Physicians, of course, often speak publicly about a health problem, adding their influential voices to important social concerns, but when they do so, they are not speaking from the vantage point of biomedicine. It is the *model* of biomedicine that interests us, not the individual physician.

Apprehending modern problems as biomedical is a potent rhetorical strategy for deflecting attention from the possible social sources of troubles, focusing instead on their supposed biological or psychological origins. Sociology identified this process years ago as "medicalization." Conrad and Schneider (1990), for example, examine the transformation of the "unruly child" into the child with "hyperkinetic impulse disorder" (HID) by tracing the application of biomedical terms to a form of deviant social behavior. Capturing "unruly" children in biomedical language exercised by the profession of medicine divested their aberrant behavior of its cultural and political significance. When the label HID is invoked, the family culture and the political arrangements it reflects are left unexamined as possible sources of a child's anxious behavior. Medicalization expresses the tenacity of naturalism and individualism in contemporary society.

Joan's narrative, however, hints at an alternative strategy for using biomedical language to apprehend a somatic trouble. Joan is not a physician. She is not licensed by the state to capture personal troubles in expert systems. Nevertheless, she appropriates clusters of words from the vocabulary of medicine and in the milieu of her personal and communal world constructs an account of her trouble. Her account begins by externalizing the source of her misery. She is not making herself sick; putatively safe environments and the supposedly safe products found in them are the cause of her sickness. Joan's theory begins with the idea of a well body encountering pathogenic environments. It is not the industrial, polluted environments of the typical contaminated community that are making her sick but the culturally defined safe and nurturing environments of homes and grocery stores. Encoded in Joan's somatic misery and the story she tells about it is the need to invert the normal logic of the sick role, deflecting attention from a clinical appraisal of the physical body to a critical appraisal of the social body. In her hands, EI becomes a lingual representation of a once healthy body protesting imperfections in the production of modern material life.

She theorizes that her sickness is caused by chemicals commonly found in pesticides manufactured for use in houses. Though her exposure to these chemicals occurred in a single incident and was not detected in subsequent blood tests, Joan is certain that her troubles started when she used a bug bomb. Moreover, Joan's theory includes an account of how the chemicals changed her body, rendering it susceptible to violent reactions from minute, subclinical exposures to unrelated chemicals found everywhere in her environment. Her pathophysiology theory keeps the focus on the external environment as the source of her misery. Finally, her treatment strategies suggest the importance of other people in the successful management of her EI. It is useful to think of MCS as a relational disease. That is, it can be successfully managed only if people and environments surrounding the sick person conform to the comparatively austere demands of the illness. Consider the well-chosen words of one woman with a long history of EI:

> More than with any other illness, what other people do or do not do affects those of us with MCS. We are at their mercy. . . . if our spouse insists on smoking, if friends and relatives won't give up their perfumes . . . if hospitals persist in using toxic cleaning products, if restaurants continue putting air "fresheners" in washrooms, . . . and on and on—there's very little we can do. . . . We can only try to protect ourselves.

Unless the person with MCS remains isolated, his or her well-being is directly dependent on the choices and behaviors of others. If people do choose to change their behaviors to accommodate the chemically reactive, they will be motivated in part by plausible, rational explanations of the need for change.

Social Representation

When another person acknowledges the body of the chemically reactive person by making some accommodation to its exacting, some might say extreme, demands, a new body is being socially represented. If MCS signals the emergence of a new body, this body becomes interesting socially and politically only when it finds individuals, organizations, and institutions willing to change their habits, routines, and policies in order to represent it. Joan's somatic trouble in a local grocery store suggests the most basic way the MCS body succeeds in securing representation: it demands it.

Joan told a story about her body, and the store clerk and manager responded to her distress. It is not known whether either person believed Joan's account of her troubles. The manager was probably motivated to assist Joan as much to remove her from his store as to relieve her of her distress, but he did so in a kind way and she appreciated the help. And through his behavior, he momentarily joined Joan in a public drama that acknowledged the reality of a sick body.

The interesting question, however, is not what happened to Joan at a local grocery store but how to, or whether society is prepared to, reorganize to prevent Joan and those like her from becoming sick. If the chemically reactive are going to live among others whose bodies have not changed, they must persuade these others that concepts of disease and environment are now coterminous, with one somehow implying the other. The social and economic costs of succeeding in this rhetorical work are understandably high.

Just how persuasive are laypersons who borrow a medical vernacular to ask others to commit substantial resources to redesign houses, workplaces, public spaces, and so on to represent a strange and troubling body? This hints at the much broader question of how institutions learn. This more abstract question will become clearer if we quickly summarize the ideas of social location and social definition.

The environmentally ill are shifting the traditional location of theorizing by appropriating the language of physician-experts to conceptualize their own somatic misery. In relocating this expert language from its professional setting to the more mundane setting of communal life, the environmentally ill are also challenging a definitional logic of medical expertise that effectively obscures the role of history and politics in the etiology of sickness by identifying the sources of their somatic disorders in the chemical culture of post–World War II America. The third and final question is a pragmatic one: So what? Who is listening and why? It is one thing to borrow a biomedical vernacular and use it to charge society with robbing you of your health while holding it responsible for your recovery; it is quite another to convince influential others that your disease claim is a legitimate one. A new theory of the body in relationship to the environment assumes political relevance if people and institutions are willing to change their behaviors in response to its logics of social culpability and demands for social changes, in spite of the medical profession's steadfast refusal to accept the new theory.

The chemically reactive are in the unenviable position of having to persuade some members of their interpersonal worlds to accept MCS as a legitimate, albeit strange, disease. Persuading others (as we will see) depends in part on the person's ability to manipulate the style and grammar of biomedicine. It is reasonable to assume that the more unusual and exotic the theory of disease and the more it requires unaccustomed changes on the part of family, friends, neighbors, and workmates, the more difficulty a person will have in convincing others of its medical legitimacy. People who accept MCS as a legitimate disorder also acknowledge their responsibility for changing personal habits that might trigger symptoms; they become accountable for both causing and abating disease symptoms. Not everyone in the interpersonal world of the environmentally ill is willing to assume this responsibility. What is striking, however, is just how many are.

Convincing people who occupy the personal spaces of the chemically reactive that ordinary environments are sources of disease might appear to be a considerably different exercise than convincing employers, government agencies, or legislatures to recognize the problem. While there are some differences, both venues require the claimant to present a carefully crafted account of the bioscience etiology of MCS, ensuring that medical nomenclature itself shapes the struggle for consensus. It is in the arenas of work and policy that MCS as a social movement begins to take shape and form.

In summary, if EI constitutes a new way of knowing the body in its relationships to the environment, it is politically important to the extent it changes opinions, social arrangements, and the distribution of resources. Limited to a subjective appraisal that something is wrong with the body's relationship to the environment, even if that appraisal is biomedical in nature, MCS is not likely to be a vehicle for notable social change. On the other hand, as the biomedical appraisal succeeds in convincing influential others that subclinical exposure to ordinary environments is the cause of disease—in spite of the efforts of the medical profession, the chemical and insurance industries, and others to deny the veracity of this claim—it becomes a moral vocabulary that justifies effective action on behalf of the sick. From this vantage point, MCS becomes a cluster of terms that succeed, albeit modestly as of this writing, in redefining the relationship of the body to the built environments of the late twentieth century.

NOTES

1. The keystone assuring the hegemony of medicine was set in place at the turn of the twentieth century, when the power of the medical institute was firmly locked into the process of social control. It was in the "promise" of certainty offered by the medical community to render understanding of human suffering and an offer to employ medical expertise in the resolution of this suffering that a deal was made. Under the leadership of the American Medical Association, the medical community offered its expertise to the state in exchange for power and control (Starr 1982).

2. This is one dimension of Parsons's "sick role" (1951, 428–47). Not surprisingly, the environmentally ill want very much to be recognized as sick, but on terms considerably different than Parsons envisaged. For the chemically reactive the issue is not simply a temporary exemption from normal role requirements but also a need to reconsider the requirements themselves. If working with fax and copying machines is making an employee sick, then modifying work routines might be necessary to accommodate him.

BIBLIOGRAPHY

Ashford, Nicholas, and Claudia S. Miller. 1991. *Chemical Exposures*. New York: Van Nostrand Reinhold.

Atkinson, Paul. 1995. *Medical Talk and Medical Work*. London: Sage.

Bauman, Zygmunt. 1993. *Postmodern Ethics*. Oxford: Blackwell.

Beck, Ulrich. 1992. *Risk Society*. London: Sage.

Berger, Peter, and Thomas Luckman. 1966. *Social Construction of Reality: A Treatise on the Sociology of Knowledge*. New York: Anchor.

Burke, Kenneth. 1973. *The Philosophy of Literary Form: Studies in Symbolic Action*. Berkeley: University of California Press.

Chemical and Engineering News. 1994. "Facts for the Chemical Industry." June, 25–30.

Chemical Manufacturing Association. 1994. Trade Advertisement.

Conrad, Peter, and Joseph W. Schneider. 1990. *Deviance and Medicalization: From Badness to Sickness*. St. Louis: C. V. Mosby.

Dossey, Larry. 1984. *Beyond Illnes*. Boulder: New Science Library.

Dumont, Louis. 1986. *Essays on Individualism: Modern Theory in Anthropological Perspective*. Chicago: University of Chicago Press.

Engle, George L. 1977. "The Need for a New Medical Model: A Challenge for Biomedicine." *Science* 196: 4286.

Foucault, Michel. 1973. *Birth of the Clinic*. London: Tavistock.

Freund, Peter E. S., and Meredith B. McGuire. 1991. *Health, Illness, and the Social Body*. Englewood Cliffs, NJ: Prentice Hall.

Geertz, Clifford. 1983. *Local Knowledge: Further Essays in Interpretive Anthropology*. New York: Basic Books.

Giddens, Anthony. 1990. *The Consequences of Modernity*. Stanford: Stanford University Press.

———. 1991. *Modernity and Self-Identity*. Stanford: Stanford University Press.

Gordon, Deborah R. 1988. "Tenacious Assumptions in Western Medicine." In *Biomedicine Examined*, edited by M. Lock and D. R. Gordon, 19–53. Boston: Kluwer Academic Publishers.

Habermas, Jurgen. 1968. *Toward a Rational Society*. Boston: Beacon Press.

Johnstone, Albert A. 1992. "The Bodily Nature of the Self; or, What Descartes Should Have Conceded Princess Elizabeth of Bohemia." In *Giving the Body Its Due*, edited by Maxine Sheets-Johnstone, 16–47. Albany: State University of New York Press.

Mitchell, Frank L., ed. 1995. *Multiple Chemical Sensitivity: A Scientific Overview*. Washington, DC: U.S. Department of Health and Human Services.

Parsons, Talcott. 1952. *The Social System*. Glencoe, IL: Free Press.

Sontag, Susan. 1989. *Illness as Metaphor*. New York: Anchor.

Starr, Paul. 1982. *The Social Transformation of American Medicine*. New York: Basic Books.

Touraine, Alain. 1995. *Critique of Modernity*. Oxford: Blackwell.

World Almanac. 1997. Mahwah, NJ: K-III Reference Corporation.

Wright, Will. 1992. *Wild Knowledge*. Minneapolis: University of Minnesota Press.

Young, Allen. 1982. "The Anthropologies of Illness and Sickness." *Annual Review of Anthropology* 11: 257–85.

Part II

||||||||||||||||||||||||||||||||||||||||||||||||||||||||||||||||||||||||

Bodies as Mediums

Introduction to Part II

When Gregor Samsa, the protagonist of Franz Kafka's *Metamorphosis*, awakens to find that his human body has morphed into that of an unctuous oversized beetle, he is forced to come to terms with his new embodied existence. Mundane activities like eating, moving about his room, or conversing with his family pose enormous challenges to his suddenly uninhabitable and alien form. His new body also brings new carnal desires and needs that repulse him, like a taste for fetid garbage and a preference for sitting under furniture. Gregor, a disembodied salesman rather disconnected from society, must learn to live in his own skin. The story of this radically morphed body/self reminds us that the human body is the *medium* that connects us to a broader cultural landscape as not only a personal and social entity but a material one as well. Because it illuminates the experiential and sometimes obdurate realities of the flesh, Kafka's tale is an apt metaphorical setting to consider how we move about the world from inside of a body.

The material body, conceived as a medium, draws from the infamous phrase "the medium is the message," coined by media scholar Marshal McLuhan. In *Understanding Media: The Extensions of Man* (1964) McLuhan sparked a radical shift in thinking that emphasized the relationship among forms of media, whether television or comic books, and the messages they conveyed. For McLuhan, "message" does not solely refer to specific content, for example, the meaning of a Myspace page, but to a "change of scale, or pace or pattern" that a new invention ushers in. Similarly, a medium is any extension of ourselves that allows us to engage, move, and change the world. A medium could be a shoe, car, microscope, telephone, or iPod. McLuhan cautioned that we tend to be distracted by the content of the medium, losing sight of the larger personal and social consequences of it. Thus, the larger idea behind "the medium is the message" is an analysis of how the characteristics of a medium play a role in societal change, not a simplistic content-over-form analysis. Likewise, body scholars have sometimes reduced the body to simple dualistic categories, playing up the self at the expense of the body. There has been a tendency to lose sight of the characteristics of material bodies. As a medium, the body is both an agent and a reflection of cultural change.

The works in this section cover a broad range of activities, from drug addiction to cosmetic surgery, yet they are bound together by a common theme of lived embodied experience. The "lived body" is explicitly connected to larger aspects of culture, where it is transformed through carrying out sets of tasks, routines, habits, and performances. In most cases, bodily adaptation is paramount. In "'Made by the Work': A Century of Laboring Bodies in the United States," historian Ed Slavishak illuminates how the material body must change to accommodate the demands of labor in a capitalist patriarchal economy, from nineteenth-century factory production to twenty-first-century service work performed by data entry clerks. The concept of a "laboring body" makes explicit how the body is a medium or tool that can masterfully perform "intricate tasks" or "challenging feats" in the context of quotas, productivity, and profit. Slavishak highlights how laboring bodies have had to adapt to the demands of the marketplace. The steel mills and coal mines of the early twentieth century required physically fit and strong, virile bodies, as the employee was often required to work rhythmically with heavy equipment (lest he fall victim to injury or amputation), whereas today's employee may work in isolation, be expected to perform emotional labor (smile!), or consume products designed to keep the laboring body productive. Over-the-counter stimulants like Red Bull, No Doze, and Blitz Caffeine Energy Gum, as well as back supports and carpal tunnel wrist braces, show how a market of consumption has emerged to meet the demands of production.

Slavishak's laboring body adds muscle and sweat to Marx's theoretical analysis of "alienating labor," demonstrating the physical and sometimes emotional consequences of becoming an extension of a grinder or a vacuum cleaner. Also implicit here is the effect of social class on the body. Poor working-class bodies, both male and female, are more likely to incur acute and chronic physical injuries while on the job. With little time off away from work, no insurance, and poor health care, the laboring body as a medium is more likely to break down, age, and degrade. In "Embodied Capitalism and the Meth Economy," anthropologist Jason Pine tells the story of how similarly vulnerable bodies are impacted by post-Fordist production, capitalism consumption, and globalization. Pine uses his ethnographic research on methamphetamine users in impoverished rural Missouri as an entry point into understanding "embodied capitalism." By way of "Wil," an unemployed crystal meth addict and father of two, we see the tangible effects of using meth and how the consumption of the drug is intricately tied to the local (and global) economy, via Wal-Mart, which is a primary employer in the area. The meth producer-consumer gets the goods to make the drug (tin foil, light bulbs, peanut butter, etc.) and the fuel that is his diet (Twinkies, Dr. Pepper, and Mountain Dew) from the place where he works. The working-poor body is shaped and constrained by living and laboring within this "complete consumer ecology."

Like Slavishak's "laboring body," which is increasingly pushed to consume in order to perform, within "embodied capitalism," Pine argues, we are all expected to tap into our own individual material resources. He calls attention to a larger cultural shift in which a new cohort of workers, Generation Y (those born between 1978 and 1992), are beginning to be defined by a heightened state of physical and mental awareness. Socialized on a cultural diet of overachieving, overscheduling, and living life on the edge, Gen Yers, like meth addicts, are mediums on overdrive. They are both the producer-consumers of late capitalism and the embodied markers of a particular cultural ethos. Just as meth bodies and those produced by the new economy believe that "risk is reward" and delight in states of nervousness and exhilaration, so, too, do "extreme bodies." In "Extreme Culture/Extreme Bodies," sociologist Mary Kosut places contemporary body practices and activities—from cosmetic surgeries to extreme body modification rituals—within a broader cultural framework. In addition to presenting an analysis of mediated texts and images, Kosut also draws from her own embodied ethnographic experience undergoing a chest hook pull. She maintains that the rise of consumer society and media culture has fueled the development of "extreme culture." Like "embodied capitalism," extreme culture is connected to a particular ethos and a set of embodied practices, routines, and consumption patterns. In these works the body is shown to be a fluid cultural and material entity that adapts to larger societal changes.

Whether it is through normative modifications such as breast implants and liposuction, or so-called extreme rituals and body marks, Kosut argues, we increasingly understand that the body can, and should, be radically refashioned, tweaked, and played with. Hence, "extreme culture" has by extension heralded an "extreme body." Similar to Gen Yers and meth addicts, extreme bodies are the product of excessive physical modification, transformation, or activity, and are also aware of, and accept, the risks that come with such intense and unusual carnal pursuits. In the words of punk godfather Iggy Pop, we are encouraged to have a "lust for life" that is realized through tweaking and transforming the body.

Of course, modifying the body to make it more beautiful or culturally acceptable is not something specific to members of Gen Y or Gen X, nor is it a uniquely American cultural phenomenon. As cultural and literary historian Sander Gilman shows us in "The Racial Nose," aesthetic surgeries have taken place across cultures for centuries. In this chapter, Gilman uses numerous historical examples to illustrate how beauty has been defined by the shape of the human nose, and in turn, how noses came to signify racial difference. The project of "making the body beautiful" is not simply about aesthetics—what happens to be deemed pretty or cute at a particular moment—but about difference, power, and domination. For example, black noses (and bodies) were said to look "savage" and "primitive" as compared to those of Dutch and English colonists and slave traders who defined and categorized Blacks as "Other." In this case, biology or difference in physical characteristics was used as evidence of the inherent inferiority of certain bodies well into the twentieth century. In addition to personifying the primitive, black noses, as well as Jewish and Irish noses, were viewed as a sign of pathology and linked to physical, emotional, and social illness. Aesthetic surgeries, cast through the lens of race and ethnicity, bring the body as medium into focus within the context of ethnocentrism and racist ideologies. Skin color, facial contours, and body shape are embodied signs of difference within what cultural critic and feminist bell hooks describes as "white supremacist patriarchy." As Gilmam demonstrates, taxonomic variations serve to justify institutional racism and promote the commonsense idea that some bodies are inherently, biologically inferior.

In "To Die For: The Semiotic Seductive Power of the Tanned Body," sociologists Phillip Vannini and Aaron M. McCright focus on skin color, in particular, the artificially tanned body. Methodologically, this chapter is based on qualitative interviews conducted with forty people who regularly unnaturally tan themselves, many through visiting salons that offer tanning beds and lamps. Here, achieving darker skin tone is not read pejoratively within the context of racial difference and inequality but rather, paradoxically, as a sign of youth, health, sexuality, and beauty. For some people who identify as white, or lighter skinned, achieving a tan is a way to make the body more beautiful. Like Kosut's "extreme body," the artificially tanned body is closely linked to other consumer-driven body projects such as dieting, tattooing, and exercising. Comparable to the rise in cosmetic surgical procedures, the growth of the tanning industry in the United States has been astronomical since the first commercial beds appeared in 1974. Today, tanning is a billion-dollar business.

Vannini and McCright examine the tanned body within a medical and a cultural framework to shed light upon the conflicting discourses and meanings of the tanning process. As many are aware, the American Medical Association and American Association of Dermatology, as well as federal agencies like the FDA, assert that tanning is physically risky behavior. Peer-reviewed medical research finds that prolonged exposure to solar UVA and UVB radiation places one at risk for all three types of skin cancer. Even artificial tanning is potentially harmful—there is no such thing as a "safe" tan. But medical discourses also compete with cultural discourses, what Vannini and McCright refer to as the "seduction frame." The seduction frame, fueled by both the tanning industry and celebrity culture, explicitly plays down the risks of tanning. In this vein, the tanned body is similar to the "extreme body" or the Gen Y "edge worker" because it accepts the risks that may accompany certain embodied practices and regimes. Risks aside, the seduction frame advances the notion that tanned skin heightens beauty, makes one look more fit, hides wrinkles, and improves overall physical and mental health.

The authors argue that the enticing image of a bronze body is appealing because it offers semiotic power, or symbolic value. Rather than signifying damage and illness, tanning aficionados see their bodies as seductive and empowered. Here we can see how the body is both a medium and a symbol. In this case, achieving darker skin is viewed as a sign of beauty and self-cultivation. Unlike racialized discourses that construct those with biologically darker skin as inferior and devalued (as discussed by Gilman), artificially tanned bodies are viewed as sexy and empowering vessels. The cultural politics of human skin underscores how the body is at once a biological and social organism.

Everyday social interaction as conceptualized by sociologist Erving Goffman takes place through a set of embodied performances and impressions that we may intentionally or unintentionally give off. As we walk through the world, our bodies are the medium through which we observe other bodies, but they are also the objects of much securitization. The bodies of women in particular are forced to contend with objectifying gazes and uninvited glances. As Vannini and McCright observe, the tanned body is at the intersection of gazes. Both the individual and the viewer clearly enjoy the voyeuristic pleasure that the sexy bronze body brings. In the last chapter in the section, "The Naked Self: Being a Body in Televideo Cybersex," embodied pleasure and mediated social interaction converge vis-à-vis televideo cybersex, where participants intentionally display their bodies as objects to be seen, felt, and enjoyed. According to sociologist Dennis Waskul, unlike traditional pornography or text-based cybersex, televideo cybersex happens through the display of images of real bodies in real time. Waskul argues that this interplay of imagery is an embodied experience, even though it is mediated through technology and the coparticipants are not in the same geographical space.

Sex, as commonly understood, is a physical communication between bodies that touch, taste, smell, grope, and ejaculate. It is also the intersection of feelings of love and desire, as well as eroticism and other complicated social meanings. Thus, sex is an interaction that entangles body, self, and society within a given context. Waskul maintains that the participants he interviewed, and the virtual actions he observed, indicate that being naked in the presence of others is a totalizing experience wherein selves are truly embodied. As compared to a static nude image, which is a pure representation, a naked body is a live medium that elicits erotic responses in other bodies. Being naked builds on cultural fantasies of casual sex and orgies in public spaces, and it brings fetishized body parts—breasts, thighs, nipples, penises—to life. In televideo cybersex you are there for the other (as an object) but also an acting subject, firmly located within a fleshy, desirous body. It is easy to dismiss online interaction as a disembodied experience, because we are not physically copresent with others in the traditional sense. However, as Waskul argues, televideo cybersex allows for another type of human experience, "total embodiment," a state in which one is embodied within an image of one's own body.

The chapters in this section highlight the adaptability of the body as medium, as well as the constraints of the material flesh. Bodies are flexible on the job, but are also vulnerable to demands of the workplace and the marketplace. They are shaped by technology, but also increasingly worked on and played with for the sake of ego and pleasure. Bodies are constructed in powerful discourses and filtered through media culture and consumer society. Yet they are also agentic, because beneath the skin we find the self.

This article gives history of labor work in the United States from the late 19th — to the early 21st Century. Labor workers bodies become the property of the business or company that is employing them. They become the machines. Health and Safety are overlooked until 1970, accidents become a burden that everyone must deal with. Men are expected to have injuries to give off the appearance of reliability & risk taking. Women & Children also work labor intensive jobs that pose risks their health. Women are categorized and "studies" say women cannot handle the labor work due to the body makeup/layout.

How the worker's body has changed overtime

7

||||||||||||||||||||||||||||||||||||||||||||||||||||||||||||||||||||||||||||||

"Made by the Work"
A Century of Laboring Bodies in the United S

Ed Slavishak

In 2004 workers at a slaughterhouse in southern Minnesota began developing cramps, tingling, and numbness in their arms and legs. The workers, mostly Spanish-speaking immigrants attracted by the availability of work in "Spamtown, U.S.A.," experienced varying degrees of debility. All worked around the plant's "head table," where pigs' heads were taken apart. By early 2008, doctors at the Mayo Clinic and Centers for Disease Control and Prevention stated that the two dozen cases—now grouped under the heading "progressive inflammatory neuropathy"—were most likely auto-immune reactions caused by a specific technique used at the head table. The men and women worked within feet of the station at which workers used air hoses to remove the animals' brains. This process, researchers explained, aerosolized small quantities of the brains, which workers then inhaled throughout their workdays. Their bodies' severe reactions to this foreign substance could be managed but not cured.

This slow unraveling of a medical mystery in a Minnesota slaughterhouse serves as a prime example of the often contentious relationship between individuals' health and the environments in which they work, the materials with which they work, and the motions that they must perform on the job. The laboring body is the place at which the abstract realm of productivity, markets, and quotas meets the tangible realm of blistered hands, tired backs, and aching feet. It is also the tool that many learn to use masterfully, performing intricate tasks or challenging feats that come only with experience and great effort.

Over the course of the twentieth century, the nature of work experiences changed drastically for the majority of the U.S. population. First, employers' use of mechanization and the assembly line meant that manual production tasks once guided by workers now became dictated by a mechanical pace. Second, service work gained increasing prominence as the American economy shifted after the 1950s. The size of the industrial workforce remained roughly steady, while the number employed in retail, health, and other service positions increased significantly. Finally, late-century management techniques driven by computerization have allowed employers to streamline workplaces even further, turning mechanical and biological feedback into quantifiable streams of data. The concept of the "laboring body," then, encompasses the steelworker tapping a furnace, the maid standing on her feet all day, the fast-food worker assembling hamburgers, and the warehouse employee dashing among mountains of packaged goods.

That the body plays a central role in work is perhaps an obvious statement, yet it is easy to lose sight of human labor in a capitalist system centered on service, global outsourcing, and automated assembly. To insist upon the physical foundation of work is to shift focus from the *results* of labor to the *demands* of labor—the everyday compromises that people make in the name of income, identity, or a "job well done." From long-haul truckers with chronic back pain and hemorrhoids to data-entry clerks with carpal tunnel syndrome, laboring bodies experience ailments and annoyances that are often hidden because they are experienced in isolation. This isolating effect has only heightened with corporate efforts to cut labor costs by demanding more from each individual within the workplace. Laboring bodies also perform work for which the resulting compensation is intangible or clandestine. The relative invisibility of unpaid domestic labor ("housework"), black-market work (such as prostitution or drug muling), and the toil of prison inmates suggests the range of situations in which laboring bodies perform outside the boundaries of "official," paid employment.

A historical look at twentieth-century labor experiences in the United States reveals several patterns that have shaped American working lives. First, this essay examines workplace hazards to chart the public "discovery" of accidents around the turn of the century. Although dangerous work was crucial to the development of the American economy before 1900, it was only around that time that journalists, reformers, and government inspectors presented working bodies as the victims of industrial progress. From this initial flurry, investigations into the dangers of work broadened to consider practically every instance in which employment strained muscles, bones, and nerves. Furthermore, the laboring body might produce, but it also consumes. From over-the-counter stimulants meant for workers on the night shift to the plethora of prostheses available on the market after 1900, companies and entire industries have gravitated to physical problems related to employment. Finally, I consider how the working body has become a symbolic asset. The *idea* of a body hard at work has the power to attract votes, the power to sell products, and the power to win symbolic struggles between employers and employees. Visual representations of "American craftsmanship" and the work ethic of everyday Americans have used bodies as shorthand to celebrate national pride and prosperity. The increasing abstraction of these images suggests that boosters of all stripes tend to find generic laboring bodies more appealing than actual, specific ones.

The Endangered Laboring Body

Examining the turn of the twentieth century highlights the period during which recent developments in work in the United States took shape. The reality for working bodies of the era was physical hazard and strain. As one steelworker told a writer for *McClure's* magazine, the industrial laborer was "a creature who seems to be made by the work, and not for it." Work shaped, stressed, and ultimately possessed bodies. Widespread mechanization in the late nineteenth century placed workers, especially those in heavy manufacturing, in close proximity to swift, heavy, and sharp machine parts. Before the safety campaigns and workers' compensation laws of the 1910s, mechanical engineers and their clients designed manufacturing processes to be economically and technically efficient. By 1900, industrialists had devised predictable, profitable systems to produce textiles, farm implements, glass, construction materials, canned food, and countless consumer goods. The sophistication of these systems and industrialists' relentless drive to get more out of them has certainly increased since 1900, but the basic characteristics of the work experiences within them could be found over a century ago. The foundation of these systems was the man, woman, or child at work—bending, pulling, lifting, and rushing to keep up.

Labor reformer Frederick Hoffman estimated in 1915 that twenty-five thousand workers died each year in workplace accidents. Four years later, the federal Bureau of Labor tallied over 1.2 million accidental job injuries nationwide. This figure, based on the reports of state compensation boards, certainly undercounted the actual number of injuries (Berman 1978). Statistics for occupational diseases are even harder to estimate due to the lack of consensus on cause and effect. Physical conditions that stemmed from work hazards often resembled ailments unrelated to the workplace. When workers downplayed their symptoms to avoid their managers' scrutiny, they further obscured the connections between aggravating substances and bodily damage (Sellers 1997).

Work was thus dangerous in a multitude of ways. The steel industry typified the experiences of workers in heavy, mechanized workplaces. Workers reported crushed arms, legs trapped between moving cars, and burns from electrical currents. Journalist William Hard wrote about the visceral experience of industrial accidents in Chicago mills in 1907. Hard noted that within such workplaces, "a human being looks smaller than perhaps anywhere else in the world." The terrifying scale of the machines matched the horrors that occurred beneath them:

> On the twelfth of last December, Newton Allen, up in the cage of his 100-ton electric crane, was requested by a ladleman from below to pick up a pot and carry it to another part of the floor. This pot was filled with the hot slag that is the refuse left over when the pure steel has been run off. Newton Allen let down the hooks of his crane. The ladleman attached those hooks to the pot. Newton Allen started down the floor. Just as he started, one of the hooks slipped. There was no shock or jar. Newton Allen was warned of danger only by the fumes that rose toward him. He at once reversed his lever and… hurried back to the scene of the accident. He saw a man lying on his face. He heard him screaming. He saw that he was being roasted by the slag that had poured out of the pot. (Hard 1907)

Newtown Allen's body had been mechanically displaced from the work process. The accident occurred at such a distance that he hardly detected it below him. Due to the scale of steel mills and the hazardous nature of the raw materials, over twenty-three *[handwritten: 2300]*   *[handwritten: 15 years   in just PA]*

hundred workers died between 1900 and 1915 in the heart of the American steel industry, Pittsburgh, Pennsylvania.

In the same fifteen-year span, over fifteen hundred workers died in the coal mines of southwestern Pennsylvania alone. The coal figures underscore the fact that work hazards were not confined to mechanized settings. More than half of coal mining victims were crushed or asphyxiated when tunnels collapsed. The dusty atmosphere of mines also resulted in explosions that produced massive single-day death tolls. Even for those untouched by traumatic injury, work in coal stamped the body indelibly. In 1902 novelist William Gibbons described an anthracite miner as a broken frame:

> The man's gait and appearance were those of an old man, although he was but little past thirty. There was a peculiarity in his walk which made him seem almost ape-like in his carriage. His head was bent, his shoulders drooped forward, his knees were crooked, while his hands hung so far to the front of his body that they almost touched his kneecaps. In appearance he resembled nothing so much as the man-ape of the tropical forest. . . . It often happens that a miner breaks down in health at forty, after thirty years in the mines. As soon as he begins to grow towards manhood, he must bow his shoulders and bend his back all day long. (Gibbons 1902)

While working, bodies belonged to the mine owner; they were one more set of tools to wield below ground. Beyond the mine, however, maimed workers had to rely on themselves, their families, or their neighbors for relief. Medical accounts of hacking coughs, persistent headaches, ringing ears, and swollen limbs suggested that mining did lasting damage.

Employers increasingly hired children and women for work that did not require the sustained muscular strength expected of adult men. Most often, these positions featured rapid movement, monotony, and filth. One of the most notorious examples of child labor from the early part of the century was the "breaker boys" who separated waste rock from coal as it traveled down massive chutes. A former breaker boy described the work in 1902:

> He rises at 5:30 o'clock in the morning, puts on his working clothes, always soaked with dust, eats his breakfast, and by seven o'clock he has climbed the dark and dusty stairway to the screen room where he works. He sits on a hard bench built across a long chute through which passes a steady stream of broken coal. From the coal he must pick the pieces of slate or rock. . . . Sitting on his uncomfortable seat, bending constantly over the passing stream of coal, his hands soon become cut and scarred by the sharp pieces of slate and coal, while his finger nails are soon worn to the quick from contact with the iron chute. The air he breathes is saturated with the coal dust. (McDowell 1902)

Young boys' size and meager wages made them desirable employees. The same held for women. Social researcher Elizabeth Beardsley Butler observed that "foreign women who ask neither for comfort nor for cleanliness nor higher wages" formed the greatest portion of the female workforce in industrial cities. Hiring supervisors chose women for particular positions based on their appearance; they assumed that pale, wiry women excelled at fast work and that only darker, stockier women could handle heavy or dirty work. Butler described female workers in a pickle plant as consumed by their tasks:

> Women, with their fingers bound with cloths to break the slip of the knife, sit at long tables emptying tubful after tubful of pickles at a fierce rate of speed. The pickles are cut lengthwise or crosswise according to their shape. Hand knives are used, but the incessant downward motion of blade and fingers looks like the vibrations of a machine. A blind haste that allows not a moment to look up or away spurs the nerves of the workers from early morning until night. (Butler 1909)

Compare that to her description of a cracker factory, in which an unbearable environment thwarted women's attempts to remain vigilant:

> Here the dough is mixed by huge metal blades . . . cut into thin sheets, and fed into the cracker-making machine. . . . At the second roller sits a girl whose duty it is to brush on the flour. The motion of her arm is quick and incessant. . . . On either side of the machine at this end are two other girls. They straighten the crackers and throw the scrappy, unformed edges of dough into a tin to be fed with fresh dough into the funnel at the other end of the room. Their workplace is not six feet from the ovens. The men say that not many of the girls can stand the work for long. In the excessive heat, with the smell of the dough, they must stare at the trays which pass slowly, continuously, beneath their eyes. They become light-headed and ill. I saw one who had been in the place three years. She was white, with a faint look about her mouth. (Butler 1909)

Government labor bureaus had long warned against women's labor as a threat to the nation's health. In 1875 the Massachusetts Bureau of Labor Statistics worried that women "break down in health rapidly" if employed. In 1888 the Maine Bureau of Industrial and Labor Statistics claimed that "woman is badly constructed for the purposes of standing eight or ten hours upon her feet" due to "the peculiar construction of the knee," "the shallowness of the pelvis," and "the delicate nature of the foot." In 1901 the United States Industrial Commission concluded that a "long workday with the machine . . . reduces the grade of intelligence" of female operators. These investigative bodies also linked injury and reproductive debility. The 1884 annual report from Maine announced "a predisposition to pelvic disease among the female factory operatives." After the turn of the century, the federal Industrial Commission concluded that women's strain on the job had "weakened the physical and moral strength of the new generation of working people" (Brandeis and Goldmark 1908).

In addition to injury, disease, and disability, fatigue received much attention in the early twentieth century as a pervasive, insidious phenomenon. Physiologists warned that fatigue accumulated over a lifetime, corroding limb, back, and brain from within. Employers designed their workplaces to bring workers to their physical extreme without affecting the accuracy of the work. Telephone operators who connected three hundred calls per hour typified an early form of service work that revolved around repetitive movements. Butler set the scene:

> The element of strain is increased sometimes by the excessive height of the switchboard, which varies from eighteen inches to thirty, and occasionally to thirty-six. . . . At the higher boards, a girl can only with difficulty reach the upper rows of jacks, unless she stands or stretches and causes delay. Stretching to either side of the three-part section of the switchboard is simplified by the system of team work. A less efficient operator will be placed between two older and more rapid hands whose duty it is to watch the board of the middle girl as well as their own, to help her out with her calls if they come in too fast, and to carry her plugs over on their own boards when they can reach more easily than she. (Butler 1909)

The teamwork model did not eliminate fatigue; it merely allowed fatigued women to finish their shift. Such a system made workers responsible for their own and their coworkers' bodies. If they could not measure up, the burden fell on fellow operators, who might very well resent the added work.

Laboring Bodies as Problems

Once investigators revealed the scope of accidents and debility in the early years of the century, a series of programs emerged with the promise of safety, financial stability, and rehabilitation. In the process each of these schemes approached the working body as a problem that, if left unsolved, would imperil the nation. From the 1910s until the end of the century, employers, reformers, and legislators debated the essential question of how workers' bodies should be understood. Did they "belong" exclusively to individuals, or could they be claimed as wards of the company and the state? The rhetoric of occupational health and safety became a vehicle through which laboring bodies were further commodified.

After 1910 employers in heavy industries crafted safety programs to improve their public image. Companies informed employees that the "best safety device known" was a careful and conscientious worker. Although safety undoubtedly had much to do with the everyday disposition of workers, corporate campaigns shifted responsibility to avoid the costs of updating machinery or improving ventilation. It was less expensive to print safety posters and award safety bonuses than to alter production. This tactic told workers that they were in charge of their bodies while on the job, even if they had no say about work conditions. Workers, meanwhile, considered their risks. Employees in some industries praised risk as a way of testing manliness, especially in occupations involving high speed or severe conditions. Western railroaders, for example, celebrated the belief that skill under pressure allowed one to avoid the worst accidents. Minor wounds were not necessarily a calamity for men who valued risk as a source of rugged identity. Slight injuries could represent experience and bravery, as in the case of Iowa trainmen who regarded missing fingers or scarred legs

[Handwritten marginalia:] When a coworker can't meet the demands from fatigue, the work falls on a coworker to finish

[Handwritten marginalia:] the risks they took on the job defined them, became part of their personality → added to the stigma that men are supposed to be tough

[Handwritten marginalia:] these are minor injuries ??

injury=
success

as evidence of maturity. Until a worker had been visibly scarred, fellow workers could consider him unreliable (Williams-Searle 1999).

This emphasis on the manliness of a body toughened by, and thus prepared for, labor extended beyond the world of male occupations. By World War I, local governments issued calls for compulsory physical training. A Newark, New Jersey, newspaper reported in September 1917 on a new law mandating physical education in public schools. A state official explained it as an attempt to improve both the workforce and the citizenry:

> This law expresses the popular will that the children and youth of the state should be so trained that physical vigor should be a support for their intellectual life, their spiritual life, their industrial life, and last, but by no means least, for their civic and patriotic life. He whose blood is red, whose muscles are hard, whose sleep is sound, whose digestion is good, whose posture is erect, whose step is elastic, whose endurance is lasting, and whose nerves are steady has just so many resources in life. Physical vigor and soundness contribute to happiness, to accomplishment, and to service to society, to state, and to country.

Here, an individual's body was the property of industry and the government. Workers were expected to devote maximum effort to upkeep and then fit themselves into a rigid system. Accordingly, workers used leisure time to keep in shape. By cultivating themselves with food and exercise, they hoped to mitigate accidents. Union newspapers encouraged exercise regimens and strict rules of hygiene to energize bodies. Workers often phrased their complaints about wages in terms of what food they could buy. Better wages, they argued, afforded better food; better food produced better work. Historians have shown that most American workers "worshipped at the shrine of fresh beef" to improve their work performance (Levenstein 1988). Also crucial were ample sleep, regular bathing, and informal exercise. Leisure hours, though scarce for those who worked sixty or more hours per week, could make the body powerful. Unions promoted boxing, replacing the emasculating effects of poor wages and monotonous work with "a more elemental concept of manhood." Boxing combined principles of strength, cunning, and honor and conveyed ability through physiques. Tug-of-war competitions at Labor Day picnics also represented ideals of strength, teamwork, and tactical thinking. As in the case of boxing, the tug-of-war was a physical activity that demanded strategy and coordination (Gorn 1986).

A different type of preparation focused on the dire economic effects of injury, disease, or death. Industrial workers turned to several options of relief before the widespread passage of compensation laws in the 1910s. First, unions pitched life insurance by pressing workers to take pride in the fact that their bodies were worth a tangible amount of money. The insurance department of the Amalgamated Association of Iron, Steel, and Tin Workers asked its members directly, "What are your chances of living twenty more years? Can you afford to tempt fate?" Second, labor leaders hoped that workers would participate in union benefit plans that paid members for the loss of work and paid members' families in the case of death. The plans' payment lists were graphically detailed—amputated arms and legs received maximum compensation, whereas eyes, hands, and feet received less. Union benefit programs were designed as stop-gap measures to keep families afloat in the immediate aftermath of trauma.

In 1909 Montana's legislature was the first to adopt a workers' compensation law. Over the next seven years, thirty-one states followed suit. Workers' compensation brought a standardized means of payment for accidents while moving the injured body from the arena of the courtroom into the shadows of bureaucracy. The programs' procedural routine and lack of contest meant that broken bodies no longer stood as public spectacles upon which judicial verdicts rested. Once industry and government incorporated a no-fault process to convert injury into a dollar value, employers could expect both workers and lawmakers to accept the inevitability of accidents. Injury became part of the workday, something for which managers could account but not a disruption that they could expect to avoid. Employers' views changed little over time. In 1978, researchers found a "strong employer consensus" nationally that nine out of ten accidents were caused by employee actions rather than unsafe conditions (Northrup et al, 1978). Critics of government regulation in the 1980s argued that employers incurred outrageous expenses to meet irrelevant safety standards. Business groups tended to echo their turn-of-the-century counterparts by declaring that no law could safeguard workers from themselves. In the 1960s injury rates in the American manufacturing sector rose by more than a third, prompting federal action. Until the passage of the Occupational Safety and Health Act in 1970, no federal standards existed for American workplaces, regardless of the goods manufactured or the services provided. Under the act, fines for workplace safety and health violations became commonplace.

The commercial market for treatment and rehabilitation represents a final effort to "fix" the working body. The earliest enterprises grew out of the trade in surgical instruments. Medical equipment manufacturers developed product lines specifically directed at workers who lost limbs, needed support in their lower backs, or required braces to keep their arms steady. Artificial limbs were the most elaborate of these products, and limb makers fought tooth and nail to claim the latest technical advances. Prosthesis companies contracted with employers to provide arms and legs in the case of accidents and advertised heavily in the labor press. In their massive, illustrated catalogues, limb makers promised readers renewed "social utility," which meant the ability to work again.

If prostheses are the most spectacular of rehabilitation products, there have also been more mundane but equally lucrative offerings. Companies that produce pain relievers and orthopedic supports have seized on the fact that working bodies need help. For several weeks in 1998, writer Barbara Ehrenreich worked for a housekeeping service to study life on the minimum wage. She found that managers stressed the importance of "working through it." Her boss advised her to manage rashes, arthritis, strained rotator cuffs, and sore feet through over-the-counter drugs and medical visits on her own time. Ehrenreich described cleaning homes as "totally asymmetrical, brutally repetitive, and as likely to destroy the musculoskeletal structure as to strengthen it." When she waited tables during the same project, she found the physical strain of service work unbearable. Ehrenreich longed to find the mythical "rhythm . . . where signals pass from the sense organs directly to the muscles, bypassing the cerebral cortex" leaving only a "Zen-like emptiness." Instead, she experienced intense back pain and relied on double doses of generic painkillers before each shift (Ehrenreich 2001).

Ehrenreich's desire to stop feeling but keep working represents a broader desire for a miracle product to mask the symptoms of aggravating work. Labor on assembly lines since the 1910s has demanded that workers move their bodies rhythmically. As auto worker Ben Hamper explained in 1986, learning such a routine is an exercise in zoning out:

> I was now ball-and-chained to a job that kept me forever in motion. That merciless minute hand relented somewhat due to the fact that there wasn't as much time to stand around clock-gazin'. Oftentimes I would get so scoped-in on my duties, so chiseled to the waltz of the rails, that I wouldn't even notice it was break time until I saw the rest of the crew peelin' off their gloves. I'd lock into the mission and stow my mind away so as not to have it interfere with the absurdity of the regimen. Entire shifts would sail by during which I hardly developed a tangible current of thought. The last thing I wanted to do was lacerate my brain with the nude truth lurking behind this mulish treadmill. (Hamper 1986)

Since the 1980s, corporate redesign of production has only increased the pressure on workers to stay robotically "on task." Labor geographers have shown that workplaces have shrunk over recent decades through owners' efforts to cut costs. Compare Hamper's description of work without contemplation to the more recent management demand for workers who are ever-alert and able to perform in small spaces. As Deborah Leslie and David Butz observe, in streamlined car plants,

> Bodily postures and the microspaces of workers are also subject to greater control under lean production. One assembly worker on the brake line noted that, in the past, "there were certain jobs where you could be comfortable sitting down and actually you could do the jobs better sitting down. . . . Now on this new line there's no chair available to you. You have to stand the whole shift." As one [car industry] researcher puts it, "If you are sitting down, you've got to get up and you are taking time to do it. You've got to be standing to make this work. To be flexible and agile in the work force, you've got to be standing." The ideal body posture of the flexible worker is a standing position, ready for action. (Leslie and Butz 1998)

The problem for workers in today's "lean" workplaces, like the experiences of Hamper and Ehrenreich before them, is that no over-the-counter remedy can change the physical demands set by management.

[handwritten margin note: the jobs numb the mind ldc they are so repetitive people do not want to think it will make the depressed]

Laboring Bodies as Symbols

Since 1900 representations of working bodies in texts (i.e., company brochures, popular magazines), in visual media (public murals, photography), and in performances (labor parades, television commercials) have attempted to determine the public face of hidden routines. Most middle-class Americans in 1910, for example, would not have known what steelmaking required of the body. Statues of steelworkers in city squares and decorative parade floats were perhaps influential in determining how city dwellers thought about men with whom they rarely interacted. In short, workers, owners, unions, and commercial associations competed to define reality. Showing that work was positive and creative encouraged investment in a harmonious economy and weakened governmental attempts to control business. Showing that the same types of work were punishing and tedious, on the other hand, pressured government to regulate.

American intellectuals of the early twentieth century worried that the hardy physiques that had advanced European settlement across the continent were disappearing. The intimate connection between individual bodies and the imaginary national body came to the foreground as vocal editorialists cautioned about the physical abilities of the United States in the new century. Social critic Henry Merwin worried that the "natural impulses or instincts" that had made the United States an agent of civilization would be "dulled and weakened" by mechanical advances (Merwin 1897). James Davis, a former iron worker who became Secretary of Labor in the 1920s, argued that American control of the world depended on physical strength. He believed that the fragile state of Americans must be repaired through exertion if they were to remain a "wrought iron race" (Davis 1922). Groups such as the YMCA, the Boy and Girl Scouts of America, and all manner of hobby clubs emerged to sing the praises of productive, laborlike leisure. Work—*or simply the idea and image of work*—became an end in itself.

Take the publications and art created by civic and commercial groups early in the century. A sense of nostalgia dominated, as shirtless men heaved basic tools and grappled with raw materials. The cover of the Union Trust Company's 1908 guide to Pittsburgh epitomized the move to simplify working bodies in order to turn them into positive symbols. In the drawing, a female allegorical figure representing the city stood over two stripped men representing the industrial workforce. The men, dressed in classical loincloths to reveal their work-hardened physiques, sat on an abstract mechanical object with a gear protruding from it. The worker to the left propped a hammer on his leg to connote generic labor. The image could be interpreted in multiple ways: as a claim that workers formed the foundation of the industrial city; as the notion that workers triumphed over machinery for civic glory; or as an argument for the essential, unchanging nature of industrial work.

Yet work did change, and business and cultural leaders responded by commemorating figures from an earlier era: skilled working men whose tasks were now performed by machinery. The class politics of the laboring body came into full resolution as boosters created a historical tale to place business owners, skilled artisans,

Figure 7.1. Classical Working Bodies. Union Trust Company, Industrial Pittsburgh, 1908.

and unskilled laborers in the same boat. They attempted to diffuse class tensions by suggesting that all workers could possess noble physiques and that even the masters of capital admired the majesty of labor. Though this flattery began in earnest around 1900, it became a persistent part of promotions that trumpeted American character, manhood, and dominance.

The perfect image for commercial groups was the triumphant, creative worker. Public murals and sculptures placed throughout American cities presented individual men engaged in indistinct work tasks. A 1904 sculpture from Pittsburgh, Daniel Chester French's *Colonel James Anderson Monument*, reveals the extent to which

Figure 7.2. Body and Mind. Daniel Chester French, *Colonel James Anderson Monument*, 1904. Courtesy of the Pittsburgh Photographic Library Collection of the Carnegie Library of Pittsburgh.

Figure 7.3. The Mechanical System. Lewis Hine, *Group of Doffers and Spinners Working in Roanoke Cotton Mills (Va.)*, 1911. Courtesy of the Photography Collections, University of Maryland, Baltimore County.

artists took workers out of actual work settings in order to focus viewers on their bodies rather than details of production. The sculpture was commissioned for the courtyard of a Carnegie Library and was thus meant to represent a noble, educated laboring class. The shirtless worker, a skilled blacksmith, sat on an anvil reading a book. In the logic of the sculpture, the worker had put down his tool, the propped-up hammer, and had picked up a book in an impromptu gesture of self-improvement. The underlying assumption of French's monument, though, was that viewers would better recognize the figure as a worker if he was stripped enough to reveal a working physique. Muscle and book formed a vision of physical and mental mastery.

By contrast, labor reformers publicized images of workers trapped in mechanical systems. Photographs of workplace interiors provided vivid evidence of the overmatch. Magazines, books, and traveling exhibits presented steelworkers dwarfed by cranes, rollers, and ladles of molten metal. Photos of workers in canning and bottling plants captured them amid massive devices that moved food and beverages at great volume. Snapshots of textile workers showed bodies cramped between machinery. A Lewis Hine photograph from 1911 showed textile workers in Roanoke, Virginia. When Hine learned that the workers were under the age of fourteen, he framed the image to place them in an overwhelming environment. Though this was not a gargantuan mill or a labyrinthine mine, the space of the cotton mill appeared threatening to the diminutive bodies. The banks of spinning machines and the ceiling filled with motorized drive

Figure 7.4. The Broken Body. Lewis Hine, *The Crippled Watchman—A Type*. From Crystal Eastman, *Work-Accidents and the Law* (New York: Charities Publications Committee, 1910).

belts created a utilitarian setting ill-suited for what middle-class viewers would have defined as childhood. Workers almost appeared as a means of gauging the machines' size; taken from the ground level at which workers spent their days, images framed humans against gears and pistons that reached beyond the upper borders.

The reformers' version of the body at work, stooped and besieged, was transformed further by catastrophes. In the first decades of the century, labor writers such as Crystal Eastman researched the "wrecks of hospital cases" and the "cities of cripples" found in industrial centers. To dramatize these catastrophes, reformers enlisted activist photographers to document amputees. Another Hine photo, *The Crippled Watchman—A Type*, presented a steelworker's lost leg as evidence of industrial trauma. The man leaned against the supports of a rail trestle in an industrial stock yard. Tracks, slag heaps, and furnaces loomed around him. Hine propped the worker against a fence, capturing his image to tell a tale of reckless industry. Such photos were meant to evoke sympathy from viewers and to exert pressure on legislators and employers (Eastman 1910).

The drastic differences between these sets of symbols led to a contest that, for all intents and purposes, has been won by commercial interests. For many, honoring American labor in popular culture means removing from the body the very characteristics that employers seek. The abilities to repeat small movements and to move at a frantic pace do not evoke the independence that most celebratory work images require. Work on an automobile assembly line, for instance, would hardly make an inspirational poster for human labor. Ben Hamper described a scene from the 1960s when he first saw what his father did at the auto plant:

> A car would nuzzle up to the old man's work area and he would be waiting for it, a cigarette dangling from his lip, his arms wrapped around the windshield contraption as if it might suddenly rebel and bolt off for the ocean. Car, windshield. Car, windshield. Car, windshield. . . . We stood there for forty minutes or so, a miniature lifetime, and the pattern never changed. Car, windshield. Car, windshield. Drudgery piled atop drudgery. Cigarette to cigarette. . . . I wanted to shout to my father "Do something else!" Do something else or come home with us or flee to the nearest watering hole. DO SOMETHING ELSE! Car, windshield. Car, windshield. (Hamper 1986)

In some occupations, symbol and practical task have merged. Employment in service positions now revolves around the ability to present a pleasant demeanor. Sociologist Arlie Hochschild referred to this type of work as emotional labor, because it requires a worker to control his or her expressions of feeling while trying to produce the proverbial "satisfied customer." Much emotional work is rooted in the necessity of an employee to become a body on display, wherein posture, countenance, and carriage are all visual cues to be manipulated in order to sell an image of attentive caring (Hochschild 1983). Unlike traditional factory workers, who could display contempt for their jobs yet receive no punishment if their output remained steady, many service employees are expected to embody engaged, agreeable servitude (MacDonald and Sirianni 1996). Waitress uniforms, for example, mark employees as subservient to those with whom they briefly interact. As a means of creating a customer-friendly experience, anthropologist Greta Paules notes, the "aggressively plain" waitress uniform renders the worker practically indistinguishable from domestic servants. Both jobs require bodily displays of industriousness and deference. The physical tolls of the work, though often quite severe, are only part of the experience of service labor (Paules 1991).

Conclusion

The laboring body has held a paradox since 1900. In the era before mechanization, it was only through strain and physical suffering that the skilled worker learned how to accomplish a task. Exertion and fatigue were essential parts of the months or years before a worker's body had adapted to work demands. As the century progressed, however, scientists and labor researchers warned that bodies *never* adapted to the pace of machines or to the fumes and substances with which they interacted (Zuboff

1988). By 2000, employers in many industries approached working bodies as fragile but malleable resources that could be augmented and adjusted with the assistance of consumer goods. The consumption side of capitalism was thus meant to negate the suffering that went into the production side. Work in the twenty-first century promises to extend the commodification of laboring bodies, as employers emphasize that employees owe it to the company to guard their own health. The implementation of "wellness at work" programs, ergonomics initiatives, and human resources safety courses all suggest that modern employers are attentive to the physical needs of their workforce. Yet these measures also serve as the latest examples of employer appropriation of laboring bodies. Once workers are enmeshed in detailed procedures, specially designed apparatuses, and lifestyle regimens, their bodies are as controlled as the layout of the workplace or the company's financial planning.

Contemporary feature films and television commercials share the assumption that for work to be inspirational, it has to be stripped of anything that grounds it in lived experience. Instead, the body at work becomes an abstract performance used to evoke ruggedness or reliability or even classlessness. Consider the scarcity of movies that focus on the physical details of a workday. Unless that work occurs in a courtroom or in an athletic venue, it rarely makes it into mainstream productions. The symbol of the laboring body appears most often as a spectacle, drawing the viewer's attention away from the realities of backs that weaken or limbs that tingle. An accurate assessment of the body's place within a global capitalist economy is, of course, far more complicated than that. Therefore, the alarming cluster of neuropathy cases from the Minnesota slaughterhouse challenges more than public health officials. Such cases remind scholars that the study of work has few definite boundaries. Understanding the body at work demands a sensitivity to economics, environment, technology, physiology, cultural practices, everyday power relationships, and the law. Above all, studying laboring bodies shows that specific experiences on the job are historical constructions, inseparable from the contexts in which they develop.

REFERENCES

Berman, D. 1978. *Death on the Job*. New York: Monthly Review Press.

Brandeis, L,, and J. Goldmark. 1908. *Women in Industry*. New York: National Consumers' League.

Butler, E. 1909. *Women and the Trades*. New York: Charities Publication Committee.

Davis, J. 1922. *The Iron Puddler*. New York: Grosset and Dunlap.

Eastman, C. 1910. *Work-Accidents and the Law*. New York: Charities Publication Committee.

Ehrenreich, B. 2001. *Nickel and Dimed*. New York: Metropolitan.

Gibbons, W. 1902. *Those Black Diamond Men*. New York: F.H. Revell.

Gorn, E. 1986. *The Manly Art*. Ithaca, NY: Cornell University Press.

Hamper, B. 1986. *Rivethead*. New York: Warner Books.

Hard, W. 1907. Making Steel and Killing Men. *Everybody's Magazine*.

Hochschild, A. 1983. *The Managed Heart*. Berkeley: University of California Press.

Leslie, D., and D. Butz. 1998. "GM Suicide": Flexibility, Space and the Injured Body. *Economic Geography* 74: 360–78.

Levenstein, H. 1988. *Revolution at the Table*. New York: Oxford University Press.

MacDonald, C., and C. Sirianni. 1996. *Working in the Service Society*. Philadelphia: Temple University Press.

McDowell, J. 1902. The Life of a Coal Miner. *The World's Work* 4.

Merwin, H. 1897. On Being Civilized Too Much. *Atlantic Monthly* 79: 838.

Northrup, H., et al. 1978. *The Impact of OSHA*. Philadelphia: University of Pennsylvania.

Paules, G. 1991. *Dishing It Out*. Philadelphia: Temple University Press.

Sellers, C. 1997. *Hazards of the* Job. Chapel Hill: University of North Carolina Press.

Watchorn, R. 1909. The Cost of Coal in Human Life. *Outlook* 92: 176.

Williams-Searle, J. 1999. Courting Risk: Disability, Masculinity, and Liability on Iowa's Railroads, 1868–1900. *Annals of Iowa* 58: 27–77.

Zuboff, S. 1988. *In the Age of the Smart Machine*. New York: Basic Books.

8

Embodied Capitalism and the Meth Economy

Jason Pine

Introduction

This essay is about desire, compulsion, and bodies. It is my attempt to re-evoke the experiences of methamphetamine users, producers, and user-producers living in the rural midwestern United States and to make them uncanny. When something is uncanny, it has the effect of being both strange and familiar. But what do rural, severely marginalized, intoxicated people have in common with "us," the urban or suburban, the educated, adequately employed, and sufficiently sober, the "mainstream"? This essay argues that it is possible to trace the excesses and intensities lived by rural midwestern meth users and cooks to a broader field of forces felt in multiple worlds, affecting not only the "abject" rural poor but also enfranchised urbanites and many others.

An ordinary description or definition of this field of forces might include familiar but surprisingly opaque words like "capitalism," "neoliberalism," and "globalization." However, rather than making these forces conform to the language that at some point was decided could sufficiently capture them, this essay attempts to bring some of the forces into relief (Stewart 2007). To do this, it is necessary to track them in their manifold incarnations as materials and places, actions and sensibilities, and, most significantly, bodies. Accordingly, this story follows meth as a cultural value back to its earlier manufacture by "freedom-seeking" biker gangs and to its contemporary production in the recombination of rural Wal-Mart products. At Wal-Mart, it witnesses the way domestic spaces and bodies are built and destroyed, and from there it picks up on alternative consumer and worker ethics that circulate in other, "cosmopolitan" areas of the country and on that global space of encounter, the Internet. In these places, it peruses products like pomegranate juice, energy drinks, and Martha Stewart furnishings to gauge the forces of marketing, style, and cultural value. It follows shifts in sensibility across generations and moves along neuropsychological pathways to track the force of affect and its rerelease in specific forms of work and consumption. It finds, in the swipe of a food stamp debit card at the checkout line of Wal-Mart, and in mass thefts of copper wire from electrical substations, the pulse of government policy and the moral hazard of big business.

Employing some of the multisited ethnographic methods described by George E. Marcus (1995), this essay creates an assemblage of routes, places, materials, actions, and sensibilities to suggest that the distinctly marked and agitated bodies of rural midwestern methamphetamine users and producers are inseparable from and incomprehensible without the broader field of forces that make them possible. It draws on the idea that bodies experience the impact of global forces in their own spatiotemporal worlds (Harvey 2000). Despite a long history of scholarly interest in the body and an ever-increasing focus on the body in everyday practices (body modification, psychopharmacology, biogenetics), academic analysis and everyday experiences of embodiment have seldom been brought together. The following is an ethnographic exploration of a particular set of experiences that have been referred to as "embodied capitalism" (Tsianos and Papadopoulos 2006). It explores how the desire to consume can become a compulsion that tugs like the internalized demands of addiction. It also explores how the compulsion to work under precarious conditions gets transformed into a physiological and affective desire for self-realization and an elusive achievement called "freedom." In this story, the bodies of rural midwestern meth users and producers register most noticeably the impacts of some otherwise underemphasized changes occurring in the practices of work and consumption throughout the United States and globally.

Manifest Destiny

Wil lives in a camper in a five-acre clearing off a gravel road that runs through the dense woods of Versailles, a small town in south central Missouri. He, his wife, and two kids, aged six and eleven, packed into the camper a couple of months ago when their trailer burned down. "And the fire wasn't 'cause of a meth lab, but it easily coulda been," he laughed, bearing a missing tooth and his good nature. "It was the bad electric wiring." Talk of wiring brought into aural relief the steady hum of the generator that Wil had placed outside to feed us light and heat by way of a dangling, naked bulb and the glowing grill of a small space heater. The generator sat behind the camper under a makeshift ceiling of blue tarp that sheltered it from the relentless, chilly rain.

Things had been going well for Wil and his family for a long run. Until recently, he had had his own cement business, a brand new trailer, and some savings toward one of the houses he and his team were building. "I raised my first kid when I was fifteen . . . and I been doing concrete work ever since," he said. Eventually, the already dark afternoon turned into nightfall and Wil talked about the years when he hooked up with a cook in central Missouri and churned out a pound of crank per week. "Crank" is the name methamphetamine inherited from biker gangs, who for many years dominated the drug's production and distribution, transporting it in the crank cases of their motorcycles. Amphetamine[1] had been the legal product of the pharmaceutical industry since the late 1930s, when Smith, Kline & French launched Benzedrine pills and inhalers, which the American Medical Association Council approved as a "pick-me-up" that would counter "certain depressive psychoactive conditions" with "a sense of increased energy or capacity for work, or a feeling of exhilaration" (Grinspoon and Hedblom 1975).[2] In the late 1960s, when the U.S. Justice Department began to scrutinize the

Figure 8.1. Trailer in South Central Missouri. Photo by Jason Pine.

extraordinarily high numbers associated with the manufacture, distribution, prescription, and sale of legal amphetamine, home-grown labs began proliferating. Then biker clubs, like Hell's Angels of Oakland, California, seized control of the market. The entrepreneurial coup of Hell's Angels is commonly attributed to its notorious leader, Sonny Barger, who transformed the club into an international organized crime organization. Significantly, despite his wild "gangster era" in which he "sold drugs and got into a lot of shit," Sonny was a media celebrity and widely esteemed as the quintessential "American rebel" (Sher and Marsden 2006, 40). Today, he is the unknown inspiration for scores of "weekend warriors."

"I was the man," Wil said, not without sarcasm. "I liked that no-one's-gonna-fuck-with-you-attitude." He explained,

> A lot of my friends were . . . "biker types" . . . outlaws, most of them. That's what I grew up with. And for me not to be associated with them, I'd feel lost. . . . The image they got, I wanted . . . they come to me cause they knew I had it . . . and that made me feel like somebody.

Wil similarly described the sensation meth gave him when he smoked it: a surge of confidence that made him feel "amped up" and convinced he could do anything, whether physical or mental. Everybody was "happy and horny," he said. People wore their genitals raw after going at it for hours. No one desired food or had time to eat; there was too much talk and getting busy with sex or housework or fixing bikes. That was usually the case for the first two or three days. Then, "everything was tunnel vision . . . far away or . . . if I concentrated on something for a while, it seemed like I was in a cave." That was Wil's experience when he did long stretches of cement work. Once he saw people lurking outside his home where there was no one. Another time, at the height of a three-week smoking binge without food or sleep, he heard the voice of his dead brother. That was the time he almost died. His body, "smelling dead," lay immobile and emaciated on the trailer floor while his senses worked overtime: "your mind ain't all there," he said.

Methamphetamine is categorized as part of a complex class of compounds that, given the limitations of current research, is clumsily called "amphetamines" (Sulzer et al. 2005). Other members of this class are MDMA or ecstasy and khat, a shrub that is heavily cultivated in Yemen (Pantelis et al. 1989). Meth is made using the compound ephedrine, extracted from the herb ephedra, used in China for thousands of years. Amphetamines interact with the neuroreceptors that regulate dopamine, which has a near-"ubiquitous" role in the regulation of emotion or affect (2007). The release of dopamine increases blood pressure, mimicking what one feels when excited or afraid. While most amphetamines inhibit the reuptake of dopamine, methamphetamine is believed to have triple potency.[3] Meth not only inhibits dopamine reuptake, but it also increases its release while, it is believed, inciting the synthesis of a new pool of dopamine available for nonreversed release. A chemist who studies rats on meth describes the drug's effects on dopamine transporters in the following layman's terms: "It's like turning a vacuum cleaner into a leaf blower."[4]

As a result, dopamine circulation is overactivated along the nigrostriatal pathway, which is associated with the coordination of motor movement. Lower amounts of amphetamine increase bodily locomotion and increasingly higher doses induce increasingly "constricted stereotypy" or "punding." Punding is the repetition of "nonspecific behavior" or the excessive iteration of the fragment of an action that is rendered meaningless in its abstraction (Rebec 1998, 517). If a rat is administered amphetamine, it chews off all the hair on its paws, bobs its head up and down, and repeatedly attempts to climb a single wall. Similarly, meth users engage in overcharged locomotor exploration, searching, and examining, but they also experience cognitive stereotypy that begins with intensified curiosity, progresses to suspiciousness, and culminates in paranoid delusions (Ellinwood, King, and Lee 2000).

This may explain why many meth users, in an act of "grooming," attempt to eliminate "meth mites" by frenetically picking at their skin or spraying it with Black Flag® to the point of laceration. It may also explain why meth users recount spending hours crouching behind blinded windows, within heating ducts, and atop trees, looking out for "meth monsters" (or the DEA). In Wil's case, a few disorienting experiences didn't change the fact that meth helped him work longer hours. It even enhanced his performance as a meth dealer:

> We always had opportunities to make it and always had our shit ready to go. We stayed
> prepared and ahead of ourselves all the time. When you're wired like that, you're not

Figure 8.2. Depressed Town in Central Missouri. Photo by Jason Pine.

missing nothin'. You know what's going on, you know what's around you. It ain't paranoia, well I guess it can fall in a category of paranoia. But, you pretty much had your game together. You was always trying to be a step ahead of everything, and we stayed that way.

Wil took a swig from his 45-ounce Budweiser®. Many "blue collar" Missourians don't drink anything but the brew of their local St. Louis–headquartered Annheiser-Busch. In the small-town bars like Hammers, "Where the men get hammered and the women get nailed," according to the fifteen-dollar t-shirts they sell, or Snappers, where speed veterans encounter crack-smoking college kids, Amstel® Light is considered fancy and effeminate. Missourians know Bud and supported Busch because Busch supported them with six thousand jobs, generous pay, and good benefits, if you live in St. Louis. But Busch recently backed out of the bargain by agreeing to a takeover by the Belgian company InBev (Allen 2008). On the map since 1852, 1 Busch Place, like many other places caught up in "globalized America," will soon turn into a landmark of what once was.[5]

A related place sits just three miles up the Mississippi River, the park that sports the sparkling, stainless steel Gateway Arch. Standing on deep foundations higher than any other U.S. monument, the structure commemorates the explorers who led western expansion in what came to be known as the nation's Manifest Destiny. According to many architects, however, Eero Saarinen was not the best choice for designing the monument. They claimed that he "abetted a culture of planned obsolescence through the architectural equivalent of novel consumer goods" (Filler 2008). In fact, Saarinen was most prolific during the 1950s, when mass production had achieved its most spectacular form to date: the car as a common commodity. Saarinen, moreover, drafted many of his architectural designs, commissioned often by corporate clients, in his studio near the world center of the great automobile boom, Detroit, home of that model of productive stability called Ford Motors and that monumental colossus called General Motors, which proved to be another bargain buster, as demonstrated in Michael Moore's eulogy for the "blue collar" town of Flint, Michigan, *Roger and Me* (1989).

Fordism was the beginning of the end of St. Louis. With mass-produced cars came "car culture" and suburbanization. Moreover, with cars and suburbs came fast-food chains like MacDonalds, shipping giants like FedEx, and mega-retailers like Wal-Mart, fueling the mass consumption of everything, especially fuel (Fox 2004). In the 1970s, the oil crisis and the failing Fordist model of geographically fixed industrial production further spurred the "white flight" that left in its wake the new "inner city" (code word for poor people of color).

In Missouri, suburban housing development was not prolific enough to transform the expansive, sparsely populated rural tracts that make up the majority of the state. In fact, much of the state is arguably the victim of the "uneven geographic development" that is central to capitalist competition (Harvey 2000). Like a struggling tenant farmer, Wil pays a true landlord rent for parking his camper in that five-acre field, where the mute carcass of his burnt trailer also sits, the ambiguous evidence of a failed crop.

> I've had some friends with families . . . and now they're homeless . . .a lot of it's family on my dad's side. . . . You ever heard of bathtub crank?.. . . . They made it too close to the furnace and the pilot light blew it up . . . lost two bedrooms, the bathroom and half the living room just making that shit. Weren't even there three weeks and lost pretty much everything they own.

There are others like Wil in Missouri and its surrounding states who engage in the risky practice of home meth production, destroying not only their homes but their bodies, most notably with third-degree burns. The choices they make have a lot to do with their desire for a better life. As the next sections will show, a better life has a lot to do with the notion of a new and improved self. First, however, it is important to look at the particularities of the rural midwestern context of meth production.

Home Is Where the Meth Is

> Myself, the best thing I ever done is peanut butter crank. You use ephedrine, creamy peanut butter, sulfur . . . I'm telling you that's good meth . . . sticky . . . if you're a smoker, you can put it in a light bulb. . . You can pretty much make it up in eight hours.

Many people like Wil in rural Missouri and neighboring Arkansas—high school educated or less, near the poverty line or lower, white and between the ages of thirty and
seventy—produce and consume their social and economic worlds with local brew,
indigenous crop, and home-made speed. Meth is as local as the Bud and marijuana;
all the ingredients, except the farm fertilizer, can be found at Wal-Mart, whose head-
quarters is near the Arkansas border with Missouri. Many individuals in Wil's extended family are employed at the three Wal-Mart stores located in the central Missouri town of Columbia, whose population is under one hundred thousand. One of
those stores is a Wal-Mart SuperCenter, a complete consumer ecology providing everything one would find in a supermarket, along with all of life's everyday goods, and
even some luxury items.

> You take the light bulb . . . you bust this end off it right here and knock it down inside.
> You clean all this white shit out—this white shit in here will kill you . . . and so you take
> salt and dump it down in there and you shake this around and the salt takes all that
> white off. . . . I take a clothes hanger, heat it up, take a torch and heat this bulb up and push
> it in and then pop a hole in it . . . and then you can actually hit off the bulb itself . . . put
> your shit down inside there and it goes around like a tornado . . . that's how I did mine . . .
> that or tinfoil . . . tinfoil's a toxin . . . your shiny side is your toxin . . . if you cook off that,
> it puts toxins on your food or anything else . . . you gotta turn it around the other way.

Creamy peanut butter, straws, tinfoil, light bulbs, and wire hangers—some might
claim that Wal-Mart, the original behemoth of retailing, by employing, feeding, and
composing the living environments of Missourians like Wil, has utterly, irrevocably
hailed them in "embodied capitalism" (Tsianos and Papadopoulos 2006). According
to this logic, individuals not only perform the specific tasks of unloading inventory,
stocking shelves, or cashiering during their documented work hours at Wal-Mart or
Annheiser-Busch; they, all of us, are constantly performing the "immaterial labor"
of ordinary, everyday consuming and marketing. That is, we help define "fashions,
tastes, consumer norms, and, more strategically, public opinion" (Lazzarato 1996).
The occult manner in which Wil consumes Wal-Mart products helps create cultural
norms while lending those products a surplus value that only other meth producer-
consumers appreciate. Lightbulbs, tinfoil, matchbooks, coffee filters, break fluid, paint
thinner, Dr. Pepper™, and Mountain Dew™ become laden with occult subcultural
meaning and value.[6]

Embodied capitalism also means that all of us, from manual laborers to managers and everyone in between, are increasingly expected to tap into our own embodied resources, such as decision-making intelligence and personality (*are you a team
player?*). Post-Fordism is marked not only by the dissolution of centralized industrial
production and the growing necessity that competitive corporations engage in multi-
national synergies of the kind belatedly embraced by Annheiser-Busch. It also means
weakened labor unions and the "neoliberal" abandonment of social welfare, in a perverse renaissance of the American dream, where "challenge is opportunity" and "opportunity" is "responsibility."[7] Most profoundly, however, the contemporary economy

constitutes a significant upheaval in everyday experience, where the way you think and feel are assessed as "productive" or discarded as nonproductive. These invasions of the body, some argue, push it to the point of "precarity" (Tsianos and Papadopoulos 2006; Lazzarato 1996).

> I had to use it to go to work . . . we stayed up for . . . I'd say a month and a half straight. I had six ounces of that shit. The rest of my guys they were always tweaked out. I'd wrap it up in Wonder Bread, in a ball, and put a bunch of them in a sandwich bag, in a cooler, or in Twinkies. . . . I had to have it for work. . . . Once you're away from it for a couple of hours, your body starts breaking down... . . . And I got sick . . . so I left that shit alone, trying to get better, but I kept smelling dead. . . . Smell like anhydrous basically, but it was a death smell. . . . I was laying on the ground for two weeks and coughing . . . and then next thing I know, I wake up the next morning and I'm ready to run a hundred miles. . . . My mom shows up to take me to the hospital, but we end up going shopping at Wal-Mart.

Wonder Bread, Twinkies, sandwich bags, and a cooler—perfect for integrating meth with working concrete. "I think a lot of people think that they gotta have it to focus, do good . . . me, I *thought* I did," Wil said, taking another swig from his 45-ounce Bud. Many meth producer-consumers in Missouri and Arkansas say similar things about meth consumption and work. Forty-four-year-old truck driver Jimmy of Heber Springs, Arkansas, says,

> Twenty years ago, it was as easy to get it as walking into Wal-Mart and buying a pack a gum. You could pull into any truck stop anywhere and say, "I'm looking for road dope" and you'd have a dozen people say, "What kind you want? I'm over here! I'm over here!" . . . I mean, if you *didn't* do it, you was an oddball.

Jimmy adds that hitting meth is "like putting rocket fuel in a Volkswagon." Randy, despite the fatigue from chemo and metastasizing throat cancer, says his home-cooked meth gave him the "jump start" and the "dough" he needed to build a new deck on his two-room house in Cedar Hill, Missouri. Twenty-two-year-old Calvin, sitting in a jail cell in Heber Springs, Arkansas, with an extra ten years of wrinkles and blemishes, says he didn't want to go to work at the factory unless he had it in his pocket. His cellmate, pockmarked and sallow thirty-year-old Henry, says he never wanted to go to work if he had it. Both of them agree that when they get out, they'll be "hittin' that coffeepot from now on." An inestimable number of meth cooks and/or users in the rural Midwest have found meth at the intersection of work and everyday consumption, as did Wil when he worked concrete:

> I mean I ate a lot a Twinkies, let me tell you, when I was doing my thing . . . those guys, when they see me eat a Twinkie they knew mud was coming or that I was getting tired. They come running up to the truck, "Where's my Twinkie?" . . . They all used, but one.

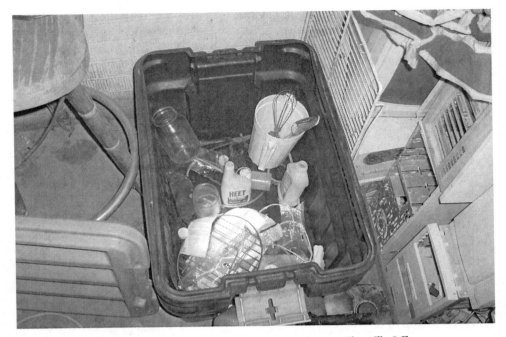

Figure 8.3. Meth Lab. Photo courtesy of Polk County, Arkansas, Sheriff's Office.

Like Wil, rural Missourians and Arkansans were dependent on local "natural" resources if they wanted to get high, make dope, or turn dope into money. Meth recipes proliferated as "mom and pop" labs sprouted and exploded in record numbers. A veritable middle-American cottage industry materialized and combusted using Wal-Mart arcana: Liquid Draino, antifreeze, radiator fluid, lithium strips from batteries, Black Flag, Solarcaine, inhalers, fish aquarium charcoal, red phosphorous from old TV sets, and, not least of them all, Sudafed. The traditional rural occupation of farming provided the additional resources, including medicated salt lick, chicken feed, and farm fertilizer. "We used to sit in the parking lot of Wal-Mart for training and see how many of 'em we could pick out," a narc says.

When federal restrictions on the sale of cold medicine containing pseudoephedrine significantly reduced home meth production starting in 2005, the rural Midwest (and many other rural regions of the United States) got ensnared in an elaborate web of global production and distribution networks. Now the product comes from somewhere else. "What we're into now is a whole other ball of wax," says one Arkansas Drug Task Force agent, "Now people disappear so quickly in this trade and then become someone else overnight." He and his partners have traced the trail to "Latinos" who import it from Mexico to Dallas, and "Asians" from the north of Texas who bring it up to Arkansas.[8] "They're filling the void with a new product: crystal meth and ice. . . . And nine times outta ten, they don't use dope. They're businessmen." The effects of "globalized America" are now registered in the rural Midwest meth economy, as local manufacture is displaced by new players, new networks, new modes of production and a new, "foreign" product. The Wal-Mart SuperCenter is yielding to the Mexican superlab, which puts out pounds upon pounds of high-grade methamphetamine with, on average, 98 percent purity. "That's a lot of product after you stomp on it, and more addictive when you don't."[9]

According to narcotics agents in Polk County, Arkansas, the younger generations, people in their teens and twenties, want the "pain pills"—Oxycontin, Zanax, and Hydrocodone.[10] "That's gold to them. Their parents don't smell it like they do marijuana. It's harder to detect and easier to transport." The Arkansas Drug Task Force agents explained that the younger generations didn't want to have anything to do with meth when it was that dirty crank, unless at an early age they were fed it by their elders. Narcotics agents working in Arkansas towns like Heber Springs, Middlebuster, and Fort Smith and in Missouri towns like Cedar Hill, Morse Mill, and Columbia recount incidences of adult users who blow meth smoke into their children's mouths "to be closer" or even force them to drink sulfuric acid when they don't shut up.[11]

If they're not that close to it, the younger generations consider crank a "white trash" or "hillbilly" drug. College students at the University of Missouri–Columbia have said they will drink and use marijuana, mushrooms, acid, and cocaine, but they draw the line at meth. They say they will even use crack cocaine, repeating the underpublicized drug consumption patterns reported during the "inner-city epidemic" of the second half of the 1980s, when the number of middle- and upper-class white crack users may have actually exceeded the total of nonwhite "inner-city" users.

According to Arkansas Drug Task Force agents, "it's all about marketing." Young people don't want a drug that "comes from a filthy trailer owned by a guy who looks like he works in a carnival, puts meth in his Dr. Pepper and drinks it." Narcs say rural meth labs are usually indescribably foul. They find excrement on the floors, buckets used as latrines, piles of dirty diapers, uncapped needles on the couch, porn, red-

Figure 8.4. Crank.
Photo by Jason Pine.

rusted guns, and all the oxidizing chemicals and run-off littering the counters, the kitchen table, and the coffee table. Homemade meth is an unwashed product that, as Wil puts it, "has the color of Mississippi mud water" (or creamy peanut butter). To young rural Arkansas and Missouri drug users, meth bares its own déclassé origins: the underskilled labor of its users (bathtub crank), the values of their "blue collar" vocations (road dope), and the banality of their unreflexive everyday consumerism (Wal-Mart).

> I lost thirty pounds in a matter of no time and I'm only a buck fifty. . . . I didn't eat and what I did eat had meth in it—Twinkies, bread. I was getting my food and my high all at once. . . . It rots your guts out . . . if you snort it, it tears your cartilage up in your nose . . . or makes your nose fall off . . . rots your teeth, and kills many, many brain cells. I wish I had all the brain cells I killed. I probably wouldn't be living in this camper.

An analogue to the desire and compulsion of meth addiction traceable in Wil's account can be found in chapter 32 of Hell's Angel Sonny Barger's self-help book, *Freedom: Credos from the Road* (2005). Entitled "Find Your Speed, Maintain Velocity, Keep on Doing It," this particular "credo" aptly captures the lethal redundancy implied in the self-destructive stereotypy that a meth-addicted body and, by extension, a stereotyped poor, rural midwesterner, performs. It is like "spinning your wheels" without going anywhere specific, just "on the road." In the introduction to his book, Barger calls this "freedom":

> The first motorcycle ride I took changed my life forever. So did serving a long-term sentence in Folsom. . . . I liked motorcycles because they were all you and nothing else. You could go as fast and far as you wanted. It was freedom all right. . . . I find jail, and especially prison, an all-American experience. Both the people who run the prisons and the inmates who are in there create their own little America, except it's an America with a much more intense set of rules, values, pecking order, privileges, routine, and punishments. . . .You have to be . . . committed to the principle of getting through life one day at a time. As a result of this system, prison gave me an invaluable perspective on freedom and survival. (Barger et al. 2005, 8–10)

When looked at within the broader field of forces animating U.S. cultural-economic life, Barger's credo reveals that the Baby Boomer (born between 1946 and 1964) is an embodied anachronism. This is because "freedom"-seeking as an end in itself, without planning for the future, is increasingly regarded as immoral, even un-American.[12] This is especially the case from the perspective of Generation Y (born between 1978 and 1992). Before taking a look at this newly active Gen Y, it is necessary to place this population in context. Barger's words demonstrate that the desire and compulsion of meth addiction and the cultural-economic world it symbolizes are linked to a more widespread sensibility that extends far beyond the rural Midwest. That sensibility is embodied by the "fast subject" (Thrift 2000) and the context that sustains and is sustained by this sensibility is the "new economy."

The New Alchemy

The arrival of crystal meth in rural Missouri and Arkansas has changed younger drug users' tastes. This new and improved product comes in the form of small clear or white shards. It is more palatable and appears less harmful. "It's clinical. And all you do is breathe in the white vapor. It's easier than smoking a cigarette." Home-cooked meth, on the other hand, is like the "moonshine of the 21st century" (Simpson 2006, 1). It recalls a "passé" form of rural poverty. Rather than market-ready moveable folkloric value, it embodies recalcitrance. This is the case because "the rural" underwent an inversion produced by the mainstreamed DIY aesthetic that began with Urban Outfitters and has culminated in Martha Stewart's tenth property, the $15-million, 153-acre, eighteenth-century Cantitoe Farm in Bedford, New York. "It's the farm as art," says Allan Greenberg, the architect she hired to restore it (Rozhon 2002).

Crystal meth is a product of the new alchemy. The naïve art of making do with whatever is at hand (or at Wal-Mart) is no match for it. Peanut butter crank is unrefined and insufficiently aestheticized; it bares its own constituent substances, the everyday household products that articulate a "middle American" body (inorganic and obese).[13] Crystal, on the other hand, like Smartwater™ or P©Mx and many other products found at Whole Foods, promises a different kind of embodiment, that of the "educated consumer."[14] Moreover, the new alchemy has helped redefine "middle-class" consumer products as the new "generic" (stigmatized, yet WIC approved). Meanwhile, Wal-Mart encourages its employees to apply for food stamps (because they qualify) and to spend their monthly benefit at Wal-Mart.[15]

In the "new economy," the origins of a product are effaced. The "fair trade" logo, for example, will signify that a banana originates not only in "approved" labor and environmental practices in Ecuador but also in concerned "fair trade" publics in Europe and the United States. Products take on as much cultural value as material value, if not more (Lash and Urry 1994). This happens when active consumers become hyperactive "voicy consumers" capable of subversion and resistance and get invited by manufacturers, designers, and marketers "to criticize, share their feelings and to interact with other consumers" (Callon 200).

Generation Y

Generation Y is the cohort born between 1978 and 1992 who are currently coming of age in the workforce. The blog *YPulse*, a youth marketing resource featured in publications such as *Forbes* and *Fast Company*, defines Gen Y by contrasting them to Gen X (born between 1965 and 1977). According to the "Youth Marketing Mega Event Conference Day One & Two Dispatch," Gen Xers are summed up by a "decaying world" of divorce, "AIDS, gangs and violence." They are "pessimistic, realistic, and nostalgic for stability" and "recycle trends, clothes styles . . . and fell [sic] there is no guarantee in finding happiness and success." The members of Gen Y, on the other hand,

- Believe they can do things on their own—starting their own business at 15, want to be famous because they think that they can because of shows like "American Idol"
- They are individuals, hopeful, entrepreneurs, optimistic, and "smarter than you."
- Extremely STRESSED generation
- They are also extremely hard to manage because they strive for so much.

YPulse gives its description of the younger generation in, above all, an economic register. It depicts an entrepreneurial personality. They are "optimistic," believe in their own potential, and "strive for so much." They are perpetually productive, but more than anything, they are perpetually producing themselves. They are what Nigel Thrift (2000) calls "fast subjects" who are "maximally creative." Unlike Gen Xers, Gen Yers do not see a "decaying" but rather a "faster and more uncertain world, one in which all advantage is temporary" (Thrift 2000, 676). They see a thrilling state of emergency rife with opportunities for self-fashioning, self-mastery, and the embodiment of success. They embody the core sensibility of the new capitalist economy.

"They're extremists, hard drivers, workaholics. . . . With an all-or-nothing personality and a history of drug experimentation, you've got a formula for disaster when this person tries crack," the director of the Cocaine Abuse Treatment Program at Columbia-Presbyterian Medical Center said of the "upwardly mobile" crack user in 1989 (Elmer-DeWitt, Beaty, and Harbison 1989). Twenty years later, the etiology of crystal meth use is not as self-evident. This is largely due, perhaps, to the fact that, when ingested, methamphetamine has a half-life up to fourteen times greater than that of cocaine. With meth, you've got a formula for deferred disaster, a formula discernable on the molecular level. In a recent study (Knutson et al. 2003), a group of scientists tracked the effects of amphetamine on "neural and affective responses to incentives" measured in dopamine levels. The incentive they used was money. The participants in the study were first shown the money, administered moderate amounts of amphetamine, and instructed to play a game not unlike casino gambling. The researchers' findings were that, contrary to the ordinary distinction between the excitement caused by the anticipation of gain and that caused by the anticipation of loss, amphetamines may regulate dopamine levels to aid in reframing potential losses as the potential *avoidance* of losses. In other words, amphetamine users are able to see "opportunities" to evade risk where nonusers ordinarily see, quite simply, risk.

Edgework

Put another way, the "fast subjects" of Gen Y are the embodiment of their own "edgework." "Edgework" is the term scholars use to describe risk-taking practices that bring the body to states of nervousness, fear, excitement, and exhilaration (Lyng 2004). As people approach the edge, "their perceptual field becomes highly focused: background factors recede from view," and their world is redefined according to "only those factors that immediately determine success or failure in negotiating the edge" (Lyng 2004, 24; Lyng 1990, 861–62).

For older generations and for many "undereducated" Gen Yers without a sense of opportunity-responsibility, meth performs the edgework for them. Its power to saturate the brain with unprecedented quantities of dopamine for the duration of an extraordinarily long half-life elongates time and redraws space "exclusively in terms of the event" (Milovanovic 2003, 122). It produces a heightened, eternal present, a hyperreality. Wil calls it "tunnel vision." Danny, a forty-year-old Austin meth dealer, calls it "TST: Tina Standard Time."[16]

The edgework performed by meth users, Gen Yers, and Gen Yers who use meth is perhaps the quintessential form of immaterial labor that fuels embodied capitalism. If your body is excited, "STRESSED," and "hard to manage," you are living, embodied proof that, in the words of neoliberals, "free people govern themselves."[17] Meth users, in fact, feel a sense of supreme self-realized sovereignty. "I felt like I was superior to society, that I was invincible because I had gotten away with so much. I would walk into a store and take what I wanted like I owned it," says 33-year-old Tim of the southern Illinois town of Quincy. "My best friend got fired from her job while buying, using register money, but she didn't believe she was fired and kept showing up," says Tiffany, a 25-year-old middle-class user in Austin. "What's mine is mine and what's yours is mine," says Heather, her 28-year-old friend, summing up the ethos of not only meth-motivated shoplifting, burglary, mugging, and identity theft but also large-scale corporate profiteering and fraud at a rising number of "underregulated" financial institutions from WorldCom (WCOM) and Enron (ENE) to Martha Stewart (MSO), and from Lehman Brothers (LEH) to Bernie Madoff (LLC).[18]

Methamphetamine's edgework summons the specialized decision-making intelligence of "extremists" and "hard drivers" who are "smarter than you," feel "optimistic," and "believe they can do things on their own," as *YPulse* describes today's most "active" generation. Methwork increases the value of fast action by redefining its worst consequences as exciting opportunities. "I was just as addicted to that 'Mission Impossible' feeling, crawling on my belly for hundreds of yards to steal that anhydrous ammonia," says Tim of Illinois. Police in rural areas across the country, in fact, have reported unusual spikes in meth-related crime. In California's Central Valley, the Agricultural Crime Technology Information and Operations Network reported a 400-percent increase in thefts in 2006. Most of the thefts were of the copper wires that carry power to irrigation systems. When a mine collapse in Indonesia, a worker strike in Chile, and the demand for industrializing metals by what investors call "emerging Asia" more than quintupled the value of copper on the London Metals Market, it is alleged that meth users began stealing it and selling it to scrap metal dealers and recyclers. It is as if, in a furious sweep of farms, electrical substations, and cellular telephone towers from California to Minnesota and from Texas to Maine, meth users are stripping bare the material foundation of U.S. industrialization (Clark 2007). Methwork is not unlike the financial markets in which it is embedded. In fact, meth's edgework, trading ruin for ruin and undoing decades of economic stability for the mainstream, precisely mirrors Bear Stearns's just-in-time hedge fund bets on subprime mortgages on the credit default swap (CDS) market, where debt is traded and coveted as if it were equity.[19] From the drugs to high finance, it's edgework, inciting a renewed War on Drugs and courting what federal regulators currently call the "moral hazard" of excessive risk (Leavitt 2008, A19).

Despite the uncertainties of contemporary cultural economic well-being, "the American people" are still bound by the "Contract with America" of 1994. The contract, according to Newt.org, offers a "national renewal, a written commitment with no fine print."[20] Indeed, the document prominently includes the Personal Responsibility Act, which entailed the drastic reduction of social welfare spending. The result is a "nonprotectionist" political economy that does not anticipate periods when a person becomes nonproductive due to accident, illness, unemployment, or age (Tsianos and Papadopoulos 2006). The future not only is not guaranteed; it is "already appropriated in the present" (ibid.). This presentist sensibility, where "all advantage is temporary" (Thrift 2000), is how capitalism feels when it is embodied. It is the embodied political-economic condition called "precarity" (Lazzarato 1996). The contemporary cultural economy, like meth, incites bodies to approach the edge, fired with the focused agility to keep a footing on the "boundary line between two physical or mental states" (Milovanovic 2003, 122). For meth bodies and the kinds of bodies produced in the new economy, risk is reward and states of nervousness and exhilaration feel like personal accomplishment, self-determination, omnipotence, and freedom (Lyng 2004).

Bodies and Precarious Renewal

The kinetics of meth and the new economy within and between bodies perhaps explains the fecundity of the broader market of crystal meth consumption that extends well beyond rural Arkansas and Missouri to a multitude of cities, suburbs, and cultural economic worlds across the United States. Take, for example, Paul, a white male in his midforties who owns with his boyfriend two new cars and a $300,000 two-bedroom home in central Austin, Texas. For him, the productive force of crystal meth gives him the embodiment of a Gen Yer:

> Young people don't use crystal . . . they don't need it . . . crystal is to regain your youth. It's needing help to stay up. Who am I gonna meet tonight? What kind of trouble can I get into? The adrenaline rush of a 25-year-old, the adrenaline rush of just life, is easy for them, you reach thirty, thirty-five, forty, forty-five, and life has become boring, to be quite honest. Gay men do not have kids to keep them young. How can I be young again? The easiest way is to find someone who has crystal meth and find a pipe and you're young again in five minutes. It's the lazy man's way to a midlife crisis.

Paul, like many others across the United States, from Orange County to Midtown Manhattan, describe their crystal meth use as an act of life renewal concretized in sex, work, sex work, housework, drug dealing, and even dissertation writing. In 2006, the federal antimeth sweep called Operation Red Fusion landed multiple Manhattan crystal meth lab busts. One arrest was of a Fulbright scholar in Columbia University's Department of History, who stated that he cooked and used crystal meth "to boost his studying" (Venezia, Martinez, and Cohen 2006). Also arrested was a vice-president of information technology at Citigroup, who cooked crystal meth in his $6,000-a-month penthouse because he couldn't find a reliable source since moving from Seattle (ibid.). "I was a million-dollar salesperson. When I was high, I could run circles around my coworkers," says Julie, a forty-year-old mother at Drug Court in Dallas. Forty-five-year-old Joey in Austin says it makes multitasking a breeze and every task more enjoyable, from cleaning the baseboards and ceiling fans to holding twelve simultaneous chat sessions on Men4Men4Sex.com and Men4SexNow.com. In the age of the digital self, the dating profile "is really a résumé" that "never sleeps. It keeps vigil day and night, dutifully holding your place in the queue of romantic prospects drummed up by the thousands of searches all over the world whose criteria you happen to meet" (Egan 2003).

Conclusion

Methamphetamine, although popular among people from a wide range of cultural-economic worlds of the United States, is not the only available resource for the kinds of productivity Wil or Julie or Paul sought. Meth is only one product within a wider narco-capitalist system that includes an array of performance enhancers, from ADHD medications (Pine 2007) to steroids to the self-help industry, systematically yielding "belabored bodies" (McGee 2007). For the fast mainstream, making it in embodied capitalism means feeling like a Monster™, Rockstar™, or a Red Bull™ and taking it Full Throttle™ down to the Redline™, or simply taking cocaine, ice, or meth.²¹ For Generation Y, it is the opportunity not to become a "brand ambassador" but to develop one's "own inner brand." In embodied capitalism, bodies, and not just those of meth users, are at once fuel and machine, resource and product, point of departure and the obstacle. They register the exertion of immaterial labor and the symptoms of precarity. Overtweaked, they bear the marks of their own edgework. When a body does not register anything anymore and is incapable of being affected, it is dead (Latour 2004). Or, does it register the ultimate intensity, that of dying? Even dying meth users risk redundancy. Their pockmarked faces, softened black teeth, and yellowed hair are already becoming the disembodied signifiers of *True Lives* requiring *Intervention*.²²

This essay has used ethnography to track embodied capitalism as a sensibility registered, in varying ways, in bodies in the rural Midwest and throughout the United States. Embodied capitalism is a relatively new concept that, paradoxically, has only been examined as an abstraction. This story has attempted to anchor it in the particularity of places and bodies, and to flesh out one of the ways embodied capitalism feels.

NOTES

I would like to thank my many inspiring colleagues at Purchase College, particularly Mary Kosut and Lisa Jean Moore, for their careful, multiple readings of this essay. Thanks also to Daniel Miller, jeff Sikes, Katie Stewart, Mishka Terplan, and, most of all, the many individuals who agreed to participate in this research. Some have successfully managed their addictions, but many, sadly, have not.

1. Methamphetamine is part of a class of drugs called amphetamine.

2. The authors cite the AMA Council on Pharmacy and Chemistry, "Present status of Benzadrine sulfate," p. 2069.

3. Sulzer (2005) notes that existing evidence that meth affects dopamine synthesis is inconclusive.

4. Personal interview with Dennis K. Miller, Department of Psychological Services, University of Missouri, Columbia, April 2005.

5. See http://www.savebudweiser.com/ for employee concerns about "jobs going overseas."

6. Rural meth users covet these for their high sugar and caffeine content.

7. The 2006 *American Dream Initiative* states, "Each of us should have the opportunity to live up to our God-given potential, and the responsibility to make the most of it. In America, anyone willing to work for it deserves the chance to get ahead." The fourth bullet point in a section entitled "New Opportunity Agenda" reads, "Every individual should have the opportunity and responsibility to start building wealth from day one, and the security and community that come from owning a home." Http://www.dlc.org/ndol_ci.cfm?kaid=86&subid=194&contentid=253993 (accessed October 12, 2008).

8. Although California is considered to be a possible origin of "imported" methamphetamine, mention of Mexico preserves the familiar meter of the "war on drugs" and immigration.

9. "Stomping on" a drug means cutting it with another substance (baking soda, laxatives, Vitamin B).

10. Xanax is for anxiety disorders, not pain.

11. The mother told Drug Task Force agents she used sulfuric acid for cleaning drains, but her six-year-old accidentally drank it. Unexpectedly, months later, the child partially regained his voice and told police his mother had forced him to drink it (personal interview with Tim Williamson, prosecutor for the 8th West Judicial District, and Officer Mike May, Mount Ida, Arizona, June 2006).

12. See note 5.

13. Townsend (1979) factors in "social exclusion" when assessing rural poverty, stating that people "can be said to be in poverty when they lack the resources to obtain the types of diet, participate in the activities, and have the living conditions and amenities which are customary, or at least widely encouraged or approved, in the societies to which they belong" (31).

14. From Smartwater: "side effects may include being called nerd, dork, geek, brainiac, know-it-all, smarty-pants, smart alek, bookworm, egghead, four-eyes, Einstein or being mistaken for the I.T. guy." Http://bottledwaterstore.com/smartwater.htm. Research that P©M conducted in 2001 found that only 12 percent of the (U.S.) population knew what pomegranates were, let alone their antioxidant quality. Http://www.healthybuzz.com/.

15. Featherstone (2004). "Wal-Mart takes out ads in [the] local paper the same day the community's poorest citizens collect their welfare checks."

16. Meth is called "Tina" among gay male users.

17. "Like Lincoln, our first Republican president, we intend to act with firmness in the right, as God gives us to see the right. To restore accountability to Congress. To end its cycle of scandal and disgrace. To make us all proud again of the way free people govern themselves." Http://newt.org/AboutNewt/FAQs/ContractwithAmerica/tabid/186/Default.aspx.

18. Bernard L. Madoff Investment Securities LLC was a private company through which, arguably, several institutions courted moral hazard, including New York University, which lost $24 million. Todd Henderson, Moral hazard and credit derivatives. University of Chicago Law School. Available at http://s.wsj.net/public/resources/documents/st_madoff_victims_20081215.html. Accessed September 27, 2006.

19. Http://uchicagolaw.typepad.com/faculty/2006/09/moral_hazard_an.html.

20. Http://newt.org/AboutNewt/FAQs/ContractwithAmerica/tabid/186/Default.aspx.

21. Energy drinks.

22. Television programs that have showcased meth addiction.

REFERENCES

Print Sources

Allen, Matt. 2008. InBev reaffirms Anheuser-Busch buyout offer. *Business Journal of Milwaukee*, June 25.

Barger, Sonny, Ralph Barger, Keith Zimmerman, and Kent Zimmerman. 2005. *Freedom: Credos from the road*. New York: HarperCollins.

Callon, Michael. 2001. Economy of qualities, researchers in the wild, and the rise of technical democracy. Available at http://www.cts.cuni.cz/seminar/callon.htm.

Clark, Korey. 2007. Metal mania: Combating the scrap metal epidemic. *Capitol Journal*, 15 no. 32, October 15. Http://www.statenet.com/capitol_journal/10-15-2007/pdf (accessed August 20, 2008).

Egan, Jennifer. 2003. Love in the time of no time. *New York Times*, September 23, Technology Section (accessed July 20, 2008).

Ellinwood, Everett H., George King, and Tong H. Lee. 2000. Chronic amphetamine use and abuse. American College of Neuropsychopharmacology: http://www.acnp.org/G4/GN401000166/CH162.htm (accessed August 28, 2008).

Elmer-DeWitt, Philip, Jonathan Beaty, and Georgia Harbison. 1989. *Time*, November 6. Http://www.time.com/time/magazine/article/0,9171,958923,00.html (accessed August 30, 2008).

Featherstone, Liza. 2004. Down and out in discount America. *The Nation*, December 16. Http://www.thenation.com/doc/20050103/featherstone (accessed August 31, 2008).

Filler, Martin. 2008. Flying high with Eero Saarinen. *New York Review of Books*, June 12.

Foster, Robert J. 2007. The work of the new economy: Consumers, brands, and value creation. *Cultural Anthropology* 22(4): 707–31.

Fox, Justin. 2004. The great paving. *Fortune*, January 26, p. 86.

Grinspoon, Lester, and Peter Hedblom. 1975. *Speed culture: Amphetamine use and abuse in America*. Cambridge, MA: Harvard University Press.

Harvey, David. 2000. *Spaces of hope*. Berkeley: University of California Press.

Knutson, Brian, James M. Bjork, Grace W. Fong, Daneil Hommer, Venkatta S. Mattay, and Daniel R. Weinberger. 2003. Amphetamine modulates human incentive processing. *Neuron* 43(2): 261–69.

Lash, Scott, and John Urry. *Economics of signs and space*. London:Sage.

Latour, Bruno. 2004. How to talk about the body? The normative dimension of science studies. *Body & Society* 10(2–3): 205–29.

Laviolette, Steven R. 2007. Dopamine modulation of emotional processing in cortical and
subcortical neural circuits: Evidence for a final common pathway in schizophrenia?
Schizophrenia Bulletin, Advance Access published on May 22, DOI. 10.1093/schbul/
sbm048.

Lazzarato, Maurizio. 1996. Immaterial labour. Trans. Paul Colilli and Ed Emery. Http://www.
generation-online.org/c/fcimmateriallabour3.htm (accessed August 15, 2008).

Leavitt, Arthur. 2008. You can't control animal spirits. *The Wall Street Journal*, August 5, p.
A19.

Lyng, Stephen. 1990. *Holistic health and biomedical medicine: A countersystem analysis*. New
York: SUNY.

Lyng, Stephen. 2004. *Edgework: The sociology of risk-taking*. New York: Routledge.

Madoff's victims. 2009. *The Wall Street Journal*, February 9.

Marcus, George E. 1995. Ethnography in/of the world system: The emergence of multi-sited
ethnography. *Annual Review of Anthropology* 24: 95–117.

McGee, Micki. 2007. *Self-help, inc.: Makeover culture in American life*. Oxford: Oxford University Press.

Milovanovic, Dragan. 2003. *Critical criminology at the edge: Postmodern perspectives, integration, and applications*. Monsey, NY: Criminal Justice Press.

Pantelis, Christos, Charles G. Hindler, and John C. Taylor. 1989."Use and abuse of khat: A
review of the distribution, pharmacology, side effects, and a description of psychosis attributed to khat chewing. *Psychological Medicine* 19 (3): 657–68.

Pine, Jason. 2007. Economy of speed: The new narco-capitalism. *Public Culture* 19(2): 357–66.

Rebec, George. 1998. Behavioral pharmacology of amphetamines. In *Handbook of substance
abuse*, ed. Ralph E. Tarter, Robert T. Ammerman, and Peggy J. Ott, 515–27. New York:
Springer.

Reeves, Jimmy L., and Richard Campbell. 1994. *Cracked coverage: Television news, the anti-
cocaine crusade, and the Reagan legacy*. Durham, NC: Duke University Press.

Rozhon, Tracie. 2002. At work on her flawless farm. *New York Times*, June 27. Http:www.
nytimes.com/2002/06/27/garden/at-work-on-her-flawless-farm.html (accessed August 25,
2008).

Sher, Julian, and William Marsden. 2006. *Angels of death: Inside the biker gangs' crime empire*.
New York: Carroll & Graf.

Simpson, Byron. 2006. Meth called the 'moonshine' of the gay community. *Out & About
Newspaper*, March, p.1. (accessed August 20, 2008).

Stewart, Kathleen. 2007. *Ordinary affects*. Durham, NC: Duke University Press.

Sulzer, David. 2005. The complex regulation of dopamine output: A review of current themes.
Clinical Neuroscience Research 5(2–4): 117–21.

Sulzer, David, Mark Sonders, Nathan W. Poulsen, and Aurelio Galli. 2005. Mechanisms
of neurotransmitter release by amphetamines: A review. *Progress in Neurobiology* 75:
406–33.

Thrift, Nigel. 2000. Performing cultures in the new economy. *Annals of the Association of
American Geographers* 90(4): 674–92.

Townsend, Peter. 1979. *Poverty in the United Kingdom: A survey of household resources and
standards of living*. London: Penguin Books and Allen Lane.

Tsianos, Vassilis, and Dimitri Papadopoulos. 2006. Precarity: A savage journey to the heart of embodied capitalism. Paper presented at the Immaterial Labor Conference, April 29–30, 2006, in Cambridge, England.

Venezia, Todd, Erika Martinez, and Stefanie Cohen. 2006. 'Crystal' palace: Exec turns his penthouse into a meth lab; Feds. *New York Post*, December 8.

WEBSITES

American Dream Initiative. Sen. Hillary Rodham Clinton, New York; Gov. Tom Vilsack, Iowa; Sen. Tom Carper, Delaware. American Dream Initiative. Democratic Leadership Council. Published July 24, 2006. Http://www.dlc.org/ndol_ci.cfm?kaid=86&subid=194&contentid=253993 (accessed October 12, 2008).

Newt.org. Larry Hunter. Contract with America, 1994. Gingrich Communications. Http://newt.org/AboutNewt/FAQs/ContractwithAmerica/tabid/186/Default.aspx (accessed August 20, 2008).

P©M Wonderful, http://www.healthybuzz.com/ (accessed January 22, 2009).

Save Budweiser.Com, http://www.savebudweiser.com/ (accessed March 2, 2009).

SmartWater, http://bottledwaterstore.com/smartwater.htm (accessed January 22, 2009).

University of Chicago Law School Faculty Blog. Todd Henderson. Moral hazard and credit derivatives. University of Chicago Law School. Http://uchicagolaw.typepad.com/faculty/2006/09/moral_hazard_an.html (accessed August 20, 2008).

YPulse Blog. Anastasia Goodstein. Youth marketing. Http://ypulse.com/archives/2006/03/youth_marketing_2.php (accessed August 20, 2008).

‖‖‖

9

Extreme Bodies/Extreme Culture

Mary Kosut

"Fran," a sixty-ish white woman with short silver hair dressed only in a black skirt, asked me, "Are you going to do a pull?" I stared at the intricate symmetrical pattern of slashes that were branded into her bare chest, and then back into her grey-blue eyes. She reassured me in a motherly way, "You don't have to do anything you aren't comfortable with. Many people wouldn't have the courage to walk through that door." I think she kept talking but I didn't hear her anymore. I just remember saying, yeah, I came all of this way and I am going to do it. (Adapted from fieldnotes 4/2/06)

As many have documented, tattooing became popularized and commodified in the later decades of the twentieth century (Sanders 1989; Myers 1992; DeMello 1995, 2000; Pitts 1998, 2003; Vail 1999; Kosut 2000, 2006; Irwin 2001; Atkinson 2003). Yet just as mini-van moms and coeds got tattooed up, more so-called extreme and unusual corporeal modifications started to surface on the fringes of American culture, beginning with the "modern primitive" body modification movement in the late 1970s and early 1980s. Fueled by charismatic leader and life-long body modifier Fakir Musafar, the modern primitive movement (based in the West Coast) enthusiastically introduced non-Western practices such as cutting, clamping, branding, scarification, and flesh hook suspension rituals to those interested in living "life in a body very differently from most around them" (Favazza 1996, 396). Thirty years later, this original movement has motivated a new generation of people who engage in embodied rituals and modifications far beyond the now safe and ubiquitous ankle tattoo or nose piercing. See the popular website *Body Modification E-Zine* (bmezine.com) for photos and testimonials of young men and women flying, cutting, and burning themselves at picnics in suburban Texas and New Jersey.

I first encountered modern primitivism in the early 1990s through stumbling upon a copy of the cult coffee-table book *Modern Primitives: An Investigation of Contemporary Adornment and Ritual* (first published in 1989). I don't know how I got the book, but I clearly recall being profoundly moved by the images inside. Visually entering an unknown world of labia piercings, split penises, sexual encasement (a practice in which the penis and scrotum are temporarily sealed in plaster), suspension rituals, and pinching ordeals (pinning the flesh with clothespins to induce pleasure/pain) changed the way I thought about my own body, and bodies in general. Like many American kids who grew up in the pre-Internet age, I was exposed to non-Western body modifications and rituals via *National Geographic's* representations of the brown-skinned primitive Other, conspicuously displayed with a lip-plate or elongated collared neck (see Lutz and Collins [1993] for a discussion). What made *Modern Primitives* so shocking was that most of the people engaging in these extremely nonnormative modifications were like me: white, American, and presumably familiar with the inside of a mall. Why would they willingly do such invasive and, from my perspective at the time, bizarre things to their bodies?

It is an understatement to say that American body modification customs have changed since my initial exposure to the world of modern primitivism roughly fifteen years ago. Evidence suggests that more people are engaging in a diverse variety of body work and body play, whether through the culturally sanctioned practice of plastic surgery or more historically nontraditional means like tattoos, genital piercings, and temporary decorative implants. For example, according to the American Society of Plastic Surgeons, the numbers of cosmetic surgical procedures (e.g., "tummy tuck," liposuction) and minimally invasive procedures (e.g. botox, laser hair removal) performed have overall increased 996 percent from 1992 to 2007.[1] Likewise, it has been estimated that 36 percent of people between the ages of eighteen and thirty-five are now tattooed in the United States (Ellis 2008). Certainly, sociologists who study deviance would draw a distinction between an upper arm lift and, for example, a facial tattoo, as the latter is an example of a physical trait "so far outside the norm, so unacceptable to a wide range of different audiences, that [it] elicit[s] *extremely* strong negative reactions" (Goode and Vail 2008, xi). However, this essay's focus is not on which contemporary body practices are culturally understood to be more or less deviant at this particular moment in history. Nor do I exclusively concentrate on extreme body modification as practiced by the modern primitives or others. Rather, I propose that seemingly incompatible and diverse body regimes and modifications can be linked because they originate from, and are practiced within, a broader framework of extreme culture. I conceptualize extreme culture as a particular set of practices, ideas, images, and commodities that surfaced in the last decades of twentieth century that revolve around the ideas of physical engagement, competition, and risk. Extreme culture developed with the rise of media culture and consumption, and is a reflection of late modern capitalism, new technologies, and globalization. The arrival of extreme culture brought an extreme ethos and an *extreme body*, one that has internalized Nike's advertising message to "just do it."

extreme culture

I employ the term "extreme body" as a conceptual tool or heuristic device, what German sociologist Max Weber (1903) called an "ideal type." At its core, an ideal type "is a concept constructed by a social scientist . . . to capture the essential features of some social phenomenon" (Ritzer and Goodman 1992, 119). Thus, the term "extreme body" does not denote any one particular modification, regime, activity, or practice. An extreme body can significantly reduce in size via gastric bypass surgery, or be modified via breast implants, rhinoplasty, or an upper arm lift for a "total body

✯makeover." Likewise, an extreme body may also skydive, hang from six large hooks, or be scarred, branded, tattooed, or amputated. An extreme body also does not indicate any one specific disposition or physicality; for example, extreme bodies can be young or old, or they may be obese or within the range of ideal or average weight. Broadly conceived, an extreme body is characterized as a distinctively malleable, flexible, and fluid entity. As such, extreme bodies engage in practices and regimes that push beyond the mundane or acceptable. Extreme bodies are the product of excessive physical modification, transformation, or activity, and also are aware of, and accept, the physical risks that come with radical carnal engagement. Even though an extreme body is an "ideal type," it is a synthesis of empirical reality—derived from images, observations, and, importantly, lived, embodied experiences.

In this article I reflect on where the term "extreme" originated and how it has filtered into the mass media, becoming a tool for advertisers, leisure and sports industries, and televisual entertainment. I argue that the emergence of extreme culture can be connected to a particular way of seeing and experiencing life inside the body that has, by extension, created a space for an extreme form of embodiment. I draw from my experiences as an embodied participant observer at a hook pull ritual conducted by Fakir Musafar, narratives from extreme sports enthusiasts, and analysis of media texts and images to call attention to the diversity of extreme bodies, and to reflect upon what they have in common. I conclude with a discussion of the boundaries of extreme bodies, and how the quest for extremeness challenges our cultural understandings of the body's limits and borders.

The Birth of Extreme Culture

> Well, I'm just a modern guy
> Of course, I've had it in the ear before
> 'Cause of a lust for life
> 'Cause of a lust for life
>
> —Iggy Pop

Throughout the twentieth century economic and social changes have shaped the patterns of American popular culture and consumption. For example, 1950s postwar America is lauded as a time of great economic prosperity and cultural stability, marked by the birth of the suburbs, family values, and rock and roll. In contrast, the 1960s were defined by the women's liberation and civil rights movements, anti–Vietnam War protests, and the tuned-in and turned-on hippie generation that broke through the staid cultural landscape that preceded it. The economically prosperous 1990s were clearly defined by the birth of the Internet and new technologies, as well as an increase in economic and cultural globalization. Within an expanding media culture, advertisers and entertainment industries began featuring activities and products touted as extreme. For example, this was the decade that introduced extreme sports (like rock climbing, sky surfing, and base-jumping), and the International

Federation of Competitive Eating (IFOCE) in 1997. The IFOCE oversaw Xtreme eating, an internationally televised "sport" in which "athletes" compete to consume fifty-four hot dogs in twelve minutes.

The early roots of the extreme culture phenomenon can be traced back as far as the 1950s when the photographer Robert Capa coined the term "Generation X" to describe the twenty-somethings he interviewed in post–World War II Europe that were grappling with an uncertain future (Ulrich and Harris 2003). Subsequently, the notion of Generation X also became associated with 1960s and 1970s subcultures, essentially denoting disenfranchised and alienated youth. By the early 1990s, Generation X signified a cohort of disaffected white teens as exemplified in the MTV series *Beavis and Butt-Head,* which debuted in 1993, and the underground film *Slacker* (1991). Unlike the hippies or Baby Boomers before them, members of Generation X (those born between 1964 and 1979) were represented in the media as lethargic, lost, and mired in ennui. The alleged X Generation became the sign of everything that was wrong with 1990s America.

By the mid-1990s, the preferred sporting activities of so-called Generation X, such as skateboarding, BMX bike riding, and snowboarding, became visible in mainstream media. This new alternative sports culture lead to the birth of the X phenomenon, including ESPN's X games and MTV sports. The lifestyle sports favored by a teen male demographic were "publicly derided as the sporting outgrowth of the short-attention spans, nihilistic desires, and aberrant world views of wayward Generation Xers" (Kusz 2004, 198). Yet, by the end of the nineties, a new image of extreme sports as a pastoral middle-class endeavor emerged within the media, divorcing the athletic activities from their negative "slacker" ethos and subcultural associations (Kusz 2004). When legendary skateboard icon Tony Hawk teamed up with McDonald's in 2003 to sell hamburgers to the youth market, it was evident that extreme sports had clearly secured a place in American corporate consumer culture. Today it is increasingly common to see middle-aged, affluent, white-collar professionals surfing and snowboarding.

The marketing potential of anything deemed or coined as extreme was unmistakably not lost on advertisers, who capitalized on the financial success of extreme sports. The national restaurant chain TGI Friday's featured Extreme Tacos, Taco Bell has Extreme Beef and Cheese Quesadillas, and Doritos currently features a flavor called Extreme Kickin' Chili. In addition to extreme food (which is typically unhealthy and high in calories), a host of body-maintenance products have been pitched under the "extreme" rubric. For example, you can reduce body odor with Right Guard Extreme Deodorant and brush your teeth with Crest Whitening Plus Scope Extreme Mint Explosion or Aquafresh Extreme Clean toothpaste. There is a long list of extreme hair care products, and Fruit of the Loom sells an Extreme Comfort Bra. Recently, extreme energy drinks have flooded the beverage market with products such as Arizona Caution Extreme Performance Energy Drink. These extreme products are diverse in form and content, but are connected by what they purport to offer—an embodied experience that involves an intense engagement of the senses that is beyond ordinary. Whether it is a larger portion size, extra flavor, whiter teeth, or more stimulation, extreme products promise more. Although the effects of these products are usually temporary, we are seemingly enticed by amplified sensations, experiences, and physical modifications.

Born out of coolly apathetic Gen X culture, the notion of extreme has been transformed and redefined in the public imagination to signify the exact opposite. Extreme is the antithesis of cool—composed, indifferent, and detached. Rather, extreme products, like extreme sports, evoke a cultural ethos characterized by a heightened level of physical engagement in the world. For purposes of this chapter, "cultural ethos" refers to symbolic forms of meaning, such as beliefs, ideas, and values that give shape to who we are, how we think about the world, and how we interact and engage within it from an embodied perspective. An extreme cultural ethos is defined by a particular way of viewing and living within the body. Consider the following quotation from a Thrill-Seekers Unlimited brochure, a Las Vegas–based company formed in 1992 that sells five-day "stunt experience extreme vacation packages" that include fire walking, bungee jumping, and an activity called "heavy weapons":

> It's a total immersion physically, mentally and emotionally for the active adult who wants to take absolute responsibility for his or her own life and break through personal barriers and comfort zones to reach a new level of expression on earth.

An extreme experience as promised above is uniquely carnal and sensate. It proposes that body and mind can and *must* be awakened to achieve a type of embodied metaphysical nirvana.

Of course, those who are attracted to extreme stunt vacations are not representative of the majority. Yet, the motivations and meanings behind these alternative and unusual embodied activities—to take charge of one's life and body, and to defy "comfort zones"—are rather ubiquitous. They occur frequently not only in reality television but also in advertisements for a host of goods and services, as in a recent commercial for the family-friendly Royal Caribbean cruise line that depicts a white, physically fit nuclear family scaling rock climbing walls and frantically bicycling to the tune of Iggy Pop's infamous drug anthem "Lust for Life." In this way, an extreme cultural ethos has accompanied the arrival of extreme products and representations, leaking into our everyday routines and consciousness, potentially shaping how we think about and inhabit our bodies.

The Twenty-First-Century Body: Consumption and Media Representations

The Consuming Body

What to do? How to act? What to be? According to sociologist Anthony Giddens (1991), these are central questions we must answer in late modern society, as traditional moorings of self-identity—family, marriage, occupation—have become increasingly less stable sites to anchor our selves. Giddens argues that because institutions and traditional ways of life have eroded, today it's up to individuals to figure out who they are. Questions of identity are continuously reflexively made and revised in the process of constructing biographical narratives, or self-stories. By extension, as we struggle to figure out our selves, "we have become responsible for the design of our own bodies" (Giddens 1991, 102). In this vein, sociologist Chris Shilling asserts that in affluent Western societies "there is a tendency for the body to be seen as an entity which is in the process of becoming," a "project" to be worked on (1993, 5). Just as we are instructed to work on our relationships, our attitudes, and our outlooks via psychotherapy, self-help books, and Dr. Phil, we are also instructed to work on the body. Natural bodies are progressively more unacceptable *as is*, and as such are a site for radical renovation and modification.

While the "body project" perspective is useful in conceptualizing an extreme body, it must be made clear that not all bodies have the means or inclination to undergo transformations. As Kleese (1999) points out, "the dimensions of choice and personal design appear to be overemphasized, or universalized" in this theory (1999, 20). Certainly, corporal identity markers such as race, gender, and sexuality, as well as class position, ground identity and shape the body today. For example, the disproportionate number of black people in the U.S. prison system illustrates how ethnicity and embodiment are inexorably connected to existing institutions and social structures. According to the independent, nongovernmental organization Human Rights Watch, black people comprise 13 percent of the national population but represent 30 percent of people arrested, 41 percent of people in jail, and 49 percent of those in prison. Therefore, it is useful to keep in mind sociologist Pierre Bourdieu's (1984) idea that the body is in essence a form of physical capital. This points to how the body can be a cultural resource or lack thereof, depending on the amount of raw material it possesses. A valued body—healthy, attractive, white, heterosexual, etc.—can by extension be more easily converted into economic, cultural, and social capital. Socially disadvantaged bodies are not as likely to have access to the privileges that make certain body projects possible.

Likewise, just as the body project is influenced and sometimes restricted by social-status variables, bodies have real material differences that can affect the ability to engage in bodily modifications and activities. It is important to highlight that the body is indeed a biological entity as well as a symbolic, social, and psychological one. For example, people who possess physical or cognitive disabilities may endure obstacles or barriers that limit the pursuit of body projects. A person's height, body type and shape, and perceived physical attractiveness constitute the biological raw material that may constrain or empower. Health may also be an influencing factor—from everyday allergies to debilitating chronic illnesses. Thus, natural or biological givens, for better or worse, essentially constrain and contour the way a body moves in the world.

Even given the obvious social and biological disparities among us, as embodied individuals we share a common historical moment in which the appearance of the body and representations of the body are particularly salient. As sociologist Mike Featherstone (1982) maintains, within contemporary consumer culture the presentation of the body, how it looks and is displayed, is tied to the consumption of commodities and services. Bodily consumption is part of a growing concern with lifestyle (Featherstone 1991, 86):

Rather than unreflexively adopting a lifestyle, through tradition or habit, the new heroes of consumer culture make lifestyle a life project and display their individuality and sense of style in the particularity of the assemblage of goods, clothes, practices, experiences, appearance and bodily dispositions. . . .

We are increasingly expected to cultivate the body's appearance not only through clothing and other material symbols, but also through anti-aging creams, health and exercise regimes, and so forth. For example, within the past decade vegan, yoga, and other "healthy lifestyles" have become trendy, ushering in a range of embodied practices and routines, and the products needed to execute them properly. Specific individual lifestyle aside, what is especially pertinent is that consistent bodily consumption is normative, if not expected. For example, if a person chooses not to dye or style his or her hair, whiten his or her teeth, follow fashion trends, or engage in diet and exercise programs, such lack of bodily maintenance can be read negatively, particularly in the case of women ("she doesn't care what she looks like"). In essence, a body that doesn't constantly upgrade and display evidence of consumption is perceived to be abnormal or suspect, and thus is likely to be devalued.

The Mediated Body

The focus on bodily upkeep corresponds with a historically new set of representations of the body in mainstream media. Analyzing media representations and meanings is important because as a source of cultural pedagogy, "they contribute to educating us how to behave and what to think, feel, believe, fear and desire—and what not to" (Kellner 1995, 1). As feminist scholars such as Susan Bordo (1993) and Jean Kilbourne (1979) have shown, advertising and pop culture representations have created particularly distorted and harmful images of the ideal female body, one that is increasingly unnaturally thin and unattainable in the real world. While 1940–1950s media representations of women favored a half-body upper torso shot that emphasized large, pointed breasts, the twenty-first-century ideal female body has been radically minimized into a prepubescent stick figure. Unsurprisingly, studies have linked body image dissatisfaction and anorexia with media representations (Botta 1999; Harrison 2000). The male body is also subject to distortion in advertising and other media that presents young, toned, tall, hairless, white men as the standard. The term "manorexia" has been coined to reflect the rise in eating disorders among young American men.

Most recently, a new set of uniquely distorted body representations has invaded the visual realm: bodies that are *interiorized* (reduced to a set of organs, blood, and tissue) and bodies that are *spectacularized* (expected to undergo radical transformations). In 2001, the network television crime drama *CSI: Crime Scene Investigation* introduced the *interiorized* body by breaking the boundaries of the flesh via digital technology and swooping camera angles. Instead of describing how a character died from a bullet to the heart, the viewer travels inside the cadaver to see a recreation of the actual piercing of the organ. The audience receives a fast-paced prime-time anatomy lesson with a soundtrack. Through this "organs'-eye" view, the liver, lung, and spinal chord become secondary characters. The *interiorized* body has become a popular standard representation as evidenced in the spin-offs *CSI: Miami* and *CSI: NY*, as well as in the medical dramas *House* and *Nip/Tuck*. These interior images effectively create a highly stylized medicalized body that can be visually assessed, diagnosed, and fixed as necessary. Because the viewer can now see how the body looks on the inside and out, surgical procedures appear less arcane and mysterious.

Likewise, the proliferation of the reality television genre has introduced a body that is potentially fixable but also uniquely performative. In shows such as MTV's *I Want a Famous Face, The Swan,* and, most recently, *The Biggest Loser,* the body is *spectacularized. A spectacularized* body is represented as a project to be worked on, but in addition, is expected to undergo an extreme transformation. For example, on *The Biggest Loser,* morbidly obese men and women compete to lose the most weight to win a $250,000 prize. The audience is invited to watch as the contestants suffer and gasp through obstacle courses and race each other in the midday sun while bogged down with the virtual fat they have recently lost. The climax comes at the end of each episode when contestants are stripped down to spandex and weighed on gigantic scales. Even though the program is steeped in medical discourse, and exercise and dietary advice, it also represents fat bodies as carnivalesque objects in the style of an old-fashioned freak show. However, it is the viewing of the spectacle in which a person loses one hundred pounds or more that is significant within the context of conceptualizing an extreme body. Such transformations, whether through multiple plastic surgeries or an ascetic dietary regime, illustrate the potential malleability of the body. The viewer is presented with tangible evidence that the body *can* be remade in a radical way, and *should* be as the results are positively life-changing and self-changing. A new self, often described by contestants as the "real me," emerges within the remade flesh.

Another example of the *spectacularized* body/self was introduced in ABC's *Extreme Makeover* (2002–2005), a prime-time reality television series that traces the radical overhaul of frumpy, lumpy bodies into firm, smooth, and improved material imitations. Typically unrecognizable due to do the scope and scale of the surgical modifications performed, the patient-transformees emerge with bright white smiles underneath flowing manes of hair as relatives and friends cheer them on with whoops and tears. Again, traditional self-help rhetoric accompanies the physical transformation. The connection between a better self and a radically better body is explicitly written in the script. For example, transformee Candace, a 29-year-old mother of two from Lincoln, Nebraska, wanted an extreme makeover because she had been called "Big Bird" and "Beeker" and had been teased all of her life because of her appearance. Candace's makeover "journey" included upper eyelid surgery, a brow lift, rhinoplasty, bone contouring above her eyes, cheek implants, lower eyelid tightening, breast augmentation, tooth extraction, porcelain veneers, and liposuction on her thighs and her stomach. She also underwent a fitness and diet routine that give her "six pack abs" and was given a new hairstyle and a fashion makeover. Candace reflected upon her transformation:

This is a permanent change—not just a physical change, but an internal change as well. And I am never going to lose that. . . . It isn't just about the plastic surgery, being alone, learning to like your self, it's about all of it, encompassed together. A life-changing experience.

Candace's mediated narrative is a salient example of the contemporary idea that individuals must take responsibility for updating their biographical narratives while working on the "body project" (Shilling 1993). The person who strives to be the Biggest Loser or endure an Extreme Makeover functions as a particular embodied visual representation—fleshy empirical proof of the extreme adaptability of the "late modern self" (Giddens 1991).

Representations of *interiorized* and *spectacularized* bodies have quickly become dominant visual frames. Given the rapid proliferation of television shows that feature such bodies, it is evident that the viewer (a type of armchair voyeur) remains to a certain extent captivated. Perhaps it is because the body is made accessible (*interiorized*), or because viewers find pleasure in watching the "before" become an "after" (*spectacularized*).

Risk and Transcendence Embodied

Dear Traveler to Inner Space:

Just a reminder, we are prepared to assemble next Saturday, April 1 between 11:30 AM and Noon for the annual Spring Spirit + Flesh Workshop & Ritual. Please arrive on time as we wish to start with an opening circle promptly at 12:00 PM. Dress comfortably and please remember to bring a flogger or two for the warm up exercises. If you do not have a flogger, we will have some floggers to borrow as well as some colorful wraps to wear for the Energy Hook Pull Dance. . . . Looking forward to an informative and ecstatic day.
—Fakir & Cleo (e-mail correspondence)

I sat on the frayed couch watching from a safe distance as the twenty or so "Spring Spirit + Flesh Workshop & Ritual" participants lined up to get chest and back hooks, third-eye piercings, and cheek skewers. We had done the opening circle, flogged each other, watched videos of Thai hook rituals, and meditated at the makeshift multidenominational altar that featured Hindu and Christian icons. Everyone was warmed up and ready to begin the main event, the hook pull ritual itself. It had been a long day and it was getting stuffy in the second-floor room with only a few windows. People were starting to sweat, even the tall guy with the shaved head wearing only a cock ring, black leather wristbands, and black lace-up army boots. The music and the

drumming, and the cacophony of screaming, laughing, and ecstatic
moans filled up the space. I wanted it to stop. I was thinking, "I wish
they would all just shut up."

My eyes focused on "Sparrow," a pale, topless woman, probably in
her midtwenties, who was wandering around with blood dripping from
the metal penetrating her chest and face. "Sparrow's" gaze seemed far
away but she appeared to enjoy pulling on the ropes attached to the
two hooks in her chest and the temporary cheek skewer piercing. Cheek
skewers look like the metal skewers you barbeque with but have tri-
angle shapes at each end, sort of like an arrow. The skewer is jammed
in one side of the face and pushed outside through the other cheek. The
center of the skewer rests inside the head so this sometimes causes the
person's mouth to gape open. I winced as "travelers" grimaced through
the process of having the skewer penetrate their cheeks. It took some
serious pressure and pushing, as they don't glide in. Fakir said, "They
will help release the tension of the mind so that we can travel more
freely outside of the constraints of the body." This is what he meant by
traveling to "inner space." (Adapted from fieldnotes 4/3/06)

Sociologists "discovered" so-called extreme body modification practices, such as full body tattooing, branding, suspensions, hook pulls, and earlobe elongation, in the 1990s (Myers 1992; Favazza 1996; Kleese 1999; Turner 1999; Sweetman 1999). Most discussions of such modifications as well as of modern primitivism, broadly considered, have centered on the common themes of spirituality and exoticism. Particularly, academics have dismissed participants as naïve postmodern pillagers who are looking for meaning or fun in the culture of the Other (Kleese 1999) or as ironic, detached consumers for whom the "modern tattoo is merely a cliché borrow[ed] from and adapting Polynesian patterns [and] Japanese motifs" (Turner 1999, 49). While the "modern primitive" label continues to be used by academics to describe the community as a whole, I assert that contemporary extreme body modifiers don't necessarily situate their body play within the original discourses of spirituality and the exotic other employed by the founding members of modern primitivism (see Kleese 1999; Turner 1999; Sweeetman 1999; Pitts 2003).

There is a new generation of extreme body modifiers who grew up in a post-Fakir, Xtreme cultural landscape, as previously described. Additionally, with the advent of the Internet and social networking sites and blogs, a rich virtual body-modification community now connects disparate groups and individuals who are interested in body play and body modifications. Although people may be engaging in the same practices as some of Fakir's original or current followers, they may perform them for different reasons and in different contexts. Discussions of overt spirituality grounded in non-Western cultural beliefs are rarely present in the virtual extreme-body-modification community, which is primarily comprised of 18–35-year-olds. Rather, I found evidence that some young people modify their bodies because they can, and because it feels good. This sort of no-nonsense approach is confirmed by 22-year-old "Aurora," who is covered in visible tattoos, has multiple facial piercings, and enjoys participating in suspensions and hook pulls:

> It is really intense. I mean, it's like scary to just let yourself go. And it can hurt . . . but just like getting a neck tattoo, or doing a pull or whatever, it hurts but it feels so amazing at the same time. All that energy that is released . . . it's my body so why wouldn't I do whatever I want with it?

I asked her if she would ever get cosmetic surgery and she said, "No, it's not for me, but if it makes people feel good, then they should go for it. Otherwise wouldn't I be a hypocrite?" After a few seconds she added, "Who knows, maybe I will be into that kind of thing someday." "Aurora" has an extreme body, as defined in this essay, because she views her own body and the bodies of others as infinitely malleable and adaptable. She accepts the pain that comes with her radical adjustments and activities, and is not detoured by the potential risks of injury or infection that could result from having large hooks inserted into her body by a nonmedical professional in an unsterile environment. Her body is raw material to be used and fashioned at will, malleable and fluid. It is the source of pleasure, identity, and embodied recreation.

Extreme Ethnography?

After speaking with Aurora and a few others in the New York City area who participated in extreme body modification rituals, and interviewing Fakir Musafar, "father" of the modern primitive movement, by phone, I decided to attend a "Flesh & Spirits" ceremony at Fakir's invitation. He strongly suggested that I "see it for myself." As a participant observer, I hoped to better understand the embodied nature of the practice and illuminate the process. I wasn't sure if I would actually do a hook pull, but made the decision to do so on site after participating in the preritual events and exercises. I surrendered myself to the moment and to an extreme ethos. In the process of seeking to understand their bodies, my gaze turned to my own. I began to visualize it as a medium, an instrument, and a site of incarnate ethnographic experience. For a day, I was both an extreme ethnographer and an extreme body modifier.

A hook pull involves pulling on or away from hooks embedded in your chest that are clamped to ropes that connect to a stationary object (like a rafter or a tree). In comparison, a suspension entails being pierced by hooks that are attached to sturdy nylon ropes, but instead of pulling on the hooks, the person literally hangs by the hooks from his or her own skin for a period of a few minutes to over an hour. This is often described as "flying" because the person is suspended off the ground. In general, hook pulls are less invasive and intense than suspensions because the participant can control the tension of the hooks and his or her feet are grounded so that the hooks don't have to bear the full weight of the body. Nevertheless, some choose to hook onto another person—so that two or more people can "dance" by creating tension between them. A few people "danced" at the ritual I attended, but I hooked onto a beam and controlled the tension of the hooks myself. Some suspensions and pulls are done privately in homes or backyards; others are executed publicly at performances that serve as art or entertainment. Of course, these rituals were originally executed in other cultural contexts, including traditional Native American cultures and different sects of Hinduism. Historically, suspensions and pulls have been performed as rites of passage, vision quests, healing rituals, or as means to achieve visions by leaving the body and communicating with the spiritual realm.

It is no coincidence that extreme body modifiers "travel" outside of their bodies and reality television contestants go on transformative "journeys." This language doesn't reflect movement in a physical sense (as in moving from here to there), but a type of figurative movement or passage beyond the constraints of a fixed body/self. The act of physical transcendence is, unsurprisingly, also present in the narratives of extreme sports enthusiasts as they pursue situations that place them in significant corporal danger. One 35-year-old rock climber recounted how he was always "chasing a moment" (Robinson 2004, 121).

> "Yeah, trad[itional] climbing is more, is about the fear . . . about overcoming fear, and its [sic] just about being out there, and hoping you get that thing. I've talked to a few people about this, and a lot of people say the same thing, your [sic] chasing . . . it's probably that you are chasing a moment all the time . . . and you get it maybe two or three times in a year, where you are absolutely on form, and you're just not scared at all, and you're just flowing, and the whole thing is a joy. . . ."

The transcendence the climber speaks of occurs when everything else, the mundane physical world, the ordinariness of everyday life, disappears through participation in risky, taxing, and often-painful activities. "Chasing the moment" is comparable to what extreme body modifiers refer to as "traveling to inner space."

Inner space, as I observed, is a moment of embodied bliss in which you are able to move beyond the physical pain and stress you are experiencing, albeit briefly. It begins with a state of throbbing, aching, intense carnality. My field notes recount what it felt like to get the hooks "thrown" into my chest:

> *Fakir takes a flap of my chest skin between his thumb and fingers and he clamps down on it like a vice. Jesus his fingers are strong. He tells me to look him in the eyes, concentrate, breathe. I smell his stale breath as his body and mine get closer, touch and overlap. The sharp thrust of a needle bursts my clamped red chest skin. Push, push—pop, and then pop through again out the other side. I think I am done. And then he works in the hooks that take the place of the needles, but after a few unsure jabs and prods. He is not gentle. . . . A dull pain turns searing. My upper chest throbs and endorphins pump through my body. I am rubbery and red; thumping heart, wet palms, flushed face. The hooks are tight—jutting out of my chest at an angle. It's so painful that it hurts to bend my head, so I can't really look at them. I am instructed to stand and rock climbing ropes are attached to each of my chest hooks. My legs wobble uncooperatively and my feet shuffle in tiny unsure steps. The*

drumming is getting louder, each beat thuds through me hard. I am guided to the rafter by a naked, balding, paunchy middle-aged white man to begin my hook pull. I can't faint, I can't faint . . . (Fieldnotes 4/3/06)

Unfortunately, I was not able to transcend the pain and travel to "ancient Egypt," as "Jerry," one of the other hook pull participants, proudly told me that he did.

After attaching the ropes that were connected to the two hooks in my chest to the large wooden beam hanging from the ceiling, I slowly edged my back at an angle with my hands on the ropes. My arms and upper torso adjusted the tension, because I was pulling my skin rather than completely suspending from it. As I continued to bend backwards the hooks in my chest started moving upwards because there was less slack in the rope. The farther that I leaned away from the rafter, the more the hooks pulled on my throbbing chest. Each little pull and tug triggered a searing pain through my upper torso. It was so excruciating that I began to feel queasy and increasingly lighter and hotter. I didn't get high off the endorphins; I felt like a radiating opened mound of matter—a metaphorical bloody side of beef that was being spun in circles. I didn't want to faint with the hooks in my chest and end up completely hanging from them with my full body weight. I waved for someone to help me get unhooked so that I would no longer be tied to the rafter. The rest is a blur. I cannot remember when my ropes were released from the beam, but obviously someone assisted me and walked me over to a couch that was about fifteen feet away. I remember sitting on the couch trying to breathe, crying a little, feeling totally freaked out (the hooks still jutting out of my chest with the ropes attached to the end sort of dangling). "Queen Bee," a voluptuous, six-foot-tall red-head with a curly afro who was dressed in S&M gear, came over to comfort me:

"Don't feel bad. Don't judge yourself. I almost fainted the first three or four times I did it too. It really hurt like hell, but I went back and did it again. You have to work at it . . . but once you let yourself go its feels like nothing you can even imagine. You have to love yourself, not judge yourself."

This postpull interaction was particularly interesting because it illuminated a "no pain no gain" ethos, and also shed light on the competitive nature of the ritual. Even though her first experience was as physically taxing and unpleasant as mine was, "Queen Bee" got back in the game, so to speak. Like extreme athletes and extreme vacation adventures, "Queen Bee" continued to endure physical pain and place her body at risk to "chase a moment." She conceptualized her body play as much like a body project, that is, something to be worked on that will probably result in a reward of some kind. Clearly, she felt satisfaction and conveyed a sense of pride in committing to a job well done (a transcendent, physically enjoyable hook pull).

To the uninitiated, extreme body rituals like flesh hook pulls may seem shocking and unfathomable. However, if you look closely you will find a marriage of both extreme sports and mainstream self-help discourses as illustrated in *Extreme Makeover* within the extreme-body-modification community. For example, practices that permanently alter the flesh, like tattooing and scarification, are often cloaked in self-help and identity-work rhetoric (Sanders 1989; DeMello 2000; Pitts 1998, 2003; Kosut 2000; Irwin 2001; Atkinson 2003). Extreme bodies are worked on as projects that express identities, or played with in a quest for a type of carnal transcendence. Through these acts, the body is placed in dangerous and possibly even life-threatening situations. Yet, within the context of an extreme culture we accept that our actions—whether attempting to scale a high cliff wall or altering the flesh via plastic surgery—might not have pleasant outcomes. As German sociologist Ulrich Beck asserts in *Individualization* (2002), everyone wants to live his or her own life, but this should be at the same time "an experimental life." If we accept the idea that life is experimental, then it is not much of a leap to conceptualize the body as experimental too. Whether through hook pulling, tattooing, bungee jumping, or using transdermal (temporary) decorative implants, the body serves as medium of play, experimentation, and transformation.

Conclusion

Radical regimes of the body have existed for thousands of years in many different forms. For example, the nineteenth-century practice of corsetry dictated that the perfect Victorian wife should "suffer and be still" while forcefully strapped into corsets as narrow as eighteen inches, making even rudimentary movement painful (Roberts 1977). While clothing that can break a person's ribs is certainly radical in terms of the physical manipulation of the body, there is a difference between a body modified by Victorian corsets and those customized by large format tattoos, breast implants, or an Extreme Thermo Rush energy drink. Obvious cultural dissimilarities notwithstanding, what the latter practices and products share in common is that they were born out of a particular historical era that is defined by media culture and capitalist consumption. The number of media texts and images advertising extreme lifestyles and modifications, as well as the body's limitless ability to be drastically manipulated, has brought the extreme body and ethos into the public imagination.

Extreme culture crystallized within a particular set of mediated texts, representations, and consumption patterns beginning in the early 1990s. The notion of Xtreme saturated mainstream American culture via embodied practices, lifestyles, consumer products, and popular media. Just as media giants ESPN and MTV cleaned up extreme sports and brought them safely to the cul-de-sacs and playgrounds for consumption, network television brought plastic surgery to the masses within the context of a digestible script that made sense, as in the television show *The Swan*, wherein a mass audience is invited to observe radical surgical transformations of real bodies from the comfort of their living rooms. The viewer watches nervously as the bandages come off and the bruises heal, revealing a person who is radically improved—inside and out.

While the idea of extreme translates to economic revenue, and as has obvious entertainment value due to its spectacular nature, the extreming of media culture suggests a larger cultural shift that is even more significant. As extreme practices and behaviors become more visible and, arguably, acceptable, what we understand as a "normal" body is redefined. When extreme practices and lifestyles become more normative, extremeness can become a quest in and of itself, for example, in the name of competition, beautification, transcendence, or for the sake of the ever-addictive adrenaline rush. The normalization of extremeness also has implications for the natural or biological body. Recently, the confirmed and suspected use of steroids by famous professional and Olympic athletes has sparked debates regarding the notion of a naturally performative body versus one that has been artificially enhanced. Likewise, new technologies assist bodies in achieving radical and historically unprecedented feats, as in reproductive therapies that result in the birth of eight babies or enable a 72-year-old woman to give birth to twins. Not surprisingly, many people are disturbed and concerned by bodies that transgress the confines of biology to such a degree. Nonetheless, the extreme ethos coupled with continued technological advancements may signal an era in which radical modifications and medical procedures currently understood as extreme begin to be viewed as "normal."

As stated earlier, not all bodies have the physical, economic, or cultural means to undergo extreme transformations or engage in extreme practices and rituals. Certainly, not all people envision the body as fluid and malleable, or feel comfortable enough to surrender to the risks involved in cosmetic surgeries, hook pulls, or mountain climbing. Yet even a cursory glance at contemporary consumer culture, mass media, and body modification trends of the past two decades illustrates that we are living in a historically unique time with respect to how we see the body's limits and borders. Today many people work on, think about, modify, and reflexively push the boundaries of their own bodies as a matter of course. As a conceptual framework or ideal type, the extreme body offers a means to begin to see how the body is continually bound and liberated by culture.

NOTES

1. American Society of Plastic Surgeons, available at http://www.plasticsurgery.org/media/statistics/loader.cfm?url=/commonspot/security/getfile.cfm&PageID=29426.

REFERENCES

Atkinson, Michael. 2003. *Tattooed: The Sociogenesis of a Body Art.* Toronto: University of Toronto Press.

Beck, Ulrich. 2002. *Individualization: Institutionalized Individualism and Its Social and Political Consequences.* Thousand Oaks, CA: Sage.

Bordo, Susan. 1993. *Unbearable Weight: Feminism, Western Culture, and the Body.* Berkeley: University of California Press.

Botta, Renee A. 1999. "Television Images and Adolescent Girls' Body Image Disturbance," *Journal of Communication* 49: 22–41.

Bourdieu, Pierre. 1984. *Distinction: A Social Critique of the Judgement of Taste.* London: Routledge.

DeMello, Margo. 1995. "Not Just for Bikers Anymore: Popular Representations of American Tattooing," *Journal of Popular Culture* 29: 37–52.

———. 2000. *Bodies of Inscription: A Cultural History of the Modern Tattoo Community.* Durham, NC: Duke University Press.

Ellis, Juniper. 2008 *Tattooing the World: Pacific Designs in Print and Skin.* New York: Columbia University Press.

Favazza, Armando. 1996. *Bodies under Siege: Self-Mutilation and Body Modification in Culture and Psychiatry.* Baltimore, MD: Johns Hopkins University Press.

Featherstone, Mike. 1982. "The Body in Consumer Culture," *Theory, Culture, and Society* 1: 18–33.

———. 1991. *Consumer Culture and Postmodernism.* Thousand Oaks, CA: Sage.

Giddens, Anthony. 1991. *Modernity and Self-Identity: Self and Society in the Late Modern Age.* Stanford, CA: Stanford University Press.

Goode, Erich, and D. Angus Vail. 2008. *Extreme Deviance.* Thousand Oaks, CA: Pine Forge Press.

Harrison, Kristen. 2000. "The Body Electric: Thin-Ideal and Eating Disorders in Adolescents," *Journal of Communication* 50(3): 119–43.

Irwin, Katherine. 2001. "Legitimating the First Tattoo: Moral Passage through Informal Interaction," *Symbolic Interaction* 12(1): 49–73.

Kellner, Douglas. 1995. *Media Culture: Cultural Studies, Identity, and Politics between the Modern and the Postmodern.* London: Routledge.

Kilbourne, Jean. 1979. *Killing Us Softly.* Media Education Foundation.

Kleese, Christian. 1999. "Modern Primitivism: Non-Mainstream Body Modification and Radicalized Representation," *Body & Society* 5(2–3): 15–38.

Kosut, Mary. 2000. "Tattoo Narratives: The Intersection of the Body, Self-Identity, and Society." *Visual Sociology* 15: 79–100.

———. 2006. "Mad Artists and Tattooed Perverts: Deviant Discourse and the Social Construction of Cultural Boundaries," *Deviant Behavior* 27: 73–95.

Kusz, Kyle. 2004. "Extreme America: The Cultural Politics of Extreme Sports in 1990s America." In *Understanding Lifestyle Sports: Consumption, Identity, and Difference,* edited by Belinda Wheaton, 119–213. New York: Routledge.

Lutz, Catherine, and Jane L. Collins. 1993. *Reading National Geographic.* Chicago: University of Chicago Press.

Myers, James. 1992. "Non-mainstream Body Modification: Genital Piercing, Burning, and Cutting." *Journal of Contemorary Ethnography* 21 (3): 267–35.

Pitts, Victoria. 1998. "Reclaiming the Female Body: Embodied Identity Work, Resistance, and the Grotesque," *Body & Society* 4(3): 67–84.

———. 2003. *In the Flesh: The Cultural Politics of Body Modification.* New York: Palgrave Macmillan.

Ritzer, George, and Douglas J. Goodman. 1992. *Classical Sociological Theory.* McGraw Hill.

Roberts, Helen. 1977. "The Exquisite Slave: The Role of Clothes in the Making of the Victorian Woman," *Signs* 2(3): 554–69.

Robinson, Victoria. 2004. "Taking Risks: Identity, Masculinities, and Rock Climbing." In *Understanding Lifestyle Sports: Consumption, Identity, and Difference,* edited by Belinda Wheaton, 113–30. New York: Routledge.

Sanders, Clinton. 1989. *Customizing the Body: The Art and Culture of Tattooing,* Philadelphia: Temple University Press.

Shilling, Chris. 1993. *The Body and Social Theory.* 2nd ed. London: Sage.

Sweetman, Paul. 1999. "Anchoring the (Postmodern) Self? Body Modification, Fashion, and Identity." *Body & Society* 5 (2–3): 51–76.

Turner, Bryan S. 1999. "The Possibility of Primitiveness: Towards a Sociology of Body Marks in Cool Societies," *Body & Society* 5 (2–3): 39–50.

Ulrich, John, and Andrea L. Harris. 2003. *GenXegesis: Essays on Alternative Youth (Sub)Culture.* Madison: University of Wisconsin Press.

Vail, D. Angus. 1999. "Tattoos Are Like Potato Chips . . . You Can't Have Just One: The Process of Becoming and Being a Collector," *Deviant Behavior* 20: 253–73.

Vale, V., and Andrea Juno. 1989. *Modern Primitives: An Investigation of Contemporary Adornment and Ritual.* San Francisco: Re/Search Publications.

The Racial Nose

Sander L. Gilman

Enlightenment Noses

In the world of nineteenth-century science, the great chain of being that was seen to stretch from the most human to the least human was also a chain of beauty, and beauty was measured by the nose. The tiny nose, the flattened nose, thus became part of the very definition of race. The difference of the too-short nose is a racial difference and racial differences are signs of character. Moreover, there was also the powerful idea in eighteenth- and early nineteenth-century anthropology that the noses of the black and the Jew were signs of their "primitive" nature. This was primarily because the too-flat nose came to be associated with the inherited syphilitic nose. In this view, flattened noses are nature's moral comment on the hygiene of a "race" in terms of both racial difference and dangerousness.

The widespread claim that the too-small nose was the ugly mark of inferior races reflected the reception of the work, at the close of the eighteenth century, of the Dutch anatomist Petrus Camper (1722–89), who "discovered" the facial angle and the nasal index.[1] The nasal index was the line that connected the forehead via the nose to the upper lip; its reflex, the facial angle, was determined by connecting this line with a horizontal line coming from the jaw. This line came to be a means of distinguishing between the human being and the other higher anthropoids.

Camper's facial angle, which connected all the races of the human species and distinguished them from the ape, was also used by many of his contemporaries and successors, such as his son-in-law, Theodor Soemmering, as a means of creating a hierarchy of the races. Camper defined the "beautiful face" as one in which the facial line creates an angle of 100 to the horizontal. According to the contemporary reading of Camper, the African was the least beautiful (and therefore the least erotic) because he or she is closest to the ape in his or her physiognomy.

Too-short noses are pathological or primitive because they are disproportionate or asymmetrical even if they are functional. They are signs of the relationship between

---

the unaesthetic and the corrupt. The shape of the nose is an essential element of that which defines the true human being. In 1811 Lorenz Oken (1779–1851), the German Romantic philosopher/naturalist, defined the notion of the beautiful face in terms clearly borrowed from Camper:

> The face is beautiful, when the nose is parallel to the spine. No face grows so, but every nose makes a sharp angle to the spine. The facial angle is known to be 80. What no one has yet observed, and what is also not observable without our understanding of the meaning of the skull, was evident to the ancient artists through their feeling. They not only made the facial angle correct, but also even exceeded it—the Romans to 96 and the Greeks, indeed, to 100. How is it that this unnatural face of the Greek work of art is even more beautiful than that of the Roman, even though the latter is closer to nature? The reason for this lies in the fact that Greek facial aesthetics represents even more the will of nature than those of the Roman; for there the nose is quite perpendicular, parallel to the spine, and thus returns from where it came. He who simply copies nature is a bungler, he is without inspiration and mimics no better than the bird's song, or the ape's gestures.[2]

Oken summarized not only the notion of the perfect face and nose, but also the way we measure and understand that face through the Kantian idealization of high art as providing transcendent models for human beauty. For Oken, bodies are not to be judged against other real bodies but against the ideal forms of bodies in art.

The black nose is the key to an understanding of the aesthetics of facial deformity in the Enlightenment. Facial aesthetics is the aesthetics of race. Even among those thinkers who advocated a relativistic aesthetics (in which each people of the world has its own standard of beauty), the meaning of facial deformity remained constant. In his *Laocoön; or, On the Boundaries of Painting and Poetry* (1766), Gotthold Ephraim Lessing (1729–81) observed, "A scar in the face, a hare-lip, a flattened nose with prominent nostrils, an entire absence of eyebrows, are ugliness which are not offensive either to smell, taste, or touch. At the same time it is certain that these things produce a sensation that certainly comes much nearer to disgust than what we feel at the sight of other deformities of body."[3] In his widely translated physiognomic study, Johann Caspar Lavater (1741–1801), who created the craze for physiognomy in the late eighteenth century, established the flattened nose as the icon of the black.[4] He cites Georges Louis Leclerc, comte de Buffon's (1707–88) *Histoire naturelle*: "All Hottentots have a very flat and broad nose, they would not have it but for the fact that the mothers feel it necessary shortly after birth to press the children's noses flat" (4:275). He also quotes Kant's essay on the "Various Races of Mankind" (1775): "The growth of the spongy parts of the body must increase in a hot and damp climate. Thick snub nose and sausage lips result. . . . [T]he black is appropriate to his climate, that is strong, fleshy, supple, but because of the rich provisions of his motherland, lazy, inactive, and slow" (4: 277). Aesthetics and character are linked to the shape of the nose. Indeed, Charles de Secondat, baron de Montesquieu (1689–1755), in *The Spirit of Laws* (1748), even weighs the appearance of the black as a justification for slavery.[5] In addition to the environmental explanation of the form of the black nose offered by Buffon and Kant, it also represents leprosy or yaws, powerfully associated in European fantasy with the "tropics" and interchangeable with the idea and image of syphilis.[6]

The Jewish Nose

The meaning read into the African's nose became interchangeable with that seen in the Jew's nose.[7] The noses of the African and the Jew were equally ugly because the Jew's physiognomy was understood to be closer to that of the African than to that of the European. Johann Caspar Lavater quoted the Storm and Stress poet J. M. R. Lenz (1751–92) to the effect that: "It is evident to me that the Jews bear the sign of their fatherland, the orient, throughout the world. I mean their short, black, curly hair, their brown skin color. Their rapid speech, their brusque and precipitous actions also come from this source. I believe that the Jews have more gall than other people."[8] The character ascribed to the Jews is written on their skin. The Jews are black "Orientals." They bear the sign of the black, "the African character of the Jew, his muzzle-shaped mouth and face removing him from certain other races," as Robert Knox (1791–1862) noted in the mid nineteenth century.[9]

Camper also saw the physiognomy of the Jew as immutable: "There is no nation that is as clearly identifiable as the Jews: men, women, children, even when they are first born, bear the sign of their origin. I have often spoken about this with the famed painter of historical subjects [Benjamin] West, to whom I mentioned my difficulty in capturing the national essence of the Jews. He was of the opinion that this must be sought in the curvature of the nose."[10] The nose defines the Jewish face and links it to the African face. The African nose and the Jewish nose became abstract "racial" signs of the character and temperament ascribed to the Jew and the African.

The assumption of the Jews' close racial relationship to or intermixing with blacks becomes a commonplace of nineteenth-century ethnology. Both non-Jewish and Jewish anthropologists of the fin de siècle write of the "predominant mouth of some Jews being the result of the presence of black blood" and the "brown skin, thick lips and prognathism" of the Jew.[11] It is not only skin color that enables the scientist to label the Jew as "black," but also the associated anatomical signs, such as the shape of the nose. The Jews were quite literally seen as black. Adam Gurowski (1805–66), a Polish count, "took every light-colored mulatto for a Jew" when he first arrived in the United States in the 1850s.[12] One of the central texts of the French Enlightenment, the *Encyclopedia* of Denis Diderot (1713–84) and Jean Le Rond d'Alembert (1717–83), argues against this source of the inherent difference in body and character of the black. The article on the "nose" contends that "most of the anatomists claim that this flatness comes from art and not from nature." Here the Encyclopedists place all of the deviant noses together: "the blacks, the Hottentots, and various peoples of Asia such as the Jews." Swaddling creates the flattened nose of the black, and the black is therefore no different from the European norm of beauty in his "natural" state.[13] The original nose, the normal nose, the healthy nose is that of the European, which may be altered through cultural interventions, but remains a sign of the universality of all human beings. This is quite different from the racial argument made in the German Enlightenment about the shape of the African nose. An echo of the Encyclopedists' argument surfaces a century later when Charles Darwin commented that the "Negroes rallied Mungo Park [the British explorer] on the whiteness of his skin and the prominence of his nose, both of which they considered as 'unsightly and unnatural' conformations."[14] Darwin sees the response of the Africans as a natural one—to them, the British nose is as ugly and pathological as the African nose is to the British. The beautiful nose is specific to the culture in which one lives. Darwin's comment ironically links nose form and skin color as comic signs when they are articulated from the standpoint of the African. The nose becomes the site for such pseudo-scientific argument on both sides of the border of racial and cultural difference. This is indicative of some of the complex associations of the image of the sunken nose.

The nose comes to signify all that is static and immutable about the African and the Jew, whether natural or cultural. In 1926 the British novelist Robert Hichens (1864–1950) allowed one of his characters to recognize the Jew by his or her nose. "'You're right. He is a Jew. Directly I was able to look really at him, to examine his face, I knew it. Not the hook-nosed Jew—the other type, the blunt-featured type.'"[15] The flat-nosed Jew reappears in numerous guises, but always as the exemplar of capital. Thus Meyer Wolfshiem, in F. Scott Fitzgerald's (1896–1940) *Great Gatsby* (1925), is described as "a small flat-nosed Jew [who] raised his large head and regarded me with two fine growths of hair, which luxuriated in either nostril. After a moment I discovered his tiny eyes in the half darkness." His nose is described as "expressive" and "tragic," capable of "flashing indignantly."[16] For ornament he wears human teeth as cufflinks, and he reduces everyone he sees to a similar commodity.

The German anthropologist Hans Günther (1891–1968) explained the competition between the "black Jews" and the "white Jews" as that of the blunt noses against the long noses. One of the sociologist Frances Macgregor's (1906–) American Jewish informants in the 1960s claimed that he wanted to show the Gentiles through his rhinoplasty that "there are nice Jews. I'll be a good-will ambassador. I can prove to people that I'm not only a 'white man' but a 'white Jew.'"[17] As we shall see, rhinoplasty in the twentieth century enabled Jews to imagine themselves as "passing" for "white." Here the model of the Jews as a mixed race is internalized as a quality of Jewish character. Becoming a "white Jew" is a psychic response to the image of the Jew in various aspects of the collective culture.[18]

Irish Noses

In the 1880s, John Orlando Roe (1849–1915) in Rochester, New York, performed an operation to "cure" the "pug nose."[19] The too-small nose he corrected was not the syphilitic nose; rather, he intervened to create new American noses out of the noses of Irish immigrants. Their new noses did not mask the sexual sins of their parents, but the fact that their parents came from elsewhere, in the case of the pug nose, from

Ireland. Roe's innovation was not only to transform his patients from "Irish" into "Americans" but also to do so without the telltale scars that revealed the work of surgeons repairing or replacing syphilitic noses. They were no longer marked in terms of contemporary racial science as "Celts" but could truly "pass" as "Anglo-Saxons."

Aesthetic surgery of the nose as practiced by surgeons such as Johann Friedrich Dieffenbach before the introduction of anesthesia and antisepsis left scars and placed patients' lives at risk because of the dangers of shock and infection. With the introduction of antisepsis and anesthesia, the scar itself remained the major "danger" for patients.[20] Scars showed that a medical intervention had taken place, and what patients came to fear most was having an operation which revealed that they had had one. The vital difference in Roe's procedure was that he operated from within the nostrils, leaving no visible scar on the skin. This powerful innovation was to change the course of aesthetic surgery. Not only was his surgical procedure innovative in the United States, but so too was the nose on which he operated.

Roe provides us with substantial information about his theory of appearance and its meaning. Based on the profile, Roe divided the image of the nose into five categories: Roman, Greek, Jewish, Snub or Pug, and Celestial. Each type of nose indicated qualities of character, following Samuel Wells's (1820–75) phrenological/physiognomic theories: "The Roman indicates executiveness or strength; the Greek, refinement; the Jewish, commercialism or desire of gain; the Snub or Pug, weakness and lack of development; the Celestial, weakness, lack of development, and inquisitiveness." For Roe, the "snub-nose" is "proof of a degeneracy of the human race." Remarkably, he finds his rationale for this in *Tristram Shandy,* which he quotes on the problem of a "succession of short noses" in a family. Roe notes that Shandy's grandfather had little choice in his mate "owing to the brevity of his nose." Roe sees this as a sign of congenital pathology that must ultimately be racially based (as it is in many ways in Sterne's novel, too). The short nose announces the degenerate race.

Roe's sense of himself as an artist (as well as a physician) can be noted in a comment made in 1905. "In the correction of all facial defects the surgeon must be not only an artist but also more or less of a sculptor, with perception of symmetry as related to the different features."[21] Symmetry and balance are concepts of the "norm" as opposed to asymmetry, which is both "ugly" and "dangerous." Charles Bell (1774–1842), the author of the classic nineteenth-century anatomical handbook for artists and one of the great surgeons of his day, shared the "prevailing opinion that beauty of countenance consists in the capacity of expression, and in the harmony of features consenting to expression."[22] Harmony is the norm, which is disrupted by the too-small nose. Symmetry is the ideal that dominates the meaning of the healthy, beautiful face in the nineteenth century and is the wellspring of the normative ideals, which the too-small nose violated. Harmony and symmetry express the universal perfection of the human countenance. All variation from an idealized norm is thus given moral meaning. (In the course of the late nineteenth century, James Shaw among others discovered that all adult faces are asymmetrical.)[23]

But Roe was not only curing the "pug nose," he was also curing the psyche. His understanding of the relationship between mind and body was clear: "We are able to relieve patients of a condition which would remain a lifelong mark of disfigurement, constantly observed, forming a never ceasing source of embarrassment and mental distress to themselves, amounting, in many cases, to a positive torture, as well as often causing them to be objects of greater or lesser aversion to others. . . . The effect upon the mind of such physical defects is readily seen reflected in the face, which invariably conforms to the mental attitude, and leads after a time to a permanent distortion of the countenance."[24] This is very much in tune with Samuel Wells's basic understanding of physiognomy. If one can cure the anomaly, the attendant changes in physiognomy that represent psychological damage can be ameliorated. If you don't look different, you will act better and be happier. And that, in turn, will be reflected in your appearance.

What does the "pug nose" come to represent for Roe, and what sort of better and happier person would not have a "pug nose"? In the context of late nineteenth-century American physiognomy and popular caricatures, it is the Irish profile that is characterized by the snub-nose.[25] The racial anthropologists of the 1880s saw the Irish as derived directly from the big-eared Cro-Magnon man with a "nose, oftener concave than straight . . . [which is] a characteristic of the modern Gaels."[26] Irish character is "bad" character. "Though the head is large, the intelligence is low, and there is a great deal of cunning and suspicion." This is written on the face of "Bridget McBruiser" for all to see. She is contrasted in the physiognomies of the day with Florence Nightingale's "English" beauty (and moral value). The Irish physiognomy is servile, marking the Irish through animal analogies as doglike, which is why the nose itself was labeled "pug." The ultimate origin of this Irish type cannot be Ireland but Africa: "While Ireland is apparently its present centre, most of its lineaments are such as to lead us to think of Africa as its possible birthplace." The Irish nose is the African nose is the Jewish nose. All such noses represent difference and are alike.

The "pug" nose defined the Irish as "black" in the racial climate of the United States.[27] This was not a social term—such as that distinguishing between the "black" (lower-class) and "lace curtain" (upper-class) groups of Irish immigrants. It is interesting, though, that the "lace curtain" Irish took this racial designation to distinguish themselves from the "dirty " Irish. Through projective identification they attempted to place themselves on the level of the aggressors and their long English noses. This idea of the blackness of the Irish did not originate as an American phenomenon. The notion of the Irish as a "black" race came from the vocabulary with which the English denigrated the Irish.[28] The constant and intense association of the Irish in Ireland and England with disease (especially diseases associated in the popular mind with dirt and sexuality) came to be defined in terms of the too-short nose. In England this was contrasted with the English nose; in the United States, with the German nose.[29] Such readings of Irish physiognomy lent power to the desire not to look Irish and to become (in)visible as English or German.

To cure the "pug" nose meant making the individual (in)visible, to allow the unregenerated "Celt" to "pass" as American. For, as Samuel Wells had commented in the 1870s, the Americanization of the Irish had caused a transformation of their character as well as their bodies: "As proof of the fact that cultivation and external influences modify configuration, look at the Americanized Celts—the Irish-Americans. The first generation born in this country shows some of the finest faces we have among us. Causes of 'arrested development' become more and more rare. Even those born and brought up in Ireland often show a decided improvement in their physiognomy after having been here a few years."[30] The modification of external signs of degeneration ("arrested development") is the goal of the surgeon. Roe's interventions were to be understood as forms of aesthetic surgery: "mainly to improve the personal appearance of the individual." Roe made better Americans by making the Irish (and the syphilitic) look "American." By eliminating the scarring that attended cutting through the skin and by operating subcutaneously, from within the nasal passages, Roe made his new Americans (in)visible.

Roe later commented that the earlier operations resulted in "exchanging a deformity for an unsightly blemish" (p.131). In an age of "passing" novels, such as Mark Twain's (1835–1910) *Pudd'nhead Wilson* (1894), a genre in which mixed-race individuals were "seen" as a social problem, the ability to "pass" as "normal" came to be a function enhanced by the cosmetician or aesthetic surgeon. Often it was the use of skin lighteners or surgery that enabled one to cross the color bar or to believe that one could cross the constructed boundary between "white" and "black." But in the fantasy of the time it was believed that such acts of "passing" were "natural" and not aided by external forces.[31] The puzzle at the heart of Twain's liberal text hinges on the ability of a light-skinned slave to exchange her child for the child of the house without there being any possibility of distinguishing between them. Neither skin color nor nose betrays the swapped children, and the master's son is raised as the slave of the slave's son. But there is, of course, a way of distinguishing the two—Twain has his eponymous hero collect fingerprints, and since each human being has different fingerprints, the confusion can be sorted out and the guilty punished. It is not the Bertillon measures of appearance but the unique qualities of Francis Galton's simultaneous discovery of fingerprints that makes people identifiable—not as members of a class but only as individuals. Part of the fantasy of the culture of segregation in the United States was that skin color alone defined race, as the African-American commentator Walter White fantasized in 1949: "Suppose the skin of every Negro in America was suddenly turned to white. . . . Would not Negroes then be judged individually on their ability, energy, honesty, cleanliness as are whites?"[32] The answer was, at least in 1949, only if they have nose jobs.

Roe's procedures made it possible to be an "American" without any "blemish." Roe's procedure turned the Irish nose into "a thing of beauty."[33] Indeed, his patients began to look like their American surgeon! With the establishment of "beauty" the patient's happiness was restored. Looking Irish was one further category of difference that was written on the body and signified a poor character and bad temperament.

In contemporary Eire there has been a continued use of aesthetic surgery to remedy "Irishness." Not rhinoplasty but the ear pin-back is the operation of choice. Michael Earley, an aesthetic surgeon based in Temple Street Hospital, Dublin, says he treats a number of children for "what is called bat ears here, or Football Association Cup ears in England, [which] is a Celtic feature which some children get badly teased about."[34] This is also a permanent part of the Victorian representation of the "jug-eared Irish."[35] It is not surprising that it has maintained its importance in Ireland, while losing it in the United States, where the Irish became "white." Although "the removal of tattoos would not be considered medically necessary, for instance," and most aesthetic surgery is not covered by the Department of Health, "things like bat ears would be done on the medical card."[36] The other common procedure that is covered on the "health card" is breast reduction. As we shall see later, the very notion of breast reduction as aesthetic surgery comes about from the model of the racialized or "primitive" breast. Young women with large breasts are seen to be unhappy for reasons other than physical ones, as one prestigious Irish surgeon noted: "It can also be awkward for them to wear fashionable clothes or mix socially."[37] One can make people happy by reducing their breast size and correcting the visibility of their ears. In this way, they become less "Irish" and more "beautiful."

Between the writing of *Little Women* in the 1860s and Roe's development of his means of curing the unhappiness attendant on the pug nose comes the introduction of antisepsis and anesthesia. It is during this period that the movement of Amy's un-happiness to the operating room took place. This moment defines the differences be-tween reconstructive and aesthetic surgery.

Thus the general question of how our society strives to "make the body beautiful" during the period from the close of the nineteenth century to our own fin de siécle is in large measure the story of how we turn to medicine to make us over and make us "happy" with our new faces and bodies. The general thesis of aesthetic surgery is that the conflict between the desire to be seen as "beautiful" or "handsome" and the dif-ficulty in achieving that end leads to a general unhappiness with one's own body. The desired beauty has a moral dimension, for the beautiful is the good. If you under-stand your body as "ugly," you are bound to be "unhappy" with your bad character. In Western society, "unhappiness" with one's body comes to be understood as a form of mental illness. In its most radical form, it can be seen in the actions of psychot-ics who compulsively mutilate their bodies; another, milder form is the desire aes-thetically to alter the body. Psychotics find themselves under the care of psychiatrists; those unhappy enough with specific aspects of their bodies seek help from aesthetic surgeons. Both the psychiatrists and the surgeons have, however, the same goals in their treatment—the amelioration of psychic "unhappiness" and the restoration (or creation) of a "happy" individual.

"Oriental" Noses—and Eyes

Ethnic difference among groups that are perceived as "ugly" and of "poor character" remains unacceptable even in a multiethnic society. One can look different, but not too different. Thus Asian-American men have been "stereotyped as being short peo-ple with flat faces and slanted eyes." To remedy this perception, some of them seek aesthetic surgery in order to "appear 'less Asian' and in the extreme to appear 'more Caucasian,'" and, one might add, to appear more erotic, as Asian men are generally imagined to be unerotic in American society. The most commonly sought aesthetic procedures, which are thought to accomplish this, are nose jobs (rhinoplasty) and eyelid surgery (blepharoplasty).[38] Asian-American women, whose "blank" look is equated in American society with "dullness, passivity, and lack of emotion," have "their eyelids restructured, their nose bridges heightened, and the tips of their noses altered."[39] (One might add that the reading of the Jewish eyelid in the early twentieth century was that it gave the Jewish face "often the expression of one who is tired, sleepy, relaxed, threatening." Therefore the Jewish glance was also seen as "conspiratorial.")[40] The shrunken nose coupled with the revealing eye take on yet other meanings as a sign of difference and visibility.

In ancient China, as in Pharonic Egypt and classical Greece, there are early records, such as the bone oracles (1334 B.C.E.), which mention "illnesses of the nose."[41] The physician Bian Qiu (407–310 B.C.E.) wrote texts in which he described how he treated the ears and eyes of patients. Likewise the physician Hua Tuo (110–207 C.E.) documented his treatment of the eyes and ears. The traditional Chinese prohibition against opening the body limited all forms of surgical intervention until fairly recently. It is only in the northern T'ang and Gin dynasty in the late 900s C.E. that medical texts begin to record the reconstructive surgery of the harelip. Aesthetic surgery is a development of "modern" China, and "modern" China can be defined as the world where Western and traditional models of treatment clash.[42] There "modern" medicine is in many ways Western medicine with a traditional inflection. As in Japan, which replaced traditional Chinese medicine *(kanpo)* with Western medicine at the end of the nineteenth century, aesthetic surgery of the eye and nose became one of the markers of the modern and the new in medicine.

In Japan as early as 1896, under the domination of Western medicine, K. Mikamo introduced a nonincision procedure to create a double eyelid, mimicking that of the Western eye.[43] His procedure was developed to create symmetry in a patient who had a single double eyelid. Its impetus was "reconstructive," though evidently its import and influence were aesthetic. From 1896 to the present, some thirty-two different procedures were developed in Japan for purely aesthetic surgery of the eyelid. The desire, well before the defeat of Japan in 1945 and the occupation of the country by the Americans, was "to have a well-defined nose; a clear-cut, double eyelid fold; and larger, more attractive breasts."

One must add that plastic surgery was recognized as a medical subspecialty in Japan only in 1975, and aesthetic surgery only in 1978. All of these procedures existed on the boundaries of official medical practice.[44] This was quite similar to the situation of aesthetic surgeons in Europe and North America. The procedures to alter the look of the eye did not change the total image of the Japanese visage. During this period the ideal form of the face as captured in Japanese traditional portraiture shifted. Traditional portraiture had emphasized the "straight eyes and nose, flat, single eyelids, and receding chin."[45] There are specific meanings associated with the "Oriental" eye and nose in binary opposition to that of the "Occidental" eye and nose. The rather wide variations in the "Japanese" visage, running from the ethnic "Japanese" to the Ainu, was evidently idealized as a pan-Japanese face in traditional portraiture. Japanese physician/anthropologists, such as Yoshikiyo Koganei (1858–1944), the head of anatomy at the Tokyo Medical School at the end of the nineteenth century, were obsessed with distinguishing "real" Japanese faces from those of the "primitive" Ainu.[46] Central to their concern were the long noses and round eyes of the Ainu (features that had virtually vanished through intermarriage by the late nineteenth century). They needed to construct the Ainu's "primitive" visage as "different" from that of the Japanese.

The emphasis on the special nature of the Japanese (and also the Chinese) face rests on the dominant theories of physiognomy that defined health and beauty in terms of the face. Charles Darwin commented that the

> obliquity of the eye, which is proper to the Chinese and Japanese, is exaggerated in their pictures for the purpose, as it seems, of exhibiting its beauty, as contrasted "with the eye of the red-haired barbarians." It is well known, as Hue repeatedly remarks, that the Chinese of the interior think Europeans hideous, with their white skins and prominent noses. The nose is far from being too prominent, according to our ideas, in the natives of Ceylon; yet Chinese in the seventh century, accustomed to the flat features of the Mongol races, were surprised at the prominent noses of the Cingalese.[47]

While "Western" scientific medicine was determining the "true" nature of the "Japanese" visage, Western surgical techniques were making that visage not *too* Japanese. In 1923 Nishihata and Yoshida presented the first study of augmentation rhinoplasty using ivory implants to alter the shape of the Japanese "sunken" nose.[48] Indeed, as traditional, nonsurgical medicine was transformed into a subordinate form of Western medicine in Meiji Japan, surgery of the eyelid and nose became commonplace signs of the advantages of Western clinical practice. The constitution of a new aesthetic ideal, that of Western art representing the Western face, meant the alteration of the eyelids in order to add the superior palpebral fold between the eyelid and brow (which is absent or indistinct in about half the population of Asia) and the introduction of augmentation rhinoplasty, innovations that radically change the morphological characteristics of the "Japanese" face. Following the lines of the Chinese creation of a unified "'Han' racial typology in the course of the nineteenth century, the Japanese created and then reconstituted idealized faces and bodies."[49]

However, it was also believed that such aesthetic surgery had quite different meanings when applied to men than it did when applied to women. The belief was that aesthetic surgery could help enhance a man's masculinity by making him a better soldier. The American surgeon Henry Junius Schireson wrote in the late 1930s that

> the effect of this [shape of the eyelid] is not only esthetically unpleasant; it is also a definite impediment to good vision. That is why the Japanese are reputedly such poor marksmen, why this highly intelligent race has so high a percentage of airplane crashes. Japanese women were the first to seek correction of this defect, for esthetic reasons. Today in military Japan the functional objective is the moving motive and thousands of Japanese men are having this correction made. . . . It is estimated that more than twenty thousand persons . . . have recently undergone this operation.[50]

The claim that the eyelid form has a negative impact on sight is nonsense, but it was evidently believed that aesthetic surgery would make more efficient soldiers and more beautiful women.

The introduction of aesthetic surgery was likewise in Japan an attempt to cure unhappiness, *jibyo,* that amorphous sense of being unwell that haunts the Japanese medical world.[51] The traditional conception of the individual in *kanpo* (traditional) Japanese medicine was one who possessed *taishitsu,* an inborn constitution. Certain constitutions manifested various forms of *jibyo.* Can one alter one's *taishitsu?* Certainly one can intervene through tonics and medicines, but changing one's constitution through aesthetic surgery became possible only when another model, that of Westernized medicine, superseded the traditional categories of *kanpo* medicine after the Meiji Restoration of 1868. Unable to open the body, traditional medicine was relegated to second-class status with the Medical Act of 1874, which demanded that all new physicians be trained in Western medicine.[52] Western medicine and surgery were given privileged status to alter and open the body and its *taishitsu.*

Following World War II and the American occupation of Japan, a resurgence of interest in creating "Western" eyes and bodies in Japan led to further developments of such procedures as well as breast augmentation using silicone injections.[53] This responded to the introduction of the Western notion of the larger breast as a sign of the erotic. Traditional Chinese and Japanese portrayals of the female breast, even such as in Kitagawa Utarnaro's nineteenth-century images of nursing mothers, stress the flat-chested look, which "carried the implication that a woman should be modest in her appearance."[54] As late as 1952 paraffin injections, and then silicone injections in 1958, were used for breast augmentation, with devastating results. Akiyama actually produced a silicone breast prosthesis as early as 1949.[55]

In today's Japan the explosion of interest in aesthetic surgery is related closely to the argument about whether aesthetic surgery can indeed create "happiness" in banishing the negative *jibyo.* As elsewhere in Asia, the search is not limited to the world of authorized medicine. Thus there are now "aesthetic salons [that] cater to Japanese women seeking a new look, a new face or a new body. . . . Yet unlike in the past, women who pay for services at these controversial places are not afraid to talk about it if only anonymously. Most seem to believe that cosmetic surgery will open career doors and put a sparkle into their social life."[56] One case report can suffice:

One 22-year-old woman, who asked to be identified only as Mariko, said she had cosmetic surgery six months ago to widen her eyes, lift her nose and chin, and slim her cheeks. She explained that since she was a teenager, she had 'hated' her own face and had been working to save money for cosmetic surgery. She put ¥1 million toward the ¥1.5 million operation and is paying off the rest in installments. Her decision to go under the knife was also prompted partly by a desire to land a job as a receptionist, and she thought having better looks would improve her chances. After the operation, she promptly got a job. A photograph of her before surgery showed a different woman, at least from the chin up. Some friends complimented her on her new look, but others pointed out the inevitable: beneath the surface, she had not changed. Her father, she claims, did not even notice that she had had surgery.

But are such patients really happy? Can you really change your *taishitsu*?

Dr. Ichiro Kamoshita, a physician who is the director of the Hibiya Kokusai Clinic, believes that women patients "are being duped by cosmetic surgery and aesthetic salon advertising that appeals to a woman's inferiority complex about her looks. Many women believe that if they improve their looks their personal relations with other people will also improve. . . . They are seeking a sense of social achievement while wishing to be lovely as a woman." Nachiko Morikawa, director of another medical clinic, noted that "they don't have a clear vision of what happiness is." The skeptical attitude of the medical profession mirrors a generation shift of attitude toward aesthetic surgery in Japan.

The changes are mirrored to a great extent in not only cultural presuppositions but in the new gender politics.[57] The ongoing popularity of aesthetic surgery in Japan has led "an increasing number of Japanese mothers [to] take their straight-A 15-year-old daughters to a cosmetic surgeon."[58] There is now a pattern of presenting procedures as gifts from parents to children, especially those seen to be "hindered by small eyes, a flat nose or a big face." In April and May, at the beginning of the school year, there is a run on aesthetic surgery for teenagers. "It was just amazing to see this many young girls at my clinic all of a sudden. I felt there was something funny going on around mid-March, so I asked my assistant to go through the files. The number [of customers], by the end of the month, had tripled [in 1997] compared with the previous year," said Fumihiko Umezawa, president of Jujin Hospital and chair of the International Cosmetic Surgery Association. "And what surprised me even more was the fact that they were the graduates of those prestigious top-ranking junior-high schools. They weren't girls dreaming of becoming a TV star or a magazine model. They were serious, innocent-looking girls with their mothers." The mother of a fifteen-year-old girl told the weekly magazine *Focus*: "Well I did feel psychological resistance [in myself], but she really wanted it and I couldn't tell her no. After all, pretty women have a better time in this world, don't they? I asked my husband to stop smoking to cover the amount necessary for her operation."[59] The daughter, on the other hand, insists that such operations are nothing special for her generation. "It's like piercing your ears. Everyone is doing it now. I cannot understand why some people make a big fuss out of it." The actual number of patients is relatively large. Forty-five fifteen-year-olds came to Jujin in March 1997, compared to fifteen in March 1996. And twenty-nine girls were treated during the holiday week in May, but there was a waiting list of an additional eighty-one. The assumption of vanity as the basis for desiring procedures is still present in Japanese medicine, but the patients are now understanding such procedures as truly "cosmetic" and not a sign of class identity.[60]

Body imagery follows the lines of political and cultural power. In Vietnam, after the American withdrawal and the reunification of the country, a detailed physiognomic study determined the relative facial dimensions of the Vietnamese so as to provide an adequate, non-Westernizing model for the relationship among the features, including the form and shape of the eyes, for aesthetic surgeons.[61] This was clearly in response to the explosion in aesthetic surgery, which remade the faces and breasts of the young women of Vietnam into "Western" faces and bodies. Although there was a lively aesthetic surgery industry in Saigon until 1975, it virtually vanished after the end of the war.

In contemporary Vietnam, the function of aesthetic surgery has become "normalized." Indeed, reports from Hanoi claim that even the criminals undergo aesthetic surgery.[62] The nose and the eye remain at the center of concern with the reconstitution of the face in today's Vietnam. "It is the opposite of the Europeans," Nguyen Huy Phan, one of the leading aesthetic surgeons in Hanoi stated to an interviewer. "Here plastic surgery increases the size of the nose, Europeanizing it. We make a superior double eyelid, with a groove, to give a livelier appearance and to awaken the glance."[63] The costs of such procedures are quite low. To have a nose rebuilt in Hanoi costs about one hundred dollars, "Westernizing" the eyelids, forty dollars. Such procedures, however, do not assure successful transformation of the psyche. "We only operate when it's reasonable, otherwise we have to send them to the psychiatrist," Nguyen Huy Phan said. Today in Ho Chi Minh City (formerly Saigon) there are a dozen mini-dirties, sometimes masquerading as barber shops and staffed by lay surgeons. Their patrons are most often men. Clinic owners say that the most popular operations are for the nose, the chin, the eyes, and the buttocks. One man even asked surgeons to bulk up his chest, which he believed would make him more attractive to women. A popular operation in southern Vietnam, too, is to have the eyes widened by creating the Western eyelid (the superior palpebral fold). Such procedures are especially popular with male stage performers. Nguyen Thu Huong, who owns one of the "beauty salons," claimed that 80 percent of the young performers of a popular drama style known as "cai luong" and some singers have paid her a visit for Westernizing procedures.[64]

The function aesthetic surgery serves as a marker of the shift to a market economy, with its claims of individual autonomy (as opposed to state control), can also be measured in the People's Republic of China with the liberalization after the death of Mao Tsetung. Ruyao Song, president of the Chinese Plastic Surgery Society, noted in 1994 that "altering eyelids is the most popular cosmetic surgery practiced at [my] Institute of Plastic Surgery in Peking, which with 400 beds is among the largest plastic surgery hospitals in the world."[65] The explosion of interest in aesthetic surgery in the People's Republic is to no little degree a sign of the increasing affluence of the general population. It has fueled an explosion of "beauty parlors [that] offer cheap cosmetic surgery promising miraculous outcomes but often mutilating their customers."[66] Ten cosmetic surgery parlors were set up in Shanghai in the early months of 1996, but when eight hundred beauty parlors opened within one year in Sichuan province's capital city, Chengdu, the municipality began to try to regulate them after numerous patient complaints.[67] In the southeastern city of Shenzhen, a "quack" named Hu Jinsong performed breast augmentation surgery in 1995 and 1996.[68] According to his account, he used a "sophisticated and top-quality" procedure, which removed body fat by liposuction and injected it into the breasts. This was supposed to reduce obesity while enhancing breast size. "The operation is simple," the ads said. "There is no hospitalization or scars and the surgery does not affect normal life and work afterwards." His patients wound up hospitalized when the procedures went horribly awry. Hu had gone to university but had no medical credentials. The most popular aesthetic surgical procedures in these new dirties are the "double-eyelid operation" and nose-bridge surgery, in which a bone graft is shaved from a patient's hip or rib to augment the existing nose. Unlike at the Institute of Plastic Surgery, aesthetic surgery in these establishments is undertaken by marginally qualified or unqualified practitioners. Even though recently China's cabinet-level State Council has put beauty parlors under the management of public health departments, abuses continue to mount. Local hospitals also participate in the beauty business, and hospital beauty centers do not need to even register with local industry and commerce administrative departments. Aesthetic surgical procedures to modify the "Chinese" eye had been widely carried out elsewhere among Chinese communities in Asia. Khoo Boo-Chai is the Singaporean surgeon who developed the modern double eyelid modification about forty years ago in the midst of the American occupation of Japan and the Korean War. He stitched along the eyelid to create a fine line of scars, which provided the appearance of a supratarsal fold. He wrote in 1963, "Our Eastern sisters put on Western apparel, use Western make-up, see Western movies and read Western literature. Nowadays, there even exists a demand for the face and especially the eyes to be Westernized."[69] The specific reason for such aesthetic surgical procedures was the ability to increase one's income or marriageability by looking more Western and thus to ensure "personal happiness."[70]

The "Asian" development of aesthetic surgery as a sign of the modern is paralleled by the focus on the alteration of the body among the new immigrants labeled by American census law as "Asian Americans." Thus, Vietnamese in the United States show a similar fascination with the newest and latest developments in aesthetic surgery. The fascination with skin lightening, nose lengthening, and eye reshaping in Japan and Vietnam today reflects the globalization of standards of beauty rooted in Euro-American stereotypes. In the case of the youth of Japan and Vietnam, the ideal is not to be "too Asian." In the United States, this desire is more directly shaped by the notion of fitting into a niche of an acceptable "American" physiognomy. As with many of the "ethnic"-specific procedures, they are undertaken by ethnic, here Vietnamese-American, surgeons. One such case, in the large Vietnamese-American community in Houston, has now made it to the courts.[71] The forty-eight-year-old Chau Truong claimed that Ho Tan Phuoc's insertion of a plastic nasal bridge caused massive infections and scarring. Her goal was to look like Dr. Phuoc's wife, "with her Vietnamese slenderness, Anglo features, and miraculously round breasts," whose image graced the Phuocs' large ad in a Vietnamese-language newspaper. "The thought of a Vietnamese-speaking doctor encouraged her. Even more alluring, there was a photo of Victoria Phuoc, bounteous in a tight pearl-colored gown, wide eyes glowing over a razor-straight, divinely symmetrical nose." The result of the surgery was the opposite: massive infection and, when the implant was removed, "a grisly, vertical dent in its place." This case and others have become the focus of debates about the politics of the Vietnamese-American community more than about medical malpractice, yet it is not accidental that keyed to a politics of appearance all of this remains linked to the ability to "pass" as not *too* Vietnamese.

A parallel development can be found in the Republic of Korea (South Korea), which has the largest single group (430) of aesthetic surgeons to be found in Asia in the 1990s.[72] The alterations of the nose and eyelid have become a major source of income for the physicians of the new economies of Asia. With the movement of Korea onto the global stage during the 1980s, the globalization of Korean advertising brought images of the Western face into the culture as part of the new middle-class ideal. In the United States, Korean Americans, like other groups of new immigrants, began to offer eyelid surgery to their teenage children "to make their eyes look 'more American.'"[73] Such ideals seem less present in Korea (or Vietnam or Japan) among the middle class. There, aesthetic surgery is a sign of middle-class rather than "American" identity, though one could argue that there is a fatal parallelism between these two ideas of imagining oneself as different. Thus, among Asian Americans in California, double-eyelid surgery has become "the gift that parents offer their daughters when they graduate from high school or college."[74] This parallels the experience of Jewish Americans in the 1960s. For the Vietnamese and Koreans in America, aesthetic surgery becomes a means of defining the flexibility of identity as opposed to its permanence.

The most striking recent literary representation of the anxiety about the composite "Asian" body in an American context is to be found in Gish Jen's novel *Mona in the Promised Land* (1996).[75] Jen ironically comments on the American construction of a "pan-Asian" body out of the varied and "different" bodies present in China and Japan. But this is possible only because the inherent comparison in the novel reflects on the function of aesthetic surgery in the acculturation of "Jews" and "Asians." Set in suburban Scarsdale in 1968, the novel chronicles the adolescence of a Chinese-American woman whose family moves into a "Jewish" neighborhood in its quest for upward social mobility. The protagonist identifies strongly with the Jews in her peer group and sees her body in terms of their anxiety about their own physical visibility. One day she and her friends sit around and discuss aesthetic surgery. "'Do Chinese have operations to make their noses bigger?' someone asks" (p. 92). Yes, Mona replies: "She too envies the aquiline line . . . in fact she envies even their preoperative noses. . . . 'You can't mean like this schnozz here?' somebody says, exhibiting his profile. . . . She nods politely. 'And your eyes too.'" She continues to explain about "operations to make singlefold eyelids into double-folds." In the course of this discussion, Gish Jen supplies an ironic environmental explanation of how and why "Oriental" eyes have their specific form, but concludes with one of the Jewish boys commenting about Mona's eyes, "You look like straight out of the Twilight Zone" (p. 93). The exoticism of the "too-small" nose and the "too-Oriental" eyes for the Jews is a clear marker of their sense of their own difference.

It is no surprise in this world as seen from Gish Jen's perspective that it is not Mona who gets the new nose or Western eyes: "Barbara Gugelstein is sporting a fine new nose. Straight, this is, and most diminutive, not to say painstakingly fashioned as a baby-grand tchotchke" (p. 124). Although Mona "admires her friend's nostrils, which are a triumph of judiciousness and taste," she herself is not moved to have aesthetic surgery. What Mona does is to convert to Judaism. But becoming a Jew in religion but not physicality, as one of the African-American characters disparagingly comments, is difficult in her world. For in order to be a "real" Jew "that nose of yours has got to grow out so big you've got to sneeze in a dish towel" (p. 137). Jewishness means belonging to a visible outsider group. For Mona this has become an insider group, which defines her sense of her own body. The role of aesthetic surgery is to reshape the external visibility of that group. Yet, as the novel shows, it is a sign of false acculturation. Barbara's nose job is faulty; it "runs extraordinarily when she cries" (p. 237). Jews with short noses remain marked as Jews in this seemingly hostile world, and the Chinese, such as Mona's physician-sister, acculturate with the rise of multiculturalism by becoming "Asian-American," a form of the alteration of identity without the alteration of the body. Happiness is becoming something else, something identifiable as "Asian" that is not too "Chinese." It is fitting in—and having a nose that enables you to do so. In the fictional world representing the imaginary body of the American Jew, the retroussé "Oriental" nose comes to be an ideal. But for the Chinese American, according to Gish Jen's portrait, it is a sign of the new "Asian" identity. One nose *does* fit all.

Black into White

Disguising of the African nose becomes a concern of American aesthetic surgeons at the close of the nineteenth century. Black was not beautiful, and those whose skin was light enough to "pass" often attempted to do so. In the United States, there was an explosion of hair straightening and skin lightening among African Americans at the beginning of the twentieth century. The drive to look less black put cosmetology, but not necessarily aesthetic surgery, at the command of those who desired to acquire happiness by approximating a "white" appearance. The cosmetologist Madame C. J.Walker (1867–1919), with her hair straighteners and skin lighteners, became the first African-American millionaire.[76] (Today in Hong Kong and Taiwan, aesthetic surgeons undertake skin lightening using methods similar to Madame Walker's.) The gradual introduction of procedures to enable individuals to "pass" as white came to play a role in the shaping of aesthetic surgery. At the end of the twentieth century, it is no longer the intent to be (in)visible but rather not to be too visible—one should not look too black or too ethnic (however that is defined).[77] Here one can apply Werner Sollors's view that self-avowed ethnic identity in the United States became possible only with acculturation.[78] Once the stigma of ethnic identity (however defined) was removed from a group, that group could begin to think of itself as ethnically distinct, but not too distinct.

Anxiety about changing the shape of the nose was rooted in notions of the permanence of racial markers. In early-twentieth-century discussions of "mixed races," it was often the "impure" physiognomy that gave a clue to the decline of the pure races through miscegenation. Thus M. L. Ettler commented in 1904 that the "lack of physical beauty in Central Europe has its roots in unnecessary racial mixing."[79] This can be seen in "disharmonies of various types" such as a "long face with a short nose."

He demands "psychical and aesthetic racial selection." For racial selection is also the perpetuation of "good" character and "appropriate" noses. In the United States and in Germany, where "racial mixing" had resulted in "mixed-race" individuals with perceived qualities of both races, there was a constant anxiety about having "black" or "Jewish" features. To be seen as "mixed race" was to be seen as being of lower moral character.

The origin of the "correction" of the black nose is masked within the medical literature. No reputable surgeon in the United States wanted to be seen as facilitating crossing the color bar in the age of post-Reconstruction "Jim Crow" and "miscegenation" laws. This is very different from the situation [. . .]of the Jews in Germany, whose civil emancipation and legal status had been clarified (if not accepted) by the same period. In 1892, the New York surgeon Robert F. Weir proposed a procedure for the restoration of "sunken noses without scarring the face."[80] This procedure altered the sunken nose through the introduction of an implant, and dealt quite explicitly with syphilitic noses. Weir also discussed the alteration of the nasal alae (wings). The operation resulted in a "parrot nose," which made his patient look "black." A further surgical intervention to shave the nostrils remedied this problem. When the Berlin Jewish surgeon Jacques Joseph (1865–1934) in 1931 reported on Weir's paper, he described it as a "method of correcting abnormally flared nasal alae (Negroid nose) by means of sickle-shaped vertical excisions."[81] Weir's procedure to reconstruct the syphilitic nose was thus also seen as an intervention to enable black noses to "pass."[82]

The history of the racial nose and early aesthetic surgery in the United States is one of understatement and dissimulation. In 1934 Jacques W. Maliniak (1889–1976) noted that "the nose has strong and easily discernible racial characteristics. In an alien environment these may be highly detrimental to its possessor. A negroid nose is a distinct social and economic handicap to a dark-skinned Caucasian."[83] Or, one might add, to someone desiring to cross the color bar. The counter-case was also true. Henry Schireson noted that one of his patients, a nurse, had massive freckles. She wished to have her freckles removed: "the excess pigmentation in the lower layers of her otherwise perfect skin was interfering with her work. In a dim light she looked to some of her patients like a mulatto."[84] Perhaps she was indeed someone trying to cross the color bar.

The discourse on "passing" in the age after the introduction of aesthetic surgery is notable in its demand for ever more strictly identifiable and immutable physical characteristics of mixed-race individuals. Thus, in a letter dated September 26, 1935, from the eugenicist Harry Laughlin (1880–1943) to Madison Grant (1865–1937), the author of *The Passing of the Great Race; or, The Racial Basis of European History* (1916), Laughlin informed him that "Stanton D. Wicks, an animal breeder from Syracuse, New York," was going to Virginia to "make some field studies on the determination or identification of 'pass-for-white individuals.' At present the Virginia law which defines a colored person as 'any one of whose ancestors are colored' has to depend in its diagnosis of pass-for-whites mainly on definite negro signs among the near blood-kin; upon associates and reputation; and lastly upon personal qualities."[85] What Wicks intends to search for are "signs of colored blood whether the criterion be anatomical, chemical, mental or temperamental—but mainly physical and chemical." Tracing the "black within" would be "applicable to other races beside the negro." If, however, the physical body can be disguised through surgery, then the identification of those "passing" can only be made through either circumstantial or "chemical" means. The need for a litmus test for race was made more urgent by the ability to alter the body surgically.

The notion of permanent racial markers becomes vital in societies that desire to impose racial classifications as social norms. Thus in South Africa under apartheid, the flare of a nostril could brand one as "black." Jack Penn (who has developed the first modern decircumcision procedure, as we shall discuss later) recounted the story of a patient who came to him with the request that he narrow her nostrils.[86] "Her nose was small and her nostrils slightly flared, but I felt it suited her face, and said so. Under the circumstances, therefore, there was no point in performing an operation which I felt was unnecessary." The young woman "burst into tears." When she had decided to marry, her abusive father shouted at her that "today no white man would marry a coloured girl." In stunned amazement, the young lass asked her father what he meant. The answer was, "Ask your mother, and look at your nose, and you will see what I mean." Her mother informed her that she was "coloured." The operation was undertaken, her "overwhelming fixation" on her nose was remedied, and the surgeon received "a letter from the Eastern Province to say that this couple was happily married." "Passing" was now possible—by a nose.

When "black became beautiful," in the 1970s, there was also a change in the meaning ascribed to aesthetic surgery for the African American. The shift to the "ethnic-specific" aesthetic surgery of the 1980s introduced procedures such as lip-thinning that were clearly attempts to approximate "white" categories of beauty. Although other black-skin-specific procedures, such as removal of the upper layer of the skin (dermabrasion) for disfiguring skin bumps (pseudofolliculitis barbae) were introduced for men, the majority of ethnic-specific procedures remained aesthetic. Rhinoplasty is still the procedure of choice. African-American clients in the 1990s (like Penn's patient in the 1960s) complain that "the base of their nose is excessively wide, particularly with regard to the rest of the face."[87] In one paper that presented the preoperative complaints of 134 "non-Caucasian" individuals seeking rhinoplasties over a period of sixteen years, the "black" noses were labeled as "wide and flat nasal dorsum, flared ala, increased interalar distance and a nasal tip with little projection and definition."[88] Thus, according to such patient observations, there seems to be the need for "tip defattening" as well as a resectioning of the base of the nose. The risk of a poor outcome of aesthetic surgery is heightened among Africans and African Americans because many have a tendency to develop raised and obvious scars (keloids).

Still, such operations are regularly undertaken, often against the objection of the families. The Jewish aesthetic surgeon Robert Goldwyn recounts the case of a "twenty-one-year-old black aspiring model" who wanted her "nose less Negroid."[89] Her family strenuously objected, as "they felt she was abandoning her heritage, in particular the family nose." Goldwyn commented that "they object to Sara for wanting a nose that is not typically black. Why deny their inalienable right to inconsistency?" The notion of a consistent racial type haunts a world obsessed with "passing." In today's America the anxiety about being seen as trying to "pass" is tied to the notion of consistency. Like the earlier risk of being scarred and thus revealing to the world one's desire to "pass," the inconsistent nose marks one as different.

Such a position can pose a true dilemma. One of the leading spokespeople for the New Critical Race theory, Patricia J. Williams, professor of law at Columbia University, notes that she is anxious about the "morality" in the "morass" of African Americans who turn to aesthetic surgery: "What made it 'the very worst kind' of assimilationism was that it was also assimilation out of the very right to coexist in the world with that most basic legacy of our own bodies. What made it so bad was the unselfconscious denial of those violent social pressures that make so irresistible the 'choice' to cut off that perfect replica of one's grandmother's nose in favor of a trendier, more 'acceptable' model."[90]

She condemns the autonomy ("self-assertion") preached by the "eager plastic surgeon" who advocated "the choice to go under the knife. 'Just say yes to yourself,' he glowed repeatedly." For her this is merely false consciousness, which is the result of the "call to conform . . . that is the perpetual risk of any socializing collective, whether family or polis." This drive to "pass" is not only the desire to "pass" as white, but to "pass" as "black." For with the emphasis on a unitary idea of "blackness" within African-American culture, the onus is not to look too "white" or too "black." Indeed "grandmother's nose" may well have been a "white" nose as well as a "black" nose, given the history of miscegenation in America. Here the problem of inconsistency turns out to be purely ideological. Goldwyn and Williams have their norms of "blackness" and do not recognize how culturally determined they are.

With the rise of a multicultural model in the United States, the meaning of the "black" nose also shifted. "New thinking on cosmetic surgery," the title of a popular essay in 1992 proclaimed, "keeps your ethnic identity."[91] Ethnic identity has value in this new world. Clients should not "have their cultural heritage erased from their faces by the wrong surgery," writes W. Earle Matory Jr., a plastic surgeon at the University of Massachusetts Medical Center. Or, as a *Living Section* essay in the *New York Times* put it in 1991, "Surgeons are learning to put the right nose on the right face."[92] The meaning of the "right face" has shifted over the past three decades.

African Americans who undertook aesthetic surgery in the 1940s and 1950s did so in order to "pass": "I don't find it advantageous," said one young African-American woman, "to have decisive Negro features. The less you look like a Negro, the less you have to fight. I would pass for anything so long as I'm not taken for a Negro. With a straight nose I could do costume work and pose as an Indian, Egyptian, or even a Balinese."[93] Such views began to shift by the 1970s, for example in the writing of the African-American surgeon Harold E. Pierce, writing in the (African-American) *Journal of the National Medical Association* about the importance of "race" as a factor in "cosmetic surgery." He found that "there are but a few required modifications in [facial cosmetic surgery]. The major difference concerns rhinoplasty."[94] Rhinoplasty, which in the past twenty years has become the aesthetic surgical procedure most frequently performed on African Americans, is usually used to correct patients' complaints of "flared nostrils, prominent tip, and/or a depressed and low nasal bridge."[95] When such perceived unaesthetic qualities are removed, "the surgeon must be careful to avoid overcorrection and creation of a nose that is racially incongruent."[96] The movement in the post-1970s period to an ethnic-specific cosmetic surgery presupposed the existence of aesthetic boundaries by which each group was defined as beautiful. Now the "black" look has become the referent.

Thomas Rees, who claimed in 1968 that the question of African Americans wanting to "pass" had to do with Caucasian ideals of beauty, came in 1986 to observe that many patients wanted to look like other "black" role models who had come to alter their appearance: "Patients are mightily impressed with the Caucasian-like transformation of the previously Negroid features of Michael Jackson, the noted entertainer."[97] One "passed" now by looking like a socially more acceptable (read: white) version of the black nose. In 1996 African Americans accounted for 6 percent, Asian Americans 7 percent, and Hispanics 9 percent of aesthetic surgeries. However, ethnic-specific aesthetic surgery among African Americans is increasing—by 2 percent from 1994 to 1997.[98] One can be "black," but "black" turns out (like "Irish" and "Jewish") to be in the eye of the beholder and the hand of the surgeon.

Whether black, Irish, or Asian, the nose that is too small or too flat has been altered by the aesthetic surgeon because of its "otherness" in relation to Western ideals. These ideals are not just concerned with beauty and attractiveness, but with markers of who is and is not acceptably human, who can and cannot be trusted. The "primitiveness" of the flat nose represents groups who are not only fit to be kept down, but who must be so treated lest they infect the dominant group. The danger of infection is always present, among other reasons, because the too-small, too-flat nose is the sign of the syphilis carried by those whose undisciplined sexual behavior is said to have crossed all appropriate boundaries.

Such beliefs and attitudes, continually propagated and strengthened by the relations of power and economic advantage among the world's peoples, create an ideal arena for aesthetic surgery, with its promise to help people "pass" as whoever they wish to be. The aesthetic surgeon operates in a world in which everyone's appearance is charged with meaning, most profoundly the meaning of who can and cannot be honored with acceptance as an equal. . . .

NOTES

1. Peter Camper, *Über den natürlichen Unterschied der Gesichtszüge in Menschen verschiedener Gegenden und verschiedenen Alters,* trans. S.Th. Sörnmerring (Berlin: Voss, 1792). See in this context Miriam Claude Meijer, "The Anthropology of Petrus Camper (1722–1789)" (Ph.D.diss., University of California, Los Angeles, 1991), and Stephen Jay Gould, *The Mismeasure of Man* (New York: W.W. Norton, 1996).

2. Lorenz Oken, *Lchrbuclider Naiurphilosopluc,* 3 vols. (Jena: Friedrich Frornmann, 1811), 3:370–71.

3. Gotthold Ephraim Lessing, *Laocoön,* trans. William A. Steel (London: Everyman's Library, 1970), pp. 89ff.

4. Johann Caspar Lavater, *Physiognomische Fragment zur Beförderung des Menschenkenntnis und Menschenliebe*, 4 vols. (Leipzig: Weidmann, 1775–78). The most recent comprehensive introduction to Lavater is Ellis Shookman, ed., *The Faces of Physiognomy: Interdisciplinary Approaches to Johann Caspar Lavater* (Columbia, S.C.: Damden House, 1993). See also Karl Maurer, "Entstaltung: Ein beinahe untergegangener Goethescher Begriff," in Rudolf Behrens and Roland Galle, eds., *Leib-Zeichen: Körperbilder, Rhetorik und Anthropologie im 18. Jahrhundert* (Würtzburg: Königshausen & Neumann, 1993), pp. 151–62; Liliane Weissberg, "Literatur als Representationsform: Zur Lektüre," in Lutz Danenberg et al., eds., *Vom Umgang mit Literatur und Literaturgeschichte: Positionen und Perspektive* (Stuttgart: Metzler, 1992), pp. 293–313; Richard Grey, "Die Geburt des Genies aus dem Geiste der Aufklarung: Semiotik und Aufklärungsideologie in der Physiognomik Johann Kaspar Lavaters," *Poetica* 23 (1991): 95–138, as well as Grey's "Sign and Sein: The *Physiognomikstreit* and the Dispute over the Semiotic Constitution of Bourgeois Individuality," *Deutsche Vierteljahrsschrift fur Literaturwissenschaft und Geistesgeschiehte* 66 (1992): 300–332; and Michael Shortland, "Barthes, Lavater and the Legible Body," in Mike Gane, ed., *Ideological Representation and Power in Social Relations: Literary and Social Theory* (London: Routledge, 1989), pp. 17–53, as well as Shortland's "Power of a Thousand Eyes: Johann Caspar Lavater's Science of Physiognomical Perception," *Criticism* 28 (1986): 379–408. Of central importance in this is the work of Barbara Maria Stafford, "'Peculiar Marks': Lavater and the Countenance of Blemished Thought," *Art Journal* 46 (1987): 185–92. See as well Stafford's books: *Good Looking: Essays on the Virtue of Images* (Cambridge, Mass.: MIT Press, 1996); *Artful Science: Enlightenment, Entertainment, and the Eclipse of Visual Education* (Cambridge, Mass.: MIT Press, 1994); and *Body Criticism: Imagining the Unseen in Enlightenment Art and Medicine* (Cambridge, Mass.: MIT Press, 1991).

5. See my *On Blackness without Blacks: Essays on the Image of the Black in Germany*, Yale Afro-American Studies (Boston: G.K. Hall, 1982), pp.19–34.

6. Winthrop D. Jordan, *White over Black: American Attitudes toward the Negro, 1550–1812* (Chapel Hill: University of North Carolina Press, 1968), p. 260n. See my *Difference and Pathology: Stereotypes of Sexuality, Race, and Madness* (Ithaca, N.Y.: Cornell University Press, 1985), pp. 131–50.

7. Camper, *Uber den naturlichen Unterschied*, p. 62.

8. Lavater, *Physiognomische Fragment*, 3:98 and 4:272–74. This reference is cited (and rebutted) in Paolo Mantegazza, *Physiognomy and Expression* (New York: Walter Scott, 1904), p. 239.

9. Robert Knox, *The Races of Man: A Fragment* (Philadelphia: Lea and Blanchard, 1850), p.134.

10. Camper, *Natüraliche Unterschied*, p. 7.

11. See the standard racial anthropology of the Jew written during the first third of the twentieth century, Hans F. K. Günther, *Rasecnkunde des jüdischen Volkes* (Munich: J. F. Lehmann, 1930), here pp. 143–49. These two quotations are taken from von Luschan and Judt.

12. Adam G. de Curowski, *America and Europe* (New York: D. Appleton, 1857), p. 177.

13 Denis Diderot and Jean Le Rond d 'Alembert, *Encyclopédie, ou dictionnaire raisonné des sciences, des arts, et des métiers, par une société des gens de letters*, 36 vols. (Geneva: Pellet; Neufchâtel: Société Typographique, 1778–79), 22:419–24, quotations on p. 420.

14. Charles Darwin, *The Descent of Man and Selection in Relation to Sex* (New York: D. Appleton, 1897), p. 579.

15. Robert Hichens, *The Unearthly* (New York: Cosmopolitan Book, 1926), p. 53.

16. F. Scott Fitzgerald , *The Great Gatsby*, ed. Matthew J. Bruccoli (New York: Scribner, 1992), pp. 73–76.

17. Frances Cooke Macgregor, *Transformation and Identity: The Face and Plastic Surgery* (New York: Quadrangle Press/New York Times Book Company, 1974), p. 99.

18. A summary of the literature on Jews and blacks is offered in the chapter "Die negerische Rasse," in Günther, *Rassenkunde des jüdischen Volkes*, here pp. 155–56.

19. John O. Roe, "The Deformity Termed ' Pug Nose' and Its Correction, by a Simple Operation," *The Medical Record* 31 (June 4, 1887): 621–23; printed in Frank McDowell, ed ., *The Source Book of Plastic Surgery* (Baltimore: Williams & Wilkins, 1977), pp. 114–19, here, p. 114.

20. Robert F.Weir (1838–94) commented in the late nineteenth century on procedures developed by the Berlin surgeon James Israel (1848–1926), the chief surgeon of the Jewish Hospital in Berlin. Israel' s procedures were developed to cure the saddle nose. Weir noted that "the scar . . . is the unavoidable result of this operation" and that the failure of the procedure sometimes "reproduces the deformity." Robert F. Weir, "On Restoring Sunken Noses without Scarring the Face," cited from McDowell, *Source Book*, p. 137.

21. Jotul O. Roe, "The Correction of Nasal Deformities by Subcutaneous Operations: A Further Contribution," *Medical Record* 68 (1905): 1–7, quotation on p. 3.

22. Sir Charles Bell, *The Anatomy and Philosophy of Expression as Connected with the Fine Arts*, 3rd ed. (London: John Murray, 1844), p. 20.

23. See my *Seeing the Insane* (Lincoln: University of Nebraska Press, 1996), pp. 188–89.

24. John O. Roe, "Correction of Nasal Deformities," p. 3.

25. Mary Cowling, *Artist as Anthropologist: The Representation of Type and Character in Victorian Art* (Cambridge, Eng.: Cambridge University Press, 1989), pp. 125–29. The image of the nose reproduced by Cowling from the physiognomic literature of the nineteenth century representing the Irish as identical with those in the "before" images reproduced by Roe.

26. John Beddoe, *The Races of Britain* (1885; rpt. Washington, D.C.: Cliveden Press, 1983), pp. 10–11 . See Nancy Stepan, *The Idea of Race in Science: Great Britain, 1800–1960* (London: Macmillan, in association with St. Anthony' s College, Oxford, 1982), p. 103.

27. Noel Ignatiev, *How the Irish Became White* (New York: Routledge, 1996).

28. Lewis Perry Curtis, *Apes and Angels: The Irishman in Victorian Caricature* (Washington, D.C. : Smithsonian Institution Press, 1971). For images of jaws and noses, see pp. 20f., 29f., and 45; and Richard Ned Lebow, *White Britain and Black Ireland: The Influence of Stereotypes on Colonial Policy* (Philadelphia: Institute for the Study of Human Issues, 1976).

29. Reinhard R. Doerries, *Iren und Deutsche in der Neuen Welt: Akkulturationsprozesse in der amerikanischen Gesellschaft im späten neunzehnten Jahrhundert* (Stuttgart: F. Steiner, 1986).

30. Samuel R. Wells, *New Physiognomy, or, Signs of Character: As Manifested through Temperament and External Forms, and Especially in "the Human Face Divine"* (1866; rpt. New York: American Book Company, 1871), p. 217.

31. Arthur G. Petit, *Mark Twain and the South* (Lexington: University Press of Kentucky, 1974), pp. 139–55, 207–10.

32. Walter White, "Has Science Conquered the Color Line?" *Negro Digest* (December 1949): 37–40, quotation on p. 37. On the problems associated with passing as white in America, see the older historical study by Joel Williamson, *New People: Miscegenation and Mullatoes in the United States* (1980; rpt. Baton Rouge: Louisiana State University Press, 1995), as well as the insightful new critical studies by Werner Sollors, *Neither Black nor White Yet Both: Thematic Explorations of Interracial Literature* (New York: Oxford University Press, 1997), and Susan Cubar, *Racechanges: White Skin, Black Face in American Culture* (New York: Oxford University Press, 1997), pp. 13–25.

33. Blair O. Rogers, "John Orlando Roe—not Jacques Joseph—the Father of Aesthetic Rhinoplasty," *Aesthetic Plastic Surgery* 10 (1986): 63–88.

34. Sylvia Thompson , "Facing Up to a Face Lift," *Irish Times*, August 22, 1994, p. 10.

35. Curtis, *Apes and Angels*. For images of big, protruding ears, see pp. 49, 54, 63, 67, and 80.

36. Yetti Redmond, "Holding Back the Years," *Irish Times*, June 8, 1992, p. 8.

37. Ibid .

38. Edward Falces and John Imada. "Aesthetic Surgery in Asians," in Eugene H. Courtiss, ed., *Male Aesthetic Sur*gery (St. Louis: Mosby, 1991), pp. 159–69, quotations on p. 159.

39. Eugenia Kaw, "Medicalization of Racial Features: Asian American Women and Cosmetic Surgery," *Medical Anthropology Quarterly* 7 (1993): 74–89, quotation on p. 74.

40. Günther, Rassenkunde des jüdischen Volkes, p. 217, with a summary of the literature on Jewish eyes.

41. M. Chien Chih Tzu Chu, *Nu Hsing Mei Yung Hsin Chih* (Taipei: Kuo chi tsun wen ku sh tien , 1995).

42. See my "Lam Qua and the Westernization of Medical Illustration in Nineteenth-Century China," *Medical History* 30 (1986): 57–69.

43. Y. Shirakabe, T. Kinusgasa, M. Kawata, T. Kishimoto, T. Shirakabe, "The Double Eyelid Operation in Japan: Its Evolution as Related to Cultural Change," *Annals of Plastic Surgery* 15 (1985): 224–41.

44. See the discussion by Naoyuki Ohtake and Nobuyuki Shioya, "Aesthetic Breast Surgery in Orientals," in Nicolas G. Georgia de, Gregory S. Georgia de, and Ronald Riefkohl, eds., *Aesthetic Surgery of the Breast* (Philadelphia : W. B. Saunders, 1990), pp. 639–53, here p. 639.

45. Yukio Shirakabe, "The Development of Aesthetic Facial Surgery in Japan: As Seen through a Study of Japanese Pictorial Art," *Aesthetic Plastic Surgery* 14 (1990): 215–21.

46. Yoshikiyo Koganei, *Beiträge zur physische Anthropologie der Aino. I. Untersuchungen am Skelet*; *II. Untersuchungen am Lebenden. Mitteilungen aus der medizischen Facultät der kaiserlich-japanische Universität zu Tokio* 2 (1983).

47. Darwin, *Descent of Man*, p. 579.

48. T. Nishihata and A. Yoshida , "Augmentation Rhinoplasty Using Ivory," *Clinical Photography* 7 (1923): 8–10.

49. Frank Dikotter, *The Discourse of Race in Modern China* (London: Hurst, 1992).

50. Henry J. Schireson, *As Others See You: The Story of Plastic Surgery* (New York: Macaulay, 1938), p. 141.

51. Erniko Ohnuki-Tierney, *Illness and Culture in Contemporary Japan: An Anthropological View* (Cambridge, Eng.: Cambridge University Press, 1984), pp. 51–66.

52. Shizu Sakai, "The Impact of Western Medicine and the Concept of Medical Treatment in Japan," in Yoshio Kawakita, Shizu Sakai, and Yasuo Otsuka, eds ., *History of Therapy: Proceedings of the 10th International Symposium on the Comparative History of Medicine—East and West* (Tokyo: Tanaguchi Foundation, 1990), pp. 157–71.

53. The meaning ascribed to the reconstructed face and its association with the "West" in modern Japan is also colored by the experience of the atomic bomb and the Hiroshima maidens. If the desire to "look American" through aesthetic surgery captured Japanese (and then Vietnamese) society from the 1950s to the 1970s, then it was paralleled in both cultures by the meaning of the scars of war and their reconstructive amelioration. In 1955 twenty-five women who had survived the dropping of the atom bombs at Hiroshima and Nagasaki were invited by a private goodwill group to receive cosmetic surgery at Mt. Sinai Hospital in New

York. They became known in the United States as the "Hiroshima maidens." Much of the surgery undertaken on this group dealt with the reconstruction and rebuilding of the face, especially the eyelids and nose. Their images were widely circulated in periodicals such as *Life* magazine, and their scarred faces (and the desire of American medicine to recuperate them) became part of a shared American and Japanese understanding of the scarred face. Disfigured by the American bombing, these faces were presented as the means by which Americans could now provide some recompense for the dropping of the first atomic bombs. The "happiness," however, seems to have been felt solely by the American physicians who performed the procedures and the public that paid for them. The results of the surgery were discussed with the women in a television interview forty years after the operation:

MICHIKO YAMOKA: After the operation—
MAYLEE: [interviewing] Good. So you were happy.
CHIKO YAMOKA: Yeah, happy.
MAYLEE: [reporting] The treatments removed much of the physical scars, but Michiko's psychological wounds are still deep. Her most horrible memory is witnessing the death of her friends, which she says was her fault. (SHOW: NEWS 9:14 A.M. ET, CNN, August 5, 1995)

The "curative" power of the surgery was experienced more by the Americans who saw the correction of war wounds in the civilian population as a form of moral correction for the action of having dropped the first atomic bombs. Facial wounds came to have complex meanings in the attempt to reconstitute "happiness." In Japan the ability to change the *jibyo* of these individuals through aesthetic surgery seemed quite limited. The surgery may have made Michiko superficially "happy," but did not change her basic sense of her psychological damage. See Rodney Barker, *The Hiroshima Maidens: A Story of Courage, Compassion, and Survival* (Harrnondsworth: Penguin, 1986).

54. Ohtake and Shioya, "Aesthetic Breast Surgery in Orientals," p. 639.

55. Y. Mutou , "Augmentation Mammaplasty with the Akiyama Prosthesis," *British Journal of Plastic Surgery* 23 (1970): 58–62.

56. Kyoko Ishimara, "Young Women Turn to Plastic Surgery, but Is a New Face Really What They're Looking For?" *Nikkei Weekly,* December 28, 1992/January 4, 1993.

57. When Western commentators imagine the Japanese body, they idealize it as un-scarred and as "Western." Thus Roland Barthes (1915–80), *L'empire des signes* (Geneva: A. Skira, 1970), fantasized about the Japanese actor Tetsuro Tanba's "Western" eyes in his 1970 study of Japanese culture. It may well be these (unoperated) eyes that came to serve as the idealized model for the contemporary Japanese face. These "Western" eyes also haunt the major shift in portraiture in postwar Japan, the *manga*, or illustrated comic book. The origins of modern *manga* can be found in the humorous illustrations of Katsushika Hokusai (1760–1849), who coined the term out of the Chinese ideograms *man* (involuntary and/or morally corrupt) and *ga* (picture). His imagery was rooted in the physiognomy of Japanese caricatures and used the conventions of representing the Japanese physiognomy as different from other "foreign" physiognomies.

58. Yoshiko Matsushita, "Mama, He's Making Eyes for Me . . . and a New Chin," *Asia Times,* May 19, 1997, p. 1.

59. One can add that precisely the same scenario can be played out in regard to young men in today's Japan. It seems clear that the shift in attitude toward aesthetic surgery is a generational one. In a recent issue of the teenage magazine *Bart* (March 10, 1997, pp. 98–103) there was an article on young men in their late teens undergoing cosmetic procedures that

cost them as much as ¥350,000 for a nose job and ¥300,000 for an eyelid procedure. This essay, accompanied by "before and after" photographs, chronicled the masculine drive for "happiness" through the Western aesthetic alteration of the too-Japanese body.

60. The physiognomy of the contemporary *manga* (and the *anime,* the animated film), however, is rooted in the animated work of Ozamu Tezuka (1926–89) from the 1950s. Influenced by American animated cartoons, such as those of Walt Disney, Tezuka developed "some of the characteristics of *manga* . . . noting that he drew the princess with big, round eyes in exotic, foreign settings." "Manga's Appeal Not Limited to Japanese Fans," *Daily Yomiuri,* December 11, 1996, p. 3; see also Frederik L. Schod, *Manga! Manga! The World of Japanese Comics* (Tokyo: Kodansha, 1986). In postwar Japan, such deracialized ("Western ") eyes came to be representative of the physiognomy of the *manga* and were read as a way of imagining a new, exotic, and happy body. The *manga* in this tradition (especially those for girls) have depicted the characters as outrageously "Western." This is certainly related to the modern tradition of the "girls' opera" (known as "Takarazuka," after a city near Osaka), which represents a fictional "Western " (actually "nowhere") world with an all-female cast (with the male characters played by the young actresses). "Takarazuka" presents a world analogous to the Occidentalist girls' comics in Japan with "neutral" (read: Western) physiognomies. Recently there have appeared very "Japanese" *manga* and *anime,* such as those by Katsuhiro Otorno. His best-known work is *Akira,* a near-future science fiction in which Japanese characters are depicted with "Japanese" eyes.

61. Le Gia Vinh, "Study of Facial Dimensions in Vietnamese Young People: Their Application into Aeshetic and Plastic Surgery," *Anthropologie* 27 (1988): 113–15.

62. Nguyen Man Phuong, "Vietnam: As Confucianism and Socialism Erode, Crime Thrives," *Inter Press Service,* October 1, 1996.

63. Pascale Trouillaud, "More Vietnamese Going under the Beauty Knife," *Agence France Presse,* November 30, 1995, 08:14 Eastern Time.

64. Le Thang Long, "Vietnamese Men Line Up for a Nip and Tuck," *Agence France Presse,* June 7, 1996.

65. Dean Lokken, "Doctor Says Cosmetic Surgery Makes Gains in China," *U.S. News & World Report,* October 17, 1994.

66. "Blinded Woman Sues Beauty Parlor," United Press International, October 14, 1996, Monday, BC cycle.

67. Alison Dakota Gee, "The Price of Beauty," *Asiaweek,* August 2, 1996, p. 38.

68. United Press International, May 1, 1996, Wednesday, BC cycle.

69. Khoo Boo-Chai, "Plastic Construction of the Superior Palpebral Fold," *Plastic and Reconstructive Surgery* 34 (1963): 74. See also Khoo's "Augmentation Rhinoplasty in the Orientals," *Plastic and Reconstructive Surgery* 34 (1964): 81.

70. The beautiful as it is understood in contemporary Chinese culture remains the symmetrical. Indeed, it defines the beautiful for the clinical practice of aesthetic surgery. See X. Wang and Z. Zhang, "Three-Dimensional Analysis of the Facial Lateral Region with Beautiful Appearance of Chinese and Its Clinical Value" [in Chinese], *Chung-Hua Kou Chiang I Hsueh Tsa Chih/Chinese Journal of Somatology* 30 (1995): 131–33 and 191. The search for happiness comes to be the search for the beauty present in the perceived symmetry of the Western face, or at least of the Asian face now reconfigured as neither Western nor too "Oriental." Naree Krajang, a Thai jazz singer, who had fat removed from her upper eyelids to make them look rounder and a nasal implant inserted in her "too-small" nose, stated that "Westerners have perfect figures, beautiful faces and shapes. . . . We want to be beautiful, like foreigners." Shiela

McNulty, "Asians Bear the Knife for Western Look," *San Jose Mercury News,* February 21, 1995, p. A1. The foreigners, by implication, are truly happy, but would everyone want to be able to cross that border into the world of the beautiful, the happy, the healthy, and the well-to-do?

71. Claudia Kolker and Dai Huynh, "A Beauty of a Dispute," *Houston Chronicle,* September 8, 1996, p. 33.

72. Steve Glain, "Cosmetic Surgery Goes Hand in Glove with the New Korea," *Wall Street Journal,* November 23, 1993, p. A1.

73. Elaine T. Matsushita, "Americans, Too: For Asian Americans, as for Other Minorities, Full Assimilation into the American Mainstream Is a Bittersweet Process, " *Chicago Tribune,* April 29, 1992, p. C6.

74. Laura Accinelli, "Eye of the Beholder," *Los Angeles Times,* January 23, 1996, p. E1.

75. Gish Jen, *Mona in the Promised Land: A Novel* (New York: Vintage, 1996).

76. Penny Colman, *Madam C. J. Walker: Building a Business Empire* (Brookfield, Conn.: Millbrook Press, 1994).

77. Blair O. Rogers, "The Role of Physical Anthropology in Plastic Surgery Today," *Clinics of Plastic Surgery* 1 (1974): 439–98; and W. E. Berman, "The Non-Caucasian (Ethnic or Platyrrhine) Nose," *Ear Nose Throat Journal* 74 (1995): 747–48 and 750–51.

78. Werner Sollors, "Theory and Ethnic Message," *MELLUS: Journal of the Society for the Study of the Multi-Ethnic Literature of the United States* 8 (1981): 15–17; and Sollors's collection *The Invention of Ethnicity* (New York: Oxford University Press, 1989).

79. M. L. Ettler, "Körperkultur und Zuchtwahl," *Politisch-Anthropologische Revue* 3 (1904/5): 624–29, quotations on pp. 635, 628.

80. Weir, "On Restoring Sunken Noses," cited from McDowell, *Source Book,* p. 139.

81. Jacques Joseph, *Nasenplastik und sonstige Gesichtsplastik, nebst einem Anhang über Mammaplastik und einige weitere Operationen aus dem Gebiete der äusseren Körperplastik: Ein Atlas und ein Lehrbuch* (Leipzig: C. Kabitzch, 1931). All quotations are from the translation by Stanley Milstein: Jacques Joseph, *Rhinoplasty and Facial Plastic Surgery with a Supplement on Mammaplasty and Other Operations in the Field of Plastic Surgery of the Body* (Phoenix: Columella Press, 1987), p. 83.

82. The "negroid nose" is one seen as one of the categories that warranted surgical intervention in contemporary Brazil today. One does not want to be seen as "too black." See Aymar Sperli, "Exo-Rhinoplasty: A New 'Old Approach' in Aesthetic Rhinoplasty," and Edwaldo Bolivar de Souza Pinto, "Rhinosculpture: Treatment of the Nasal Tip, Columella, and Lip Dynamics," both in the online *Brazilian Journal of Plastic Surgery,* October 31, 1996 (www.plasticsurgery.org). Both of these essays list "negroid nose" as one of the nasal forms to be "repaired."

83. Jacques W. Maliniak, *Sculpture in the Living: Rebuilding the Face and Form by Plastic Surgery* (New York: Romaine Pierson, 1934), p. 55.

84. Schireson, *As Others See You,* p. 276.

85. Harry Laughin Papers, Box C-2-1, Truman State University, Kirksville, Mo.

86. Jack Penn, *The Right to Look Human: An Autobiography* (New York: McGraw-Hill, 1974). See D. H. Walker, "The History of Plastic Surgery in South Africa," *Adler Museum Bulletin* 11 (1985): 6–11.

87. W. Earle Matory Jr., "Aesthetic Surgery in African-Americans," in Eugene H. Courtiss, ed., *Aesthetic Surgery* (St. Louis: Mosby, 1991), pp. 170–84, quotation on p. 174.

88. W. Earle Matory Jr. and Edward Falces, "Non-Caucasian Rhinoplasty: A Sixteen-Year Experience," *Plastic and Reconstructive Surgery* 77 (1986): 239–52.

89. Robert M. Goldwyn, *Beyond Appearance: Reflections of a Plastic Surgeon* (New York: Dodd, Mead & Co., 1986), pp. 200–201.

90. Patricia J. Williams, *The Rooster's Egg* (Cambridge, Mass.: Harvard University Press, 1995), pp. 238–39.

91. Jenny Choi , "New Thinking on Cosmetic Surgery: Keep Your Ethnic Identity," *Self*, December 1992, p. 43.

92. Elisabeth Rosenthal, "Ethnic Ideals: Rethinking Plastic Surgery, " *New York Times*, September 25, 1991, p. C1.

93. Macgregor, *Transformation and Identity*, p. 92.

94. Harold E. Pierce, "Cosmetic Head and Face Surgery—Ethnic Considerations," *Journal of the National Medical Association* 72 (1980): 487–92. See also the earlier essay by R. S. Flowers, "The Surgical Correction of the Non-Caucasian Nose," *Clinics of Plastic Surgery* 1 (1977): 69–87.

95. Matory and Falces, "Non-Caucasian Rhinoplasty."

96. P. E. Grimes and S. G. Hunt, "Considerations for Cosmetic Surgery in the Black Population," *Clinics in Plastic Surgery* 20 (1993): 27–34, here p. 31.

97. Thomas D. Rees, "Discussion of W. Earle Matory Jr. and Edward Falces, "Non-Caucasian Rhinoplasty: A Sixteen-Year Experience," *Plastic and Reconstructive Surgery* 77 (1986): 252.

98. Maudlyne Ihejirka, "More Ordinary People Seeking Plastic Surgery," *Chicago Sun-Times*, March 30, 1997, p. 38.

|||||||||||||||||||||||||||||||||||||||||||||||||||||||||||||||||||||||||||||

11

To Die For

The Semiotic Seductive Power of the Tanned Body

Phillip Vannini and Aaron M. McCright

Get undressed—but be slim, good-looking, tanned!
—Michel Foucault, *Power/Knowledge* (1980)

Broadly interpreted, sun worship is an old cultural practice. People throughout history have turned to the sun for a wide variety of activities designed to purify or embellish their souls and bodies (see Douglas 1966). Sun gods from the Greek Apollo to the Egyptian Ra populate world mythologies that place the sun at the center of life. Aesculapian health clinics over two millennia ago attempted to cure the ill with sunbathing, and Native American Pawnee dancers of the Bear Society believed the sun gave them healing powers (Randle 1997). A more diffuse and secularized strain of solar worship exists in the contemporary United States.[1] For instance, municipalities all over the nation attempt to lure prospective businesses and workers to their areas by advertising the total number of sunny days they enjoy each year. People often attempt to cure stress and fatigue by taking vacations in warm, sun-caressed locations and resorts (see Desmond 1999). To most, a "lovely" day has sunny weather, while an "awful" day is filled with rain and clouds. We often seek out companionship with those whom we believe have a "sunny" personality. And a lucky few of us may meet that special person and say, "You are the sunshine of my life."

It is becoming increasingly common for a number of people in our society to actively seek a suntan year-round. While many people tan under the sun, greater numbers each year patronize tanning salons or purchase their own private tanning beds, lamps, and tanning lotions to bronze their skin. In other words, more people are shifting their preference from the real sun to a simulated sun—the tanning lamp. The first tanning salon in the United States opened in 1978, and today the United States has more than fifty thousand salons operating in an industry with twenty-eight million users who generate over $4 billion in gross revenues a year (Palmer et al.

From *Symbolic Interaction*, Volume 27, Number 3, pp. 309–332. © 2004 the Society for the Study of Symbolic Interaction. Reprinted with permission of the University of California Press and the Society for the Study of Symbolic Interaction.

2002). With mounting awareness of the risks associated with extensive exposure to carcinogenic ultraviolet (UV) radiation and with the increasing total market value of body enhancement products and services, the practice of artificial tanning has gained enough significance to warrant empirical scrutiny.

In another study (McCright and Vannini 2004), we observed two competing "stories" or frames (Goffman 1974) about artificial suntanning within public discourse: a medical frame and a seduction frame. The competition between these two frames provides the dynamic context in which we may more completely understand why people artificially tan their skin in the contemporary United States. We begin the following section by briefly noting the historical significance of the practice of tanning and artificial tanning and the established medical frame through which many in the public interpret tanning. Since artificial tanning is linked closely to other "projects" of the body such as fitness, fashion, dieting, piercing, and tattooing, we then discuss how the existing literature on the sociology of the body helps to account for this embodied practice. We end this section by identifying the emerging seduction frame and noting the competition between the medical frame and the seduction frame. After discussing our methodology and analytic framework, we report and reflect on in-depth interviews with forty artificial tanners. We conclude by drawing together our observations and offering a brief reflection on the semiotic power (Wiley 1994) of the body.

Artificial Tanning in Sociohistorical Context

Popular enthusiasm for the sun and suntanning has varied much across both time and space. Eighteenth-century European upper-class ladies, for example, shunned the sun and used parasols and cosmetic powder to display pale skin. At that time tanned skin connoted humble class origins, as most unskilled workers and farmers would be tanned from protracted sun exposure during the workday. With the passing of time and with the transition from a production society to one based on conspicuous consumption (Veblen 1899), the meaning of tanned skin changed. As early as the 1920s, tanned skin began to connote upper-class taste and an affluent lifestyle (Holubar and Schmidt 1994). As the popularity of leisurely outdoor pursuits such as lawn tennis, swimming, golf, and sunbathing brought the bodies of the wealthy outside to play, the pale body began to signify confinement to indoor workplaces and lack of discretionary income. The shift from the symbolic to the semiotic realm had begun to emerge: bronzed skin was no longer merely indexical of exposure to UV rays; it connoted sign-value.[2]

Enticed by Coco Chanel's famous pronouncement, "The 1929 girl must be tanned. A golden tan is the index of chic!" America's love affair with suntanning officially began in the 1930s. With the popularization of the bikini swimsuit in the late 1940s and 1950s and the romanticization of the southern California lifestyle, it was not long before Hollywood stars and fashion models began to show off their bronzed bodies and rave about their tans (Randle 1997). Whereas the first advertisement for a tanning lamp appeared as early as 1923 in *Vogue* magazine (Randle 1997), the artificial tanning business only began to gather meaningful popularity in the 1980s in North America and western Europe. The widespread emergence of tanning salons and the rise of retail sales of tanning lamps coincided with the invention and distribution of more technologically advanced lamps capable of delivering UV light five times as intense as that of normal sunlight (National Institute of Health 1989). According to the Indoor Tanning Association (2004), the professional indoor tanning industry now employs more than 160,000 employees and has a total annual economic impact in excess of $5 billion.

The Medical Frame

Over the past two decades a critical mass of physicians and health professionals, medical associations (e.g., American Medical Association, American Association of Dermatology), medical organizations (e.g., American Cancer Society, Skin Cancer Foundation), and federal agencies (e.g., National Cancer Institute, Federal Trade Commission, Food and Drug Administration, Centers for Disease Control and Prevention) have begun to pay attention to the phenomenon of tanning, artificial tanning in particular. This collective is responsible for promoting a major frame through which many in the general public interpret artificial tanning. Medical frame proponents claim that decades of peer-reviewed research finds that prolonged exposure to solar UVA and UVB radiation and occasional sunburns are risk factors for all three types of skin cancer: basal cell carcinoma, squamous cell carcinoma, and melanoma. These proponents further claim that artificial tanning devices also expose people to UVA and UVB radiation, and the preponderance of existing peer-reviewed empirical research finds that use of artificial tanning devices also increases the likelihood of contracting skin cancer (see, e.g., International Agency for Research on Cancer 1992; Swerdlow and Weinstock 1998; Westerdahl et al. 2000).[3] They argue that this heightened risk is present across the population of artificial tanners, from male adults to female teenagers, and is especially acute for people with fair skin, light hair color, and blue or green eyes (see, e.g., Demko, Borawski, and Debanne 2003; Randle 1997; Swerdlow and Weinstock 1998).

Thus, medical frame proponents claim that artificial tanning is an extremely risky behavior. At the very least, they argue, the indoor tanning industry must be regulated so that a company can proclaim that its products produce a "safe" tan with "no harmful rays" and "no harmful or adverse effects." At the most, individuals should refrain from using the products and services of the indoor tanning industry to protect themselves from unnecessary exposure to known carcinogens (and thus an increased risk of skin cancer). The American Academy of Dermatology has publicly discouraged the practice of artificial tanning, and the American Medical Association also has requested a ban on the sale of artificial tanning equipment (AMA 1994). We now turn to the sociology of the body literature before identifying a key competitor with the medical frame—the seduction frame.

Sociology of the Body

The sudden emergence and consequent rapid growth of what has come to be known as the sociology of the body (see, e.g., Falk 1994; Featherstone 1991a, 1991b; Featherstone, Hepworth, and Turner 1991; Frank 1991; Richardson and Shaw 1998; Shilling 1993; Turner 1991, 1996) prompted one symbolic interactionist (Strauss 1993) to remind us that it was George Herbert Mead who first advanced much of what we now consider novel theorizing about this topic. We largely concur with Anselm Strauss that Mead's (1934) pragmatist philosophy contained the genes of our contemporary nondualistic thinking about the body. There is no body without an agentic, reflexive, and semiotic self (Wiley 1994), and interaction is first and foremost an interaction of signifying bodies. Through our bodies we perform, express, and (re)present ourselves, and others judge our appearances and performances. The body is both a subject and an object of action, and it is through our self-directed action and reflection that we communicate with others (Mead 1934; Peirce 1960; Strauss 1993).[4]

We understand artificial tanning as a body practice that "serve[s] to enhance, promote, denigrate, destroy, maintain or alter performances, appearances, or presentations" (Strauss 1993:121). In addition, we see tanning as a form of communication occurring through the body and entailing "cooperative activity with others and [being] the basis of shared significant symbols (Mead 1934), giving meaning to what one feels, sees, hears, smells, and touches" (Corbin and Strauss 1988:54). The tanned body derives its meanings from its position as both a subject (through its relation with a self and others) and an object (to the self and to others). Following Strauss, we can therefore say that there is "action *on* the [tanned] body, *toward* the [tanned] body, or *with respect* to the [tanned] body" (Strauss 1993:120; emphasis in original), and consequently performances *by* the tanned body and appearances *of* the tanned body. The symbolic and semiotic properties of such bodily performances and appearances stand in a reflexive relation to a semiotic self that evaluates meanings associated with the past untanned "Me" and, through a present agentic "I," acts toward an ideal future tanned "You" (Wiley 1994).

Gregory Stone (1962) and Erving Goffman (1959) identified the importance of managing bodily appearance and impressions through careful manipulation of the semiotic power of objects such as clothing, props, and settings. More recently, symbolic interactionist studies on the body have highlighted the meanings of performances and practices as varied as tattooing (Sanders 1989; Vail 1999) and exhibitionism in sexually charged Internet-mediated communication (Waskul 2002). These studies document the contemporary social trend toward a presentation of the self that takes place through actual or virtual, permanent or temporary modification of the body or body parts. Barry Glassner (1988, 1989) also noticed this trend and advanced the argument that the seductive power of images typical of postmodern culture has resulted in the boom of fitness programs and facilities, in the expansion of dieting clinics and programs, and ultimately in the widespread acceptance of plastic surgery. In essence ours is an image-centered culture based more than ever before on the power and widespread acceptance of seduction[5] as a form of strategic interaction (Baudrillard 1990a, 1993). In the contemporary United States, tanned white skin may connote that its possessor is a healthy, relatively affluent, sociable, physically fit, and attractive person, for example, and because the value of this object empowers, enhances, or endows the appearance of an enselfed body, we can say that tanned skin has not only a symbolic meaning but also semiotic power.

The Seduction Frame

Consistent with Glassner's (1988, 1989) argument on fitness and selfhood, we have documented the emergence of a seduction frame through which many in the general public interpret artificial tanning (McCright and Vannini 2004). This seduction frame is promoted explicitly by individuals (e.g., tanning salon owners and employees) and organizations (e.g., Indoor Tanning Association, National Tanning Training Institute, International Smart Tan Network) in the indoor tanning industry and implicitly by much of popular culture (e.g., beauty professionals, celebrities, and popular magazines).[6] Seduction frame proponents claim that regular bronzing of the skin will increase a person's physical attractiveness and overall mental and physical health. They claim that a suntan will heighten your physical beauty, help you look more athletically fit, and improve your self-esteem and self-confidence. In addition, they argue that sunlight may help people live longer, healthier lives since sunlight provides vitamin D, affects more than a hundred bodily functions, and is believed to increase longevity. Contrary to most existing scientific evidence, seduction frame proponents claim that sun exposure and tanning does not cause skin cancer. Indeed, these groups argue that suntanning dramatically reduces the risks of many other types of cancer. Ultimately, seduction frame proponents claim that artificial tanning is smart or good, because it is the most rational (i.e., efficient, standardized, and controlled) way to reap these seductive benefits.

The seduction frame encompasses some of the most common characteristics associated with postmodern society, such as the culture of the seductive image (Baudrillard 1993; Glassner 1988, 1989) and expressive personal appearance (Featherstone 1991a, 1991b). It connects the tanned body's appeal to a political economy of bodies and consumer objects and its meanings assume sign-value and symbolic-exchange value (see Baudrillard 1968). By tanning, the self plays with the authenticity of its body. The body technology of artificial tanning seemingly serves to liberate the white self of its pale appearance and enables the tanned white self to achieve a mythical seductive authenticity. In the seduction frame, then, the tanned self achieves its semiotic seductive power through its appeal for a voyeuristic crowd of both intimates and strangers. Consequently, the tanned self derives its self-esteem through the narcissistic realization of its semiotic power.

The triadic relation between the self, the body, and society is a semiotic one (Wiley 1994). However, the meanings that this semiotic relation may assume are largely dependent on the various frames through which people interpret how the tanned self is performed. We have identified the core elements of two competing frames. The medical frame highlights long-term costs and avoided risks and embodies coercive/repressive discursive power (e.g., "No, you shall not!"). On the other hand, the seduction frame highlights largely short-term costs and desired risks and embodies productive power (e.g. "Yes, you shall!"). While the essence of these frames is relatively stable, we argue that they nonetheless result from ongoing, contested processes that are similar to the dynamics of social movement framing processes (Benford and Snow 2000). The medical frame competes with the seduction frame for the definition of tanning practices. Tanners differentially internalize the essence of these two competing frames, and this evolving competition continues to influence their perceptions and negotiations of tanning practices.

Methods and Data

The data we analyze in this research consist of forty qualitative interviews with artificial tanners. The interviews were semistructured and nonstandardized (Denzin 1989). The length of interviews varied between thirty and sixty minutes. We occasionally interviewed more than one individual at a time when friends said they would not mind talking to us together. We gave each participant the option to terminate the interview at any point and the freedom to refuse to answer any question. We granted confidentiality to everyone who agreed to participate, and we report only pseudonyms below.

We contacted tanners through snowball sampling. We initially asked for volunteers in several large upper-level sociology classes at one midsized public university in the Pacific Northwest to put us in touch with friends or family members who artificially tanned and who would not mind speaking to us. Later we managed to contact five more male tanners in a different city in the Pacific Northwest. In addition we contacted a tanning salon manager and another tanning salon worker, both of whom introduced us to artificial tanners of various ages and backgrounds. Our sample consisted of twenty-three women and seventeen men. The ages of tanners ranged from eighteen to fifty-two, but most were between twenty and thirty years old. All were of white European background, except for two men who were Japanese. We collected basic background information about each participant, such as age, place of birth, places of recent residence, and ethnic and class background. There was some socioeconomic diversity among tanners, but all had what could be considered a middle-class background. Finally, we taped, transcribed, and coded interviews for similarity and variability among themes (Denzin 1989).

We approached interviews from the angle of social semiotics; that is, besides asking artificial tanners about their own practices, we asked them to interpret the meanings of tanning. In doing so, we intended to learn how tanners give meaning to tanned bodies. For example, we asked artificial tanners questions such as "What does a tanned body communicate about a person?" and "What does a pale body communicate about a person?" Peter Manning (1987) suggested that researchers can combine semiotics and fieldwork and that the results can maximize the interpretive value of research. We derive inspiration from Manning's work by asking ourselves how our research subjects are *"oriented* to the messages" (Manning 1987:43) they communicate to others through their bodies and through what frames they exchange these messages. Precisely, we asked our research subjects what they intended to communicate about themselves through their tanned bodies and what information they could learn about others by simply looking at their tanned bodies. However, we also deviate from Manning's conceptualization, as we rely on Peircean rather than Saussurean semiotics.

Norman Denzin (1992) suggested that symbolic interactionism must develop a more refined approach to the theoretical and empirical study of signs and sign systems and must link that semiotic approach to the critical study of the operation of ideological systems. Social semiotics provides researchers with such a framework (Gottdiener 1985, 1995; Hodge and Kress 1988; Vannini 2004). Social semiotics is based on pragmatism and American semiotics (e.g., Peirce 1960)—as well as on critical linguistics (Halliday 1978)—and opposes formalism, idealism, and European structural semiology (e.g., Saussure 1959). There is a sharp difference between social semiotics and semiotics. Social semioticians follow both Peircean pragmatism and a critical epistemology and believe that meaning arises out of social interaction. Semioticians instead are formalists and idealists and believe that meaning arises out of the structure of signs and sign systems. In short, social semioticians share much with symbolic interactionists (Vannini 2004), as they also believe that power plays a crucial role in the process of assigning meaning to signs, which is known as semiosis. Because semiosis always takes place in a context (known as an exosemiotic context) bounded by specific historical, political, economic, and cultural relations, the construction, exchange, and interpretation of signs are shaped by heterogeneous relations of power. Therefore, when interpreting tanners' own interpretations, we paid close attention to the positioning of meanings within discursive frames and within the power configurations that characterize these frames.

Talking with Artificial Tanners

Becoming an Artifical Tanner

Medical studies have found that people begin artificially tanning at young ages and continue to tan with highly variable frequency (Cokkinides et al. 2002; Demko, Borawski, and Debanne 2003; Geller, Colditz, and Oliveria 2002; Knight, Kirincich, and Farmer 2002; Mawn and Fleischer 1993; Young and Walker 1998). The women in our sample began tanning earlier than did the men. In general, younger (i.e., ages twenty to thirty) women started artificially tanning during their first few years of high school, whereas younger men began tanning as late as the senior year in high school or even later, during their early twenties. The older women in our sample (i.e., over thirty) started tanning in their thirties and forties, which approximately coincided with the late 1980s and early 1990s. None of our informants began frequenting tanning salons before the late 1980s. The earliest a participant began tanning was at age twelve; accompanied by her mother in preparation for a family trip, she later quit tanning and did not begin again until her late teens.

As technologies became widely available with the rise of consumer demand in the 1980s, tanning salons relied on a rapidly expanding body-consumer culture to increase business volume. Following Featherstone (1991a), we suggest that the practice of artificial tanning has coupled the traditional concept of self-preservation of the body with a newer vision of the body as a sign of youth, pleasure, and self-expression. This trend partially resulted in the commodification of the body, which works in different ways across different age groups. For older consumers, a tanned skin may be desirable because it helps to conceal age spots and skin blotches and also makes it difficult to perceive skin wrinkles—thus providing an illusion that it halts the aging process. However, the obvious biochemical fact is that extensive tanning actually accelerates the aging of the skin (but visible signs of this are evident only in the long term, long after the short-term benefits of tanning cease). Younger consumers who may not yet be interested in slowing the signs of aging interpret tanning differently as it helps to highlight muscular tone, thus making one's silhouette seem thinner. Physical appeal and self-expression play an important role in the development of adolescents' identities, and in light of the sharp increase in teenage buying power it is not surprising that they constitute a large segment of the tanning market (see Danesi 2003).

We investigated the interplay of motives and age by inquiring about the first tanning salon experience. In their narratives, interviewees emphasized the uncomfortable feeling they associated with lying on a coffinlike bed. For example, Kristi reported:

The first time was freaky; God, I can still remember how freaked out I was. To begin with, you walk into this tiny room where there is little or no furniture except for the bed. And it *stinks* in there, I mean . . . *Ew!* It literally smells like burned up flesh. You know, they have fans, and I guess they try and clean it all up before a customer walks in, but it still smells like they have literally been burning up bodies in there. And if you get past that like I kind of did, you lie on the glass bed and you know how you have to close yourself in, right? Well it felt like I was dead and that was my coffin. It was hot in there, I began getting really sweaty and impatient, and when I got up my skin was all icky. It felt really weird.

The sense of sacrifice documented above points to the asceticism present in tanning. Within the seduction frame, beauty, fitness, and health are not perceived as natural properties but rather as the fruit of hard work. Interestingly, this self-discipline goes hand in hand with the hedonism and narcissism underlying the contemporary concern with body appearance enhancement (Featherstone 1991a). The preoccupation with the seductive body generally reflects a new ethic that calls for every body to be aesthetically pleasing and relatively healthy and condemns the unfit, the smoker, and now the pale as the new deviants (see Edgley and Brissett 1990).

Women tanned more frequently than did men, although frequencies varied greatly. One needs both time and money to use a tanning salon, and these resources vary across individuals and time. Moreover, people often buy tanning salon packages that end up structuring their attendance. For example, some tanning salons sell monthly passes for unlimited tanning, whereas others sell session-based packages that can include from as few as five sessions to as many as twenty.[7] Some salons also sell yearly passes and often use incentives to lure patrons to return. For example, a salon may use a point system that allows a patron to tan more cheaply as he or she tans more frequently throughout the year. In spite of these incentives, most tanners' schedules are inconsistent. A typical tanner, for instance, may go to a salon as often as three or four times a week during a "peak" period and then discontinue tanning for as long as two months. Tanners must decide on the costs and benefits of different types of investment. Some of the students we interviewed admitted tanning less at times during the semester when studying is a priority. Older tanners, such as some parents we interviewed, told us that they could not afford to go to tanning salons when large and important family expenses took precedence. Clearly, tanning is a form of investment in one's physical capital that must be understood within larger socioeconomic dynamics.

Habitual, or "heavy," tanners (sometimes referred to as "tanorexics" or "tanaholics") are a minority, but it is difficult to estimate the size of this group. In fact, whereas we spoke to only three young women who *admitted* tanning as often as two or three times a week approximately every week, there may be a discrepancy between admissions and the truth. In our interviews with salon workers we discovered a different reality, as the following excerpt from Laura's comments testifies.

> You know, I have to tell you that at my salon we had two conflicting priorities, I guess you could say. On one hand, we're in business to make money, but on the other hand, we know that some people are just getting sicker and sicker as a result of coming in. We give people disclaimers, we warn them about not coming in too often, and whenever we found it necessary we can simply not let someone in because they look just *too* tanned. When I was working [at the salon] I had a pretty good number of ladies, some quite older than the average girl who comes in, who would try and come in every day, and I mean *every* day. And I don't know how many times I saw them try to come in more than once a day. If I happened to be working the second time they'd show up I'd send them home, but I know that they would come in later on when I was off and tell a coworker of mine that that was their first of the day. And if that didn't work out they would go over across the street to one of the other salons in the area.

Every commodity and service produced in a capitalistic society has the potential of being addictive because of its seemingly endless supply. Consumer products and services have seductive qualities, but as Baudrillard (1990b:73) explained, "the age of hidden persuasion is over." Instead, seducers openly display their symbolic-exchange value (Baudrillard 1990b:73). Tanners, for example, uncover their bodies and display their bronzed skin for everyone to see: hiding tanned skin would be senseless. Furthermore, the body lies at the center of all addictions because the logic of endless consumption may serve to push away, at least illusorily, death (Baudrillard 1993). While none of the people we interviewed admitted to having an addiction problem, almost all of them told us they had friends or acquaintances who may be tanaholics. For example, twenty-year-old Janet told us that she recently had an animated argument with her roommate who, according to Janet, needed help to stop her incessant tanning.

Everyone with whom we spoke identified certain peak tanning times that largely coincided with the following seasons: the arrival of spring, the arrival of summer, and the weeks before the winter holiday season. The arrival of spring and summer motivated our artificial tanners in similar ways. In warm weather, individuals spend more time outdoors and wear more skin-revealing clothing:

> Justine: You know how it is, I mean for us girls, we normally wear less in the summer or spring than in winter, and it just looks bad if you're as white as snow in the middle of June or July.

> Bryan: Well, when summer comes around you want to look a little nicer and wear shirts or stuff like that. I like to work out and lift weights, and sometimes I can do that outside in our house's backyard. But sometimes I'll end up just working out at the gym, so you can't really get tanned unless you go to a salon. Besides, if you go to a salon you get to even your tan up. It sucks when you have tan lines.

Of course, these seasonal occasions have strong social implications for the presentation of the embodied self. Goffman (1959, 1963, 1967, 1969) taught us that agency plays a central role in bodily performance. By controlling and monitoring their bodies in order to maximize the benefits of social interaction, tanners make strategic use of the semiotic power of their skin. Performing the embodied self at a wedding, a prom, or any social event requires that one look one's best at a time when the norms contained in the "shared vocabularies of body idiom" (Goffman 1963:35) are most intense and demanding.

One would assume that when it is sunny and warm outside tanners would prefer sunbathing to tanning salons, but this is not always the case. The *arrival* of the warmer months (which in the Pacific Northwest occurs usually around mid-April) requires that skin be ready for the upcoming hot summer days. For many artificial tanners, the spring season and very early summer are times of intense salon attendance. When summer weather brings continuous sunny days, then the need to artificially tan slightly decreases, but it does not disappear. At this time, many artificial tanners will frequent salons *in combination* with sunbathing, so that artificial tanning *prepares* one to sunbathe when sunbathing is possible and also *enables* one to tan when it is not. As stated above, a few individuals in our sample tan year-round, and even those who do not, feel there are a number of benefits in tanning during the cold months of the year. For example, those who tan around Christmastime do so to prepare for holiday trips, family reunions, or various social occasions (such as New Year's Eve parties). Furthermore, the few who tan more during autumn and winter do so because they enjoy the feeling of warmth associated with tanning on otherwise cold, bleak days or simply because they just want their skin bronzed at all times.

We asked our informants if they would consider stopping tanning at some future date. A few, mostly women, admitted they would not quit in the foreseeable future. Others told us they had neither thought about it nor believed they might quit when time or money becomes scarce or when their priorities change. Megan, quoted below, is a young woman whose skin was oddly orange-colored and marked with spots and moles.

> Megan: Yeah, I guess . . . I could stop one day. I know that it's not good for you. I mean my mom got skin cancer because of it . . .
> Interviewer: You mean your mother right now has skin cancer because of tanning too much?
> Megan: Oh yeah, and she lives in Hawaii, and so she tans outside a lot too, and the doctor told her it's basically because of tanning too much. Anyways, I know that I don't have it yet, so I guess I can always stop when I start to see moles popping up on my skin.

As we discuss in depth below, perceptions and behaviors such as these are enabled or motivated by the alluring power of the interpretive frame that individuals use to assign meaning to signs. While psychology can explain individual risk-taking behavior, the social conception of risk and the culture-dependent evaluation of costs and opportunities associated with choices and action outcomes lie in the semiotic power of the interpretive frame that artificial tanners use. In simple words, Megan, whose disposition may be shocking to us, is simply choosing the seduction frame because it is more appealing to her than the medical frame.

Motives

We found one underlying motive for artificial tanning: the enhancement of one's appearance. Informants clearly linked body image with self-esteem. With no exceptions, our informants told us that tanned skin improves their looks in different ways (see Netburn 2002). For example:

> Kate: It's better brown and fat than white and fat!

> Amber: It makes me look thinner, I mean, I'm sure a lot of women have told you that it makes them look like ten pounds less.

> Immanuel: Well, I actually used to have acne when I was younger and obviously I hated that. I heard that tanning would clear up my skin, so I started doing it and I kept on doing it and I like myself better now.

> Ted: It's kind of cool cuz it helps you bring out your definition. . . . It just saves you so much work at the gym cuz it really makes you look more shaped and lean, you know.

As we discovered, informants believe that tanning improves their appearance in many ways. Some tanners like to wear gold jewelry or bright-colored clothing, and tanned skin enhances the contrasts. Others like to be outside in the spring and summer, and tanned skin makes them feel more comfortable at the pool, on the beach, or anywhere where other people may be tanned. Some women find themselves dating after a failed marriage and believe that tanning—together with dieting and cosmetics—gives them an edge in the dating scene. No matter what the specific strategy is, tanners' ultimate goal is to manage the impression they make by looking more seductive to others and themselves. The semiotic principle on which this conduct is based is rather simple: an object (tanned skin) connotes positive characteristics such as youthfulness, sexiness, sociability, affluence, and healthfulness. Tanners then use these meanings of bronzed skin in a variety of ways beneficial to them. The most evident of these ways is the use of tanned skin in strategic (seductive) interaction (see Goffman 1969).

Possibly the most common purpose of artificial tanning is to obtain a "base tan," which helps one to prepare for more tanning.

> Krissi: What I do a lot of, is go to a salon to get a base. Like, when spring comes around and I have a plan to go on a trip, like last year for example. Before I went to Hawaii I bought a package of ten tans at a salon to get a base before going to Hawaii, so that I could get there and tan outside and not get burned . . .
> Interviewer: So you didn't get burned?
> Krissi: Yeah I did actually. I got burned here and in Hawaii [laughs]. But that's because I tanned too fast, I mean before leaving, and when I got to Hawaii it was so nice that I spent too much time outside [laughs].

Managers of artificial tanning salons know that many patrons come in to get ready for suntanning immediately before times of the year when road trips are common. The salon workers we interviewed told us that salons will often offer considerable discounts around spring break and before long weekends such as President's Day or Memorial Day. Tanners believe that by "getting their skin ready" for a major suntan they will avoid burns—an idea they find appealing. Not only are burns painful, but being burned during a holiday trip may cause them to look unsightly (and even incompetent) and thus stay away from the pool or the beach where the action is. While this interpretation seems guided by the seduction frame, it also illustrates the apparent influence of the medical frame.[8]

When asked if they preferred results obtained through artificial tanning to those obtained through sunbathing, most of our informants chose the former. Some suggested that a "real" suntan looks more natural—but only insofar as it is uniform, and many admit that a uniform suntan is very difficult to achieve. Others claimed that an artificial tan is more even, is easier to control by going to a salon regularly, and is safer. In addition to appearance enhancement, artificial tanning offers a relatively wide variety of advantages especially in comparison to natural sunbathing. Informants, both male and female, agreed on the following about sunbathing: it takes too much time; it is boring lying outside just to get a good tan; it demands privacy; it requires adequate space, which may not always be available; it is much too dependent on the presence of good weather; and it often causes tan lines (while on a private tanning bed one can freely tan in the nude).

In sum, the simulation (tanning lamp) becomes more efficient than the real (sun) (see Baudrillard 1983), and artificial tanning guarantees quick and efficient results, privacy, and predictability. The only problem for almost everyone is the somewhat mythical orange boundary line:

> Justine: I don't think there's that big of a difference between a real tan and a fake bake [artificial tan]. I mean, like I said, I think fake-baking is more convenient, but then you gotta be real careful about it. I'm sure you've seen these girls at the gym who just look like oranges. Seriously, don't they have any friends to tell them it looks stupid? That's where you gotta draw the line, when it looks fake . . .
>
> Interviewer: But wait, it *is* fake!
>
> Justine: Yeah, but the problem is when it *looks* fake.

Justine's declaration is quite interesting when examined from a symbolic interactionist and dramaturgical perspective. As Goffman (1959) explained, there is a clear difference between impressions we give and the impressions we give off. While an audience and a performer tacitly agree that the performer is strategically managing a certain front, they are also participating in an information game in which the performer reveals more information about himself or herself through nonintentional than through intentional communication. The impression given off here is that one is "trying too hard." Health, indeed, is an important component of the seduction frame. When one's skin is too tanned, it serves as a reminder that tanning is also a health risk. This also illustrates the efficacy of the medical frame for the interpretation of tanned skin. With tanning there are socially agreed on conventions about what is and what is not aesthetically pleasing. Through social interaction people create aesthetic norms (Becker 1982) on the fashionableness of shades of tanning much like they create norms on the appropriateness of clothing for specific contexts (Stone 1962). And finally, in relation to the authenticity of a false object (artificially tanned skin), one need only think that it is not the use of technology in itself that invalidates authenticity but rather how technology is used (as in the case of a body that is *too* tanned) (Grossberg 1992).

An additional concern for artificial tanners who debate whether to rely on the sun or the tanning lamp involves which one provides a longer-lasting tan. Most informants believed that a real suntan can stay on longer than a "fake bake," but many were also concerned about getting burned while sunbathing. Thus most salon customers follow a controlled progressive-increment routine under the lamp. They may, for example, start out with a ten-minute session to build up a tan and then move gradually to twenty minutes and then level back to fifteen minutes to maintain it. Salons generally enforce these practices depending on the initial skin tone of a customer. A fair-haired and fair-eyed patron is usually instructed to take it easy on the bed. However, these judgments are left completely to the subjective discretion of those who own their own lamps for home use. One young man who owned such a machine said, "Yeah, I don't care. I'll do forty minutes. Sometimes it feels so nice that I nap in there."

A small minority of interviewees believed they suffered from seasonal affective disorder (SAD) and that exposure to light and warmth during the winter helped them to combat their despondent moods.[9] Only one informant, however, was diagnosed with SAD by a physician. All of those who mentioned this motive told us that it was only a secondary reason, however.

Of Real Beauty and Symbolic Seduction

Many artificial tanners with whom we spoke acknowledged that tanning is part of a much larger "package" that includes commercial bodily practices related to health, fitness, and beauty. Katherine, in response to the interviewer's question about how much money she spent on her "tanning habit," said:

> I put in more than I should, I guess. But you know it's really hard to say. I mean, shouldn't we include the tanning lotions, moisturizers, and accelerants that go with it? I guess it's all part of a package that has to include money spent on makeup, hairdos, paying for the gym, health foods, and more stuff like that.

This is the package about which Featherstone (1991a, 1991b) and Glassner (1988, 1989) wrote. The body plays a central role in our postindustrial economy, and tanning is but another practice that is quickly becoming as common as fitness and exercise. Tanners, then, do not simply get their skin bronzed; they also attempt to make it smooth, toned, young, and healthy-*looking*. Sex appeal and sexuality play some role in the seduction frame, but it is important to emphasize that a tanned body is also meant to connote ambition, success, and *fitness*—that is, the ability to fit in—the various contexts of a postmodern society governed by the logic of seductive images (Featherstone 1991a, 1991b).

Because we are interested in the interplay of gender, seduction, and embodied interaction, we decided to explore the extent to which tanners were conscious of their body image. We discovered a number of gender differences. Female tanners seemed to spend much more money than did male tanners, as one might expect from having knowledge of gender expectations of physical attractiveness in our culture. But, more interestingly, some of the men admitted feeling no shame in violating gender expectations.

> Steve: I guess us guys are not supposed to be so much into our own looks, but, whatever, I like myself better when I'm tanned.
> Interviewer: Do your buddies give you a hard time?
> Steve: Sure they do. They're all like, "Hey dude, did you go tanning yet?" and stuff, but they're just dumb asses, and they say that just to be cool and tough but then they go

and do it too. I'd say about half the men in my [fraternity] house tan. I still think that we spend way less money than girls do, though, cuz we don't normally buy all that crap they buy.

Judging from our sample, men who tan understand that there are cultural norms that discourage them from being excessively concerned with their appearance, especially with having a "pretty boy" look. But at the same time, they see tanning as similar to weightlifting, a more traditionally masculine activity. All the men we interviewed worked out more or less regularly and found nothing "effeminate" about tanning. This is an interesting finding because it highlights the link between tanning, health, fitness, and beauty within the common seduction frame. Our interviews with men revealed that tanning has become more normative over time for men. For example, Kazuhiro said:

I lived in London for a while, after I moved out of Japan, and then after that I moved to the States. So I guess I could tell you what it's like to tan in three different countries if you want. But let me tell you that when I moved to the States a few years ago I stopped tanning at first. Here, everybody made a huge deal about tanning, I mean all my guy friends thought tanning was gay and only chicks do that kind of stuff. But then after a while I started working out and hanging out with different people, and I guess that's about the time more men started tanning too, so I started doing it again.

Gender is a performance (Butler 1990), and these young men perform their androgynous identity. This is not an uncommon finding; others have observed how images of masculinity increasingly acknowledge male concern with appearance (Bancroft 1998). A recent pop culture buzzword is *metrosexual*, which refers to an urban man with refined taste and a strong aesthetic sense who spends substantial time and money on his appearance and lifestyle. We believe that the metrosexual concept, much like the diffusion of tanning among males, is another sign of the pervasiveness of the seduction frame in our culture. To validate this interpretation, we discussed the issue of men who artificially tan with our female informants. Only two women, both of whom are young, told us they thought it was "weird" that men tan. They thought a man should have a more rugged look, not look like a "smooth-skinned pretty boy." None of the other female tanners found it intrinsically strange that men tan, and many explicitly expressed their preference for tanned skin in men—thus underlining the change in gender expectations. Many young women told us that men who tan are also likely to work out, dress nicer, and in general take better care of their appearance and have better taste than—as one female informant put it— "men sitting at home on their couch drinking beer and watching football."

All of our interviewees believed that tanned skin is attractive skin, but we wanted to understand how they generated that belief. In other words, aside from our knowledge that some people find that tanning is fashionable, we were interested in actual interpersonal exchanges between tanners and their acquaintances. It is through discourse that individuals shape meaning (Blumer 1969), and we were obviously interested in learning about specific instances of interaction. We discovered that tanning is often a topic of conversation among friends (and especially among female friends). Sometimes tanners will drive to a tanning salon together; sometimes they will consult with one another on the best products to purchase, the most effective types of lamps, and the frequency and length of sessions, and so forth. But this "tan talk" also works in other important ways.

> Interviewer: So, does anyone actually tell you, "Oh you look nice, you must have been tanning!"
> Jessica: Oh yeah, totally. I get it a lot actually, and I can so tell the difference of people's reactions when I'm pale. Just not too long ago I was at my parents' house and my mom saw how pale I was and she told me to get a tan. But that's just one example. My friends, for example, will tell me stuff like "You look nicer when you're tanned" or "Hey I haven't seen you in a while, you look so good tanned like that."
> Paula: My kids tan. Both the boys and the girls. And I tell them to.
> Interviewer: You tell your kids to get tanned?
> Paula: Oh yeah [laughs]. They look so much better when they're tanned.

We discovered that tanners receive positive feedback from different types of people: close friends and acquaintances, family, and romantic partners. Of course, this finding should not shock anyone; we are all aware that we derive our sense of self and our body image from interaction with others (Cooley 1964; Mead 1934). But this feedback loop does not always work in the same way. Most female partners explained that the feedback they receive comes mostly from other females. Justine said:

> I usually get that [positive feedback] from my girlfriends. Sometimes my sister may have said something to me, but it's usually friends. Not guys. Guys don't notice that. And if they do, they won't tell you. Guys—that's my theory—they look at the big picture, at the "package," you know what I mean? If a girl has a nice body, she's dressed well, and she looks cute a guy will be like "Oh yeah, she's hot," but I don't know of guys who will focus on a girl's tan and see that apart from the rest. Don't get me wrong, it has to be there though, it's really important. You don't wanna look really really good all around but then be pale, cuz then guys will notice that.

We tested Justine's idea with other female tanners, and they corroborated it. For example, Cassidy told us, "Yeah, I agree with that, totally. And on top of that I'd add that even though we girls may do it to get guys' attention, we also do it to get girls' attention. I mean, not in a sexual way, but there is always that kind of competition among girls, you know."

Evidently, then, what matters to a tanner is the point of view of a reference group of significant others (Shibutani 1961). This obviously varies among individual tanners and is largely dependent on social networking strategies. From the perspective of the semiotic self (Wiley 1994), the tanner's self poses a future "You" as an ideal self and uses past "Me's" as references for present action. This semiotic and reflexive self then uses the technology of artificial tanning to reach an ideal state of tanned authenticity.

Everyone in our sample thought that tanned skin connotes health and that a pale complexion signifies illness and poor health. This is clearly ironic as recent medical evidence points out that tanned skin is indexical of rapid aging and possibly even cancer. But medical discourse is not very convincing or compelling among tanners. We asked our informants to reflect on this issue. Katja's insightful statement raises a central point of this article:

> Well, yeah, you're right, it should mean it is sick, but people believe things that fit their version of reality rather than what is actually real. Beauty gives you power, and especially at our age we're more interested in sexual stuff, and appearance, and attractiveness than health. And so younger people take more risks, I've learned in my intro psychology class, and I agree with that.

Through tanning—and the enhancement of appearance that tanning is believed to give—the body assumes seductive power. This seductive power is dependent on the semiotic meanings associated with tanned skin, and we have called this the semiotic seductive power of the human body.

In our interviews we were also interested in learning what channels are influential in the diffusion of messages that reinforce the value of tanning. Without much surprise we learned that most of our interviewees see tanned people on television and in music videos, films, magazines, and advertisements and therefore learn that "tan is in." While it would be a mistake to conclude that every fashionable person tans, one is hard-pressed to pick up a copy of *Self* or *Cosmopolitan* or *Fitness* and find a pasty-looking celebrity.[10]

Health, Risk, and Technology

In line with existing medical research on the phenomenon of artificial tanning, we found that despite awareness of the risks associated with both natural and artificial tanning, our interviewees were not particularly cautious about their practices (see Coupland and Coupland 1997; Knight, Kirincich, and Farmer 2002). For example, almost no one said they wore goggles under the lamp. Goggles play a critical role in protecting eyes from potential damage, but they also leave unappealing shades of paleness around the eyes. Approximately half of the people in our sample claimed to use some kind of lotion to protect from burns, but many believed that this clashed with their ultimate goal. As Chris put it: "Why would you put protective lotion over your body when you're paying to get tanned?" In fact, there are lotions marketed to artificial tanners. Many of these, despite promising to maintain a tan while protecting skin from burns, seem to have harmful effects on top of the damage caused by lamps (Palmer et al. 2002). While every one of the tanners we interviewed told us they try to tan in moderation (the definition of moderation is highly subjective, though), almost everyone experienced a burn at one time or another. Burns ranged from minor annoyances that would abate within a few days to major dermatological problems that required medical attention. In addition to what people told us, two female interviewees were noticeably burned when we spoke to them.

Medical discourse on sunburns, the risk of cancer, and the risk of premature aging seemed to matter little, however. Most of our respondents had collected information about the side effects of tanning from a variety of sources, including salon workers, popular magazine articles, Internet articles, television, and their friends. But just about everyone seemed to downplay this risk. As one young man said: "What can you do these days that does *not* cause cancer?" Much of this risk-taking behavior was explained to us as a form of "getting the best out of life" and "doing your body a little bad and a little good at the same time." This disposition seems to corroborate our argument about the power of the seduction frame. Tanners are not unaware of an alternative interpretation (the medical frame); they simply prefer to interpret tanning within the seduction frame. In their analysis of medical discourse and sunbathing, Coupland and Coupland (1997) reached a very similar conclusion: health is important, but the appearance of being healthy is more important even if it is detrimental to physical health. This makes especially good sense within the seduction frame: seduction, after all, is a play of *appearances* and signs, as Baudrillard (1990a) opined.

Few of our informants had direct experience with tanless lotions. Tanless lotions are different from accelerants in that they basically work like a skin dye, allowing one to look tanned without tanning artificially or naturally. While tanless lotions have few side effects, apparently their results are not always satisfactory. Few of our informants had tried tanless lotions, but many of them had a friend or an acquaintance who made regular use of the products and as a result looked "funny" and even "ridiculous" because of their uneven orange or waxy brown tone. We even learned of a young woman who had apparently become "addicted" to tanless lotions and could not leave the house without applying copious doses of her favorite brand.

Besides fostering (and being fostered by) a new relation with our body, artificial tanning evokes the picture of a body increasingly shaped by technological practices. We asked our interviewees to interpret for us the fine line between the real and the artificial through an admittedly complex question.

> P.V.: Do you believe that what is natural is beautiful, or do you believe that what is artificial is beautiful?
> Katie: Well, both I guess. We always say that what is natural is beautiful, but then we try to re-create whatever is natural through technology. If I said that what is artificial isn't beautiful, after all, I'd contradict myself, you know, why would I tan?

Indeed, this was a difficult issue to investigate, but just about everyone claimed that the line between the natural and the artificial is difficult to draw. In a very pragmatic fashion Katie and others explained to us that they do what makes them feel good, and technology and commerce are driven by this need for the improvement of life. Clearly, however, this "need," so typical of the seduction frame, is linked to issues of political economy and material power. If beauty becomes a commodity, then do we not live in a society in which even physical beauty is socially stratified? The answer is yes according to both Bourdieu (1984), who wrote about how physical capital lies at the foundations of a political economy of bodies, and Baudrillard (1968), who explained how desire and consumption are socially stratified. The following reflection by Simone corroborates this argument.

> You know, I definitely think so, look how much money goes into looking good, from wearing the right clothes to buying a gym membership, to tanning passes. You need to pay a price to be beautiful in our society. I mean there definitely are people who are poor and are still beautiful, but you just won't see them on TV or at the movies.

Most of the people we interviewed seemed to agree on this point. There was, however, considerable disagreement over the "so what?" element of this scenario. Some reflected on this situation from a position of politically progressive liberalism and condemned the marriage of commercial interests and beauty, whereas others simply told us "this is the way things are." Perhaps biased by our own adherence to feminist ideals, we asked both men and women if this situation is fair at all to women, who are pressured to tan more than men (and engage in related body practices from dieting to wearing makeup). While we encountered a variety of answers, from the more conservative to the more politically emancipatory, we were intrigued with the issue raised by Katja:

> OK, I have thought about this one. I consider myself a feminist, a moderate feminist, but a feminist. So why do I do all these things I do to look better? And why do so many women do all these things they do? My take on it is this, if beauty gives us power, then great. I don't know if it is men or women or both that make up all these ideas that we have in our mind, but if a woman gains power over a man in any way, then it's good for women, right? How many guys do you know that go gaga over some girl and will do anything for her? Beauty gives you power.

Here Katja raises critical issues of agency, culture, and the gendered stratification of social structure. While we abstain from tackling ideological reflections on her statement, we come away with the understanding that while social forces shape bodies, bodies also agentically shape these social forces. The issue, therefore, is one of *body power* as well as of power *over* bodies, that is, a question of bodies as subjects of social action and bodies as objects of social action, and of the blurred boundaries separating these oppositions.

Conclusion: Semiotic Power and Seduction

We have argued that the semiotic properties of the medical frame are not as powerful as those of the seduction frame. Meaning possesses semiotic power (Wiley 1994), and the frames through which we interpret the meaning of objects also possess semiotic power. Meaning and interpretive frames derive their semiotic power, at least in part, by alluring, charming, and seducing us to believe. Just as we are seduced to believe in the power of the meaning of freedom, justice, and equality, we are equally seduced to believe in the power of the meaning of beauty. Through the seduction frame the tanned self is allured by the semiotic power of tanned beauty. The medical frame is less compelling because it does not hold an equally strong power to seduce the self into belief.

The human body assumes symbolic meaning and also semiotic power through social interaction in a specific context. Through social interaction in the context of postmodern culture—and within the seduction frame in particular—artificial tanners are constantly told that they look "good," "sexy," "beautiful," "young," "healthy," and so forth. Through the mechanism of the looking-glass self (Cooley 1964), these tanners conclude that their appearance is pleasing to others. Because beauty is a valued characteristic in our society, feeling beautiful is directly associated with a more positive self-concept, and such a positive self-concept directly and positively motivates an individual's conduct (Gecas 1991). Therefore, the semiotic seductive power of the tanned body has value for its possessor.

The semiotic seductive power of one's tanned body also has value for others. Not only do people like being looked at, but they also like looking at beautiful, young, healthy, and fit others. This is the idea of scopophilia, more or less explicitly present in the work of Goffman, Baudrillard, and Foucault. The voyeuristic pleasure of the "gaze" is clearly evident in sexual encounters (Waskul 2002) as well as in public and less sexualized encounters (Goffman 1963). The pleasure of the gaze and the frequency and social acceptability of gazing are stronger in a postmodern society where seductive images of the body and of consumer products float abundantly (Featherstone 1991a, 1991b; Glassner 1988, 1989). Perhaps a bit narcissistically, artificial tanners—and arguably many of us in general, whether we tan or not—like to seduce as much as to be seduced. Seduction, as we argued, is a play with meanings and appearances of material objects and of the embodied self.

The self is a sign, as Peirce (1960) believed. In our postmodern culture the self signifies much meaning through changing body images and constantly shifting bodily practices—and thus mostly through surfaces rather than depths. The relation among the body, the self, and society therefore assumes great theoretical importance in postmodern society. But contrary to some of the excesses of postmodern theory, we believe that such a triadic relation is not governed by the illogical play of floating signifiers. The body, much like the self and society, is not just made of fluid meanings but instead is an "empirically verifiable and objectively real thing" (Waskul, Douglass, and Edgley 2000:377). For all its playing with appearances and meaning after all, the tanned self/body is at risk of cancer and death, aging and disease. The importance of a theoretical approach to the body-to-self-to-society (Waskul, Douglass, and Edgley 2000) relationship lies in the need to tease out the relation among dynamics of semiotic reflexivity, historical contingence, individual agency, bodily processes, and matters of sign-value in the context of a political economy of embodied selves and enselfed bodies.

In this article, we have attempted to specify that the body-to-self-to-society relation is dependent on two closely interrelated forces: the semiotic power of meaning and the power of seduction. We are not alone in suggesting that symbolic interactionists ought to pay more attention to issues of the semiotic power of meaning. Norbert Wiley (1994) and Eugene Rochberg-Halton (1986) reminded us that symbolic interactionists too often neglect the contributions of Charles Sanders Peirce to a semiotic and pragmatic theory of meaning. Peircean ontology holds the key for a reflexive approach to the study of the self and the semiotic power of meaning (Wiley 1994). What is needed is an extension into the terrain of the power of embodied seduction, and we hope this article represents a step in that direction.

NOTES

1. Our research focuses almost exclusively on Caucasians, or whites, in the United States. While some people of color have also begun to artificially tan their skin in recent years, the more prevalent historical trend has been for people of color to "whiten" or bleach their skin to conform to European-based notions of beauty.

2. We argue that the difference between the symbolic and the semiotic is to be found in the sign-value of an object. In itself bronzed skin is merely an index (Peirce 1960) of a natural phenomenon, sunburn. But in a specific historical, political, economic, and cultural context tanned skin *connotes* value.

3. Excessive exposure to UV light is also linked to photosensitivity, photo-aging, pseudophorphyria, eye damage, photo-aggravated disease, pruritus, nausea, immunosuppression, polymorphous light eruption, and the formation of basal and squamous skin cell carcinomas and middermal elastolysis. Even the use of most tanning lotions and accelerators is linked to a higher risk of contracting hepatitis and aplastic anemia (see Palmer et al. 2002).

4. Furthermore, while Mead reminded us that though we may produce disparate symbolic meanings out of our bodily action and our embodied interaction, the human body is still anchored in physiological processes that lead to such material events as birth and death. This is not a backward way of reintroducing outdated notions of biological determinism but a way of reminding ourselves that the symbolic and the material are interconnected. The body, as socially constructed as it may be, is still subject to illness, such as skin cancer, and ultimately death (Charmaz 1995; Frank 1991).

5. Seduction is not necessarily a sexual practice. More generally, "seduction" means alluring, charming, and even enticing someone to believe by attraction and charm. Artificial tanners seduce not through sex but through play with meanings. Seductors and seductresses undermine the certainty of meanings through which their tanned bodies are to be interpreted. By doing so, tanned selves lead the objects of their seduction to ask themselves, What is really going on around here? Is this a real fit, healthy, and "naturally" beautiful body? Is this the body of an affluent, ambitious, popular, and successful self?

6. It is important to recognize that the practice of artificial tanning may become more or less fashionable over time. Anecdotal evidence suggests that some may now view tanning as passé and already replaced by the use of tanless lotions or sprays (now offered by a growing number of salons) or even by the permanent alteration of one's skin color, which is becoming increasingly common among both whites and nonwhites. Arguably, this succession of

substitutions of simulations with other simulations is indicative of the continuous movement toward the fourth order of simulacra hypothesized by Baudrillard (1983, 1993). Yet, a "retro" return to pale, pasty skin is also feasible. In sum, what is certain is that the presentation of the tanned self assumes meaning and power within the seduction frame, symptomatic of a contemporary society in which power is based on stimulation as much as domination (Baudrillard 1968, 1990a; Foucault 1980).

7. Prices vary considerably due to the range of collateral services. Some packages, for example, include manicure, pedicure, hair removal, and nail sessions, or even enrollment in fitness classes.

8. Medical frame proponents, however, are quick to claim that a base tan is nothing but a burn on top of which other burns will accumulate (see Spencer and Amonette 1998).

9. This, of course, raises questions related to the social construction of SAD that we cannot pursue here because of space constraints.

10. One young woman pointed out a possible link between larger racial issues and the tanning of Caucasian people. This self-professed fan of rap and hip-hop went as far as to say, "I wish I was black." No other interviewees brought up similar issues, however.

REFERENCES

American Medical Association (AMA). 1994. *House of Delegates Interim Meeting, Resolution 217.* Chicago: American Medical Association.

Bancroft, Angus. 1998. "The Model of a Man." Pp. 26–38 in *The Body in Qualitative Research,* edited by J. Richardson and A. Shaw. Aldershot: Ashgate.

Baudrillard, Jean. 1968. *Le systeme des objects.* Paris: Gallimard.

———. 1983. *Simulations.* New York: Semiotext(e).

———. 1990a. *Seduction.* New York: St. Martin's Press.

———. 1990b. *The Transparency of Evil.* London: Verso.

———. 1993. *Symbolic Exchange and Death.* Thousand Oaks, CA: Sage.

Becker, Howard. 1982. *Art Worlds.* Berkeley: University of California Press.

Benford, Robert D., and David A. Snow. 2000. "Framing Processes and Social Movements." *Annual Review of Sociology* 26:611–39.

Blumer, Herbert. 1969. *Symbolic Interactionism.* Englewood Cliffs, NJ: Prentice Hall.

Bourdieu, Pierre. 1984. *Distinction.* London: Routledge.

Butler, Judith. 1990. *Gender Trouble.* New York: Routledge.

Charmaz, Kathy. 1995. "The Body, Identity, and Self." *Sociological Quarterly* 36:657–80.

Cokkinides, Vilma, Martin Weinstock, Mary O'Connell, and Michael Thun. 2002. "Use of Indoor Tanning Sunlamps by U.S. Youth, Ages 11–18 Years." *Pediatrics* 109:1124–30.

Cooley, Charles. 1964. *Human Nature and the Social Order.* New York: Scribner's.

Corbin, Juliet, and Anselm Strauss. 1988. *Unending Care and Work.* San Francisco: Jossey Bass.

Coupland, Nikolas, and Justine Coupland. 1997. "Bodies, Beaches, and Burn-Times: 'Environmentalism' and Its Discursive Competitors." *Discourse and Society* 8(1):7–25.

Danesi, Marcel. 2003. *Forever Young.* Toronto: University of Toronto Press.

Demko, Catherine, Elaine Borawski, and Sara Debanne. 2003. "Use of Indoor Tanning Facilities by White Adolescents in the United States." *Archives of Pediatrics and Adolescent Medicine* 157:854–60.

Denzin, Norman. 1989. *The Research Act*. Englewood Cliffs, NJ: Prentice Hall.

———. 1992. *Symbolic Interactionism and Cultural Studies*. Cambridge, MA: Blackwell.

Desmond, Jane. 1999. *Staging Tourism*. Chicago: University of Chicago Press.

Douglas, Mary. 1966. *Purity and Danger*. New York: Praeger.

Edgley, Charles, and Dennis Brissett. 1990. "Health Nazis and the Cult of the Perfect Body: Some Polemical Observations." *Symbolic Interaction* 13:257–79.

Falk, Pasi. 1994. *The Consuming Body*. Thousand Oaks, CA: Sage.

Featherstone, Mike. 1991a. "The Body in Consumer Culture." Pp. 170–96 in *The Body*, edited by M. Featherstone, M. Hepworth, and B. Turner. Newbury Park, CA: Sage.

———. 1991b. *Consumer Culture and Postmodernism*. London: Sage.

Featherstone, Mike, Mike Hepworth, and Bryan Turner, eds. 1991. *The Body*. Newbury Park, CA: Sage.

Foucault, Michel. 1980. *Power/Knowledge*. New York: Pantheon.

Frank, Arthur. 1991. "For a Sociology of the Body." Pp. 36–102 in *The Body*, edited by M. Featherstone, M. Hepworth, and B. Turner. Newbury Park, CA: Sage.

Gecas, Viktor. 1991. "The Self-Concept as a Basis for a Theory of Motivation." Pp. 171–88 in *The Self-Society Dynamic*, edited by J. Howard and P. Callero. Cambridge: Cambridge University Press.

Geller, Allan, Graham Colditz, and Susan Oliveria. 2002. "Use of Sunscreen, Sunburning Rates, and Tanning Bed Use among More than 10,000 U.S. Children and Adolescents." *Pediatrics* 109:1009–14.

Glassner, Barry. 1988. *Bodies*. New York: Putnam.

———. 1989. "Fitness and the Postmodern Self." *Journal of Health and Social Behavior* 30:180–91.

Goffman, Erving. 1959. *The Presentation of Self in Everyday Life*. New York: Anchor Books.

———. 1963. *Behavior in Public Places*. New York: Free Press.

———. 1967. *Interaction Ritual*. Chicago: Aldine.

———. 1969. *Strategic Interaction*. Philadelphia: University of Pennsylvania Press.

———. 1974. *Frame Analysis*. New York: Harper and Row.

Gottdiener, Mark. 1985. "Hegemony and Mass Culture." *American Journal of Sociology* 90:979–99.

———. 1995. *Postmodern Semiotics*. Cambridge, MA: Blackwell.

Grossberg, Lawrence. 1992. *We Gotta Get Out of This Place*. New York: Routledge.

Halliday, Michael. 1978. *Language as Social Semiotics*. London: Arnold.

Hodge, Robert, and Gunther Kress. 1988. *Social Semiotics*. Ithaca: Cornell University Press.

Holubar, Karl, and C. Schmidt. 1994. *Sun and Skin*. Vienna: Verlag der Osterreichischen Arztekammer.

Indoor Tanning Association. 2004. "About ITA." Available at http://www.theita.com/page.php?ArticleID55. February 4.

International Agency for Research on Cancer. 1992. *Monograph on the Evaluation of Carcinogenic Risks to Humans: Ultraviolet Radiation*. Vol. 55. Lyon, France: IARC.

Knight, Matthew, Anna Kirincich, and Evan Farmer. 2002. "Awareness of the Risks of Tanning Lamps Does Not Influence Behavior among College Students." *Archives of Dermatology* 138:1311–16.

Manning, Peter K. 1987. *Semiotics and Fieldwork*. Newbury Park, CA: Sage.

Mawn, V., and A. Fleischer. 1993. "A Survey of Attitudes, Beliefs, and Behavior Regarding Tanning Bed Use, Sunbathing, and Sunscreen Use." *Journal of the American Academy of Dermatology* 29:959–62.

Mead, George Herbert. 1934. *Mind, Self and Society.* Chicago: University of Chicago Press.

National Institute of Health. 1989. "Sunlight, Ultraviolet Radiation, and the Skin: A National Institute of Health Consensus Development Conference Statement." Bethesda, MD: U.S. Department of Health and Human Services, *Public Health Service* 7:1–23.

Netburn, Deborah. 2002. "Young, Carefree and Hooked on Sun Lamps." *New York Times,* May 26, p. 9.1.

Palmer, Richard, Joni Mayer, Susan Woodruff, Laura Eckhardt, and James Sallis. 2002. "Indoor Tanning Facility Density in Eighty U.S. Cities." *Journal of Community Health* 27:191–202.

Peirce, Charles S. 1960. *Collected Papers of Charles Sanders Peirce.* 6 vols. Cambridge: Harvard University Press.

Randle, Henry. 1997. "Suntanning: Differences in Perceptions throughout History." *Mayo Clinic Proceedings* 72:461–66.

Richardson, John, and Alison Shaw, eds. 1998. *The Body in Qualitative Research.* Aldershot: Ashgate.

Rochberg-Halton, Eugene. 1986. *Meaning and Modernity.* Chicago: University of Chicago Press.

Sanders, Clinton. 1989. *Customizing the Body.* Philadelphia: Temple University Press.

Saussure, Ferdinand de. 1959. *Course in General Linguistics.* Trans. Wade Baskin. New York: McGraw-Hill.

Shibutani, Tamotsu. 1961. *Society and Personality.* Berkeley: University of California Press.

Shilling, Chris. 1993. *The Body and Social Theory.* London: Sage.

Spencer J., and R. Amonette. 1998. "Tanning Beds and Skin Cancer." *Clinical Dermatology* 16:487–501.

Stone, Gregory P. 1962. "Appearance and the Self." Pp. 86–118 in *Human Nature and Social Process*, edited by A. M. Rose. Boston: Houghton Mifflin.

Strauss, Anselm. 1993. *Continual Permutations of Action.* New York: Aldine de Gruyter.

Swerdlow, A. J., and M. A. Weinstock. 1998. "Do Tanning Lamps Cause Melanoma? An Epidemiologic Assessment." *Journal of the American Academy of Dermatology* 38:89–98.

Turner, Bryan. 1991. "Recent Developments in the Theory of the Body." Pp. 1–35 in *The Body*, edited by M. Featherstone, M. Hepworth, and B. Turner. Newbury Park, CA: Sage.

———. 1996. *The Body and Society.* 2d ed. Thousand Oaks, CA: Sage.

Vail, Angus. 1999. "Tattoos Are like Potato Chips . . . You Can't Have Just One." *Deviant Behavior* 20:253–73.

Vannini, Phillip. 2004. "Toward an Interpretive Analytics of the Sign: Interactionism, Power, and Semiosis." *Studies in Symbolic Interaction* 26:151–176.

Vannini, Phillip and Aaron McCright. 2004. "To Die For: The Seductive Semiotic Power of the Tanned Body." *Symbolic Interaction* 27:151–176.

Veblen, Thorstein. 1899. *The Theory of the Leisure Class.* London: Macmillan.

Waskul, Dennis D. 2002. "The Naked Self." *Symbolic Interaction* 25:199–227.

Waskul, Dennis, Mark Douglass, and Charles Edgley. 2000. "Cybersex: Outercourse and the Enselfment of the Body." *Symbolic Interaction* 23:375–97.

Westerdahl J., C. Ingvar, A. Masback, N. Johnsson, and H. Olsson. 2000. "Risk of Cutaneous Malignant Melanoma in Relation to Use of Sunbeds." *British Journal of Cancer* 82:1593–99.

Wiley, Norbert. 1994. *The Semiotic Self.* Chicago: University of Chicago Press.

Young, Janice Clark, and Robert Walker. 1998. "Understanding Students' Indoor Tanning Practices and Beliefs to Reduce Skin Cancer Risks." *American Journal of Health Studies* 14:120–27.

12

The Naked Self
Being a Body in Televideo Cybersex

Dennis D. Waskul

In any form of interaction, the body becomes an object to one's self and others, presenting itself as an acting subject and a viewed object. This characteristic of the body is explicit in sex, making it a distinctively and pleasingly embodied experience, for in order to have sex a body is necessary. In sex our bodies become objects for the purpose of pleasure in our partner(s) and ourselves. Yet sex is not merely about bodies; it is inextricably infused with subjective meaning. As Simmel (1950:131) suggests, "Sexual intercourse is the most intimate and personal process, but on the other hand, it is absolutely general. . . . [T]he psychological secret of this act lies in its double character of being both wholly personal and wholly impersonal." For these reasons, sex is an ideal context for examining the interplay between the objective and subjective qualities of the body and the self and how these are mediated by situated social interaction.

Cybersex is a form of experience that makes these relationships especially salient. After all, the Internet is among the most dislocated and disembodied contexts for real-time human interaction. "The body—or its absence—is central to contemporary notions of 'cyberspace,' 'the Internet,' 'virtuality': computer-mediated communications (CMC) are defined around the absence of physical presence, the fact that we can be interactively present to each other as unanchored textual bodies without being proximate or visible as definite physical objects" (Slater 1998:91). On the Internet, participants interact with others in separate electronic space removed from the immediate presence of the body. Because sex requires a body, cybersex participants must evoke them, and in this process the role and nature of the body is necessarily magnified. In text-based cybersex, participants evoke a subjective semiotic body through typed words. In televideo cybersex, participants interact through digital cameras that display live images of their bodies. Thus televideo cybersex participants evoke the body as an image; they quite intentionally display their bodies as *objects* to be seen. What

---

From *Symbolic Interaction*, Volume 25, Number 2, pp. 199–227. © 2002 the Society for the Study of Symbolic Interaction. Reprinted with permission of the University of California Press and the Society for the Study of Symbolic Interaction.

is the relationship among bodies, selves, and society in these complex erotic forms of social interaction? What can these relationships tell us about the interplay among bodies, selves, and society in everyday life?

Cybersex and the Body: Textual Enselfment and Video Embodiment

"Cybersex" has rapidly become a catch-all term used to refer to an enormous range of computer-mediated sexually explicit material, including adult CD-ROMs, interactive games, and pornographic sound, image, and video files often available over the Internet (Robinson and Tamosaitis 1993). However, in spite of these commercial uses of the term, we find that cybersex is only marginally related to pornography and is more squarely situated in a specific kind of interactive erotic *experience*.[1]

Among experienced cybersex participants, little ambiguity exists as to what constitutes cybersex. It refers strictly to erotic forms of real-time computer-mediated communication. Through typed text or live video (and sometimes spoken voice) cybersex participants meet one another for erotic encounters in the ether of computer-mediated environments. Regardless of the form, however, cybersex always entails meeting someone else in these decidedly liminal "places" where real people interact with other real people for the purposes of sexual arousal and gratification. This study is concerned only with televideo cybersex—casual and usually anonymous televideo sexual encounters between participants who do it for fun.[2]

Although televideo cybersex entails considerable text communication, it differs from text cybersex in that one can *see* the other person(s) involved in live streaming video. By using relatively inexpensive digital cameras and client software, in televideo live images of one's partner accompany "hot chat." What they look like, what they are (or are not) wearing, where they are, their moment-by-moment expressions, and what they are doing (often to themselves) are all apparent. For this reason, televideo contrasts with text cybersex: *it is an embodied experience.* Televideo cybersex participants embody themselves in the images that represent them. Indeed, the purpose of televideo cybersex is to see images, the bodies of other people, and to be seen.

Thus one cannot, as in the case of text cybersex, simply create a body of unbounded dimensions and attributes. In televideo the body is not a "pure object of meaning" (Waskul, Douglass, and Edgley 2000:394); instead it is presented as an object—a visible *thing*, an image attached to the corporeal person, put on display with the intention of being seen for the purposes of giving and receiving sexual attention or arousal.

The Object and Subject Body: Sex, Objects, and Sex Objects

I make myself flesh in order to impel the Other to realize *for herself* and *for me* her own flesh, and my caresses cause my flesh to be born for me insofar as it is for the Other *flesh causing her to be born as*

flesh. I make her enjoy my flesh through her flesh in order to compel
her to feel herself flesh.

—Jean-Paul Sartre, *Being and Nothingness*

Being treated as an object—a physical body—is a necessary part of human sexuality.[3]
In sex we have little choice in this matter of being an object, but neither do we have this
choice in any other form of interaction. The very nature of personhood is to be both
perceiver and perceived, subject and object. Indeed, "the self has the characteristic that
it is an object to itself" (Mead 1934:136). Likewise, the body is always both a noun and a
verb; we inhabit an object body (noun) that is subjectively experienced in embodiment
(verb). Although symbolic interactionists have studied the dual nature of the object/
subject self, comparatively little investigation has explored the nature, extent, and processes by which the body adheres to this same quality and the relationships between
the objective/subjective body and the self as it is experienced in situated contexts.

Until the early 1990s interactionist literature had largely ignored the body and its
relationships to the self, often latently implying (if not overtly stating) that the body is
little more than a container for selfhood or a thing to which a self is affixed (Waskul,
Douglass, and Edgley 2000).Traditional interactionist literature often saw selfhood as
"something housed within the body of its possessor . . . for he and his body merely
provide the peg on which something of collaborative manufacture will be hung for a
time" (Goffman 1959:252–53). Ironically, to conceive of the body as merely that in or
on which selfhood is contained or affixed is tantamount to equating the body with
the self and thus potentially undermines Mead's (1934:136) essential argument that
"we can distinguish very definitely between the self and the body. . . . [T]he parts of
the body are quite distinguishable from the self."

Interactionists were not alone in the tendency to turn a blind eye to the body.
Until quite recently the body has been conspicuously absent throughout sociology
(Shilling 1993; Smith 1990). Human agency has been equated with consciousness (if
at all), and there has been comparatively little serious consideration of this process
in relation to the corporeal body (Holstein and Gubrium 2000; Turner 1991). Over
the last decade the body has become the subject of considerable sociological interest,
owing significantly to the work of Michel Foucault and the scholars in medical and
feminist sociology. Yet a lingering conceptual chasm remains between sociological
theory and the body—a substantial divide that often makes the physical body a sociological enigma. However, a solid interactionist foundation exists in which we may
situate "both the body and the mind in the interpretive practices by which meaning is assigned to experience" (Holstein and Gubrium 2000:198) and thus answer the
challenge posed by Anselm Strauss:

> What is required is a set of related concepts—a conceptual framework—that will bring
> the body into line with characteristically human activities: how they are carried out,
> managed, and the contexts in which they take place and that affect these activities. *Ac-
> tion/interaction is where our focus should be.* The challenge is to relate body to this focus.
> (1993:108; original emphasis)

While the body may be *present* as an empirical *object,* its meaning and our ability to conceive of it is no more or less innately determined by the qualities of its "thing-ness" than any other object. In fact, "the body cannot be a direct object to itself: It is an object only to some actor" (Strauss 1993:110). This "actor" can be an individual or a group of individuals who act toward the body in some fashion (Strauss 1993). It is through a process of interpreting, assigning meaning, and internalizing these interactions that we come to indirectly interpret, know, and understand the body. In this way, as Mead (1934:136) might argue, the body can be an object unto itself but only insofar as a self is involved: "bodily experiences are for us organized about a self." It is "the self [that] makes possible the body as meaning" (Gadow 1982:89), for only by virtue of a self may we see and act toward our bodies as others might. We decorate it through clothing, adorn it through accessories, have sex with it through masturbation, and, in extreme duress, even kill it through suicide. In other words, we may extend Mead's overall point: the body and the self are not merely two separate entities; we can only experience either of them indirectly and symbolically by taking the role of the other.

The body and bodily states are experienced only indirectly in a process by which corporeal objective and subjective conditions are socially shaped. "Physiological sensations are only the raw material out of which bodily experiences are socially constructed" (Cahill 2001:47). As Mason-Schrock (1996) contends, transsexuals explicitly illustrate this relationship among the body, the self, and society. They believe they are born into the wrong body and must look elsewhere for signs of their true gendered selves. But it would be a mistake to understand this problem as limited to transsexuals and others in similarly extreme conditions. For all of us, the conceptual frameworks by which we interpret the body, the language we use to describe it, the narratives we tell about it, the situations in which we find it, and the definitions we impose on it have an influence on the body as an object and mediate how we experience it as a subject. While we may often apprehend the body in various physiological states—in sexual arousal, a drug high (Becker 1963, 1967), pain (Baumeister 1989), critical illness (Frank 1991), or any other corporeal condition—these are experiences, mediated by social structure, culture, interaction, and social situation.

We may argue that the body is experienced as an object and made meaningful as a subject through the same processes and symbolic capacities by which we acquire a self. As Mead (1934) points out, young infants have no selves but acquire them through interaction with others combined with the characteristically human symbolic capacity to take the role of the other with increasing degrees of sophistication. Thus the capacity for selfhood rests in our ability to see ourselves as others might, and as Strauss (1993) suggests, the same may be said for the body. Just as there is "a dynamic relationship between the acting self (subject) and the viewed self (object)" (Strauss 1993:112), so too is there a dynamic relationship between the acting body (subject) and the viewed body (object). To extend Mead's argument, we are born into a body, but we are not born with the capacity to understand that body as an object, to see it as others might, to assess what that body is, what it means, its parts, and its relationship to the whole being. The body, therefore, comes to acquire meaning in a symbolic process that is no different from any other object.[4]

However, the body is a special kind of object, "because it must represent the self in a special sense" (Strauss 1993:111). Because selfhood is symbolic and cannot be directly observed, it is all too easy to directly equate the self with the body and remain oblivious to distinctions between the two and to the broader relationships among bodies, selves, society, and the situations in which we interact. "Embodiment connotes personification, but it also can refer to the body itself as the materialization of otherwise invisible qualities. . . . [T]he body continues to be an omnipresent material mediator of who we are or hope to be" (Holstein and Gubrium 2000:197), and therefore this tendency to equate body and self is not entirely without merit.

To be sure, an immediate and undeniable relationship exists between the self and the body. This relationship takes vivid form when the severely stigmatized body negatively affects the self (see Goffman 1963b). More generally, a body is an obvious and necessary prerequisite to having a self; one can hardly speak of a self that has no body (after all, the loss of a body is tantamount to death; a self without a body is not a person; in common parlance we only refer to people as bodies when they are dead). As Simmel (1950:322,344) suggests, the body is our "first property." We unconditionally possess our body, it obeys our Will, and others may categorize it as belonging to us alone. But even so, "body and self, though inseparable, are not identical" (Gadow 1982:86). The body does not represent the whole of the self, and the self is not a physiological component of the body. As William James reminds us:

> Our bodies themselves, are they simply ours, or are they *us?* Certainly men have been ready to disown their bodies and to regard them as mere vestures, or even as prisons of clay from which they should someday be glad to escape. ([1892] 1961:44)

While Strauss argues that the distinction between the body and the self "is *only* an analytic artifact" (1993:113; original emphasis), we can remain this conceptually casual only if we ignore the significance of the body in relation to the self (Goffman 1963b; Mason-Schrock 1996) or the degree to which the body can become an independent object or subject completely detached from the self in social situations (Waskul, Douglass, and Edgley 2000). In addition, the increasing prevalence of social interaction technologies makes it possible to transcend the empirical shell of the body, thus severing its traditional connection to the self and the situatedness of both in social contexts. Technologies of communication, especially interaction on the Internet, make it increasingly possible to dislocate selfhood from the body, precariously situating and/or dislocating one or the other from the context of interaction. In some cases, these technologies permit the body to be "enselfed" (Waskul, Douglass, and Edgley 2000); in others (such as televideo cybersex) it permits participants to embody the self. These separations potentially relocate the subject *and* object of interactions and potentially transform or expose relationships between them.

Nudity and the Net: Voyeurs and Exhibitionists

It is easy to imagine what goes on in televideo cybersex. Participants meet one another in televideo environments (sometimes one on one, sometimes in groups), disrobe (partly or completely, if they are not already naked), display their bodies before others, and comment on what they are seeing. This experience typically leads to sexual arousal, self-touching, and masturbation—all of which participants usually (but not always) put on display for others to see. Often these provocative encounters become an emergent "conversation of gestures": one participant disrobes and flaunts his or her body; if pleased, the other participant may say so, disrobe, and do the same. One participant may begin to masturbate, inviting the other to join in. This conversation of gestures continues until its climactic conclusion. Couples (heterosexual or homosexual) will sometimes connect with individuals or other couples. Most often these erotic encounters occur between people who do not know one another and intend to have casual and immediate sexual gratification. Once satisfied, the interaction typically ends and participants disconnect. However, in spite of various differences, the eroticism of televideo cybersex emerges from a process of intentionally displaying one's body before others in an explicitly sexual manner.

On the surface, televideo cybersex may appear similar to other forms of public or semipublic nudity. It would seem to share much in common with nude beaches (Douglas 1977), nudist resorts (Weinberg 1965, 1966, 1967), the naturist movement (Bell and Holliday 2000), Finnish saunas (Edelsward 1991), streaking (Toolan et al. 1974), and the practice of exposing female breasts at Mardi Gras in New Orleans (Forsyth 1992). Like those who engage in other forms of semipublic nudity, televideo cybersex participants blatantly violate obvious cultural norms. In addition, cybersex occurs in an environment that shares a similar "liminal" (Turner 1969) stigma-suspending quality with other forms of public nudity. "Clothing modesty is a *ceremony* of everyday life that sustains a nonintimate definition of relationships, and with its voluntary suspension relationships are usually [redefined]" (Weinberg 1966:21; original emphasis). The Finnish sauna, like nude beaches, resorts, Mardi Gras, and televideo cybersex, "represents a symbolic separation from the ordinary, a liminal period characterized by separate space, separate time, and separate activities" (Edelsward 1991:193). This separation and liminality is marked by physical, temporal, normative, and symbolic territories. Televideo cybersex occurs in the already liminal world of "cyberspace," a place without space. On the Internet participants, from the comfort of their "space" at home (where nudity is permissible), interact with others in a semipublic "place" (where nudity is generally not permissible).

The Internet juxtaposes these "spaces" and "place," and thereby creates a natural environment for liminality: a place separate from one's space where the ordinary norms of everyday life easily may be suspended. In the final analysis, however, televideo cybersex differs markedly from other forms of public nudity (if we can call it "public" at all). Unlike saunas, nude beaches, and resorts, where nudity is purposely antierotic (Douglas 1977; Edelsward 1991; Weinberg 1981), the nakedness of televideo cybersex is intended to be read sexually. In the former, participants rigidly practice "studied inattention" (Douglas 1977:108), or what Goffman (1963a) calls "civil inattention." In contrast, televideo cybersex participants do not desexualize their nudity, they do not practice "civil inattention" toward the naked bodies of others, and they do not loathe the opportunistic gaze of those who may be watching. Instead they revel in attention. Unlike naturism, there is no "problematic relationship to sex" (Bell and Holliday 2000); nudity and sex are irrevocably intertwined. Nudity in the context of televideo cybersex has nothing to do with "a 'philosophy' which is all about bodies in nature" (Bell and Holliday 2000:127). It does not entail defying social norms and values (Toolan et al. 1974) or the freedom of naturism (Douglas 1977), and it does not involve a lifestyle among others who share strong bonds of solidarity (Edelsward 1991; Weinberg 1965, 1966, 1967). In televideo cybersex, being naked is undeniably and unambiguously about *sex*. Stripping and being seen nude is meant to be erotic, and there is no pretense of other motivation.

The eroticism of televideo cybersex is related to the pleasures of voyeurism and exhibitionism. However, in the objectified sense of the terms, the participants in this study are *not* true voyeurs or exhibitionists. Voyeurism is the practice of observing others in sexually arousing activities or postures. "Most of us are voyeurs to some extent or at some times: we enjoy looking at people, their visual depiction, or reading about sexual activities" (Kupfer 1983:94). Likewise, exhibitionism is the practice of putting our bodies on display as an object to be seen for the purposes of sexual arousal and attention. We are all exhibitionists to some extent or at some times: we enjoy being looked at, made to feel desirable, sexy, and attractive. Although sexual gazing and being looked upon makes up part of our sex lives, they do not substitute for our actual physical participation. Certainly exhibitionism and voyeurism often aroused participants in this study, but the experience was interactive. Because participants could see and respond to each other, little gap existed between what they watched and how it aroused them (and vice versa). Therefore, the voyeurism and exhibitionism of televideo cybersex closely approximates the voyeurism and exhibitionism of *any* sexual experience.

If the majority of participants in this study are not true voyeurs or exhibitionists, then what accounts for the eroticism of cybersex? How do televideo participants play with the natural tendencies of voyeurism and exhibitionism in their experiences of cybersex? Because both voyeurism and exhibitionism are focally related to the body, what are the implications and consequences of this experience on the self? Because televideo cybersex participants explicitly display their bodies as objects for the subjective sexual interpretation of voyeuristic glare, to what extent may we conclude that televideo cybersex is merely a playful extension of the same social processes by which all bodies are experienced in the interstices of being both object and subject?

Sexuality, Alter-sexuality, and Cybersex

In this study I use televideo cybersex as a strategic lens to allow us to see, further understand, and contemplate relationships among the body, the self, and situated social interaction. Sexuality may not be the direct topic of interest in this study: however, it is essential to address it. "Sexuality" is a general term that potentially can refer to almost anything that we may regard as sexual in relation to the person. Yet "sexuality" is commonly used in specific and concrete ways. We commonly speak of *"our* sexuality," or *"their* sexuality," but seldom do we think of it as merely *"a* sexuality." Thus people often assume that sexuality is connected directly to the person, as something that, although influenced or shaped by others, is within individuals and pertains to their bodies with regard to sex. Given that computer-mediated interaction is a distinctively dislocated and disembodied form of interaction, framing sexuality in this way poses serious problems for the study of sex on the Internet.

As Rival, Slater, and Miller indicate (1998:301), the cardinal attraction to sex on the Internet is the "license simply to float pleasurably through a shamelessly eroticized space." The key point, however, is that

> these pleasures and transgressions evidently depend upon *a clear separation of sexuality from "real life"*: they are without commitment or consequence; the material resources on which they depend (finance, technology, symbolic capital, labour) are obscured from view and experienced as beyond any scarcity. . . . [T]here are no material cares or dangers (including disease); no enduring commitments; performance is unproblematic; desire is inexhaustible, as is desirability (everyone is desired and included). Bodies neither fail, nor make non-sexual demands. (Rival, Slater, and Miller 1998:301; emphasis added)

In short, the dislocated and disembodied nature of computer-mediated communications makes cybersex an experience that potentially expresses a sexuality separate from and transgressive of the person, the body, and everyday life.

For these reasons, it remains unclear whether cybersex participants act out vicarious fantasies directly related to their sexuality or merely engage in cybersex as a form of communicative play only marginally related to sexuality. Whether we can ever tell the difference between the two is even more unclear. On the Internet, an otherwise heterosexual female could "go gay" for a fifteen-minute cybersex encounter. Possibly her lesbian cybersex experience is related to her sexuality, but equally possibly, it may not be. In fact, Slater's (1989:99) research on sexpic trading on Internet Relay Chat (IRC) found that "most informants were clear that one of the greatest pleasures and attractions of the IRC sexpics scene was not so much the direct indulgence of their own desires as a fascination with the diversity of human sexuality." Slater (1998:106–7) cites at length participants who find "both sexpics and cybersex very boring" and states, "Both are merely occasions or opportunities for other pleasures of the scene." Clearly these kinds of situations raise complex questions, but at the very least they suggest the need to conceive of the relationship between sexuality and cybersex differently.

In addition to an expression of sexuality, cybersex may constitute a form of *alter-sexuality*, referring to sexual experiences that differ from those in "real" life. They are a special category of sexual experiences that stand over and against, bounded within a sphere of experiences that can be comfortably maintained as separate and distinct from everyday life and may not be related directly to a person's "real" sexuality. Alter-sexuality is a kind of liminal experience in which both intimacy and sexuality may be reinvented in the context of loosened temporal, physical, and normative constraints.

How can we frame sexuality so that it may be dynamic enough to include the enormously varied and rich experiences that are made possible in cybersex? We may look to Goffman for a promising approach to framing sexuality and alter-sexuality in relation to cybersex. For Goffman (1959:252–53), the self "is a *product* of a scene that comes off, and it is not a *cause* of it. The self, then, as a performed character, is not an organic thing that has a specific location. . . . [I]t is a dramatic effect arising diffusely from a scene that is presented, and the characteristic issue, the crucial concern, is whether it will be credited or discredited" (original emphasis). Similarly we can argue that sexuality is the product of a scene that comes off, not a cause of it. Sexuality is a dramatic effect arising diffusely from the presented scene, and the crucial issue is whether sexuality is credited or discredited, not whether it is a genuine part of the individual. Framing sexuality in this fashion obliterates the problem of connecting cybersex to the person. As Goffman (1959:252) might argue, "while this [sexuality] is . . . *concerning* the individual, [it] does not derive from its possessor, but from the whole scene of his action, being generated by that attribute of local events which renders them interpretable by witnesses."

For the purposes of this research, sexuality is something that we *do*, not something that we *are*. Thus this research focuses on how participants "do" sexuality in televideo cybersex, with specific attention to how it is related to the body, the self, and situated social interaction.

Methods and Data

Methods

Open-ended qualitative interviews with televideo cybersex participants generated the data for this study. I spent several months and uncounted hours exploring and generally "hanging out" in televideo environments where people meet, chat, and watch each other in real time.

I accessed televideo environments that participants explicitly used for sexual purposes and invited them to contact me (via televideo) for a live online interview. Whenever possible, I avoided soliciting specific individuals for interviews so as not to disrupt the social and sexual context of these erotic environments. All respondents agreed to participate, were informed of the nature of the study, were guaranteed anonymity, and were given an opportunity to ask questions. Participants were told that they could withdraw from the interview at any time.

An unstructured nonstandardized interview strategy was used (Denzin 1989; Lincoln and Guba 1985) in which interview questions emerged from the responses of participants. This method of data collection relies on a conversational style that allows the discussion to flow from a participant's perspective (although sometimes the researcher refocused the direction of the conversation). This interview style also allows for tremendous flexibility and a free-flowing format that adds comfort and familiarity to the interview process. Moreover, it approximates the informal conversational structure of most online chat and televideo environments, making it quite useful for dealing with the sometimes delicate and potentially embarrassing issues involved in the experience of cybersex.

Because televideo cybersex participants are not particularly accessible for research, large samples are difficult to obtain. Even in adult televideo chat environments, not all participants are interested in sex or in answering intimate questions from a researcher. Still, over four months, I conducted thirty-one interviews. Interviews lasted between fifteen minutes and one hour. All participants in this study identified themselves (or could be recognized) as adults. Twenty-four participants were male, and seven were female. Nineteen identified themselves as heterosexual, six as homosexual, and six as bisexual. No additional identifying information was asked of the participants. Of course, given the size of the sample, the findings are merely suggestive.

Collecting Data on the Horny:
Ethics and the Role of the Researcher in Televideo Cybersex

I encountered unique ethical and methodological problems in interviewing televideo cybersex participants. All interviews were live and conducted via televideo. The sexual interests and motivations of participants sometimes made managing the interview difficult. In truth, because most of the participants were naked at the time of the interview, their erotic motivations could not be easily ignored. I was fully clothed (and thus the deviant within these environments) and the participants' nudity did not bother me. But in some cases the nudity and motivations of participants created circumstances that interfered with the research.

At no time did I lead participants to believe that I was interested in sex play, nor did I evince any pretense that the interview would turn into an opportunity for such activity. I "advertised" my interests in conducting interviews by using televideo identifying fields. For example, I often used the screen name "conducting research," or simply "research." Some televideo systems allow additional fields to provide identifying information (e.g., to advertise interests and preferences and to select participants whose interests are similar). I used these additional fields to invite participants to contact me for an interview. Of course, all interviews began with a briefing to make my motivations clear, to explain the nature of the study, and to answer questions.

Usually these taken-for-granted methodological practices make the purposes of the interview relatively clear, and they communicate what participants can expect. Still, during several interviews, it became necessary to politely remind participants that I was *not* conducting participant observation; that I was interested only in their thoughts, ideas, and contributions to understanding televideo cybersex. In short, it sometimes became necessary to tell respondents that I would not have televideo cybersex with them. In most cases respondents would jokingly dismiss their invitations, explaining that they were just kidding around, and legitimize their advances to me as a part of the playfulness of televideo. However, some participants would continue to use the interview as an opportunity for sexual arousal. For example, some would make certain the camera was focused squarely on their fully aroused genitals, others would try to entice me by behaving in a sexually provocative manner, and still others would try to seduce me in the process of answering interview questions. I do not wish to overstate this problem. The majority of participants were very helpful and cooperative. However, I found it necessary to discontinue five interviews. Although the frequent nudity, flirtation, and overt sexual playfulness did not bother me, my research demanded that participants were aware of the purposes of the interview, and although they may have had ulterior motives, they had to show a willingness to accommodate to my research purposes. At the very least, complex ethical issues surround this kind of erotic Hawthorne effect. At one level, continuing an interview with a participant who is merely "getting off" from being watched during the process of data collection raises ethical questions. In these circumstances, I am no longer just a researcher; I am a participant in an erotic episode regardless of my actual intent, action, and awareness. At another, more realistic level, these kinds of situations cannot be avoided in research such as this. One cannot interview naked people in erotic circumstances and expect to be anything less than a participant (of some kind) in a sexual encounter. Of course televideo cybersex participants will look at me, and I will look at them and understand that this interaction will arouse some participants.

In doing this kind of research, one must be prepared for situations like these. Playfulness, flirtation, and promiscuous online sex is exactly what this study focuses on, and therefore I could not expect to remove those elements from the data collection process and still claim to be studying the same thing. I can only imagine how much more difficult this research might have been if I were a female. As a male, I caught the fancy of some females, but generally, few females are found in these televideo environments and they are rarely as boorish as the men. Although it would be misleading to generalize, I encountered these problems only with a *few* gay men. If I were a female, however, there is little doubt that I would have been inundated with an excessive amount of male attention, and the nature of this problem would have multiplied exponentially.

As a final comment, scholars cannot conduct honest firsthand research on sexual behavior and not confront their own sexuality. Admittedly, I was naive to this fact during data collection. In retrospect, it is obvious that I used my role as "sociologist," and to a lesser degree "husband," to bracket my sexuality and suspend it from the context of my investigations in televideo cybersex. I am left to wonder if my research would not have been better if I were a participant, knowing it would have been much different. But even so, it would be doubly naive to suggest that my sexuality did not influence the people who chose to participate in this study, the questions I asked them, the responses they gave me, the data I have chosen to include in this article, and how I have framed my discussions of it. Is there a tinge of bias in my work? Does my status as a married heterosexual man latently taint my attempts to understand and communicate the nature of televideo cybersex? An honest answer would have to be "yes," although it was not intended. I interviewed persons of a wide range of sexualities, and each interview varied in length and depth. Thus differences in the amount and quality of data do in fact exist. Married women who identified themselves as heterosexual were far more willing to answer my questions at length, allowed more time for the interview, and provided the most detail in their accounts of televideo experiences. Perhaps I showed these women greater interest. Or perhaps they were just more interested in me; maybe women in general are more willing to discuss sexuality. Heterosexual men volunteered for the study but gave notably short responses and far less detail. Were they uncomfortable talking about such things to another man? Or was I less interested in hearing what they had to say and hence crippled in my ability to elicit further comments? Homosexual and bisexual men willingly participated in the study but here too often gave curt answers. Would I have gotten more descriptive replies if I had identified myself as homosexual or bisexual? In retrospect, my sexuality *has* influenced this research and become a part of this study.

Televideo Cybersex: Being a Body and Ephemeral Self-Reduction

Televideo cybersex is a hybrid form of erotica—part pornography and part live erotic entertainment. It is pornography to the extent that participants see or hear objective and computer-mediated sexually explicit sounds and images that are dislocated from the people they represent. People look at and listen to sexual sounds and images, giving televideo cybersex much the same voyeuristic appeal as any other kind of pornography, with the added twist of being live, fully interactive, and starring honest-to-goodness "amateurs."

What I like most is seeing hot studs!

It's just for fun. I like looking at other people. More like a game to see if you can guess what they're gonna look like with no clothes on.

Of course, I find the whole thing with televideo exciting and men are the reason. . . . It is exciting from one click to the next to see what is going to pop up in front of you.

I'm just like most males, I get hard just watching a pretty girl putting on a show.

Because televideo cybersex participants are not just watching but also being watched, the experience becomes more than pornography. They are live erotic performers and consumers, casual voyeurs, and exhibitionists all at once. The televideo cybersex norm is "you can watch me in exchange for me watching you"—a norm that can cause uneasiness. One woman explained, "I've only done it [televideo cybersex] for two different guys, but I didn't feel comfortable doing it so now I just flash a booby here or there."

Why would anyone feel compelled to show her body in a circumstance that makes her uncomfortable? All participants seem acutely aware of a very simple reciprocity, or "gift exchange" (Simmel 1950:392–93), that underlies the experience. Like nude beaches, there is in televideo cybersex a "reciprocity of nude exposure" (Douglas 1977:138). As Simmel (1950:392) points out, "Once we have received something good from another person . . . we are obliged ethically; we operate under a condition which, though neither social nor legal but moral, is still a coercion. . . . I am caused to return a gift, for instance, by the mere fact that I received it." Thus to the extent that participants are curious, interested, or aroused by what they see, they may feel compelled to make an equivalent exchange—to return the "gift"—so that they may continue to watch. As one participant stated, "I'd rather watch than show, but people want to see me in return for me seeing them."

Although being watched makes some televideo cybersex participants uncomfortable, for the vast majority, it makes the experience fun, exciting, and erotic. Many participants are excited by the simple fact that someone wants to see their naked bodies. As one man explains, "Knowing that someone wants to watch you is a turnon." Or, as simply stated by another, televideo cybersex involves a kind of looking-glass eroticism: "Being watched makes me feel sexy that someone would want to even watch." Similarly, for other participants the interactions that ensue while being watched make the experience exciting. For example: "I prefer to be watched and know I'm watched, with audience participation and involvement."

The Eros of Stripping, Being Naked, and the Naked Self

Stripping and being seen naked is what televideo cybersex is all about. Stripping exposes the "body's erotic generators" (Davis 1983:51)—genitals and other body parts that have been culturally sexualized (buttocks, breasts, legs, and other sexual generators ordinarily kept covered or concealed). The mere sight of them can be very arousing. Consequently, in nonsexual circumstances where nudity is sometimes required, such as medical examinations, others evoke dramaturgical techniques to neutralize the power of erotic generators or create distance between the body and those who are looking at it (Henslin and Biggs 1971; Smith and Kleinman 1989). Thus simply exposing one's "erotic generators" for the viewing pleasure of someone else can be erotic for several related reasons. First, it excites those who are watching and in doing so interactively stimulates our exhibitional imaginations. Second, it is the quickest way to turn *any* situation into a sexual one. Third, it is part of the condition of sex, and therefore we commonly associate it with sex. Indeed, "there is a strong element of sexuality in nudity and the very fact of the genitals being uncovered suggest[s] symbolically that they are more accessible" (Bryant 1982:26).And fourth, revealing what is normally concealed is in-and-of-itself a rush, a "sneaky thrill" (Katz 1988), or a feeling of liberation that comes from blatantly violating a cultural norm.[5]

If that were not enough, stripping reduces the self to an object. As one man indicated, sexual nudity with others fosters full embodiment; the self and the body are unified in a moment of negotiated sexual pleasure:

> Showing yourself in an excited state separates me from the real world. It becomes a focus, no reality, just a sexual moment and a focus on your sexuality. A focus on the sexual organs and also the body seen through the eyes of others.

"Just the act of removing one's clothes can help strip away symbolic identity and work roles, allowing one to become merely a body, which is the prerequisite for sexual pleasure" (Baumeister 1991:38). Stripping involves a "break through identity boundaries" (Davis 1983:51), in which we dispose of "all the grand, complex, abstract, wide-ranging definitions of self and become just a body again" (Baumeister 1991:12). A male participant refers to this identity breakthrough:

> I enjoy the freedom of being nude. I have a stressful vocation and it seems the pressures come off with the clothes. . . . Many of us are defined by what we wear. This causes others to pull on you or give you more to do. Such as a doctor 's outfit, a nurse 's outfit, etc. When naked there is no distinguishing way of identification or anything to link me or anyone else to work. Nudity is a great equalizer. Freedom to just be comes to the front.

For this reason, sex in general and stripping in particular "must at least have the potential of being one of life's boundary experiences" (Davis 1983:xx).Because stripping and being seen nude breaks through identity boundaries, many televideo cybersex participants claim to get much more than a mere orgasm from the experience. Precipitated in part by a viewing audience, *being* naked becomes an experiential state separate and distinct from the clothed world. Furthermore, nakedness is a condition in which one can *be* that is separate and distinct from the clothed selves of everyday life. Unlike nudity in private, being naked in semipublic places becomes a state in which one is placed as a social object—literally a thing—a body to be seen. Thus one becomes a "naked self," an objectified nude body presented for the purpose of being seen and interpreted as a sexual body.

Playing with the Object/Subject Body: Erotic Looking Glasses and the Reenchantment of the Sexual Body

By virtue of the naked self, many televideo cybersex participants are quick to point out "being naked" provides not only sexual benefits but also a variety of other benefits such as increasing appreciation for and assessment of their bodies:

> When someone is turned on by watching me, it makes me feel that I'm sexier than I truly believe I am. . . . It's nice to get compliments on . . . the body. . . . I just think it's sexy that people can masturbate and think of me, little ol' me.

Having a few dozen guys tell you how hot you are, etc., really gives you a great outlook on how you see yourself sexually. Positive reinforcement!

For these participants, the excitement that others receive from seeing them nude is repaid unto the self by the indirect yet comforting knowledge that one's body *is* appealing and desirable. Although a common theme for most participants, this reenchantment of the sexual body assumes special importance for those who, for various reasons, claim to be disenchanted with their bodies.

For some participants, this disenchantment has to do with perceptions of their appearances, especially with regard to age and weight—cultural standards of beauty and sexiness that refer directly to assessment of the corporeal body. The body may be disappointing to the self, but the sexual attention the individual receives in televideo cybersex serves to undermine that disappointment and reenchant the sexual body. As one man states, "It feels good when others compliment me. I feel like, even though I am overweight, I am accepted by them." A female participant explained that her weight normally disenchants her feelings of physical attractiveness. She also indicated an acute awareness that many men in televideo cybersex will merely tell her what she wants to hear to get what they want (presumably, a sexual performance). But interestingly, she voluntarily suspended her suspicions of deceit and found the trade-off is worthwhile because the attention she received served to reenchant feelings of sexiness and physical attractiveness:

[To be seen naked] feels wonderful! Of course, it makes me feel like he desires my body. I know in my head that he is going to say what I want to hear so he can get what he wants, but in turn I get what I want. . . . As you can see, I'm a pretty good size woman. I'm not uncomfortable about it on here. I feel as desirable as the ladies who are much smaller than me. As a matter of fact, I feel very sexy and seductive on here.

Others experience more ambiguous disenchantment and make vague reference to "self-esteem"—a self-imposed assessment of their selves, of which the body is merely a part. Like the participants cited above, the sexual attention to their bodies that they receive is repaid unto the self, but in this case the appearance of the body is less significant than the value they attribute to the self. In these conditions, the self is disappointing unto itself, but because the body and the self are inescapably connected, the positive sexual attention to the body increases the value they attribute to the self, as one woman indicated: "I enjoy most the emotional uplift I get from people telling me I am beautiful. I need to feel that I am still attractive. . . . It's just good to have people tell you [that] you are still attractive especially when I have a low self-esteem."

All of these participants suggest that at times the ways they conceive of the body and self is disenchanting and being naked in televideo cybersex reenchants these internal conceptions of the self and body. However, for some participants, the source of disenchantment has less to do with these kinds of intrapsychic assessments of the body and self and more to do with interpersonal social relations. In fact, overwhelmingly these participants connected the problem to marriage and long-term partnerships. For some, the problem is related to the routinization of their normal sexual activities and the desire for a different experience: "My main reason for being here is to be sociable, hoping to meet that Mr. Right even though I'm married and have a very active routine sex life at home.The routine part sucks!" For other participants, the problem is related to the monotonous "mono" of monogamy and the desire for someone different: "I've been in a long-term relationship for almost five years, and this way I can remain faithful to that while still getting off with hot guys from around the world." For many televideo cybersex participants, monotonous routinization of monogamous sexual relations intersects with their experiences of body and self and disenchants them.

Davis (1983:119) argues that "marriage seems almost intentionally designed to make sex boring." Long-term sexual relationships also tend to make our bodies boring. In time, being seen nude by one's lover becomes so commonplace or taken for granted that sexual generators simply run out of gas or otherwise lose their erotic power. When our own nudity no longer generates appreciative erotic power, a classic looking-glass (Cooley [1902] 1964) process may compel us to feel undesirable, unattractive, inadequate, and thoroughly unsexy. Thus some participants find televideo cybersex helpful in refueling a connection to their corporeal sexual body and the power of that body to generate eroticism:

> I've been with my wife for so long now that our bodies aren't as exciting as they once were. Our sex life is OK, but without that special quality I sometimes feel like a piece of furniture around the house. When someone is excited about seeing me in all my nudity I suddenly feel sexually awake again.

> Hubby is older than I am. He knows nothing of this. I'm not a complainer, but he does not have the passion or the desire, or at least he doesn't know how to show me. . . . It's hard for him to tap into the part of my brain that triggers the stimulation. I'm a very erotic person. The feeling of being naughty is a turn-on too. See I'm bad, but I love it.

These participants claim "therapeutic" value to the experience of interacting with others as a naked sexual object. This "nude therapy trip" is a relatively common theme among nude beachers also: "[A] lot of people got into traditional nudism for the nude therapy trip, a kind of commonsense, self-help therapy" (Douglas 1977:158).The use of nudity as a therapeutic tool in self-help groups, although not a common practice, is documented (Symonds 1971).To the extent that one attributes "therapeutic value" to the revealing of intimate secrets, being seen nude before others would constitute a dramatic context for such "therapy." More specifically (and less ideologically), being naked before others is a novel condition that shrinks selfhood to the body. A person sheds normal abstract and multifaceted symbolic layers of selfhood with the clothing as he or she becomes a body to be seen. Such a situation begs for interpretation and a redefinition of self that can be harnessed for "therapeutic" purposes, regardless of whether this occurs in the formal context of a self-help group (Symonds 1971) or in more casual experiences such as nude beaches and televideo cybersex.

For other participants, televideo cybersex offers little more than a new and novel mechanism for exploring and cultivating sexuality. For them, nudity is simply a condition of televideo cybersex, and the eroticism engulfs the experience of being naked. The novelty of the medium and the unique circumstances of being seen and interacting with others in the nude combines to form a potentially powerful erotic experience that builds from fantasies of promiscuous casual sex, orgies, and similar circumstances in which one's body is offered up as a piece of semipublic property. Thus first-timers and those who have just recently discovered "the joys of televideo sex" state:

> I just tried this on a friend's advice and last night I met a guy named ———. I mean to be honest, I have never been to that height before, even in actual sex. I had several orgasms, no man has done that before.

> Can I tell you a secret? I get more turned on here than I do with my husband.

Regardless of the specific motivations and personal benefits that televideo cybersex participants claim, all indicate that being naked in the presence of others reduces the whole of the self to the body. Being naked in the presence of others is a totalizing experience wherein selves are truly embodied. Awareness shrinks to the body and the immediate present (Baumeister 1991). Thus televideo cybersex does not remove the self but rather shrinks it down to a bare minimum. "The minimum self that a person can have is the body" (Baumeister 1991:17).

Further, selfhood not only shrinks to the body but also is made into an object—a naked sexual body to be looked at and commented on. Clearly these participants play with the experience of being object/subject and in the process often gain much more than just sexual gratification. In televideo cybersex "the body becomes a focus of interaction and hence a key constituent of the 'me' of the experience" (Glassner 1990:222). Yet these erotic naked episodes provide looking glasses to experience the body and thus create a space "where the 'I' does stand a chance, where one can both participate in and respond to the informational overbearance of the body" (Glassner 1990:223). As these participants indicate, the tension between the acting body and interpreting self (the "I") and the viewed body (the "me") functions as a kind of personal ritual of self-renewal (Davis 1983): by manipulating the relationships between them, one may temporarily enfeeble the self by being a body in order to return to selfhood reaffirmed.

Just Another Body: The Face, the Self, and the Body

Although selfhood may shrink to its bare minimum, that "shrinking" is only temporary, ephemeral, and squarely situated in the liminal online environment. In everyday life we can rarely separate the body so clearly from the self, and therefore in everyday life we remain far more accountable for what we do with, to, and by our bodies. It should be no surprise, then, that in "real life" these participants rarely, if ever, indulge in this kind of explicit and promiscuous sex play. As one woman reported, "I would not dare flirt like this in public. The men seem more open and flirtatious as well." A male participant expressed the same sentiment: "There is no way in hell that I'd do anything like this in real life!" In televideo cybersex being a body is a prerequisite for preserving the integrity and dignity of the self. Although long-term friendships and intimate real-life relationships can and do sometimes emerge from televideo encounters, most of the time the experience is fleeting, anonymous, and casual. Being seen naked (and often masturbating) in anonymous and casual semipublic social situations is, after all, taboo, and therefore, as Douglas (1977:58) reported with regard to nude beaches, many people are "afraid of being seen by friends or associates and branded a weirdo or a sexual pervert." So as not to implicate the self in the promiscuous virtual encounters, great efforts are usually taken to keep identity detached from the body. Because televideo cybersex participants can control the angle and zoom of the digital camera, this delicate dramaturgical task is most commonly achieved by simply not showing one's face. As one man explained, "It's all very anonymous, at least for me. I rarely show my face, therefore I am just another body. Once I show my face, it becomes too personal—I'm not just a body anymore!"

As televideo cybersex participants have discovered, a body without a face is a body without a self: it is "just another body."[6] Televideo cybersex participants are not the only ones to have learned this. Parts Models, a New York agency that specializes in modeling body parts, does not supply models for erotica, but when asked to find a female, fifty to sixty years old, willing to expose her nude chest for a health article in *Self* magazine, the editor claimed: "I screened the magazine very carefully and once they assured me they wouldn't use the model's face it was no problem" (Norwich 1987:51). David Roos of Gilla-Roos, Ltd., an agency that also specializes in parts modeling, described a similar circumstance: "We just shot a commercial for an airline. They wanted a 'chubby man who would stand in the water. Naked.' Of course we found their man, . . . but only because everything would be exposed except his face" (Norwich 1987:53).

Clearly the face occupies a supreme position in connecting or disconnecting the self with the body. One's face is the most identifiable feature of one's body and self; it is the single human physiological feature that concretely conjoins the corporeal body with the self. Although the face is just another part of our bodies, we tend to regard it as more uniquely ours than any other part. Significantly, the face is the one part of the body that is almost always seen naked, and therefore televideo cybersexmakes it extremely vulnerable. Because the face represents the most critical identifier of who we are, some fear recognition. As one woman stated, "I am afraid to show my face. I live in a small town and someone could notice me." A man said, "I do show my face, but not when I am getting to know someone. . . . I am well known in my community and also around the state where I live. You never know who might be online and checking in." Indeed, as this man makes poignantly clear, the vulnerability of "showing face" makes even the safest sex potentially risky:

> I don't show my face at first. I started doing that after an embarrassing situation with a coworker not long after installing the camera and software. . . . I had been putting on a show for someone with no cam for several days. A guy at work finally told me it was him [and he] wanted to play in real time. It was very embarrassing. . . . Since then, I've just felt more secure not showing face. [I] still do show face, but only after I'm sure I don't know the other person.[7]

Many televideo cybersex participants are concerned that their images can be saved, reproduced, and distributed. The images can be collected and used to incriminate the self. These men manage their anxieties by concealing their faces:

> I don't show my face because [the image] can be saved.

> I don't show my face just to protect my privacy. If this could not be saved, I would show my face more.

Not "showing face" conceals the greater and most significant aspect of one's identity, thereby making the process of being a body experientially complete. By detaching the face from the body, televideo cybersex environments often become a virtual meat locker of neck-down naked people. No two bodies are alike, of course, but without a self or an identity attached to them, they are *just* penises, breasts, buttocks, and torsos, making the experience exceedingly impersonal.

Some participants dislike the impersonal element of televideo cybersex; others thrive on it. As one participant indicated, those who like the impersonality refer to the need to be a *thing* from time to time: "Yes, it's impersonal and therefore not very fulfilling. But sometimes being impersonal is exactly what I crave! To simply be seen, looked at, desired, and for someone to comment on what they are seeing."

Those who dislike the impersonal virtual meat locker of televideo cybersex state that sex (even on the Internet) is much more fun when shared with a person rather than a mere object This point would seem obvious, but it is often overlooked. For example, the cultural critic Mark Dery (1922:42–43) claims that "the only thing better than making love *like* a machine, it seems, is making love *with* a machine." Dery is wrong. No matter how technologically advanced or expensive, or what geewhizzery it promises, machines and objects are no match for people in sexual affection. Almost everyone would rather have sex with a person because machines do not and cannot have a self, as some televideo cybersex participants remind us:

> Most of the time, I personally do not continue to carry on conversations with men who will not show me their face, with a few exceptions. However, it does become very impersonal when all they want from you is to help them masturbate, without ever seeing their face or expressions. I have connected before and just watched without feeling any sense of connection at all. [In these situations it was] very impersonal, and I wondered if the satisfaction they felt was comforting at all.

It's a bit impersonal. When I get to know the other person more, I show face.

My face is my best feature. How can people tell that you are happy doing what you do online if they can't see your expressions? The eyes, they are not alone as gateways to the soul, all language of the body shows the soul's words and wishes. . . . [Showing your face] lets people into your world a little more. . . . [T]o let them look into more of my world through my face and my expressions, brings them closer to the reason that I am masturbating online—not because I'm horny, or want attention, but because it makes me feel good to share the experience.

While nudity in and of itself transforms one's self and body into a unified object, nudity in the context of these semipublic televideo environments makes the objectification even more extreme. Objectification results in part from the medium itself. Televideo lacks the qualities of touching and feeling another body, and therefore, as one man described, televideo cybersex is "like looking at a live magazine." Even more, being a body is also a function of the social context. Social taboos against nudity and masturbation in public and semipublic places lead participants to conceal their identities and to present themselves as *only* a body or body part—a detached penis, vagina, or pair of breasts. At one level, being a body acts back unto the self in an erotic looking-glass process of ritual self-renewal. At another level, when one presents oneself as a body with no self, everything that makes one sexy, desirable, and interesting is stripped away, and having sex with a selfless body is not much different from having sex with any other object.

The Gendered Body in Televideo Cybersex

Although "you can watch me if I can watch you" may be the norm of televideo cybersex, in practice the sexual exchange is rarely this egalitarian. By virtue of their bodies some people have more power to "call the sexual shots" and many can command a performance without having to do so themselves. In televideo cybersex this power is undeniably available to *women*.[8] Further, although all women have this power, the more attractive they are, the more sexual power they may wield.

Because there are fewer women than men in casual televideo cybersex environments, men compete with other men to attract the interest of women, and this competition can get fierce. As one man casually remarked, "The fight for attractive people is awful." Key ways that men attempt to attract women are through advertising themselves by their screen names, or nicks, and, when additional fields are available, providing detailed descriptions of their physical features and special talents. Thus screen names and identifying fields become spaces for men to boast about themselves. Consider, for example, the following listings (all of which have been modified to protect participants' anonymity):

HardWood
BadMAN
BoyinNylon
HungDude
25 year old STUD
Fit, BIG COCK
Very Submissive
8" plus a lil' more
6', 185, Muscles, HUNG
Cum watch me j/o
Spank me!
Cute and playful!

Women are far less likely to advertise their physical features but instead tend to advertise their *preferences* so as to attract the right applicant for the job. The following are
examples of such listings (again, modified to protect the participants' anonymity):

BeHARD
Bi_ANN
Drippingpussy
Want HOT men
Prefer petite
4 BIG cock
I like BIG dicksl
Tempt Me-NO MEN!
Must be CUT!

Beyond attracting the initial attention of a woman, a man must be prepared to please
her and in many cases to listen, obey, and follow her instructions. With so many men to
choose from, women do not need to tolerate someone they find rude, offensive, unimag-
inative, ugly, uncooperative, or otherwise inadequate. In addition, the distance afforded
by the computer-mediated context adds an element of safety—for all participants, not
just women. Not surprisingly, many women feel a sense of liberation that is related to
this combination of distance, control, and what seems to be a reversal of sexual power:[9]

> It's sometimes empowering cuz I know I have the power to block someone I don't like
> or whatever.

> I think it's liberating. I have more power to choose and flirt with men without worrying
> about physical repercussions to me. It is functional.

> Being watched is erotic, and if they make me feel like a piece of meat, I have control.

> You choose who you want to see you, so you have a good idea how it will turn out.

Like other aspects of televideo cybersex, this privilege and power comes at a cost, which, unfortunately, ends up making televideo cybersex more *like* the everyday micropolitics of sex than a departure from them. Because men compete with other men for the attention of women, some men become too brazen, rude, and just plain offensive. Consequently, women sometimes find the heightened attention excessive. As one woman explained, "I think it is harassing sometimes the way they are so bold to just say or show something without knowing who or what is on the other end!" Another participant made the situation clear: "I think it's appalling. How worse could you treat someone than as a slab of tuck-flesh to be beaten off for?" One woman has gone so far as to categorize men on televideo according to how annoying their behavior is. She described the kind of excesses that women commonly encounter in these environments:

> I kinda got an order of which I perceive these men who are clamoring for attention. 1. Normal: fully dressed, at work or home, for chat or looking for love. 2. Semi's: without shirt with a big grin, usually married waiting to play with someone who is willing. 3. Regulars: showing nothing but their penis with an erection waiting for an orgasm (some are there every day). Some say they have two or three orgasms a day. Wow. They must never have real sex. 4. Kinkys: either doms, subs, bis, each are wanting something out of the ordinary in order for them to become excited. 5. Pervs: these are some sick mf's. They do ungodly things with their bodies, want to do really sick things—for example, shove a Pepsi can up his ass (I couldn't believe it), have sex with animals, etc . Overall it is very exciting when you are dealing with types 1, 2, and sometimes 3. But when it comes to the last two they harass the shit out of you, bothering you the whole time . . . until you finally have to just put them on your ignore list.

The naked body is, in glaring clarity, a *gendered* body.[10] Many social roles can be shed along with the clothing worn to play them, but some roles are permanently fashioned into our skin—and the more of that skin we show, the more salient that role becomes. While McCormick and Leonard (1996:110) claim that in cyberspace "we are freed from our physical bodies," that so-called freedom (see Waskul, Douglas, and Edgley 2000) is no more or less possible to obtain in televideo environments than in everyday life. In fact, it should be no surprise that the traditional micropolitics of sex become paramount—even exaggerated—when genders interact in the nude on the Internet, or anywhere else.

Conclusion

Computer-mediated communication is a dislocated form of interaction that occurs in a social "place" without necessary connection to geographic "space," where the activities of participants and experiences of self are not necessarily contained or affixed to corporeal bodies (Waskul, Douglas, and Edgley 2000).These characteristics create a context in which online interaction may assume unique forms that have the potential to challenge traditional understandings of self, body, and social situations and the relationships among them.[11] As previous studies have indicated, the dislocated nature of online interaction may be related to experiences of "ultimate disembodiment" (e.g., Waskul, Douglas, and Edgley 2000). As this study suggests, the same quality of the medium may also allow for experiences of "total embodiment"—a condition in which one is embodied within an image of one's own body. In the final analysis, computer-mediated communication is like all other forms of human interaction: it is *emergent* from the purposes of the communication within *situated* contexts that are *negotiated* with others. Although important, the medium is just one of many variables that intersect with the experience of online interaction.

In any scene of interaction, the body is both an experienced subject and a viewed and acted-upon object. How that body appears affects the definition of the situation, the interactions that transpire, and the scene that ensues. Consequently, most of the time we are quite conscious of how others view our bodies, and although we may sometimes intentionally manage that image, we *always* make certain that we have *some* clothing on when in public or in the public view.

At a very young age we are socialized to society's proscriptions and prescriptions concerning the situations, circumstances, and purposes of allowable and forbidden genital exposure (Henslin and Biggs 1971). We learn that only three general categories of persons can legitimately approach the naked body of someone else: authorized sex partners, medical practitioners, and the parents of very young children. We also learn that all these persons must be very careful about *how* they approach the naked body: parents and sex partners must be careful lest they be guilty of rape, abuse, or misconduct; medical practitioners make certain to use elaborate dramaturgical tactics to assure that the context is desexualized and, if possible, the person is detached from the body completely (Henslin and Biggs 1971; Smith and Kleinman 1989). In addition, the treatment of and deference to the naked body is deeply ritualistic, and by adhering to these rituals the naked body achieves a sacred status.[12]

Beneath the facade of clothing is a sacred sexual body—compartmentalized segments of flesh that we may touch only in private and share only with the closest of intimates. This body is protected by stringent rules and filled with profound meaning to the individual, to those who may see it, and to the larger culture. Under normal circumstances, access to the sacred naked body of others means power and privilege and therefore connotes specific rights and responsibilities. The naked body is surrounded by rules that protect it from being profaned, that dictate who may approach it and under what conditions, and what may (and may not) be done in these circumstances (Durkheim [1912] 1965). As Goffman (1971) and Durkheim might suggest, adherence to these rituals maintains the "sacred" sexual body as an object of ultimate value, and while threats of profanation occasionally may occur, we can comfortably maintain the sacredness of the naked body so long as we abide by the rules.

A large part of the eroticism and feelings of liberation that come from televideo cybersex stems precisely from the cultural heresy of breaking these rules. Participants may reap the benefits and remain relatively safe from the potential consequences of revealing what is normally secret and profaning and what is normally sacred. By revealing their naked body, participants create an intensely personal interaction, yet suspend the self as a spectator by concealing their identities. Thus televideo cybersex participants reap the same benefits as fitness enthusiasts—"an intimate and holistic marriage between self and body" (Glassner 1990:221). However, to achieve this benefit, televideo cybersex participants reduce the whole of the self to the body and thus profane the sacred and assure that the complex and multidimensional self is made into an image to be seen and therefore not a person at all.

In both text and televideo cybersex, the body is a *virtual* object of which one may only be a *spectator*. Significantly, participants themselves are spectators unto their own bodies, as they must see and respond to the images of their bodies and thus act toward, manage, and interpret that image as others might. In most televideo cybersex environments the image of one's own body appears in a window beside the images of others and is clearly visible to the individual as a mirrorlike reflection. Participants must manipulate the images of their bodies in order to prevent "showing face" and to assure the appropriate camera angle, zoom, and focus necessary to perform the "conversation of gestures" inherent in the mutual masturbation of televideo cybersex. These erotic looking glasses of televideo cybersex influence how one conceives of one's self and body, but this does not differ fundamentally from the ways in which the body manifests itself in everyday life. Instead televideo cybersex simply exaggerates it. In any scene of interaction the body will be placed as a social object and we will most often manipulate its appearance—as is essential to the overall definition of the situation and the self we claim within it. By virtue of literal and metaphorical looking glasses, we manipulate how others perceive the corporeal body in everyday life through clothing and cosmetics, and in doing so, in everyday life the body assumes a virtual ontological status not much different from the images sent and received by televideo cybersex participants.

Like everyday life, in these televideo interactions others symbolically reflect the body back onto the self; these reflections influence how the self conceives, appreciates, and apprehends the body. Hence we can understand the body as an object and subject distinct from the self. However, it would be a mistake analytically to sever the connection between selfhood and body. The boundaries between the self, the body, and situated social interaction will never be clearly demarcated, and any attempt to do so would lack credibility. A better approach is to understand the varied dynamics of the relationships among bodies, selves, and the contexts in which both are located. In a culture seemingly obsessed with bodies, it would be a serious mistake to ignore these and the myriad other relationships among the body, the acting individual, and society.

I do not argue that self and body are separate and distinct entities but rather that one does not automatically imply the other and that neither are simple innate things that the individual has. Surely, the body, unlike the self, is an empirical entity that can be observed, measured, and seen to exist in time and space independent of our own conscious awareness of it. But even so, what that body means is no more or less innately predetermined or any more or less socially shaped than any other object. As the participants in this study have illustrated, the body is not just a thing that exists; it is something that people read, interpret, present, conceal, and make meaningful in an ongoing negotiated process of situated social interaction.

Acknowledgments: This article has benefited from the immediate contributions of Charles Edgley (not the least of which is the title itself) and from his long-term personal, intellectual, and creative influences that I cannot delineate here in a manner that reflects my true gratitude. I also wish to acknowledge the insights, assistance, and support of Mark Douglass and the suggestions of the four anonymous reviewers for *Symbolic Interaction*. Special thanks to Kathy Charmaz, Jamilah Nixon Mathis, Aimee Messer, Kerry Beck, and Christopher Schmitt for their generous editorial assistance, which greatly improved this article.

NOTES

1. Researchers overlook this fact. Many define cybersex as broadly as possible to support the notion that it is common, widespread, and usually a problem (or at least a potential problem that may cause disaster in participants' lives). For example, in a recent book on cybersex addiction and recovery, Schneider and Weiss (2001:7) define cybersex sweepingly as "any form of sexual expression that is accessed through the computer or the Internet." Researchers such as Schneider and Weiss (2001) and Cooper, Delmonico, and Burg (2000) fail to distinguish between *looking at* pornography online and *participating in* cybersex and thus exploit the ambiguities of the term to support their preconceived conclusions about "cybersex compulsivity."

2. Televideo has been used widely for the pursuit of profit in the Internet pornography industry (Lane 2000). "Live" webcam performances are a relatively common and apparently lucrative service for the entrepreneurs of virtual pornography. However, these webcam services differ from televideo cybersex in that its performers are paid to put on a show, the audience pays to watch, and the performers can rarely if ever see their customers. Those that pay the fee can "peep" in on the show and sometimes communicate with the performer through typed text, but there is little interactivity and the motives of the performer(s) are at least partly financial. This study focuses on persons who use televideo for sex, for fun, and for free (not considering ISP fees, cost of the digital camera, and cost of the client software) with other participants who are doing the same.

3. Although "sex object" has become a stigmatizing label, being treated as an object—a physical body—is a necessary part of sexuality. Many feminists argue legitimately that patriarchal social and cultural structures reduce women to mere objects. I do not ignore this criticism by feminists but suggest that there is a fundamental difference between being *made* into an object and choosing to *be* an object. The former is domination; the latter is a necessary element of sex.

4. It would seem that Mead was quite aware of this point: "It is perfectly true that the eye can see the foot, but it does not see the body as a whole. We cannot see our backs; we can feel certain portions of them, if we are agile, but we cannot get an experience of our whole body. . . . The mere ability to experience different parts of the body is not different from the experience of a table. . . . The body does not experience itself as a whole" (1934:136).

5. "Social theorists have resisted strongly the recognition that deviance is not merely a re-action against something negative in a person's background but a reaching for exquisite possibilities. . . . [D]eviant persons also appreciate the economy of doing evil for characterizing the self generally: it is literally wonderful. Through being deviant for a moment, the person may portray his or her general, if usually hidden, charismatic potential" (Katz 1988:73).

6. A fascinating exception appears in *Le viol* (1934), a painting by the Belgian surrealist René Magritte. In this surreal anatomical rearrangement, a woman's face and body are one and the same: a portrait of a face that is a woman's torso wrapped in hair; eyes are represented by breasts, the nose by a belly button; the mouth is a patch of pubic hair. Not surprisingly, this painting has been subject to substantial feminist criticism for the manner in which it "fragments the female by turning her into a sexual body" (Gubar 1989:49). Some have argued that the female face is erased by the torso, making her sightless, senseless, and dumb, an abject and obscene artistic rendition of female submission and servitude (Gubar 1989). According to Gracyk (1991:125), it is "one of the most graphic subordinations of a woman to an object, for it reduces her to genitalia." What is fascinating about this image (and the controversy surrounding it) is that few seem to ponder whether Magritte intended to (super)impose a *body* on a face, a *face* on a body, or *both*. When critics look at *Le viol* they see a body in place of a face—one dimension of Magritte's surreal and philosophical riddle. It is interesting that they do not see a face in place of a body, or both at once. Even if Magritte had not intended, *Le viol* impressively mines the fascinating relationship between bodies and faces—one part of the object and subject of embodiment—revealing (at the very least) the taken for granted cultural tendency to see the image as one thing and not another.

7. Televideo cybersex participants reverse the traditional expressive order of the body normally experienced in the ritual of courtship. Usually, lovers become familiar with one another's faces first and genitals last. As these participants indicate, in televideo cybersex genitals come first and faces are seen last, if at all.

8. Obviously this section refers strictly to heterosexual one-on-one televideo cybersex. I am confident that the relationship differs among couples that connect with other couples, gay men, and gay women. In each category, the distribution of sexual power is likely to assume different forms in relation to the body and the context of interaction. I focus here on one-on-one heterosexual encounters for several reasons. First, these are the most common sexual relations in televideo cybersex. Second, a full analysis of sexual preference in relation to televideo cybersex is not necessary for my overall argument; this one component is sufficient. Third, and most significantly, I had no difficulty collecting data from gay men, but gay women and couples were not at all interested in talking to me, and therefore I have little data on them. Apparently gay women and couples are all too familiar with the deceptive tactics of heterosexual men who often try to cop a peek or con them into a brief encounter. Such tactics are not uncommon. One participant in this study gloated when she told me how she used pictures in a magazine (combined with a slight blurring on the focus of the cam) to temporarily con people into thinking she was something she was not. Of course, the picture did not move and therefore the con was short-lived, but deceitful tactics such as these have made gay women and couples *very* suspicious and almost impossible for this man to interview.

9. This perception of feminine sexual liberation and power in televideo cybersex is actually far more complicated than suggested here and is experienced as real for reasons that are more legitimate than this analysis suggests. Although I am skeptical about much of what passes for "sexual freedom" in cybersex, it is worth reminding ourselves that we are a society in which women continue to be punished or otherwise found guilty for actively seeking

sexual pleasure and overtly acting on sexual desire, as opposed to "following their hearts" (Williams 1989:209, 259–60). Further, at least some of the controversy over contemporary high-tech, easy-access, in-the-comfort-of-your-home pornography is attributable to the fact that it is now brought not only into locations where children might wander but also "into the domain of traditional female space" (Williams 1989:283). There is little doubt that sex and pornography on the Internet pose unprecedented opportunities for women to indulge sexual interests. Where else do women find "license simply to float pleasurably through a shamelessly eroticized space" (Rival, Slater, and Miller 1998:301)? Where else do women find equivalent opportunities to explore sexual interests and desires without paying the price of stigma, punishment, and shame charged by the sexual double standard? In short, the analysis presented here is critical of the extent of sexual freedom given the form in which it appears on the Internet, but even so, I have to acknowledge that the freedoms expressed by the women in this study are quite real even if the forms of those sexual expressions adhere to what appears to be the same old androcentric sexuality.

10. A similar analysis could be done on the role of race and age in the body politics of the nude in televideo cybersex. Just as one's gender cannot be removed by clothing, neither can race or age (although the latter can be faked to some extent). Many televideo cybersex environments displayed relatively common themes that build off race and age stereotypes. Particularly evident are fantasies of the experienced (and often dominant) elder mistress with her boy-toy and fantasies that build on the mythical girth of the African penis.

11. What is unique about online interaction and cybersex is that the corporeal body is located in one place and a symbolic representation of it is located elsewhere. This, in itself, is not without precedence (see Flowers 1998), but the quintessence of cybersex—the remarkable interaction among the corporeal body, its virtual representation, and the situated communicative context—surely is. In reference to erotic CD-ROM "games," Williams (1989:312) describes the body in these virtual environments as "felt to be in two places at once. . . . [P]leasure consists in a body that is uncannily both *here . . . and there*. . . . [T]here is a sustained simultaneous dividedness of attention and blurring of the distinction between the virtual bodies on screen—one of which is now presumed to be 'my' own—and my own 'carnal density' here where I sit before the screen" (original emphasis). As this study seeks to emphasize, this body—precariously perched in "two places at once"—is not only a unique characteristic of cybersex; it is also what makes the experience ideal for the kind of social psychological analysis that can fundamentally inform or transform the ways in which we think about bodies, selves, situated social interaction, and the nature of personhood because it renders opaque relationships that are normally quite transparent

12. This is overly simplified. Both the naked body and the clothed body may be considered "sacred" (in the Durkheimian and Goffmanian sense). The naked body achieves sacred status as a result of the rules that govern it and the deference to which it is treated. But the deference and rules regarding the treatment of the naked body exist and persist because *clothing* is "one of the most basic and pervasive symbols of civilization" (Douglas 1977:39–40). It is basic and pervasive because it is, in part, through clothing that we physically and symbolically transcend ourselves. Clothing fails to cover the body. It is merely a partial synthetic exterior skin with the delightful capacity to accentuate specific parts of the body while concealing others. Although man comes into the world "covered in a skin. . . . [he] soon discovered that he could make himself not only one additional skin, but practically as many as he liked, an endless variety of them, to meet his every need and fancy" (Langner 1991:4–5). Of course, these "skins" are produced in societal, cultural, and institutional contexts, in accordance with those

formal and informal social mandates. Consequently, "adornment creates a highly specific synthesis of the great convergent and divergent forces of the individual and society" (Simmel 1950:344). Through clothing, in part, we are no longer akin to the animal world but to the world of gods, spirits, and society (Langner 1991). Hence the source of sacredness of the naked body lay in its ever-present potential to subvert society itself—an antisacred—because it is the *clothed* body that is sacred to social order.

REFERENCES

Baumeister, Roy. 1989. *Masochism and the Self*. Hillsdale, NJ: Erlbaum.

———. 1991. *Escaping the Self: Alcoholism, Spirituality, Masochism, and Other Flights from the Burden of Selfhood*. New York: Basic Books.

Becker, Howard. 1963. "Becoming a Marijuana User." Pp. 41–58 in *Outsiders: Studies in the Sociology of Deviance*. New York: Free Press.

———. 1967. "History, Culture, and Subjective Experience." *Journal of Health and Social Behavior* 8: 163–76.

Bell, David, and Ruth Holliday. 2000. "Naked as Nature Intended." *Body and Society* 6 (3–4):1274D.

Bryant, Clifton. 1982. *Social Deviancy and Social Proscription: The Social Context of Carnal Behavior*. New York: Human Sciences Press.

Cahill, Spencer. 2001. *Inside Social Life: Readings* in *Sociological Psychology and Microsociology*. Los Angeles: Roxbury.

Cooley, Charles H. [1902] 1964. *Human Nature and the Social Order*. New York: Scribner's.

Cooper, Al, David Delmonico, and Ron Burg. 2000. "Cybersex Users, Abusers, and Compulsives: New Findings and Implications." Pp.5–29 in *Cybersex: The Dark Side of the Force*, edited by A. Cooper. Philadelphia: Brunner-Rutledge.

Davis, Murray. 1983. *Smut: Erotic Reality/Obscene Ideology*. Chicago: University of Chicago Press.

Denzin, Norman. 1989. *The Research Act: Theoretical Introduction to Sociological Research Methods*. Englewood Cliffs, NJ: Prentice Hall.

Dery, Mark. 1992. "Sex Machine, Machine Sex: Mechano-Eroticism and Robe-Copulation." Pp. 42–43 in *Mondo 2000*. New York: HyperPerennial.

Douglas, Jack. 1977. *The Nude Beach*. Beverly Hills, CA: Sage.

Durkheim, Emile. [1912] 1965. *The Elementary Forms of Religious Life*. New York: Free Press.

Edelsward, L. M. 1991."We Are More Open When We Are Naked." *Ethnos* 56 (3–4):189–99.

Flowers, Amy. 1998. *The Fantasy Factory: An Insider's View of the Phone Sex Industry*. Philadelphia: University of Pennsylvania Press.

Forsyth, Craig. 1992. "Parade Strippers: A Note on Being Naked in Public." *Deviant Behavior: An Interdisciplinary Journal* 13:391–403.

Frank, Arthur. 1991. *At the Will of the Body: Reflections on Illness*. Boston: Houghton Mifflin.

Gadow, Sally. 1982. "Body and Self: A Dialectic." Pp. 86–100 in *The Humanity of the Ill: Phenomenological Perspectives*, edited by V. Kestenbaum. Knoxville: University of Tennessee Press.

Glassner, Barry. 1990. "Fit for Postmodern Selfhood." Pp. 215–43 in *Symbolic Interaction and Cultural Studies*, edited by H. Becker and M. McCall. Chicago: University of Chicago Press.

Goffman, Erving. 1959. *The Presentation of Self in Everyday Life.* Garden City, NY: Doubleday Anchor.

———. 1963a. *Behavior in Public Places: Notes on the Social Organization of Gatherings.* New York: Free Press.

———. 1963b. *Stigma: Notes on the Management of Spoiled Identity.* Englewood Cliffs, NJ: Prentice Hall.

———. 1971. *Relations in Public: Microstudies in Public Order.* New York: Basic Books.

Gracyk, Theodore. 1991. "Pornography as Representation: Aesthetic Considerations." Pp. 117–37 in *Pornography: Private Right or Public Menace?*, edited by R. Baird and S. Rosenblum. Buffalo, NY: Prometheus.

Gubar, Susan. 1989. "Representing Pornography." Pp. 47–67 in *For Adult Users Only: The Dimensions of Violent Pornography*, edited by S. Gubar and I. Hoff. Bloomington: Indiana University Press.

Henslin, James, and Mae Biggs. 1971. "Dramaturgical Desexualization: The Sociology of the Vaginal Examination." Pp. 243–72 in *Studies in the Sociology of Sex*, edited by J. Henslin. New York: Appleton-Century-Crofts.

Holstein, James, and Jaber Gubrium. 2000. *The Self We Live By: Narrative Identity in a Postmodern World.* New York: Oxford University Press.

James, William. [1892] 1961. *Psychology: The Briefer Course.* New York: Harper and Brothers.

Katz, Jack. 1988. *Seductions of Crime: Moral and Sensual Attractions in Doing Evil.* New York: Basic Books.

Kupfer, Joseph. 1983. *Experience as Art: Aesthetics in Everyday Life.* Albany: State University of New York Press.

Lane, Frederick. 2000. *Obscene Profits: The Entrepreneurs of Pornography in the Cyber Age.* New York: Routledge.

Langner, Lawrence. 1991. *The Importance of Wearing Clothes.* Los Angeles: Elysium.

Lincoln,Yvonna, and Egon Guba. 1985. *Naturalistic Inquiry.* Newbury Park, CA: Sage.

Mason-Schrock, Douglas. 1996. "Transsexuals' Narrative Construction of the 'True Self.'" *Social Psychology Quarterly* 59 (3):176–92 .

McCormick, Naomi, and John Leonard. 1996. "Gender and Sexuality in the Cyberspace Frontier." *Women and Therapy* 19 (4):109–19.

Mead, George Herbert. 1934. *Mind, Self, and Society.* Edited by C. Morris. Chicago: University of Chicago Press.

Norwich, Casmera. 1987. "Parts Plus," *Photo/Design* (July–August):51–54.

Rival, Laura, Don Slater, and Daniel Miller. 1998. "Sex and Sociality: Comparative Ethnographies of Sexual Objectification." *Theory, Culture, and Society* 15 (3–4):295–321.

Robinson, Phillip, and Nancy Tamosaitis. 1993. *The Joy of Cybersex: An Underground Guide to Electronic Erotica.* New York: Brady.

Sartre, Jean-Paul. 1956. *Being and Nothingness.* New York: Philosophical Library.

Schneider, Jennifer, and Robert Weiss. 2001. *Cybersex Exposed: Simple Fantasy or Obsession?* Center City, MN: Hazelden.

Shilling, Chris. 1993. *The Body and Social Theory.* London: Sage.

Simmel, Georg. 1950. *The Sociology of George Simmel.* Edited by K. Wolff. New York: Free Press.

Slater, Don. 1998. "Trading Sexpics on IRC: Embodiment and Authenticity on the Internet." *Body and Society* 4 (4):91–117.

Smith, Allen, and Sherryl Kleinman. 1989. "Managing Emotions in Medical School: Students Contacts with the Living and the Dead." *Social Psychology Quarterly* 52 (1):56–69.

Smith, Dorothy. 1990. *Texts, Facis, and Femininity: Exploring the Relations of the Ruling.* London: Routledge.

Strauss, Anselm. 1993. *Continual Permutations of Action.* New York: Aldine de Gruyter.

Symonds, Carolyn. 1971. "A Nude Touchy-Feely Group." *Journal of Sex Research* 7 (2):126–33.

Toolan, James, Murray Elkins, Derek Miller, and Paul D'Encarnacao. 1974. "The Significance of Streaking." *Medical Aspects of Human Sexuality* 8:152–65.

Turner, Bryan. 1991. "Recent Developments in the Theory of the Body." Pp. 1–35 in *The Body: Social Process and Cultural Theory,* edited by M. Featherstone, Mike Hepworth, and B. Turner. London: Sage.

Turner, Victor. 1969. *The Ritual Process: Structure and Anti-Structure.* Ithaca: Cornell University Press.

Waskul, Dennis, Mark Douglass, and Charles Edgley. 2000. "Cybersex: Outercourse and the Enselfrnent of the Body." *Symbolic Interaction* 23 (4):375–97.

Weinberg, Martin. 1965. "Sexual Modesty, Social Meaning, and the Nudist Camp." *Social Problems* 12 (3):311–18.

———.1966. "Becoming a Nudist." *Psychiatry* 29 (1):15–24.

———. 1967. "The Nudist Camp: Way of Life and Social Structure." *Human Organization* 26 (3):91–99 .

———.1981. "Becoming a Nudist." Pp. 291–304 in *Deviance:An Interactionist Perspective,* edited by E. Rubington and M. Weinberg. New York: Macmillan.

Williams, Linda. 1989. *Hardcore: Power, Pleasure, and the "Frenzy of the Visible."* Berkeley: University of California Press.

Part III

||||||||||||||||||||||||||||||||||||||||||||||||||||||||||||||||||||||||||||

Extraordinary Bodies

Introduction to Part III

As we have stated in the introduction to *The Body Reader*, our aim is to collect essays that illustrate the significance of bodies, as objects invested with social meanings and as embodied actors that challenge and transgress the boundaries of culture and the flesh. The types of bodies collected in this section, the hairy, leaky, scarred, transsexual, and disabled body, are notable for their transgressions beyond what is socially expected and/or desired. And yet, the title of this section, "Extraordinary Bodies," obviously begs the question, what is an ordinary body? Could the case not be made that all bodies are extraordinary? Surely, all of social life is about confronting the recalcitrance of the materiality of the body. Bodies are stubborn and disrupt the flow of business as usual in both intended and unintended ways, and social institutions attempt to wrangle and moor bodies to particular rituals and routines. And yet, the body rarely remains docile and predictable throughout the life course. It gets sick when it's not "supposed to," becomes pregnant when we don't want it to, leaves traces behind when stealth is attempted, and erupts despite requirements of civility and silence. Indeed, it seems like our bodies act out of the bounds of ordinariness, the expectations and taken-for-granted assumptions of bodily composure and performance, much more than they can be contained by these norms. At times, we all have extraordinary bodies, and when we are able, we must tame and discipline these bodies or endure the penalties of embarrassment, shame, and exclusion.

All bodies, then, are potentially extraordinary bodies, but it is our reactions to their extraordinariness that set the limits of socially desired visions of ordinariness. The definitions of ordinariness and extraordinariness are thus dialectical and the terms are co-constitutive. This is not to say the terms are meaningless. Quite the contrary, it is the movement back and forth between ordinariness and extraordinariness that helps to guide our social behavior and corporeal borders. Over time and in different cultural contexts, what counts as ordinary and extraordinary might vary. Even with these variations, however, there is a consistent social purpose of extraordinary bodies as instructive to the normative.

Human agency is also at play in the traffic between ordinariness and extraordinariness. It is not merely the structural position of these bodies that creates their extraordinariness, but also their participation or resistance in social circumstances. The rewards and punishments that accrue on the basis of our fit into the standards of decorum or social acceptability might seduce us into certain bodily shapes, sizes, presentations, or expressions. We attempt to morph our own bodies into the contents of that which is socially acceptable or deemed "natural." Or we might be resistant and bring our otherwise unwelcome bodies into view in social situations that communicate the message that they do not belong. Perhaps it is the extraordinary body and its social interpolation that acts as a governor for our presentation of self whereby we regulate our minute and mundane activities of daily life within an internalized set of standards. Sometimes we stray outside of the contours of ordinariness, on purpose or by accident, but we rarely linger there without social commentary.

In "Manscaping: The Tangle of Nature, Culture, and Male Body Hair," sociologist Matthew Immergut compares the hairiness of male bodies and the management of "excessive" body hair to the landscaping movement and the ways in which we construct the idea of nature. The grotesque of the natural environment in its overgrown, weedy, and wild geography is brought under control through manicuring and designing. But at the same time, the resulting pedicured landscape is supposed to appear natural. This practice is comparable to creating the hairless and smooth male body, Immergut argues, which is a contemporary norm in certain heterosexual circles. Male bodies are worked upon to make them appear naturally hairless, thereby bringing into view the extraordinary hairy body, which is in need of intervention to become socially (and sexually) acceptable. Immergut maintains that experiencing the glory of the great outdoors in a national park is a simultaneously natural and cultural event. Similarly, when we admire the glistening smooth skin of a masculine Adonis, the interplay of nature and culture collide.

Sociologist Lisa Jean Moore's "Incongruent Bodies: Teaching While Leaking" is a deeply personal account of leaking breast milk during a class lecture. This essay demonstrates the ways in which bodies reveal themselves as flesh and fluid at unexpected moments. The extraordinary experience of body fluids spilling from the self-contained borders of our skin creates opportunities for breaches of social scripts. A professor revealing her status as a nursing mother is then compared with revelations about one's sexual identity. Both circumstances enable students to read the professor's body as a text. When bodies don't do what they are as supposed to do, and can't contain "information" that is distracting to business as usual, extraordinary opportunities arise to investigate normative assumptions about how bodies are to look, act, and perform in specific environments.

In "Envisioning the Body in Relation: Finding Sex, Changing Sex," anthropologist Eric Plemons examines the social and medical history of transsexualism and sex reassignment surgery in the United States. He argues that a transsexual body is always a body in relation to other bodies. In other words, in order for the "transsexual" body to be identified and treated, there needs to be a medical discourse that defines and describes this type of body. Through his fieldwork and reading of medical records, Plemons demonstrates how the "natural body" is constructed in a "surgical imaginary." Surgically modifying the genitals is a practice that is about form and function as much as it is about social identification and normative constructions of sex and gender. It is not so much that the transsexual body is an extraordinary body as it is extraordinary that medicine has such a difficult time visualizing social desire as part of the medical practice. Surgeons' efforts to make something look natural presumes that there is a normative natural genital, and denies the range of variation of all human genitalia.

The excerpt from Jarvis Jay Masters's book *Finding Freedom* is entitled "Scars," a first-hand account of Masters's experiences living on death row. While a departure from some of the more academic pieces, this essay illustrates the ways in which Masters, a poet and Buddhist philosopher, sees the interconnectedness of his fellow inmates through their scarified bodies. The extraordinary pain and suffering inscribed on these male bodies through wires, knives, fists, and extension cords are shocking in their ubiquity in the exercise yard of the prison. His fellow inmates have been brutalized throughout their childhood, their bodies standing as testaments to histories of abuse. However, these men normalize the violence and their marked and "healed" bodies are contained, like their feelings, by walls and fences to shield themselves and others from having to acknowledge greater social problems.

"Slippery Slopes: Media, Disability, and Adaptive Sports," by anthropologist William Peace, introduces us to the world of adaptive sports, specifically skiing. Some might believe that within a variety of athletic venues, bodies with disability are conspicuously absent. However, as Peace's essay aptly argues, this absence is not so much about the individual body's desire or ability as much as the social structure's highly coordinate system of discrimination that displaces such bodies. Peace's auto-ethnography and qualitative interviews with fellow disabled athletes interprets the ways in which disability is socially defined and transgressed. The physical differences that these bodies experience are not what prevent them from the exhilaration of sport; rather, it is structural limitations that constrain them. Through first-hand accounts, Peace illustrates the commonalities between bodies that succeed at physical challenges, revealing the constructed nature of extraordinariness, ability, and disability.

Manscaping

The Tangle of Nature, Culture, and Male Body Hair

Matthew Immergut

The first time I took a razor to my body was in college. Not to my wrists or face, but to my stomach. I had this creeping feeling of disdain for the hair growing there. So I locked the bathroom door, grabbed a blade, and scythed the personal scourge. When I finished, I stroked my smooth abdomen and felt proud—like a suburbanite gazing with satisfaction across his freshly mowed lawn. Yet, I was also ashamed of my newly manicured body because it seemed to raise questions about my masculinity—after all, what kind of "guy" shaves his gut? Shouldn't I be celebrating my hairy virility? What I didn't fully realize hiding behind my bathroom door in the 1990s was that I was mired in the middle of a shift in cultural attitude toward male body hair. The days when chest hair and chains were sexy were disappearing, replaced by a new hypersmooth hetero-man.

In this chapter, I am interested in exploring this newly deviant hairy "heterosexual" male body and the meanings given to those threadlike segments of keratin sprouting from his skin. What I am particularly interested in exploring is how the contemporary stigma of male body hair has become symbolically linked with all forms of unwanted or grotesque nature. What's my evidence? "Manscaping." Popularized by the television show *Queer Eye for the Straight Guy*, manscaping involves waxing, shaving, lasering, or simply shaping any hairy region of the male body below the head. This connection between manscaping and landscaping is not linguistically arbitrary, a simple humorous flourish, but rather, as I untangle below, reflects a culturally pervasive story about "man" against an untamed "nature." More specifically, appropriating the work of social theorist Mikhail Bakhtin, I argue that the practice of manscaping represents an effort to control the grotesque, messy, and boundary-breaching hairs of the male body in order to cultivate an alluring but nonetheless "natural" and distinct human self.

No doubt, women as well as nonwhites have long been associated with a chaotic natural realm in Western intellectual history, and nature has often been construed as an unwieldy feminine force (Adams 1993; Gard 1993; King 1990; Merchant 1980; Plumwood 1993). As such, these "others," their bodies, and their hair have been subjugated to a variety of "civilizing" regimes—including the long-standing normative demand for hairless women (Toerien and Wilkinson 2003; Toerien, Wilkinson, and Choi 2005). Yet increasingly body hair seems to be attaining egalitarian status as a manifestation of nasty and wild nature regardless of the body it sprouts from—and this includes white males. But, you might ask, Do we really want to talk about the body tribulations of white men? And isn't it about time they had a taste of their own medicine? No, I'm not interested in bemoaning the pains of modern men nor celebrating what might be a justified comeuppance. Rather, I'm interested in exploring what this body practice reveals about contemporary understandings of, attitudes toward, and relationship with nature.

The sociological premise that underlies such an investigation is that seemingly mundane bodily practices such as plucking eyebrows or styling hair reflect larger sociocultural arrangements (Conboy, Medina, and Stanbury 1997; Hope 1982; Weitz 2004). I've just stretched this idea to argue that mundane bodily practices can also provide a window into larger cultural currents that define what it means to be human in relationship to the nonhuman world. More than a decade ago eco-feminist Ynestra King said, "there is a terrible confusion about our place in nature" (King 1990). Man-scaping, as far as I can tell, discloses the continuation and possible intensification of this confusion.

A few words about methods are in order. There is very little extant research specifically on men's body hair. When male body hair is addressed—usually in passing—scholars tend to hold a view of male body hair as a marker of ideal masculinity (Luciano 2001; Toerien and Wilkinson 2003; Pope, Phillips, and Olvardia 2000; Synott 1987). My first task, therefore, is to present evidence that such a perspective is outdated and that the new hetero-norm is hairlessness. The data I use, as you will see below, are quite heterogeneous, gleaned from a variety of sources such as Internet sites, newspapers, circulating images of men in popular culture, the latest men's depilatory technologies, and so forth. I also performed informal interviews with aestheticians at waxing salons and laser hair removal centers and engaged in limited participation in their services—ouch. Once gathered, this textual- and image-based material was analyzed for nature-based themes in a research method known as discourse and document analysis (Rapley 2007). Two important caveats need to be made here. First, on the basis of deduction from the data, I claim that the men I'm talking about are "heterosexual."[1] I did not, however, conduct interviews or distribute a survey in order to assess sexual preference or other identity variables (which, by the way, I think would make an excellent student research project). Second, I am constructing a fairly big argument on limited data—more empirical research needs to be done. Nevertheless, I consider this a theoretical and exploratory essay, aimed at playfully opening up a space to consider these changing body practices and aesthetics and what they might tell us about the relationship between human embodiment and nature in late modernity. Before getting into this thicket of male body hair, I need to present some concrete evidence that hairy men are truly endangered.

Making the Case for Endangered Hairy Male Bodies

In 1987 sociologist Anthony Synott wrote an excellent article on the sociology of hair in which he proposes a "theory of opposites." Simply stated, in North America and Britain opposite sexes have opposite head- and body-hair norms. "Hair is not just hair, it is a sex symbol" writes Synott, addressing this difference relative to body hair,

> and voluminous chest hair is therefore the equivalent of long, glossy, wavy head hair on a woman. Hence the availability of paste-on chest hair. Women seem to feel the same as men about male body hair. . . . Conversely, both men and women are extremely upset by chest hair on women; again, the glory of one gender is the shame of the opposite sex. (393)

Certainly this theory of opposites reflects body hair norms during the time he was writing. Yet the adage, "the glory of one sex is the shame of the other," does not seem viable when one looks at male bodies today. Rather, when it comes to body hair, the shame of one gender now seems to be the shame of the other as well.

To begin making this case, let's look at some numbers. According to the American Society of Plastic Surgeons (ASPS), in 2000 laser hair removal—a very expensive yet effective hair removal technique—was the second most popular noninvasive procedure undertaken by men: 133,142 men, to be more precise (Cooper 2006). Still in second place in 2006, the number of men getting their hair zapped via laser increased to 173,000 (ibid.). Of course, we don't have identity variables for these numbers, and therefore we might assume, as one salon owner told me in a thick Russian accent, "it's a gay thing . . . gays, they have beautiful bodies but they want no hair on the body." However, a manager of a fairly upscale laser center had a different take: "we're seeing more straight guys all the time. It's not just a gay thing anymore." Even though she admitted to not having records of the sexual preferences of her client base, she did assure me she had excellent "gay-dar."

Stepping away from the numbers, consider the now-iconic image of Burt Reynolds in a 1972 *Cosmopolitan* centerfold. This image of Burt reclining across a bear skin rug, cigar in mouth, hand poised over genitals, represented a significant cultural moment— here was a man posing almost completely naked in a traditionally female centerfold. Burt's body became a marker of the feminist movement's progress at equalizing the sexes as well as a signifier of the incorporation of men into an expanding consumer market (Bordo 1999). What's interesting to me, however, is Burt's body hair. No paste-on chest pieces here, just his raw hairiness and animal virility on display. Now reflect on the male icons of contemporary popular culture. Compare a hairy Burt Reynolds to completely hairless Brad Pitt. Or for that matter, simply try to find any body hair on any male model in any contemporary magazine—chances are you won't. Actually, what you are likely to find, if you observer closely, is once-hairy male sex symbols becoming increasingly hairless such as David Hasselhoff and John Bon Jovi.

Although there have been no opinion surveys about men's body hair recently, public forums also provide substantiation of this shifting bodily aesthetic. Begin with this Dear Abby column from 1979:

Hairless in Hilo: Dear Abby: I've never seen a problem like mine in your column. I'm a 33-year-old normal man except that I have absolutely no hair on my chest, arms or legs. And that is where I want hair the most. I have plenty of hair on my head and a thick growth in my pubic hair, so I know I can grow hair, but I'm so ashamed of my hairless body I avoid going to the beach. Is there some kind of treatment I can take to promote the growth of hair where I want it? I am miserable in my hairless state. I want to be like other guys. (quoted in Synott 1987, p.392)

Now put Hilo and his hairless dilemma next to this recent internet posting by SM:

SM: I wish I was stuck in the 70's where hair was cool and hot. It drives me mad when I hear most women talk about a man they once dated and were horrified to see that he was covered with hair. That's when I usually shy away. I dread the famous "let's all go in the spa!" shouted at parties. Sometimes I brave it anyways but I'd be lying if I said I wasn't nervous as hell.[2]

Although SM presents himself as "excessively" hairy, he is not alone. Internet chat rooms are full of supposed heterosexual men ruminating about the sexual appeal of everything from shaved chests to seal-slick pubic areas.

Newspapers and magazines also provide ample support for the disappearance of hairy men. As an example, consider this op-ed piece by Megan Daum in the *San Francisco Chronicle*:

my adolescent sources and the grooming industry say men aren't just "the new women"; they're the new seals. . . . it's no secret that larger numbers of men are getting their body hair waxed and lasered off. (Daum 2006)

Even though Daum is in San Francisco and therefore might not appear representative, major news outlets from the *New York Times* (see Newman 2007) to Internet magazines (Mondschein 2008) have documented the hairless-man trend. Even Canadians have taken note, as journalist Georgia Binks writes,

somewhere along the line, after Samson, a few after Rapunzel, and about 30 years after the musical *Hair* hit the Broadway stage in the 1960s, hair became ugly. Not all hair, of course—but body hair. Everything from back and leg hair to pubic hair. And it's not just a female obsession anymore. (Binks 2005)

The list of articles, images, and evidence reaches way beyond what I've presented here. However, the more interesting question is, What's going on? Where have all the Burts gone? Why have some facets of American mainstream culture seemingly embraced the ideal of baby-butt-smooth men?

It's challenging to pinpoint the exact cultural factors that contribute to this desire for a hairless body, but I can suggest a few. The rapid spread of muscle culture has played a part (Moore 1997; Klein 1993). Body hair covers up the hours of labor men have spent working out and working up their muscles—or getting "buff," which literally means "to polish or shine." Writing about the growing trend of body hair removal for heterosexual Greek men, Helena Smith says, "What's the point of working up a sweat to acquire macho muscles if they are hidden behind a mat of body hair?" (Smith 2000). A cultural obsession with youth and youthfulness also probably has contributed to this hairless movement. If hair sprouting from the body is one of maturity's first biological markers, then to grow hair is to grow older and, thus, in a culture that reveres the *appearance* of youth, body hair must go—for men and women over, say, age twenty-two. More philosophically, the youthful-fit-hairless body also suggests a pervasive denial of mortality—perhaps with every hair plucked, zapped, or shaved one has had a little triumph in a greater war against death (Becker 1973; Shilling 2003). On a more mundane but nevertheless very powerful level, hetero men are simply the newest consumers to be drawn into an increasingly intensifying beauty market. Ever since Burt's appearance in the 1970s, men and their bodies, as Susan Bordo (1999) argues, have been increasingly drawn into an "ever-widening vortex of late-twentieth-century consumerism" (18). Besmirching male body hair and then providing a product to resolve this "problem" seems like a "natural" progression of the market.

Then there is the increasing influence of gay culture on straight men (Gill, Henwood, and McLean 2005; Shilling 2003). Of course there is no singular "gay culture" nor any standardized perfect gay body (Hennen 2005; Connell 2005; Monaghan 2005). Nevertheless, the gay ideal with the most sway on the hetero male, as Monaghan (2005) points out, is the "young, blond, smooth-skinned, gym-buffed model type." The extremely popular show *Queer Eye for the Straight Guy*, in which five gay men give total makeovers to straight men, represents a cultural crystallization of this influence.

Very often makeovers included what Kyan Douglas, the grooming guru, calls "manscaping"—trimming, shaving, waxing, or shaping male body hair. As *Queer Eye's* popularity demonstrates, manscaping—the practice and the term—appears to have gone mainstream.

More than muscles, youth, mortality, and expanding markets, I'm interested in this landscaping connection. I suspect that this linking between lawn care and male body hair is more than a simple metaphor, but a manifestation of subterranean roots beneath the cultural landscape. Like a well-manicured lawn, the male body and its hairs have become the site of cultivation—pulling out and clipping back the unwanted to create the desired aesthetic. Like landscaping, manscaping entails human alteration of the external environment, only that environment is not a lawn or land but skin. So too, an expanding market offers various mechanical and chemical technologies for converting a weedy body into the dermal garden of one's dreams. The proverbial weed-whacker has its bodily counterpart in the Mangroomer: The Essential Do-It-Yourself Back Shaver, while chemical herbicides to rid one's lawn of noxious weeds, such as Roundup, have their parallels with products such as Nair for Men.

Whether engaging in landscaping or manscaping, what both practices express is a deep desire for control over land and body. To state the matter differently, the act of manscaping, like landscaping, embodies an enduring effort to control nature. But what is the nature of this nature?

Constructing Nature and Hairy Bodies

The body is a bio-physical entity but is also, significantly, a social creation. The same can be said about "nature." There is a bio-physical reality being referenced when we talk about nature, but the way in which we know and talk about that reality is deeply shaped by our historical and sociocultural position. For example, a photographer, hunter, and real estate developer will understand the same open field bustling with deer quite differently—the photographer sees a natural wonder ("take a picture"), the hunter a five-point buck ("pull the trigger"), and a real estate developer future profits ("bring in the bulldozers"). These differences aren't based on what's "out there" but on social values, meanings, interests, and identities (Greider and Garkovich 1994; Fine 1998). In other words, nature is socially constructed—which also means there's no singular Nature, only multiple natures (see Nash 1982; Oelschlaeger 1991; Murphy 1997; Taylor 2003; Williams 1980; Smith 2001; Cronon 1995; Demeritt 2002; Fine 1998).

Rather than simply an interesting academic insight, this idea that nature is more human product than natural entity has serious environmental and political implications—for the way a group defines a specific nature will influence its feelings and direct its behavior. Consider the simple linguistic shift between calling the same geographic location a "swamp" versus a "wetland." These two names given to the same spot carry very different valuations and direct differing courses of action: namely, draining versus protecting.

Ideas of nature have also been used as ideological weapons to support the interests of the socially powerful. From the justification of European conquest by labeling indigenous peoples "wild savages" to the scientific racism that secured European superiority on the basis of "natural" skull size differences, the annals of Western history are rife with such examples of the naturalization of social injustice (Sale 2006; Bell 2004). Much of this ideological use of nature stems from a culture/nature dualism at the center of the Western worldview (Peterson 2001; Oelschlaeger 1991; Plumwood 1993; Davidson and Smith 2006; Devall and Sessions 1985; Ruether 1989; Gard 1993; Spretnak 1994). Rather than simply descriptive of the way the world is, this dichotomous worldview is normative—a socially constructed organization of life into mutually exclusive categories in which everything of value resides on the culture side and includes male, mind, reason, spirit, and human, while the devalued side of nature is associated with female, bodies, flesh and fluids, emotions, matter, and animals.

Much of Western history attests to the naturalization of this socially constructed schema as women, indigenous people, and nonwhites were consistently marked as more natural than cultural, more emotional than rational, more animal than human, more savage than civilized, thereby legitimizing their subjugation.[3]

Although certainly not as politically nefarious, hairy male bodies, from this dualistic perspective, are slipping or have slipped into the natural side of the equation. Manscaping, therefore, represents one more modern practice for reestablishing a bulwark against nature, an effort to mark oneself and one's body clearly on the cultural and human side of the equation. In other words, contemporary hairy and hairless males are simply being subsumed within a familiar culture-nature schema—hairless bodies on the culture side and hairy bodies on the nature side.

Sure, this makes sense. Yet, one problem with this dichotomous equation is the pervasive love of nature in the larger culture. We can observe the ever-expanding markets for nature's goods, a growing outdoor recreation and ecological tourism industry, a large section of the entertainment world devoted to the wonders of the wild, and a diverse and increasingly powerful environmental movement. Each of these uniquely testifies to a pervasive desire to protect and connect with rather than escape from or dominate the natural world.

We can account for this, in part, by loosening a strict culture-nature dichotomy and positing that in contemporary society natures are proliferating—in any context multiple natures will be produced and circulated for different purposes. In the case of body hair there are (at least) two prominent natures at work: alluring and grotesque. Alluring nature gains its status from being under some form of physical or symbolic control—nature that stays put, so to speak. Grotesque nature is any form of nature that blurs or breaks the symbolic or physical boundaries established by humans—nature that doesn't stay put. Body hair on men is now being symbolically linked with a grotesque nature and thus hairy bodies have become grotesque bodies.

Grotesque and Classical Bodies

I'm drawing this distinction from the work of Russian social theorist Mikhail Bakhtin's (1984) typology of the grotesque and classical body. From his historical studies of sixteenth-century European literature, Bakhtin locates the grotesque body within the context of pre-Lenten medieval carnivals. The carnival was a time for the breaching of established social codes in which "normal" social interactions were subverted—a time of communal feasting and debauchery in which traditional status and class hierarchies were broken down as nobleman and peasant joined in mutual celebration. This type of communal revelry also included public release of the body and its shared functions, displays of excess and indulgence, and comic expression that reinforced, rather than excluded, a human and fleshy (*carn*) commonality. Rich or poor, high or low, the carnival was a ritualized moment of social equalization in which there was a collective recognition that every human and nonhuman animal eats, shits, bleeds, and dies.

From this research, he draws a portrait of the grotesque body as one that penetrates outwards into the world as well as allowing the external world inside (27). Examining grotesque imagery Bakhtin writes,

> Special attention is given to the shoots and branches, to all that prolongs the body and links it to other bodies or to the world outside. . . .The grotesque body . . . is a body in the act of becoming. Thus the artistic logic of the grotesque image ignores the closed, smooth, and impenetrable surface of the body and retains only its excrescences (sprouts, buds) and orifices, only that which leads beyond the body's limited space or into the body's depth. (316–18)

The grotesque body is a body in constant interchange with its surroundings: a body that is in continual intercourse with other human bodies, the bodies of nature, and the cycles of death and renewal—in other terms, a type of "ecological body" (Gardiner 1993; Bell 1994).

With the disintegration of the medieval world and the birth of the modern social order emerged a new "bodily canon" of the "classical body." Counter to the grotesque's interpenetrating openness, the classical body is a sealed, closed, individual sphere (321). The classical body is, according to Bakhtin,

> an entirely finished, completed, strictly limited body, which is shown from the outside as something individual. That which protrudes, bulges, sprouts, or branches off . . . is eliminated, hidden, or moderated. The basis of the image is the individual, strictly limited mass, the impenetrable façade. The opaque surface and the body's "valleys" acquire an essential meaning as the border of a closed individuality that does not merge with other bodies and with the world. (320)

This is the modern "bourgeois ego," according to Bakhtin, a sense of identity based on maintaining an embodied distinction from everything else.

The revelry in the grotesque—in gorging and drinking, in the excesses of the "lower stratum" of bodily life—is deemed dirty, crude, and repulsive to classical sensibilities. "The classic body does not spit. It does not sweat. It does not cry," writes Michael Bell (1994). "It is dirty even to speak of excrement, urine, vomit, ejaculate, and menstrual blood except in polite, disdainful, or scientific language which sanitizes and distances material truth, like plastic wrapping around a supermarket chicken" (73). To follow Bell's imagery of the plastic-wrapped chicken, the archetypal modern expression of the classical body can be found in Barbie and Ken: no openings to stick things in, no protruding genitals that leak fluids out, no nipples, and absolutely no body hair, just sleek, nonbiodegradable, and seamless plastic.

Grotesque Bodies and Grotesque Nature

The hairy male body has become a type of grotesque natural body. It's a body emblematic of a boundary breaching and wild nature and therefore anathema to contemporary-classical aesthetics. No doubt, the physical characteristics of body hair have contributed to this label as grotesque. Body hair breaks borders. Like the shoots of a plant, it pushes beyond the surface of the skin and, at times, reaches beyond the confines of the skin completely as it lands in the shower drain, furrows into a bar of soap, or lodges in food. Body hair also disperses the sweat and odors of the body outward. It is, however, not only its capacity to cast outward but its ability to bring in the outside world by catching smells and other particles that makes body hair particularly susceptible to classical repulsion and efforts of management. Body hair, in other words, can be interpreted as an organ of grotesque interchange between the body and its surroundings. Although head hair has many similar characteristics, only body hair has gained a kind of grotesque status and therefore is seen as in need of contemporary-classical regimes of control—i.e., manscaping.

Popular texts and images clearly attest to male body hair as grotesque. For instance, classical bodies are premised on a sealed purity, a hygienic standard that depends upon the exclusion of all things deemed filthy. Body hair, in that it breaches the boundaries of this enclosed sterility, evokes repulsion from contemporary men and women aiming to adhere to classical standards. "In contemporary Western culture," write Toerien and Wilkinson (2003) on the normative demands of hairlessness for women, "only women's body hair is routinely treated as a cause for disgust, much like other body products (such as blood, faeces, sweat or odours) that are thought to be unclean" (338). For current research, these scholars surprisingly overlook the growing egalitarian status of body hair as filth for both genders. "When it comes to armpits, it is absolutely necessary to maintain the hair growth," advises a "Hair on Men's Body" Internet column, "plus women are totally averse to men with bad body odor. Bushy armpits generate heavier perspiration. . . . Taking care of your body hair is the first step towards better personal hygiene" (Jurgita 2003). Or consider the promise of "better hygiene" as a selling point for Nair for Men.[4] According to an Internet article on the importance of shaved male parts, "pubic hair collects sweat and other body fluids that give off strong odors. The warm moist pubic hair provides ideal conditions for bacteria and fungus to grow."[5] Increasingly, body hair is achieving an egalitarian status as unhygienic—a place for mushrooms, bacteria, and other contaminating natural elements to nest and grow. Hairy body parts are thus polluted body parts, and hairless body parts are pure body parts for both men and women striving for classical bodies.

The contaminating potential of body hair runs deeper than issues of hygiene, however. The grotesque quality of body hair threatens to disrupt a much deeper and more cherished human-animal boundary. In the classical-contemporary imagination, body hair appears as a reminder of our connection to other "dirty" creatures, a repulsive memento of our common animal nature. "I have never been a fan of the hairy back," writes Lisa Daily (2006) in her e-article, "Manscaping: The Battle against Hair." "Or hairy shoulders. Most women I know aren't. Frankly, we would like our guy to have more than one degree of separation between him and the banana-eaters down at the zoo." "The hairy bear-y Male," opens a Hair on Men's Body advice column, "a majority of women loathe the sight of an excessively hairy man. They may usually pass him off as some bristly creature" (Jurgita 2003). "If you look like a sasquatch, then you will need to either shave or wax your body hair," counsels the Midlife Bachelor,

> A sasquatch is a large hairy beast (also known as "Big Foot") that supposedly lives in the wilderness of North America. A sasquatch has thick hair everywhere—like a bear . . . women do not like the sasquatch look! My point—if you are a sasquatch, it is time to get yourself waxed. Shave that back and chest, at the very least.[6]

Sasquatch, apes, bears, bristly creatures—this type of discourse reveals body hair's potential to disrupt a culturally enduring division between humans and nonhumans.

Sure, Darwin made a pretty strong case about our shared evolutionary history, and scientific studies keep discrediting each of the boundaries we've set up to distinguish ourselves from other creatures (see Falk 2007; Peterson 2001). Yet, manscaping seems to reflect a historically and culturally pervasive desire to maintain our humanness through denial—as if by removing body hair women and men are echoing the tortured assertion of the *Elephant Man* (1980), "I am not an animal! I'm a human being!" To not remove these grotesque strands, to let body hair go undomesticated, therefore, is to risk being absorbed back into a primal animalistic and inhuman state.[7]

Inherent in this fear of being stigmatized as a grotesque animal is the creeping fear of the wilderness: after all, where do these inhuman creatures dwell but beyond the edges of society? I am not talking about the wilderness popularized by the environmental movement—an ecologically delicate landscape and refuge for poetic and even mystical encounters (see Cronon 1995). Rather, body hair is symbolically tied to a pre-Romantic, older, and more chaotic nature, one that has the potential to powerfully disrupt an orderly civilization (Merchant 1980). This is the wilderness of the early Puritan settlers of North America, who, guided by their cultivated sensibilities and a religious script that included dominion and visions of a sacred garden, set out to cut down and take control of a "cursed" and "chaotic" landscape whose wilds threatened to pollute and possess their bodies and souls (Finch 2001; Nash 1982).

Yes, most Puritans and the wilderness they knew may have disappeared, but a Puritanical attitude toward male body hair echoes in the acts of modern manscapers. Consider Kyan Douglas's definition of manscaping: "manscaping is trimming/shaving/waxing hair to maintain it so it doesn't look like fur, a sweater or worst of all, a forest."[8] Or how about this Internet advice: "if your chest/naughty bits are lost in the wilderness rather than shave, try relaxing the hair a little bit" (Renzi 2007). Reflect on the implicit association with body hair, wilderness, and the desire for dominion in a review of Norelco's new Bodygroom razor for men: "Norelco is *blazing a path* through the largely *unexplored* world of men's body-hair removal with the release of Bodygroom, a new electric razor designed to *clear-cut dense thickets* of chest, back and even pubic hair—without the nasty irritation" (Creamer 2006; italics added). Associated with either a threatening forest or a creature dwelling in the wilderness, hairy male bodies demand civilizing. Just as landscaping cuts back the disorderly and chaotic—even tall grasses can have dangers such as snakes and ticks lurking about— manscaping tames body hair that has become the symbolic repository of all forms of unwanted wilderness. This wilderness demands control because, like all things grotesque, it constantly threatens to creep across or violently dislocate humanly constructed boundaries. Manscaping therefore seems to reflect a recent chapter in an old story about an ongoing struggle to civilize the wild; the only difference is that the attitudes and efforts once primarily reserved for controlling an external savage nature have become focused on the hairs of male bodies.

Of course, in most cases removal of body hair is not for moral purity but for sexuality—manscapers are not repressed Puritans nor classically aristocratic bourgeoisie but sexually liberated moderns, right? Maybe. As critical theorist Herbert Marcuse

(1966) argued, human sexuality does have socially revolutionary potential. Yet, the culture industry of capitalism transfigures and tames this sexual potential by transforming sex into one more commodity for consumption—witness the multi-million-dollar pornography *industry*. Commercialized and therefore controlled, the apparent sexual freedom that bombards modern men and women is deeply enmeshed with expanding forms of social domination. From this perspective, manscaping with the motive for sexual appeal seems part of this ever-escalating effort of advanced capitalism to domesticate all dimensions of sexuality (and nature). Like a well-manicured lawn, manscaping seems to reflect a commercialized and market-regulated obsession with classically styled, purified, individuated bodies—bodies that are about looking good rather than about indulging in wild pleasure.

To pull this tangle together, male body hair has become a symbolic crystallization of a boundary breaching, animalistic, and wild nature—in a singular term, grotesque nature. As such, the stigma of body hair runs deeper than the skin. Similar to the classical bourgeois-ego fretting about contamination of his pure body or the Puritan worrying about the potential moral stain caused by the wilderness, body hair reflects a type of character flaw—like the neighbor who becomes suspect because he allowed his lawn to grow dense with overgrowth. Manscaping efforts are therefore aimed at control over these grotesque hairs—an effort to transform an uncomely personal wilderness into a well-presented garden. Manscaping, stated differently, can be interpreted as a recent chapter in the ongoing struggle for power over a grotesque nature; a well-manscaped body is a demonstration of control and possession of a distinctly human self.

Classical bodies are not bodies free from nature, but they are bodies ideally composed of an alluring nature. The weedy and wild grotesque elements of the body must be tamed, but the result must appear natural. "Natural Hair Removal" products, for example, promise the use of natural ingredients (read "alluring nature") to remove unwanted hair (read "grotesque nature") as well as promising that the results will look "natural." Hairless classical bodies also desire to commune with and protect an alluring nature—to frolic in emerald rainforests rather than tangled hellish jungles, to protect wetland treasures rather than putrid swamps. Alluring nature, whether on the body or outside the body, is thus premised on a physical and symbolic domination—at root, desired and alluring nature is premised on dominion. Grotesque nature, whether bodily or external, is despised because it disrupts and breaks the symbolic and physical boundaries we've put in place.

Manscaping is, therefore, not simply an effort to distance oneself from nature—after all, the term "manscaping" implies a cultivated nature, not freedom from nature. Rather, shaving and plucking is a reaffirmation and a bulwark to establish the boundary between an alluring controlled-civilized natural body and a grotesque uncontrolled-uncivilized natural body. For those with enough money to afford laser hair removal, mastery over body hair has almost been accomplished. As long as body hair resiliently resurfaces, however, so too does an older chaotic and disobedient nature—a disconcerting reminder that complete control has not yet been achieved.[9]

Conclusion

For women, this battle against the wilds of body hair has been going on for quite some time—for so long that hairless women seem "natural." This may have something to do with a long-standing Western legacy of associating women with the frenzied passions of nature's forces and conceptualizing women's bodies as highly grotesque and messy, and therefore threatening to rational male order (Kristeva 1982; Shildrick 1997). Due to this association, women and their bodies were, from the perspective of men, seemingly in need of greater emotional and physical management. Hairlessness therefore became a type of external sign that expressed an inner self-containment and, more importantly, a mark of being under the control of a man's "civilized" dominion. Considering manscaping, however, we are faced with a strange transfiguration in which men seem to be doing to themselves what they demanded of women as well as women making those demands on men. Clean up those grotesque, disorganized, spongy, leaky, and animal bodies!

At one level, this transformation could simply be seen as an expansion and incorporation of men's bodies into the beauty market. Linking a grotesque nature to male body hair is simply a convenient symbolic tool to stigmatize this male body part and provide new commodities to rid one of this natural nastiness. After all, human conceptions of nature have long been a convenient tool for condemnation as well as idealization. However, I have a theory that the use of this nature is less about symbolic convenience and more about a larger cultural disquiet.

In the face of ecological anxiety induced by issues as overwhelming and potentially disruptive as climate destabilization, one response is an intensified desire to control the body. A number of highly respected sociological theorists make a similar claim, such as Anthony Giddens (1991), who argues that the rapid and destabilizing social forces of late modernity have facilitated an intense focus on personal identity and the body. In her work *The Body Project* (1998), Joan Brumberg outlines how larger social anxieties coalesce around adolescent girls' bodies—the body becomes central to her identity, its alteration the only site of control. No doubt, social anxiety consolidates around those who are most vulnerable, but ecological anxiety—the anxiety produced from the increasing awareness of an environmental crisis—seems more egalitarian and democratic. Why? Well, simply put, environmental problems don't respect borders. The hazards of climate change or radioactive clouds all transgress their point of origin, crossing over national, class, race, status, and gender boundaries. Certainly pollution follows the poor and socially marginalized (Bullard 2005, 2000, 1993; Bernier 2007). But because we are all living in what Ulrich Beck (1992, 1999) calls a "World Risk Society," everyone remains susceptible, even future generations. These environmental hazards penetrate their way into the everyday world, opening up an entire spectrum of questions about the safety of basic necessities such as food, water, air, and shelter (Edelstein 2000).

So, as the biosphere spins out of control and the old chaotic metaphors for nature return, the body becomes a locus of increasing control. The logic goes something like this: "I might not be able to be in command of an erratic atmosphere but at least I can have some control over my physical being." The body has become the great new hope for dominion at a time when the external natural world seems to be returning with a primordial vengeance. The average man might not be able to exert much influence over these uncontrollable elements of outside nature —and the men that do have the power to change it don't seem very interested in doing so—but if this chaos can be symbolically shifted to the body, then some feeling of control is within grasp. The contemporary manscaping trend is one example of this intensified desire for power over an increasingly chaotic nature. As body hair has become the symbolic repository of a grotesque nature, modern manscapers set upon their body hair with religious zeal and razors to conquer this vestige of natural chaos, to beat back the disquiet caused by a hostile wild, to cultivate a pure body on an increasingly polluted earth.

Now, I am not promoting an antimanscaping campaign or a hairy revolution for environmental sustainability as if by "returning" to some idea of the "good old hairy days" when Burt Reynolds was lying on a bearskin rug could somehow reestablish ecological harmony. Such a move seems silly and has been attempted unsuccessfully by the men's movement in the 1990s—in particular by Robert Bly, who implored "the sanitized, hairless, shallow man of the Judeo-Christian corporate world" to get in touch with his "Wild" and "Hairy Man" (Bly in Ross 1992). Bly's return to hairy nature was an effort to resolve a particular male crisis, not an environmental crisis. So, too, while possibly well-intentioned, much of this manly return was laden with sexist, antifeminist, and ethnocentric sentiments (see Ross 1992). The increasingly stigmatized status of body hair does make it more likely to become a form of dissent to classical body regimes, but stopping manscaping will not accomplish a great deal of ecological good.

What I am proposing is a more modest examination of all types of body projects and practices—from plastic surgery to exercise regimes—in the context of ecological crisis. Drawing out such interconnections and implications may prove not only intellectually interesting for those engaged in body studies but also, for those ecologically engaged scholars and activists, such studies may illuminate what Max Oelschlaeger (1994) has termed the "paradox of environmentalism" (p. 21): After more than three decades of progressive environmental changes why do we appear closer than ever to an ecological meltdown? Manscaping, as far as I can tell, reveals that even with more than three decades of ever-increasing environmental consciousness, there is still a persistent and possibly mounting bewilderment about our embodied relationship to other creatures and our place in the biosphere. This confusion may continue, in part, to thwart even the best-intentioned economic, technological, and legal changes for a sustainable future.

NOTES

1. The quotation marks around "heterosexual" should forewarn you that this term is highly contested and that human sexuality cannot fit into a neat homo-hetero binary.

2. Accessed May 2007, http://www.skinema.com. Also, a simple Internet search brings up a plethora of heterosexual male body hair discussions. For two examples visit http://www.jurgita.com/articles-id142.html or http://www.carefair.com/Men/Does_She_Mind_1934.html.

3. Although at certain points in modern European history there appears a romantic celebration (often patronizing) of a feminized nature (Merchant 1980) and the "noble savage" (Sale 2006), with the progress and spread of civilization, the idea that triumphed was that nature was to serve culture, animals to serve humans, women to serve men, savages to serve the civilized, and nonwhites to serve whites. Human exceptionalism and distinction, in other words, is a master ideological variable in the domination of nature as well as in different forms of social domination, oppression, and injustice (Spretnak 1999; Adams 1993; Conboy, Medina, and Stanbury 1997).

4. Accessed May 2008, advertisement available at http://www.lovehoney.co.uk/product.cfm?p=1337.

5. Accessed May 2008, http://www.bodyhairremovalnews.com/Men-Shaving-Pubic-Hair-Quiz-Show.htm.

6. Accessed May 5, 2008, http://www.midlifebachelor.com/makeover/makeover-appear-hygiene7.html.

7. Recall your grade-school days and those pictorial representations of the "evolution of man." The posters—probably duplicated in Time-Life books on evolution—show that not only does primal man move from quadra- to bipedal, from a crude club to a refined spear, but he also evolves from hairy to hairless. Although this representation of man's evolution may strive to *describe* the "facts" (i.e., humans were hairier back then and have become progressively less hairy), in the popular imagination this description has become prescription, and the line between facts of body hair and its value becomes fuzzy. The following excerpt from an Internet discussion about body hair illustrates this point:

> I think that our antipathy against body hair is an evolution thing. Maybe in the past people who didn't have a lot of body hair were considered to be more evolved.... So maybe it is an instinctive way of us humans to remove body hair because we don't want to look like our ancestors (whether they were apes or just heavily haired humans).

Rather than neutral or descriptive, this statement, like so many other public discussions about evolution, is implicitly linked with a value-laden notion of progress—as a species we're not simply evolving but moving toward the "good." Body hair is therefore a primitive marker, a sign that progress has not been made and that hairy men are evolutionary left-behinds in need a civilized shaving or waxing to enter the ranks of homo sapiens.

8. Douglas, Kyan, 2003, "Interesting Questions, Facts, and Information," *FunTrivia* (online 2006). Available at: http://www.funtrivia.com/en/Television/Queer-Eye-for-the-Straight-Guy-10553.html.

9. Although stigmatized, grotesque male body hair does have its place in the public eye—quite often as comic relief. To take one example, in *The Forty-Year-Old Virgin*, actor Steve Carell plays the role of Andy, an earnest yet socially awkward guy who lacks experience with women. In what has become a somewhat classic yet painful scene, Andy, with the guidance of his coworkers who are dedicated to getting him laid, has his chest and stomach hair waxed. Finding humor in grotesque expressions, as Bakhtin argued, helped level social distinctions as well as differences between earthiness and society. Unlike this "laughing with," the new genre of male body hair humor seems more like a "laughing at"—a form of corrective humor aimed at patrolling the border of the acceptable. In this case, body-hair humor reinforces the increasingly normative demands for a hairless male body.

When not the source of humor, media representations of hairy men often appear as morally suspect and primitive characters. Witness the majority of men on the television show *The*

Sopranos, which revolves around the daily life of New Jersey mobsters. Tony Soprano, played by James Gandolfini, is a contemporary incarnation of grotesque excess—prone to violent emotions, excessive eating and sexuality, and a good deal of body hair. He is the embodiment of all the rejected elements of a classical body and a civilized life. Nevertheless, judging from the ratings, rather than repellent he appears to be a point of popular fascination and possibly idolization. This might be, in some measure, because each of his grotesque characteristics contains what Stallybrass and White (1986) call "the imprint of desire." These grotesque elements, seemingly cast out as the Other to civilization, "return as the object of nostalgia, longing and fascination. Placed at the outer limits of civil life, they become symbolic contents of bourgeois desire" (191). Tony Soprano is an object of fascination because he blurs the distinction that has been constructed between a classical humanity and an uncivilized animal nature.

REFERENCES

Adams, Carol J., ed. 1993. *Ecofeminism and the Sacred*. New York: Continuum.

Bakhtin, Mikhail. 1984. *Rabelais and His World*. Bloomington, IN: Indiana University Press.

Beck, Ulrich. 1992. Risk society: Towards a new modernity. In *Theory, Culture, and Society*. Translated by M. A. Ritter. Edited by M. Featherstone. London: Sage.

———. 1999. *World Risk Society*. Malden, MA: Polity Press.

Becker, Ernest. 1973. *The Denial of Death*. New York: Free Press.

Bell, Michael. 2004. An invitiation to environmental sociology. In *Sociology for a New Century*. Edited by C. Ragin, W. Griswold, and L. Griffin. Second ed. Thousand Oaks, CA: Pine Forge Press.

Bell, Michael M. 1994. Deep fecology: Mikhail Bakhtin and the call of nature. *Capitalism, nature, socialism* 5 (4):65–84.

Bernier, C. J. Correa. 2007. *Toxic Wastes and Race at Twenty: 1987–2007*. Cleveland, OH: United Church of Christ Justice and Witness Ministries.

Binks, Georgia. 2005. It's a Smooth World. *CBC News*, March 25.

Bordo, Susan. 1999. *The Male Body: A New Look at Men in Public and in Private*. New York: Farrar, Straus, Giroux.

Brumberg, Joan. 1998. *The Body Project: An Intimate History of American Girls*. New York: Random House.

Bullard, Robert. 1993. *Confronting Environmental Racism: Voices from the Grassroots*. Cambridge, MA: South End Press.

———. 2000. *Dumping in Dixie: Race, Class, and Environmental Quality*. Jackson, TN: Westview Press.

———, ed. 2005. *The Quest for Environmental Justice: Human Rights and the Politics of Pollution*. San Francisco: Sierra Club Books.

Conboy, Katie, Nadia Medina, and Sarah Stanbury, eds. 1997. *Writing on the Body: Female Embodiment and Feminist Theory*. New York: Colombia University Press.

Connell, R. W. 2005. *Masculinities*. 2nd ed. Berkeley: University of California Press.

Cooper, Lasandra. 2006. *Cosmetic Surgery for Men Tops 1 Million, Says American Society of Plastic Surgeons*. American Society of Plastic Surgeons 2001 [cited July 2006]. Available from http://www.plasticsurgery.org.

Creamer, Matthew. 2006. Norelco puts the man in manscaping: Testosterone-fueled site for Bodygroom plays up the "optical inch" in attempt to steer clear of metrosexuality. *Advertising Age*, May 15, 45.

Cronon, William. 1995. The trouble with wilderness; or, Getting back to the wrong nature. In *Uncommon Ground: Toward Reinventing Nature*. Edited by W. Cronon. New York: Norton.

———, ed. 1995. *Uncommon Ground: Toward Reinventing Nature*. New York: Norton.

Daily, Lisa. 2006. "Manscaping: The Battle against Hair." Available online at http://click.laval-ife.com/dating/feature/article/manscaping-the-battle-against-hair/rHSA/27764/p1.

Daum, Meghan. 2006. Surveying the cultural manscape. *San Francisco Chronicle*, Sunday, April 16, 8.

Davidson, Joyce, and Mike Smith. 2006. "It makes my skin crawl...": The embodiment of disgust in phobias of "nature." *Body & Society* 12 (1):43–67.

Demeritt, David. 2002. What is the "social construction of nature"? A typology and sympathetic critique. *Progress in Human Geography* 26 (2):767–90.

Devall, Bill, and George Sessions. 1985. *Deep Ecology: Living as if Nature Mattered*. Salt Lake City, UT: Gibbs Smith.

Edelstein, Michael R. 2000. "Outsiders just don't understand": Personalization of risk and the boundary between modernity and postmodernity. In *Risk in the Modern Age: Social Theory, Science, and Environmental Decision-Making*. Edited by M. J. Cohen. New York: St. Martin's.

Falk, William. 2007. Chimps like us. *The Week*, December 28, 35.

Finch, Martha L. 2001. "Civilized" bodies and the "savage" environment of early New Plymouth. In *A Centre of Wonders: The Body in Early America*. Edited by J. M. Lindman and M. L. Tarter. Ithaca, NY: Cornell University Press.

Fine, Gary Alan. 1998. *Morel Tales: The Culture of Mushrooming*. Cambridge, MA: Harvard University Press.

Gard, Greta, ed. 1993. *Ecofeminism: Women, Animals, Nature*. Philadelphia: Temple University Press.

Gardiner, Michael. 1993. Ecology and carnival: Traces of a "green" social theory in the writings of M. M. Bakhtin. *Theory and Society* 22 (6):765–812.

Giddens, Anthony. 1991. *Modernity and Self-Identity*. Stanford: Stanford University Press.

Gill, Rosalind, Karen Henwood, and Carl McLean. 2005. Body projects and the regulation of normative masculinity. *Body & Society* 11 (1):37–62.

Greider, Thomas, and Lorraine Garkovich. 1994. Landscapes: The social construction of nature and the environment. *Rural Sociology* 59 (1):1–24.

Hennen, Peter. 2005. Bear bodies, bear masculinity: Recuperation, resistance, or retreat? *Gender & Society* 19 (1):25–43.

Hope, Christine. 1982. Caucasian female body hair and American culture. *The Journal of America Culture* 5:93–99.

Jurgita. 2003. *Hair on men's body* [Online], 10-26-2006 [cited March 2007]. Available from http://www.jurgita.com/articles-id142.html.

King, Ynestra. 1990. Healing the wounds: Feminism, ecology, and the nature/culture split. In *Reweaving the World: The Emergence of Ecofeminism*. Edited by I. Diamond and G. Orenstein. San Francisco: Sierra Club Books.

Klein, Alan M. 1993. *Little Big Men: Bodybuilding, Subculture and Gender Construction*. Albany: State University of New York Press.

Kristeva, Julia. 1982. *Powers of Horror: An Essay on Abjection*. Translated by L. Roudiez. New York: Columbia University Press.

Luciano, Lynne. 2001. *Looking Good: Male Body Image in Modern America*. New York: Hill and Wang.

Marcuse, Herbert. 1966. *Eros and Civilization*. Boston: Beacon.

Merchant, Carolyn. 1980. *The Death of Nature: Women, Ecology, and the Scientific Revolution.* New York: HarperSanFrancisco.

Monaghan, Lee F. 2005. Big handsome men, bears, and others: Virtual constructions of "fat male embodiment." *Body & Society* 11 (2):81–111.

Mondschein, Ken. 2008. *History of Single Life: Public Hair.* Nerve 2007 [cited June 2008]. Available from http://www.nerve.com/regulars/singlelife/006/.

Moore, Pamela L., ed. 1997. *Building Bodies.* New Brunswick, NJ: Rutgers University Press.

Murphy, Raymond. 1997. *Sociology and Nature: Social Action in Context.* Boulder, CO: Westview Press.

Nash, Roderick. 1982. *Wilderness and the American Mind.* New Haven, CT: Yale University Press.

Newman, Andrew. 2007. Depilatory market moves far beyond the short-shorts. *The New York Times*, September 14, C3.

Oelschlaeger, Max. 1991. *The Idea of Wilderness: From Prehistory to the Age of Ecology.* New Haven, CT: Yale University Press.

———.1994. *Caring for Creation: An Ecumenical Approach to the Environmental Crisis.* New Haven, CT: Yale University Press.

Peterson, Anna L. 2001. *Being Human: Ethics, Environment, and Our Place in the World.* Berkeley: University of California Press.

Plumwood, Val. 1993. *Feminism and the Mastery of Nature.* London: Routledge.

Pope, Harrison G., Katharine A. Phillips, and Roberto Olvardia. 2000. *The Adonis Complex: The Secret Crisis of Male Body Obsession.* New York: Free Press.

Rapley, Time. 2007. *Doing Conversation, Discourse, and Document Analysis.* Thousand Oaks, CA: Sage Publications.

Renzi, Dan. 2007. *How was your day, Dan?* 2005 [cited March 2007]. Available from http://danrenzi.typepad.com/stuff/2005/04/after_letting_m.html.

Ross, Andrew. 1992. Wet, dark, and low, Eco-Man evolves from Eco-Women. *Boundary 2* 19 (2):205–32.

Ruether, Rosmary Radford. 1989. *Gaia and God: An Ecofeminist Theology of Earth Healing.* New York: HarperSanFrancisco.

Sale, Kirkpatrick. 2006. *Christopher Columbus and the Conquest of Paradise.* Second ed. New York: Tauris Parke Paperbacks.

Shildrick, M. 1997. *Leaky Bodies and Boundaries: Feminism, Postmodernism, and (Bio)Ethics.* New York: Routledge.

Shilling, Chris. 2003. The body and social theory. In *Theory, Culture & Society*, second ed. Edited by M. Featherstone. London: Sage.

Slater, Candace. 1995. Amazonia as Edenic narrative. In *Uncommon Ground: Toward Reinventing Nature.* Edited by W. Cronon. New York: Norton.

Smith, Helena. 2000. Why Zorba can't keep his hair on: Today's Greek gods go late-night loitering in beauty parlours. *New Statesman*, July 10, 12.

Smith, Mark. 2001. The face of nature: Environmental ethics and the boundaries of contemporary social theory. *Current Sociology* 49 (1):49–65.

Spretnak, Charlene. 1994. Critical and constructive contributions of ecofeminism. In *Worldviews and Ecology: Religion, Philosophy, and the Environment.* Edited by M. E. Tucker and J. A. Grim. Maryknoll, NY: Orbis Books.

———. 1999. *The Resurgence of the Real: Body, Nature, and Place in a Hypermodern World.* New York: Routledge.

Stallybrass, Peter, and Allon White. 1986. *The Politics and Poetics of Transgression*. Ithaca, NY: Cornell University Press.

Synott, Anthony. 1987. Shame and glory: A sociology of hair. *The British Journal of Sociology* 38 (3):381–413.

Taylor, Sarah McFarland. 2003. Nature. In *Religion and American Cultures: An Encyclopedia of Traditions, Diversity, and Popular Expressions*. Edited by G. Laderman and L. Leon. Santa Barbara, CA: ABC-CLIO.

Toerien, Merran, and Sue Wilkinson. 2003. Gender and body hair: Constructing the feminine woman. *Women's Studies International Forum* 26 (4):333–44.

Toerien, Merran, Sue Wilkinson, and Precilla Y. L. Choi. 2005. Body hair removal: The "mundane" production of normative femininity. *Sex Roles* 52:399–406.

Weitz, Rose. 2004. *Rapunzel's Daughters: What Women's Hair Tells Us about Women's Lives*. First ed. New York: Farrar, Straus, Giroux.

Williams, Raymond. 1980. *Ideas of Nature*. London: Verso.

Disruptive Bodies

　L Disrupt

　　　　－to break apart
　　　　－ To interrupt the normal course or unity of
　　　　－ To throw into disorder

interrupt thought : How do we interpret bodies?

　1) Significance － the meanings/identities we give the physical/material bodies

　2) Subjectification － how we take the significance and give it meaning within a specific context.

"Leaking" body → material body, but also what is revealed about the body.

Congruent → harmonious, similar shape/size

Incongruent → incompatible, when our expectation do not align with the outcome.

||||||||||||||||||||||||||||||||||||||||||||||||||||||||||||||||||||||||||||||||

14

Incongruent Bodies
Teaching While Leaking

Lisa Jean Moore

Coming of age intellectually in the explosive queer worlds of the 1990s San Francisco Bay area, I found my early academic training and experiences astonishing. New vocabularies, identities, morphologies, and possibilities constantly emerged and abated. My doctoral and postdoctoral education, as well as my adjunct teaching, were so all-encompassing that I took for granted my ongoing consciousness-raising. I came to believe the entirety of "the academy" (colleagues, students, scholars, researchers) also underwent profound internal transformation of consciousness about queerness, bodies, gender, and positionality. And I could not have been more pleased to be hired seven years ago by a CUNY school. The College of Staten Island (CSI). My entire family delighted in the move to New York City—a place, I felt, that would also support the intellectual and political work of interdisciplinary LGBTQ studies. However, I soon discovered that Staten Island was somewhat of an anomaly among the New York City boroughs—a homogenous, provincial, conservative, secessionist island in a vibrant, diverse, progressive metropolis. And forget about postmodernity, intersectionality, and postcoloniality. I still wonder if modernity has actually arrived on Staten Island, as there are many vestiges of the pre-modern. For example, when the Pope died, the flags on my public and secular campus were at half mast for two weeks.

As many assistant professors can attest, the first year in the classroom is difficult. At CSI, it was grueling. My carefully detailed lesson plans were rendered irrelevant. My assumptions about the students' cultural, visual, and reading literacy were totally misguided. Each class session seemed to devolve into anecdotal personal stories' enabled and even embellished by my own insecurities; I felt as if I had no control of the class. It was as if Angela's uncle from New Jersey were as much an expert on race as June Jordan. And although incredibly challenging, that first year taught me an invaluable lesson. It was through these embodied experiences that I now understand the teacher's body, my body, creates a simultaneous (and often unexpectedly parallel) lesson plan for students and colleagues. My body, without any intentional or conscious instruction,

From *Feminist Teacher*, Volume 17, Number 2, pages 95–106. © 2007 University of Illinois Press. Reprinted with permission of the University of Illinois Press.

leaked. It became a vehicle for students to inquire and learn about "sociology" of bodies, genders, race, and sexualities, despite my well-constructed syllabi or overheads.

The scholarship of anthropologist Mary Douglas contends that "the body provides the basic scheme for all symbolism" (163). These bodily symbols located in/on the body represent profound socio-cultural markers. As Douglas writes, "I suggest that many ideas about sexual dangers are better interpreted as symbols of the relation between parts of society as mirroring designs of hierarchy or symmetry which apply in larger social systems" (4). When my body leaks, it creates and disrupts meanings. It disrupts the socially expected bounded rationality of members of the academy. Attributions of meanings to bodily fluids are made through larger socio-cultural processes. The feminist philosopher Margrit Shildrick finds that female bodies are constructed within bio-medical and bio-ethical discourse as leaky; the female body is messy, unbounded, shifting, porous, flexible, and unpredictable. Indeed, anthropological fieldwork demonstrates the cross-cultural experiences of a woman's body as polluting because of its leakiness: "a bleeding vagina and dripping nipples testif[y] to its inability to remain in control" (Tsoffar 10). Shildrick and Price argue that this leakiness contaminates rational and bounded spaces: "As the devalued processes of reproduction make clear, the body has a propensity to leak, to overflow the proper distinctions between self and other, to contaminate and engulf" (3). These types of collective representations are transmitted through social interactions within the classroom as well.

In my case, dominant social meanings of my body are taken for granted by my students—my professor is a woman, which means she is heterosexual. Furthermore, students have related to my breast milk. The milk indicates to them certain beliefs about familial and gender relations; it says look, she is a mommy. However, there are subversive meanings embodied by my body—I am a lesbian, I reproduce and survive outside of heterosexual relationships. At the same time, through tactical omission, I comply with the maintenance of dominant normative meanings of my body. I dance between congruence and incongruence—both deliberately and inadvertently. I adhere to an embodied performance that is congruent to the students' taken-for-granted beliefs about me because it is useful. But through my inadvertent slip or leak of information, there is the unexpected revelation of the subversive meaning of my body. The jolt of incongruence—that I do not have a phallus and that I am a "real" woman who has babies and leaks breast milk—throws into question the very taken-for-granted beliefs about my sexuality, my students' desire, and the ongoing negotiation of power relationships.

Being Congruent

This essay, culled from processes of self-reflection, explores how my body is incongruent to my students and my colleagues. Incongruence occurs when what others expect about the progressive logic of someone's body conflicts with the anticipated biography. In my life, when incongruence is revealed, it creates both humorous and painful experiences for me and some of my students. But these moments of incongruence are rarely planned or intended. Rather, as this essay details, these revelations of incongruence are often spontaneous, irrational, and somatically initiated.

Furthermore, this bodily incongruency is a dialectical process. In many instances, members of the college community perceive my body as incongruent. This type of incongruence happens when my body's appearance and actions do not match who I am, aspects of my identity. This is a complicated process because in many ways my body is socially congruent; it reproduced, for example. But because of my sexual identity, and because of the institutional disembodiedness of the academy, my body and my self become incongruous. In turn, I experience my own body as incongruent to the environments and relationships of the academy.

And even though my experiences of teaching at an urban commuter campus populated by predominantly white-ethnic, working-class, first-generation college students has greatly improved since my first year, I still find myself reflecting back to seven years ago and the initial and ongoing process of "coming out"[2] to students. I assumed my students presumed me to be heterosexual. And perhaps as a means of self-defensiveness, I presumed them to be homophobic. Although I can acknowledge these as assumptions now, they felt real to me at the time and as a result became real in the way I behaved toward my students and how I interpreted their behavior to me.

Since my academic training was highly influenced by cultural studies, studies of the body, and queer theory, I felt very aware of my own performance in the classroom, during office hours, and with my colleagues. For example, I knew and still know how my body, through a compassionate nod of the head or an empathetic patience expressed with verbal and physical coaxing, can be comforting to students as we discuss challenging materials about racism and sexism. However, as a white, female, thirty-something body on public display for 150 students during a three-course semester, I was not prepared for the nonverbal data mining of my personal life incited by bodily "clues." Nonverbal data mining was unabashedly confirmed by follow-up questions. For example, after I wore my grandmother's wedding ring for a week, a student who barely knew me asked me if I had gotten engaged. Or an outfit that revealed my tattoo on my ankle would lead to inquiries about the disciplinary style of my parents. During office hours, a student pointed to a photo of a male friend holding up his Barbra Streisand tickets with a handwritten caption: "The closest I will ever come to my idol." She asked if he was my husband. Students wanted information—in some ways they were hoping my body would leak. Despite these fairly consistent desires or questions to understand what my body meant, it has been the incongruence that my body represents to students that I find the most intriguing.

This exercise of self-reflection reminds me of the experience of thumbing through old photo albums. You see yourself in a previous time with the awareness that you lived through what is captured on film or in memory. "How did I ever think that hair color was attractive?" Or "Look how young I looked and so thin." And "I remember that day like it was yesterday. It poured." Your biography, the story of your body, is mediated by the passage of time and the ability to look back and evaluate and interpret that which has happened. This essay, like autobiography, is partial; it is a collection of stories I am able to remember and chose to share. As I reflect back to my early days as an assistant professor, I harshly judge myself. Much like the criticism of previous outfits and hairstyles, I wish I had done some things differently as a new professor. I wish I could be more proud of the behaviors I uncover. I wish I could have had more courage or boldness. But I also understand that my untenured status and the lack of security with my role as a mother disabled me from accessing my strengths.

Seven years ago, when I started my first tenure-track job, after completing a post-doctoral fellowship in California, having a baby, and surviving a trans-continental move, I was a nursing body to a six-month-old baby girl. I was a queer body in a two-mom family moving to New York City. I was, and to some extent still am, a highly anxious and madly-in-love mother unable to fully comprehend the intensity of passion I feel for my daughters.

But I am also public property with a professional obligation to the City University of New York. And my body has become a text to be read by new audiences. As a nursing body carrying a breast pump to campus, I was read as heterosexual. And as a pregnant body two years later, I was read as heterosexually active and married. At present, as a woman who is "read" as feminine and a mother of two girls on a highly normatively gendered campus, I occasionally come out as a lesbian when I feel safe.

Although I had never been one to hide or misrepresent my identity or embodied self, somehow the new professorial appointment, the repressive norms of Staten Island, and the freshness of motherhood placed me in an environment where the stakes of coming out seemed too high. So, I began the process of allowing myself to "pass" as a traditionally feminine/straight woman. I acquiesced to passing for this more socially acceptable identity on several occasions because it seemed like a far easier task than using my body as a tool of transgressive education. But despite this consent to passing, which enabled my students to maintain the congruent and intact image of Professor Moore, my body revealed information that led them to more chaotic images.

Clearly it was and is not only students who are "tricked" by my body. There is a legacy of heterosexism and male domination evident in the structural arrangements of most academic institutions, including CSI and CUNY. From "spousal" hires, punitive maternity policies, and discriminatory benefit packages, the structural conditions under which academics labor are not democratic. These structural conditions are reinforced by micro-interactional communications between hierarchically placed faculty members. For example, as I recall in this story, simple queries into the well-being of a child can reveal heterosexist assumptions.

Incongruence as Cognitive Dissonance

My first week on campus, an older tenured psychology professor asks me how old my daughter is. "She is six months old," I respond, pleased by her interest.

"Oh, how lovely. So is your husband with her now?" She queries.

"No, I am not married."

"Oh, I understand. So your boyfriend, partner, whatever you call the baby's father . . ." Expectantly smiling. She wants to assure me that she is current on the breadth of possible relationships I could have with the father of my child.

"No. My daughter has two mothers," I awkwardly reply.

"I don't understand, dear." She looks puzzled but does not allow her beaming smile to crack.

"I am a lesbian and my daughter has two mothers. My girlfriend is home with our daughter right now." Red-faced and hurrying, she quickly picks up her pace down the hallway.

"Oh, very nice."

Clearly, to use psychological terms, she was experiencing cognitive dissonance, a discrepancy between her taken-for-granted perception about who I am and the integration of new information—my embodiment of difference. How can this incongruency be reworked into her assessment of me and possibly ease her obvious embarrassment? I may never know this because we have never spoken since this interaction.

Later in the semester, I pass an older sociology professor in the hallway.

She stops me as we pass. "How is your semester going?"

"Fairly well. I am glad I ran into you. I wanted to ask you a question. We are reading Adrienne Rich today in Sociology of Women and I am thinking of coming out to the students. When I was an adjunct in California I did, and it was a good experience for the students to sort of then think of compulsory heterosexuality or positioning themselves on the lesbian continuum."

She shook her head, "Oh, I wouldn't. I don't think they will like you then and you might get bad teaching evaluations."

I was in shock but also ashamed for having asked. I thanked her and tried to figure out why I was also so annoyed. On the drive home from campus, after teaching Rich and not coming out to my students, I realized that I was irritated because my senior colleague had been teaching on this campus for twenty years and had normalized a discriminatory practice without any resistance.

My colleagues, institutionally located in the heteronormative academic institution, perpetuate the conditions of a closeted campus. They each participate in creating an environment that tolerates hostility to gay and lesbian faculty, and, as a result, students. Worse, they instructed me to do the same. And although the faculty at CSI actively co-construct the campus environment, many faculty members seem to be disinterested in, oblivious to, or unable to examine their own homophobia. It seems to me that faculty are not as able to participate in the interactive processes of personal or intellectual transformation as my students. And I do not feel as forgiving of their insults and ignorance as I do those of my students. Thus the remainder of this essay interprets my relations with students.

Incongruence through Leaking

As I continue my process of self-reflection, the first few years on campus seem to be overflowing with experiences of my incongruent body. During my second semester teaching at CSI, I was assigned to teach GREC (Gender, Race, Ethnicity, and Class). Because this course meets the general education requirements of the college's degree-granting programs, a broad range of students enroll. On the eighth week, I screened a thirty-minute clip from *It's Elementary,* a documentary film that shows teachers introducing age-appropriate gay and lesbian lesson plans and the bias awareness effects of such lessons. After the clip, I asked the students for their impressions. Up until this point of teaching I had never specifically asked students anything about sexuality. Nor had I revealed my identity as a lesbian or as a mother.

A male student raised his hand and said, "Clearly the movie shows how gay people should never be parents." As a first-year professor, already warned about the importance of the students liking me and feeling the necessity of teaching in an inclusionary and participatory dialogic fashion, I probed.

"Well, that is an unusual interpretation of the film—what do others think?" I asked, hoping to be rescued by another student.

"Yeah, I agree. I mean come on; things are just going too far. These kids are going to be so confused. I mean, I think it is just selfish for gays or lesbians to have children. That is just going to screw up the kids."

As I nodded, I became increasingly upset. I also imagined the lovely scent of my baby daughter's head that I would see later that day after zooming across the bridge in hopes of making it to her in record time. Since I was wearing a blue silk top, it took only a split second for me to realize that let-down[3] had occurred. My bra felt entirely soaked through, even though I had carefully changed nursing pads before class, and droplets of milk cascaded, fully formed, down the front of my shirt. The linoleum tile in front of my foot had a perfectly formed puddle of milk. Students in the front row were instantly glued to my breasts, seemingly in awe of my freakishness. I attempted to cover myself with some papers and announced that class was over even though we had an hour left. As I gathered up my things, the whispering increased. An older woman, a returning student, came up to me. "Oh, Professor, the same thing happened to me when I was away from my baby. It just means that you need to feed them," she said. A few other students nodded. "You just need to get home," she added.

"My husband always told me he could tell when I needed to feed the baby, because my boobs got humongous," another student interjected.

As I write this, I still feel a pang of humiliation. What was most striking about my breasts leaking milk down the front of my professional attire is how my students quickly reasserted the dominance of a heteronormative model of my body and identity. According to them, let-down occurred because it was time for my body to feed the baby—it was the natural logic of my body clearly establishing that it is natural for mothers to feed their babies in spite of their careers.

Three years later, after the pregnancy and birth of my second daughter, I was teaching a course called Birth and Death. During a lecture about childbirth, one of my favorite students, Nicola, asked me what my very recent birthing experience was like.

"It was very fast. And as much of our reading explores, it was mismanaged by the hospital." I began explaining how I was disregarded by the medical resident when I arrived at the hospital insisting that the baby was coming. The resident did not believe me and would not put me in a room. My daughter was born forty-five minutes after I arrived, practically landing on the floor. During the story, my usual vigilant self-protectiveness lapsed. It was cathartic to discuss the birth, still fresh in my mind, with an academic spin; I remember using the terms medicalization, medical model, and paternalism. Then somewhere I got lost in the story. I told my class how I kept yelling at my girlfriend to go and get the doctor. I reflected how I was so angry because I just didn't feel she was being aggressive enough—typical of her calm and unassuming nature—probably one of the reasons we have been together so long.

After an audible gasp, I regained consciousness. I looked around the room and said, "Well, I guess I just revealed information that some of you didn't know."

Antoinette asked, "Are you telling us you are gay?"

I nodded.

"How could that be? I thought you were married. I thought I saw you and your husband on campus."

I shook my head.

Fatima, one of my repeat students, a twenty-five-year-old Liberian woman, started to cry in astonishment. She said, "Professor Moore, I can't believe you never told me. I thought we were close. I just can't believe you didn't tell me." It was clear to me that Fatima felt betrayed, as if I had slighted her or insulted our connection.

The next day during office hours my student Isabella, an older woman from Barbados, stopped by to tell me that in her Geography class, one of the male students was telling the class how Professor Moore was a "dyke." She went on to recount how he was encouraging other students to go to my office and look at my photos on my door, see my children, whom he said "were bought at the sperm bank."

The lioness quality of motherhood overwhelmed me and I lost my head. "Who said that?" I blurted out with no compunction, no sense of discretion or anonymity. Isabella said it was one of the white guys.

In the class of forty, there were five white men. I asked her which white guy and she responded, "I don't know. They all look alike to me."

During our next class, I was still unclear how I would deal with the students. But when I arrived in class, the anger and feelings of protectiveness of my daughters swelled.

"I shared some information with you in our last class. It was personal information, and I felt as if you were capable of respecting that. But, unfortunately, it has come to my attention that you do not deserve to know that information. Now, I am used to garden-variety homophobia, but the fact that someone in here said something about my daughters is not acceptable. They come to campus with me sometimes and I don't want them to be exposed to hatred when I can control it. I am so disgusted with this situation that I can't teach today." And I left the class.

At the time, leaving class seemed like an act of self-preservation. They had hurt me and in some ways frightened me. I wanted them to experience the consequences of their actions. And from my present vantage point, I honestly cannot say that I wish I had done things differently. But leaving the class limited the potential for productive conversations with students. It cut off the possibility of confronting homophobia and of exploring the power of raw emotions in consciousness-raising. I did not allow myself or the students a space to work through the feelings that were upsetting the classroom. I have reason to believe that much could have been accomplished if I had been braver.

I could not have been more surprised when I arrived at the following class. My students greeted me with a bouquet of flowers and a card. I still have mixed feelings about the students' card. Many of my friends thought it was very thoughtful of the students. However, I felt awkward and exposed, as if my succumbing to the anecdotal pleasures of the classroom established an environment of familiarity that degraded my pedagogical relationship to my students. Did they learn anything beyond "we hurt our professor's feelings and have to say we are sorry"? Did they understand the larger institutional legacy of condoning homophobia and heterosexism? Did they understand how their own assumptions of me, the fact that they were shocked, were based in processes of normative socialization by powerful hegemonic matrices of domination? As each semester unfolds, I find myself working through these questions with surprising results.

And what happened in those classes is neither static nor finite. There are ripple effects of leaking and the aftermath. Several students from these two classes continued to work with me for the remainder of their undergraduate careers and beyond. Fatima, now in graduate school for sociology, continued to come to my office to check in and share stories about her daughter. To this day, whenever she calls or emails, she always asks about my girls with deep sincerity. Isabella, a devout Christian, works at a social service agency in Manhattan and reminds me that "Jesus still loves me" whenever we speak.

(In)Congruence through Packing

Within the gendered power relations of the university and the relative powerlessness of the new untenured professor and lactating first-time mom, I was attempting to establish my legitimacy. In order to conform to what I believed were the normative demands of my job, I worked to appear to my students as a rational, stable, and integrated self/body. To be clear, I wanted there to be congruence with what these particular students expected a professor to be. In a sense, my performance in front of the classroom illustrates multiple examples of "Ontological Packing." Ontological Packing is a method for supporting dominant meanings around the body in order to maintain power in a phallocentric hierarchical structure. One of the outcomes of Ontological Packing is ascribing meanings to bodily fluids, sexuality, and gender.

The term "packing" refers to the action of wearing a concealed detachable phallus (often shaped and modeled after an actual penis, but not always) and retaining some of the symbolic and material power that comes with having and using a phallus. I am using the term phallus to suggest the material and symbolic celebration of male generative power often to the exclusion or denigration of female generative power. Since the phallus is symbolic, it is transferable (Butler, *Bodies*). To be clear, I did not and do not wear a dildo when I teach. Furthermore, I am not pursuing female masculinity nor do I have the desire to pass as a man. Rather, the act of teaching, reproducing, and parenting while being a female without a male member (of the family or otherwise), can be understood through the metaphor of packing a phallus.

As a professor, I retain a sense of phallocentric power of being the rational knower and firm disciplinarian. As a mother, I have used the product of the phallus to generate, create, and sustain a family. But in actuality, in my personal life, there is no "real" phallus. There is incongruency between my public persona and my personal life, and this incongruency can be revealed when my body (breasts or mouth) leaks. So although it is true that I wield phallocentric power, there is no presence of an actual man in my life. However, my students believe, until it is revealed otherwise, that there is an actual man in my life who enables me to do the things I do. I have allowed the assumptions about the supposed man in my life, my heteronormativity, to persist because they enable me to maintain legitimacy in my social position as professor and mother.

Incongruence as "Disequilibriating Jolt"

Coming out to my students is a "disequilibriating jolt" (Bordo, "Reading") for my students.[4] This disequilibriating jolt is created through a series of social interactions and creates opportunities for "unpacking." Something out of place creates havoc in one's perception of the situation. The moment of recognition of embodied incongruence creates this jolt that may destabilize the classroom dynamics, the students, and their teachers.

As in my case, the jolt leading to a display of embodied incongruence was preceded by two leaks. The first leak felt out of control of my conscious mind. My breasts leaked despite every ounce of conscious will that struggled to contain the milk. This leak established further proof of my normative status in the students' mind. The second leak—the leakiness of my mouth—created a jolt for the students. It revealed the incongruence of my body and identity for the students. It is difficult to know if this leak was motivated by some subconscious desire to subvert the taken-for-granted. Whatever the motivation, the outcome of leaking bodily information challenges the students' perception of their teacher and transforms the dynamics of the classroom.

As I stated earlier, in the classroom, a teacher's body and its embodied performance have the potential to provide stability to the classroom environment. In particular, when teaching sociological topics that often inspire deep consciousness-raising and self-reflection, the teacher's embodied use of tone, voice, and body language may comfort students or encourage them to reveal things in a "safe" space. The disequilibriating jolt of revelation of an incongruent body has the potential to disrupt the harmonious flow of social exchange. Students may feel betrayed, while at the same time there is the potential for them to further examine the depth of their own socialization, as Fatima and Isabella continue to do.

Incongruence as Liberatory

Acknowledging the incongruence and working through the messiness in its aftermath has enabled a liberation of the self. Because of leaking through my mouth and my breasts, aspects of my self, my identity, emerged in the classroom. Parts of my self were now free—the mothering self and the lesbian self. My personal liberation was also public—it was collectively negotiated in the context of that class. Each time a new semester begins, there is the potential for liberation; there is the possibility the self/body will emerge within the negotiations of new social relationships. However, as the dynamics of social power change, my own calculation of relative risk changes and I may deliberately reveal aspects of myself. That is not to say that I do not continue to conceal parts of myself, nor that students do not experience body incongruency as the body leaks. For example, now that I am tenured, I feel comfortable taking more risks in the classroom. And although I rarely discuss my sexual identity or my girlfriend, it often is clear that I do not have a male partner. Tenure provides a safety net for certain admissions in the classroom, but not all. I may not fear for my job security, but I do still fear for my personal security and the security of my children, who often accompany me to campus.

In the academy, the body has historically been inscribed by its relationship to the phallus. In my case, the interpretation of the emerging representations of feminine power, for example the breast milk, are immediately interpreted as evidence of some heterosexual and/or phallocentric relationship. This interpretation of breast milk as evidence that the professor is really a (married) mommy creates a level of comfort in the classroom. Leaking breast milk reasserts congruence of embodied gender normativity. Bodies doing "naturally" gendered things have the power to reduce the threat of a smart, young, feminist professor. And although it may be true that some students were attempting to be empathetic to me during let-down, they were doing so within a familiar script of heterosexuality that evoked our "husbands." Even though I was a feminist professor, I was more like them than they might have thought. Was this shared heterosexual experience the basis of their understanding? The process of comforting me through an embarrassing event was couched in a shared identification based on false assumptions of my "lifestyle"—which in effect led me further into the closet. Would they have comforted me had they known the "Truth"?

When the "Truth" was revealed, the incongruence required some unpacking, deconstructing, and disassembling of prevalent taken-for-grantedness. The processes of unpacking force students and colleagues to reconsider their previous interpretations. They question the truth of what occurred, and they can feel betrayed—as Fatima did. But if we are both committed to the relationship, students can and do recover from their betrayal. I want to be extremely clear, however, that this is not a simple or short process. Our relationship has lasted for over seven years, and Fatima and I do not strictly connect during my on-campus office hours during the semester.

Over time, professors' bodies provide material and cultural resistance to the taken-for-granted assumptions about social order, specifically heterosexual paradigms, socio-cultural constructions of race, expressions of hegemonic masculinity, and beliefs about able-bodiedness. Incongruent bodies are clearly exceptionally powerful pedagogical devices, but at the same time, it is often painful, tiring, and potentially dangerous when students are jolted into unpredictable social relations.

Although leakiness has traditionally been depicted in pejorative terms, Shildrick's work attempts to resurrect leakiness as an asset in times of post-structural subjecthood, belonging to a subject that is nomadic rather than stable. Despite the academic pressures to maintain the self as a bounded subject, bodies spill from their containers and disrupt distance from students that may be desirable in the classroom. But in some ways, the leakiness humanizes faculty to students. There is a potential to enable more openness to lectures and key concepts. And although there is the risk of the *Oprah* phenomenon, incongruent bodies as they emerge in everyday, real-life classrooms are not a "guest spot" on the syllabus. Rather they are unpredictably emergent and require some unplanned integration into the pedagogical context of a shared classroom experience. Bodies are recalcitrant and relentless, they are not fleeting secondhand stories or retellings of what someone saw on the History Channel over the summer. And as such, bodies become texts that are read and re-read, interpreted and misinterpreted by students, colleagues, and selves. In my own case, I forced myself to integrate the text of my body into the classroom.

All bodies leak and have the potential to disorder and modify the classroom milieu. Using one's body, intentionally or otherwise, to disrupt normativity has the potential to be a profound consciousness-raising experience. The challenge of embodiment and the corporeality of bodies is that bodies behave in unpredictable ways. We cannot always choose when we want to deploy or erase our body for educational purposes. Nor can we always finesse the interruption our corporeality presents to a class.

In conclusion, my experiences of embodied teaching at CSI have taught me that indeed bodily symbols located in/on the body represent profound socio-cultural markers. Some of these bodily symbols are bodily fluids or semi-conscious utterance— both leaks. One process of meaning attribution to bodily by-products occurs either overtly or tacitly through classroom interactions. Meaning attribution to the body is deeply embedded within the context of gendered power relations, and these relations inform the meaning of the body. When incongruent bodies are produced in classroom interactions, they are fertile ground for deconstructing these gendered power relations.

NOTES

1. Although I do allow students to share their personal stories as a way to explore how these are not private troubles but publicly produced and maintained (à la Mills), it is clear to me that many students have been encouraged to see sociology as some form of group therapy. It seems to me that this deep desire to share one's personal story, particularly stories of sex and gender, is mediated by the reality entertainment and talk show medias. For example, in my first semester, two students came to tell me that they liked my class because it was just like they were on *Oprah*.

2. As I age, due to the pervasiveness of heteronormativity, I have come to understand coming out as a process that requires constant articulation and work on the parts of all social actors. As a young college student, coming out to my parents, family, and friends was seen as a "stage" and easy for them to forgive, ignore, or explain away. As a young adult within a long-term, live-in relationship with a woman, coming out as queer or lesbian was taken more seriously as an identity claim. My identity needed to be managed by others. My partner had to be integrated into my family and friendship network. As a mother with two school-age children, coming out is more complex. It now involves vulnerable others (my children) whom I do not want to confuse by passing, and I simultaneously do not want to endanger as "freaks." Furthermore, they frequently come out on my behalf. On a recent return plane trip to New York from Nashville, Tennessee, my older daughter (age six) had to sit in a different row. I overheard her telling the elderly couple who were her seatmates that she had two mothers. After my initial reflexive instinct to sink down in my seat, she called out to me, "Mommy, how old are you? And how old is Mom?"

3. When women are nursing, let-down often happens when a baby has latched on to the nipple and triggered the milk to flow. But let-down can also occur when a woman gets very emotional, thinks about her baby, or hears a baby cry.

4. To be clear, the disequilibriating jolt outlined by Bordo refers to the film *The Crying Game* and the revelation of Dil's penis.

REFERENCES

Bordo, Susan. *The Male Body: A New Look at Men in Public and Private*. New York: Farrar, Straus, Giroux, 1999.

———. "Reading the Male Body." *The Male Body: Features, Destinies, Exposures*. Ed Laurence Goldstein. Ann Arbor: University of Michigan Press, 1994. 265–306.

Butler, Judith. *Bodies That Matter: On the Discursive Limits of "Sex."* New York: Routledge, 1993.

———. *Gender Trouble: Feminism and the Subversion of Identity*. New York: Routledge, 1990.

Douglas, Mary. *Purity and Danger: An Analysis of the Concepts of Pollution and Taboo*. New York: Routledge, 1996.

Shildrick, Margrit. *Leaky Bodies and Boundaries: Feminism, Postmodernism and BioEthics*. New York: Routledge, 1997.

———, and Janet Price. "Openings on the Body: A Critical Introduction." *Feminist Theory and the Body: A Reader*. Ed. Janet Price and Margrit Shildrick. New York: Routledge, 1999. 1–14.

Tsoffar, Ruth. "The Body as Storyteller: Karaite Women's Experience of Blood and Milk." *Journal of American Folklore* 117 (Winter 2004): 3–21 .

15

Envisioning the Body in Relation
Finding Sex, Changing Sex

Eric Plemons

[handwritten note: ☆ author uses "transgender" as a medical term]

On December 1, 1952, the *New York Daily News* ran a pair of cover photos. On the left was a woman with deep red lipstick and coiffed blonde hair. On the right was a smiling young army cadet with his hat gallantly tipped to one side. The headline above the photos read, "Ex-GI Becomes Blonde Beauty." George Jorgensen, the young army cadet, had traveled to Denmark to undergo sex reassignment surgery—or a "sex change" operation—and returned to the United States as the "blonde beauty," Christine Jorgensen. Popularly known as the first American transsexual, Christine Jorgensen's widely publicized return to the United States sparked a series of debates that continue today.

The practice of body modification certainly did not begin with the advent of reconstructive surgeries like those involved in sex reassignment. From tattooing and piercing to circumcision and rhinoplasty, people change, mark, and reconstruct their bodies in many different ways for many different reasons. But piercings, circumcisions, and nose jobs are not front-page stories—not even in the 1950s. So what makes sex reassignment surgery so distinct from other ways that people make and remake their bodies? Answering this question requires a critical engagement with some of our most fundamental—but, as it turns out, deeply complex—ways of thinking about people.

This essay explores transsexualism and sex reassignment surgery in America through two lenses: the social and the medical. While it will be analytically useful to separate the social from the medical, it will also be clear that an engagement with each depends on an understanding of the other. In other words, the *what* of transsexing is inseparable from its *how*. Medically speaking, the *how* of changing sex involves a patient interacting with psychotherapy couches, white coats, green scrubs, and lots of paperwork. In this medical frame, transsexualism is conceived as a problem in the physical body that can be effectively treated through medical and surgical intervention; it is not a problem with the way the patient feels. Surgeons don't operate on feelings; they operate on actual skin, actual flesh, actual bodies. Socially speaking, the *how* of transsexualism is absolutely about feelings, norms, and expectations. It is a feeling of not belonging, of not quite fitting in, that leads a person to seek interventions to change his or her sex. It is a feeling of fear and anxiety that produces the extraordinary forms of regulation that determine who is and who is not allowed access to these interventions. In examining the meeting of feelings and flesh, I will show that the sexed body is always a body in relation—to its mind, to its society, and to its self.

In the case of transsexualism, as in so many others, bodies are the sites at which the divergences between social and medical signification converge and are renegotiated. In the ethically debated processes of changing sex, scientifically backed medical claims, deeply felt personal emotions, and widely held social beliefs all come together to inform the way we think about health and sickness, sex and gender, bodies and selves. These radically distinct kinds of knowledge meet under the sign of *transsexualism* and bring with them their own histories, associations, and modes of authority. And whether you agree or disagree, object to or support the knowledge claims made in any one of these registers—medical, personal, social—it is crucial to see how their contestations make and remake the bodies of people called "transsexuals" every day.

My look through the social lens will begin with a brief history of the condition of transsexualism in the United States and the way it is diagnosed and treated. I argue that a centrally important way to analyze the social conception of transsexuality is to look at the means and mediums by which it is regulated. One of the best ways to understand the fears and anxieties that a thing produces is to look at the rules and regulations meant to control that thing. In this case, it is looking not just at the number of rules but at the content of these rules—*what* they actually require people to *do*—that provides insight into how we understand the relationship between bodies and selves, sexes and genders.

With this understanding of the kinds of evaluation required, of how proof of transsexualism is produced, and of the network of experts brought to bear on whether access to medical interventions should be allowed, we next turn to the medical interventions themselves. By looking at what doctors do in order to "change sex," we get a picture of how and where "sex" is located in the body. In addition, we'll look critically at the nature of surgical intervention and what kinds of sex surgeons have in mind when they have scalpels in their hands.

Before I begin the task I have laid out, I want to say a word about abstraction. Abstraction is a valuable analytic tool for lots of reasons, not least of which is that it can help us think of new ways to engage things that seem to be stultifyingly familiar—things like bodies. It is critical to remember, however, that while we may talk about "the body" as an abstract concept, "the transsexual body" does in fact exist. The policies and modes of thinking that I discuss here impact the daily lives of real people who, in addition to being transsexual, have lives as complex and mundane as anyone's. As scholars of "the body" we must never forget that bodies are the material shape of people—and further, that "the body" can include both the generality of every body in the world and the specificity of *your* body, seated and reading.

Some History:
Why Transsexualism Is a Medical Problem and Why It Matters

Every disease, disorder, and treatment has a unique history. This history includes the time and place where it was first recognized and named, all the people who have been involved in producing knowledge about it, and the modes of thinking about health and wellness that have animated their actions. Transsexualism is no different. Though gender variation and cross-gender behavior have existed in various forms throughout history, the concept of transsexualism as a pathological incongruence between the body and the mind has only been around since the 1950s. Like all things related to social identity and bodily practice, gender variance can only be understood in reference to a particular place and time. The (very) brief account of transsexualism and sex reassignment surgery in the United States that follows is an effort to place this mode of gender variance and the institutional response to it in the context of twentieth-century America.[1]

Christine Jorgensen's return to the United States in 1952 garnered floods of media attention and sparked debates among the general public and doctors alike. Some physicians and ethicists considered it wildly unethical to surgically remove healthy tissue on the basis of the demands of these new "transsexual" people whom they considered patently insane. Others saw surgery as the potential cure to a problem of gender variance that had not been successfully treated by any other mode of treatment. At the forefront of this second group of physicians was Dr. Harry Benjamin.

Dr. Benjamin was a German-born endocrinologist practicing in San Francisco, California, in the 1950s. Prior to her historic surgery, Dr. Benjamin had been treating Jorgensen as well as several other patients with hormone replacement therapy. Basically, hormone replacement therapy supplies male-bodied patients with increased amounts of estrogen and female-bodied patients with increased amounts of testosterone.[2] Benjamin initiated this treatment because he believed that the physical changes enacted by hormone replacement could ease the psychological distress felt by his patients. After Jorgensen's transition became front-page news, Benjamin's office was flooded with letters from people all over the country who desperately wanted hormonal and surgical treatment. It was he who coined the term "transsexual" to describe the newly identified disorder, which he described as a "unique illness distinct from transvestism and homosexuality, perhaps conditioned by endocrine factors, and *not amenable to psychotherapy*" (emphasis mine) (Benjamin 1954: 219). In his groundbreaking book *The Transsexual Phenomenon* (1966), Benjamin broke from a significant body of previous research that had defined transsexualism as a psychosexual disorder. Instead, he defined it as an exclusively medical one. He wrote,

> Psychotherapy with the aim of curing transsexualism, so that the patient will accept himself as a man . . . is a useless undertaking. Since it is evident, therefore, that the mind of the transsexual cannot be adjusted to the body, it is logical and justifiable to

attempt the opposite, to adjust the body to the mind. If such a thought is rejected, we would be faced with therapeutic nihilism. (1966: 116)

This conception of the problem remains the crux of the diagnosis and treatment of transsexualism today. The mind and the body are conceived as radically distinct and at odds with one another. This configuration reflects Descartes' influential claim that the body and mind are distinct entities. While the definition of transsexualism both assumes and asserts the disconnection of body from mind, it also relies upon their intimate connection. This tension in the conceptualization of the disorder is evident in its exceptional diagnostic and treatment protocols.

As with any other disorder, transsexualism is diagnosed in reference to a codified set of symptoms. In this case, however, the process of diagnosis is a complicated one. This is the case because although transsexualism is still defined as a medical disorder, it does not have, nor has it ever had, medical symptoms. There are no tests to run, no samples to analyze, no tissue to examine to find transsexualism. In fact, it cannot be diagnosed through medical means at all. Instead, symptoms for this medical disorder are found in the form of stories. Psychotherapists evaluate patients on the basis of stories patients tell about their lives. In other words, the mind tells the story about the body that the body itself cannot tell. But it is crucial to understand that these are not stories about aches and pains, or bodily dysfunction. These are stories about the patient's emotional feelings about his or her body in particular situations and at particular times. They are stories about childhood toys and clothing, about puberty and dating, about sexuality and friendship, about roughhousing and quiet contemplation. In other words, transsexualism is diagnosed through stories about the experience of living in a gendered body. It is a problem not of the body alone but of the body *in relation*. More on this in a moment.

This diagnostic scheme—beginning with psychotherapy and ending in medical intervention—has remained relatively unchanged since 1979 when the Harry Benjamin International Gender Dysphoria Association (HBIGDA)—an international group of experts on the care of transsexual people—first published their Standards of Care,[3] a set of guidelines that instructs caregivers how to diagnose and treat people who seek medical interventions to change their sex. According to the Standards of Care, once a person has been evaluated by a psychotherapist and assigned the diagnosis of transsexual (also known as severe gender identity disorder), that person can then be approved for access to hormones and then to surgeries. The therapist identifies the disorder and then refers patients to physicians and surgeons to treat it. This act, in effect, provides an institutional bridge between the body and the mind, and positions this disorder as one that proves Descartes' point, and at the same time confounds it.

While the complications and contradictions of the current diagnostic and treatment scheme may be obvious, the medical designation of the disorder is no accident and is no small detail. Because transsexualism is defined as a body problem, the surgery used to treat it is framed as a necessity rather than a desire. This difference marks the distinction between "aesthetic" and "reconstructive" surgeries. Aesthetic surgeries are typically described as elective or cosmetic procedures like rhinoplasty or liposuction. They are surgeries that are requested by the patient but do not remedy an existing health problem. Reconstructive surgeries are those that work to restore the body's normal functioning after disease or accident (Gilman 1998). Examples of reconstructive procedures include restorative skin grafting or bone structure repair. The distinction between these two types of procedures in reference to transsexuality is an important one. I offer an example of another kind of surgical intervention into bodily gender to illustrate what is at stake in the distinction between aesthetic and reconstructive surgeries, and what these classifications tell us about the relations between body and mind.

Jan, a female-bodied person, wants to undergo surgery in order to increase the size of her breasts to an extremely large EEE size. Breast augmentation or "enhancement" (notice the positive language here) is considered an aesthetic procedure that can be performed on the basis of a patient's desire. In this case, the mind and the body, which in the case of the transsexual are unproblematically recognized as being separate and distinct Cartesian entities, are assumed to exist in this woman in untroubled harmony. Jan is making a request to alter her sex characteristics, to be sure, but her desired alteration is not understood to indicate a psychological problem or a medical disorder. Jan will not need a therapist's approval to access the surgery that she desires. She is free to go to the market and find a doctor who will perform that surgery for her. The American appreciation of large breasts makes Jan's desire a legitimate one that reflects the gender values of those around her.

Clay, another female-bodied person, wants to undergo surgery to remove existing breast tissue completely and approximate aspects of a male chest. However, Clay cannot simply go to the surgeon and buy his services. The desire to radically remove breast tissue and either move existing nipples or maintain nipple position (the procedure depends on preoperative breast size and skin quality) in order to approximate male sexual characteristics is not one that reflects social values. Common understandings of gendered bodies are so opposed to such an action that the only way it can be reconciled is by calling this desire pathological and demanding that its pathology be recognized through a formal diagnosis of transsexualism. The fact that Jan is free to alter her secondary sex characteristics through an unmediated negotiation with her surgeon and that Clay is not marks sex reassignment as a site of exception. It is not the fact of surgical intervention into sexed and gendered body parts that elicits a social response; rather, it is the kind of surgical interventions involved that does so. Penis enlargement surgeries are fine; penis removal surgeries are not. The kinds of anxieties that sex reassignment surgeries provoke are made visible in the complex processes required to gain access to it.

It is plain to see from this example that some desires to alter the body through surgery are deemed acceptable and some are deemed pathological. This example is a clear illustration of the ways in which ideas about the medical and the social constitute each other. What counts as sickness and what counts as its cure are not questions of biology and chemistry alone, but are rather intimately tied to—and thus can be analyzed as reflections of—our social understandings of what bodies are and what they ought to be. But what ought a sexed body be? It is clear that living in the world as a sexed and gendered body includes things that don't show up on medical charts: things like feelings, sense of belonging, desire, and so much more. How can doctors find sex in order to change it? In the next section I offer a theoretical frame in which we might engage these questions, and then look at some concrete examples of where and how ideas about natural sexed bodies are made.

"Sex" as a Medical Category

If it is a series of norms, expectations, and beliefs that give meaning to the idea of a healthfully gendered body, it is medical knowledge that is called upon to create healthful gender through the production of recognizable sex. The idea that these things—sex and gender—are distinct entities that somehow exist in an analogous relationship to body and mind is far from obvious. Indeed, it is difficult to explain just how a change in the body impacts a person's sense of self if we abide by the notion that body and mind are separate. But the fact is that while the psychotherapist who diagnosed the disorder may be concerned with a patient's sense of self or "gender identity," physicians and surgeons do not operate with "feelings" and "experience" as their primary concerns. In this diagnostic and treatment scheme they have been tasked to "change sex," and just how they do that bears elaboration. French philosopher and historian Michel Foucault offers an effective way to approach this problem.

In *The Birth of the Clinic* (1963), Foucault aimed to denaturalize the idea that the human body is a totally formed object whose mysteries are waiting to be uncovered by ever more sophisticated modes of scientific analysis. He argued instead that the "medical gaze"—or modes of seeing the body from its whole surface to its tiniest core parts—actively produces the body as an object that is apprehensible to us. Our ideas about the nature of the body come not from the object itself but from a rigorous training in how to see, interpret, and thus constitute what is concealed therein. These forms of knowledge, situated in particular historical moments and traditions of thought, are *produced by* rather than *revealed by* human practice. Following this line of argument we might ask how something as complex, as intimate, as social as sex becomes locatable on the body. In the next section I examine the kinds of interventions that doctors make in order to help a patient change sex. What will be made clear in the analysis that follows is that while we may think of sex and gender as deeply internal characteristics, the fact of their production is overwhelmingly concerned with the surfaces of the body.

If we were to believe the childhood lesson that what makes boys boys and what makes girls girls are penises and vaginas, respectively, it would follow that changing sex would be considered primarily a genital affair. In fact, medical interventions meant to change sex involve hormonal as well as surgical interventions. Further, the category "sex reassignment surgery" describes a whole host of procedures that include operations on the genitalia but are not limited to them. Though any of these operations may be performed for a number of conditions, they are only considered "sex reassignment" when they are performed on a person who has been diagnosed as

transsexual. In addition to genital and chest reconstructions, male-to-female transsexuals may have operations to raise the pitch of their voice,[4] to shave down a prominent Adam's apple, to reconstruct their hair patterns, or to soften their jaw line or
brow. Female-to-male transsexuals may choose to have operations to produce a more
square jaw line or prominent brow, or may have implants that approximate more defined musculature, such as pectoral or calf implants. This list of procedures is not
just declarative; it is indicative. In other words, it doesn't simply answer the question,
what do doctors do to a body in order to change its sex? This list also tells us how and
where doctors and surgeons locate sex in the body. It turns out that no one characteristic can stand alone as the fact of sex in a body—not a penis or a vagina, a jaw
bone or a bald spot.

As you can see from the list above, the idea of sex becomes materialized onto the
surface of the entire body; the size, shape, and texture of an array of body parts become indicators of sex. Whereas sex is often thought of in terms of genitals and hormones alone, here we see that sex is dissolved into so many divisions of musculature,
fat distribution, bone structure, hair patterns, and genital potential. Katharine Young
describes the ways in which personhood extends to and encompasses the physical
body:

> Individuating marks are so described on the surface of the body that personhood ap-
> pears to thin out over the broad expanses of the body and to condense in its puck-
> ers, whorls, slits, nipples, invaginations, and outpouchings. The deciphering gaze skips
> and scrutinizes, swept over planes and mounds, hollows and hummocks, to stick on the
> dense, folded, concentrated structures, especially where they cut into the body. (Young
> 1997: 84)

This is the body of a person, made and unmade by structures and folds, protrusions
and recesses. Sex characteristics, it seems, are in the body's details. We can classify
these characteristics into two categories: those that happen on the surface of the body
and those that change the shape of the surface itself. The first group of characteristics
can be changed through the ingestion and/or injection of sex hormones, the second
group through surgical intervention.[5]

Artificial sex hormones can enter the body through transdermal patches and topical creams, but they are most often ingested in pill form or injected directly into a
muscle. With the extended use of artificial sex hormones, the adult transsexual body
undergoes many of the same changes that take place in an adolescent body during puberty. Hormones change body hair patterns, voice pitch, skin texture, muscle
mass, breast and genital development, and fat distribution. They also cause emotional
changes that vary widely from person to person. Some people find that hormones
give them a feeling of euphoria. Many others experience hormonal transition as a
very self-conscious and stressful process. While this "second puberty" may be changing their bodies in a way that will ultimately be pleasing to them, it involves all of the
physical and social discomfort that puberty entails. Even welcome changes are hard
to adapt to and involve learning to relate to and recognize one's body in new ways.

Because hormone therapy is generally administered to adults, there are some aspects of puberty that hormone replacement therapy does not enact. For example, skeletal changes that frequently occur during adolescent puberty do not occur during hormone replacement in adulthood. The width of a person's hips does not change and neither does his or her height, although the perception of these characteristics is absolutely dependent on gender. One could, for example, go from being a "man" of average height to being a rather tall "woman," and vice versa. In everyday life, the bodily changes enacted by sex hormones are the characteristics that most often determine whom we perceive to be men and whom we perceive to be women. It is a body's shape, its sounds, its hair (or lack thereof) that signal its sex in casual interaction. We don't ask to see people naked before we decide which pronoun to use to refer to them. In spite of the fact that a body's sex is constituted by this multitude of factors—shapes, smells, sounds, and textures—the genitals are the body parts around which imaginaries of sex and changing sex are organized.

You don't have to be a surgeon to have an idea of what is involved in a surgical change of sex. Because our culture locates sex characteristically in genitalia, we are raised to think of genitalia as extremely important, very private, and extraordinarily sensitive. Many of us are told from a very young age that genitals are what make girls and boys different, and we use this differentiation to build a host of social expectations of ourselves and others. Later in life, we find that the differences between boys and girls involve much more than the shape of genitals. We find out that *Men Are from Mars and Women Are from Venus* (Gray 1993), and the world around us is dedicated to reminding us how men and women think, feel, and relate to the world—differently. This is all based on the very simple childhood lesson: *boys have a penis and girls have a vagina.* Although most of us know that behavior and personality are based on more than just the bodies we are born into, many still firmly believe that the genitals hiding in everyone's jeans are more than just body parts like hands or eyes. Many people believe that genitals play a large part in making us who we are. And so for many people, the idea of slicing, removing, reforming, and stitching these parts is unthinkable. Surgeons, however, think about it a lot.

Surgeons who perform sex reassignment surgeries (SRS) define their goals and evaluate their outcomes in terms of two kinds of results: aesthetic and functional. That is, they want to know what "natural" genitals look like and what they do, so that they can reproduce this natural-looking and natural-acting body through surgical reconstruction. But what does a natural body look like? Like you? Like me? If every body is different from every other, how do surgeons decide which model of the natural to follow? A scene from my ethnographic research among surgeons offers one answer to these questions.

In a surgical workshop on male-to-female genital construction, a well-known surgeon, Dr. A, narrated a video presentation of his newly developed procedure. After the presentation, another prominent surgeon, Dr. B, commented that the *mons pubis*—the mound of flesh just above the genitals—was malformed in the examples provided. Dr. A replied that as a gynecologist, the *mons* in the postoperative patients looked "pretty good to me" and that he had not had any patients complain about the results of the

procedure. Dr. B countered, "I'm sure no one is complaining, but if you take out an anatomy book and compare it to what you've done here, you'll see that it doesn't match."

Dr. B was asserting that there was something that the anatomy book could tell
all of us that the five-by-eight-foot image of postoperative genitalia projected on the
screen at the front of the room was somehow obscuring from view. He asserted that
he was able to see something in this image that others were not seeing—including the
other silent surgeons in the room, and indeed Dr. A's noncomplaining patients themselves. Dr. B suggested that his training and expertise allowed him to view the body
with distinct attention for each of its structures. In other words, he saw it *better*. This
is an example of Foucault's "medical gaze" in action. The superiority of this surgeon's
vision was not left up to subjective determination but was produced by the invoca-
tion of a higher authority to which we might all make reference not just conceptually
but *visually*. There existed an image of the natural to which we must all defer.

The anatomy book is a genre of depiction that is distinguished from other sorts
of medical texts by its overwhelming focus on the visual. Anatomical drawings are
conscientiously made as composites or generalized bodies. In this way they can be
understood to look like and represent all bodies, rather than being a rendering of one
body in particular (Vandam 1997). As such, the anatomy book is a form, and its individual illustrations are both the result of the norming of bodies and, as demonstrated
in the example above, a powerful means by which normal/natural bodies are produced. These representations are descriptive, not proscriptive. They illustrate (and in
some cases explains in words) what structures look like and how they are positioned
in relation to each other. They do not give the necessary and sufficient conditions under which a lump of flesh is classifiable as a particular body part. Rather, they illustrate and thus help to produce the natural body and its parts. It is this authoritative
representation of the natural and normal body to which Dr. B made reference.

Anatomical illustration may provide surgeons like Dr. B a visual depiction of the
body, but they cannot depict its functions. In other words, the images are very good at
representing structure, but not so good at representing action. If deference to universal
form comes in the shape of the universal anatomical atlas, where do we find ideas about
the universal functions of the body's parts? Many organs have a perfect function: the
heart moves the blood, the kidneys rid it of contaminants. As functional body parts by
definition, the internal organs can be replaced without much anxiety over their form.
For example, the value of an artificial heart is in its ability to pump the blood, not in
how closely it matches the appearance of a natural heart. The case of genital reconstruction is, I would argue, distinct from other kinds of organ replacement in its attention to the *look* of the body part in question as well as its activity. Most importantly, sex
reassignment surgery is distinct from other kinds of organ replacement in the means
by which the "right activity" of the organs involved is medically determined.

What Dr. B's comments make clear in the register of the surgical is equally true in
other modes of experience: the genitals are a peculiar kind of spectacle: even when
you're seeing them, you're not seeing them. The social realities enabled by and signified in the genitals cannot be simply represented in illustrations, photographs, narratives, or numbers. How could we possibly explain the link between a photograph,

drawing, or measurement of a penis and what it means to have a penis? Or desire a penis? To lose one? Or to long for one? It is wildly inadequate to say that the genitals are socially complicated body parts. As saturated sites of meaning making around which so much of our lives is organized, their intactness and recognizable form is one of the very conditions of our intelligibility as people. But surgical texts about SRS do not include identity, desire, or recognizability as genital functions. Anatomical illustrations do not depict the senses of selves that are at stake in the form and function of the genitals. But surgical categories do delineate other standards of form and function. Attention to what is included in these categories demonstrates how the natural body is constructed in the surgical imaginary.

Since the genitals fashioned during sex reassignment surgery are not capable of making babies, their medical function becomes read entirely through the social. By this I mean that the medical creation of sex is all about gender. Here again, the body is not considered alone as a bounded unit with systems that work more or less well. It is, instead, a body in relation. Let me explain what I mean.

Surgeons have two kinds of functional goals when reconstructing genitals in SRS: urinary and sexual. Urinary goals include the basic requirement that the reconstructed genitals should allow the patient to control his or her bladder and to expel urine through an unobstructed opening. But they are also concerned about the gendered bodily posture when patients are urinating. Male-to-female patients should be able to pee in a sitting position; female-to-male patients should be able to pee while standing. The fact of how a body is positioned while peeing has nothing to do with the healthy function of the urinary system but is instead centrally concerned with creating a properly gendered social body that can act in gendered spaces, such as public restrooms, in acceptable and common ways. To our previous list of characteristics in which sex is made locatable on the body, we can add a series of bodily postures that those characteristics make possible.

Sexual function goals are also highly gendered. These goals are primarily fashioned around imagined futures of (hetero)sexual intimacy, especially penetrative intercourse. As a result, surgeons aim to create a body that can only be said to sexually "function" in relation to another body with which it comes into particular forms of contact. Thus the neo-phallus (or newly constructed penis) must be both long enough and rigid enough to allow penetrative intercourse. The neo-vagina must have an opening and cavity that can accommodate penetrative intercourse. It is clear from these goals that medical notions of the way bodies work are deeply tied to social ideas about what bodies ought to do. Sex is not simply about genital structures and bodily features but is tied to what those features and structures say about a body in relation to other bodies.

Conclusion

The transsexual body is thus always a body in relation. The multiple surfaces, textures, sounds, thicknesses, and soft spaces by which it became knowable to Dr. Benjamin in 1953 still bear a complex relation to its insides, the dark and unknowable internal space where deep feelings and self-perception reside. When we interrogate the conception of transsexuality as an asymmetry between body and mind, we find that the very premise of this model—that body and mind are distinct—is troubled both through the social lens and through the medical. The body is not simply an object made up of structures and chemicals that can be known and wholly understood through the medical gaze. It is also a complex social object whose parts and characteristics become meaningful and knowable only in relation to multiple other forms of knowledge and knowledge-making practices.

Transsexualism, both as a diagnostic category produced through story telling and a series of medical practices aimed at making an internal self evident on the surfaces of the body, demands that we think critically about knowledge about the body, how it is made, and what interests are supported by its production and application. This essay is an effort to think through the way social and medical ideas about the body intersect and are negotiated in the idea of changing sex, and in the very stuff of the sexual body. As a condition whose definition begins with a story and ends with surgical sutures, transsexualism is an exceptional site from which to interrogate the binary opposites that structure much of how we think about and understand people: body versus mind, science versus belief, gender versus sex, health versus sickness. Negotiations over these ideas and the powerful changes they make possible do not just impact bodies; they change people's lives. Inside the operating room and out. Standing in line for prescriptions. Making sense of their own life stories. Learning to live in relation to other people, other bodies.

NOTES

1. For a thorough history of transsexualism in the United States see Meyerowitz 2002.

2. Every person has a naturally occurring combination of estrogens and testosterone in his or her body. Hormone therapy is intended to recalibrate the balance of these hormones in order to produce desired sex-specific effects.

3. In 2005 the HBIGDA changed its name to the World Professional Association for Transgender Health. The group's mission statement and institutional affiliations remain unchanged.

4. Testosterone lowers vocal pitch because it causes the vocal chords to thicken. Once the chords have grown, they do not shrink back. Therefore, male-to-females who take estrogen do not experience a rise in vocal pitch, but female-to-males who take testosterone do experience a drop in vocal pitch.

5. Not all people who identify as transsexual choose to undergo all of these treatments. The following description is meant to serve as a general indication of what kinds of interventions are available and performed in the name of sex reassignment.

REFERENCES

Benjamin, Harry. 1954. "Transvestism and Transsexualism as Psycho-Somatic and Somato-Psychic Syndromes." *American Journal of Psychotherapy* 8: 219–30.

——. 1966. *The Transsexual Phenomenon*. New York: Julian Press.

Foucault, Michel. 1963. *The Birth of the Clinic*. New York: Vantage.

Gilman, Sander. 1998. *Creating Beauty to Cure the Soul*. Durham, NC: Duke University Press.

Gray, John. 1993. *Men Are from Mars, Women Are from Venus: A Practical Guide for Improving Communication and Getting What You Want in Your Relationships*. New York: Harper Collins.

Harry Benjamin International Gender Dysphoria Association. 1990. *Standards of Care, 5th Edition*. Harry Benjamin International Gender Dysphoria Association, Inc.

——. 2001. *Standards of Care, 6th edition*. Harry Benjamin International Gender Dysphoria Association, Inc.

Meyerowitz, Joanne. 2002. *How Sex Changed: A History of Transsexuality in the United States*. Cambridge, MA: Harvard University Press.

Vandam, Leroy D. 1997. "Some Personal Reflections on Anatomic Illustration with Particular Regard to Regional Anesthesia." *Anesthesia & Analgesia* 85: 691–96.

Young, Katherine. 1997. *Presence in the Flesh: The Body in Medicine*. Cambridge, MA: Harvard University Press.

||||||||||||||||||||||||||||||||||||||||||||||||||||||||||||||||||||||||||||||||||||||

16

Scars

Jarvis Jay Masters

I remember the first time I really noticed the scars on the bodies of my fellow prisoners. I was outside on a maximum-custody exercise yard. I stood along the fence, praising the air the yard gave my lungs that my prison cell didn't. I wasn't in a rush to pick up a basketball or do anything. I just stood in my own silence.

I looked at the other prisoners, playing basketball or handball, showering, talking to one another. I saw the inmates I felt closest to, John, Pete, and David, lifting weights. I noticed the amazing similarity of the whiplike scars on their bare skin, shining with sweat from pumping iron in the hot sun.

A deep sadness came over me as I watched these powerful men lift hundreds of pounds of weights over their heads. I looked around the yard and made the gruesome discovery that everyone else had the same deep gashes—behind their legs, on their backs, all over their ribs—evidence of the violence in our lives.

Here were, America's lost children—surviving in rage and in refuge from society. I was certain that many of their crimes could be traced to the horrible violence done to them as children.

The histories of all of us in San Quentin were so similar it was as if we had the same parents. Though I was a trusted comrade of most of these inmates, and to a few of them I was their only family, normally I wouldn't dare intrude on their private pain. Even so, I made up my mind that I would bring John, Pete, and David together to talk about their scars. These men had probably never spoken openly of their horrible childhood experience. I doubted that any of them would ever have used the word "abuse." They looked hardened to the core, standing around the weight-lifting bench, proud of their bodies and the image they projected.

It occurred to me, as I approached them, that such a posture of pride symbolized the battles they had "made their bones" with. This was prison talk for "proved their manhood." At one time I had been hardened as well and had made my own denials. The difficulty I would have in speaking with them would be interpreting the prison language we all used when talking about our pasts. Shucking and jiving was the way to cover up sensitive matters.

From *Finding Freedom: Writing from Death Row*, pp. 65–71, by Jarvis Jay Masters © 1997 Padma Publishing. Reprinted with permission of Padma Publishing.

John was a twenty-eight-year-old bulky man serving twenty-five to life for murder. I had met him when we were both in youth homes in southern California. We were only eleven years old. Throughout the years, we traveled together through the juvenile system until the penitentiary became our final stop.

When I asked him about the scars on his face he said, "They came from kickin' ass and, in the process, getting my ass kicked, which was rare."

John explained that his father had loved him enough to teach him how to fight when he was only five years old.

He learned from the beatings he got. In a sense, he said, he grew up with a loving fear of his father. He pointed to a nasty scar on his upper shoulder. Laughing, he told us that his father had hit him with a steel rod when John tried to protect his mother from being beaten.

Most of us had seen this scar but had never had the nerve to ask about it. As we started at it, John seemed ashamed. Avoiding our eyes, he mumbled a few words before showing us his many other scars. He could remember every detail surrounding the violent events that had produced them. I realized that these experiences haunted him. Yet as he went on talking, he became increasingly rational. He had spent more than half his life in one institutional setting or another, and as a result he projected a very cold and fearsome, almost boastful smile. He wanted nothing of what he shared with us to be interpreted, even remotely, as child abuse.

This was especially apparent when he showed us a gash on his back that was partially hidden by a dragon tattoo. It was a hideous scar—something I would have imagined finding on a slave who had been whipped. John motioned me closer and said, "Rub your finger down the dragon's spine." I felt what seemed like thick, tight string that moved like a worm beneath his skin.

"Damn, John, what in the hell happened to you?" I asked.

There was something in the way I questioned him that made John laugh, and the others joined in. He explained that when he was nine his father chased him with a cord. John ran under the bed, grabbed the springs, and held on as his father pulled him by the legs, striking his back repeatedly with the cord until he fell unconscious. He woke up later with a deep flesh wound. John, smiling coldly, joked that that was the last time he ever ran from his father.

David and Pete recounted similar childhood experiences. Their stories said much about how all of us had come to be in one of the worst prisons in the country. Most prisoners who were abused as children were taken from their natural parents at a very early age and placed in foster homes, youth homes, or juvenile halls for protection, where they acquired even more scars. Later in their lives prisons provided the same kind of painful refuge. It is terrifying to realize that a large percentage of prisoners will eventually reenter society, father children, and perpetuate what happened to them.

Throughout my many years of institutionalization, I, like so many of these men, unconsciously took refuge behind prison walls. Not until I read a series of books for adults who had been abused as children did I become committed to the process of examining my own childhood. I began to unravel the reasons I had always just expected to go from one youth institution to the next. I never really tried to stay out of these places, and neither did my friends.

That day I spoke openly to my friends about my physical and mental abuse as a child. I told them I had been neglected and then abandoned by my parents, heroin addicts, when I was very young. I was beaten and whipped by my stepfather. My mother left me and my sisters alone for days with our newborn twin brother and sister when I was only four years old. The baby boy died a crib death, and I always believed it was my fault, since I had been made responsible for him. I spoke to them of the pain I had carried through more than a dozen institutions, pain I could never face. And I explained how all of these events ultimately trapped me in a pattern of lashing out against everything.

But these men could not think of their experiences as abuse. What I had told them seemed to sadden them, perhaps because I had embraced a hidden truth that they could not. They avoided making the connection between my experience and theirs. It was as if they felt I had suffered more than they. That wasn't true. What they heard was their own unspoken words.

Eventually, we all fell silent around the weight-lifting bench, staring across the yard at the other men exercising.

John and I spoke again privately later. "You know something?" he said. "The day I got used to getting beaten by my father and by the counselors in all those group homes was the day I knew nothing would ever hurt me again. Everything I thought could hurt me I saw as a game. I had nothing to lose and just about everything to gain. A prison cell will always be here for me."

John was speaking for most of the men I had met in prison. Secretly, we like it here. This place welcomes a man who is full of rage and violence. He is not abnormal here, not different. Prison life is an extension of his inner life.

Finally, I confided to John that I wished I had been with my mother when she died.

"Hey, didn't you say she neglected you?" he asked.

John was right, she had neglected me, but am I to neglect myself as well by denying that I wished I'd been with her when she died, that I still love her?

Slippery Slopes
Media, Disability, and Adaptive Sports

William J. Peace

The history and scholarship of mass media have conspicuously ignored the images commonly associated with disability in American society. This is unfortunate because the media is complicit in distorting the cultural perception of disability (Riley 2005). For decades disabled Americans have grown increasingly appalled, offended, and angry about the way they have been exploited by the media. Dominant images associated with disability are largely negative. Stereotypical portrayals of disability abound, as do feel-good stories. Here I refer to archetypical ninety-second television news segments or 500-word stories in national newspapers that focus on the "remarkable," "heart warming" tale of a disabled person. Disabled athletes in this regard provide the media with endless fodder and great visuals: the paralyzed person, blind person, or amputee who finishes a marathon or performs some other "miraculous" feat. What is celebrated is not the athletic or personal achievement but rather the ability of a disabled person to "overcome" a physical deficit; the more profound and visible the disability, the better the story. The negative portrayal of disabled people is not only oppressive but also affirms that nondisabled people set the terms of the debate about the meaning of disability.

The antiquated images of disability have resonated with the general public and reinforced economic, political, and social oppression experienced by disabled people. Thus the media has contributed to and expanded the gulf between disabled and nondisabled people. This divide and the inequities associated with disability are rarely discussed. Thanks to the Internet, technological advances, laws such as the Americans with Disability Act (ADA), and rapidly aging Baby Boomers, disabled and nondisabled people are interacting more than at any other time in American history. The interaction between those with and those without a disability has led to conflict and misunderstanding. Disabled people have rights, civil rights guaranteed by the ADA, and are not hesitant to assert them.

Disabled people have embraced a social model of disability that is based on the belief that disability is a social malady. The social model of disability is at odds with what the average American has been taught about disability: that the primary problem disabled people have is a physical or cognitive impairment. In contrast, disability scholars assert that a bodily deficit is used to justify the prejudice, discrimination, and oppression associated with disability. Scholars in the humanities and social sciences such as Simi Linton (1998, 2006), Paul Longmore (2003), Rosemarie Garland Thomson (1997), and others have firmly established that disability is a social construct. Disability cannot be studied in isolation or on a case-by-case basis because it is part of the social structure of American society. This theoretical shift has had a seismic impact on the disability community and was spearheaded by innovative disability studies scholars. For those with disabilities, the scholarship produced by the aforementioned scholars provided them with a way of understanding disability that was empowering. For the first time in American history, people with disabilities understood that the discrimination they encountered was not of their own making and began to think of themselves as a single, united, and oppressed minority group.

The media and general public have yet to acknowledge the social model of disability. Thus when disabled people such as myself embrace the slogan "Disabled and Proud" and assert our civil rights, the average citizen does not know how to respond. The result is a culture clash, disabled versus nondisabled, one that is being worked out in the media, online, and in adaptive sport programs across the country. The sporting arena is of particular interest because the presence of disabled people is unexpected there. It is assumed that a physical or mental deficit precludes not just an interest in sports but the ability to participate. Conceptually, the disabled body from an athletic standpoint is devalued, as are the lives of disabled people. It is assumed that disabled people should not be skiing, kayaking, or playing a sport. Instead, they should be focused on an all-out effort to "fix" their bodies and return to normal (Christopher Reeve's quest for a cure to spinal cord injury is a perfect example). The fundamental dichotomy between disabled and nondisabled people forms the core of this chapter. I will detail why adaptive athletic programs are important and how adaptive athletes undermine disability-based prejudice. My research is based on interviews I conducted with adaptive athletes, bloggers, and adaptive sport program co-coordinators in the northeastern United States between 2006 and 2008. I will also draw on my experience as a novice adaptive skier and kayaker.

A Primer on Disability Activism and Disabled Bodies

Disability studies is among the newest fields in American academia. In my estimation, disability scholarship as it is known today began with the publication of the *Body Silent* by Robert Murphy in 1987. I consider this book the Magna Charta for all disabled people. While other scholars such as Irving Zola and Irving Goffman had studied disability for many years, Murphy was the first prestigious scholar based at an Ivy League institution to critically examine disability from a cultural perspective. Murphy did something in the *Body Silent* that no other person had done before: he bared his soul and body and evocatively convinced others that the main problem people with disabilities encounter is not their disability but the social consequences it generates. Given this new perspective, people with disabilities began to "demedicalize" their bodies and push for civil rights legislation while disability studies scholars published ground-breaking books like Nancy Mair's *Waist-High in the World* and Rosemarie Garland Thomson's *Extraordinary Bodies*. The central idea that would emerge from the incipient disability studies field was the belief in a social model of disability. This is the fundamental principle that created and has sustained the disability rights movement. The social model of disability is not complicated: in essence it holds that society disables people with physical and cognitive disabilities. Disability is something imposed on top of a physical impairment that is used to unnecessarily isolate and exclude disabled people from full participation in society.

The origins of disability studies can be found in the 1960s civil rights movement, and the epicenter for disability rights was the San Francisco Bay Area. The efforts of one man, Edward Roberts, known as the "father of the independent movement," stand out. Roberts is remembered for his political prowess and razor-sharp wit. For example, after learning that his doctor had characterized him as a hopeless vegetable, he remarked that if he had to be a vegetable he wanted to be an artichoke—prickly on the outside but with a big heart inside, one that could call on all the other vegetables of the world to unite. Roberts helped lay the foundation for disability pride from which disability studies would emerge. The notion of disability pride is something that is hard for an able-bodied person to grasp. I know this, as do many other disabled people who have been told overtly and covertly that they are inherently defective and incompetent. Family, friends, and strangers deliver this message as efficiently as a Federal Express package. Roberts was among the first generation of people with a disability to escape institutionalized life and embrace an identity tied to disability. In a letter Roberts sent to Gina Laurie he stated that he was "tired of well-meaning non cripples with their stereotypes of what I can and cannot do directing my life and future. I want cripples to direct their own programs and be able to train others cripples to direct new programs. This is the start of something big—cripple power" (Roberts circa 1970).

For people with disabilities, Roberts became a powerful symbol for all that was wrong with America's perception of disability. He was the Jackie Robinson of the disability rights movement, the single individual around whom others could rally. Like Jackie Robinson, Roberts did not single-handedly end baseless discrimination. He was part of a much larger social movement that produced cataclysmic changes in terms of civil rights. Each civil rights movement was associated with tragic events or charismatic figures: Jerry Rubin was the face of the Students for Democratic Society and encouraged male college students to burn their draft cards. The women's movement burned bras, and Gloria Steinem founded *Ms. Magazine*. The Vietnam War is tied to Lyndon Johnson, the fall of Saigon, and the My Lai Massacre. Martin Luther King, Jr., is remembered for his powerful speech "I Have a Dream" and tragic assassination.

What is absent from Americans' general understanding of civil rights is a disability component. Disability rights as civil rights is not a connection people make. Disabled people are an invisible minority and are not considered to be a "distinct and insular minority group." In spite of the fact that I have not walked in over thirty years, I can readily understand why people do not connect disability rights and civil rights. Eighteen years ago the ADA was passed, and since that time the Supreme Court has muddied the meaning of disability in an effort to limit the scope of the law. The definition of disability contained in the ADA was broad by design and was the end product of a generation of lawmaking. The intent of the ADA was to protect the civil rights of all people who were perceived to be disabled. The legislative process to protect the rights of people with disabilities began in 1968 with the Architectural Barriers Act and concluded with the ADA. During this era, 1968 to 1990, fifty acts of Congress were passed designed to protect or enhance the rights of people with a disability (Longmore and Umansky 2001). In spite of all this legislation, the legal definition of disability has not changed since 1973 when it was included as Title V, part of the Rehabilitation Act that barred discrimination against disabled people in programs that receive funding from the federal government. As outlined in the Americans with Disability Act, an "individual with a disability is defined as someone who: (i) has a physical or mental impairment which substantially limits one or more of such person's major life activities, (ii) has a record of such an impairment, or (iii) is regarded as having such an impairment."[1]

Since the ADA was passed, the Supreme Court has used the definition of disability as it relates to the phrases "substantial limitation," "major life activity," and "regarded as" to narrow the number of people who are considered to be legally disabled. At a theoretical level I understand what the Supreme Court is trying to do: identify exactly who is disabled and entitled to protection under the law. However, creating a precise definition of disability is exceptionally difficult and highlights that disability is a complex construct. There are a multitude of factors involved—social, political, economic, and legal—that make it difficult to identify what all people with a disability have in common. There is a seemingly endless array of disabling conditions and no agreement as to what disability means to this wide cross-section of people. Until we can identify what it means to be disabled, people with disabilities will continue to struggle to defend their civil rights. Thus the Supreme Court will continue to rule as it has and limit the scope of the ADA because it perceives disability to be a medical or physical deficit alone.

In utilizing a medical model of disability, the Supreme Court has ignored the broader ramifications of disability. Here I refer to the fact that disabled people are as a group uniformly poor, unemployed, and lacking a basic education. This troika puts disabled people at a distinct disadvantage before they exit their homes and bars too many from pursuing a rewarding life. The result is that the Supreme Court has not only narrowed the scope of the law but also splintered and butchered our understanding of what it means to be disabled. This has led me to tease my friends that what medical science failed to do—cure my paralyzed body—the Supreme Court did. In the court's view my disability is "mitigated" by the fact that I use a wheelchair and all people whose impairments can be alleviated by medication, glasses, or other devices are generally not disabled and so do not come under the protection of the ADA. In short, the Court determined that disabled people are not a distinct and insular minority group. Thus people who are paralyzed, deaf, blind, diabetic, or missing a limb have nothing in common! This is hard for me to fathom.

the Idea of mitigated is interesting.

Since the Supreme Court narrowed the definition of disability, I do not consider the ADA a mandate that protects the civil rights of disabled people. The ADA was about far more than ramps for wheelchair users, braille for the blind, and closed captioning for the deaf. The ADA was intended to protect anyone who experienced discrimination because he or she had what was perceived to be a disability. According to Silvia Yee of the Disability Rights Education and Defense Fund, the ADA was "built on the conviction that disability prejudice is a fundamental force behind the exclusion of people with disabilities from a myriad of social and economic opportunities." In Yee's estimation there was no question that disability prejudice existed and that the phenomenon was "not widely understood or truly accepted among the political and social institutions that are counted upon to put anti-discrimination laws into practice" (Yee 2007).[2]

Adaptive Sports: Undermining Stigma Associated with the Disabled Body

Too many people fail to realize that the dichotomy between disabled and able-bodied is a fallacy. Life is simply not that definitive. Under the law, I am not disabled. I am a teacher, writer, father, and provider for my son and have been since he was born. Provided I can enter a building or my employer is willing to make a "reasonable accommodation," there is no reason why I cannot work. My ability to work and care for myself is not compromised by my physical deficit: partial paralysis. Yet when I sit in my wheelchair, a device that supposedly mitigates my disability, I remain the symbolic representation of disability. I am regularly asked, "What happened to you?"— a question that assumes a significant flaw exists. The person asking this question is making a statement about my disability. He or she is telling me that there is something inherently "wrong" with my body. Such a person is also curious or, in some cases, fearful. The tacit understanding is that I am not a fully functioning adult capable of living independently. Even if capable, the only reason I can function "normally" is that I am a remarkable person, one who puts all those other disabled people to shame. All this is called into question when disabled people participate in adaptive sports. It is the only environment in which people with a wide range of disabilities interact not only with one another but with able-bodied people as well.

A nuanced view of disability too often requires personal experience with disability. In part, this is why historian Paul K. Longmore (1995) has argued that the first phase of disability activism centered on civil rights while the second phase has been a quest for a collective identity. In this regard, disability rights scholars have been particularly successful. A cursory glance at the literature published in the last ten years reveals a bevy of exceptionally well-written memoirs and theoretical analyses. For example, Linton's *Claiming Disability* was the first comprehensive account in disability studies that provided the groundwork for terms and concepts in the field and linked them with identity politics. Disability as a cultural identity is well understood by disability studies scholars but has not as yet been incorporated into the multicultural curriculum. Leonard Davis, an influential disability studies scholar, has noted that faculty members who mandate the inclusion of African American, Latino, and Asian American texts and novels do not support the inclusion of works about disability (Davis 2002). In contrast, people outside of academia have embraced this literature and disability culture. Disability culture is created by people with disabilities and is based upon the disability experience. Carol Gill, a disability rights activist, has written that disability culture involves "the pleasure we take in our own community," maintaining that "the assertion of disability pride and the celebration of our culture are a massive assault on ablecentric thinking. It also really rocks people when we so clearly reject the superiority of nondisability" (Gill 1995:98).

I contend that the divide between disabled and nondisabled people is innately tied to the body and individual difference. According to Bérubé, disability "is a category whose constituency is contingency itself" (Bérubé 1998:x). For disabled people it is obvious why nondisabled people resist thinking about disability: the fear of disability itself. It is equally obvious why this fear must be overcome: nondisabled people perceive disability as inherently negative. Corporal variation is perceived to be deviant; there is a divide between normal and abnormal, disabled and nondisabled. Disabled people know a different reality, one in which "there's no line dividing us. There are shades of ability, varying talents that surface in surprising places. This is true for physical and cognitive disabilities. Most of us, in the course of our lives, discover we have abilities or affinities for some things and lack talent elsewhere, so this idea that a certain class of people lack value or ability to contribute inevitably underestimates and wastes human potential" (Olson 2007).

Like many disabled people, I embrace an identity that is tied to my body. I have been made to feel different, inferior, since I began using a wheelchair thirty years ago and by claiming that I am disabled and proud, I am empowered. A skeptic at heart, I have always craved tangible proof that disability rights have advanced. In part this is why I am critical of disability studies. How can disability rights scholars determine whether progress has been made? The proof I sought became evident two years ago on a ski trip to Vermont. My son had never skied and I had not seen an adaptive sit ski since I was in college. In the late 1970s one adaptive sport, wheelchair basketball, was dominant (I was on my college team). Modern sit skis do not resemble the model I saw in college, and I will never forget the first time I skied in 2006. I had no conception that a veritable technological revolution had taken place. As I looked around I saw an overcrowded room filled with people. Near me I saw people with a host of physical disabilities: amputees, people with cerebral palsy, the blind, and paralyzed people. I also saw many people with cognitive disabilities such as autism, Down Syndrome, and a host of behavioral disorders. Adaptive skiing had come of age, and it was clear that any person who desired could ski.

Adaptive skiing involves the use of specialized equipment that is as diverse as disability itself. Broadly, adaptive skiing can be broken down into basic groups. Two-trackers are adaptive skiers who use archetypical equipment, stiff plastic boots, and two skis along with ski poles. An adaptive skier who can ski in this manner usually has a cognitive impairment such as autism or Down Syndrome. Other two-trackers include visually impaired skiers. Sometimes these skiers wear a bright orange bib that identifies them as "Blind Skier" and they ski with a person whose identical bib identifies him or her as "Blind Guide." The blind skiers I have observed wore this type of bib and skied with a sighted skier who guided them as they skied. Three-tracker adaptive skiers usually have one leg. These skiers ski on one leg and instead of traditional ski poles use poles that have an outrigger or small ski attached to the bottom. The outriggers are used to control speed and direction. They are also used to brake. Four-tracker adaptive skiers ski on two skis and carry two outriggers. A person who has cerebral palsy or walks with a cane or uses crutches is often a four-tracker.

Mono-skiers are the elite of adaptive skiers, and the rigs they use are akin to Ferraris. Prominent mono-skiers such as Kevin Bramble are on the cutting edge of technology in the ski industry and not only participate in the Paralympic Games but also appear in Warren Miller ski films and the popular X-Games broadcast on ESPN. A typical mono-skier is paralyzed in his or her lower extremities, has good torso control, and possesses excellent upper body strength. If the reader has ever seen a seated adaptive skier whiz by, the skier is probably using a mono-ski. A similar device, a bi-ski, exists for those adaptive skiers who cannot master a mono-ski. However, the prestige factor among adaptive athletes is greatly reduced when one uses a bi-ski. The bi-ski is like a mono-ski but has a lower center of gravity and two specially made skis making it easier to master because the two skis actuate independently and the skier is much closer to the ground.

The above clinical description does not convey the effort and knowledge needed to ski. It also does not convey the fear I felt when I skied the first time. Skilled volunteers determined the correct rig for a novice such as myself to use. Selecting the appropriate rig is the most important decision an adaptive skier makes. My first season skiing I used a mono-ski. To mono-ski one sits in a small plastic bucket seat that is connected to a single ski with a basic suspension system. To balance and turn one uses two outriggers. What I did not anticipate was exactly how tightly I had to be strapped into the bucket. My body was strapped into the bucket tighter than one's feet in ski boots. The volunteers kept telling me a tight fit was required and the key to success. They also joked that there is no such thing as too tight. I simply tried to focus on being able to breathe. The entire process of getting into the bucket, selecting outriggers, and getting ready takes about an hour for a novice. As I headed outside with two volunteers in tow I was extremely nervous. Having two experienced people at my side helped, but those first few trips up the ski lift and down the slopes were nerve-wracking experiences. By the end of the first season of skiing, I was not only able to enjoy myself but also became aware of what was going on around me. I also learned that I enjoy skiing for many reasons. First, the view from the top of the ski lift was a sight to behold, especially early in the morning. Second, skiing was a physical challenge I could share with my son. It also helped that we each like to go very fast. Third, I liked to socialize with skiers, who struck me as open-minded free spirits. My presence was readily accepted and I felt as though I was an ordinary, nondisabled person. Finally, the bar was packed and the people who helped me ski drank high-quality micro-brewed ale.

Between 2006 and 2008 I skied at least once a month and talked to adaptive skiers and all those affiliated with the adaptive ski programs I participated in. I learned that adaptive sports in general and adaptive skiers in particular were important because they shed light on the dichotomy between the way people who can and cannot walk perceive disability. Among paralyzed people such as myself, a wheelchair and mono-ski are alternate forms of locomotion. Depending upon the environmental setting, they can be a superior or inferior means of movement. At heart a wheelchair and mono-ski are culturally constructed technological devices that empower the human body. As such they affirm how remarkably adaptable the body is. A wheelchair or mono-ski is a type of human adaptation, a process that was recognized by Charles Darwin and tied to disability by Kenny Fries in his memoir *The History of My Shoes* (Fries 2007). Fries wrote about two interconnected stories, one that concerned Darwin and the other about his struggle to understand the meaning of disability. While this may seem to be a tenuous connection, bodily fitness and disability are directly related. The human body is continuously evolving via variation and adaptation, but it is society that determines how a given variation is perceived. In the case of the disabled body, all adaptive athletes know there are advantages to their physical deficit. For instance, Fries found that his shoes, leg braces, and abnormal gate made him a better mountain climber than an able-bodied person. Likewise, when skiing I use the muscle spasms in my torso caused by bumpy terrain to my advantage in terms of balancing on the edges of my skis.

A great deal of stigma is associated with a wheelchair, which can be characterized as a portable social isolation unit (Murphy 1980). In my experience, when I get out of my wheelchair and am active athletically, this diminishes the stigma and isolation associated with disability. The adaptive sport a person with a disability participates in is not as important as the physical activity itself. This is why many disabled people such as myself are drawn to adaptive sports. Physically departing their wheelchair negates negative stereotypes associated with disability. For example, one man told me,

> The minute people see a wheelchair they think of all the things that cannot be done. They consider my life a quasi tragedy. The younger and more physically fit the person using a wheelchair is the worse that person's life is thought to be. If you are a guy, they think you can't have sex or push a chair on anything other than a sidewalk. People assume I live in a nursing home. If you are a disabled woman then you cannot give birth or raise a child. This skewed viewpoint is really hard to overcome—people are conditioned and raised to think this way. There is a fundamental philosophical difference between those that walk and those that do not. I see my wheelchair as a powerful means of freedom while those that can walk see it as horrible, a fate worse than death. In some ways this is why I like to get out of my wheelchair as much as possible. I bike, kayak, sail, and ski. When you are doing a sport, regardless of what it is, people see you as capable, you do not need to be a Paralympian. When active I am transformed from being thought of as a pathetic human in a wheelchair whose life sucks into an average person. (interview with a disabled male, age thirty-two)

For disabled men and women who have come of age in the post-ADA world, there is growing frustration and anger about the law, specifically the gap between what the ADA is supposed to do and the reality they experience. Many ski lodges I have been to are grossly inaccessible. They have met the letter of the law; specifically, they have made "reasonable accommodations." However, these accommodations do not mean that ski resorts seek to be truly inclusive. Discrimination, though increasingly uncommon, exists in part because the bodily image associated with skiing does not include the presence of disabled people. All ski resorts have a clientele and an image they project to draw customers. Thus even at resorts where adaptive skiers abound, corporations do not place great value on adaptive ski programs. The severely limited number of employees hired to coordinate adaptive programs evidences this. The ski resorts I have been to in New England are reliant upon well-trained, poorly paid, and overwhelmed employees. They are also dependent upon a large staff of volunteers. The adaptive programs I have skied at usually have a staff of less than three or four full-time employees. The archetypical person who coordinates an adaptive ski program is a recent college graduate. Stress, long hours, and substandard pay insure that most adaptive program coordinators do not work for more than a few ski seasons.

The adaptive skiers I have met are a dedicated group who love the physical and social dimension of the sport. It is one of the few activities that disabled people participate in that permits social networking. Thus it should be no surprise that adaptive sports and athletic competitions have played a major role in the disability rights community. Some of the largest disability-related organizations in this country and abroad can trace their origins to adaptive sport. In adaptive sports, the Paralympic movement is easily the largest international competition for people with physical disabilities. Other well-known programs include the Wounded Warrior Project, Disabled Sports USA, Adaptive Sports Association, Special Olympics, and the American Association of Adaptive Sport Programs, to mention but a few prominent groups.

Among accomplished adaptive skiers, adult men and women between twenty and twenty-five years old, ski resorts are a safe haven, a place to let loose and not only be among their peers but also develop personal and professional relationships. One young man told me,

Skiing is the one place where I am not looked at with pity or scorn by other people, especially by older people who just don't get how or even why a paralyzed person would want to ski. What, I wonder, do they expect me to do? Sit at home with a lap blanket? When I am out skiing with friends I am just another guy out on the slopes. I just happen to be using a mono-ski. I have even been asked by nondisabled people if they can rent sit skis. No idiots asks, "What happened to you?" which is rude and pisses me off. No one asks a person who can walk this sort of question. Imagine if I asked someone why they were fat or if I went up to a woman and asked her why she had small breasts or a big ass. The best part of skiing is that a lot of people, snowboarders for example, know mono-skiers can really rip it up. I don't like the attitude of snow boarders and hate it when they stop and sit down in the middle of a slope, but to these guys I am cool. The X Games helped a lot in this regard as does the fact a lot of skiers dislike snowboarders. The thing is that when I ski I feel equal to others. I can't tell you how many times I have people yell at me "go for it dude" and I am dumb enough to try and show off. We are all just having fun and I am just another dude sharing the same space. (interview, male, twenty-one)

When I skied I noted that many married couples participated in adaptive programs. The couples I spoke with all felt at ease, that is, their relationship was accepted. For those married or involved in an intimate relationship with a disabled person, such a union is subject to intense public examination. In my experience, it is common for nondisabled people to question why an able-bodied person would consider having a relationship with someone who has an obvious physical deficit. Friends and strangers alike will ask couples intrusive questions that are rude. For example, every nondisabled woman I have been intimately involved with has told me that the first question female friends ask about the relationship is, "Can he have sex?" Apparently the fact that I have a son is not adequate proof of my reproductive ability. Such inappropriate questions place a nondisabled and disabled couple at a distinct disadvantage in that mixed couples are public property, their physical and personal relationship open to scrutiny. Those couples that do not have a disability are exempt from comparable inquiries. One woman who was married to a paralyzed spouse told me,

I love to see my husband play sports. I feel as though we have a mixed marriage—he is paralyzed and I am not. By mixed marriage I think what we experience is like what a married black man and white woman went through in the 1950s—that sort of thing was just not socially acceptable. I hate it when people give me that look of pity or want to put a halo over my head for being married to a man in wheelchair. My husband uses a wheelchair, he is not in wheelchair. To me, there is a big difference. I lose no matter what—if I get flowers it is not an ordinary event but as though I deserve them 'cause I am married to a disabled guy. The funny thing to me is that I am not into sports at all. He is a much better skier than I am. He has been skiing for ten years and I finally relented and am learning how to snow board. At the end of the day I am so sore I can barely walk while he is zooming by at a million miles an hour. When people see this, that they know he is a far more skilled athlete, can go on a double diamond while I am still on a bunny hill and holding onto a rope toe as though my life depended upon it makes others think. (interview with female, midtwenties)

The mission statement for most adaptive ski programs focuses on quality-of-life issues and empowerment. For example, New England Disabled Sports at Loon Mountain in Lincoln, New Hampshire, aims to enhance the quality of life of individuals with disabilities through outdoor education. It is believed that participation in outdoor activities in a supportive, boundary-free environment will endow participants with the opportunity to conquer physical challenges that enable them to build self-esteem and confidence. I appreciate the sentiments expressed but know that adaptive skiing is well beyond the economic means of many disabled people. The cost of a mono-ski is prohibitive for many. There are a small number of companies that manufacture adaptive ski equipment. For example, a basic entry-level mono-ski made by

Freedom Factory costs $2,600, and two outriggers cost $375. A mono-ski used by a skilled adaptive skier who races can double or triple this amount and often exceeds $5,000. For those who cannot afford to own their own adaptive equipment, all programs rent specialized equipment. Every adaptive program I have participated in has a sliding pay scale and does its best to be inclusive. The cost of adaptive equipment also limits many programs that have tight budgets. The ski season in New England is short, unpredictable, and with the price of gas and lodging, an expensive proposition. Adaptive programs in New England charge disabled skiers between $75 and $110 a day to ski. On average I estimate a weekend of skiing for a disabled person would cost about $500 (this includes gas, an inexpensive motel, food, and ski equipment rental). Adaptive skiing in western states such as Colorado, Utah, and Wyoming is twice as expensive as in New England and restricted to elite skiers.

In spite of the cost, the number of disabled people participating in adaptive sports has increased significantly in the last decade. Although no federal laws such as Title IX, which has helped female athletes, exist, disabled people who cannot afford to ski can find other easily adaptable sports such as kayaking. Disabled kayakers such as myself can afford not only to purchase a reasonably good kayak but also to inexpensively modify it with dry cell foam and duct tape that costs no more than $50. For instance, my kayak cost $500, and required ancillary equipment such as a life vest, paddle, and roof rack brought the total up to about $1,000. This amount is the equivalent of two weekends of skiing or a deposit on a mono-ski. The cost of renting a kayak for one day is half the price of a mono-ski. A disabled person with a limited budget is more likely to be able to afford to purchase or rent a kayak. Kayaking offers disabled people the same feeling of empowerment that skiing does. One kayaker told me economics were a major factor in his decision to paddle instead of ski.

> It took me two minutes to figure out skiing was too expensive. Kayaking is my sport. I am pretty new to kayaking but can get places where I could never dream of being when using my wheelchair. For example, I recently camped on an island in Long Island Sound. Being on the water is relaxing and after using a wheelchair for most of my life it is a different movement. But the best part of kayaking is the feeling of equality. When on the water I am just another kayaker—no one knows I use a wheelchair. I am not Mr. Cripple, a living symbol of how life can go wrong. Shit, why are people so stupid when it comes to disability? No other place in American society offers me the sense of equality as when I am out on the water. I truly feel liberated when I am in my boat. Sometimes when I paddle I really wish I did not have to return to the dock and get back in my wheelchair and the hassles associated with it. (interview with male, forty-five years old)

Conclusion

In this chapter I have constantly referred to the disability rights movement and a number of influential disability studies scholars. While I have tried not to be biased, it must be apparent that I am drawn to the disability rights movement. There are two reasons for this: first, in spite of the important contributions disability studies scholars have made, in my estimation the field has lost its soul. I do not question the dedication, effort, and contributions made by disability studies scholars. There is no doubt their work is important and intellectually rigorous. I am also aware that the place of disability studies in academia is by no means secure. Opposition to disability studies within academia is an ongoing problem because some scholars perceive disability as degrading or as watering down the integrity of identities. Given this, disability scholars have focused on the important job of securing a place in higher education where disability is perceived to be a form of human diversity as well as an intellectual endeavor. These efforts are critical but contain one flaw I cannot overlook: disability studies scholars have not done enough to empower the people they study. People with disabilities are the most overlooked, disenfranchised, and stigmatized minority group in American society. Given this reality, I think every disability studies scholar must make a practical contribution to the lives of the disabled people they study. Jim Charlton in *Nothing about Us without Us* (2002) has chronicled the history and legacy of exclusion familiar to disabled people past and present, and this is exactly the sort of oppression disability scholars must work to end.

Second, thanks to the Internet, people with disabilities are communicating daily if not hourly and are not as isolated as they once were. People with disabilities have embraced the Internet with gusto and have formed a vibrant cyber community. Disability studies scholars have also embraced the Internet, but their communication and scholarship is restricted and exclusionary. This is a significant problem. For example, the journal of the Society for Disability Studies, *Disability Studies Quarterly*, can only be read by members. Membership costs $95 a year. This is far too costly when one considers that dozens of disability-related blogs and websites exist that are free to all who can access the Internet. The exclusive nature of disability studies scholarship is particularly unfortunate. I worry about those who could benefit the most from disability studies but are unable to read the work intended to empower them. In my estimation this highlights how far disability studies has distanced itself from the disability rights movement. Disability studies is more than an intellectual endeavor. I know this, as do many disability scholars who are not only engaged scholars but activists as well. It is imperative for all academics, activists, universities, independent living centers, bloggers, and cultural institutions to work together and demonstrate the relevance of postsecondary education. This type of action-oriented scholarship and activism can only enhance the quality of life for all people—those with and those without disabilities.

NOTES

1. This definition is from Title I of the 1990 Americans with Disabilities Act. Retrieved August 2008 from the U.S. Department of Justice Americans with Disabilities Act, ADA homepage. Available at http://www.eeoc.gov/types/ada.html.

2. Both quotations in this paragraph are from the Disability Rights Education and Defense Fund website, which is available at http://www.dredf.org/publications/civil_rights_to_human_rights.pdf.

REFERENCES

Bérubé, Michael. 1998. "Foreword: Pressing the Claim." In *Claiming Disability*, edited by Simi Linton. New York: NYU Press. Pp. vii–xii.

Davis, Leonard. 2002. *Bending over Backwards: Disability, Dismodernism, and Other Difficult Positions*. New York: NYU Press.

Fries, Kenny. 2007. *The History of My Shoes*. New York: Carroll & Graf.

Gill, Carol. 1995. "The Pleasure We Take in Our Community." *Disability Rag*, September/October.

Linton, Simi. 1998. *Claiming Disability: Knowledge and Identity*. New York: NYU Press.

———. 2006. *My Body Politic: A Memoir*. Ann Arbor: University of Michigan Press.

Longmore, Paul K. 1995. "The Second Phase: From Disability Rights to Disability Culture." *Disability Rag*, September/October.

———. 2003. *Why I Burned My Book and Other Essays on Disability*. Philadelphia: Temple University Press.

Longmore, Paul K., and Lauri Umansky. 2001. *The New Disability History*. New York: NYU Press.

Mairs, Nancy. 1997. *Waist-High in the World: A Life among the Nondisabled*. Boston: Beacon Press.

Murphy, Robert. 1980. *Body Silent*. New York: Norton.

Olson, Kay. 2007. "Updated: CNN, Developmental Disability, and Institutionalization." The Gimp Parade, August 1 (http/www.thegimpparade.com).

Thomson, Rosemarie Garland.1997. *Extraordinary Bodies: Figuring Physical Disability in American Culture and Literature*. New York: Columbia University Press.

Riley, Charles A. 2005. *Disability and the Media: Prescriptions for Change*. Hanover, NH: University Press of New England.

Roberts, Edward. Ca. 1970. Letter to Gina Laurie, University of California, Bancroft Library Special Collections.

Yee, Sylvia. 2007. "From Civil Rights to Human Rights." Disability Rights Education and Defense Fund, available at http://dredf.org/publications/Civil_rights_to_human_rights.pdf.

Part IV

|||||||||||||||||||||||||||||||||||||||||||||||||||||||||||||||||||||||||||||||||||

Bodies in Media

Introduction to Part IV

We live in an era that is crowded with a plethora of representations of the body. Oversized bodies advertise clothing on the sides of buses and buildings, television programs like *L.A. Ink* feature tattooed bodies, and avatars or virtual bodies allow us to live our Second Life in cyberspace. Google's "image" search option is an indication of the importance of visual culture in modern life, and our thirst for representations of certain bodies—from the hooded naked prisoners of Abu Ghraib to paparazzi shots of celebrity genitals. Every time we open a magazine or turn on a computer we are presented with messages about the body. Implicitly and explicitly, we learn which bodies are beautiful, fit, and sexy, and which bodies are undesirable, unhealthy, and even dangerous. The media, from local news to national ad campaigns, tells us how to care for our bodies ("Perfect Abs in 7 Days"), what to put in them (Atkins diet, South Beach diet), and what to put on them (Coach bags). Media representations of bodies have an effect on all of us to a certain degree because the media is one of the primary agents of socialization. Today some children may learn more about the body (their own and others) from the media than from the significant adult figures in their lives. In this context, all of the works in part 4 examine how the body is visualized in mass media, and how these representations create dominant cultural narratives about the body.

In the United States, the ideal female body as represented in the media and the real fleshy female body are at odds. The "average" American woman is roughly 5'4" and between 140 and 160 pounds, while the typical model is likely to be at least five inches taller and forty pounds thinner. It is not surprising that many women of diverse ages are preoccupied, if not obsessed, with measuring up to such an implausible ideal. Not only is a woman expected to be thin, but she is also expected to be firm and cellulite free, trimmed very near to the bone. It is significant that the archetype of the ideal slender body has grown increasingly thinner throughout the 1980s and 1990s. This body, contrasted with the curvaceous and busty 1950s female body, illustrates how standards of beauty and femininity vary over time and are culturally constructed. Not surprisingly, studies show that with rising norms of thinness, body image dissatisfaction and eating disorders have increased among women (Wykes and Gunter 2005).

Recently, the seldom-visible fat body has surfaced from the margins, where it has become a televisual star in series like MTV's *Fat Camp* and *Celebrity Fit Club*. In these popular representations, the fat body is shown as inherently flawed and something to be fixed. If the underweight body is represented as the dominant ideal, the image of the fat female body is the opposite, evoking revulsion and disgust. As author Le'a Kent asserts in "Fighting Abjection: Representing Fat Women," the idea that "fat is beautiful" is a rather deviant one. Whenever the fat body becomes visible in contemporary culture, it is likely to be pathologized and medicalized, seen as a sign of the spoiled identity of the person within it. Kent argues that the fat body is never portrayed in the media as effective, powerful, or sexual. Using examples from two fat-affirmative magazines, *FaT GiRL* and *Women en Large*, she critically examines how oppositional readings of fatness make it possible to rewrite the fat female body. Kent shows us how alternative media can be an important tool to interrogate and subvert dominant images and narratives.

In "Hey Girl, Am I More Than My Hair? African American Women and Their Struggles with Beauty, Body Image, and Hair," communications professor Tracey Owens Patton also analyzes hegemonic standards of beauty and their relationship to body image. Like Kent, she examines how dominant beauty standards marginalize entire groups of women who do not fit normative expectations, in particular, those defined by a white European model. Popular mainstream representations of Black women such as the oversexed Jezebel, the tragic mulatto, and the matronly mammy figure illustrate that ideas of black beauty and social inequality are inextricably bound. Owens Patton unravels the complexity of hair straightening from slavery to contemporary media representations. She argues that when Black women are presented as beautiful in the media, they tend to have straighter hair and lighter skin. This sends the message that only certain Black bodies are beautiful—those that embody whiteness. Just as Kent argues that fat identity is bound by marginalizing images and rhetoric, Owens Patton asserts that Black women are held captive by dominant white beauty standards. Although it is difficult to do so, Black women must continue to resist and rewrite Eurocentric body ideals that convey the binary message that black body = ugly and white body = beautiful.

Representations reflect and reify powerful social and political messages regarding not only beauty and body image but also deviance and fear. As sociologist Barry Glassner asserts in *The Culture of Fear: Why Americans Are Afraid of the Wrong Things* (2000), mass media effectively creates moral and social panics through portrayals of certain issues and people as threatening, in particular Black men and teen moms. Rather than focus on addressing how to remedy social problems and the larger social conditions that support them, such as failing public school systems and lack of health care, media attention is directed towards certain deviant individuals. In "Images of Addiction: The Representation of Illicit Drug Use in Popular Media," sociologist Richard Huggins analyzes how the bodies of drug addicts are visualized and constructed across a range of popular media, from ad campaigns sponsored by the British government to artistic portrayals. Representations of addiction frequently focus on the material body of the addict, which becomes a symbolic map for the perceived social significance of drug use and addiction. He argues that there is a relationship between "embodied deviance" in the form of IV drug use and larger notions of social control, social order, and the overall health of the social body. For example, Huggins examines how a "war on drugs" campaign uses images that show the degradation of a female user's body to illustrate how drugs will rob women of their beauty and youth, thereby tapping into gender stereotypes. This representation also makes a connection between bodily decay and community decay and disintegration. Media campaigns such as these demonstrate, again, how larger social problems are reduced to carefully constructed images of certain individuals and their visually problematic bodies.

As the chapters in this section underscore, women's bodies in particular are subject to dominant visual regimes and media scrutiny. While men's bodies are certainly constructed and represented as per the cultural construction of masculinity (see Immergut, this volume), women's bodies are more vulnerable to dominant social texts and images within the context of patriarchy. Simply put, women's bodies are controlled, restricted, and defined in a way that men's are not. In "The Ana Sanctuary: Women's Pro-Anorexic Narratives in Cyberspace," clinical psychology doctoral candidate Karen Dias examines how women who are struggling with anorexia can potentially find refuge from the surveillance and regulatory mechanisms of control of the public sphere. Because women's bodies are often subjected to relentless scrutiny and inspection in spaces and places in the built environment, cyberspace provides a virtual location for some women to share their stories with others in a safer location. Rather than analyze pro-ana websites as promoting or causing eating disorders, which is common in the media and professional medical community, Dias focuses on how the women themselves discuss their embodied experiences. She argues that through pro-ana narratives we can see how dominant cultural scripts about anorexic bodies are reproduced, negotiated, and/or resisted. Just as the body is a site of struggle (and resistance), so there are also struggles over where and how women's embodied stories can be told. Like Le'a Kent and Tracey Owens Patton, Dias argues for an alternative reading of media representations of bodies that are outside the bounds of "normal."

Media representations instruct us which bodies should be emulated and which bodies should be avoided and controlled. As we have seen in this volume, certain bodies are pathologized and medicalized while others are represented as the ideal standard of physical and emotional well-being. We can learn a great deal about our culture through analyzing how bodies are mediated, but just as importantly, it is imperative to reflexively consider which bodies are missing in media representations (Casper and Moore 2009).

REFERENCES

Casper, Monica J., and Lisa Jean Moore. 2009. *Missing Bodies: The Politics of Visibility*. New York: NYU Press.

Glassner, Barry. 2000. *The Culture of Fear: Why Americans Are Afraid of the Wrong Things*. New York: Basic Books.

Wykes, Maggie, and Barrie Gunter. 2005. *The Media and Body Image*. Thousand Oaks, CA: Sage.

cite
her name , date of
pub for book , title,
editors of book , pg
numbers

hegemonic : dominant

18

Hey Girl, Am I More Than My Hair?

African American Women and Their Struggles with Beauty, Body Image, and Hair

Tracey Owens Patton

Throughout history and to the present day, African American women have challenged White definitions of beauty. What or who is considered beautiful varies among cultures. What remains consistent is that many notions of beauty are rooted in hegemonically defined expectations. While definitions of beauty affect the identities of everyone, this article focuses on African American women and the intersection between beauty, body image, and hair. Specifically, this article looks historically at how differences in body image, skin color, and hair haunt the existence and psychology of Black women, especially since one common U.S. societal stereotype is the belief that Black women fail to measure up to the normative standard. Two theoretical frameworks guide my analysis of beauty standards: Afrocentric theory and standpoint theory. I argue that the continuance of hegemonically defined standards of beauty not only reifies White European standards of beauty in the United States, but also that the marginalization of certain types of beauty that deviate from the "norm" is devastating to all women. Further, the unrealistic expectations of beauty and hairstyle reify the divisions that exist between African American and Euro American women.

First, in order to understand African American women and the intersection between beauty, body image, and hair, this article juxtaposes beauty standards of African American and Euro American women, reviewing them through historical and current lenses. Second, I consider the theoretical frameworks of standpoint theory and Afrocentric theory as a means to elucidate beauty issues. Third, aspects of body, image, and race are discussed. Finally, I explore the possibility of redefining standards of beauty and "normality" through Black beauty liberation.

[handwritten: hegemonic based on white beauty]

From *National Women's Studies Association Journal* 18:2 (2006), pp.24–51. © 2006 NWSA Journal. Reprinted with permission of The Johns Hopkins University Press.

An Historical Review of Beauty: Black Beauty vs. White Beauty

> I want to know my hair again, the way I knew it before I knew that
> my hair is me, before I lost the right to me, before I knew that the
> burden of beauty—or lack of it—for an entire race of people could
> be tied up with my hair and me.
>
> —Paulette Caldwell, "A Hair Piece" (2000, 275)

Beauty is subject to the hegemonic standards of the ruling class. Because of this, "beauty is an elusive commodity" (Saltzberg and Chrisler 1997, 135), and definitions of beauty vary among cultures and historical periods. Beauty issues and subjection to dominant standards are not the sole domain of Black and White women. For example, while all cultures have had, and continue to have, various standards of beauty and body decoration, the Chinese practice of foot binding was one that forced women to conform to beauty ideals that reified patriarchal privilege and domination. "The Chinese may have been the first to develop the concept that the female body can and should be altered from its natural state. The practice of foot binding clearly illustrates the objectification of parts of the female body as well as the demands placed on women to conform to beauty ideals" (Saltzberg and Chrisler 1997, 135).

An example of other types of beauty being rendered "voiceless" is found in Fiji. After the export of American television shows to Fiji, the rates of anorexia and bulimia increased exponentially. Further, the women of Fiji, who tend to have larger, rounder body shapes and are brown-skinned, not only became very conscious of the fact that their body shape did not meet Euro American standards, but their skin did not as well (Lazarus and Wunderlich 2000). While this article focuses on beauty standards between Black and White American women, this Fijian incident shows that adherence to White standards of beauty, as well as to American standards of beauty, can be exported to other countries with, in this case, devastating consequences. The following literature review historically chronicles some of the effects two co-cultures, Black women and White women, have faced in relation to beauty issues and body image.

Black Beauty

Women of color looking for answers through an introspective gaze or through their communities in order to counter White hegemonically defined standards of beauty is not a new occurrence. Historically and into modern times African American beauty has been disparaged. As much of the literature on African American women and beauty has pointed out, African American women have either been the subject of erasure in the various mediated forms or their beauty has been fraught with racist stereotypes. According to Michèle Wallace,

> The black woman had not failed to be aware of America's standard of beauty nor the
> fact that she was not included in it; television and motion pictures had made this

information very available to her. She watched as America expanded its ideal to include Irish, Italian, Jewish, even Oriental [sic] and Indian women. America had room among its beauty contestants for buxom Mae West, the bug eyes of Bette Davis, the masculinity of Joan Crawford, but the black woman was only allowed entry if her hair was straight, her skin light, and her features European; in other words, if she was as nearly indistinguishable from a white woman as possible. (1979, 157–8)

While mediated images of beauty have become more diverse (e.g., Tyra Banks, Naomi Campbell, Tomiko, Alex Wek, and Oprah Winfrey), "biases against Black women based on their physical appearance persist" (Jones and Shorter-Gooden 2003, 178) and many Black women do not feel "free" from mediated beauty standards. Some historically popular yet recurring negative manifestations of African American beauty include the oversexed Jezebel, the tragic mulatto, and the mammy figure.[1] Therefore, it is clear that the notions of Black beauty and Black inferiority are inextricably bound.

Given the racist past and present of the United States, there are several identity and beauty issues that African American women face. Since 1619, African American women and their beauty have been juxtaposed against White beauty standards, particularly pertaining to their skin color and hair. During slavery, Black women who were lighter-skinned and had features that were associated with mixed progeny (e.g., wavy or straight hair, White/European facial features) tended to be house slaves and those Black women with darker skin hues, kinky hair, and broader facial features tended to be field slaves. This racist legacy and African American internalization of this White supremacist racial classification brought about what Jones and Shorter-Gooden have termed "The Lily Complex." This complex is defined as "altering, disguising, and covering up your physical self in order to assimilate, to be accepted as attractive. . . . As Black women deal with the constant pressure to meet a beauty standard that is inauthentic and often unattainable, the lily complex can set in" (2003, 177). The desire to change her outer appearance to meet a Eurocentric ideal may lead her to loathe her own physical appearance and believe that "Black is not beautiful . . . that she can only be lovely by impersonating someone else" (177).

According to Greene, "the United States idealizes the physical characteristics of White women and measures women of color against this arbitrary standard" (1994, 18). To challenge White beauty as the stereotypical de facto standard against which all women are measured, middle-class and lower-middle-class Black women formed Black Ladies societies to uplift the race to a level equal to or exceeding that of a White woman.

To achieve this, it seemed necessary to make her more of a lady, more clean, more proper than any white woman could hope to be. As if to blot out the humiliation of working in the white woman's kitchen all day, of being virtually defenseless before the sexual advances of white men, black women enacted a charade of teas, cotillions, and all the assorted paraphernalia and pretensions of society life. It was a desperate masquerade which seemed to increase in frenzy as time went on. . . . Black women began to turn their heads in Charlotte Forten's[2] direction, even if their economic circumstances prevented them from imitating her standard of living. Many fewer looked to the examples of Harriet Tubman and Sojourner Truth, whom no man in his right mind would want, except, perhaps, patient Uncle Tom. (Wallace 1979, 156–7)

Wallace challenges the concept of assimilation.[3] Creativity in hairstyling can be a challenge to assimilationist notions of beauty (regardless of style worn) because it can challenge perceived expectations. When hair must be straightened for employment or for social mobility, it can be seen as assimilationist—subscribing to dominant cultural standards of beauty. However, as Orbe and Harris noted, in an organizational situation an organizational member must balance her identity. "Just as [a] young woman must negotiate her identities, so must an organizational member who comes from an underrepresented racial/ethnic group. Some organizational members may feel their racial/ethnic identities become less important as they climb the ladder of success" (2001, 192). However, engaging in organizational social mobility does not mean that one will automatically assimilate or substitute her cultural, racial, and ethnic identity for that of the majority culture. Rather, women can take creative measures in surviving the organization and being true to one's self. One way is with appearance. While individually not all African American women valorize White beauty standards, African American women have had to invent their own beauty measures. In utilizing the uniqueness of African hair textures, which range from the kinky curls of the Mandingos to the flowing locks of the Ashanti (Byrd and Tharps 2001, 1), Blacks have been very creative in hairstyling. In the early fifteenth century hairstyle for the Wolof, Mende, Mandingo, and Yoruba signaled age, ethnic identity, marital status, rank within the community, religion, war, and wealth (2–4). Hairstyling sessions were a bonding time for women. A hairstylist always held a prominent position in these communities. "The complicated and time-consuming task of hair grooming included washing, combing, oiling, braiding, twisting, and/or decorating the hair with any number of adornments including cloth, beads, and shells. The process could last several hours, sometimes several days" (5–6). The most common hairstyles the Europeans encountered when they began exploring the western coast of Africa in the mid-1400s included "braids, plaits, patterns shaved into the scalp, and any combination of shells, flowers, beads, or strips of material woven into the hair" (9). During this time period hair was not only a cosmetic concern, but "its social, aesthetic, and spiritual significance has been intrinsic to their sense of self for thousands of years" (7). Realizing the prominence hair played in the lives of western Africans, the first thing enslavers did was shave their heads; this was an unspeakable crime for Africans, because the people were shorn of their identity (10).

Throughout the centuries of slavery scarves became a practicable alternative to covering kinky, unstyled hair or hair that suffered from patchy baldness, breakage, or disease. For example, in the eighteenth and nineteenth centuries, because slaves did not have traditional styling tools and were not given combs, they developed new hair implements. One development was a "sheep fleece carding tool" (13), which was used to untangle their hair. Additional household hair care included "bacon grease and butter to condition and soften the hair, prepare it for straightening, and make it shine. Cornmeal and kerosene were used as scalp cleaners, and coffee became a natural dye for women" (17). Hairstyles were often determined by the kind of work a slave performed. If one was a field slave and lived in separate slave quarters, "the women wore head rags and the men took to shaving their heads, wearing straw hats, or using animal shears to cut their hair short" (13). If a slave worked directly with the White population, e.g., barbers, cooks, housekeepers, they often styled their hair similarly to that of Whites. For example, house slaves were required to have a "neat and tidy appearance or risk the wrath of the master, so men and women wore tight braids, plaits, and cornrows" (13). Black male slaves, like upper-class White males, chose to wear wigs in the eighteenth century or "styled their own hair to look like a wig" (13).

Emulating White hairstyles, particularly straight hair, signified many things in the Black community. First, straighter hair was associated with free-person status. Light-skinned runaway slaves "tried to pass themselves off as free, hoping their European features would be enough to convince bounty hunters that they belonged to that privileged class" (17). Emulating Whiteness offered a certain amount of protection. Second, lighter-skinned straighter-haired slaves "worked inside the plantation houses performing less backbreaking labor than the slaves relegated to the fields" (18). Because of this, these slaves had better access to clothes, education, food, and "the promise of freedom upon the master's death" (18). However, the "jealous mistress of the manor often shaved off the lustrous mane of hair, indicating that White women too understood the significance of long, kink-free hair" (19).

Thus, as has already been shown, adopting many White European traits was essential to survival, e.g., free vs. slave; employed vs. unemployed; educated vs. uneducated; upper class vs. poor. Issues of hair straightening were hotly contested in the Black community. The practice was viewed as "a pitiful attempt to emulate Whites and equated hair straightening with self-hatred and shame" (37). The most vocal opponents of hair straightening were W. E. B. DuBois and Booker T. Washington (see Byrd and Tharps 2001, 37–40)—both men were light-skinned Black males with wavy hair—and Marcus Garvey. All of these men had influence in the African American community. With regard to the issue of hair, Garvey proclaimed, "Don't remove the kinks from your hair! Remove them from your brain!" (38). However, most Black women felt straightened hairstyles were not about emulating Whites but having modern hairstyles. Madame C. J. Walker was one of the more popularly known hairstylists who helped African American women achieve modern hairstyles.

In the twentieth century, the 1905 invention of Madame C. J. Walker's hair softener, which accompanied a hair-straightening comb, was the rage.[4] Hair straightening was a way to challenge the predominant nineteenth-century belief that Black beauty was ugly. According to Rooks, "African Americans had long struggled with issues of inferiority, beauty, and the meaning of particular beauty practices. . . . [Walker] attempted to shift the significance of hair away from concerns of disavowing African ancestry" (1996, 35). Walker's beauty empire, therefore, not only contributed to higher self-esteem among the Black community, but also created a new job industry for those who attended her beauty schools.

Hair straightening has continued to be a controversial beauty move by some in the African American community, particularly after the 1960s and 1970s "Black is Beautiful" social movement. For example, Malcolm X spoke out against hair straightening due to the belief he had that hair straightening caused Black people to feel ashamed of their own unique beauty, as well as the belief that hair straightening emulated White standards of beauty. However, hair straightening, as Taylor challenged, "has taken on such racialized significance that participation in the practice can be a way of expressing black pride rather than a way of precluding it" (2000, 668). Additionally, straightening one's hair is not synonymous with racial shame or "acting white." Jones and Shorter-Gooden argued that "not every woman who decides to straighten her hair or change the color of her eyes by wearing contacts believes that beauty is synonymous with whiteness. Trying on a new look, even one often associated with Europeans, does not automatically imply self-hatred. It is possible to dye your brown tresses platinum and still love your Blackness" (2003, 178). While blond straightened hair and colored contacts are still controversial and seen as assimilationist to many in the African American community, hair-straightening also may be an expression of creativity or for employment reasons. As Wallace noted, "White features were often a more reliable ticket into this society than professional status or higher education. Interestingly enough, this was more true for women than it was for men" (1979, 158). In addition to straightened hairstyles, other hairstyles that African American women use in order to define their own beauty include afros, braids, dreadlocks, and knots. All of the aforementioned hairstyles carry with them signs of beauty, boldness, rebellion, self-confidence, spiritual consciousness (Jones and Shorter-Gooden 2003, 187) and whether intended to or not, a challenge to White beauty standards.

African American and Latina women have adopted many strategies when confronting White standards of beauty from society in general, as well as from African American and Latino men in their communities: "Latino and African American men seem more often than white men to link long hair with attractiveness for women of all ages" (Weitz 2001, 672). The three most common standards of White beauty in the United States that women are subject to include: (1) women's hair should be long, curly or wavy—not kinky—and preferably blond; (2) women's hair should look hairstyled—this requires money and time; and (3) women's hair should look feminine and different from men's hair (Weitz 2001, 672). Due to the fact that beauty is subject to the social conditions of racism, sexism, and classism, few women are able to attain such nebulous standards. Through the development of strategies, African American women demonstrate Disch's claim that "expectations for what constitutes femininity and masculinity are frequently affected by race, class, culture, and other factors. The freedom to be the kind of woman or man a person might like to be is greatly curtailed by sexism, poverty, racism, homophobia, and other cultural constraints and expectations" (1997, 20).

White Beauty

Saltzberg and Chrisler noted that "beauty cannot be quantified or objectively measured; it is the result of the judgements of others" (1997, 135). However, it is fair to say that in the United States, and in many countries that are influenced by the United States (largely through mediated forms), the current standard of beauty is a White, young, slim, tall, and upper-class woman, and some take extraordinary measures in order to meet such standards.

> Constituting itself as the site of absolute presence, whiteness functions as an epistemological and ontological anchorage. As such, whiteness assumes the authority to marginalize other identities, discourses, perspectives, and voices. By constituting itself as center, non-white voices are Othered, marginalized and rendered voiceless. Whiteness creates a binary relationship of self-Other, subject-object, dominator-dominated, center-margin, universal-particular. (Yancy 2000, 157)

Adherence to White beauty standards also can be traced throughout the centuries and since many of these beauty standards largely, but not exclusively, affected White women, the standards mentioned below can be juxtaposed against African American beauty standards. As Saltzberg and Chrisler illustrated, sixteenth-century European women "bound themselves into corsets of whalebone and hardened canvas. A piece of metal or wood ran down the front to flatten the breasts and abdomen. This made it impossible for women to bend at the waist and difficult to breathe" (1997, 136). In the seventeenth century, the waist was still cinched, but fashions were designed to enhance the breasts. "Ample breasts, hips, and buttocks became the beauty ideal, perhaps paralleling a generally warmer attitude toward family life" (136). In the eighteenth century, corsets were still worn; however, the introduction of large crinolines exaggerated the smallness of the waist and made movement difficult (The Victorian Era, n.d., n.p.). In the nineteenth century, wearing corsets and, paradoxically, dieting to gain weight, became popular in Europe and North America. Physicians and clergy spoke against the use of corsets because the tight lacing often led to "pulmonary disease, internal organ damage, fainting (also known as 'the vapors'), and miscarriages" (Saltzberg and Chrisler 1997, 136). In the twentieth century and twenty-first century, beauty trends continue to fluctuate.

For example, in the 1920s slender legs, hips, and small breasts were popular. "Women removed the stuffing from their bodices and bound their breasts to appear young and boyish" (Saltzberg and Chrisler 1997, 136). In the 1940s and 1950s, the hourglass shape (e.g., Marilyn Monroe) was popular. In the 1960s, a youthful, thin body and long, straight hair were popular. In the 1970s, a thin, tanned physique and the "sensuous look was 'in'" (137). In the 1980s, the mesomorph body type was preferred (thin, but muscular and toned body) with large breasts. In the 1990s, two dichotomous beauty images prevailed: (1) the heroin-chic, gaunt, waiflike body with some breasts and (2) the very thin body with large breasts. "Small breasts [were] a disease that required surgical intervention" (137). In the beginning of the twenty-first century, youthful, slim body types with large breasts are still preferred.

There are several things learned from this brief history of body image. First, women were subjected to hegemonically defined standards of beauty. Second, history, and our knowledge of history and women, in general, privileges and largely traces Euro American body-image issues. Third, women currently continue to be held to hegemonically defined standards of beauty. For example, modern beauty standards encompass tattoos, piercing (belly button, chin, ear, eyebrow, labia, nipples, nose, tongue), high-heeled shoes, tight jeans, curlers, perms, straighteners, diet aids, lipo-suction, plastic surgery, botox injections, skin lightening, and gastric bypass. All of the above are costly, but the physical costs of altering the body to attain hegemonic standards of beauty can range from breast cancer ("silicon leaks in some implants have resulted in breast cancer" [Saltzberg and Chrisler 1997, 137]), to anorexia, buli-mia, and emotional stress.

Finally, it is clear from these beauty standards that not all types of Whiteness are valued. Many Euro American women cannot measure up to the White normative standard of beauty promoted—beautiful, blond-haired, slim, tall, virginal, and upper-class. Because of this exclusionary standard of beauty, not all Euro American women emulate the stereotypical White woman—only a few women are privileged to be in this "beautiful" club. Those Euro American women who deviate from this standard of whiteness are displaced like ethnic minority women for their departure from "pure" White womanhood.

Media Stereotypes: Body Image, Hair, and Race

Historically, the relationship between African American women and their hair goes back to the days of slavery and is connected with the notion of the color caste system: the belief that the lighter one's skin color, the better one is and that straighter hair is better than kinky hair. This thinking creates a hierarchy of skin color and beauty that was promoted and supported by slave masters and slavery. The woman with the wavy hair was considered more attractive and had "good" hair, as opposed to the woman with the kinky hair who had "bad" hair. The notions of "good" hair and "bad" hair come from the social construction of beauty standards. According to Wallace, "the black community had for quite some time been plagued by color discrimination. The upper echelons of black society in particular tended to rate beauty and merit on the basis of the lightness of the skin and the straightness of the hair and features" (1979, 158). These notions are still maintained in some portions of the African American community and in the media.

In the media, many of the African American women who are glorified for their beauty tend to be lighter-skinned women who have long, wavy hair. However, this reification of the beauty standard does not come solely from the African American community but also from the Euro American community, which promotes the ac-ceptable standard of beauty. All one has to do is pick up a hairstyle magazine for Af-rican American women and see that many of the models have very light skin (some models could be mistaken for Euro Americans), some have blue or green eyes, and most of them have long, straight or wavy hair. A few notable exceptions include Tyra Banks, Naomi Campbell, Tomiko, and Alex Wek. Despite these exceptions, it is important to note that while these models may have their own definition of beauty, the media may promote or single out a more Eurocentric-looking model because Euro American standards of beauty are paramount and mediated standards of beauty promote adherence to whiteness.

The performance of beauty comes to us through a variety of mediated images that we are bombarded with daily. These messages of beauty largely encompass ways in which women can make themselves look better, skin products that can tone, redefine, and take away age. Subsequently we learn that beauty is one of the defining characteristics of a woman. For example, among the numerous beauty products advertised on television are hair products. Most often the hair commercials show Euro American women tossing their bouncy, shiny, long, straight hair. Even humorist Erma Bombeck observed that,

> After watching supermodels Cindy Crawford and Christie Brinkley push what appear to be pounds of hair off their face over and over again there would be no time to do anything else. These people can't carry a package, eat hot dogs, wave, or shake hands. Every second of their lives is consumed with raking their fingers through their hair and getting their sight back. (Wilson and Russell 1996, 82)

This image, while directed toward Euro American women, impacts African American women, because it is often not our image that becomes the vision and standard of beauty. We are socially constructed through language and mediated images to believe that what makes a woman beautiful is not her intelligence or her inner beauty but her outer beauty.

Historical Resistance: Body Image, Hair, and Race

As James Baldwin said, "The power to define the other seals one's definition of oneself" (n.d., n.p.). Whether intended or not, hair makes a political statement. To counter hegemonic Eurocentric standards of beauty Black women in the past and present continue to create resistant strategies as their beauty was not and is not predominantly represented. The resistant strategy used by Africans and African Americans was in the counter-hegemonic creation of unique hairstyles that showcased both Black beauty and creativity whether it was through the use of curls, dreadlocks, plaits, scarves, waves, weaves, wigs, and ornamentation in the hair. Popular resistant strategies were most visibly seen during the Black Power movement that simultaneously promoted the "Black is Beautiful" campaign.

For example, as bell hooks indicated, the Black Power movement of the 1960s challenged white supremacy in many areas, and one area briefly challenged was hair. What this social movement did with slogans such as "Black is Beautiful" was work to "intervene in and alter those racist stereotypes that had always insisted black was ugly, monstrous, undesirable" (1995, 120). The Black Power movement raised and challenged the ingrained stereotypes of beauty that were and are perpetuated by Euro Americans. The movement also examined the psychological impact such beauty standards had on African American girls and women. The Black Power movement first "sought to value and embrace the different complexions of blackness" (hooks 1995, 121). This meant that African Americans would examine the racist notions behind the divisive color caste system.

Second, the Black Power movement agenda allowed for an examination of children who suffered discrimination and who were "psychologically wounded in families and/or public school systems because they were not the right color" (122). This allowed for an examination of the effects of the color caste upon children. Third, African American women stopped straightening their hair. This means that there was a decade of acceptance for "natural" hairstyles. Fourth, many people who had stood passively by observing the mistreatment Blacks received on the basis of skin color, "felt for the first time that it was politically appropriate to intervene" (122). Finally, in addressing issues of skin color and hair, African Americans could "militantly confront and change the devastating psychological consequences of internalized racism" (122). Hair, therefore, became one of the tools or mechanisms that African Americans could utilize in order to confront the damaging Eurocentric standards of beauty that African Americans were unable to attain. For a brief moment, African Americans were able to create and reify their own standards of beauty.

However, the progressive changes made during the Black Power movement eroded as assimilation became more dominant in the late 1970s and throughout the 1980s. As African Americans were told that the key to American success was through assimilation of hairstyle and dress, many African American women began to press or chemically straighten their hair again and "follow the latest fashions in *Vogue* and *Mademoiselle*, to rouge her cheeks furiously, and to speak, not infrequently, of what a disappointment the black man has been" (Wallace 1979, 172). Many women found that it was easier to don wigs, weaves, or undergo expensive chemical processes in order to replicate mainstream hairstyles rather than wear their hair in an afro, braids, or dreadlocks which may convey a political statement or socioeconomic status. According to hooks, "once again the fate of black folks rested with white power. If a black person wanted a job and found it easier to get it if he or she did not wear a natural hairstyle, etc., this was perceived by many to be a legitimate reason to change" (1995, 122).

Consequently, White standards of beauty became the norm and became further reified by both African Americans and Euro Americans in their communities and through mediated images. Assimilation, in essence, made African Americans more socially mobile. This assimilation also "meant that many black folks were rejecting the ethnic communalism that had been a crucial survival strategy when racial apartheid was the norm and were embracing liberal individualism. . . . Consequently, black folks could now feel that the way they wore their hair was not political but simply a matter of choice" (hooks 1995, 123). Not everyone saw African American hairstyles as a "freedom of choice." This can be seen from the Euro American reaction to braids and cornrows at work. In addition, the color caste system was back in place. This system pitted light-skinned African American women against dark-skinned African American women. African American men once again returned to valuing highly desirable white or lighter-skinned women who had long hair, as opposed to lighter-skinned or darker-skinned African American women who may have chosen to wear shorter or natural hairstyles. The return to the overt and internalized system of assimilation to the Euro American standard of beauty not only created rifts between African American women but also pitted African American and other women against one another.

In the 1990s through the present, African Americans have begun to use a resistive strategy of acceptance. In this counter-hegemonic turn, beauty differences within the Black community are considered good, because one is being creative in their own individual beauty standard, rather than looking for outside acceptance. According to Susan Taylor (20/20, 1998), editorial director of *Essence* magazine, African American women have not traditionally seen themselves represented positively in any mediated form, so African American women create their own standard of beauty. Because of this counter-hegemonic creation, there is a wider range of beauty norms among African American women and more acceptance of different body types and weights. Some of the African American women interviewed for the 20/20 segment said that they do not concern themselves with weight, but rather they look at the whole package: hair, disposition, dress, style, and the way a person carries herself (1998). With this counter-hegemonic strategy in place, this approach begs the questions: who determines difference? and who determines which differences matter? These questions are best answered using standpoint theory and Afrocentric theory because they allow for a cultural critique of hegemony and beauty.

Black Beauty Liberation: Challenging Hegemonically Defined Beauty Norms

Say it Loud, I'm Black and I'm Proud!
—James Brown, "Say it Loud, I'm Black and I'm Proud," 1969

Signified meanings over time by people, groups, and politics become fixed to a group and can impact identity. Rather than being fluid, identities become trapped in the marginalizing rhetoric that initially erected the boundary. Boundaries not only define the borders of nations, territories, communities, and imaginations of the mind, but also they define the limits of space, place, and territory (Cottle 2000). One marginalized demarcation point is understanding and appreciation of difference—appreciation of African American beauty. The boundaries of beauty become deeply entrenched and thus are accepted as "common sense." The fictions and narratives about African American women exist, but without thoughtful understanding and knowledge, the dialectical tension between body image, hair, and race will continue to exist and contribute to oppression and marginalization. In order for bridges of understanding to be built, the boundaries of beauty need to be redefined and the borderland of marginalized beauty needs to be centered.

How do we transcend the interlocking system of domination that reifies the hegemonic order to the detriment of all women? Marable found that "the challenge begins by constructing new cultural and political identities, based on the realities of America's changing multicultural, democratic milieu" (2000, 448). According to Moon, "it might be more useful to think of identity as a habit rather than an essence. Identity-as-habit is an idea that allows both for the ingrainedness of habits (as anyone who has attempted to break a long-term habit can attest) and for the possibility of movement away from such habits" (1998, 324). One way to enact "identity as habit" is to think of African American women and the intersections between beauty, body image, and hair through the lens of womanism and Black beauty liberation.

Standpoint theory and Afrocentric theory support a womanist critique of beauty, body image, and hair. Both theoretical perspectives are important in allowing for a critique of marginalizing Eurocentric beauty standards. First, standpoint theory allows for a centering of individual experience and allows for a space for that story to be told. This space for alternative narratives and experiences allows room for acts of oppression and resistance to be exposed. Standpoint theory also considers how social categories, like gender, race, sexuality, and socioeconomic class influence our lives. Finally, standpoint theory allows one the ability to validate the self by resisting participation in the continuance of the hegemonic order.

Second, Afrocentric theory is complementary to standpoint theory because it allows for a centering of Black people and Black experiences. Just like in standpoint theory, Afrocentric theory allows room for acts of oppression and resistance to be exposed. In this case, it allows the centering of Black beauty and counter-hegemonic experiences to be exposed. Afrocentric theory also allows room for the possibility of diversity in beauty and diversity in beauty standards among this group. Rather than this theory being rigid, Afrocentric theory is used in a dynamic way that allows one to be able to look at the beauty diversity within Black women, instead of treating all Black women as a monolithic group. Just like in standpoint theory, Afrocentric theory allows one the ability to validate the self by resisting the continuance of hegemony. Finally, Afrocentric theory allows one to see the diversity among Black women in terms of body image, body size, hair, and skin color because of the focus on valuing the personal experience, allowing one to name and define her own experience(s). As Delgado aptly stated, Afrocentric theory "embraces an alternative set of realities, experiences, and identities" (1998, 423). Through embracing alternatives, Afrocentric theory shatters the myth that Black women constitute a monolithic group because one is allowed to be considered intragroup diversity.

In using the standpoint/Afrocentric theoretical matrix, the ideas behind Alice Walker's womanism are complementary because womanism also advocates the inclusion of the traditionally oppressed and marginalized, as well as promotes consciousness raising for both the oppressor and oppressed. Womanism recognizes that society is stratified by class, gender, ethnicity, race, and sexuality, however, the placement of race, the importance of race, and the experiences ethnic minority women have had to deal with regarding race and racism are central and key points in womanism. (Patton 2001, 242–5)[5]

It is through this framework that I offer a womanist liberatory Black Beauty Liberation campaign. Much like the "Black is Beautiful" campaigns of the 1970s, African American women need to be liberated from the confines of White-dominated standards of beauty. A womanist Black Beauty Liberation campaign would encompass a Black or woman of color whose beauty issues (e.g., body image, hair, and race) are brought in from the margin to the center in an attempt to honor the beauty in her that has been reviled, rebuffed, and ignored. To be a Black beauty liberationist means that you are not identified with the powers that be, but rather directly challenge the White supremacist hegemony that has kept your beauty and your body invisible, marginalized, and stereotyped.

To create a revolution of beauty it is not enough that "creative" style challenges to White beautification be accepted only by celebrities or by "radical" professors. The acceptance of these marginal groups still means that the majority of women are marginalized based on White supremacist beauty standards. In the standpoint/Afrocentric theoretical matrix, the visible invisible center is decentralized. A direct challenge to hegemonic beauty standards comes under critique as Black women define their beauty standards—not the White center defining it for them.

For example, in a commodification of the Other through Whites setting the beauty norms then coveting aspects of etherized beauty, while at the same time rejecting the Other, we find that many White women are incorporating Black beauty standards into their regime, for example, injecting collagen into their lips to get the full effect that African American women have naturally, tanning in order to achieve the natural brown skin of African Americans, and padding the derrière in order to have a fuller backside. What these few differences show is that beauty concerns and the expectations of living up to and fulfilling the stereotypical socialized role of "woman" is something that unites women since we all have to endure the scrutiny. Without understanding and respecting beauty differences in general, women face alienating and stereotyping one another, rather than becoming a united force. As Wallace noted "white men, white women, black men, and black women are just an accumulation of waste—wasted hope and wasted cockiness, born of insecurity and anxiety, which help to keep us all in our respective places" (1979,130). We need to understand the implications and history behind the standards of beauty. "Being a Black woman in the United States is necessarily different from being a White woman because of the different histories that lie behind each social identity or point of intersection, but alliances can be formed across these differences if both parties consent to the repression of difference involved" (Fiske 1996, 93). By resisting ascribed identities, we may begin to challenge the notion of beauty as it is currently defined because we are critically and actively challenging hegemony. Through the standpoint/Afrocentric matrix we are able to challenge the hegemonic narratives that confine beauty into binaries of White-beautiful, Black-ugly.

Such liberatory stances against White supremacist beauty have taken place; however, it is now time to directly challenge the assimilated beauty standards that are continually promoted through the media. Reality TV shows like *Extreme Makeover* and *The Swan* attempt to produce the same type of woman—one who maintains hegemonic beauty standards—that no woman can naturally attain. Through an oppositional beauty gaze an appreciation of Black beauty has flourished in children's books [e.g., *Happy to Be Nappy (Jump at the Sun)*, by bell hooks; *Nappy Hair* by Carolivia Herron] and in hairstyles beyond straightened styles (e.g., afros, dreadlocks, and twists are again considered stylish for Black musical artists, athletes, and on college campuses). However, these venues are not enough to promote the feeling of beauty acceptance on a large scale. With liberation comes a critical transformation. "Liberation means challenging systemic assumptions, structures, rules, or roles that are flawed" (Harro 2000, 463). Through liberation and challenging the systems of domination that exist in regard to body image, hair, and race, a recentering of marginalized beauty can begin. For example, Black communities have already taken smaller steps that have led to some success in redefining beauty whether through lawsuits or in their own practices. In order to be a liberated self, White hegemonic beauty needs to be challenged. Instead of succumbing to the White supremacist status quo, African American women need to continue to challenge the norm. We need to demand the same recognition of diversified Black beauty. As Spellers noted, "Silencing the stories of marginalized groups aids in the creation of a dominant discourse. By studying personal stories, the tendency to naturalize one's experiences of reality as a universal experience of reality becomes minimized and we come to understand that there are different ways of knowing" (1998, 72). Through acknowledging and recognizing that other forms of beauty exist in the world beyond white supremacist definitions, we come to understand that there are different types of beauty in the world. One of the more immediate effects of beauty challenges can be seen in mediated diversity largely on "Black" television shows on UPN: *Girlfriends* and *Kevin Hill* both showcase a variety of hairstyles and skin colors. And *Ally McBeal* was the first "White" show that featured an African American female main character with naturally curly, non-straightened hair.

Beauty Identity: To Begin Again

Challenging and redefining the self, ingrained identities, and White hegemony is very difficult. "These stereotypes and the culture that sustains them exist to define the social position of black women as subordinate on the basis of gender to all men, regardless of color, and on the basis of race to all other women. These negative images also are indispensable to the maintenance of an interlocking system of oppression based on race and gender that operates to the detriment of all women and all blacks" (Caldwell 2000, 280). Debunking the myth of what is beauty would require Euro American women to say "the hell with what men think" and African American women would have to say "the heck with what all of White culture thinks" (Wilson and Russell 1996, 85). This is quite a difficult position for all women and even more so for African American women because African American women have to challenge an entire race of people and system of thought. As a society, we seem to forget our rhizomatic past (Gilroy 1993); a past that is impacted by the diasporic connections between people and cultures. For example, much of what once was African or African American culture is now mainstream and worldwide: pierced ears, nose, nipples, and other body parts come from the twelfth century and were introduced to Euro Americans once Africans were enslaved; music (spirituals, gospels, jazz, rock, bluegrass, country, rap, and hip hop) all have origins in or have been influenced by African or African American culture. "No matter what a woman does or doesn't do with her hair—dyeing or not dyeing, curling or not curling, covering with a bandana or leaving uncovered—her hair will affect how others respond to her, and her power will increase or decrease accordingly" (Weitz 2001, 683). Until we critique the message of stereotypical standardizations of beauty, African American women, and all women in general, and the disparagement of their beauty, we will never get past the wall of misunderstanding, sexism, and racism. As hooks stated, "Everyone must break through the wall of denial that would have us believe hatred of blackness emerges from troubled individual psyches and acknowledge that it is systematically taught through processes of socialization in white supremacist society" (1995, 131). We will not only continue to cause self-esteem and psychological damage to women and to African American women specifically, but we will continue to pass on our sexist and racist ways to generations of young people. We have all seen the devastation that societal standards of beauty wreak upon women: psychological damage, loss of self-esteem, anorexia, bulimia, sexism, racism, ignorance, and lack of communication. The language, verbal and nonverbal, as well as the reification of White standards of beauty needs to be challenged and will continue to be challenged as women create their own standards of beauty.

NOTES

1. For a thorough analysis of stereotypes, see Donald Bogle's (2001) seminal book, *Toms, Coons, Mulattoes, Mammies, and Bucks: An Interpretative History of Blacks in American Films.*

2. Charlotte Forten of Philadelphia was "one of the tiny minority of free, educated black women of the nineteenth century." She came from a middle-class abolitionist family "who did not differ appreciably from their well-off white neighbors in demeanor and values." She was a teacher at an integrated grammar school in Salem "charged with teaching the Negroes all the necessary rudiments of civilization . . . until they be [sic] sufficiently enlightened to think and provide for themselves." Despite her status, she suffered racist incidents from Whites and berates herself for not being worthy enough or intelligent enough. Although her "contemporaries described her as a handsome girl, delicate, slender, attractive, whereas she saw herself as hopelessly ugly" (Wallace 145, 147–9).

3. Yep defines assimilation as a "view [that] directs the marginalized person to try harder and harder to adhere, obey, and follow the rules of the dominant group—rules that he or she can never fully and completely participate in creating" (80). Martin and Nakayama (2000) state that "in an assimilation mode, the individual does not want to maintain an isolated cultural identity but wants to maintain relationships with other groups in the new culture. And the migrant is more or less welcomed by the new cultural hosts. . . . When the dominant group forces assimilation, especially on immigrants [or U.S. ethnic minority groups] whose customs are different from the predominant customs of the host society, it creates a 'pressure cooker'" (2000, 207).

4. Madame C. J. Walker did not invent the hot comb. Marcel Grateau, a Parisian, used "heated metal hair care implements as early as 1872, and hot combs were available in Sears and Bloomingdale's catalogues in the 1890s, presumably designed for white women" (Princeton n.d.).

5. Alice Walker created the term "womanism." Walker's definition of womanism found in Smith states that "womanist comes from the word 'womanish': Opposite of 'girlish,' i.e., frivolous, irresponsible, not serious. A black feminist or feminist of color. From the colloquial expression of mothers to daughters. 'You're acting womanish,' i.e. like a woman. Usually referring to outrageous, audacious, courageous, or willful behavior. Wanting to know more and in greater depth than is considered 'good' for one. Interested in grown-up doings. Acting grown-up, being grown-up. Interchangeable with other colloquial expression: 'You're trying to be grown.' Responsible. In charge. Serious" (1983, xxii). A womanist or Black feminist critique makes one aware of the exclusive nature of feminism as it has been popularly articulated by White, educated, middle-class women (Wood 1994). Womanists believe that challenging patriarchal oppression and sexism is equally important with fighting against racism. Therefore, articulating a type of feminism that shows how the twin oppressions of racism and sexism are interrelated is paramount, as both are necessary in fighting against a system built on oppression.

REFERENCES

20/20. 1998. "Black Women, White Women and Weight." Television Broadcast, May. New York: American Broadcast Corporation.

Allan, Janet D., Kelly Mayo, and Yvonne Michael. 1993. "Body Size Values of White and Black Women." *Research in Nursing & Health* 16:323–33.

Allen, Brenda J., Mark P. Orbe, and Margarita Refugia Olivas. 1999. "The Complexity of Our Tears: Dis/enchantment and (In)Difference in the Academy." *Communication Theory* 9(4):402–29.

Asante, Molefi K. 1998. *Afrocentricity.* Trenton, NJ: Africa World Press.

Asante, Molefi K. 1991. "The Afrocentric Idea in Education." *Journal of Negro Education* 60(2): 170–80.

Baldwin, James, n.d. Just Above My Head, quoted in Tijuana Murray, "Differences and Blurred Vision." *In Life Notes: Personal Writings by Contemporary Black Women,* ed. P. Bell-Scott, 1994, 396. New York: W. W. Norton.

Berkie, Ayele. 1994. "The Four Corners of a Circle: Afrocentricity as a Model of Synthesis." *Journal of Black Studies* 25:131–49.

Bogle, Donald. 2001. *Toms, Coons, Mulattoes, Mammies, and Bucks: An Interpretative History of Blacks in American Films.* New York: Continuum.

Brown, James. 1969. "Say It Loud, I'm Black and I'm Proud!" *Polydor.* Retrieved from http://www.lyrics.com/.

Butler, Judith. 1995. "Melancholy Gender/Refused Identification." In *Constructing Masculinity,* eds. Maurice Berger, Brain Wallis, and Simon Watson, 21–36. New York: Routledge.

Byrd, Ayana D., and Lori L. Tharps. 2001. *Hair Story: Untangling the Roots of Black Hair in America.* New York: St. Martin's Griffin.

Caldwell, Paulette M. 2000. "A Hair Piece: Perspectives on the Intersection of Race and Gender." In *Critical Race Theory: The Cutting Edge,* eds. Richard Delgado and Jean Stefancic, 275–85. Philadelphia: Temple University Press.

Clifford, James. 1997. *Routes: Travel and Translation in the Late Twentieth Century.* Cambridge: Harvard University Press.

Cottle, Simon. 2000. "Introduction to Media Research and Ethnic Minorities: Mapping the Field." In *Ethnic Minorities and the Media: Changing Cultural Boundaries,* ed. Simon Cottle, 2–30. Philadelphia: Open University Press.

Crago, Marjorie, Catherine M. Shisslak, and Linda S. Estes. 1996. "Eating Disturbances Among American Minority Groups: A Review." [Electronic version] *International Journal for Eating Disorders* 19(3):239–48.

Delgado, Fernando P. 1998. "When the Silenced Speak: The Textualization and Complications of Latino/a Identity." *Western Journal of Communication* 62(4):420–38.

Disch, Estelle. 1997. "Social Contexts of Gender." In *Reconstructing Gender: A Multicultural Anthology,* ed. Estelle Disch, 19–20. Mountain View, CA: Mayfield Publishing.

Faludi, Susan. 1991. *Backlash: The Undeclared War Against American Women.* New York: Crown Publishers.

Fiske, John. 1996. *Media Matters: Race and Gender in U.S. Politics.* Minneapolis: University of Minnesota Press.

France, David. 2001. "Law: The Dreadlock Deadlock." *Newsweek,* September 5. Retrieved from http://www.msnbc.com/news/622786.asp (accessed September 5, 2001; site now discontinued).

Gilroy, Paul. 1993. *The Black Atlantic: Modernity and Double Consciousness.* Cambridge: Harvard University Press.

Greene, Beverly. 1994. "African American Women." In *Women of Color: Integrating Ethnic and Gender Identities in Psychotherapy,* eds. Lillian Comas-Diaz and Beverly Greene, 10–29. New York: The Guilford Press.

Harro, Bobbie. 2000. "The Cycle of Liberation." In *Readings for Diversity and Social Justice: An Anthology on Racism, Anti-semitism, Sexism, Heterosexism, Ableism, and Classism,* eds. Maurianne Adams, Warren J. Blumenfeld, Rosie Castaneda, Heather W. Hackman, Madeline L. Peters, and Ximena Zuniga, 463–69. New York: Routledge.

hooks, bell. 1995. *Killing Rage.* New York: H. Holt & Company.

Jones, Charisse, and Kumea Shorter-Gooden. 2003. *Shifting: The Double Lives of Black Women in America.* New York: HarperCollins Publishers.

Lazarus, Margaret, and Renner Wunderlich. 2000. *Beyond Killing Us Softly: The Impact of Media Images on Women and Girls.* Motion picture. Dirs. Margaret Lazarus and Renner Wunderlich. Cambridge, MA: Cambridge Documentary Films.

Lester, Regan, and Trent A. Petrie. 1998. "Physical, Psychological, and Societal Correlates of Bulimic Symptomatology among African American College Women." *Journal of Counseling Psychology* 45(3):315–21.

Lorde, Audrey. 1997. "Age, Race, Class, and Sex: Women Redefining Difference." In *Race, Class, and Gender: An Anthology,* eds. Margaret Andersen and Patricia Hill Collins, 177–84. Belmont, CA: Wadsworth Publishing.

Marable, Manning. 2000. "Beyond Racial Identity Politics: Towards a Liberation Theory for Multicultural Democracy." In *Critical Race Theory: The Cutting Edge,* eds. Richard Delgado and Jean Stefancic, 448–54. Philadelphia: Temple University Press.

Martin, Judith N., and Thomas K. Nakayama. 2000. *Intercultural Communication in Contexts.* Mountain View, CA: Mayfield Publishing Company.

Molloy, Beth L. 1998. "Body Image and Self-Esteem: A Comparison of AfricanAmerican and Caucasian Women." *Sex Roles: A Journal of Research* 1–11. Retrieved from http://www.find-articles.com/cf_0/m2294/n7-8_v38/20914081/ print.jhtml.

Moon, Dreama. 1998. "Performed Identities: 'Passing' as an Inter/cultural Discourse." In *Readings in Cultural Contexts*, eds. Judith N. Martin, Thomas K. Nakayama, and Lisa A. Flores, 322–30. Mountain View, CA: Mayfield Publishing.

National Association of Anorexia Nervosa and Associated Disorders. N.d. Retrieved from http://www.anad.org/facts.htm (accessed December 5, 2003; site now discontinued).

Orbe, Mark P., and Tina M. Harris. 2001. *Interracial Communication: Theory into Practice*. Belmont, CA: Wadsworth/Thompson Learning.

Patton, Tracey O. 2001. "Ally McBeal and Her Homies: The Reification of White Stereotypes of the Other." *Journal of Black Studies* 32(2):229–60.

Patton, Tracey O. 2004. "Reflections of a Black Woman Professor: Racism and Sexism in Academia." *Howard Journal of Communications* 15(3):185–200.

Princeton. N.d. "Walker Display." Retrieved from http://www. princeton.edu/-mcbrown/display/walker.html (accessed February 22, 2002; site now discontinued).

Rooks, Noliwe. 1996. *Hair Raising*. New Brunswick, NJ: Rutgers University Press.

Saltzberg, Elayne A., and Joan C. Chrisler. 1997. "Beauty Is the Beast: Psychological Effects of the Pursuit of the Perfect Female Body." In *Reconstructing Gender: A Multicultural Anthology*, ed. Estelle Disch, 134–45. Mountain View, CA: Mayfield Publishing.

Smith, Barbara. 1983. "Introduction." In *Home Girls: A Black Feminist Anthology*, ed. Barbara Smith, xxii. New York: Kitchen Table: Women of Color Press.

Spellers, Regina E. 1998. "Happy to be Nappy! Embracing an Afrocentric Aesthetic for Beauty." In *Readings in Cultural Contexts*, eds. Judith N. Martin, Thomas K. Nakayama, and Lisa A. Flores, 70–8. Mountain View, CA: Mayfield Publishing.

Taylor, Paul C. 2000. "Malcolm's Conk and Danto's Colors; or Four Logical Petitions Concerning Race, Beauty, and Aesthetics." In *African American Literary Theory: A Reader*, ed. Winston Napier, 665–71. New York: NYU Press.

Turner, Valerie. 1994. "Part Two: Searching for Self." In *Life Notes: Personal Writings by Contemporary Black Women*, ed. Patricia Bell-Scott, 77. New York: W. W. Norton.

Victorian Era, The. N.d. "The Victorian Era." Retrieved 22 February 2002, from http://www. media-awareness.ca/eng/med/class/teamedia/body/lookll.htm (site now discontinued).

Wallace, Michele. 1979. *Black Macho and the Myth of the Superwoman*. New York: The Dial Press.

Weitz, Rose. 2001. "Women and Their Hair: Seeking Power through Resistance and Accommodation." *Gender & Society* 15(5):667–86.

West, Cornel. 1994. *Race Matters*. New York: Vintage Books.

Wilson, Midge, and Kathy Russell. 1996. *Divided Sisters: Bridging the Gap between Black Women and White Women*. New York: Anchor Books.

Wood, Julia T. 1994. *Gendered Lives: Communication, Gender, and Culture*. Belmont, CA: Wadsworth Publishing.

Yancy, George. 2000. "Feminism and the Subtext of Whiteness: Black Women's Experiences as a Site of Identity Formation and Contestation of Whiteness." *The Western Journal of Black Studies* 24(3): 156–66.

Yep, Gust A. 1998. "My Three Cultures: Navigating the Multicultural Identity Landscape." In *Reading in Cultural Contexts*, eds. Judith N. Martin, Thomas K. Nakayama, and Lisa A. Flores, 79–85. Mountain View, CA: Mayfield Publishing.

‖‖‖

19

Fighting Abjection
Representing Fat Women

Le'a Kent

Fat is Beautiful. Or, as the name of one fat girl's publication puts it, *I Am So Fucking Beautiful.*[1] What are the effects when fat women begin to say such things? More important, how do they manage to say such things? Beginning to publish and circulate images valuing the fat female body (or even beginning to value one's own fat female body) in what Eve Kosofsky Sedgwick has called a "fat abhorring world of images," a world in which fat women are charged with "concentrating and representing 'a general sense of the body 's offensiveness,'"[2] requires radical confrontation with the representational status quo. It requires undermining the process of abjection that makes fat women's bodies synonymous with the offensive, horrible, or deadly aspects of embodiment. It requires finding a way of representing the self that is not body-neutral or disembodied (and therefore presumptively thin), but intimately connected with the body in a new vision of embodiment that no longer disdains the flesh. This vision of embodiment doesn't obsessively seek the good, thin body (a body good only because it is marked by the self's repeated discipline), but instead redefines the good body and also the good self. By insisting that the body's desires should mark the self as well and that the good self is the self so marked, this new vision of embodiment shifts the relationship between self and body. Shifting the relations of embodiment gives fat women a way to stop living their bodies as the "before" picture and to begin to have a body thought valuable in the present.

My interest in these questions is not, of course, strictly academic. Growing up with a miserably fat mother (or perhaps merely a miserably dieting mother), maturing into an eating-disordered teenager, and ultimately ending up in a body most fat activists would place on the small end of "fat" (fat enough to suffer street harassment, but thin enough not to suffer medical harassment—fat enough to have to shop in special stores, but thin enough that those stores can still be found in shopping malls), I've gone across borders my teenage self could not imagine. I got fat, but somehow I still exist. "The worst" has happened, and it's not that bad.[3] I'm "imprisoned" in a fat body, yet somehow, as the fat activist writer Marjory Nelson would say, "I'm home free." During my dieting days, I endlessly told myself and was endlessly told that becoming fat would mean being drowned in flesh—that once I was fat, no one would be able to see (or love, or want, or respect) me. And yet, it hasn't happened. With the help of fat feminist friends, with the help of books such as Kim Chernin's *The Obsession* and the fat activist anthology *Shadow on a Tightrope*, I found a way to think and live my fat body in the present. According to all cultural "wisdom" (and just watch what happens to self-valuing fat women on talk shows if you don't believe me), I must be deluded—I am impossible, I am living in a state of denial, and I must sooner or later come to my senses and resume loathing my body, if only for my "health."

My impossibility is different from the impossibilities of fat women who were fat children, and different again, in its white-middle-class-ness, from the impossibilities of fat women of color, but no less impossible for all that.[4] The narrative I have told, of moving from self-loathing and body obsession to a gradual acceptance of a fat female body, is common if not banal. Fat women who were fat as children seem to bear a different set of scars, inflicted by medical institutions and critical families.[5] Fat women of color often tell of simultaneously encountering racism and fat oppression after growing up in more fat-affirmative home cultures.[6] Nevertheless, in mainstream conceptions of the self and the body, the self, the person who one *is*, is presumptively thin—and the hard-won realization that one can live as a fat subject is nothing short of transformative.

The transformation from dieting teenager to Fat Girl is difficult. So difficult, in fact, that one woman I spoke to at a reading for the book *Women En Large: Images of Fat Nudes* said she was working on a manual for how to live as a fat woman. It's a good idea. A manual is necessary first of all as a counterweight to shelves and shelves of diet books, and second as a means of scraping together the cultural resources needed to live as a fat woman. Little in late-twentieth-century U.S. culture has given any inkling that it might be possible to *live* as a fat woman. Die as a fat woman, yes. Die *because* you're a fat woman, unquestionably. It is all too easy to find images of fat shot through with warnings about one's impending death—images of revulsion, images in which fat bodies are fragmented, medicalized, pathologized, and transformed into abject visions of the horror of flesh itself. In contemporary culture, the fat body generally becomes visible only at the margins, if at all, and only when written into a pathologizing narrative in which fat is a cause of ill health and a symptom of poor behavior. This narrative creates fatness as a "spoiled identity,"[7] an identity that can communicate only its own failure, an identity for which all other narratives are impossible. The fat body is never portrayed as effective, as powerful, or as sexual. Recent fat liberationist cultural production defies these limits, rewriting the fat body to challenge both abject images of the fat body and the horror of the body itself.

Everywhere and Nowhere: Abject Representation, 1994–95

To understand how contemporary fat women's representations combat prevailing visions of the fat body, it is necessary to understand something about how prevailing representations work. Unfortunately, one can choose from many recent examples. The presentation of fat bodies as pathological began a distinct resurgence in late 1994, spurred on by two events. The first was the widely reported discovery of the "obesity gene." That the gene discovered was not a human gene but a mouse gene and that the gene accounts for only a fraction of severe obesity even among mice were technicalities, less widely reported.[8] Among endless reports suggesting that soon fat people could be wiped out by a genetically engineered pill or shot, these details were overlooked. The second event was former surgeon general C. Everett Koop's "Shape Up America" plan, given pseudogovernmental legitimacy both by Koop's prominence and by the concurrent publication of an NIH "study" (in fact a selective review of already-existing research, done by a committee stacked with interested parties from the weight loss industry) endorsing yo-yo dieting. Weight loss programs Jenny Craig and NutriSystem were reportedly among the concerns funding Koop's venture.[9] *Time* magazine heralded Koop's initiative with a cover headline, "Girth of a Nation." For fat people, the allusion to D. W. Griffith's film *Birth of a Nation* was perhaps sickeningly appropriate. Just as his white actors in blackface enacted a white fantasy of freed slaves, so in this article people not fat were photographed in lurid colors, and with distorting fisheye lenses, gulping down Doritos, Budweiser, and ice cream while sprawled before the television. In a single photograph, *Time* encapsulates the fat-abhorring narrative: fat people are freakish slobs who have no self-control (and they're driving up our health care costs).[10]

The February 1995 issue of *Life* magazine offers perhaps the most paradoxical example of this eruption of concern about fatness, if only because, despite its headline ("Twenty-eight Questions about Fat"), and despite the fact that "Fat" is the single largest word on the cover, the article within contains very few photographs of fat people. The cover features a thin woman pinching significantly less than an inch of her well-tanned abdominal fat; the question "do men and women gain weight differently?" refers to a photograph of the boxer George Foreman and the ballerina Margaret Tracey; and another photocaptioned "Fat Floats" pictures thin women doing aquarobics.[11] Fat is incessantly referred to, and just as incessantly erased.

Literal erasure and extreme fragmentation characterize the few representations of fat people in the magazine. The chin of a liposuction patient protrudes from the surgical draping. Some fat calves appear to be exercising in an institutional-looking gym. A fat man is captured in the background, overwhelmed by the foregrounded presence of the Duke University Rice Diet Program's sign.[12] All of these photographs are small, less than one inch by two inches, making the fat man (the only full-body photograph of a fat person in the entire magazine) less than half an inch tall as he walks past the sign of his own erasure. Other representations of fat in the article include a cross-section of a clogged artery, presumably from a fat person, although the source is not pictured. The lead-in to the caption reads "Fatty Tubes"; according to text below, "a 1993 study based on autopsies of 1,532 teenagers and young adults found that all of them had fatty patches in their aortas."[13] Thus fat is a contamination threatening everyone: yet the placement and caption of the photograph imply that arterial fat is always a consequence of body fat, a conclusion that the study itself does not support.

In an issue supposedly devoted to fat, the largest photograph of an actual fat person is a two-by-three-inch thermogram of a fat woman next to the story description in the table of contents. This thermogram, a visual representation of the temperature of various parts of the body—ranging from a purplish blue at the coolest parts, through greens and yellows, to a deep red and white in the warmest parts—is, in effect, a brightly colored pseudoscientific, psychedelic blob. Evidently, "What do fat people actually look like?" is not one of the twenty-eight questions considered. Yet the thermogram is significant as an example of the fat body as sign, and always sign of the same thing—lack of self-control, leading to disease. The medicalizing filter shaping that representation makes it difficult to read this body any other way. The depiction certainly undermines the subjectivity of this particular fat woman, who is erased to the point that the narrative of illness is the only narrative the thermogram can support.

Many other examples of the paucity of and prejudice in representations of fat people could be drawn from television, magazines, newspapers, and movies. This pattern has been noted by scholars and fat activists alike. When *FaT GiRL* surveyed members of its editorial collective about fat representation, the consensus was that fat women are invisible to mainstream media. Replies included "There are no fat reporters on TV news"; "I don't think we're represented at all, except in Jenny Craig ads, where you'll notice there are no fat people really"; and "Invisible." Other interviewees cited portrayals of fat women "as fools and objects of disgust"; "as out of control"; "as undesirable and unnecessary"; "As pathetic, helpless slobs. Tragic, ugly, lazy characters with no self control"; and "as sick, lazy, and slobs."[14]

To these observations, I would add the significant genre of the "before" picture in weight loss advertisements, both print and televised. The before-and-after sequence gets to the heart of mainstream fat representation and the resulting paradoxes and impossibilities of fat identity. Here the fat person, usually a fat woman, is represented not as a person but as something encasing a person, something from which a person must escape, something that a person must cast off. The fat body is once again caught up in a narrative of erasure. Typical of this genre is an advertisement for "Medical Weight Control" that appeared in the *Los Angeles Weekly* in late 1994.[15] In this drawing, the before and after pictures are collapsed into one, with a rather manic-looking thin woman clad in aerobics gear emerging triumphant from the body of a fat woman, like a butterfly emerging from its cocoon. (A radically fat-affirmative reading might note the similarity between this image and the science fiction standby of the alien bursting forth from its human host.) The fat body is stiff, stationary, dressed in an unbelievably frumpy gingham dress, and has no head. "Imprisoned in every fat man," after all, "a thin one is wildly signaling to be let out."[16] In this scenario the self, the person, is presumptively thin, and cruelly jailed in a fat body. The self is never fat. To put it bluntly, there is no such thing as a fat *person*. The before-and-after scenario both consigns the fat body to an eternal past and makes it bear the full horror of embodiment, situating it as that which must be cast aside for the self to truly come into being.

In short, in the public sphere, fat bodies, and fat women's bodies in particular, are represented as a kind of abject: that which must be expelled to make all other bodily representations and functions, even life itself, possible. I borrow this idea of the abject from the feminist psychoanalyst Julia Kristeva. In *Powers of Horror,* she explains that the process of abjection is the act of primal repression that founds subjectivity and begins a sedimentation of identity around the newly forming self. The abject sets up the categories of self and not-self, but it is an expulsion of something internal to the self. In this process, according to Kristeva, "I expel myself, I spit myself out, I abject myself within the same motion through which 'I' claim to establish myself." In this way, "the one haunted by abjection is set literally beside himself." The abject is "what life withstands . . . on the part of death."[17] The abject is that revolting physicality, that repellent fluidity, those seepages and discharges that are inevitably attached to the body and necessary for life, but just as necessarily opposed to a sense of self. Kristeva also argues that in this psychological expulsion, the abject is consigned to a repeatedly retrieved past, placed in a representational "land of oblivion" that is nonetheless "constantly remembered."[18] Abjection is thus characterized by revulsion, fear of contamination, association with the deathly aspects of the body, a repeated expulsion that marks the self's borders, consignment to the past, and constant reevocation. Within mainstream representations of the body, the fat body functions as the abject: it takes up the burden of representing *the horror of the body itself* for the culture at large.

The fat body represents the corporeality and inevitable death of all bodies—a condition that, like plaque in the arteries, is universal but must be fought constantly and repeatedly, and is projected onto fat bodies.[19] The fat body is linked with death, and allowing fat into the body is thought to inevitably court death (the increasing concern about dietary fat in recent years may thus be read both as a displacement and as an intensification of the abjection of the fat body). The subject of the before and after pictures literally stands beside her abjected fat self, or drags herself out of it. Through the normative practice of dieting, millions enact the abjection of their fat bodies. The parallel between Kristeva's abject subject and the vomiting bulimic is too obvious to dwell on. The fat body rings the margins of the good self, haunting them as it helps create them. The fat body must be repeatedly evoked at the margins, drawn in and then expelled, in order to continue taking the weight of corporeality off thin bodies—playing much the same role as that taken by the female body in relation to the male, according to Elizabeth Grosz's analysis in *Volatile Bodies.* Because the fat body is the abject that makes possible the consolidation of the good body and the good self, it remains in a marginal state even when, as in *Life,* it is allegedly the focus of attention. As in the before and after pictures, the fat body is endlessly present in its representation as *past.* It is drawn back, recalled, referred to again and again, only to be cast out again; and through that casting out, it forms the margins defining the good body, the thin body that bears the mark of the self's discipline. In the article discussed, the fat body is evoked by the captions in order to be displaced by the photographs, invoked by the title in order to be displaced in the body of the text, or invoked under the sign of its own erasure (whether through dieting or through death).

Strategies for the Abject: FaT GiRL and Women En Large

Clearly, the cultural process of abjection outlined above makes the idea of a *fat person* almost unthinkable. Fat is culturally and psychologically opposed to the self, not part of the self. To represent and affirm themselves as fat women, to put a self in the fat body, to envision their own existence, fat women producing fat liberationist culture must counteract the effects and the dynamics of abject representation. If the process of abjection means that the fat body is pushed to the margins, placed in the past, linked with death, envisioned as a crypt in which the (presumptively thin) self is in danger of withering away, and made to bear the horror of corporeality, then the process of fat-affirmative representation must counter or undermine these moves. Because the process of fat abjection is so central to ideas of proper selfhood in our culture, fat-affirmative representation often must create new modes of self and new ways of seeing and being in the body. At the very least, the fat body can no longer function solely as a symptom of the weakened self. It must be written out of this narrative and into others. The ultimate goal is to reunite the self and the body, as the self within is implicated in the fat body's desires. For this reunion to occur, the body hatred at the heart of the mind-body split must be set aside, and the body no longer abjected from the self.

FaT GiRL and *Women En Large,* the two examples of fat-affirmative cultural production I discuss, are among the latest ventures in a tradition of fat activism that is over twenty years old. In a foreword to the 1983 anthology *Shadow on a Tightrope: Writings by Women on Fat Oppression,* Vivian Mayer dates the feminist fat liberation movement, and therefore its body of cultural production, to the 1973 founding of the Fat Underground.[20] According to Mayer and to a recent interview with Judy Freespirit, an early member, the Fat Underground was founded as a radical alternative to the National Association to Advance Fat Acceptance, whose position on civil rights for fat people Freespirit characterizes as "do[ing] volunteer work for the Cerebral Palsy Association to show fat people were nice."[21] The Fat Underground had ties to feminist, lesbian, and leftist journals and published feminist analyses of fat oppression in *off our backs, Sister, Issues in Radical Therapy, Plexus, Hagborn, Conditions 6, Common woman,* and *Out and About.*[22] Fat liberation pieces were published by Fat Liberator Publications, a private photocopy press run by various members of the Fat Underground, through 1980.[23] *Shadow on a Tightrope* itself, probably one of the best-known and most enduring fat liberationist texts, includes pieces written between 1972 and 1982 and is something of a touchstone for the editors of both *FaT GiRL* and

Women En Large, and several writers in the first two issues of *FaT GiRL* mention reading *Shadow* when they were younger.

Earlier in this essay, I noted that late 1994 was marked by a resurgence of anti-fat discourses in the popular press. Not entirely coincidentally, late 1994 also witnessed a burgeoning of fat-positive publications featuring women, among them the first issue of *FaT GiRL: The Zine for Fat Dykes and the Women Who Want Them* and a book titled *Women En Large: Images of Fat Nudes.*[24] Although they differ considerably, both publications set forth a vision of fat women explicitly opposed to mainstream (non) portrayals.

Many of the authors in *Shadow on a Tightrope* are lesbians, and many were involved in various incarnations of lesbian feminism. The connections between lesbian activism, feminist activism, and fat activism continue to the present day, inspiring publications such as *FaT GiRL,* a quarterly magazine dedicated to political, erotic, and creative portrayals of fat dykes. *FaT GiRL* lists "angry," "feminist," and "political" as some of its founding adjectives (along with *"fleshy,"* and, of course, "found next to your vibrator"),[25] and the interview with Judy Freespirit is included in its first issue. On the zine's masthead, the publishers proclaim: "Submit your daily experiences getting from here to there; your fictional explorations; your whimsical reminiscences; your sarcastic diatribes; your songs of laughter and tears of anger and pain; your non-linear meanderings; your artistic endeavors: wood cuts, drawings, photos, rubber stamps, cartoons; your hard-hitting investigative journalism; your hot sexual forays from the perverse to the sublime, your tales of gender play; news; reviews; announcements; letters; gossip and encouragement."[26] Such a publication clearly draws on a mixed heritage as it responds to earlier feminist fat liberationist texts and to the proliferation of lesbian pornography, magazines, and zines of the 1980s and early 1990s.[27]

In contrast with *FaT GiRL's* deliberate avoidance of a slick style, *Women En Large* is a glossy book of photographs of fat nude women, with essays and poetry by and about them. Laurie Toby Edison, a photographer, and Debbie Notkin, a writer and activist, formed their own press, Books in Focus, to publish it.[28] Notkin's roots are in feminist and fat activism and in the science fiction community, but not specifically in lesbian politics (although several of the women pictured are lesbians and one, April Miller, is also on the editorial collective of *FaT GiRL).* The essays in *Women En Large* concentrate mainly on substantiating the phenomenon of discrimination against fat people, as well as asserting and proving that fatness is largely genetically determined, and therefore a phenomenon and identity just as stable and valid as any other. While *FaT GiRL* can be characterized as a radical approach to fat liberation ("we're here, we're fat, get used to it"), *Women En Large* is a more liberal, identity-based document, seeking a justification for fatness in the individual's genetic code, the biological bedrock of contemporary visions of identity ("fatness is genetic, so stop discriminating against us"). That *Women En Large* is willing to argue with anti-fat assertions and to justify fatness, while *FaT GiRL* refuses to argue those points, affects how the two publications combat mainstream representations of fat women.[29]

Women En Large includes forty-one "images of fat nudes" bracketed between a brief foreword and two concluding essays. The photographs and essay topics chosen were determined by a need to contradict mainstream images at the level of content. Because fat women are usually pushed to the margins or not represented, they are here at the center. Because fat women are often thought to be essentially the same," Edison and Notkin strongly emphasize diversity, especially with respect to age, size, race, and abledness. Because fat women are thought to eat all the time and to never exercise, food is never shown or mentioned in the book and women are shown stretching and dancing. Because fat bodies are thought to be inherently perverse, the photos are "not intended to be erotic."[30] Because fatness is often thought to arise from laziness, bad eating habits, or other such culpable behavior, Notkin argues at some length in the first essay, "Enlarging: Politics and Society," that fatness arises from each individual's genetic makeup, and is thus out of her control.[31]

In the text and in a talk accompanying a slide show of photographs from the book,[32] Edison and Notkin emphasize the realness, the factuality of fat women and of Edison's photographs of the women. Every photographic decision is justified by their priorities of accurate representation—showing the women as they really are, showing them in their real variety, showing them as human. The women are photographed in their homes so we can see that they have lives. The women are photographed exercising because fat women do exercise. The women are photographed with musical instruments because they play them. These representational choices also attempt to work against mainstream stereotypes of fat people as slovenly, sedentary, or stupid.[33] The fat body in *Women En Large* is definitely not an uninhabited shell, nor a prison, nor perverse.

The essays in *Women En Large* concentrate on constructing a solid identity for fat women: an inevitable identity for which they are not to blame, for it is based on genetic immutability. Notkin sees medicalizing discourses as the major enemy of fat subjectivity, but she also relies on them, marshaling scientific citations to debunk the assertion that fat people are inherently unhealthy. What is inherently unhealthy, she argues, is yo-yo dieting and the inhumane stresses that a prejudiced world inflicts on fat people.[34] However, in engaging so extensively with the medical model, in rewriting the fat body using genetics as an identity technology, Notkin, like purveyors of mainstream representations, treats the fat body as a symptom—not of sloth and gluttony, but of a genetic difference. While this argument is a distinct improvement on mainstream discourse, by contributing to a sense that the fat body needs extensive explanation in a way that other bodies do not, it sets itself at odds with the photographs' assertions of value and beauty.

The text of *Women En Large* directly and effectively counteracts images of abjection that constitute the mainstream representation of fat, both by simply representing fat women and by contradicting the medicalized linkage of fat with death, but it does not take issue with the fundamental split between body and self. The fat body is presented as beautiful, but apparently with the hope that it will become irrelevant, that the reader, guided by the homey interiors of the photographs, will ultimately come to realize that "we're all the same underneath" and stop unjustly punishing fat people for a benign genetic difference. Thus, although the fat body is no longer positioned as the abject, the body itself is still severed from identity. Who these women "really" are resides not in their embodiment, not in the flow of desire issuing from the fat body, but in their musical instruments, their house plants, their hobbies, or their poetry. The text downplays the fat body made visible in the photographs, in effect maintaining the mind/body split, maintaining the presentation of fat as symptom, and maintaining some of the mainstream erasure of the fat body.

In some of its more parodic or enigmatic photographs, *Women En Large* does attack the dynamic of abjection as well as the content of mainstream representation. One photograph in particular—that of Cynthia McQuillen cradling a human skull in front of her crotch—asks the question, "Is this what this body really is?"[35] Rather than writing fat in from the abject margins by asserting a sameness (as do most of the other photographs in the book), it overtly performs abjection, parodying the usual terms of fat representation and challenging the dynamic itself. Here McQuillen appears, like the woman pictured in *Life* magazine's thermogram, behind the sign of death; but she looks from beyond it, locking eyes with the viewer to confront and unsettle the process of abjection. Clearly, the self is in this body, alive and very much affronted by the juxtaposition. The alienness of the bony skull next to her rounded flesh and the life in her look expose the falseness and the violence of normatively abjected representations of fat women.

Such counterabjection characterizes much of *FaT GiRL*, which humorously emphasizes fat as an assertion of the physical, reclaiming the fat body to make it into a comedic weapon. But *FaT GiRL* isn't just about comedy. It's also about, as the cover of the second issue declares, "stories, reviews, smut, comics, resources, and more!!!" By relying on a parodic strategy of counterabjection, by rewriting the fat body as particularly powerful, and by eroticizing the fat body, *FaT GiRL* acts against mainstream abjection, undercutting both the dynamic of abjection and the denigration of the body in the mind/body split.

Rather than simply *not* subjecting the fat body to abjection, *FaT GiRL*'s representations often destabilize the process of abjection through recipes for counterabjection—political acts in which the fat girl performs a literal abjection in order to make fun of mainstream culture's obsession with abjecting fat bodies. In counterabjection, the abjected substance is not shamefully denied but proudly displayed, in order to affront the culture at large. This is an abjection with a difference. A prime example is the recipe for a "Fat Girl Revenge Cocktail":

ingredients:

one quart brightly-colored kefir (yogurt drink)
one teaspoon syrup of Ipecac (vomiting agent)

Drink the kefir. Upon approaching desired target (diet centers are good places), swallow the syrup of Ipecac. Position your mouth so it's facing your target. When your stomach begins to heave, aim quickly, and fire. Most effective if done in broad daylight.[36]

Rather than being the agent of abjection, here the diet center becomes the target of a literal abjection. Rather than assert reasonably, as *Women En Large* does, that dieting is unhealthy, here *FaT GiRL* does to the diet center what the diet center would do to fat girls (or would have fat girls do to themselves). Rather than abjecting her own fat body, the Ipecac-taking fat girl is abjecting diet culture. In this public abjection (best done in broad daylight, as opposed to the secretive vomiting induced by fear of fat) the diet center and not the fat girl is made to bear the mark of revulsion. In the revenge cocktail, a performance of a literal sick-making, the analytic point and its embodiment in the body of a fat woman are fused.

Through its expelling force, the fat body is a direct political agent. The fat body is similarly empowered and written as agent rather than symptom throughout *FaT GiRL*. A second political action tip suggests that when harassed "about being fat or looking pregnant" (an assertion of fat as symptom if there ever was one—based on the assumption that heterosexual reproduction is the only excuse for the fat body), the fat girl should perform the symptom to excess and act out a monstrous birth:

> Turn your back and look downward (giving them the misleading impression that they've made you feel humiliated and horrible about yourself), and stuff whatever you might be carrying into your clothing. Then, turn the tables on your unsuspecting victim(s) by clutching your bulging, padded gut and stumbling towards him/her with an arm outstretched, moaning and grunting: "Help me! I'm going to have my baby!" . . . The piece-de-resistance comes when you squat and grunt and give birth to whatever you were able to stash away under your clothes. Best results if you can pull it out from between your legs—especially if you pre-plan the action and have a bloody barbie [sic] doll, used tampon. . . . And remember, the more the merrier ! (Friends having multiple simultaneous births makes for a more blessed event.)[37]

Distracting the harasser with a false performance of fat shame, the fat girl then enacts a parodic abject birth. The appearance of shame here functions not to entrap the fat girl but to snare her audience; and in giving birth to the bloodied Barbie doll, she expels and degrades one significant artifact of fat-hating beauty culture.

A slightly different, but no less assertive, mode of fat physicality is expressed in the lyrics to the *FaT GiRL*–theme polka (itself a dance associated with rotundity): the superhero Fat Girl threatens, "Shut up or I'll sit on you!"[38] In addition to affirming the unashamed fat body, this last manifestation also recuperates the common childhood taunt, "What are you going to do? Sit on me?" *FaT GiRL* attributes lack of power not to the fat body itself but to the shame that the fat person is made to feel. When fatness is performed without the shame, the taunt—an accusation of powerlessness that writes the fat body as unable to defend itself—becomes a threat. In imagining this powerful and unashamed body, *FaT GiRL* writes the self back into the fat body as a *fat self*—as a person particularly shaped and empowered by fat; a self whose body is effective, defining, and pleasurable; a self whose body is not a symptom but a weapon. The narrative of abjection is replaced by a narrative of attack.

It is also significant that in its rewriting a fat embodiment, *FaT GiRL* is frankly erotic, whereas *Women En Large* attempts (or at least claims) to avoid eroticism.[39] In its concern with counteracting myths about fat women at the level of content, *Women*

En Large avoids representations of sexuality or of eating, fearing that it will reinforce those myths. *FaT GiRL,* on the other hand, revels in writing the fat body into forbidden sexual scripts. In picturing fat women feeding pastries, grapes, and ice cream to each other in its premiere issue, the zine enacts an erotic spectacle unimaginable in mainstream representation or in *Women En Large.*[40] The photos of eating accompany a discussion feature called "Fat Girl Round Table," but the zine also features erotic pictorials. In presenting fat bodies in sexual acts, fat women actively desiring other fat women, fat women in S/M scenarios, *FaT GiRL* appropriates sex as a joyous way of rewriting the fat body. It uses the erotic to envision a good, pleasurable body in which there is an interplay between the body's desires and the self's expressions—the good body is rewritten as the body that can tell the self its desires, act on its desire, provide pleasures. Suddenly the disciplined body, the dieting body, the subject of "self-control" seems empty and impoverished.

Several of the erotic short stories in the magazine focus on S/M, presenting the sexual scene as a story in which the top rewrites the previously loathed fat body into pleasure and desirability. These stories typically involve a scenario in which the fat woman is the bottom; by giving up control to the top she provides an opportunity for the top to convince the bottom that her body is an object not of loathing but of beauty, pleasure, and lesbian desire. One particularly clear example of this pedagogic scenario is "Thank You Note to a Top," by Drew:

"You've got a beautiful body," she says and I don't believe her. I let the whip that's slicing across my back drown her out. I don't want to hear this right now. . . .

I was having such a good time before she started talking about my body. . . .

"Don't you believe me, baby? This is some sweet stuff you got. . . . You better believe me. You better believe every word I tell you." I can't tell if she's angry or not and I don't have a safeword tonight. "You've got a beautiful body," she repeats, testing me.

"Yeah, well, I grew it myself," I spit, thinking how much I hate it when Tops lie.

She pauses, looking into my tear-blurred eyes, and repeats slowly, "You grew it yourself. You learned how to love yourself enough to eat and sleep and work and play and give pleasure to yourself and other women, didn't you? And that's what you're doing now, you know." She's got four fingers in me now, pumping slowly in time with her words. I know the whip is still there, but I can't really feel it anymore. My mind is trained on her words.

"This is a body for loving women with, isn't it, and you're giving it to me, aren't you, baby? Aren't you?" . . .

Months later we are making out like teenagers in her truck and I remember to thank her for giving me my body back that night. When I bottom, I give my Top access to my pain, even the pain she didn't cause. And in that vulnerable state, my child-self exposed, I can finally hear those good truths: You're so good. You're beautiful. I'm proud of you. I want you.[41]

In this story, Drew clearly intends the S/M scene to rewrite the negative messages of childhood. In childhood, the narrator was involuntarily powerless and the messages of body hatred were written into her before she could know to reject them. Now, by voluntarily becoming powerless again, she can allow the top to rewrite these messages, using the pleasures and intensities of the body to reinforce them.

The non-S/M eroticism in *FaT GiRL* is just as crucial for rewriting the body and the self. Repeatedly, fat women are shown in the throes of sexual and sensual pleasure—eating, laughing, dancing, masturbating, sunbathing, and having sex. Here, unlike in *Women En Large*, all the pleasures in the catalogue of activities are mediated through the body. The fat body is not just an indifferent vehicle for the self, but a sensual surface with different potentials for different bodies.

This fat body is not marginal or coincidental, but central. It is also highly visible. The *FaT GiRL* theme polka likens Fat Girl the superhero to Superman, only

Fat Girl can't live out no clark kent lies
girdles, corsets, vertical stripes, there is no disguise
she's omnipresent she 's an omnivore
you know you can't hide from Fat Girl.[42]

Identity and selfhood are thematized in light of this omnipresent visibility as well: "Just as we see gender and race before we see an individual, we see FAT. Oh my God it's a FAAAAAAAAAAT dyke! How people react to your identity is wrapped up in your physical presentation. . . . When you claim your dykehood you are demanding a public sexual persona. Fat women have a sexuality? Hard bodies only. Are you Height/Weight Proportionate? . . . Do you fit? How wide are your hips? Where do you fit in? How do you fit in relation to me; what does that say about my identity?"[43] While seeming to maintain the opposition between "physical presentation" and "an individual," Max Airborne also suggests the troubling power of the fat woman: by claiming a sexual identity for herself, she inevitably introduces questions about others' identities. When the abjection of the fat body within mainstream representation is what founds the good body and solidifies identity for the thin self, it is not surprising that when the fat body refuses to stay at the margins, other identities will be disturbed as well.

Simply by representing fat women, both *Women En Large* and *FaT GiRL* trouble the usual construction of embodiment, in which the self is presumptively thin and the fat body is made to stand in for the abjectness of flesh itself. While *Women En Large* attempts to counteract representations of fat women as the abject by correcting the medical and cultural assumptions that anchor them, it ends up reinstating the fat body as symptom. Moreover, by avoiding potentially negative images the book fails to write the fat body out of the narrative of medical symptom and into a narrative of sexual pleasure. *FaT GiRL's* strategies make it possible to rewrite the fat body as a site of sexual pleasure, after first reiterating and parodying the conventions of mainstream representation. *Women En Large's* content-based strategy results in splitting the body from the self, though the fat body is no more opposed to the self than is any other body. In *FaT GiRL*, by contrast, the fat body is rewritten as being particularly useful—a weapon, a site of political comedy, and an erotic object all in one. *FaT GiRL* thus not only puts a fat self in the fat body but begins to combat the denigration of the body itself. Once the girl within can be either fat or thin, the presumptively thin self of fat abjection will be displaced in favor of a diversely embodied subjectivity that can no longer afford to disdain the flesh.

NOTES

1. *I Am So Fucking Beautiful* is a zine that was produced in the mid-1990s, by Nomy Lamm of Olympia, Washington. It is dedicated to the exploration and affirmation of being a young, fat, feminist woman.

2. Michael Moon and Eve Kosofsky Sedgwick, "Divinity: A Dossier, a Performance Piece, a Little-Understood Emotion," in *Tendencies,* by Sedgwick (Durham: Duke University Press, 1993), 217.

3. I was overjoyed when I first read Marjory Nelson's formulation of this sentiment in "Fat and Old: Old and Fat," her contribution to *Shadow on a Tightrope*: "I realize that the 'worst' has happened to me. All that I've been warned about and worried about has occurred. The knowledge frees me. I know who I am. I'm fat and I'm old, and I'm home free" (in *Shadow on a Tightrope: Writings by Women on Fat Oppression,* ed. Lisa Schoenfielder and Barb Wieser [Iowa City: Aunt Lute, 1983], 236).

4. For discussions of differences between being a fat woman in a white community and being a fat woman in an African American community, see especially Chupoo Alafonte's and April Miller's remarks by Debbie Notkin in "Enlarging: Politics and Society," in *Women En Large: Images of Fat Nudes,* ed. Laurie Toby Edison and Notkin (San Francisco: Books in Focus, 1994), 94, 104. Fat African American women published in fat liberationist sources generally seem to agree that while fat women are more accepted and are found more attractive in African American communities, the anti-fat discourse of white culture is very difficult to avoid. In "Oh My God It's Big Mama!" *(FaT GiRL,* no. 1 [1994]: 14–20), Elizabeth Hong Brassil discusses the fact that although she is Vietnamese, with recognizably "Asian" facial features and an olive complexion, people often assume she is white because contemporary American images of Asian women fetishize their slimness. Fat liberationist women of color seem to bring to the fat liberationist project considerable strengths in the differences of their home cultures' ways of viewing the body; the project of examining fat liberationist cultural production as a site where these differing ideas of embodiment do battle with white mainstream representation is critical and yet to be done.

5. For accounts of fat women who were fat as children, see Lynn Mabel-Lois, "We'll Worry about That When You're Thin"; Terre Poppe, "Fat Memories from My Life," and Lynn Levy, "Outrages," in Schoenfielder and Wieser, *Shadow on a Tightrope,* 62–66, 67–70, 79–81, as well as Max Airborne, "My Life as a Fat Child," *FaT GiRL,* no. 2 (1995): 48–49.

6. See in particular Queen T'hisha's and Chupoo Alafonte's remarks in Notkin, "Enlarging," 106, 94.

7. Michael Moon uses this phrase when he asserts, in a discussion with Eve Sedgwick, that "at a certain active level of human creativity, it may be true that the management of spoiled identity simply is where experimental identities, which is to say any consequential ones, come from" (Moon and Sedgwick, "Divinity," 225). While Moon's insight is acute, I would also like to point out that Moon is certainly not the first to use the concept of spoiled identity to describe fat identity. The phrase was used in 1983 as part of a section title in *Shadow on a Tightrope* ("A Spoiled Identity: Fat women as survivors . . .").

8. See *Food for Thought: Networking Newsletter for the Size Rights and Anti-diet Community*, February 1995, and the January/February 1995 issue of *Rump Parliament* for further discussion of the anti-fat campaigns. One example of the media come-on surrounding the mouse gene discovery was provided by the ABC network. Advertisements for a story run on the program *20/20* on February 3, 1995, asked, "Could the discovery of the obesity gene mean a cure?" and contained a video of a fat person getting a shot in the arm, implying that the program would address how the discovery of an obesity gene (in mice?) could lead to a "cure" for fatness. In fact, the bulk of the segment focused on a new "therapy" combining two previously known appetite suppressants, which sometimes resulted in the less-than-revolutionary loss of 10 to 15 percent of body mass. This was the ill-fated phen/fen combination, pulled from the market in 1997 because of its serious side effects.

9. K. and R. Stimson, "Countdown to International No Diet Day," *Food for Thought*, February 1995, 2, and Lee Martindale, "U.S. Gears Up for International No Diet Day" (press release issued by *Rump Parliament Magazine*), February 1995.

10. Philip Elmer-Dewitt, "Fat Times," *Time*, January 16, 1995, 59–61; see the photograph by Chip Simons, 58–59.

11. Bob Adelman, "The Boxer and the Ballerina: George Foreman and Margaret Tracey" (photograph), *Life*, February 1995, 63; Gerd Ludwig/Woodfin Camp & Associates, "Fat Floats " (photograph), *Life*, February 1995, 68.

12. J. Bolivar/Custom Medical Stock, "No Miracle" (photograph), *Life*, February 1995, 64; Nina Berman/SIPA Press, "A Leg Up" and "Let Them Eat Rice" (photographs), *Life*, February 1995, 62, 70.

13. Lisa Grunwald, Anne Hollister, and Miriam Bensirnhon, "Do I Look Fat to You?" *Life*, February 1995, 60.

14. "Chew on This!" *FaT GiRL*, no. 1 (1994): 2.

15. "Medical Weight Control" (advertisement), *Los Angeles Weekly*, December 30 , 1994–January 5, 1995, 50.

16. Cyril Connolly, quoted in Grunwald, Hollister, and Bensimhon, "Do I Look Fat to You?" 64.

17. Julia Kristeva, *Powers of Horror: An Essay on Abjection*, trans. Leon J. Roudiez and Alice Jardine (New York: Columbia University Press, 1982) 3, 1, 3.

18. Ibid., 8.

19. In this respect, fat is like the body fluids (fluid bodies?) usually assigned the role of the abject. Like body fluids, whose "control is a matter of vigilance, never guaranteed" (Elizabeth Grosz, *Volatile Bodies: Toward a Corporeal Feminism* [Bloomington: Indiana University Press, 1994], 194), fat is envisioned as that which inevitably contaminates everyone (even the apparently healthy adolescents), but must nevertheless be the object of an eternal struggle.

20. Vivian Mayer, foreword to Schoenfielder and Wieser, *Shadow on a Tightrope*, x.

21. A. Hernandez, "Judy Freespirit: A. Hernandez Talks to One of the Fore-mothers of Fat Activism," *FaT GiRL*, no. 1 (1994): 6.

22. Lisa Schoenfielder and Barb Wieser, bibliography in Schoenfielder and Wieser, *Shadow on a Tightrope*, 241–43 .

23. Lisa Schoenfielder and Barb Wieser, preface to Schoenfielder and Wieser, *Shadow on a Tightrope*, xviii–xxi.

24. See Lee Martindale's editorial (p. 1) in the January/February 1995 issue of *Rump Parliament* for further discussion of the connections between the two. It is Martindale's contention that the growth of fat and anti-diet activism, combined with the Federal Trade Commission's

recent crackdown on misleading diet advertising, spurred the diet industries to design and fund former surgeon general Koop's "Shape Up America" plan .

25. *"Fat Girl* Is . . .," *FaT GiRL,* no. 1 (1994): overleaf of cover.

26. *"Fat Girl* Is a Political Act," *FaT GiRL,* no. 1 (1994): 1.

27. The combined heritages of *Shadow on a Tightrope* and *FaT GiRL* suggest a connection between gay and lesbian activism and fat activism, if perhaps not, as Michael Moon declares, "a profound and unacknowledged historical debt" (Moon and Sedgwick, "Divinity," 234); Moon's assertion that fat liberation is "a movement much younger than gay/lesbian liberation" (making the historical debt long-standing) is open to debate. Though I take issue with the claim that the debt is unacknowledged (especially if the current blossoming of fat liberation is considered), it seems clear that there are tactical debts, as well as tactical similarities, between the two movements and commonalities in the situations that gave rise to each. Recent lesbian theorists in particular have described the position of the gay or lesbian person within the heterosexual symbolic order as one of abjection. Diana Fuss argues that gays and lesbians are an "indispensable interior exclusion" in such an order ("Inside/Out: Introduction," in *Inside/Out: Lesbian Theories, Gay Theories,* ed. Fuss [New York: Routledge, 1991], 3), and Lynda Hart uses this analysis to launch her own discussion of "the invention and circulation of 'lesbians' as a haunting secret" *(Fatal Women: Lesbian Sexuality and the Mark of Aggression* [Princeton: Princeton University Press, 1994], ix). Judith Butler's theorization of the abject is perhaps most resonant with an account of fatness as abjection . For Butler, "The abject designates . . . precisely those 'unlivable' and 'uninhabitable' zones of social life which are nevertheless densely populated by those who do not enjoy the status of the subject, but whose living under the sign of the 'unlivable' is required to circumscribe the domain of the subject" *(Bodies That Matter: On the Discursive Limits of "Sex"* [New York: Routledge, 1993], 3). The connections Butler makes between abjection and a sense of uninhabitability, as well as her connections between abjection and repetition, apply well to the fat body and to the re-petitive, yet never fully successful, process of dieting.

28. Notkin, "Enlarging," 112. That Edison and Notkin had to form their own press to get *Women En Large* published speaks to a certain level of fat-phobia.

29. In "Divinity," Moon and Sedgwick discuss the distinction between ontogenic and anti-ontogenic stances, which Shane Phelan examined earlier in *Identity Politics: Lesbian Feminism and the Limits of Community* (Philadelphia: Temple University Press, 1989). In both cases, the argument for an anti-ontogenic stance "that does not begin by positing an origin or ex-planation for difference" grows out of gay and lesbian political movements and holds that succumbing to the impulse to explain implies that one has accepted a nonprivileged status— things that are seen as normal, natural, and right never need explanation. The analysis of Phelan and others is explicitly Foucauldian, as they note that "explanations" usually involve submitting oneself to disciplinary apparatuses such as psychiatry or medicine.

30. Cookie Andrews-Hunt and Tara Hughes, "New Book, *Women En Large,* Shows Beauty of Fat Women," *Seattle Gay News,* January 27,1995,10.

31. Notkin, "Enlarging," 92–101.

32. Debbie Notkin and Laurie Toby Edison, lecture, Elliott Bay Books, Seattle, December 10, 1994.

33. Notkin, "Enlarging," 91.

34. Ibid., 92–101.

35. Laurie Toby Edison, photograph in Notkin and Edison, *Women En Large,* 61.

36. "Recipes: Fat Girl Revenge Cocktail," *FaT GiRL,* no. 1 (1994): 25.

37. "Helpful Hint: Hysterical Pregnancy and Insta-Birthing," *FaT GiRL*, no. 1 (1994): 40.

38. Max Airborne, *"Fat Girl: A Polka by Max Airborne,"* *FaT GiRL* no. 1 (1994): 41.

39. Laurie Toby Edison, quoted in Andrews-Hunt and Hughes, "New Book, *Women En Large*, Shows Beauty of Fat Women," 10.

40. "Fat Girl Roundtable," *Fat Girl*, no. 1 (1994): 33–40.

41. Drew, "Thank You Note to a Top," *FaT GiRL*, no. 1 (1994): 26–27.

42. Airborne, *"Fat Girl: A Polka, "* 41.

43. "Will I Sit on You and Squash You?" *FaT GiRL*, no. 1 (1994): 14.

REFERENCES

Adelman, Bob. "The Boxer and the Ballerina: George Foreman and Margaret Tracey" (photograph). *Life*, February 1995, 63.

Airborne, Max. *"Fat Girl: A Polka by Max Airborne."* *FaT GiRL*, no. 1 (1994): 41.

———. "I Was a Fat Kid" (cartoon). *FaT GiRL*, no. 1 (1994): 8.

———. "My Life as a Fat Child." *FaT GiRL*, no. 2 (1995): 48–49.

Andrews-Hunt, Cookie, and Tara Hughes. "New Book, *Women En Large*, Shows Beauty of Fat Women." *Seattle Gay News*, January 27, 1995, 10.

Berman, Nina, and SIPA Press. "A Leg Up" (photograph). *Life*, February 1995, 62.

———. "Let Them Eat Rice" (photograph). *Life*, February 1995, 70.

Bolivar, J., and Custom Medical Stock. "No Miracle" (photograph). *Life*, February 1995, 64.

Brassil, Elizabeth Hong. "Oh My God It's Big Mama!" *FaT GiRL*, no. 1 (1994): 14–20.

Brassil, Elizabeth Hong, and Max Airborne. "Two Fat Dykes." *FaT GiRL*, no. 1 (1994): 31–32.

Butler, Judith. *Bodies That Matter: On the Discursive Limits of "Sex."* New York: Routledge, 1993.

"Chew on This!" *FaT GiRL*, no. 1 (1994): 2.

Drew. "Thank You Note to a Top." *FaT GiRL*, no. 1 (1994): 26–27.

Edison, Laura T., and Deborah Notkin. *Women En Large: Images of Fat Nudes.* San Francisco: Books in Focus, 1994.

Elmer-witt, Philip. "Fat Times." *Time*, January 16, 1995, 59–61.

"Fat Girl Is . . .," *FaT GiRL*, no. 1 (1994): overleaf of cover.

"Fat Girl Is a Political Act. " *FaT GiRL*, no. 1 (1994): 1.

"Fat Girl Roundtable." *FaT GiRL*, no. 1 (1994): 33–40.

Fuss, Diana. "Inside/Out: Introduction." In *Inside/Out: Lesbian Theories, Gay Theories*, ed. Fuss, 1–10. New York: Routledge, 1991.

Grosz, Elizabeth. *Volatile Bodies: Toward a Corporeal Feminism.* Bloomington: Indiana University Press, 1994.

Grunwald, Lisa, Anne Hollister, and Miriam Bensimhon. "Do I Look Fat to You?" *Life*, February 1995, 60.

Hart, Lynda. *Fatal Women: Lesbian Sexuality and the Mark of Aggression.* Princeton: Princeton University Press, 1994.

"Helpful Hint: Hysterical Pregnancy and Insta-birthing." *FaT GiRL*, no. 1 (1994): 40.

Hernandez, A. "Judy Freespirit: A. Hernandez Talks to One of the Foremothers of Fat Activism." *FaT GiRL*, no. 1 (1994): 6.

Kristeva. Julia. *Powers of Horror: An Essay on Abjection.* Translated by Leon J. Roudiez and Alice Jardine. New York: Columbia University Press, 1982.

Levy, Lynn. "Outrages." In *Shadow on a Tightrope: Writings by Women on Fat Oppression,* edited by Lisa Schoenfielder and Barb Wieser, 79–81. Iowa City: Aunt Lute, 1983.

Ludwig, Gerd, and Woodfin Camp and Associates. "Fat Floats" (photograph). *Life,* February 1995, 68.

Mabel-Lois, Lynn. "We' ll Worry about That When You' re Thin." In *Shadow on a Tightrope: Writings by Women on Fat Oppression,* edited by Lisa Schoenfielder and Barb Wieser, 62–66. Iowa City: Aunt Lute, 1983.

Martindale, Lee. Editorial. *Rump Parliament,* January/February 1995, 1.

Mayer, Vivian F. Foreword to *Shadow on a Tightrope: Writings by Women on Fat Oppression,* edited by Lisa Schoenfielder and Barb Wieser, ix–xvii . Iowa City: Aunt Lute, 1983.

Moon, Michael, and Eve Kosofsky Sedgwick. "Divinity: A Dossier, a Performance Piece, a Little-Understood Emotion." In *Tendencies,* by Sedgwick, 215–51. Durham, N.C.: Duke University Press, 1993.

Nelson, Marjory. "Fat and Old: Old and Fat." In *Shadow on a Tightrope: Writings by Women on Fat Oppression,* edited by Lisa Schoenfielder and Barb Wieser, 228–36. Iowa City: Aunt Lute, 1983.

Phelan, Shane. *Identity Politics: Lesbian Feminism and the Limits of Community.* Philadelphia: Temple University Press, 1989.

Poppe, Terre. "Fat Memories from My Life." In *Shadow on a Tightrope: Writings by Women on Fat Oppression,* edited by Lisa Schoenfielder and Barb Wieser, 67–70. Iowa City: Aunt Lute, 1983.

"Recipes: Fat Girl Revenge Cocktail." *FaT GiRL,* no. 1 (1994): 25.

Schoenfielder, Lisa, and Barb Wieser. Preface to *Shadow on a Tightrope: Writings by Women on Fat Oppression,* edited by Schoenfielder and Wieser, xviii–xxi. Iowa City: Aunt Lute, 1983.

———, eds. *Shadow on a Tightrope: Writings by Women on Fat Oppression.* Iowa City: Aunt Lute, 1983.

Stimson, K., and R. Stimson. "Countdown to International No Diet Day." *Food for Thought: Networking Newsletter for the Size Rights and Anti-diet Community,* February 1995, 2.

"Will I Sit on You and Squash You?" *FaT GiRL,* no. 1 (1994): 14.

‖‖‖

20

Images of Addiction
The Representation of Illicit Drug Use in Popular Media

Richard Huggins

It is not I who became addicted, it is my body.
—Jean Cocteau, *Opium*, 1930

Introduction

This chapter examines images of illicit drug use, in particular injecting drug use, and focuses on the ways in which the body of the addict is represented and constructed across a range of popular media forms. Through such an analysis I argue that there is a significant relationship between images of "embodied deviance"—in this case in the form of injecting drug use—and notions of social order, social control, and the "health" of the social body in contemporary societies. Focusing on images of drug use and drug users, on how people use, take, and experience drug use, rather than, for example, perceptions of crime associated with drug use or wider aspects of "junky culture," it is possible to conceive of, understand, and interpret drug use as very much a set of actions that takes place through and within the lived body and is constructed in concert with that body. Focus is placed on the material body of the addict and how, in turn, this body can act as a kind of symbolic map not just for the social significance of drug use and addiction but for broader notions of deviance and social and bodily disorder. One maps on to the other and back again, and the centrality of the symbolic form is enhanced by the social and spatial location of the addict at the margins of our societies (Fraser 1996; Pile, Brook, and Mooney 1998).

This chapter draws on recent developments in the sociology of the body and social theory (Berthelot 1986; Brook 1999; Burkitt 1999; Cregan 2006; Crossley 2001; Ettorre 1998; Featherstone 2000; Featherstone, Hepworth, and Turner 1991; Howson and Inglis 2001; Nettleton and Watson 1998; Newton 2003; Shildrick 2002; Shilling 1993, 2001, 2003, 2007; Turner 1984, 1992, 1996, 2006; Synnott 1993; Williams and Bendelow 1998). In particular there has been a reawakening of interest in the notion of the body as a metaphor for larger social groups and organizations such as community, region, or nation. Turner, for example, has argued that we have witnessed the rise of the "somatic society" in which "our major political and moral problems are expressed through the conduit of the human body" (Turner 1996:6). In addition, the chapter draws on the work of Douglas (1966), Grosz (1994) Kristeva (1982), and Turner (1992, 1996, 2006) to explore the persistence of and fascination with images of the addict's body and the structure, focus, and impact of these representations and images. Douglas's (1966) focus on the significance of boundaries, purity, danger, and cleanliness provides a valuable framework for the analysis of the production of meaning within images and representations in the context of broader ideological concerns (Nead 1992). It highlights the importance of stable categories, impermeable boundaries, and borderlines for the maintenance of order and emphasizes the perceived threats that transitional and transgressional actions and behaviors make to that order. Such an emphasis on pollution and purification is particularly relevant to discussions of the addict's body, and injecting drug use as the act of injecting drugs into the body both is a clear transgression of boundaries and has been conceptualized as a form of internal pollution through which "the internal environment of our bodies is destroyed" (Warbuton 1978: 309). Furthermore, one popular and recurrent key term in drug argots (both street and professional) is to talk about becoming, getting, and staying "clean" as an outcome of detoxification and abstinence.

Mapping "Embodied" Deviance: Images of Addiction

Images of addiction and the symbolic meaning of drug use are highly reliant upon discourses that focus on the body and parts of the body, and, to some extent, the power of many representations of the drug user stems from such a fascination. Different types of media outputs, for example in literature, film, photography, popular journalism, commercial advertising, and government information, can be shown to focus on several persistent and recurrent themes that appear central to the construction of the ideas of addiction and of the addict. It is through these images that the notion of "embodied deviance" can be mapped. By this I mean a notion of "deviance" that is constituted through the willed or unwilled action of the body and is displayed on the skin and through the actions, movements, and corporeality of the addict's body. Thus, it is not so much an issue of individual behavior but the manifestation of behaviors classified as "deviant" (both in the form of drug use but also in other ways, notably sexual and criminal) through the actions of and on the body.

Turner's idea of the "somatic society" (Turner 1984, 1992, 1996, 2003), in which political problems and social anxieties are frequently transferred to the body, is significant in relation to the analysis of images and representations of drug use and addiction. In these terms the body can be seen to act as a metaphorical map of social problems and communities, public spaces, and, in particular, the margins (of the body and society) and the marginalized (bodies and social groups). The case of addiction is even more complex as—for many—drug use *is* an actual social problem and not simply a metaphorical one. But I maintain that such representations and discourses do not, simply, reflect how things are or may be but that the close relationship among representations, social meanings, and actual practices conflates around notions of the addict in mutually reinforcing ways (Huggins 2006).

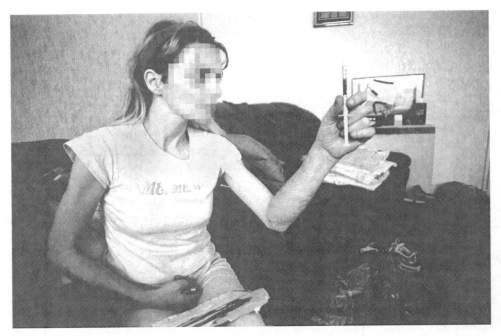

Figure 20.1. The Addict's Body in Chaos: Headline and Lead Photograph, *Guardian* Newspaper (UK), Tuesday, 13 April 2004, page 1.

Analysis of images of the addict and addiction across a range of popular media forms reveals a set of recurrent themes that can be seen to map this notion of embodied deviance: first, that the central focus of discourses about drug use tend to center on the body and, in particular, on the effects of drug use on the body's physical integrity and, as such, drug use is measured or conceptualized through its internal and external effects on the body; second, that the addict is represented as occupying the margins of our societies in both social and geographical terms; third, that the notion of the drug user and addict as "other" has been a consistent feature of the representation of the addict throughout the history of the representation and regulation of drug use: and fourth, that representations of the addict focus on the body, as both "other" and its margins, in ways that reflect both the perceived social otherness of the addict and the social marginalization of the drug user. In figure 20.1 we can see ready examples of such fascination with the body and its decay through drug use. The ulcerated arms of the female addict are clearly displayed as part of a "warning" narrative of the effects of injecting drug use.

It will be immediately apparent that the focus here is on the ways in which images of both substance use and substance users work within "political, normative and discursive regimes" (Shilling 2003: 203) for and by those who are (apparently) warranted to identify and classify actions and behaviors as problematic (Valentine and Fraser

2008). Importantly, the body can be seen to act as a metaphor or set of metaphors for wider social and political organization and perceived threats to the organization and order of any given society (Douglas 1966). Turner (1991) argues that social theory has tended to conceptualize the body in three main ways. The first approach sees the body as actualized in sets of social practices through which the body is constantly produced, regulated, and sustained. The second approach stresses the signification role of the body and conceptualizes the body as a system of signs. Here the body acts as the carrier of social meaning and symbolic value. The third approach, while still focusing on the body as a set of signs, argues that the body stands for or expresses relations of power within a given society. For Turner such approaches explain the central significance of the body and the interplay of meanings between physical and biological *actual* bodies and ideas and beliefs about the body, society, and social order. Such an approach can be used to explain, for example, how different conceptions of the diseased body can signify changing social and power relations and not simply new medical "discoveries" (Turner 1996).

Important as these insights are in terms of understanding aspects of the social significance of drug use, they do not pay sufficient attention to the actual role of the body in bringing into being the act of drug use and as the location of the notion of addiction. The nature and notion of addiction is a highly contested one in and of itself (Booth Davies 1997; West 2006), and it may be the case that one of the most significant complications of interpreting "addiction" is precisely *caused by* this very embodiedness.

So while it is possible and important to explore and analyze social and cultural constructions of addiction and the social significance of substance use, it is less possible to reduce this activity to a set of socially constructed actions or acts, as this does not take enough account of either the role of the body or the corporeality of drug use and its experience. Furthermore, addiction cannot be adequately explained or interpreted through sociological theory and methods such as symbolic interaction, discourse analysis, or communicative action. Important as these approaches and frameworks are for analysis of the social meaning of substance use, drug use itself is not constituted at this level or in this way. Indeed, it is important not to conflate analyses of discourses about and signifiers for drug use, and associated cultural meanings, with actual embodied drug use.

Even if we take the more structural arguments that suggest that addiction is or may be either a response to or a condition of mass consumer society, of modernity, or an outcome of the rise of the individualized society (Giddens 1991; Levine 1978; Reith 2004; Sulkunen 2009) this still does not explain how, why, and what addiction is and how it is constituted through and in the body—we need to study the actual body to achieve that.

So while we can, perhaps, identify contextual factors—such as the historical, social, political moments—that may lead to the development of substance misuse as a social and cultural phenomenon, this does not adequately explain the role of the body in drug use and human action (Merleau-Ponty 2004 [1948]; Crossley 1995). Indeed, addiction, whatever "it" is or may be, takes us to the very edge of our theoretical and sociological frameworks of understanding and demonstrates the limitations of much theorizing in engaging with the sensational and sensuous body and its relationships to human action and behaviors.

All this does not, of course, mean that one cannot analyze aspects of drug use and addiction from and through established sociological methods or theory. Rather, it suggests that in order to gain a fuller understanding, of both drug use and reactions to it, we need to relocate analysis onto the body and recognize more directly that it is actual bodies that enact substance use. It is important to investigate the "addicted" body and what such individuals say about their bodies (in relation to drug use) and how they corporeally experience and constitute their drug use. In addition, the language, discourses, and images that others use to describe, frame, code, and respond to the addict's body are highly significant.

It is important to note that unlike many other acts, injecting drug use is either something one—through the body—has experienced or it is not. Although aspects of drug use can be seen as a performance, the act itself cannot be simply performed. It is experienced as an individual act even though it is accompanied by a series of social patterns and possesses a collective meaning and significance. Injecting drug use is an action or an activity enacted at and through the body, a form of bodywork that is then experienced at the level of the body. Thus the experience of drug use itself is not one that arises out of ideological forms or discursive practices or even power relations, though these are all important in explaining forms, historical occurrence and specificity, the social and political significance of drug use, and the popular and official responses to drug use and users. It does not provide for a framework that explains the intrinsically corporeal nature of drug use and addiction.

How then can we approach drug use and addiction? It seems to me that the discussion so far should encourage us to concentrate on two distinct, but interrelated, approaches. The first are those insights provided by the notion of the "somatic society" (Turner 1996) in which the imagery and symbolic role of the body are central. The second is to focus on the physical and lived body of the addict—on how addiction is constituted by the actions of the body, in pursuit and use of prohibited substances, and also by the actions of the substances in question on the body. This includes the "performance" of the body in the theater of addiction in terms of drug administration and substance use and the physical marking of the body and body parts (internally and externally) with the signs and effects of drug use and the effects of the nature of administration and injection techniques.

Images of Addiction: The Centrality of the Body

Doolie sick was an unnerving sight. The envelope of personality was gone, dissolved by his junk-hungry cells. Viscera and cells, galvanized into a loathsome insect-like activity, seemed on the point of breaking through the surface. His face was blurred, unrecognisable, at the same time shrunken and tumescent. (Burroughs 1977:58)

As stated earlier the body is central to images and narratives of addiction, and such images circulate widely through many media forms. Burroughs's key novel *Junky* (1977)[1] provides an excellent example of how the body of the addict is narrated through body images and metaphors. He explores how these narratives map onto wider social concerns and anxieties. Burroughs's characters are physically different from nonusers and look sick or diseased, their bodies bearing a set of marks of difference and addiction that manifests as deconstruction of the human body either into disease, subhumanity, or animal-like incarnations.

> His veins were mostly gone, retreated back to the bone to escape the probing needle. For a while he used arteries, which are deeper than veins and harder to hit, and for this procedure he bought special long needles. He rotated from his arms and hands to the veins of his feet. A vein will come back in time. Even so, he had to shoot in the skin about half the time. But he only gave up and "skinned" a shot after an agonising half-hour probing and poking and cleaning out the needle, which would clot with blood. (Burroughs 1977:42–43).

These powerful literary motifs are echoed in first-hand accounts of drug use collected by the British government as part of its *Talk to Frank* campaign.

> My friend has become dependent on it, he takes about 9 grams on his own per day and has become what I can only describe as a vegetable. He used to weigh about 13 stone and he now weighs about 8 stone.

> He has lost all control of his regular bodily functions like peeing, pooing, he has virtually gone see through with no colour to his skin at all. He has no strength at all, his muscle mass has been reduced to zero.[2]

In such discourses the body and the fluids it contains and expels, or in the case of addiction, ingests through consumption and injection, frequently act as metaphors and signifiers of order, disorder, orderliness, safety, danger, and threat. If we extend such analysis we can identify a range of metaphors of drug use, including disease, demonization, weakness, flaw, and decay. Such metaphors and representations reveal significant assumptions about normal (and "abnormal") behavior. In this way the addict's body may be seen as an example of how the body can be understood as a set of maps and metaphors for the wider social body, as the ravaged body of the addict is depicted in ways that aim to discipline and to promote antidrug messages. Furthermore, the centrality of the body to a "somatic society" and contemporary social theory attests to the very fact that the body has become a "problem." The regulation of the body and groups of bodies appears to be both more difficult and more desired for both individuals and authorities. The status of the self, the body, and the individual is less fixed in an era of multiple, competing, and uncertain identities. In this bodily *milieu* it is perhaps no surprise that interest should focus on the representation of all sorts of bodies across space and time.

While I acknowledge the complex and ambiguous construction of representations and their multiple meanings (Drotner 1992), I would also maintain that representations are important sites for the investigation and analysis of social, cultural, and political power and that there are important patterns in such images and representations across both time and different media (Freedberg 1989; Hall 1997; Hartley 1992). In the specific case under consideration here is the added complexity that representations and images of addiction try to render that which is invisible, and predominantly experienced as an embodied set of sensations, visible (Hickman 2002; Shilling 2007) through the presentation of symbolic notions of social and individual decay, marginalization, and assorted threats to the established order.

Images of the addict, addiction, and its associated actions are repeatedly found in popular media and cultural outputs across literature, film, television, advertising, public information campaigns, and newspapers. In this section I focus on some examples of such imagery and explore these images in relation to the theories and ideas introduced in the earlier part of the chapter.

If we take some of the key motifs of addiction and drug use we can see the emphasis placed on the body of the addict in the narration of these issues. Thus the body is represented through images that stress desolation, decay, the making of holes in the skin, the medication of the individual and society, the emergence from the body of blood and the spread of "contaminated" blood and associated blood-borne viruses through populations of users and nonusers, and the sequential breakdown of the body and body parts in terms of veins, teeth, skin, and then the major organs.

The close interplay and overlap between photographic representations and discursive constructions of problematic drug use can be further illustrated with reference to a series of photographs by Eugene Richards and Donna Ferrato entitled "Sex Workers." In this series, Richards's (2000) picture "Crack Annie," Brooklyn, 1988, is both illustrative and representative of the highly deviant notion of "crack whores" that emerged in the late 1980s and early 1990s in the United States and that became a powerful image of the degeneration of the American inner city (Green, Day, and Ward 2000). Richards's picture is accompanied by the following caption: "A young woman addicted to crack. There's no sensuality here, there's no pocket money to be earned. This is simply one of the consequences of a terrible addiction" (Richards 1990:34).

Now this is obviously going to be true for many crack users and again the aim here is not to argue that there are not links between drug use and sex work or that these links are not problematic. However, the point might be made that representations like those of Richards overlook the actual nature and experience of drug use by addicts and neglect the possibility that drug use is experienced in different ways by different users and may not always create problems for users in the ways imagined (Green, Day, and Ward 2000). I would further maintain that the images used, found, and employed often demonstrate highly recurrent themes and content, even to the point of the repetition of certain body actions and positions. For example, women and their bodies are often represented in specific ways in images of drug use just as they are in official and unofficial narratives of drug use and in interview data from the field.

The representation of women in drug photography reflects a series of key themes that are often associated with the women in other contexts and narratives. These include vulnerability, in this case to drug use, sexual availability or unreliability, drug use as something done to them by, usually, men, and the decay or threat of decay of the "natural" physical and bodily state (including beauty and youth).

Rarely are women depicted as anything but (knowing or unknowing) victims who possess little or no autonomous power or agency. Just as women are seldom represented as autonomous actors with agency in crime narratives (official, unofficial, and fictional), so they are seldom represented as dealers, instigators, or introducers to substance use. So while some research has demonstrated that some female heroin users are first injected by their male partners, it is a surprise that such research can be directly associated, in the same article that reports it, with vampires, "dope-fiends," and heroin injecting (Tompkins and Sheard 2007:17).

> Those who inject heroin often say that the heroin rush is better than sex, and many female heroin users are first injected by their male partners. Both vampire and drug fiend carry a ghostly pallor, sunken cheekbones, a haunted look of despair and self-loathing . . . symbolic of the prison of addiction and dependency.

The set of images discussed in this chapter, though far from exhaustive, is characteristic of the type of images that tend to dominate representations of what is sometimes called heavy-end drug use (Brain, Parker, and Bottomley 1998). The photographers, commentators, legislators, and those charged with delivering public policies appear to be drawn to the apparently desperate and destructive aspects of such drug use and are happy to focus on a mixture of sex, drugs, and criminality. Resonant and powerful as such images are, they illustrate the limited utility of photography in reporting and portraying "life" and aspects of the social precisely because the focus tends to be always on the margins, the danger and the destruction.

Katovich (1998:277) notes that although the focus of the "war on drugs" periodically changes, the images rarely do, and he argues that the "reality of illegal drugs as social objects has always been dependent on how people agreed to define such objects" and the substantial meaning of illegal drugs emerges in the process of creating responses to them. For Hickman (2002:122), such strategies of envisioning addiction do not emerge from a void and have a long history that reflects a range of social and historical processes. One central theme throughout is that of the "other," which often acts as central in representations of drug use, and cultural products frequently demonstrate the composite effect of representations that place the war on drug outside of U.S. or Western borders, construct the drug user and dealer as depraved and deranged, and avoid engagement in the social, political, and legal factors that shape drug use (Boyd 2002; Kohn 1997).

In 2004 an antidrug campaign was launched by the Metropolitan Police across London using billboards, public house beer mats, and flyers showing six pictures of a female drug addict. These images were derived from police photographs taken over an eight-year period, and they map the physical effects and impacts of her drug use, her transformation from a "pretty blonde" to a "cadaver in a wig." This Metropolitan Police campaign was directed at the capital's estimated forty-five thousand crack cocaine "addicts" with accompanying slogan "Don't let drug dealers change the face of your neighbourhood."[3] This was an undeniably powerful campaign, visually striking and full of impact. However, it draws heavily on the suggestion that there is not much worse for a woman than to prematurely age and lose her looks, and it utilizes a marketing strategy that draws on gender stereotypes emphasizing that drugs make individual women *look bad*, unlike substances used to enhance physical appearance. The images also highlight the metaphorical links among the body, physical damage, and damage to community order and integrity. Such campaigns raise interesting issues about drug use and embodiment, bodily pleasures, and perceived risks. The campaign overtly links both bodily decay and community disorder through the representation of the (perceived) effects of individual drug use and the possibility of community decay and disintegration.

Images of drug use frequently suggest strong geographical links between drug use, urban spaces, and social order, indicating that drugs and their availability are somehow written into the geography of the city. Burroughs (1977) notes that in ways similar to how a geologist can read a landscape for signs of oil, a junky can read the cityscape for signs of junk. These signs are located in areas of the city where artificial and prosthetic body parts can be found—limbs, wigs, and dental mechanics—along with body-masking substances such as perfumes, essential oils, and pomades, locations in which "dubious business enterprise meets Skid Row" (Burroughs 1977:111). Thus "certain signs indicate the near presence of junk. Junk is often found adjacent to ambiguous or transitional neighborhoods" (Burroughs, 1977:111). Such representations resonate with the discursive and social construction of space in contemporary cities around crime and drug use. The notion that "junky downtown" (Lees 1998:246) streets are clearly mapped out in geographic space is a focus of a number of studies conducted in recent years that explore the processes through which social space and specific urban environments become viewed as "dangerous places" (Fraser 1996; Lees 1998; Pile, Brook, and Mooney 1998) or more complex "drugscapes" (Tempalski and McQuie 2008). There is here a close relationship between certain types of representations (literary, academic, criminal justice) that demonstrate the close interplay among lived experience, such representations, discursive practice and social and political attitudes, values, and public policy. Furthermore, such discussions also alert us to the way in which city spaces can be termed representational spaces in which certain images and representations tend to be displayed (van Loon 1997).

In similar ways others have shown how the body of the racial other (Murji 1999; Sharma and Sharma 2000) is employed in the construction of urban space as one that can be characterized as racially contested and as a consequence "dangerous" in particular ways (violent, predatory crime, drug use, social disorder) for certain groups (police officers, forces of "law and order," the "good citizen"). These are powerful narratives and they are reflected back to us in official discussions of the "drug problem."

The norms and values of the poorest communities are anti-authoritarian and tend towards lawbreaking, therefore are open to drug use. Because of this organisations which might challenge drug use either do not exist or are not supported by local people. (Home Office 2003:4)

Fitzgerald (2002:380) argues that the images found in drug photography reproduce drug users as "strange, suffering and powerless victims" creating problems for drug users who may wish to deviate from the identity of suffering or mobilize new or different identities for political or other purposes, and he notes that there is rarely a face "for an ordinary, living drug user, only a suffering or a monstrous, freakish, diseased Other." In many ways these recurrent images are critical as they can be seen as categorizing the drug user as someone who looks *like this*.

Figure 20.2 illustrates how the image of the addict can come to represent a site of social order and chaos as reflected in bodily disorder and chaos. In what Fitzgerald (2002:369) calls "drug photography" we can further explore the tensions, complexities, and problems of "making visible" a social problem (through, for example, social realism in film or documentary photography as well as the meanings of these representations [socially, politically, morally]).

As Fitzgerald (2002:374) argues, "There is a tendency in drug photography to attempt to make images of dark, seedy, secret worlds resulting in the 'Othering' of the individual and in the development of a range of preexisting, citational images of drug use that then come to inform and define what might be called the landscape of authentic drug photography." For example, in figure 20.2 the injecting drug user is portrayed as the ultimate symbol of both addiction and individual and collective moral, social, and political collapse.

For Weimar (2003:268) the "symbols associated with addiction helped separate drug users from mainstream society. Arguably the most recognizable and powerful symbol of addiction is the hypodermic syringe, a symbol that denotes heroin addiction." Such images focus on bodily damage, deprivation, blood, and injection. In these ways, these images utilize dominant framing techniques and thus, "rather than just depicting a technical method of drug administration, the images of the injecting scene has a number of functions" (2002:379). It can be a form of narrative disclosure, it can categorize, individualize, or isolate a character. Importantly, the injection scene effectively distances the drug users from "normality." The power of the image of the injecting drug user is critical to establishing the absolute violation of self and the social. For many (Duterte et al. 2003; Manderson 1995; Vitellone 2003), images of injecting drug use arouse immediate waves of discomfort and distaste as the syringe acts as the ultimate boundary violation, reinforcing Douglas's idea of pollution and taboo, and as such delineates the boundary between social inclusion, exclusion, and deviance.

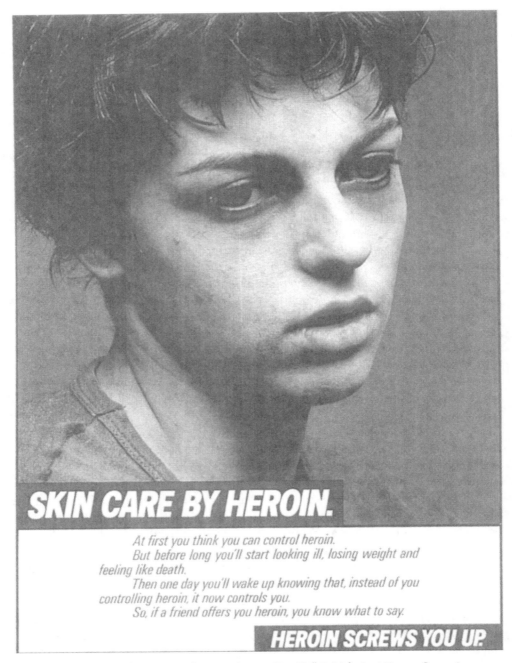

Figure 20.2. Embodied Drug Use: "Heroin Screws You Up," British Anti-Drugs Campaign (Television and Poster), Mid-1980s.

Conclusion

Images of addiction that feature the body and body parts in various states of decay, decomposition, and distress are often powerful and shocking. The addict's body is frequently presented as a series of certain types of bodies that are usually sick, diseased, contagious, criminal, medicalized, and pathologized. The body as both spectacle of horror and fascination. Social and cultural theory—in its widest sense—provides a useful set of analytical frameworks and ideas for consideration of the social significance of the body, but we need to keep the "real" and lived body clearly in sight too. These images vary over time and, perhaps, have different meanings and values attached to them in different media, but the central image remains constant—one in which the unruly and undisciplined body becomes disfigured by the use of dangerous intoxicants and unhygienic administration methods.

This chapter has focused on the analysis of images of addiction and of the addict's body as a way of exploring both the significance of and the representational power of the body and body images and the ways in which representations of addiction and the addict work to both create and recreate persistent and recurrent images of the addict that reinforce notions of drug use and social disorder. In this sense the addict's body becomes one that symbolically represents a set of social anxieties and concerns about not just bodies but the wider community and social order. Images of drug use are or can be mobilized as part of the overall process of disciplining the self in line with "intensified mandates for self-control" where attempts are made to expel unhealthy meanings of the self through acts of patrolling the borders of identity via projections onto the physical figure of the drug user (Crawford 1994:1347). I think these trends can only become more intense in the multiple media cultures of contemporary society as the tensions between unrestrained consumption, the personal and the self, and social order and discipline become ever more pronounced.

NOTES

1. Burroughs is one of a number of authors we could focus on here, including, for example, Irvine Welsh, *Trainspotting* (1993), Hubert Selby Jr, *Requiem for a Dream* (1979), Nelson Algren, *The Man with the Golden Arm* (2000), or, more recently, Stephen Elliot, *Happy Baby* (2005).

2. See Talk to Frank: Your Stories, http://www.talktofrank.com/article/aspx?id=244. Last accessed 31 October 2008.

3. See London Metropolitan Police, "Drugs Action and Advice," available at http://www.met.police.uk/drugs/advertising.htm.

REFERENCES

Berthelot, J. (1986), "Sociological Discourses and the Body," *Theory, Culture, and Society*, 3, 3, pp. 155–64.

Booth Davies, J. (1997), *The Myth of Addiction*, 2nd edition. London, Routledge.

Boyd, Susan (2002), "Media Constructions of Illegal Drugs, Users, and Sellers: A Closer Look at *Traffic*," *International Journal of Drug Policy*, 13, pp. 397–407.

Brain, K., Parker, H., and Bottomley, T. (1998), *Evolving Crack Cocaine Careers: New Users, Quitters, and Long-Term Combination Drug Users in N.W. England*. London, Home Office.

Brook, B. (1999), *Feminist Perspectives on the Body*. London, Longman.

Burkitt, I. (1999), *Bodies of Thought: Embodiment, Identity, and Modernity*. London, Sage.

Burroughs, W. (1977), *Junky*. London, Penguin.

Cocteau, J. (1990), *Opium: The Diary of His Cure*. London, Peter Owen.

Crawford, R. (1994), "The Boundaries of the Self and the Unhealthy Other: Reflections on Health, Culture, and AIDS," *Social Science and Medicine*, 38, 10, pp. 1347–65.

Cregan, K. (2006), *The Sociology of the Body*. London, Sage.

Crossley, N. (1995), "Merleau-Ponty, the Elusive Body, and Carnal Sociology," *Body and Society*, 1, 1, pp. 43–66.

Crossley, N. (2001),. *The Social Body: Habit, Identity, and Desire*. London, Sage.

Crossley, N. (2007), "Researching Embodiment by Way of 'Body Techniques,'" *Sociological Review*, 55, pp. 80–94.

Douglas, M. (1966), *Purity and Danger*. London, Routledge.

Drotner, K. (1992), "Modernity and Media Panics" in Skovmand, M. and Schroder, K., *Media Cultures: Reappraising Transnational Media*. London, Routledge, pp. 42–64.

Duterte, Micheline, Hemphill, Kristin, Murphy, Terrence, and Murphy, Sheigla (2003), "Tragic Beauties: Heroin Images and Heroin Users," *Contemporary Drug Problems*, 30, pp. 595–617.

Ettorre, E. (1998), "Re-Shaping the Space between Bodies and Culture: Embodying the Biomedicalised Body," *Sociology of Health and Illness*, 20, 4, pp. 548–55.

Featherstone, M. (ed.) (2000), *Body Modification: An Introduction*. London, Sage.

Featherstone, M., Hepworth, M., and Turner, B. (1991), *The Body: Social Process and Cultural Theory*. London, Sage.

Fitzgerald, John (2002), "Drug Photography and Harm Reduction: Reading John Ranard," *International Journal of Drug Policy*, 13, pp. 369–85.

Fraser, P. (1996), "Social and Spatial Relationships and the 'Problem' Inner City: Moss-Side in Manchester," *Critical Social Policy*, 16, pp. 43–65.

Freedberg, D. (1989), *The Power of Images*. Chicago, University of Chicago Press.

Giddens, A. (1991), *Modernity and Self-Identity*. Cambridge, Polity.

Green, A., Day, S., and Ward, H. (2000), "Crack Cocaine and Prostitution in London in the 1990s," *Sociology of Health and Illness*, 22, 1, pp. 27–39.

Grosz, E. (1994), *Volatile Bodies: Toward a Corporeal Feminism*. Bloomington, Indiana University Press.

Hall, S. (1997), *Representation: Cultural Representations and Signifying Practices*. Buckingham, Open University Press.

Hartley, J. (1992), *The Politics of Pictures: The Creation of the Public in the Age of Popular Media*. London, Routledge.

Hickman, T. (2002), "Heroin Chic: The Visual Culture of Narcotic Addiction," *Third Text*, 16, pp. 119–36.

Home Office (2003), *Drugs and Community Development*. London, Home Office.

Howson, A. and Inglis, D. (2001), "The Body in Sociology: Tensions Inside and Outside Sociological Thought," *Sociological Review*, 49, 3, pp. 297–317.

Huggins, R. (2006), "Mapping Addiction: Embodiment, Drug Use, and Representation" in D. Waskul and P. Vannini (eds.), *Body/Embodiment: Symbolic Interaction and the Sociology of the Body*. London: Ashgate, 165–80.

Huggins, R. (2007), "Systemic 'Normalisation'? Mapping and Interpreting Policy Responses to Illicit Drug Use" in Manning, P. (ed.), *Drugs and Popular Culture: Drugs, Media, and Identity in Contemporary Society*. Devon, UK, Willan, pp. 260–78.

Jacobson, C. (1999), "Junkies and Speed Freaks," *Creative Review*, 19, 9.

Katovich, Michael (1998), "Media Technologies, Images of Drugs, and an Evocative Telepresence," *Qualitative Sociology*, 21, 3, pp. 277–97.

Kohn, M. (1997), "The Chemical Generation and Its Ancestors: Dance Crazes and Drug Panics across Eight Decades," *International Journal of Drug Policy*, 8, 3, pp. 137–42.

Kristeva, J. (1982), *Powers of Horror: An Essay on Abjection*. New York, Columbia University Press.

Lees, L. (1998), "Urban Renaissance and the Street: Space of Control and Constestation" in Fyfe, N. (ed.), *Images of the Street: Planning, Identity, and Control in Public Space*. London, Routledge.

Levine, H. (1978), "The Discovery of Addiction," *Journal of Studies on Alcohol*, 39, 1, pp. 143–77.

Manderson, D. (1995), "Metamorphoses: Clashing Symbols in the Social Construction of Drugs," *Journal of Drug Issues*, 25, 4, pp. 799–817.

Merleau-Ponty, M. (2004) [1948], *The World of Perception*. London, Routledge.

Murji, K. (1999), "White Lines: Culture, 'Race', and Drugs" in South, N. (ed.), *Drugs: Cultures, Controls, and Everyday Life*. Sage, London, pp. 49–65.

Nead, L. (1992), *Female Nude: Art, Obscenity, and Sexuality*. London, Routledge.

Nettleton, S. and Watson, J. (1998), *The Body in Everyday Life*. London, Routledge.

Newton, T. (2003), "Truly Embodied Sociology: Marrying the Social and the Biological?" *Sociological Review*, 51, 1, pp. 20–42.

Pile, S., Brook, C., and Mooney, G. (eds.) (1998), *Unruly Cities? Order/Disorder*. London, Routledge/Open University.

Plumridge, E. and Chetwynd, J. (1999), "Identity and the Social Construction of Risk: Injecting Drug Use," *Sociology of Health and Illness*, 21, 3, pp. 329–43.

Reith, G. (2004), "Consumption and Its Discontents," *British Journal of Sociology*, 55, 2, pp. 283–300.

Richards, E. (2000), "Crack Annie," *Aperture*, 160, Summer, p. 2.

Richards, E. and Ferrato, D. (1990), "Sex Workers," *Aperture*, 121, Fall, pp. 30–35.

Sharma, S. and Sharma A. (2000), "'So Far So Good . . .': *La Haine* and the Poetics of the Everyday," in *Theory, Culture, and Society*, 17, 3, pp. 103–16.

Shildrick, M. (2002), *Embodying the Monster: Encounters with the Vulnerable Self*. London, Sage.

Shilling, C. (1993), *The Body and Social Theory*. London, Sage.

Shilling, C. (2001), "Embodiment, Experience, and Theory: In Defence of the Sociological Tradition," *Sociological Review*, 49, 3, 327–44.

Shilling, C. (2003), *The Body and Social Theory*, 2nd edition. London, Sage.

Shilling, C. (2007), "Sociology and the Body: Classical Traditions and New Agendas," *Sociological Review*, 55, S1, pp. 1–18.

Shiner, M. and Newburn, T. (1997), "Definitely, Maybe Not? The Normalisation of Recreational Drug Use amongst Young People," *Sociology*, 31, 3, pp. 511–29.

Sulkunen, P. (2009), *The Saturated Society: Governing Risk and Lifestyles in Consumer Culture*. London: Sage.

Synnott, R. (1993), *The Body Social*. London, Routledge.

Taubin, A. (1995), "Chilling and Very Hot," *Sight and Sound*, 11, pp. 16–19.

Tempalski, B. and McQuie, H. (2008), "Drugscapes and the Role of Place and Space in Injection Drug Use–Related HIV Risk Environments," *International Journal of Drug Policy*, 20, 1, pp. 4–13.

Tompkins, C. and Sheard, L. (2007), "Bodily Harm," *Druglink*, Jan/Feb, pp. 16–17.

Turner, B. (1984), *The Body and Society*. Oxford, Blackwell.

Turner, B. (1991), "Recent Developments in the Theory of the Body" in Featherstone, M., Hepworth, M., and Turner, B., *The Body: Social Process and Cultural Theory*. London, Sage.

Turner, B. (1992), *Regulating Bodies: Essays in Medical Sociology*. London, Routledge.

Turner, B. (1996), *The Body and Society*, 2nd edition. London, Sage.

Turner, B. (2003), "Social Fluids: Metaphors and Meanings," *Body and Society*, 9, 1, pp. 1–10.

Turner, B. (2006), "Body," *Theory, Culture, and Society*, 23, pp. 223–29.

Turner, P. (ed.) (1985), *American Images: Photography 1945–1980*. Harmondsworth, Penguin.

Valentine, K. and Fraser, S. (2008), "Trauma, Damage, and Pleasure: Rethinking Problematic Drug Use," *International Journal of Drug Policy*, 19, pp. 410–16.

van Loon, J. (1997), "Chronotopes: Of/in the Televisualization of the 1992 Los Angeles Riots," *Theory, Culture, and Society*, 14, 2, pp. 89–104.

Vitellone, N. (2003), "The Syringe as Prosthetic," *Body and Society*, 9, 3, pp. 37–52.

Waldby, C. (1996), *AIDS and the Body Politic: Biomedicine and Sexual Difference*. London, Routledge.

Warbuton, D. (1978), "Internal Pollution," *Journal of Biosocial Science*, 10, pp. 309–19.

Weimar, D. (2003), "Drugs-as-a-Disease: Heroin, Metaphors, and Identity in Nixon's Drug War," *Janus Head*, 6, 2, pp. 260–81.

West, R. (2006), *Theory of Addiction*. Oxford, Addiction Press/Blackwell.

Williams, S. and Bendelow, G. (1998), *The Lived Body: Sociological Themes, Embodied Issues*. London, Routledge.

Young, J. (1971), *The Drug Takers: The Social Meaning of Drug Use*. London, Paladin.

Young, J. (1981), "The Myth of Drugtakers in the Mass Media" in Cohen, S. and Young, J. (eds.), *The Manufacture of News: Social Problems, Deviance, and the Mass Media*, revised edition. London, Constable, pp. 326–34.

||||||||||||||||||||||||||||||||||||||||||||||||||||||||||||||||||||||||||||||||

21

The Ana Sanctuary
Women's Pro-Anorexic Narratives in Cyberspace

Karen Dias [1]

In this paper I explore cyberspace as a space in which women who are struggling with anorexia can potentially find sanctuary from the surveillance and regulatory mechanisms of control of the public sphere. I explore the narratives of women who create and visit pro-anorexia, or pro-ana, websites. Taking seriously the voices of these women can be viewed as a transgressive act, in contrast to hegemonic biomedical and psychiatric discourses of anorexia that portray women with eating disorders as "irrational" and "in denial" of their behavior, and pathologize and medicalize their experiences. However, through their narratives we see how dominant cultural scripts about their bodies are reproduced, negotiated, and/or resisted. We can also observe women's engagement in the interpretation of their own experiences. The transient and fluid nature of pro-ana websites (in response to the backlash they receive) also illustrates the resilience of the women who seek them out and (re)create them. Just as the body is a site of struggle (and resistance), so too there are struggles over where and how women's stories of their body can be told.

Given that women's bodies and experiences of embodiment are subjected to relentless surveillance in the public sphere (Bray and Colebrook "Haunted"), cyberspace can potentially provide a space for women to meet safely as opposed to traditional public spaces and places in the built environment.[2] Cyberspace can be conceptualized as an alternative space for women with eating and body issues, one that may serve as a sanctuary.[3] Since the public realm is regulated by banishing from sight behaviors that are considered abnormal, repugnant or deviant (Duncan), cyberspace can provide a space to escape the scrutiny of others (though perhaps not self-scrutiny), as well as the opportunity to interact with others struggling with eating disorders. This could be helpful since the early stages of anorexia are usually marked by extreme isolation, secrecy, and disconnection. Ironically, cyberspace is a public space. While in contemporary Western culture, not interacting within

---

From the *Journal of International Women's Studies*, Vol. 4, #2, April 2003, pp. 31–35. © 2003 Journal of International Women's Studies. Reprinted with permission of the Journal of International Women's Studies.

the public spaces of society is considered abnormal and unhealthy, occupying public spaces and revealing one's abnormality or deviance is considered equally if not more unhealthy (Bankey). The backlash these websites have received from the media and professionals in the field, which I will discuss later in this article, has been extensive. The stigma and shame that come with both diagnostic labeling and society's misunderstanding of eating "disorders" contribute to women's need to find creative ways to connect and find support. In contrast to the dominant discourses of anorexia and eating disorders in general, my research is informed by these women's narratives in an attempt to access alternative definitions and understandings that they may have of their own mental states (Parr 183).[4] Narratives may embody, reproduce, and/or alter cultural scripts; they may also push at the boundaries of what is unsayable and untellable in particular contexts (Chase 24). What women struggling with anorexia may not be able (or ready) to say to family, friends or professionals, they may be able to say in the safer and less confronting space of cyberspace.

Third Wave Feminism

The issue of body image has been named as a central issue in third wave feminism because all women, feminist or not, "offer heartfelt and complex emotions on the topic" (Richards 198). Third wave feminists have directed much of their attention to the impact that popular culture has on their subjective experiences, rather than adopting legal or political strategies, because they see "the media and entertainment industries [are their] most visible 'oppressors'" (Richards 198) and an analysis and critique of popular culture as important to the political struggle towards female empowerment. Popular culture, "fueled by feminist backlash and capitalism, has focused a great deal of attention on young women and their bodies," propagating contradictory messages (that often use co-opted feminist language) of female control and agency alongside images of unattainable feminine beauty (Carter 120-1). For many young women, their bodies have become "arenas for feelings [they] don't deal with, for unresolved traumas and injustices" (Edut xx). The epidemic of eating disorders and body dissatisfaction among women in Western industrialized countries (and increasingly globally) reflects the consequences of these contradictions. Third wave feminists' narratives, like those of pro-anorexics, illustrate the dilemmas young women today face in negotiating culture's stifling emphasis on hegemonic feminine beauty ideals while trying to enact agency through negotiations of their identities.

A question I grapple with in my research is whether women's behavior on these websites may be considered feminist without being overtly political, and conversely whether it can be considered political without being overtly feminist. I see this dilemma as a central tension in third wave feminism, especially in regard to the second wave critique that young women today are self-absorbed and inactive (Baumgardner and Richards 86) and apathetic to the work of the second wave (Walker xxxi). Third wave feminists are attempting to "contest a politics of purity that would separate political activism from cultural production" (Heywood and Drake, "We Learn" 51) and recognize the importance of individual experiences and personal narratives to speak to social and political dynamics. Third wave feminists address the "need for greater acceptance of complexities, ambiguities, and multiple locations, and highlight the dangers of reduction into dichotomous thinking" (Pinterics 16). They locate their theory in everyday experiences, involving the negotiation with and recognition of multiple identities and femininities. Though third wave feminism may not have a clear definition of itself or of feminism, it is a movement that is encouraging and creating solidarity among women on the basis of challenging dominant power relations. This article reflects upon the connection and solidarity created through pro-anorexia websites which may serve to challenge and subvert these power relations.

Methods

The notion of "ethical" Internet research is a current and ongoing topic of debate. The Internet provides many ambiguous areas in terms of what constitutes ethical research of widely accessible material. Because many on-line sites are openly accessible to the public, obtaining informed consent is often not done.[5] However, care needs to be taken to exercise that the "fair use" of contributions to public forums respects participants' privacy and protects them from harm. My research is a feminist poststructuralist discourse analysis of the data I have collected from various pro-ana websites since September 2001. For the purposes of this article I have chosen to highlight narratives that illustrate one major theme that emerged continually on these websites: alternative discourses of anorexia and eating disorders in general. In order to guarantee participants' confidentiality, I have removed all names and pseudonyms. I have only accessed publicly available information from pro-ana websites; that is, I have not accessed any forums or chat rooms that required a password, pseudonym or my participation. I have not asked participants any direct questions, nor have I directly interacted with them in any way. Though most of the links to the websites I am referencing are no longer active—for reasons I will address later in this article—I have chosen not to provide any links in referencing my sources in order to further protect the women's privacy, referencing them anonymously. I have, however, referenced some narratives that derive from a forum provided by an eating disorder support organization discussing pro-anorexia websites. This organization is not connected with, nor allows, links to any pro-anorexia websites.

I also want to acknowledge the controversial nature of this subject matter. I have professional work experience as a counselor working with this group, as well as personal experience with disordered eating. I have sensitivity and empathy towards women with eating disorders, which I bring to my work as a social scientist and researcher. My intent, by putting these women's narratives at the center of my research is to listen to and take seriously their voices; voices which are subversive because they exist.

Pro-Anorexia Websites

Pro-anorexia (or pro-ana) websites are a genre of websites disseminating information about eating disorders, primarily anorexia nervosa, and providing girls and women with a forum to discuss and share information about ana.[6] There is usually a warning on the first page, alerting viewers that the site contains pro-anorexia information, to enter at their own risk, and not to enter if they are recovering from an eating disorder.

> Welcome to this Pro-Ana (Mia)[7] Support Group. We are about encouragement, support, and assistance, to others like us who live with an ED and suffer with the problems that go along with it. . . . This site does not encourage that you develop an eating disorder. This is a site for those who ALREADY have an eating disorder and do not wish to go into recovery. Some material in here may be triggering. If you do not already have an eating disorder, better it is that you do not develop one now. You SHOULD leave. (Anonymous, Pro-Anorexia Site, 25 Oct. 2002; emphasis in original)

Most sites make it quite clear that their purpose is to support those who are struggling with an eating disorder, and to provide a space, free from judgment, where they can share ideas and offer encouragement to those who are not yet ready to recover. Some of the homepages of these websites display images of emaciated and skeletal bodies.

The primary purpose of these sites seems, on first contact, to to be to promote and support anorexia, including detailed "how to" sections. These sites tend to have common features such as: bulletin boards and chat rooms; diaries (website owners post their diaries online, often keeping viewers up-to-date daily on calorie intake or avoidance, relapses, recommitments, *etc.*); tips and tricks (*e.g.* ideas for dieting, food avoidance, distractions from hunger, *etc.*); trigger pictures or thinspirations (pictures of ultra-thin, emaciated bodies to inspire loyalty to the regime and distractions from hunger); and, links to other pro-ana sites, often in the form of web-rings.[8] Some also have poetry, lyrics, stories, treatment information and general information about anorexia, and related issues.

Most of the images of thinness and emaciation common on the sites are mainstream pictures of celebrities or fashion models, sometimes collages of both. Some mimic themes commonly found in advertising, such as dismemberment, where bodies are hacked apart, and certain body parts are focused upon.

If the models and celebrities were not familiar to us, it would be very difficult to discern between the "deviant" bodies of the anorexics and the "normal" and "acceptable" bodies of the models. All of the images highlight the glaringly contradictory messages women receive about appearance and their bodies.

Backlash and Flaming

Pro-anorexia websites have caused a huge uproar in the media, the medical community, among parents of anorexics and among recovering anorexics. In July 2001 an American eating disorder advocacy group, ANAD (Anorexia Nervosa and Associated Disorders), made pleas to servers like Yahoo to take down these sites, with 115 sites shut down four days later (Reaves). Many other servers followed suit, with several sites disappearing daily. It is very difficult to locate pro-ana sites consistently—sites found one day are often shut down the next. All the original twenty-seven sites I have been researching since September 2001 are now gone. Yet new sites keep emerging, sometimes only accessible to those that apply directly to the site-owner—one strategy these women use to avoid having their sites shut down. The women visiting these sites are well aware of the animosity towards them. Many sites post letters from the media that condemn their behavior, sometimes as a form of inspiration to keep going. The ability to resist and subvert the policing of web servers and critics attests to the fluidity of these spaces and the resilience of their users. The paradox of theorizing these sites as potential safe spaces for these women to meet and support each other is that ultimately these women do not have control over these spaces.

In mainstream media critiques of pro-ana sites, the website owners are blamed for causing and promoting a "deadly disease," and the "horrors" of the contents of their sites are displayed and discussed. What are absent from these critiques are the women's own voices, as well as mention of the broader and more complex historical, political, and social factors contributing to the epidemic of eating disorders in the first place. The following comes from a forum user, not a journalist:

> You people are seriously sick! You're nothing but slaves to the media. You say you do this for YOU to make yourself feel better. Bullsh*t. You wouldn't feel bad about yourselves if you didn't have a distorted perception of perfection. You people need to do a hell of a lot more than lose weight, you need to get some self-esteem. Go to counseling. Being thin is not going to make you happy. Everyone has problems and you think being anorexic is going to make them easier?? . . .The makers of this site ought to be ashamed of themselves. (S.C. a.R.E.D. Forum User, 2001–2002; emphasis in original)

Congruent with medical and psychiatric discourses about the "irrational" and "distorted" (individual) thinking patterns of those with eating disorders, we are left with the impression that the problem lies here, in these individual women and the "outrageous" practices that they endorse via the Internet.

The assumption, evident in most popular notions about eating disorders, is that these women are conforming to dominant notions of femininity. The American Psychiatric Association's diagnostic criteria for anorexia nervosa outline women's refusal to maintain a "normal" body weight, intense fear of gaining weight or becoming fat, and disturbance in the way body weight or shape is experienced.[9] Yet what is not acknowledged is the extreme fat prejudice in Western society, and the intolerance for a diversity of sizes and shapes that may drive women and girls to extreme behaviors to avoid discrimination:

> Let me tell you something. . . . I've been fat all my life (it hasn't been that long, I know. I'm only 15), but now I'm trying to change that. People with ED's are everywhere. I realized this when I had one (bulimia). I know two girls, not including myself, that are bulimic, and at least one that is anorexic. I live in a TINY town, and it is very uncommon to find so many people in the same age group that are suffering from the same things. I never knew about my friends' problems; and even though I do now, we never talk about them. Being overweight and being teased, left out, criticized, etc. can screw up a little girl's mind. I wouldn't tell anyone to do what I do, but if they do it on their own, they have their reasons. All my friends with ED's, including myself, are happier thin than they were fat. Insults and cruelty are easier to handle if they come from yourself. (S.C.a.R.E.D. Forum User, 2001–2002)

What is also not discussed are the normative dieting and weight loss behaviors that may also be viewed as conforming to hegemonic notions of femininity, but in ways that are socially sanctioned and seen as legitimate.

> Let me tell you girls, I am in great shape, but NOT anorexic. I am 5'4 120 lbs. There is not an inch of fat on me. I eat healthy and work out regularly. I have a wonderfully fit & curvaceous body. I am proof that you can have a great body and not starve yourself into a bony skeleton. (S.C.a.R.E.D. Forum User, 2001–2002)

Rarely mentioned or taken into consideration in mainstream interpretations of these websites are other possible causes of their behavior, aside from conformity and "slavery to the media," such as sexual or physical abuse, oppression, discrimination, harassment, violence, or trauma.[10]

Pro-Anorexia Narratives

What does it mean that these women are exposing very personal narratives of their struggles with their bodies, in a very public space?

> Why am I doing this, letting my self be vulnerable to the world wide audience of the web? because I want to help people battle this, and I want to win my own battle. I don't know if this will actually help anyone, and I don't expect too many people would be that interested in my insanity but I don't care what people think I am going to say my peace. ***Plus I can be totally anonymous*** (Anonymous)

These women, unlike the portrayals of them as being in denial, are actually quite articulate and seemingly aware of their circumstances:

What does pro-ED (pro-ana) mean to me?

People with eating disorders are isolated and surrounded by people who don't understand what we think or feel. . . . Some of us need our EDs still and aren't ready to recover. Eating disorders are dangerous, and ignorance compounds that. We can't go ask for safe advice from non-EDs without a risk of being hospitalized or shunned. Pro-ED to me means understanding that there's no shame in how we are, and acceptance that this is how we will continue to be for an indefinite period of time. It means support for us so we don't have to deal with this alone. It means nonjudgmental help so we can survive and remain as safe and healthy as possible while maintaining the behaviors we still need to keep. Pro-ED to me does not mean recruiting, encouraging or teaching others to be anorexic, encouraging excessively dangerous practices, or starving to death. (Anonymous)

Some of the themes illustrated in these narratives came up repeatedly on pro-anorexia websites: not feeling understood by those around them; feeling out of control; feeling isolated and in pain; using the eating disorder as a form of coping and a security blanket; recognizing that they still need that security blanket even though they are aware of the potential dangers of anorexia; needing support and connection; feeling ambivalent towards both ana and recovery; and, resisting dominant interpretations of their experiences of disordered eating.

In speaking about this phenomenon with therapists who work with this population and women who have recovered from eating disorders, I have heard such comments as:

- "Well, it is not like this has not been going on behind closed doors anyway. It is probably shocking to those who were not previously aware of this behavior."
- "Even before these websites it was possible to get plenty of tips and tricks from books, movies, magazines, biographies, and other girls."
- "When I was going through my eating disorder it certainly would have been comforting to have people to talk to before I was ready to get help."
- "These websites seem to defy the behavior typical of anorexics, who usually keep their behavior very secretive."

In the therapeutic community it is increasingly recognized that there are different stages of readiness for change.[11] In the early stages of anorexia, before a person is ready to accept help, treatment is usually not very successful. This means that women typically do not get support unless they are forced into treatment or until they speak to a professional. The support that these women provide one another on the Internet around this issue is something quite new.[12] Women can access less intimidating support before they are ready to take the step of seeking face-to-face support.

One of the assumptions evident in the hostile critiques of these websites is that the young women's "deviant" behavior is going on because they are not under the supervision of "legitimate" authorities. However, it is widely known by professionals and those suffering with eating disorders that tips and tricks are widely available through autobiographies, textbooks, health care practitioners, and the media, and that competition and tips flourish in endorsed treatment settings. The following extract is from an interview between a researcher and a pro-ana website owner:

> Q: Many of your sites have links to pro-recovery websites. . . . Do you find that even pro-recovery websites can be triggering, or helpful in maintaining your disorder?
>
> A: Yes . . . as a matter of fact, the first site i went to was [URL removed]. by far that is the most triggering site i've been to, its made by an EX-anorexic. and it's a RECOVERY site. i learned more from that site than any PRO site could offer. (Anonymous; emphasis in original)

Another major paradox with eating disorders is that in order to access treatment, women have to be clinically diagnosed by a physician and often have to meet rigid criteria for diagnosis and admittance. In other words, if their health is not seriously compromised and their weight is not low enough, they do not qualify for treatment unless they can afford private services. Many girls and women I have worked with were well aware of this pattern, and many actually avoided seeking treatment for fear of rejection. Many who are quite ill are turned away from services because doctors determine that their condition is not immediately life-threatening. The success rate of treatment programs for anorexia is very low—not solely the result of the failure of specific treatment techniques, but largely because once anorexia reaches a critical and chronic stage it is much harder to recover.

Studies of recovery from disordered eating have been conducted almost exclusively within a medical model that seeks causes for, and evaluates treatment of, clinically diagnosed eating disorders.[13] The studies assume that there must be causes for eating disorders and that their discovery will solve the problem of recovery. They also assume that professional intervention is essential to the recovery process. However, many recovered anorexics say the events, people, and processes outside therapy were generally those most relevant to their recovery (Beresin et al.). What is almost completely absent from the literature is a focus on positive outcome indicators, that is, the factors that are most likely to assist recovery. The focus on the negative, that is, what might prevent recovery is because positive outcome indicators tend to resist measurement. They are most likely to come in narrative form, with all its complexities (Garret). Also absent in almost every study are the patients' own words. Clinical studies of anorexia and recovery which have trusted patients' ideas and given them voice have provided far richer understandings.[14]

One phenomenon common on these websites is a practice common in Narrative Therapy—the externalization of the "eating disorder voice" (Epston et al.). Clients are sometimes encouraged to separate the voice that encourages the destructive behavior of the eating disorder from themselves, in order to gain some psychological distance and recognize that the eating disorder does not define them. This technique is used on pro-anorexia websites when participants name ana a friend and/or enemy that they all have in common and toward whom they feel ambivalent. It is often illustrated, as is sometimes the case in narrative therapy, in the form of letter writing:

This is a letter I wrote to my Anorexia. I've never posted here before, and I think this pretty much sums up my problems, my thoughts and feelings. Please post a reply. I feel so alone and attacked. I need someone to understand.

Dear Ana,

I feel trapped by you. . . . Where is the love you promised? The acceptance? When will I feel like I'm finally in control? Why is it that the more I control what I eat and weigh, the more out of control I feel? As I peel away the layers of fat, the old problems resurface . . . the depression, the loneliness, the cutting, the insomnia. Why can't I just be normal? Lose another pound, wear a smaller size, feel a new bone . . . you are all I have left . . . now I'm addicted to you. You are a mirage. A vision of something that doesn't exist. . . . You are my only friend, my biggest enemy. I worship you, and you destroy me . . . (S.C.a.R.E.D. Forum User, 2001–2002; emphasis in original)

The second narrative shows that this woman sees through the illusion of control that Ana promises; the more she tries to control what she eats and weighs, the more out of control she feels. Many of the narratives demonstrate that even though the women recognize that they are not yet ready to recover, there is some ambivalence about recovery.

Since the original Sanctuary was wiped out I've kinda let things slide again. . . . I'm working on starting all over again. . . . I'm going to avoid the "tips and tricks" angle because of the controversy and because there are enough sources of this already on the internet. . . . What I'd like to see this place become is a kind of meeting ground. Those of us with EDs know what it's like living with them and we also know just how lonely keeping all of this inside us can be. I'd like to see this become a place where we can meet each other, offer support and a shoulder, joke around, etc. . . . What I don't want to see is a place where you have to pretend, argue, justify behaviors, defend yourself. We do enough of that in everyday life. (S.C.a.R.E.D. Forum User, 2001–2002)

What comes through these narratives most of all is the desire to find a space in which they can meet, free from judgment, to support each other and break the isolation they feel.

Unlike the mainstream interpretations of these women's behavior as pathetic or malicious, and as attempts to harm themselves and others, these narratives paint quite a different picture. They illustrate these women's struggles, emotional pain and searching for acceptance and connection, as well as an ambivalence towards recovery. Some show us that these women are very aware of their own situation, as well as looking out and caring for others. There is also evidence of the tension between the desire to go public with their stories (in this case via the media) in order to effect some change in societal awareness, and the fear of how these stories may be distorted and misrepresented as deviant. The contents of these websites and the women's narratives illustrate the contradictions and paradoxes inherent in their situation. The boundaries of the "safe space" are constantly threatened.

Anorexic Nation has been shut down, yet I bet within seconds you could find a site that tells you how to make a bomb, or has child pornography or about a million other crimes. Yet, sites like "Anorexic Nation" are eliminated. What's wrong with this picture? I like this site and hope it stays up, and to hell with the people who don't get it or won't get it. (S.C.a.R.E.D. Forum User, 2001–2002)

Anorexia is certainly not to be taken lightly as its effects can be extremely harmful and potentially fatal. However, considering the high failure rate for traditional biomedical treatment methods and the paradoxes around access to treatment, perhaps it is time to reexamine the approach we take as a society to these "disorders."

Third Wave Feminist Bodies

Feminist theories of eating disorders that address women's agency contribute greatly to reconceptualizing the meaning of eating and body disturbances in women. Elizabeth Grosz has called anorexia a protest against the social meaning of the female body. Contrary to popular notions of anorexia as the result of slavish observance to patriarchal feminine ideals, Grosz asserts that it is "precisely a renunciation of these 'ideals'" (40). She even goes so far as to label feminine practices in certain contexts as "modes of guerilla subversion of patriarchal codes, although the line between compliance and subversion is always a fine one" (144). Feminists have also argued that the anorexic ultimately harms herself; that these women are getting ill rather than getting organized (Ellmann). Certainly this is ultimately true, and anyone working in this field or who has been affected by an eating disorder is only too well aware of the very real dangers of eating disorders to body, mind and spirit. Yet anorexic behavior, though contradictory, serves a greater purpose than simply self-abnegation or compliance to hegemonic ideals.

Third wave feminism offers further insight because of the contradictory nature that has come to define this wave of feminism. "Contradiction [is] . . . a fundamental, definitional strategy, a necessary, lived, embodied strategy" (Heywood and Drake, Introduction 8), as young women's experiences today are "diverse, fragmented, and embody a lived messiness" (ibid 2). Many women, in trying to make sense of this messiness, have turned the focus inward, to the body, and have started from a place where they hold a degree of power and control (Richards xxii). The narratives in third wave collections, like the narratives on pro-anorexia websites, describe individual women's struggles with their identities as well as the contradictory nature of what each of them finds empowering. As Edut states, "in a world that still tries to assume our identities, we rebel with an outward expression of self . . . in all its messy complexity" (xxi). Thus, although pro-anorexia website users do not (overtly) declare their motives to be either feminist or political, their behavior can be read as strategic acts of agency.

Through this article I have demonstrated that there is much more depth and meaning in women's pro-anorexia narratives than may be obvious by listening to dominant interpretations of their messages. Biomedical and psychiatric discourses can no longer point the finger at individual psychopathology in the face of mounting evidence of the broader historical, sociocultural and political connections with this increasingly global cultural epidemic. If we look beyond the supposed individual pathology of such "deviant" behavior, we can detect alternative discourses of resistance. We can also see individual agency in these women's attempts to reach out to one another and create safe, nonjudgmental spaces. Though pro-ana sites do appear to visually reinforce hegemonic norms by showing mainstream images of acceptable female beauty alongside images of deviant bodies, their very presence in public spaces and their ability to resist and subvert pressures to behave creates something of a parody of these impossible norms and demonstrates their agency pose in spite of the backlash. The judgmental responses of practitioners in the field of eating disorders separate the girls and women who do not want help from those who are ready to seek help. These simply reinforce dominant binaries of good/compliant girl and bad/resistant girl that have historically been used to pathologize and silence women. These websites should be positioned within this new wave of feminism, a feminism that ignores these binaries through positing a multiplicity of voices and agencies.

NOTES

1. Graduate Student, Department of Women's Studies and Gender Relations, University of British Columbia, Canada. For comments contact Karen Dias or diaskaren@hotmail.com. I would like to acknowledge Dr. Isabel Dyck for her ongoing support and guidance with this project.

2. This new alternative public space is not available to everyone, as access to technology and necessary skills effectively replicates class divisions within virtual spaces, tending to reinforce existing inequalities and propagating dominant ideologies. As well, the cost of access to the Internet contributes towards class divisions as well as racial ones; the vast majority of the Internet's users are white and middle-class. Moreover, the "real" identities of its users can never be fully known. In cyberspace it is possible to represent yourself as a different age, race, or sexual orientation, providing users with unprecedented possibilities for controlling the conditions of one's own self-representations. Virtual reality encounters provide an illusion of control over reality, nature, and, especially, over the unruly, gendered and race-marked, essentially mortal body (Balsamo; Kolko *et al.*; Stone). For the purposes of this article, I assume that the narratives collected are from girls and/or women struggling with eating disorders. I will use the term "women" throughout the paper to include girls and women although I am mindful that I cannot know the demographics of the women I am studying with any certainty.

3. In fact, one pro-anorexia site is titled "The Anna Sanctuary," suggesting a safe space where women who are pro-anorexia can meet without the judgment they would receive in a "real" public space.

4. This is one of many ways that these new cultural texts may be read, and in doing so I have chosen to focus on narratives taken from these sites that illustrate these alternative discourses.

5. For the purposes of this paper I follow the Medical Research Council of Canada, which outlines specific instances in which informed consent is not required: (1) For information collected indirectly from subjects from existing records in the public domain. (Appendix 1) (2) For research about "a living individual involved in the public arena . . . based exclusively on publicly available information, documents, records, works, performances, archival materials

or third-party interviews. . . . Such research only requires ethics review if the subject is approached directly for interviews or for access to private papers" (Appendix 2, Article 1.1c); (3) For research involving "observation of participants in . . . public meetings . . . since it can be expected that the participants are seeking public visibility" (Appendix 2, Article 2.3).

6. It is difficult to know at any given time just how many of these websites exist; the Eating Disorders Association estimates that the internet contains at least 400 pro-ana sites (Reaves).

7. Some websites also refer to mia, which is short for bulimia, or coe, which is short for compulsive overeating.

8. Websites about eating disorders fall into three general categories: (1) *Medical*: those that disseminate medical, psychiatric, and psychological information about eating disorder diagnosis and treatment, etc., or details about professional organizations; (2) *Support*: individuals who are struggling with an eating disorder, in recovery, or have recovered or organizations that provide information and/or support around eating disorders; (3) *Pro-ED*: sites providing non-judgmental support for individuals currently engaged in eating disorders and not in recovery. Web-rings are clusters of websites that have information on similar topics. Through a web-ring you can connect directly with other topically related sites without going through a search engine.

9. (1) Refusal to maintain body weight at or above a minimally normal weight for age and height (*e.g.* weight loss leading to maintenance of body weight less than 85% of that expected, or failure to make expected weight gain during period of growth, leading to body weight less than 85% of that expected); (2) Intense fear of gaining weight or becoming fat, even though underweight; (3) Disturbance in the way in which one's body weight or shape is experienced, undue influence of body weight or shape on self-evaluation, or denial of the seriousness of the current low body weight; (4) In postmenarchal females, amenorrhea, *i.e.* the absence of at least three consecutive menstrual cycles

10. For more on this see Herman; hooks; Kearney-Cooke and Striegal-Moore; Lovejoy; Thompson; Wooley.

11. A set of therapeutic techniques increasingly used in the treatment of eating disorders is "Motivational Enhancement Therapy," which recognizes various stages of "readiness for change" (Prochaska *et al.*). In the earliest stage—pre-contemplation—the anorexic is not yet ready to take steps towards "recovery." At this stage traditional treatment is not very effective. Many do not reach out for support during this stage, suffering in secrecy and isolation.

12. There are a number of autobiographies and memoirs that describe the experience of anorexia and other eating disorders (Apostolides; Hornbacher; Liu; MacLeod). While these texts provide insight into the anorexic experience, they differ from the websites in a number of ways. Firstly, they are often written post-recovery. Secondly, the women on these websites may not have access to connections or resources that would enable them to get their story into the mainstream through endorsed and privileged means such as publication. Thirdly, these stories are not welcomed or encouraged and are often choppy and disjointed owing to the backlash these websites receive and the subsequent shutting down.

13. Recovery studies on eating disorders are accounts of long-term follow-up studies of patients treated for anorexia nervosa. The earliest example was written by in 1954 and the latest review article counted 30 such studies since then. Follow-up studies of bulimia nervosa have only recently begun to appear in the literature (Herzog *et al.*).

14. For more on this see Beresin *et al.*; Bruch; Chernin.

REFERENCES

American Psychiatric Association. *Diagnostic and Statistical Manual of Mental Disorders.* Washington, DC: American Psychiatric Association, 1994.

Apostolides, Marianne. *Inner Hunger: A Young Woman's Struggle through Anorexia and Bulimia.* New York: Norton, 1998.

Balsamo, Anne. "Forms of Technological Embodiment: Reading the Body in Contemporary Culture." *Feminist Theory and the Body.* Ed. Janet Price and Margrit Shildrick. London: Routledge, 1999. 278–89.

Bankey, Ruth. "La Donna e Mobile: Constructing the Irrational Woman." *Gender, Place, and Culture* 8.1 (2001): 37–54.

Baumgardner, Jennifer, and Amy Richards. *Manifesta: Young Women, Feminism and the Future.* New York: Farrar, Straus and Giroux, 2000.

Beresin, Eugene, et al. "The Process of Recovering from Anorexia Nervosa." *Journal of the Academy of Psychoanalysis* 17 (1989): 103–30.

Bordo, Susan. "Feminism, Foucault, and the Politics of the Body." *Feminist Theory and the Body.* Ed. Janet Price and Margrit Shildrick. London: Routledge, 1999. 246–57.

Bray, Abigail, and Claire Colebrook. "The Haunted Flesh: Corporeal Feminism and the Politics of (Dis)Embodiment." *Signs: Journal of Women in Culture and Society* 24.1 (1998): 35–67.

Bruch, Hilda. *Conversations with Anorexics.* New York: Basic, 1988.

Carter, Claire. "Negotiations with Femininity: 'The Personal is Political' Revisited in Third Wave Feminism." *Views from the Edge* 11.1 (2002): 110–28.

Chase, Susan. "Taking Narratives Seriously: Consequences for Method and Theory in Interview Studies." *The Narrative Study of Lives: Interpreting Experience* 3 (1995): 1–26.

Chernin, Kim. *The Hungry Self: Women, Eating and Identity.* New York: Harper & Row, 1985.

Duncan, Nancy. *BodySpace.* London: Routledge, 1996.

Edut, Ophira, ed. Introduction. *Body Outlaws: Young Women Write about Body Image and Identity.* Seattle: Seal, 1998. xvii–xxii.

Ellmann, Maud. *The Hunger Artists: Starving, Writing, and Imprisonment.* Cambridge: Harvard UP, 1993.

Epston, David, Fran Morris, and Rick Maisel. "A Narrative Approach to So-Called Anorexia/Bulimia." *Journal of Feminist Family Therapy* 7.1/2 (1995): 69–96.

Garret, Catherine. "Recovery from Anorexia Nervosa: A Sociological Perspective." *International Journal of Eating Disorders* 21 (1997): 261–72.

Grosz, Elizabeth. *Volatile Bodies.* Bloomington: Indiana UP, 1994.

Herman, Judith. *Trauma and Recovery: The Aftermath of Violence from Domestic Abuse to Political Terror.* New York: Basic, 1997.

Herzog, David, et al. "Outcome in Anorexia Nervosa and Bulimia Nervosa: A Review of the Literature." *The Journal of Nervous and Mental Disease* 176 (1988): 131–43.

Heywood, Leslie, and Jennifer Drake. Introduction. *Third Wave Agenda: Being Feminist, Doing Feminism.* Ed. Leslie Heywood and Jennifer Drake. Minneapolis: Minnesota UP, 1997. 1–20.

———. "We Learn American Like a Script: Activism in the Third Wave; or, Enough Phantoms of Nothing." *Third Wave Agenda: Being Feminist, Doing Feminism.* Ed. Leslie Heywood and Jennifer Drake. Minneapolis: Minnesota UP, 1997. 40–54.

hooks, bell. *Sisters of the Yam: Black Women and Self-Recovery.* Boston: South End, 1993.

Hornbacher, Marya. *Wasted: A Memoir of Anorexia and Bulimia*. New York: HarperCollins, 1998.

Kearney-Cooke, Ann, and Ruth Striegal-Moore. "Treatment of Childhood Sexual Abuse in Anorexia Nervosa and Bulimia Nervosa: A Feminist Psychodynamic Approach." *International Journal of Eating Disorders* 15 (1994): 305–19.

Kolko, Beth, Lisa Nakamura, and Gilbert Rodman, eds. *Race in Cyberspace*. London: Routledge, 2000.

Liu, Aimee. *Solitaire*. Lincoln: Universe.com, 2000.

Lovejoy, Meg. "Disturbances in the Social Body." *Gender and Society* 15.2 (2001): 239–61.

MacLeod, Sheila. *The Art of Starvation*. New York: Schocken, 1982.

Medical Research Council of Canada, Natural Sciences & Engineering Research Council of Canada, and Social Sciences & Humanities Research Council of Canada. Tri-Council Policy Statement: Ethical Conduct for Research Involving Humans. 3 Mar. 2002. <http://www.nserc.ca/programs/ethics/english/policy.htm>

Parr, Hester. "Bodies and Psychiatric Medicine: Interpreting Different Geographies of Mental Health." *Mind and Body Spaces: Geographies of Illness, Impairment, and Disability*. Ed. Ruth Butler and Hester Parr. New York: Routledge, 1999. 181–202.

Pinterics, Natasha. "Riding the Feminist Waves: In with the Third?" *Young Women: Feminists, Activists, Grrrls*. Ed. Candis Steenbergen. Spec. issue of *Canadian Women's Studies* 20.4/21.1 (2001): 15–21.

Prochaska, James, Carlo DiClemente, and John Norcross. "In Search of How People Change: Application to Addictive Behaviors." *American Psychologist* 47 (1992): 1102–14.

Reaves, Jessica. "Anorexia Goes High Tech." *Time Magazine*, 31 July 2001. <http://www.time.com>.

Richards, Amy. "Body Image: Third Wave Feminism's Issue?" *Body Outlaws: Young Women Write about Body Image and Identity*. Ed. Ophira Edut. Seattle: Seal, 1998. 196–200.

Stone, Allucquère Rosanne. "Will the Real Body Please Stand Up? Boundary Stories about Virtual Culture." *Cyberspace: First Steps*. Ed. Michael Benedikt. Cambridge: MIT UP, 1991. 81–113.

Thompson, Becky. *A Hunger So Wide and So Deep: A Multiracial View of Women's Eating Problems*. Minneapolis: Minnesota UP, 1994.

Walker, Rebecca. "Being Real: An Introduction." *To Be Real: Telling the Truth and Changing the Face of Feminism*. Ed. Rebecca Walker. New York: Anchor Books, 1995. xxix–xl.

Whittle, David. *Cyberspace: The Human Dimension*. New York: W.H. Freeman, 1997.

Wooley, Susan. "Sexual Abuse and Eating Disorders: The Concealed Debate." *Feminist Perspectives on Eating Problems*. Ed. Patricia Fallon et al. New York: Guilford, 1992. 171–211.

About the Contributors

PATRICIA HILL COLLINS is Distinguished University Professor of Sociology at the University of Maryland, College Park. She is the author of numerous books, including *Black Feminist Thought: Knowledge, Consciousness, and the Politics of Empowerment* and, most recently, *From Black Power to Hip Hop: Racism, Nationalism, and Feminism.*

KAREN DIAS is a doctoral candidate in Clinical Psychology at Widener University, in Chester, Pennsylvania. In 2003 she received her master's degree in Women's Studies at the University of British Columbia in Canada, where she focused her research on women's mental health issues, particularly eating disorders.

H. HUGH FLOYD, JR., is Professor and Chair of the Sociology Department at Samford University in Birmingham, Alabama. His research focuses on the environment, health, and family dynamics. He is coauthor of *Bodies in Protest* with Steve Kroll-Smith.

ARTHUR FRANK is Professor of Sociology at the University of Calgary, Alberta, Canada. He is author of *At the Will of the Body, The Wounded Storyteller: Body, Illness, and Ethics,* and *The Renewal of Generosity: Illness, Medicine, and How to Live.* He is an elected fellow of the Royal Society of Canada.

SANDER L. GILMAN is Distinguished Professor of the Liberal Arts and Medicine at the University of Illinois in Chicago and the director of the Humanities Laboratory. A cultural and literary historian, he is the author or editor of over sixty books, including *Making the Body Beautiful* and, most recently, *Fat: A Cultural History of Obesity.*

GILLIAN HADDOW is a sociologist and Innogen Research Fellow at the University of Edinburgh, Scotland. Her research focuses on genetic health and the effects public consultation has on the governance of large-scale DNA databases. Other research interests include the democratic mandate of genetic interest groups and the regulation of cytoplasmic embryos and xenotransplantation.

RICHARD HUGGINS is Assistant Dean of Social Sciences and Law at Oxford Brookes University, where he teaches research methods and the politics and sociology of crime. He is currently completing a book on British approaches to drug use and control (forthcoming from Willan, 2010) and working on the third edition of a jointly authored textbook, *Politics: An Introduction,* for Routledge. Recent publications include *New Media, New Politics* (coeditor).

MATTHEW IMMERGUT is Assistant Professor of Sociology at Purchase College, SUNY. He works in the fields of environmental sociology as well as sociology of religion. Along with research on environmental conflicts, his most recent work investigates contemporary religious and secular ascetic practices.

KRISTEN KARLBERG is a medical sociologist who studies pregnancy and technologies. Her interests within this discipline include bodies, gender, and genetics.

LE'A KENT is a doctoral candidate in English at the University of Washington with research and teaching interests in twentieth-century U.S. literature and culture. She has written on lesbian pornography, male consumerism, and antigay legislation.

MARY KOSUT is a sociologist and Assistant Professor of Media, Society, and the Arts at Purchase College, SUNY. Her areas of research include the body, art worlds, and consumption. Her essays on tattoo art, body modification, and academic culture appear in journals such as *Deviant Behavior, Journal of Popular Culture,* and *Cultural Studies—Critical Methodologies.*

STEVE KROLL-SMITH is Professor of Sociology at the University of North Carolina, Greensboro. He is the coauthor of *Bodies in Protest* with H. Hugh-Floyd and *Volatile Places: Communities and Environmental Controversies* with Valerie J. Gunter.

JARVIS JAY MASTERS is a widely published African American Buddhist writer living on San Quentin's Death Row. He is author of *Finding Freedom: Writings from Death Row.*

AARON M. MCCRIGHT holds a joint academic appointment in the Department of Sociology and the Lyman Briggs School of Science at Michigan State University. He is coeditor (with Terry N. Clark) of *Community and Ecology: Dynamics of Place, Sustainability, and Politics.*

LISA JEAN MOORE is a medical sociologist, Coordinator of Gender Studies, and professor at Purchase College, SUNY. She is the author of *Sperm Counts: Overcome by Man's Most Precious Fluid* and the coauthor of *Missing Bodies: The Politics of Visibility,* both from NYU Press.

TRACEY OWENS PATTON is Associate Professor in the Department of Communication and Journalism and the COJO Director of Graduate Studies at the University of Wyoming. Her research focuses on the interdependence among race, gender, and power and how these issues interrelate culturally and rhetorically in education, media, and speeches. Her essays appear in the *Journal of Black Studies, National Women's Studies Association Journal, Transformations: The Journal of Inclusive Scholarship and Pedagogy,* and *Women's Studies in Communication.*

WILLIAM J. PEACE is an anthropologist and Independent Scholar. He is author of *Leslie A. White: Evolution and Revolution in Anthropology* and the forthcoming *Bad Cripple.*

JASON PINE, a professor in the Anthropology and Media, Society, Arts Departments, Purchase College, SUNY, studies aesthetics, affect, and embodiment in alternative economies. He has conducted fieldwork in the United States (rural and urban methamphetamine production and consumption) and in the southern Italian city of Naples. Additionally, he studies the aesthetics and political economy of virtual world-building in Second Life and broader cultural investments in design, from the arts to biotechnologies. His essays appear in *Public Culture, Journal of Modern Italian Studies,* and *Law, Culture, and the Humanities.*

ERIC PLEMONS is a doctoral candidate in the Department of Anthropology at the University of California at Berkeley. His research engages the production and circulation of expert knowledge about gender-variant bodies. He is currently working on a project investigating the variation of surgical techniques used in sex reassignment surgery around the world.

BARBARA KATZ ROTHMAN is Professor of Sociology at Baruch College, City University of New York. She is the author of *Laboring On: Birth in Transition in the United States,* with Wendy Simonds and Bari Meltzer Norman, and *Weaving a Family: Untangling Race and Adoption.*

ED SLAVISHAK, Associate Professor of History at Susquehanna University, is the author of *Bodies of Work: Civic Display and Labor in Industrial Pittsburgh* (2008). He is preparing a study of photography, tourism, and dereliction in the Appalachian Mountains.

PHILLIP VANNINI, Associate Professor, School of Communication and Culture, Royal Roads University, Victoria, British Columbia, is author of *Body/Embodiment: Symbolic Interaction and the Sociology of the Body* with Dennis Waskul and *Material Culture and Technology in Everyday Life: Ethnographic Approaches.*

DENNIS WASKUL is Associate Professor of Sociology at the University of Minnesota, Mankato. He is author of *Self-Games and Body Play: Personhood in Online Chat and Cybersex,* editor of *net.seXXX: Readings on Sex, Pornography, and the Internet,* and co-editor of *Body/Embodiment: Symbolic Interaction and the Sociology of the Body.* Dennis has published extensively in the areas of symbolic interaction, sociology of the body, sociology of the senses, sexualities, and computer-mediated communications.

Index

CPSIA information can be obtained at www.ICGtesting.com
Printed in the USA
LVOW09s0921100715

445573LV00001B/1/P